THE
COMPLETE
SMOKING
DIARIES

THE
COMPLETE
SMOKING
DIARIES

Simon Gray

GRANTA

Granta Publications, 12 Addison Avenue, London W11 4QR

First published in Great Britain by Granta Books 2013

This book consists of four previously published volumes:
The Smoking Diaries, first published by Granta Books in 2004 and published as
The Smoking Diaries Volume 1 in 2008; *The Year of the Jouncer*, first published by
Granta Books in 2006 and published as *The Smoking Diaries Volume 2:
The Year of the Jouncer* in 2008; *The Last Cigarette*, first published by
Granta Books in 2008 and published as *The Smoking Diaries Volume 3:
The Last Cigarette* later in 2008; *Coda*, first published by
Granta Books and Faber and Faber in 2008 and published
as *Coda: The Smoking Diaries Volume 4* in 2009.

A CIP catalogue record for this book is
available from the British Library.

1 3 5 7 9 10 8 6 4 2

ISBN 978 1 84708 848 2

Typeset by M Rules

Printed and bound by CPI Group (UK) Ltd, Croydon, CR0 4YY

CONTENTS

Simon Gray, London, 2002

INTRODUCTION

'Piero de' Medici had the sculptor make in his courtyard a statue of snow, which was said to be very beautiful,' said Vasari in his *Lives of the Artists*. I'm fond of this story, apocryphal or not. Michelangelo's Snowman. It might well have been his greatest work, but, like a theatre performance, you had to have been there to have seen it, it was unreproducible. Theatre lives only in the present tense: writing or acting for theatre is the art of feigning spontaneity. What could be more spontaneous than this:

> My plan is to get down some thoughts and memories of Alan, but I don't think I can start today, not on the first day, with the pigeons hopping, and the little birds with yellow chests etc., one of which is now sharing my drink. Best let it happen when it happens, tomorrow perhaps, or later in the week, let it sneak up. Today the thing is just to be here, back here at the usual table, my yellow pad in front of me, free to go wherever – although I think I must make a pact with myself to lay off the subject of my age, and my physical deterioration, it's really time I outgrew all that, it's not becoming in a man nearing seventy, although I must confess that now I see those words actually on the page, 'nearing seventy', I find myself gaping at them.

This reads like dialogue in a play, part of a monologue spoken directly to the audience. In the course of his extended soliloquies the nature of the speaker is revealed little by little as a not-quite-solipsistic, sometimes bitter, often loving, amiable, humane, vulnerable, intelligent, droll, melancholy, curmudgeonly protagonist called 'SIMON GRAY' – an almost entirely convincing characterization of the writer Simon Gray.

If I say 'almost' it's because what Simon achieves is so beguiling and so difficult. The passage above (from the beginning of *The Year of the Jouncer*, the second volume of *The Smoking Diaries*) is like Paul Klee's drawings: the pen never seems to leave the paper. Taking a line for a walk – Klee's famous description of drawing – is easier than writing. You can sketch a line following the brain's instructions in real time, but you can't write words as fast as they occur to you. It takes a good actor to convince you that the words he's speaking have just come to mind; it takes a virtuoso writer to give the same impression on the page. 'Hold on!' Simon tells the reader, as if we – or he – were getting the wrong idea about what he's saying. Or 'No!' when he wants to contradict himself. Or 'wait until fresh and vigorous, vigorous? Hah! Well, until fresh, fresh? Also hah!' when he's trying to dissect the past, or giving a cautionary message to his audience: 'but it's never too late, it is always said, never too late to change. Oh yes, it is . . . I would certainly go forth and do good in the world, if only my vices would let me. Alas, I am what I am, alas. Know what I mean?' He writes as if memories and the act of recording them are occurring simultaneously, achieving spontaneity with an artlessness that's supremely artful.

If the diaries are a series of dramatic soliloquies, they're accompanied by their stage directions. The scene is always set meticulously: weather, architecture, furniture, supporting cast, who are often the cats, Tom and Errol, the dogs, George and Toto, and always the wife, Victoria. And the location of the action – the act of writing – is always described. It's on planes: 'I'm only going on like this because we're on the verge of taking off'; at a desk in Suffolk: 'it's now three in the afternoon, my lights are on, the rain is drizzling down, and I'm cold'; in a bar in Barbados: 'Can I, in all conscience, keep my table at the bar while I have lunch at a table in the restaurant?'; in a café in Crete, in a hotel room in New York or at a smoker's table on the pavement in Holland Park Avenue.

Once the scene is set, like an actor tackling a long soliloquy, Simon fills his lungs (ironic for a would-be ex-smoker) and words fly out of him as if he has discovered the secret of circular breathing: on cricket, tyranny, racism, sharks, rats, dogs, cats, flies, DTs, childhood, sex, murder, friendship, death, the power of fiction, lesbian fantasies, Harold Pinter (his temper and, more surprisingly, his gentleness), C. P. Snow, Simon Callow, Alan Bates, Tom Stoppard, Nathan Lane and more. It's the literary equivalent of the way in which thoughts come unbidden into your mind when you're lying half awake in the early morning or drifting unmoored during the day.

The momentum of the diaries – what I suppose you could call the 'plot' – is provided by the successive renunciations of Simon's greatest pleasures: alcohol and smoking. 'Start stopping smoking NOW' is an injunction that proves as painful to follow as the prospect of renouncing life itself:

> in short –
> in short
> and in short
> I am afraid.

Simon's writing for the theatre is invariably warm and approachable – a paradox given that his tone is sharp, his politics unregenerate, his central characters often rumpled wrecks whose alcohol intake is auto-destructive and whose nicotine consumption is probably poisoning half the street. His early plays were grotesques in the style of Joe Orton, but then he appropriated the classicism of Racine. We see a character in a room: doors open, people enter and leave and, by a remorseless accumulation of incident, that character's doom is sealed.

His plays have an ascetic, classical, conservative form yet contain (or restrain) characters whose emotions spill out in a prodigal disorder. The form of the diaries is unrestrained but they are no less plays than his plays, even though they feature a sole protagonist whose emotions, of course, spill out in a prodigal disorder. It seems odd that there aren't more playwrights, besides Alan Bennett, who take to prose in the intervals between plays, given that those intervals tend to be long. Writing a play is so precariously difficult; it's the literary equivalent of juggling with crockery in a high wind while tightrope-walking over a deep gorge. Character and story have to be revealed through action rather than description and have to be introduced by sleight of hand. Confrontations, love affairs, battles, deaths and births have to be engineered as if each action inevitably and effortlessly followed another, and – hardest of all – an audience has to be left with the impression that the characters exist independently of the writer and that the play has come to life spontaneously.

Some novelists think that writing plays is an easy option: the literary landscape is littered with the corpses of plays that were dead at birth – James Joyce's *Exiles*, Virginia Woolf's *Freshwater*, William Golding's *The Brass Butterfly*, Muriel Spark's *Doctors of Philosophy* and, notoriously, Henry James's *Guy Domville*. On the opening night, like many playwrights, James was too nervous to watch his own play, so he missed the reception of the line 'I'm the last, my lord, of the Domvilles', to which a wit in the gallery responded, 'It's a bloody good thing you are!' He arrived backstage during the curtain calls and, reassured by applause for the actors, he stepped on to the stage and was drowned by a tsunami of booing.

It's a story that Simon would have relished. He falls with masochistic gusto into riffs about the agonies of a playwright ('a combination of fool and criminal') watching his own play:

> I feel like a criminal forced to sit with the jury and witness my own crime, witness myself committing it, and then showing it off. One of the things that might strike other people as odd, but doesn't strike me as odd, which is the oddest part of it, is that my sympathies, no, more than my sympathies, my whole digestive system and nervous tract, are with the jury, at least its hostile members.

Or there's the story that he tells of a drunken director who 'stumbled down the aisle and tumbled over the seats, often with a lighted cigarette in his mouth'. Things go from worse to terrible and

> of course the producer, who was devoted to the play, made periodic attempts to fire the director but was thwarted by the director's agent, who pointed out that the playwright had director approval, and as the playwright and the director were one and the same it would be a question of asking him to fire himself, which he was unlikely to do, as he got on so well together.

When I first read this my simmering smile erupted into a bark of laughter.

And what joy there is in his account of trying to type up his day's writing when the letter 'h' on his typewriter had started sticking, leading to an h-less paragraph about the loss of his 'ligtness of touc'. The writing is crafty – moments of pain are subverted by explosions of comedy; and the whirling free association never becomes wearisome because it's spiced with irresistibly vivid turns of phrase – a woman has 'a voice you could grate cheese on'; a pile of dead insects looks like 'toast crumbs'; the loss of a friend is 'a bit of grit in my inner eye'. For all that he's voluble, irascible and wholly unclubbable, he's always wary of boring you.

Wit and spontaneity prevent the diaries from ever being infected by the Pooterish tone that tends to afflict any conversation with oneself. With Simon there's always self-mockery or self-condemnation, or at the very least self-disgust – 'I've just re-read the above paragraph. It is disgusting.' Often with diarists evasion, self-justification and self-recrimination amount to self-defence – *quand je m'accuse, je m'excuse* – but Simon's confessions aren't larded with self-pity. Memories, such as of his girlfriend – or to be more accurate 'his first fuck' – are anatomized for their reliability, and the narrator is interrogated and found wanting:

You had no sex with her?

That's it. Yes.

What form did this no sex take?

When I'd peeled my trousers down to my knees, and rolled my underpants down to my trousers' crotch, I lay on top of her and bucked about, yelping.

Or, writing about his mother, he charges himself with neglect: 'I . . . thought about the kind of son I was, who would deprive his dying mother of a few more minutes, that's all she'd claimed . . . I still don't know why I wouldn't stay.'

The problem with most diaries is that, if true, they're never quite true enough. Cocteau said that 'A journal exists only if you put into it, without reservation, everything that occurs to you.' Simon follows Cocteau with somewhat more wit and considerably less self-regard in writing frankly of sexual desire, failure, fantasy and jealousy; of his loneliness and of what he regards as his nastiness:

> the truth is that I'm nastier than I used to be back when – back when I was sixty-four, for instance, when I was nastier than I was at sixty-two and so forth, back and back, always the less nasty the further back, until I get to the age when I was pre-nasty, at least consciously, when the only shame I knew was the shame of being found out which was when I was, well, about eight, I suppose.

He writes too about his addictions. Ill health may have forced him to give up alcohol and smoking but he couldn't resist the addiction of writing, even at 3 a.m. after a sleeping pill, two Co-proxamol and a Broadway opening night.

Under the whole book runs a strong but barely sounded *obligato*: the love for his wife, Victoria. Perhaps it's this that prevents him from writing more biliously – 'unchoke me from this hatred that comes on me like a sickness more and more' – but his invocation to himself doesn't inhibit him from describing the *New York Times* theatre critic as having 'an unhappy prose style, aiming to be simultaneously colloquial and elegant it comes out in a bit of a muddle, here snobbish and there vulgar, and sometimes both in the same sentence' in a marvellously drawn and painfully recognizable passage about putting on one of his plays – *Butley* – on Broadway.

Simon's diaries – like those of Pepys and Virginia Woolf and Joe Orton – give the feeling of a life spilling out indiscriminately, innocent of self-censorship, as if the life is being lived through the diaries. He takes life as he finds it, without seeking to improve it or to moralize about it. '– in other words you can learn nothing from experience, at least in my experience.' There are few who can write about their experience with such charm, such honesty and such self-knowledge.

Richard Eyre
June 2013

THE
SMOKING
DIARIES

Volume 1

The Smoking Diaries

For Dena

PART ONE

HAPPY BIRTHDAY, SWEETHEART

So here I am, two hours into my sixty-sixth year. From tomorrow on I'm entitled to various benefits, or so I gather – a state pension of so many pounds a week, free travel on public transport, reduced fees on the railways. I assume I'm also entitled to subsidiary benefits – a respectful attention when I speak, unfailing assistance when I stumble or lurch, an absence of registration when I do the things I've been doing more and more frequently recently, but have struggled to keep under wraps – belching, farting, dribbling, wheezing. I can do all these things openly and publicly now, in a spirit of mutual acceptance. Thus am I, at sixty-five and a day. Thus he is, at sixty-five and a day, a farter, a belcher, a dribbler and a what else did I say I did, farting, belching, dribbling, oh yes, wheezing. But then as I smoke something like sixty-five cigarettes a day people are likely to continue with their inevitable 'Well, if you insist on getting through three packets, etc.' to which I will reply, as always – actually, I can't remember what I always reply, and how could I, when I don't believe anyone, even my doctors, ever says anything like, 'Well, if you will insist, etc.' In fact, I'm merely reporting a conversation I have with myself, quite often, when I find myself wheezing my way not only up but down the stairs, and when I recover from dizzy spells after pulling on my socks, tying up my shoelaces, two very distinct acts. No, four very distinct acts, each separated by an interval longer than the acts themselves. Naturally, like most people of sixty-five and a day I only grasp my age, the astonishing number of years I've completed, by these physical symptoms – within, the child, about eight years old, rages away – I wish it were all reversed, that I had the appetites, physical stamina, and desirability of a healthy eight-year-old, and the inner life of a man of sixty-five and a day as I imagine it to be from the point of view of an eight-year-old – calm, beneficent, worldly-wise and brimming with tolerance, not to mention forgiveness, yes, I need to be in touch with my inner adult, is the truth of the matter, who has always been lost to me except as an idea. But the truth is that I'm nastier than I used to be back when – back when I was sixty-four, for instance, when I was nastier than I was at sixty-two and so forth, back and back, always the less nasty the further back, until I get to the age when I was pre-nasty, at least consciously, when the only shame I knew was the shame of being found out which was when I was, well, about eight, I suppose.

TWO FRIENDS IN A PLIGHT

What's the date? Well, it's Friday midnight the week before Christmas, and this is what happened this evening – at about the time when Victoria and I were vaguely preparing to cross the road to dinner at Chez Moi, there was a ring on the doorbell. We froze, she in her study, I in mine, waiting for the bell to ring again or for the bell ringer to go away – we have a policy, since we were mugged on the pavement outside the house, never to answer the door in the evening unless we know for certain who's there. The bell didn't ring again. 'Any idea who that might have been?' I bellowed huskily (pretty exact description – my voice, when used normally, is low and broken from fifty-seven years of smoking but when raised it comes out husky), 'Did you get a look?' – sometimes she pops into the bedroom when the doorbell rings, and peeks down from the window – no, she said, she'd seen a shape at the frosted glass in the front door, but couldn't tell anything, not even the sex, it had only been a glimpse, really, from the top of the stairs. 'Well,' I said, 'did you get a sense? Did you hear the footsteps? Could it have been a policeman?' I have a dread of policemen at the door, bearing bad news, a hangover from the years when my children were at that sort of stage – Lucy's first car, Ben's tendency to stray into unprotected areas, unprotected from himself, in some cases – yes, it could have been a policeman, Victoria said, but then it could have been anyone, as she hadn't heard anything, but I was suddenly convinced that I had, that I'd heard the heavy tread, with something slow and deliberate in it, of a policeman, though now I come to think of it, it would have to have been a policeman from another age, a policeman from *Dixon of Dock Green*, if not Dixon himself, the policemen of these days don't have a heavy tread, for one thing they don't wear constabulary boots, they wear light, smart shoes that probably cause them to pitter-patter lightly along, in twos or threes or even little packs of four or five, towards some pop star whose Internet habit they are investigating – clearly, then, if I'd thought about it, the heavy tread I hadn't heard hadn't belonged to a policeman, but not having thought about it and now actually assuming our bell had been rung by a policeman, actually picturing him in his helmet, heavy jacket, enveloping blue trousers, and his large boots, we crossed the road to Chez Moi and saw, as we entered, the Pinters, Harold and Antonia seated at a table facing the door, in the second room.

'I came across a moment ago, and rang your bell, to see if you wanted to join us,' Antonia said. 'I saw somebody through the glass at the top of the stairs, so I knew you were in.' We reminded her of our policy of never answering the door until we know who is at it, without of course explaining that I'd mistaken her tread, which I hadn't actually heard, for that of a policeman from a distant epoch, but it struck me as unusual, not to say unprecedented, for her to have rung the doorbell, and there was something in Harold's manner, subdued and soft in his greetings –

'The thing is,' he said, almost as soon as we'd sat down, 'I might as well tell you, I've just discovered – well, today in fact, that I've got cancer.'

The world went immediately upside down and into a spin. In all the years, etc., the standing order of things is that I'm the one that gets ill, hovers now and then at death's door, and he is the robust one, seeming almost to get more robust with the passing of time – furthermore it's always been a condition, an absolute condition, of my relationship with him, as I've understood it, that he should still be in the world when I leave it, just as he was when I entered it.

He went through the stages of the treatment that lay ahead for him – that he would begin it two days after Christmas, then there would be a break of three weeks during which the poisons would be at their business of attacking the cancer, then another all-day session followed by another three weeks, by which time there would be, he noted matter of factly, certain physical changes, his face might alter in shape, his hair might fall out – 'But of course you know the procedure,' he said to me, 'from Ian. How's he doing?'

'Not too well,' I said, and gave him the information Ian had given to me, just last night as a matter of fact, and also in Chez Moi, at a table around the corner from the one we were now sitting at – I tried to be crisp and impersonal, and stopped myself saying, 'But of course his isn't anything like yours, his is far worse' – which would be true inasmuch as I understand the matter, Harold's cancer being local, in his oesophagus, Ian's being all over the place, in his liver, his lungs, probably now also in his lymph – but I didn't think he'd want me to offer consolation by stressing the direness of Ian's plight – direness of Ian's plight! Christ! What a phrase – I've never used it before in my life, where did it come from, direness, plight, when I mean that actually I think he's dying.

How will Harold manage?

He'll manage well, I think. With endurance, resolution. Grit. He has a lot of that, thank God.

ON HOLIDAY

I talked to Rollocks for a short while, about the moon, which was three quarters full, or a quarter empty, depending on your temperament, and then we talked about cricket, the tragic decline of West Indies cricket, then what it is like to find ourselves in the computer age. Rollocks is perhaps five years younger than me, but older in terms of dignity, bearing, manner of speech. He brought me a specially chilled diet coke. The bar is empty, apart from Rollocks, who never presides over any customer but myself, as far as I can make out. His hours begin at 11 p.m. and end at 7 a.m., and his function is to provide all-night service to a clientele who tend to be in bed as he arrives on the premises, and to be about to rise as he leaves them. I can't say that the clientele is all elderly – quite a few are much younger than me, but they seem to settle into elderly habits, early days, early nights. I don't imagine that they even notice that everyone else does as they do, or that they do as everyone else does, but often, when I walk around the grounds at half-past midnight, I find every light in the apartments and cottages is out, and the hotel takes on the aspect of a large nest, humming with sleep – and then later there are Rollocks and I in the bar, where we too follow a pattern – a short conversation, he brings the diet coke, I write. Last night I wrote a letter to Harold. I don't remember now quite what I said – I know I mentioned Rollocks, and then went into a little bit about the hotel and I wrote about the weather, and the mosquitoes, all of this uneasily, as I was trying to find my way towards the central issue, the state of Harold's health – wondering how the treatment was going, how his appetite was, whether his temperature had dropped, etc. – and from there I went into my own feelings when I'd been ill to the point of death five years ago, that I'd found it unbearable to be with people because they seemed to me to be coming from another country, or rather that I'd been exiled to another country and they were paying me brief, troubled visits, then back they went to where I'd once belonged – and then I found myself refining – or possibly coarsening – this thought by adding that actually I'd felt I was under arrest for a rather sad crime, that in some sense the exile was, or seemed to be, a moral one. I'm not sure that this was an appropriate line to take – how can it be helpful to a man perhaps mortally afflicted to have it suggested that he might actually be in the throes of committing some social offence? Well, I've already posted the letter – I know I've posted it, so why did I suddenly start looking for it – I actually picked up my hat as if the letter to Harold I know I've posted might nevertheless be under it. Why did I bring the hat down anyway? It's a straw hat, I wear it to keep the sun off my head, and although I'm outside, it's two in the morning, no sun, just a quarter moon, as I believe I've already –

So a little pause, to light a cigarette, a sip of diet coke, calm restored. I've put the hat on my head – Ian's hat actually, that he wore to cover the effects of chemotherapy and has been passed on to me – not quite true that I claimed a few days after his death. When I was told that he'd wanted me to have something, he probably meant from his library, but I immediately asked for his hat, on which I keep far too attentive an eye, clasping at it when it's windy, fearful I might forget it when I've taken it off on the beach, now wearing it at night in the bar. I'll have to get over this, I'm bound to lose it, it's in the nature of straw hats to detach themselves from you eventually, much better to accept its loss now and adopt a more sensibly careless attitude to it, thinking that I can always get a new one. Of course, the thing about Ian is – no, I can't remember him, not at the moment, his expressions, voice, etc., all I can remember is his coffin being carried down the aisle, then being loaded onto the hearse. He was quite a tall man, as tall as me, and the coffin looked too small – but then that's often the way with coffins, miracles of packaging, a body with all those knobs and joints and so forth packed away. Well, his hat is on my head. I'll try to hang on to it.

GOOD MORNING

I had to get up at 6.30 this morning for a pee – on the way back to bed I popped on to the terrace for a quick gander at the breaking dawn which, as it turned out, wasn't breaking, the light was grey, and the pale trees and the shrubbery shifting about irritably in a sharp wind, the only signs of human life a strange and stooped figure on the beach, moving spectrally between a couple of beach-beds under one of the charmingly shaped (like a coolie's hat) straw and wooden-poled little edifices that provide a circle of shade only a few feet from the sea – there are only three of these shelters, which are not only delightful to look at but delightful to be under – a small shelf for drinks encircles the pole, altogether a home from home – and they are much prized and competed for – now the rules of the hotel, I should explain, regarding beach-beds, chairs, etc. are really quite simple, indeed there is only one clear rule, when it comes down to it – first come, first served, but on a day-to-day basis, in other words you can't keep your cherished location for the length of your stay, you have to establish your claim to it every morning – thus the spectre in the 6.20 a.m. gloom – he was staking his claim for the day, though he seemed to be doing rather more than that, stooping now over this bed, now over that, kneeling at the table on the pole, bowing to the sea – he was wearing the hotel dressing gown, a short number with greyish blue and white stripes, institutional, a prison or hospital sort of thing that nevertheless in the context conferred on him a sort of authority, and made it seem as if he were performing a ceremony of a ritualistic nature, a blessing perhaps –

I peered closer and realized that he was elderly, older than me even, and by quite a bit, and that what he was doing was elderly business, exactly the sort of thing that I've been doing for a few years now – and it gets worse and worse – when I try to sort myself out somewhere, picking things up, putting them down in order to pick something else up for reasons unknown, putting it down, stopping to work out a puzzle to do with, for instance, the whereabouts of a towel that one had thought one had adjusted a moment ago, but now seems to have vanished from the scene of the action, on and on it goes, fiddling, fussing, farting around – and superstition comes into it somewhere, the fear that if one hasn't got every detail – as when he kept edging a bed inches sideways from one end, going to the other end and inching it back again, pushing it forwards, pulling it backwards, standing to inspect it, making a further adjustment – was this one for his wife, slumbering in their room, unaware that her husband was fretting and fiddling at inches and angles for her sake, would she even notice when she came to the beach the exact arrangement of her bed, and how could she notice, really, as there was nothing specific for it to be exact to, unless of course she'd provided him with exact instructions – my bed is to be precisely at such an angle to the sea/sun when we come down at 8 a.m. sort of stuff, no, these impulses were coming from *within* him, and mine come from within me, synapses or whatever they are that control these matters, going into a muddled repeat mode, doing almost the same thing again and again, the deep-laid purpose, if there is one, is never to finish the inessential task – no, that's not true, getting out of the house is sometimes essential, when I have to meet people or go to the dentist across the street, but getting out of the house – making it from my study to the pavement without going back for something it turns out I haven't forgotten can take ten to fifteen minutes, which I fill by performing inessential tasks again and again – put my spare spectacles in the case for safety's sake, take them out again straight away for future convenience's sake, decide to swap spare spectacles for the ones I'm using, decide to swap the spare spectacles I'm not using for the ones I've just made spare – I become increasingly desperate during all this, crying out, 'What am I doing? Why am I doing this?' generally culminating in a scream, a husky scream, because of my smoking,

'God, I hate myself!' So I found myself hating the old guy who seemed really to be doing a studied and detailed imitation of me. I watched him walk a few steps away from the benches, stop, turn, crouch clutching his knees (I can't do this . . . joints too stiff), peer at the bench, then back for some more rearranging, then away only a few paces this time, and back, at it again. Finally, he made it to the path above the beach that will take him back to his snoozing wife – or mistress, young, vibrant, preparing herself for a pre-breakfast frolic, while her man – 'my man' – is out there, not hunting/gathering, but fiddling and faddling for her sake – perhaps the realigning was really to give himself angles from which he can peer between her legs or down into her breasts. But I don't think so. Nothing of the eager scamper, the driven scuttle, in the way he groped his way through the greyness, across the lawns towards his room – or somebody else's room, his legs looked as if they didn't care much where they took him, as long as it was somewhere very close. As he tottered around the palm trees and out of sight, I had an impulse to zip – a word I like to use for my own totter – down the stairs, across the lawn to his nest, snatch up his towels, zip back up here, thus providing Victoria and myself with four towels instead of the usual two, and further providing somebody else with the opportunity of marking out the most desired spot on the beach, and further providing the possibility of the most magnificent row after breakfast when he and his wife come to loll in their rightful place, and find two others, I'd hope of the same age, but of different nationalities, two elderly French versus two middle-aged Scots would be best, but really I would accept any combination – the impulse didn't pass. I took it to bed with me, and nourished it a while as I lay with my arms wrapped around my wife, who was deeply asleep and mumbling slightly. Now that I've written this, I'll spend the rest of the day reading. I feel a strong need for what in my Cambridge days, my Leavis days, was considered a life-enhancing book, though I'm not sure what sort of book a life-enhancing book would be, when it comes to it. Or even what enhancing means when connected to a book. I suppose it must have spiritual implications. The only writer who actually changed my life for the better in any practical and measurable way was Hank Janson, who gave me what I had for a sex life when I was twelve years old – at that age I had no idea of what was to be found between a girl's legs, but partly assumed, mystically assumed, it would be a prettier, daintier, more feminine version of what was to be found between my own, and I couldn't imagine, of course, how they could interact, hers and mine. So Hank Janson – the titles alone drove my blood wild – *Torment for Trixy – Hotsy, You'll Be Chilled* – and on the cover a vivid blonde, blouse ripped, skirt hitched up to her thighs, struggling sweetly against chains, ropes, a gag – and in the top right corner set in a small circle, like a medallion, the silhouette of presumably Hank himself, trench coat open, trilby tilted back, a cigarette hanging from a corner of his mouth.

UNDER THE INFLUENCES

His real name was Frances Stephen or Stephen Frances, one or the other surfaced in the newspapers when he was on the run in – when would that have been, roughly? the year Hank Janson was on the run, well, it was when I was fifteen or so, and as I was born in 1936, 1936 + 15 = 1951. Yes, that's about right, 1951. Now what the thing was about Hank Janson was that he was –

Start again. Hank Janson.

I kept my Hank Janson library squirrelled away in different nooks and crannies of my bedroom, some under a loose floorboard, and as an extra security measure, I tore the covers off and concealed them between the pages of the books, so I naturally assumed that this secret cache was entirely unknown to my mother, who never mentioned that she knew about it except once, obliquely. She came into the dining room where my brother Nigel and I had just started our breakfast – a meal my mother cooked before dressing for the day – generally she wore a flapping dressing gown over an almost transparent nightie, so I suppose, on reflection, I could have found out what was to be found, or rather not to be found, between a girl's legs by dropping to my knees – but of course both Nigel and I kept our eyes averted, from each other as well as from her, as she flung herself into and out of the dining room talking constantly and comically or reproachfully, pausing to gesture with her cigarette, laughing at something she'd said –

Now the thing about Mummy, Mummy and me, well, actually it was I whom she frankly –

Frankly, I was the one she loved to fondle, the one she made sit on her lap, whose legs she stroked, whose hair she ruffled, the nape of whose neck she kissed, etc., and so forth, while Nigel and his father (well, our father, but I tended to see them as a twosome) stood or sat by with the appearance of disdain for all these displays of full-blooded passion – yes, that was it – Mummy and I were the adoring couple, Nigel and Daddy were a pair of disapproving relatives – great-uncle and uncle perhaps, though that doesn't work out – oh yes, it does if you see Daddy as Mummy's uncle, and Nigel as mine, everything slots into place, anthropologically speaking – is anthropology the right science for these delicate matters, or should we be thinking of psychiatry here – well, these days, of course, one should be thinking of column inches in the *Mail on Sunday*, with myself portrayed as Mummy's toy boy, and Nigel and Daddy as the jilted lovers bonding. There is one memory, though, that abruptly and discordantly intrudes itself into the family idyll. There I was, hunched on the lavatory, brooding over my latest Hank Janson, when the door burst open, and there was my father.

'Get out,' I ordered, speaking from a self I didn't know I owned.

'Sorry,' said my father, and got out . . .

When I eventually came out of the bathroom on to the landing, I could hear their voices from the bedroom, he was talking quietly, with brio, a lively mutter, not his usual tone or style at all, and she was gasping with suppressed laughter – the obvious effort to maintain low audibility being from tact, I like to think, although they both knew the acoustics of the house well enough to know what carried where. I don't know exactly what I anticipated – scenes, showdowns, confiscations certainly, worst of all a long morbid conversation, anyway not parental laughter, my doting Mummy laughing at her wanking (this word didn't exist at the time, at least in my circles) son, so I was at first mortified, then relieved, then mortified again but in a – not comfortable, of course not, but – but secure sort of way. Loved. I can't remember how I sidled into view at breakfast time, so I assume it was as usual, Mummy's long legs scissoring her in and out of the dining room – Daddy didn't have breakfast with us, he had it in bed – this was the marital routine, Mummy down at seven to make a cup of tea, take it up to Daddy with the newspapers and the post, then she'd slip back into bed, then downstairs to make our breakfast, then in term time Nigel and I off to school, he to St Paul's, I to Westminster, and Daddy, shortly afterwards, off to the Belgrave Hospital, near the Oval, where he was the pathologist. We lived in Oakley Gardens, Chelsea, now a swank address, but then a slummy, no, not slummy, a down-at-heel professional classes neighbourhood at a time when the professional classes, particularly doctors, were overtaxed and underpaid, and my father, for instance, hard pressed to pay our school fees. England of half a century ago, depleted by war, only just emerging from rationing, restricted in travel (sixty pounds per annum per adult), long orderly queues on the pavements outside the butcher's, the fishmonger's, the sweet shops, I could go on listing the deprivations of this victorious nation, because they were all around us, affecting every aspect of our lives, but of course they were, for Nigel and myself and all those of our age and younger, the natural conditions of life, as were the daily civilities – the calm, the sense of safety. There was a working-class estate, the Peabody Buildings, directly behind the small backyards of the houses along our side of Oakley Gardens, and there was Chelsea Manor Street with its 'bombed outs' living on council estates, and a small cluster of prefabs at one end – so a continuous if accidental mingling of classes, but I never once, in the seven years we lived there, heard an obscenity on the street, let alone saw a violent gesture, though occasionally, when going up Chelsea Manor Street to swim in the public baths, Nigel and I would be encircled at an unintimidating distance by a group rather than a gang of working-class boys of our age or older, and jeered at for being posh – and that was it, the class war, as experienced by the two Gray brothers half a century ago, when there really were visibly defined classes, working/lower, lower-middle, middle, upper-middle, and upper . . . but enough history, enough sociology, back to 47 Oakley Gardens, sometime in 1951, to the breakfast that followed my mortification on the lavatory, Daddy upstairs in bed with his tea, post and papers, Mummy now downstairs, flying about in her transparent nightie, cigarette hanging from the side of her mouth – but no, that's not the breakfast I'm after, it's a subsequent breakfast, some weeks or possibly even months later. She stalked into the dining room, head held high – an ominous sign – in her hands a plate for Nigel, a plate for me, she flung the plates down with a flourish, drew on her cigarette with a flourish, released a long cloud of smoke. 'That filthy man Hank Janson has run away,' she said. 'Did you know that?'

Impossible to describe the effect of those two words – Hank and Janson – coming from her lips. It was mysterious, omniscient, terrifying. How did she know? How? In retrospect, I can see that Mummy being my mother, and having heard from father Daddy about the presence of the book (he couldn't have seen the cover, given my posture) over which I'd been bent, with warm wings brooding, as the Jesuit poet, Gerard Manley Hopkins, once described his own solitary labourings – no, no, it was God in the poem, God who did the brooding, with warm wings, ah, my dear! Nothing to do with my sort of brooding at all, although some critics have hinted that the strain of Hopkins's celibacy might have given rise to the explosive, ejaculatory nature of his verse – now what was I? Oh, yes, Mummy and her 'That filthy man Hank Janson has run away!'

'Where to?' Nigel said at last, thus seeming to demonstrate not simply a lack of surprise, but the possibility of a vast reservoir of knowledge – at the very least of some of the circumstances that would have caused Hank to run.

'He's wanted for writing lewd and disgusting and obscene books,' our mother replied, at an angle to Nigel's question, 'wanted by the police.' And by me, too, for the same thing. She jabbed her cigarette at us, and left us to it.

There followed a brief squabble as to whose hoard she'd unearthed. 'Not mine,' said Nigel confidently, 'I've only got one, and it's behind the wardrobe, I've pushed it so far back I can hardly get at it myself.' He'd done this on purpose, he explained, because he was trying to give up Hank Janson because he was trying to get into the St Paul's rugger colts, and because he was preparing to take Communion. 'Well, it's not me,' I said, although it obviously was, my Jansons squirrelled into so many corners that Mother would have needed little inspiration to turn up one of them within a minute or so, once she'd decided to search –

or perhaps she always did a search, a routine search, but didn't grasp the significance of what she turned up until her husband reported to her what he'd observed of their son on the lavatory, and the *Daily Mail* reported to her that the writer Janson was on the run – these days, of course, he would have been protected by Index on Censorship, PEN, Amnesty International, Writers in Prison.

In fact, he made it to Spain. I know this because I sat next to his agent – he'd been my agent too, for a brief period – on a London bus one afternoon, about thirty-five years ago. I can't imagine the context in which Janson's name came up, we certainly didn't know each other well enough to trade information about our youthful sexual habits – anyway he told me that Janson had fled to Spain, where he had written novels about the Spanish civil war which always contained one scene of bondage, not of the former playful, fanciful kind, in which there was merely male dominance over sweetly rebellious femininity – the Spanish bondage was gritty, nasty, cruel – political, in other words – heroic Republican guerrillas, female rather than feminine (beautiful nonetheless), brutalized by Franco's thugs, beaten, raped, murdered – he (the agent) had been astonished by the change in tone and style, but the thing was, he said, that the passion in the politics was quite genuine – these novels, which he'd written under his real name – Stephen Francis or Francis Stephens – were serious works, properly researched and constructed, bits of dialogue in Spanish. One or two – I think he mentioned a trilogy – had been published in hardback. He still lived in Spain, prospered there in fact – it was where he'd always wanted to go, just as he'd always wanted to write the novels he was now writing, so actually he was grateful for his enforced exile, grateful that he'd been hounded out of the dark little office in Soho where he'd dictated the saucy and ebullient works of his early phase to a middle-aged woman who was now his wife – no, I don't believe this last bit, I've added it on to my memory of the conversation – why? – but that his amanuensis was middle-aged, yes, that makes perfect sense, I can accept that, though it's far more entrancing to think that she was in her twenties, sitting with her legs crossed, skirt hitched, stocking top visible, a blonde curl tumbling over her forehead, bent over her pad as her pen flies across the page – and Hank, his feet propped on his desk, hat tilted to the back of his head, cigarette hanging from the corner of his mouth (like Mummy), rapping out his sentences – 'fought like a wild cat' – 'her arms up behind her back' – 'bound them tightly together with the stockings I'd unclipped from her suspenders' – 'lay there on the floor, panting, eyes flashing fury' – 'stared down at the two softly heaving mounds' – 'gentle slopes of' – 'as she opened her mouth to scream I' – 'fastened it behind her neck with my –' he was a small man, the agent said, with crinkly brown hair, and I'll bet he married his secretary, whether the agent told me he did or not, and they live in a grand little villa outside Malaga, perhaps – I'm glad he came out on the Republican side, though the handcuffs aspect of his writing seems more falangist – but really there is probably little connection between a man's sexual obsessions and his political inclinations – think of Kenneth Tynan, a theatre critic of the sixties and seventies (twentieth century), a prominent supporter of all left-wing and libertarian causes, who devoted the last decade of his life to spanking women, thinking about spanking women, brooding endlessly about spanking women – but perhaps that is libertarian, though probably not left-wing, because whatever you think about spanking women –

– a few yards from where I'm sitting, writing this, is

AN UNTROUBLED MIND

a very fine-looking, stiff-backed old gentleman, with fine white hair and a calm and steady gaze. His smile is cryptic and serene. He is holding a magazine, which he now and then consults, but mainly his gaze is fixed ahead, making it seem not only calm and steady, but inward-looking, as if his past were some vast landscape that he can keep unfolded, his to survey and command. His wife is possibly younger than he, perhaps a decade younger, but then his stillness and nobly contemplative air make him seem ageless, while she looks as if she's been at the same age for most of her life – perhaps since she met him, took control of all the trivial problems of his days and nights – she's stout, stubby – yes, a little stub of a woman, with a small, ugly, determined face, hair cut brutishly short, her eyes bulging slightly, her brow dark and heavy – not exactly angry, rather furiously anxious – she has dreadful varicose veins, knobs of them on her calves, she stumps about in flip-flops, baggy shorts, tending to her seraphic husband, bringing him plastic cups of water, removing the magazine as soon as he loses interest in it, which is almost immediately, putting it back in his hands, helping him out of his chair and into another chair – tending, tending, furiously and anxiously tending, occasionally talking to him in abrupt sentences, sometimes with a whiny tone, sometimes eagerly, pointing out, for instance, that the hotel isn't a hotel, it's composed of small chalets, each one containing a bedroom and a bathroom and a balcony – he gives her a condescending and rather empty attention while she utters these imbecilities – after all, they are inhabiting one of the chalets themselves, and the one they inhabit must look pretty much like all the other chalets, how dare she disturb this distinguished consciousness to so little purpose, is the thought that goes through one's mind as off she goes, to find him an unwanted towel, or take his walking stick from the back of the chair, propping it beside him or putting it between his legs so that his hands can fold around its top – and then once or twice she presses affection on him – Victoria reports that she saw her once bend suddenly, while she was fiddling about his person, and kiss him full on the lips, then fiddle a bit more before kissing him fully on the lips again – this from a little dog of a stumpy woman to a man contemplating the eternities within – once I saw her take him by the hand and lead him gently to the edge of the lawn, then down the path that leads to the opening to the beach, then several yards across the sand, the two of them toddling hand in hand, it was most poignant, the childlikeness of it. I've just glanced over his shoulder as I passed (deliberately, I must admit) behind him and saw the cover of the magazine that he was holding passively in his lap. It's called *Bravo Spain*, and is evidently a travel/tourist publication, clearly without meaning to him, and it occurs to me that he has Alzheimer's, or one of its variants, and that all her dogged, furious tending, her changes of tone and sudden open and passionate and tender displays of affection are attempts to compensate externally for all he has lost, and no doubt is still losing within – how hopeless it all is, really, there's no getting away from it when one sees such things – the things people do to the very end and then past the very end – and, you know, I can't imagine them married, or young, or in middle age or even the year or so back when he started to go, and when I try, the question persists unworthily, 'Whatever did he see in her?' to which she provides the answer in virtually every one of her actions – if I look elsewhere there is affection to be seen among the many elderly couples in this hotel, hand-holding, caressing, and at night dancing to the unmusical bands and groups – a different one for each night of the week. – it's half past one in the morning, I am at my table, Rollocks is laying the breakfast tables, the sea growls and rustles a few yards away, and I wonder how Harold is. There was a piece in the paper this morning – Saturday – we get the papers here a day late, so it was Friday's *Times* or *Telegraph*, announcing that Harold had cancer of the oesophagus, and then giving a brief account of his life and achievements that read as if it were a compressed combination of a promotional release and an obituary – ghastly to come across it, even though I'd been warned by someone who phoned from London yesterday – I'm not going to write tonight, I shall sit here sipping my diet coke, smoke a cigarette, listen to the sea. First I shall write down one word at the beginning of the next line on my yellow pad, and start from there tomorrow. The word I shall write is –

BOOKS

Oh, yes. So books. What books? I left London in such disarray that I couldn't believe we'd get to the airport, let alone to Barbados – when it came to packing books I flung what was nearest to hand on to the bed for Victoria to pack, and then, of course, when she was unpacking them and I saw from our balcony all those ideal spots for reading – on the lawns, on the beach, in the bar where I'm writing this, on the balcony itself – well, there's a biography of Cardinal Richelieu, the only book I brought with some deliberation. I picked it up with pleasure until I twigged that I didn't want it at all, the book I'd chosen with a degree of consideration was the wrong book, I'm not in the slightest bit interested in Cardinal Richelieu (well, I am – but only the slightest bit), the chap I'm keenly interested in is Talleyrand, now and then Bishop Talleyrand, who began his political career by taking holy orders, receiving Voltaire's blessing almost simultaneously, and went on to survive the catastrophes of France, in fact could be found near the centre of the catastrophes of France from the end of the Ancien Régime through the revolution, through the Empire, then through the Restoration, then through the Republic – he should have been executed once or twice every decade – 'a shit in silk breeches,' Napoleon called him, perfectly accurately, it seems to me, but Napoleon ended up on St Helena, in the custody of a mean-spirited (or strait-laced, depending on your point of view) English civil servant while old Talleyrand was around to welcome Louis XVIII, Napoleon III, how did he do it, is what I want to know, how did he get away with it, playing with fire almost all his life, burning everybody but himself? Now this is a pathetic account of Talleyrand's life, everything I know about him has gone into a fog, which the book on him would have dispelled if I'd brought it, rather than the book on Richelieu, about whom I'm content to remain in a fog – in fact, apart from a general outline of his life, much muddled by my having seen four or five film versions of *The Three Musketeers*, about the only hard fact I remember is that he suffered from piles, towards the end of his life could scarcely rise from his bed, and when compelled to do so by reasons of state, would have to be carried. There is a very important book – that's what we say these days when wishing to draw attention to what we believe to be a good film, book, play, exhibition, we say that it's 'important', as, for instance, an 'important' new play by so and so (me, for instance), we usually say it in an important manner, our voices becoming grave, heavy, episcopal, so what exactly do I mean when I write that there is a very 'important' book about piles waiting to be written – I think I mean that piles might be found to have affected the course of history now and then – no doubt Richelieu, given his steely mind, his patience and his ambition, would have made the decisions he made if he'd been piles-free, but Napoleon at Borodino, a few hours before the battle which led on to the disaster of Moscow, lingering in his tent, hoping his piles would quieten down so that he could be out and about on his horse, which he couldn't bear to mount – you see how one could go on from there – for want of an ointment – there's one currently on the market called Anus-oil, or very nearly that, which is quite soothing, I believe – for want of a tube of Anus-oil the battle of Borodino was lost – drawn, actually, I think, but a strength-sapping draw, and so the unplanned diversion to Moscow – the rest is history. Yup. Now to move with piles into a different field, take Gary Cooper in *High Noon*, a film recognized as a complete turkey when it opened for try-out showings in the Midwest, audiences laughing, jeering, walking out as jaunty, heroic, sunny even, Gary Cooper strode down the streets of his little town, a parody of the classic Western sheriff – the reason he looked so implausible, however, was that all through the shooting he'd been crippled by piles – every step a torment, which he'd tried to disguise by assuming a bogus jauntiness whenever he could manage it – generally he could do one take in this mode, and that was the take the director felt obliged to use. Well, after the first try-out showings, and the public's response, the producers were in despair, should they can the whole affair and leave Gary Cooper to dwindle into the Hollywood twilight, another star who'd ended in a feeble and melancholy twinkling down? They repaired to the editing room to see if they could find any scenes that actually worked, hoping to build from there, useless, useless, all they had was Gary's piles-driven gait, simultaneously cramped and bow-legged, his face grimacing in agony, his eyes tortured – until somebody – either the director or the editor, though I suppose it might have been the producer – suddenly saw that in the problem lay the solution. They spliced all the scenes in which Gary's piles were at their most inflamed, and looked at what they'd got – the nobly tortured, stoically enduring sheriff that marked a significant if not actually an important turning point in the history of the Western – downhill, in my view, being the only person I know who found the film phoney and inflated on my first viewing and before I knew the facts, but my opinion is neither here nor there in this account, which is concerned with pointing out the crucial part played by piles in the transformation of the film from out-of-town turkey to an Oscars-all-round triumph, with a treasured place – allotted to it by the usual collection of people I'm inclined by nature to disagree with – in the history of the cinema, etc. – though it should be added that further acknowledgement must be made to the magical powers of the editing room, where they added the magnificent theme song sung by Tex Ritter, and the shots of the ticking clock – you can see that it's just been stuck in, the clock, because it's completely bald, so to speak, no human form comes near it, no shadow falls upon it, we just cut to it whenever the director needs to jack up the tension – but mainly the success of the film has to be attributed to Gary's piles, just as Napoleon's failure in Russia has to be attributed to piles – and there are many other stories to be unearthed, I truly believe – what about Coleridge's piles, for instance – discover if there's a connection between the piles, the laudanum and the great hallucinatory poems, 'Ancient Mariner', 'Kubla Khan' – the laudanum, taken to escape the pain from piles, giving him the hallucinations that inspired the poems – was the man from Porlock his dealer, possibly, come to report that his supply had run out, so no more inspiration, no more Kubla. I could go on in this vein –

Oh. I've just come back from a swim – as I was cavorting towards shore, doing my very favourite thing in life, rolling myself underwater, down and down, then bobbing up again, then lolling on my side for a while before dipping back down – I have many of the instincts, though none of the grace, of a porpoise, I believe – I saw a kindred spirit, a recumbent porpoise, toes turned up, arms stretched out, head cushioned on the water. It was the wife of the man with Alzheimer's, the Alzheimer widow, as I've come to think of her, not fussing and worrying and scowling, but taking her ease in the ocean, lolling to the manner born – she got out, quite a difficult manoeuvre on this beach, as there is a steep shelf, and the waves can tumble you about, mixing you into a rush of pebbles and sharp little rocks – but her sturdy, varicosed legs carried her up over the shelf onto the shore, where she picked up a stone, took aim, I thought at first at me, but she swung it well away, across an unpeopled patch of water, with accuracy and skill – it skipped and skipped, it must have done four long skips, then a sequence of shorter ones before going under. She watched it do this with close attention, then turned, and stumped off up the beach. The little incident gave me great pleasure, even more when I passed her a few minutes later, her damp head pressed on Mr Alzheimer's chest. He gazed smiling over her head, benignly unresponsive – then she set about sorting him out, pushing his sunglasses further up his nose, exchanging his magazine for a book, getting him a cup of water –

AUDEN BY MOONLIGHT

Almost the worst part of my book-packing was that I hadn't brought any poetry at all – apart from Ian's, that is, but Ian's is for another kind of reading, to do with him as much as his poems – Wordsworth and Hardy are the two poets I've especially wanted to read, and some Keats, I had a yearning for Keats and also Pope – so I phoned a friend in New York, and asked her to send an anthology, any anthology really that you can lay your hands on quickly, I said, it's really quite urgent, and this is what she sent – the *Oxford Book of English Verse*, edited by Christopher Ricks, which could hardly fail to serve the purpose, and which I now have before me on the table in the bar, and into which I have been dipping and delving for some hours – the last hour with some difficulty, as the electricity suddenly cut off, as it does from time to time in Barbados, and I've had to read by the light of the moon (a mere sliver), two candles, and an oil lamp, all furnished by Rollocks – well, the moon-sliver wasn't furnished by Rollocks, of course, he provided just the candles and the lamp, and frankly they didn't produce much in the way of illumination, more a smoky pool that drew to it moths and mosquitoes and other rubbish on wings, but I was so in need of poetry that I'd probably have made do with my lighter, and the glow from my cigarette – I started with Ricks's Preface and Introduction – I scarcely ever read prefaces and introductions to anthologies of poetry, assuming that the collection will make its own argument, no need to apologize or explain, here they are, these poems as opposed to those poems, have a good time – but this time – it was when we still had the electricity – I settled down to both, really settled, clamped on my glasses, lit a cigarette, put my elbow on the table, my left thumb on my left cheek – my en garde position for serious reading – and read. The preface was a two-minute job, but the introduction was the real thing, full of zing and zest, chirrupy, affable and informative, occasionally sinister into the bargain – he tells us to

admire Matthew Arnold for the way he 'made friends with the
necessity of death' for example, which reminded me of that chap in
Muswell Hill, or was it Crouch End, who kept the bodies of his
victims in his armchairs, and some of their heads in the fridge –
Nielsen, I think the name was – Ricks seems to have been around as
long as I have, reviewing here, there and everywhere, Professor of
English here (Cambridge), there (Oxford) and everywhere (Harvard,
Yale, Princeton etc.) – if I ever run into him I'll tell him how much
I like his selection, I've already come across lots of things I'm either not
familiar with, or had forgotten – the Hardy is very good, and the Keats,
but then there are a couple of poems at the end, by contemporaries, that
are – well, they're not terrible, exactly, not in themselves, but in the
company they're keeping they seem unworthy, well, worthless in fact –
friends of Ricks, perhaps? but on the other hand there's less Auden than
usual, even if there's still too much, but then any Auden is too much,
as far as I'm concerned – in fact it was while I was scowling down at
'Musée des Beaux Arts' that the lights went out, as if the hotel generator
were connected to my consciousness, which also went out as soon as it
encountered the first line – I used to nag away at Ian about it, 'About
suffering they were never wrong, the Old Masters' – how can you be
right or wrong about suffering? And as for 'the Old Masters' – well, the
old masters, whoever they were, were young, or anyway alive when
they painted their paintings, they weren't being old masters, or masters
of anything except the palette to hand, the canvas in front of them –
so I would nag away at Ian, hey, what about the horse at the end,
scratching its 'innocent' behind against a tree, what would a 'guilty'
behind be like? Well, let's not go into that, especially when discussing
Auden, keep focused on the horse, 'indifferent' to Icarus falling out of
the sky – but it wouldn't be indifferent, this horse, because it wouldn't
have seen – if you've ever looked at the Brueghel he claims he's writing
about you can see the horse not seeing – and not seeing is not at
all the same thing as being indifferent – and as for Auden in his bar
on 39th Street or whichever New York street he was on, brooding
on 'the low, dishonest decade' – decades can't be low or dishonest,
it's a crap historian's or journalist's phrase, OK between blinks but
falling apart the moment you bring a spot of attention to it, ask a few

questions – how does he rate himself in terms of lowness and dishonesty, as he sits in his bar on 39th Street, that's a question, a real poet's question, also what's he drinking, how much has he drunk, what about his friends – people he knows something about – what are they up to, where are they in fact, with the bombs about to fall, etc., and as for 'Stop all the Clocks', all I can say is it's the appropriate poem for the film, *Weddings and a Funeral* – no, that's not fair, the poem on the page isn't as bad as the poem in the film, the page poem is written as a blues number, it's got a real jump and beat to it, the film poem rolls out like a sermon, reverential and syrupy – and anyway, I've got to face it, almost everybody I like and a lot of people I admire, like and admire Auden, I used to admit as much as I nagged away at Ian, nagged frenetically away, even claiming once I had evidence to prove Auden was autistic – what evidence? Ian asked, – well, I said, he liked to pick his nose and eat it in front of people, and then, well, the poems! I said triumphantly, take 'In Praise of Limestone' and off I went – 'Actually, Auden stinks,' he said, out of nowhere, during one of our very last conversations, 'but his forms, you see, the way he could play about with forms' – and that was it, for him, as a practising poet there was an astonishing skill to be admired and studied. If you weren't a poet and were after meaning, sense and feeling you went to, for instance, Wordsworth on the one hand, Pope on the other, but if you had a technical interest in rhyme schemes, etc., for their own sake, and for the sake of your own practice, then Auden was worth your while – and so we left it at that, for the rest of his life, or at least of my time with him.

TERRITORIAL IMPERATIVES

It is raining – more accurately it's just finishing raining, all the colours washed out, the beach, the trees, the lawn, looking dun-coloured, drab. In spite of the rain the predators were down in the early hours, marking their beds and chairs with towels that are now soaking – but of course the old hands know that this doesn't matter, when the sun comes out the towels (they're green) will dry out in minutes and there will be their beds waiting for them, all prepared – we've had our own spot, at the back of the lawn, separated from the sea by a path and a low wall – not really a wall as the top is separated from the bottom by evenly spaced little pillars, which leave evenly spaced little gaps, through which you can see the sand, the sea, the rafts and boats, people swimming and of course those three prized spots, one of which I saw the old guy fussing over at 6.30 the other morning – I consider ours to be the best spot in the hotel, really, as you not only have this view in front, but also you can keep an eye on all the people on the lawn – and it's become accepted among the lawn community that these are our places, two beds, one low wooden table for Victoria's beach-kit, and a white stool-like table for my cigarettes and ashtray – yesterday a group of three arrived from London mid afternoon, and took the last three beds, which were directly behind us, OK beds but lacking our versatile view – there was something about them that made me immediately uneasy, a woman of about my age, small, and ginger-grey hair, a pretty freckled face with a shrewd and determined look to it – she had an orange hat which she put on and took off regularly, according to some plan to do with how much sun was good for her head and hair, but she seemed to be doing it almost to the minute, as if she'd worked it out mathematically – I pegged her as the ringleader, a woman of steely calculation, designated moves – beside her was a rather slovenly young woman – early forties, probably a daughter, wearing an unbecoming pink hat, cloche-shaped, that pushed her ears down – couldn't really see her face, she wears very large dark glasses, but her body, white, soft and formless, spills all over her bed, and her green bikini bottom has a touch of the nappy about it – there is also a useless-looking man, husband and father, I assume, who comes and goes to report on his success or failure in accomplishing missions appointed by the other two – he came back to say to the daughter that he hadn't been able to find her sunscreen, went off to look for it again in the small zip bag to be found, the mother said, on a shelf in the cupboard, that's where she thought she'd put it, had he thought to look there – he was already on his way. When Victoria and I went for a swim the mother was training her gimlet eyes on a book – I couldn't catch the title, it blends too much into the background design of the cover – but as I say I had my doubts, my suspicions, and cast a look back at them as we stepped on to the sand, and again just before we plunged into the sea – a lovely swim, lovely and long, out to the rafts, towards the next hotel along, an unhappy-looking place, on the skids I bet, with only one bed occupied, listless waiters standing with their trays hanging down by their sides, and then back to our beach, sliding under the moving ropes for the buoys – I'm very bad at this, always misjudging, coming up so the rope scrapes my back or catches my heel, infuriating as I'm mildly allergic to the algae that accumulate on the rope, and so get stripy little rashes on my back and heels. It's inexplicable, as I swim easily under water, love to be there, under water, and it's also infuriating because Victoria glides under them with a few effortless movements of the hips and arms – it's to do with my being over-buoyant (stomach full of bubbles from diet cokes, probably), I should force myself to dive deeper, not just go a few inches under as I immediately, but without realizing it, bob a few inches back up – but going under the ropes, even when there's a stingy rash to show for it, is part of the fun – so out we came from the sea, full of high spirits and the joys of the sea, had a brisk shower under the palm tree and then sauntered across the lawn to our beds, where I noticed immediately my small, white stool-type table had gone, the ashtray lying upside down on the grass, contemptuously discarded. Of course, my cigarettes and lighter, my personal markers, I'd left on the table at the bar, so theoretically, legally, down to the meanest letter of the law, but against every conceivable spirit of it, I had no clear entitlement, beyond the fact that every one of the lawn's occupants knew that the table was lodged in our territory, and belonged to us – specifically to me – I looked towards the group behind, straight at the boss, and then at the small, stool-type table placed where no small, stool-type table had been placed before – there was a tall full glass on it, a straw in it – then looked again at the boss. She had her orange hat on, her eyes, lifted from the book, stared straight at mine, unblinkingly bold, not to say hard, her lips twitched imperceptibly, her eyes went back to her book, fastened there, as with her free hand she lifted her orange hat from her head and put it beside her drink.

So. So I knew. I told Victoria I knew. This morning I rose at half past seven (thinking 'but what's the use?'), peered down from the balcony through the rain, and saw draped over the backs of our beds three green towels. On the white stool of a table was a small bag, presumably waterproof, and on the other table, the small wooden one, some tubes of sun lotion. I trudged through the rain to some beds further down, laid the three green towels on the two beds and the chair, put down some unreadable paperbacks (literally, they've been used so often as markers, on wet days and dry, that now the pages are stuck together, saving them from being found unreadable for the usual reasons), trudged back to the room, dried myself, joined Victoria in bed, where I lay with my arm under her sleeping head – thinking on the one hand of Auden's utterly ghastly 'Lay your sleeping head, my love/Human on my faithless arm' – what is 'human' doing here, what other kind of head would his love have – better not go into that – 'faithless arm' – '*faithless* arm'!, etc. (the worst thing about Auden, I'm coming to realize, is that his lines stick – how come I can quote reams of him, and only fragments of Hardy? And then to misquote Eliot!) and on the other hand how to punish the squatters on our rightful beds, in a hotel where no dog-turds are available owing to an absence of dogs – but there is a cat – a nice cat, marmalady, but a touch withdrawn – and, oh, monkeys – there are monkeys at the top of the garden, by the tennis courts, but wouldn't I arouse suspicion if I were to be seen scraping up monkey turds? especially if they turn up later under the green towels of the squatters.

I'm looking at them now, orange hat, pink hat and useless husband, sitting in a row, in our places, facing the sea, reading their books – almost certainly trashy books, from the rapt expressions on their faces – pink hat has just taken off her pink hat, to release a pack of hair so coarsely and bogusly ginger that it must be natural, nobody could do that to their hair deliberately, not at that sort of age, in this sort of hotel –

Mrs Alzheimer is sitting a bit behind them; she is doing a watercolour. Mr Alzheimer is sitting bolt upright beside her, his face wearing its usual expression. On his feet, a pair of enviable blue canvas shoes, beneath them natty white socks that come up to just above his ankles. He has nothing to read in his hands, which are folded calmly into his lap. I think she is talking as she dabs her brush onto the pad. I think I'll get up and stroll behind them, perhaps I'll hear a snatch –

Of course I couldn't loiter, so I only got one sentence. 'Well, why don't you work at it then?' she said, quite ill-naturedly, but I couldn't tell whether she was talking to Mr Alzheimer or herself. I must find Victoria. Time for a swim.

NEWS FROM HOME

I'm a bit shaken. Distressed would be a better word. This afternoon was mainly more rain until about 4.30, when the rain stopped, the sun almost came out, we were thinking of another swim when the telephone rang. It was the receptionist to ask if I was Simon Gray. I said I was. There was a package, she said, just delivered by FedEx. I went down and collected it, puzzled – disconcerted even – the only person who would FedEx me a package of anything would be my agent, Judy Daish, and she would certainly have phoned to tell me it was on its way, and furthermore have told me what was in it – anyway I'd asked her not to be in touch unless she had some good news, which means, if you think about it from another angle, that I'd been in receipt of a steady flow of bad news –

The package was, in fact, a large, brown envelope, which contained a small white envelope in which there was a letter from Harold. He was writing in response to my letter of a week or so ago – tapped it out on his Olympia portable, he said in his opening sentence, warning me of typos and spelling mistakes to come – it is a page and a half long, and on a separate sheet of paper there is a lovely poem by Alan Ross called 'An old man looks at a cricket match'. The first part of the letter contains a few comments about this and that in my letter and then comes at the centre of the letter, at the heart of it, an account, a terrible account of the state of his health, a concentrated paragraph of pain and bewilderment, typed out on his Olympia portable, with poignant little typos but all his misspellings corrected, the words crossed out xxxx and rewritten –

Now I must tell myself that Harold has not tapped out on his Olympia portable an announcement of his death. He has merely put down, with characteristic clarity, the ordeal that he is undergoing at the moment – the fact that he cannot eat properly, cannot drink (even water) properly, that trying to do either causes him great discomfort, and is sometimes physically impossible. The sentence that most disturbs me – us – Victoria and myself – is that his doctors are completely baffled that this condition should have returned, and more ferociously than before.

I shall stop now. I might go on with this in the morning. I might not – when it comes to it, there isn't much to say – the thing about a close and long friendship – friendship, what an odd word that suddenly looks, as I write it down. Friendship.

SHIP AND HOOD

So that's the word I see when I sit down at the table this morning. Friendship. Looks more normal in the daylight, flowed easily out of the nib, and so I can put down brotherhood, and look at it. Hood, what does it mean, the hood in brotherhood. Well, I suppose the ship in friendship has something to do with making – it has an Anglo-Saxon feel to it, *schiffen* or *schlippen* to do with making, could it be? – I was very bad at Anglo-Saxon, considering it a waste of time because it involved a lot of learning, no chance at all of flannelling through the exam, which, as a consequence I nearly failed (this was at Dalhousie University, Nova Scotia). I wish now – as is always the way with these things – that I'd worked at it, so that I could, for instance, know rather than guess that the word *schiffen* means to make, or is a past participle, made – and so avoid having to check it when I get home – I don't believe I'll be able to get hold of an Oxford Concise here at the hotel – so I'll have to settle for the guess, and turn my attention to the hood in brotherhood, about which I haven't a clue – fatherhood, motherhood, brotherhood – sisterhood – other words with hood as a suffix, I can't come up with a single one, but then I am in Barbados, the morning is balmy, my mind a muddle of passingly agreeable thoughts, and dark ones lodging deeply – hood, hood, come on, come on – riding hood, Little Red Riding Hood, why would a little girl walking through the woods to visit her granny be wearing a riding

hood, and what is a riding hood – in as much as I can visualize it, I see
it as dark and sinister, as sported by the four horsemen of the Apocalypse,
for instance, or the Ku Klux Klan, is there something in the story I'm
failing to remember, an explanation of Red Riding Hood's wearing
a red riding hood, it can't be that Hood is her surname, Red and Riding
her Christian (given, they try to compel us to say, these days, in case
we offend a Muslim) names – highly unlikely, Red is a name for Irish-
American baseball players, Riding as a middle name? Well, I suppose it's
possible, no odder than my own, come to think of it, Holliday, though
actually Holliday is my third name, not my middle name, Simon James
Holliday Gray is how it goes, so Simon James Holliday Riding Gray? I
like it – Simon James Riding Holliday Gray? – but it's a translation, isn't
it, now I come to think of it, it has a German or Slavic or Scandinavian
feel to it – the woodsman, the granny – Grossmutti? – the wolf, the wolf
waffle, no, that was Luftwaffe, wolves come into the Nazis somewhere,
I'm sure of it – no good going on with this, again wait until I get home,
there'll be a book, quite a few books, no doubt, giving the antecedents
of nursery stories, as well as all kinds of analyses, Freudian, etc. –
disclosing what the wolf really intends when he says, ' All the better to
eat you with, my dear' to L.R.R. Hood, or Ms Hood – abandon these
futile speculations and take the full word 'brotherhood' in all the
meanings it has for you, leave it at that, which is quite enough.

But of course I've started thinking about Piers, over a decade
younger than Nigel and me, and dead – how long is it now? four years,
five years, that long? The unfairness of it. Though what is fairness – On
the day that he was born –

Born. Whenever I remember it, it's always in a slack sort of way, Nigel
then about twelve, myself ten and a bit. We're playing cricket on the
pavement outside the house, and my mother – *our* mother – comes out.
She is wearing a hat, looking elegant and in a hurry. She stops, though,
to announce with a smile that she has just given birth to a baby boy, we're
going to call him Piers, isn't that exciting news, now she's off to meet
Daddy, we haven't seen each other for a long time – this is how the scene
idles through my mind, and though it's self-evidently wrong, it's always
seemed right enough in feeling – actually, as I think about it properly, I
now see that it's a conflation of two memories, the later one, to do with

the announcement of Piers's birth, mixed up with the early one, when I was about four and a half, Nigel six and three quarters therefore – we're playing in the snow outside our grandparents' house in Montreal, 4047 Vendôme Avenue, our aunt Gertrude is in attendance somewhere but I can't see her in memory, all I see clearly is Mummy, dressed in her fur coat, carrying a small suitcase, walking hurriedly past us, her face averted. We ran over to her, she stopped, we asked where she was going, she said she was going to get some milk, she really couldn't stop, she said, smiling a smile that meant something terrible, and off she went. Then we were told by Gertrude to go inside, where Grandma was waiting to tell us that the milk, so to speak, was back in England, with Daddy. Gertrude was a small, thin, wiry woman, with a sharp voice, often irritable or exasperated, doing her best against the grain of her temperament and possibly ambitions, to look after her brother's two children, for whom she had little natural affection, I suspect, but towards whom she had a strong sense of duty. Grandma, apart from being short, was quite the opposite, a roly-poly, playful, laughing – sometimes hysterically laughing – magnificat of a grandmother, who perpetually sucked peppermints (to conceal the sherry on her breath, I now know), who adored me, and whom I adored being adored by. She used to tickle me until I nearly fainted, bundle me about the bed, and hold me into her breasts, enveloping me with her wonderfully pepperminty smell, with its magic additive – Grandpa.

Stopped there this morning. Can't write tonight. Too much of the sun, though of course I sat in the shade as always, but then I must have spent a total of two hours in the sea, the sun beating down on an unprotected and salty head, so I'll just sit for a while, drink a diet coke, smoke a few cigarettes, go to bed. Try not to think too much. Probably can't anyway. The inside of my head feels soft and thoughtless, with a muzzy ache going round its rim. Leave a space for tomorrow. Then Grandpa.

*

GRANDPA THEN

He was in his late sixties when we came to Canada. He was short, he had sticking-out ears, he was bow-legged, he always had his hair crew-cut, bristly grey it stood in a bundle of stubbles straight up from his head. His Scots accent was still as strong as the day he and his wife – good God, I've just this second realized I don't know Grandma's Christian name, let alone her maiden name – anyway, they left Greenock for Canada at the turn of the century. He was a personal secretary to a steel mogul, working in Toronto, or was it Ottawa? from Monday to Friday, returning to Vendôme Avenue late on Friday night, an event much dreaded by me as I occupied his bedroom, and he would carry me from his bed to a sofa in the sitting room, which I found frightening, or to loving slaps and tickles on Grandma's bed, which I found entirely satisfactory, of course, especially snuggling into the doting comfortableness of her – the dread was of the actual removal, the rough, almost violent picking-up, the stiff, indifferent carrying, as if I were logs, the abrupt dropping down – joltingly, if it was on to the sofa, more complicatedly unpleasant, if on to Grandma's bed, never near her, but at the foot, or on the side, in both cases close to the edge. There was no communication between us that I recall, no warning before he jerked me from sleep, no warning before he dropped me –

The truth is – was – that poor old Grandpa wasn't wanted in the marital, and I was, and it was a shortish journey from the sofa to his marital, and my little legs made it often, and what did he have but his bachelor's bed, kept insultingly warm for him by me. He tried his best, though, during the short weekends and vacations, to be a Grandpa, taking us on Saturday mornings to a palatial soda fountain, for ice-cream sodas and milkshakes, and spending half-hours with us in the garden on Sundays, throwing baseballs and Canadian footballs to us – probably rather stingingly now and then when throwing to – at – me. He was a gruff man, reserved, seething with unreleased energy, his bow-legged gait rapid and forceful, 'full of vim', as Grandma used to say, with one of her long, tipsy giggles – well, of course he was full of it, with nowhere to put it, being Scots, Presbyterian, faithful, honourable, etc. – except once, into me, with a strap. He'd been in some other room – his bedroom, perhaps, lying, staring at the ceiling, no, no, it was evening, that was the point, a Saturday evening, past my bedtime, I was frolicking on the bed with Grandma, the game being that she would order me to bed, i.e. the sofa, I would pretend to go, then dart back, slide under the bed, reappear where least expected, allow her to catch me and tickle me into helplessness, be ordered to bed – we were at it for hours, it must have seemed to Grandpa, tormenting hours for him, blissful for me, and jolly, jolly, jolly for old Grandma, the wife he was never not in love with, every second of his life since he'd clapped eyes on her at a Greenock bus stop. He erupted into the room, wielding a strap. He seized me by the nape of my neck, ran me into our shared bedroom where he swung me about with one hand, flailed at me with the strap with the other, yelping out half-sentences to do with teaching me to go to bed when I'm told – time I learnt – Grandma stood at the door, swaying, pleading, crying out with the blows that it was her fault, we were only playing, stop James, please stop – and Gertrude, shocked and silent, grappling with different duties and devotions – to the nephew to which she was an unwilling guardian, to a father she revered, to a brother she worshipped – of course, I didn't really know what she was grappling with, didn't know then (too busy with yelps, screams and sobs of my own) and I don't know now. She'd had a fiancé, a pilot shot down in the first year of the war, but the only photograph she ever showed us was of herself and our father, children at a lake, both grinning in bathing suits that in her case really looked like a suit, he in one with straps over his shoulders – Gertrude gave us our breakfast, lunch and tea, took us to the doctor and the dentist, walked us in our early days to school, read to us in our early days at bedtime, but of Gertrude I know almost nothing – in fact I don't know even that she was an unwilling guardian, she might have come to care for us deeply as Mummy sometimes claimed, when feeling called upon to defend the decision to take us to Montreal after war had been declared and when the U-boats were freshly on the rampage, and then to bring us back just before the war's end, when the U-boats were still on the rampage, but the question here, whether our parents wanted us back or Gertrude and our grandparents wanted us gone, I no longer have a hope of answering. Mummy in later life propounded one or the other, according to her mood – 'No wonder they wanted to get rid of you, is *this* how you behaved?', sometimes separated by no more than a few sentences from 'We had to risk bringing you back when we did, we were missing out on your childhood, you see,' her eyes filling with tears, her voice shaking with what often turned out to be laughter so that – so that really –

Grandpa taught me to swim in the lakes one summer, when I was five. He'd taught Nigel in the summer the year before. That summer he taught me. Held me firmly under my stomach, encouraged me to kick and to strike out with my arms – this wasn't for graceful or stylish swimming, strictly functional, for survival. The moment when he let me go and I didn't for once flounder and sink, but remained in the water, held up by my own mysterious forces and moving an inch or two was the most ecstatic of my life. So Grandpa gave us our swimming, Gertrude gave us our reading, Grandma gave me all the love I needed – and more. 'All you can eat – and more!' reads the sign outside some of the hamburger joints in the States – but the comparison doesn't hold, to be offered more hamburgers than you can eat induces nausea. More love than you need – well, there's no such thing, in a Grandma's case, my Grandma's case. My appetite grew by what it fed on, needing more cuddles, rollings about on the bed, swallowings up in round flesh and rich pepperminty and something else smells – and a jealous Grandpa to boot.

We were sent back to England some months before the war ended, but I remember almost nothing about it – of the leave-taking, last cuddles, etc., nothing of the trip to New York, or of being put on the boat by Grandpa and Gert, of the journey itself nothing, until I come to my mother's face, appalled, as she took in the two thugs, crew-cut, ears sticking out, with Canadian accents, who'd come back in place of the English moppets she'd checked up on outside 4047 Vendôme Avenue, on her way to get the milk.

From Grandma, Grandpa and Gert we got Christmas cards and birthday cards, five dollars inserted, until we'd grown up. I visited them once when I was in my early twenties, stopped by for lunch on my way from London to Halifax, Nova Scotia. Grandma was in her mid-seventies, and though there was no question of my getting any rollings about on the bed, or ticklings and hysteria, there was still something in her eyes when she looked me over from top to toe, and then took my hands in hers and gave them a long, suggestive squeeze. 'Oh, I can tell from these you're a writer,' she said, 'these have never done a day's work in their life, and don't intend to.' And she turned her round, shiny old face up towards mine, and laughed into it a great gust of peppermint and what I could now identify as sherry, which made me feel quite dizzy, really, and a little loose at the knees. Apart from that, I don't think she spoke much. Grandpa sat at one end of the table in the kitchen, I sat at the other, his two women sat between, one on either side, though Gert didn't do much sitting, she either served, or stood waiting to serve, a Black Cat or a Craven A held between fingers that trembled. Her face was gaunt, her eyes sunk, her voice hoarse, she seemed very ill, but of course I didn't know her well enough to ask after her health. Grandpa and I did most of the talking, he asking thoughtful, Scots-type questions in his strong Scots accent about the make of the aeroplane I'd flown in from London, the state of the English economy, which I answered with lies and guesses and other Cambridge mannerisms. I didn't think of how he'd once thrashed me with his belt – perhaps he did, though, and wistfully. The three of them died a couple of years later, within months of each other, from unrelated illnesses, although they were probably connected deaths in the sense that whichever had gone first would have been the crucial prop removed, the other two would follow, of necessity. Gert was the first, of cancer, in her early fifties, Grandpa next at eighty-six – working almost until he died, his employers under the impression that their Scots dynamo was still in his sixties; then Grandma of liver, I suppose, a bit more lingeringly and expensively than the other two, although Grandpa's life savings were almost entirely used up on Gertrude's medical bills, which were enormous – he must have believed that property was theft, or a waste of capital, or provided career-debilitating security, anyway, for whatever reason, he rented every house they lived in, including 4047 Vendôme Avenue, and he died penniless. Grandma's bills in a nursing home were paid for by their son, my father, who, having moved back to Canada himself (Halifax, Nova Scotia), was able to afford them. I suddenly find myself remembering other stuff about our time in Montreal, to do with Gert and her Black Cat which was cork-tipped, and about smoking, that I was a heavy smoker in Montreal by the time I was seven, but I don't have the desire this evening – a lovely evening, sun hovering before sinking, a light breeze, the sea a trifle turbulent from an earthquake somewhere or other, I'm going down to the beach.

Just back. The red no-swimming flags are up. I decided to ignore them in favour of a bit of rough and ready surfing, using my stomach as a surfboard, well, surf-tub, getting a kind of bum's rush onto the beach, where I rolled onto my front, heaved myself to my feet, lunged back into the waves. I did it lots and lots of times. Then saw in today's (yesterday's) *Telegraph* a review of Harold's sketches at the National, in one of which he also performed – reviewer said Harold had lost a lot of hair, looked frail, had also lost some of his commanding presence – was this necessary? Could he not simply have reviewed the sketch, with a courteous nod to his acting? but today's today, even in yesterday's *Telegraph*, and we don't do that these days.

SIGNIFICANT SPEECH

The dreadful thing about this most necessary (so I believe) holiday, is that I can't afford it. I'm overdrawn at the bank, in debt all over the place, have pretty well no income. On the other hand I don't really mind. Some years back I would have minded. But some years back I could have afforded it. Even the bar bill, when I was a four-bottles-of-champagne a day man. But that was some years back. Now I don't have a bar bill, worth speaking of. But even though it's not worth speaking of (diet cokes, fruit juices now and then) I can't afford it. But as I don't mind, why think about it? Think instead about the –

Alzheimers, really? What about them? Yes, the thing is that there they were, the two of them, this late afternoon, sitting at the far end of the bar, where it opens out to an expansive view of the sea, the waves crashing a few feet below, against the rocks and the wall. They were facing another couple, elderly, English, with a table not exactly between, because the other couple were sitting at it, the Alzheimers quite a bit away from it, which gave the impression that the Alzheimers, formal and stiff, were being interrogated. Or that they were doing the interrogating. My plan (which I executed) was to drift around them in a roundabout fashion, picking up any audible scraps of chat. I had to get quite close to hear anything, as the sea was loud, the voices low and the conversation, when the non-Alzheimers were speaking, free flowing, unstructured, and when you could hear it nearly meaningless. In fact, the first sentence I understood was spoken by Mrs A. Her voice had a bark to it – her social voice, I suppose – and she has a tendency to 'ink' her 'ings', as for example, now, as she said: 'You weren't thinkink of stayink there, then?' They chattered back that no, they'd had a good look around, it hadn't suited them, but they'd liked the pool, the grounds – obviously all this about a hotel that's recently opened to incredulous applause on the island – applause because it's smart, handsome, comfortable, etc. and so forth. Incredulous because it's plonk in the middle of Barbados, miles from the sea, and who wants to be in Barbados if you can't be up to your waist within minutes of leaving your room – 'I wouldn't stay there,' said Mr A, in a clear judicious voice, 'not if I can be staying here. All this –' he gestured with his stick, stiffly but quite dramatically towards the vast and billowy etc., over the rim of which the sun etc. – 'all this! *And* we've got a pool,' he stabbed upwards with his stick – 'into the bargain.' Mrs A looked at him with controlled lasciviousness. 'That's right, he didn't like it at all, did you, Humphry?' Humphry, whose accent I now identified as Canadian, confirmed that no, not at all, he hadn't liked it, wouldn't stay there for a single night. 'Nice lunch, though,' he added, 'worth going for a lunch.' So. So. Mr Alzheimer hasn't got Alzheimer's. Not only is he capable of speech, he's capable of opinionated speech. Of course, the fact that he's Canadian might have given rise to the misunderstanding, in that one sometimes feels, not that Canadians can't remember, but that they look and behave (some of them only, of course, and even they only sometimes) as if they haven't got that much to remember – not burdened by too much history (Europe), nor animated by too much aspiration (USA) might be a rush-to-judgement historian's way of looking at Canadians, though about the quickest, funniest, wisest man I know is Canadian – though actually he's Jewish, his name is Louis Greenspan and basically he comes from Poland – his father was a rabbi who specialized in circumcision (he developed the knack shortly after arriving in Halifax, Nova Scotia, and discovering that there was a shortage of rabbis in this field) – in 1938 he was only just restrained by members of his family from returning to Poland because he'd had enough of Canadian anti-Semitism – which doesn't mean that he preferred the German variety, only that he hadn't much of a nose for the future. But to get back to Humphry – no, there's nothing to get back to, really, except an entirely fresh burst of speculation – Humphry is a super-rich Canadian recovering from a stroke – how about that? suits the rearranged facts – and his wife, the late Mrs Alzheimer, is probably, given her displays of almost gloating physical affection, only recently his bride – so Humphry is a widower, and she – given also the impression she conveys of long familiarity – possibly an employee – secretary, perhaps? Long-time nurse of the long-time ailing now defunct first Mrs Humphry – or – or – well, there's another guest we should take a look at, turned up this morning in a red cap, white blouse, red pantaloons, red woollen socks, and black sandals – turned up on the beach in this outfit, a man of about fifty, a New Yorker from the sound of him, and quite definitely the sort of chap most easily described by the sort of word one isn't allowed to use any more – faggoty, queer, pansy, etc. – there are distinctions between them, I know, but he sort of blends them all together – oh, hag-fag probably gets it all in a hyphenated one, as he hangs out with a dwarfish and dour middle-European lady, who a few days ago was hanging about with a young – well, much younger than she is – rather jolly woman whom one would have taken for her niece if they hadn't spoken to each other in English, with thick but distinctly different accents – hag-fag, by the way, had a natty little camera with him, which he pressed into the hands of one of the waiters, then perched himself on the wall, the sea behind and virtually under him, and posed for a picture of himself. Just himself. In his red socks, black sandals, red pantaloons, white blouse, red cap – his hag abandoned under a palm tree on the beach – I'm going to stop this. I'm coming to the end of the pad, we go home the day after tomorrow (Monday) so I shall leave the remaining page open for last-minute pensées – or leave it blank, perhaps.

As Mr A passed me in the bar after lunch he pointed with his stick to the ice bucket which contained a bottle of water, and said, 'I can see you're a man who knows how to live,' thus reviving memories of myself of six years ago, sitting at the same time of day with a bottle of champagne in the bucket. Mrs A was nowhere in sight. So Mr A from immobile and mute, to garrulous and roaming. I found more grace and nobility in him when he had Alzheimer's.

When I was changing into my swimming trunks in the bedroom, I caught my naked self in the mirror. Great stomach drooping, like a kangaroo's pouch, though without the opening at the top, thank God – when I stretched my arms out, their pits seemed to have dewlaps, or would wattles be the word? Old. Old's the word.

Came across a discarded section of *The Times*, several days out of date – a medical supplement, in this issue dealing with cancer of the oesophagus, Harold's cancer. Horrible reading – hideous statistics. Hope Harold doesn't come across it, or he'll think he's a goner. Why would they publish statistics of that sort – presumably the medical profession knows them, and current and future patients will be demoralized by them – they certainly can't be helpful, can they?

Every night there's a lizard, light grey lizard, about three inches long, on the wall of our terrace, chasing a black moth around the lamp. Every night they go around and around the lamp, in loose, zigzaggy circles.

Beside me on the table as I write this last sentence on the back of the last page of the pad, there is an envelope addressed to Rollocks containing some money and a note thanking him for looking after me. I add that I look forward to seeing him next year. Well –

PART TWO

LAST CIGARETTES

Well, here I am, back in London, dizzy and faint from jet lag, or possibly from all the usual remedies, etc. that Victoria has pressed on me to counteract jet lag, or possibly from all the cigarettes I've smoked to make up for the cigarettes I couldn't smoke from the time we passed through security at Barbados airport to the time we got out of Gatwick – a matter of twelve hours, most of them spent conscious, not smoking – most odd that I never mind, in fact scarcely notice, not smoking when I'm officially forbidden from doing so, but the moment I'm a free man I smoke virtually double to make up for the long period of obedience. Ian was probably killed by cigarettes, a fate he accepted stoically enough – a wry shrug, a little grunt of laughter – until it was on him. Even then he accepted the logic of it, as a natural consequence of a self-destructive and therefore unnatural habit, but to the end he couldn't or wouldn't stop. Another friend of mine, another close, good friend died from cigarettes – emphysema, in his case – but he tried to stop as soon as he became ill – he spent the six or seven years in which his lungs shrivelled fighting, and losing, the battle against his addiction, thinking that it would follow the same pattern as his battle against alcohol, in which he'd ultimately triumphed – a heroic tussle, it had been, his tussle against alcohol, entailing many squalid capitulations along the way – he was a great presence for me when I had to stop drinking for ever, never ever patronizingly the forerunner, always treating me as I longed to be treated, as the only man who'd ever had to give up alcohol – so he died dry, sober, full of hatred for the old drinking self that had wasted twenty years of his life, and still waging a pitiful last campaign against his smoking self – giving up on his deathbed. It was a chosen death, as a matter of fact, he was offered either a few months lingering helplessly, rasping out short, stabby breaths, or a double or so ration of morphine and an immediate release. It was a decision he made in clear consciousness, to that extent an enviable death, but it was slightly marred, in my view, by his wife's odd sense of style. As he was slipping from the scene, she pressed into one hand a glass of whisky, and between the fingers of the other, a lighted cigarette, thus turning him in the last moments of his life, when too enfeebled to resist but still conscious enough to be aware, into an advertisement for the two things that had destroyed his life. Though I suppose if he'd been photographed and circulated, he might have served as the ghastliest of warnings – look what I've done to myself, and with both hands – she described the doing of it, the getting of the lighted cigarette between his fingers, the curling of his fingers around the glass – she'd poured the whisky in after she'd got the glass firmly settled, she said – I asked her with what tenderness I could muster why she'd done it, well, she said, well, that's how she remembered him in his heyday, when she first met him (both in their mid-forties, divorced, with children), for her he'd been the most glamorous, flamboyant, chain-smoking, whisky-guzzling – and that's how she'd go on thinking of him, that's how he'd like to have gone out, didn't I think so? 'He wouldn't have been seen dead –' I wanted to say, but couldn't, as actually he had been, pretty well – also she was brimming with grief, exhilarated with it, as people sometimes are when they assist a loved one to cross the line, and she had a theatrical background (her father had been famous in musical comedy) and so what could I say – well, volumes, really, but I didn't, hoping that a brief silence would also be a deep and eloquent one. 'I knew you'd approve,' she said, confirming Wittgenstein's remark, which I usually think is nonsensical, that our understanding of the world depends on the way we interpret the silence around us. And mine wasn't even around her, it went down the telephone line, straight at her. But can we say that she misinterpreted it, and thus failed to understand the world, or at least the world inasmuch as I wanted her to understand it, hence *my* world? Am I saying that she misunderstood my world because she failed to understand my silence? But can a silence be mine, or yours, or his or hers, surely a silence down the telephone is the telephone's silence, open to any interpretation, and she decided to interpret the telephone silence in terms of her world (i.e. her grieving impulse to create a glamorous last image of her dying/dead husband) which leads me to assume that *he* must have been silent when she arranged the cigarette and the drink in his hands, incapable one assumes of vocal consent or protest – El Cid springs to mind here, strapped dead on to his horse to lead the charge that drove the Muslims from Spain, played in the film, both dead and alive, by Charlton Heston, who defined the distinction between these two states by being noisy when alive, mute when dead, but actually more eloquent dead than when alive – and you could say that my friend was eloquent in death, but it wasn't his own eloquence, it was his wife's, who offered it up for an interpretation that I completely understood and that I could meet only with a silence of my own which she completely failed to understand but assumed she'd interpreted correctly – though think of it this way, if she'd asked me to interpret my own silence with a simple question, i.e., 'Why are you being silent, Simon?' most likely I'd have said, 'Oh, I'm only being silent because – because um – I can't think of anything to say – um – just thinking – imagining him there – dying, dead, a cigarette between his – and a glass of Scotch, was it, why Scotch, by the way? His drink when he drank was vodka or gin, though admittedly when those weren't available anything alcoholic would do, I remember his breakfasting once off the dregs of his last bottle of gin and about a quarter of a pint of port, mixed into a coffee mug –' and so from there we would have escaped from the attempt to understand each other's world through the interpretation of each other's silences, by swapping anecdotes about the beloved dead when in his heyday as a smoker and a drinker. *Requiescat.*

All of the above was written – and is being written – onto a yellow pad by a Cross ballpoint pen (pleasantly heavy) held, in the classic handwriter's grip, between the thumb and forefinger of my right hand – which brings to mind Keats's astonishing line from 'The Fall of Hyperion, A Dream', I think it is – 'When this warm hand my scribe is in the grave'. In my case it is likely to be dead in the grave because, in my left hand, held between the two middle fingers in the classic smoker's grip, is a cigarette. But of course I smoke with my right hand when it's not busy with a pen. So I'm killing myself with both hands, although not simultaneously, I'm glad to say . . .

*

My mother died of cancer when she was fifty-eight. She began to be ill on the first night of my first play, and died during the last week of its run. In accordance with her instructions – 'If I get ill, my dear, I don't want to know that I'm going to die until it's all over!' – she was led to believe that she was suffering from an entirely predictable recurrence of her war-time tuberculosis, and that with rest and patience she would soon be back on the tennis court – she was a formidable player, even in her fifties, smoking not only between sets but between games, and sometimes – when she was serving – during them. (In Halifax she'd taught the young ladies of Dalhousie University how to play hockey, had raced up and down the pitch wielding a hockey stick, occasionally removing the cigarette from her mouth to blow the whistle which hung around her neck – it was an extraordinary and famous spectacle, from which Nigel and I, both students, used to avert our eyes as we hurried past to the library or lectures) – well, as I was saying, when she was dying she was told all that was needed was what was needed the first time she had tuberculosis, patience and rest – though every so often when she was in the middle of a lively sentence, there was a look in her eyes, vague and appalled – the words would stop and she would lie back, – her arms and legs had become sticks, her face gaunt, her eyes sunk, and her stomach – 'My dear, how ridiculous! I look pregnant!' – but she maintained her belief that she would shortly become well right up to the last days, when she was given enough morphine to keep her either comatose or hallucinatory. In one of her last lucid spells she said, 'I'll tell you one thing, Si, I've learnt my lesson! I'm never going to smoke another cigarette.'

My father never learnt his. He died in the same hospital – Charing Cross – under the supervision of the same doctor. One afternoon I came in to find him agitated, knotting the end of his sheet with his fingers, turning his face one way and the other on his pillow, muttering. When I asked him what was up, was he OK, he wouldn't answer at first, then finally whispered that they'd taken his cigarettes, he didn't know what to do to get them back. I asked the matron where his cigarettes were. 'Well,' she said, 'we think his smoking probably contributed to his illness.' 'But you say he's dying.' Yes, she said, he was dying. 'Then why not let him have his cigarettes?' 'Because they're bad for him.' 'But if he's dying –' 'Because he smoked.' But what did that matter now? 'It matters because he shouldn't smoke.' And so forth, for quite some time, until I took it up with the doctor – an old friend of my father's – who countermanded the matron's orders. I sat beside him and held his free wrist as he smoked the first of his recovered cigarettes. He gave me such a smile, a smile of such gratitude, that I felt I'd at last become a son to him, and a bit of a father too. A day later an aneurysm burst, and he began to drown in his own blood. He was saved into a quicker death by his friend the doctor, who gave him a lethal shot of morphine, just as he had done for my mother. Piers was with me for the death. Nigel, flying in from Montreal, arrived half an hour too late. As the three of us stood around his bed, wondering what to do, what exactly was the procedure, etc., a nurse arrived with a tray of food. 'Now eat it all up,' she said as she put it down beside his bed and flashed him a nursey smile. 'Make sure he does,' she said as she went out. 'He needs it.' They took him away eventually, and we took away the things he'd had beside his bed, his spectacles, a book, his package of cigarettes, and a rather bulky gold lighter, that I suppose was a present from someone or other.

I am in my sixty-sixth year and I have smoked heavily for fifty-nine of those years. I began in Montreal – no, I need a break here. Light up, settle back, watch something on television.

YOUNG AND PUFFING

We were part of a street gang run by a girl called Carole, who at nine was three years older than me, and was almost certainly the most beautiful girl, as her name suggests, in the whole world. She was at the centre of numerous dramas which culminated in her hauntingly tragic death – slain by a traitor (usually Nigel) or shot for being a nurse or an Apache princess who strove to bring peace to all the tribes, and always, in the magical moments of her going, stretched out on the pavement of Vendôme Avenue, her small, perfectly oval face and her eyes – I can't remember her eyes, her face, in fact I can't remember anything about her except that her name was Carole, and that I was deeply in love with her. There were six or seven of us in this gang, and I have a suspicion the rest of them, including the girls if there were any other girls, played the robust and manly parts – the murderers, enemy warriors, defenders – while I played the close companion in her life, the tender mourner at her death, the one who at the very end held her hand as she smoked her last cigarette, which I would take from her fingers when her head lolled sideways, her eyelids closed, and suck on mournfully. In those days in Montreal everybody smoked. Grandpa chain-smoked, Gert smoked Craven A and Black Cat – neither of them filter-tipped as filter tips hadn't been invented, but one of them, perhaps both of them, cork-tipped, a strip of cork lining the outside bottom end (the cork making it the bottom end), so that the cigarette wouldn't get stuck to the heavily lipsticked lower lip – Gert wore heavy lipstick in all circumstances. I'm not sure, now I come to think of it, that Grandma smoked – I can see Grandpa with his cigarette, it used to jut out of the side of his mouth, but not jauntily, more as if it were a necessary implement, like a pencil – and I can see Gert smoking, the smoke all around her face, causing her to cough a great deal – she used to cough her smoker's cough through the smoke – but Grandma – perhaps not everybody smoked, after all – but then she had the peppermints –

Everybody in the gang smoked, of course. Not that we were allowed to – although it's hard, given that smoking wasn't then thought to be a health hazard, to see quite why we weren't. It must have been a matter of decorum, a marking off of one of the stages of growing up – short trousers, long trousers, cigarettes –

Anyway, our smoking was exhilaratingly furtive, the deep, dark, swirling pleasures of the smoke being sucked into fresh, pink, welcoming lungs, it took me just three or four cigarettes to acquire the habit and you know there are still moments now when I catch more than a memory of the first suckings-in, the slow leakings-out when the smoke seems to fill the nostril with far more than the experience of itself, and I regret the hundreds and hundreds or thousands of cigarettes that I never experienced, inhaled and exhaled without noticing – of course it's a truism that a cigarette is at its best after a swim, after a fuck, after a meal and with the first cup of coffee in the morning – but their specialness is connected to the event, they are context smokes, not relished as the smokes of childhood were relished, which carried with them most of all the whiff of the smoking experiences to come . . . There were financial difficulties. Our pocket money was a quarter (twenty-five cents) a week, out of which we had to buy a comic book – Captain Marvel, or Captain Marvel Junior, or Batman – candy bars, cigarettes. On the other hand, in Montreal, as opposed to anywhere in England, we could get all those commodities – when we got back to England we couldn't believe that rationing was actually rationing, having heard the word only as a muddling threat from Gert when we failed to eat whatever was on our plate – 'If you were in England you wouldn't have that on your plate, because of rationing, so eat it up!' – the muddle coming, of course, from our not wanting it (fish and greens especially, in my case) on the plate at all, so that rationing, clearly intended to sound a bad thing, couldn't help sounding in its particular application a good thing. When we finally came up against the word in its true meaning – in its 'Is this all we're getting?' meaning, 'and you're jolly lucky to get that, I had to queue hours for it, and it's only because I get on so well with the butcher – you're not in Canada now, you know! You're in Hayling Island.' – our mother always said 'Hayling Island' rather than England, and Canada rather than Montreal, for psychological reasons – to make us feel the cramping-downness of our changed situation.

But we knew where we were, and where we no longer were. Canada was Grandma and Gert and Grandpa (a bully over the fish and greens, which he once tried to cram into my stomach by force) and candy bars and cigarettes and comic books, and the gang on the streets after school, and almost no supervision – Hayling Island was no cigarettes except when we could cadge them from the American soldiers based nearby, who also gave us candy bars and even the occasional comic book – and also, in cold weather, lifts to school. They were exceptionally kind, and asked no favours in return. These days their easy generosity and enjoyment of us would no doubt arouse suspicions, possibly even investigations. When they left, about a year after Nigel and I arrived, we spent days searching their barracks for mementoes and trophies. On the floor in a corner I found a yellowed, bloated copy of *The Adventures of Sherlock Holmes*, the first book –

book, actual book – I read, and I read it from cover to cover, again and again – so there is that, the most important of all the favours that came my way from those kindly young Americans. It's only now, of course, as I write about them, that I realize how *young* they were, nineteen, twenty, that sort of age, seen now from my mid-sixties when once I saw them from my ten years or so. I wonder if the one who left Sherlock Holmes is still alive. Well, why shouldn't he be, he'd only be coming up to about seventy-five – almost in my own age group, when I think about it, in fact he could have been sitting at one of the tables in Barbados, or sunning himself on the beach, after a successful life in crime, or a famous author, or indeed it could have been Ken Annakin, who directed lots of long, popular films – *Those Amazing Men on their Flying Machines* was one, I think. Annakin was there in Barbados during our first week, a plumpish man with a pack of grey hair springing up at the front and then, mysteriously, down again at the back – some Hollywood coiffeur's trick, I suppose. He always had a few copies of his recently published autobiography on his table at lunch-time, others he'd placed in the window of the small shop, among the bikinis and beach-wraps, etc. If he's there next year I'll ask him if he was in the American air force, and if he was, was he by any chance based in Hayling Island in 1944, and if he was, did he happen to leave behind a copy of *The Adventures of Sherlock Holmes*, and if he did could I take this opportunity to tell him how much I owed him – also, while the thought is with me, should I take copies of my own books to Barbados next year, if we're lucky enough to get there? I feel there is a 'No' to all the above questions – was it Annakin who directed *The Longest Day*, by the way? I think it was. So. Inconclusive. What? What is inconclusive? I don't know.

AM I, IN FACT, INNOCENT?

It was Nigel who put the question directly to our father. 'We want to know if you're withholding our rations.' He did actually use the word 'withholding'. I like to think I supplied him with it, but I don't think I did, he came to it by himself, indignation and suspicion possibly enlarging his vocabulary. Our mother responded with a crisp slap across his chops, or his buttocks, depending on availability, and asked him, how did he dare! – he didn't, after that. Have I put this down yet – Mummy was a zestful slapper and cuffer, the first blows were a shock as Gert never hit, and Grandpa only on that one occasion, when of course it was Grandma he was hitting, she the sinner, I merely the sin, but for Mummy hitting was an instinctive reaction, that induced in us appropriately instinctive reactions – we learnt to duck, bob, weave and skip, so that if she connected we came to accept it as our failure of reflex, just as if she missed she accepted it as her failure – she never followed up, except when really incensed, although she would frequently find occasion to aim a slap again almost immediately, so that some conversations were physically chaotic affairs, punctuated by laughter and exclamations of pain. I suppose these days a mother like Mummy would be spending a lot of time in the courts and jail even, but we live in exceptionally stupid days, nasty and stupid, in which phrases do the work not only of thinking but of feeling – 'an innocent child', we invariably say, when we all know somewhere in our systems that there isn't, and never has been, such a creature. The other day a Frenchman, who dragged his unruly son out of a restaurant on to the pavement and slapped him sharply on the bottom, was reported to the police by passers-by, spent a few nights in jail 'to teach him a lesson', and has to return to face trial. This happened in Scotland, of course, and in Edinburgh, more of course – but some good may come of this, it might teach the French to stop romanticizing the Scots, they only do it to get at the English, with whom they actually have far more in common – at least in terms of cultural achievement, native wit, intelligence –

But what's my increasing distaste for the Scots – I'm half-Scot myself, or half Scottish or half-Scottie, whichever is the most offensive – got to do with the question – what question? Oh yes, is one closer to innocence when old than when young? Well, take your own case – yes, take my own case, am I closer to innocence now, at sixty-five and a few months, than I was when I was eight and a bit? A fatuous question, and I didn't even ask it – I've just checked and nowhere do I ask it, which is lucky as how could I possibly answer it, not knowing what innocence is even, when it comes down to it – on the other hand

I did write that it's a state that has to be achieved – yes, I did, alas – but do I really believe that one day, through hard spiritual work, I might be able to say, 'There! Innocent at last, thank God!' when it's quite obvious, virtually a law of nature, that every day I increase the aggregate of bad things I've done and thought, and even though I do fewer and fewer as I have less and less energy I'm still by definition growing less and less innocent, though it also seems to be a law of nature that I mind less and less – scarcely notice it, in fact, thank God! – for instance, I still feel worse about helping Nigel to kill a rat (already dying, probably poisoned, so it was for its own sake of course) when I was eight than about something vile that I did this morning which if I remember it this evening I'll let pass with a wince, if that – more likely a blink – most likely, though, I won't remember it. But supposing our moral systems aren't like our gastric systems or livers, don't just decay but are subject to sudden bursts of rejuvenation, perhaps ahead of me lies an Indian summer of shame and guilt, before the winter blankness sets in – complete indifference to the world and any suffering I've caused in it – which might in some respects – in my calm smile, my steady gaze – resemble the blankness of innocence – I can hear their voices, 'He was so sweet in those last months, so gentle, simple, childlike –' and also the voice they couldn't hear, the thin cold jeer, acid leaking out of the withered bladder of my spirit, who would have thought the old man had so much piss in him, etc., let us not speak of the wisdom of old men, etc. – have I ever met a wise old man, think, think – well, what about the very, very old man who lived on the edge of a cliff, and looking out one day saw a very, very young man poised to jump. So he went out and saith unto him, 'Why, why are you about to dash yourself down to your death?' And the young man saith, 'Well, the world stinks, all its inhabitants stink, there is no good in it, there is no good in me, why should I go on living, why, why?' So the old man saith unto him, 'Come, come into my little hut, and we will talk a while, grant me this wish, at least, for your soul's sake.' And the young man went with him unto and into his hut, and they talked a while, a very very long while, and then they came out of his hut, and they both threw themselves over the cliff. This story was told by the Reverend Stancliffe, Reverend what? Stancliffe, Henry, Thomas? anyway, Dean of Westminster, he told it to the boys of Westminster school, in Westminster Abbey, some fifty years ago. I can't remember anything else about his sermon, except that it began: "'Everybody for himself!" said the elephant, as he danced among the chickens'. It's the only story I know about the wisdom of old men. Blake's God is an old man with angry cheeks. And Larkin's old men – well, we shall find out, won't we?

But to get back to Mummy, 'innocent' is certainly a word I'd use for her oaths-and-blows style of parenting. It came to her perfectly naturally, and was therefore the naturally perfect way to regain full contact with her two sons – after all when we'd last seen her, heading for the milk, I had been nearly four, Nigel five, when we next saw her I was nearly nine and Nigel ten. Of the five years in which she wasn't a practising mother, she'd spent one and some months in hospital with tuberculosis, and the three and a bit before that driving an ambulance on the RAF station where my father was a medical officer – so she'd seen – they'd both seen – a number of wounded, dying and dead young men, and she'd nearly died herself – so a lot of life lived without us, a substantial gap in our relationship to fill, and her clouts, cuffs, smacks, etc. were an effective way of filling it – after the first assault, which took us by surprise and shocked us to tears, we enjoyed, no, loved – loved, although we'd never have admitted it, but what was it we loved? The intimacy, that was it, the knockabout intimacy of it, within a month we were closer to her than we'd been to poor, undemonstrative Gert during the years of her dogged attentions. Our father, on the other hand, only struck once, and that was in cold blood, ritualistically, with a shoe, in the manner of a schoolmaster with no relish for this aspect of his job – though of course no longer an aspect of a schoolmaster's job, but a jailable offence – and here, I swing to an apparently contradictory position.

MR BROWN AND MR BURN

I'm with the jailers when it comes to the schoolmaster floggers – well, not all of them, I was beaten a few times at Westminster, perfectly reasonably it seemed to me, even while it was going on, and though I didn't enjoy the pain, I more than enjoyed the distinction it conferred on me, moving amongst my peers, my bum smarting but my head held high – not a manly figure, nor a boyish one, something decidedly girlish, possibly – a punished princess, yes, the sexual thrill came not with the beating, but after it, in a delicious sense of how I was being perceived, perceiving myself as a self perceived, honoured, desired – which is not, of course, how I may have been perceived at all, contemptuously or disgustedly may have been how I was perceived – depending on the sexual and emotional make-up of the perceivers, some of whom were no doubt capable of complicated combinations of contempt, lust, disgust etc. for posturing and knowing fourteen-year-olds. The schoolmaster I would like to see jailed – like him still to be in jail as I write this, which means he would have done fifty-four years inside as he first set about me when I was eleven, at a prep school in Putney called Glengyle, where Nigel and I were sent after we'd moved from Hayling Island to Oakley Gardens, in Chelsea – was known to me then, as he is known to me now, as Mr Brown. As known to me then he was a very long man, with a long face, long, broken yellow teeth, and a mop of brown hair. For the first term or so he was perfectly pleasant, even, I might say, a bit of a fan of mine – laughed at my jokes and read bits of my essays out, was sympathetic to my problems with maths, and when Nigel and his generation had moved on to their public schools, made me captain of the football team. But then arrived Mr Burn, about whom I have written a few times, and so here, to save myself from the embarrassment of remembering him all over again, let me find the passage – quote myself to myself –

Mr Burn was round and short and he always smelled of sweet powders, different combinations of powders, I suppose, as the powdery smell, and the intensity of the tickle in my nostrils, varied from day to day. His face was always pale, but dully pale from the powder, and his lips were red, nearly crimson. It was like a toned-down clown's, Mr Burn's face, with the large, pale sweet-smelling cheeks, the full red lips, and the coal-black eyes that flickered over you, if you were me, taking in every desirable aspect of your body, and flickering into you to take in all that part of you that you prayed was concealed from all the eyes in the world, including God's eyes,

because it was the shameful part of you, the part that was most
shamefully you. He had splayed feet and asthma, and would paddle
with a soft, rolling gait between the aisles, wheezing as his eyes
flickered from this boy to that until they developed the habit of
flickering only at me – of course they took in every other boy in the
room too, took in their awareness of him. I was the target though.
I knew it from my hot flushes, the prickling of my scalp.

Yes, that pretty well holds, at least in that it revives the memory of
slightly thrilled nausea in me, <u>now</u>, at the thought of myself as prey to
this exotic predator who stalked the aisles of Glengyle Prep, his dark eye
fixed under its hooded lid – but what I'm really concerned with here
is not the effect he had on me, but the effect he had on Mr Brown, who
turned on Mr Burn's arrival at Glengyle from the affable chap I
described above into a flogger (he used a gym shoe, his own, and he
had a large foot) – no, no, more than flogger, flogging became an
addiction, and I was the bottle he preferred it to come in – every other
boy he flogged now and then, me he flogged at least once a day, twelve
savage strokes – by the third, one couldn't believe one could get to the
fifth – added to this the strain of the posture, and the sense of
proffering oneself, and the further sense one had of Mr Burn loitering
in a corner of the room, or his face at the window – and the sure
knowledge that whatever Mr Brown was doing he was doing,
unwittingly possibly, for Mr Burn, who never ever laid a hand on me,
of course, except tenderly and insinuatingly –

Something of the nature of this relationship I understood at the time,
and I still have within me the same understanding, not an understood
understanding, but when I try to bring an experienced – more
experienced – intelligence to the matter I'm no further forward, the old
muddled conviction is, as I say, still there in all its freshness, and the
fact is I still have no idea what went on between them, those too utterly
dissimilar (and young! young!) men, one tall, thin, boyish and never
really very bright but a lover of sports, and without, I feel sure, any
lust for boys in him, the other short, portly, authoritative, musical,
contemptuous of sports (but he liked to watch me play, turned out in

the coldest weather, to watch me put on a special turn of speed for him) – they might have been designed in their symmetrical opposition, by a novelist or a film director – and when they weren't teaching or fondling in the one case, thrashing in the other, they kept each other company. Mr Brown stooping low to catch all Mr Burn's husky murmurings – Mr Brown, as spellbound by Mr Burn's words as I was, had the same thrilled sense that this alien creature had him in its power, and had like me to succumb to its commands – 'But you must give him a flogging, my dear Mr Brown,' I imagine him saying, rather unimaginatively as of course he would have used his Christian name, but then I never knew Mr Brown's Christian name – 'Flog him for his own good, for your own good, my own good, my will be done, my dear and my darling Mr Brown.'

Mr Brown's formalized brutalities became known to my parents, made known somehow and in such terms that they acted swiftly by taking me away within a week and Mr Burn, who might even have been the source of their information, though of course by circuitous routes, came one evening to the house, at his own invitation, to inform them that he'd seen to it that Mr Brown was leaving Glengyle under a cloud, that he, Mr Burn, would be taking me – a remarkable and precocious boy, who needed the closest attention – under his wing. This was reported to me years later by Mummy, who shuddered at the recollection, interrupting herself with exclamations of 'the most revolting, the most repellent – and make-up! I could see he wore make-up!' – I was confined to my room while this conversation was taking place, but I could hear their voices coming from the sitting room, all three of them so familiar, there seemed to be no pauses, rather as if it were a complex musical piece, each voice coming in on an overlap, my mother's loudest, Mr Burn's low, huskily intense, my father's also low, an interrogative mutter, almost. Nigel came into my room, gravely excited – 'What's going on?' he said. 'What have you done?' I hated him for his normality, that he was always untouched by such defilements – a word I use now that describes accurately what I couldn't put a word to then – that the conversation in the room below was a defilement that I had brought on myself by being me – the conversation went on and on, suddenly became louder as it moved to the

landing, then even louder as it moved away from me down the stairs, Mr
Burn's voice now quite different in pitch, at a pitch I'd never heard
before, high, desperate, wheedling, then the slamming of the front door.
Then the parents' tread up the stairs. Then my father came into the
room. I don't think Nigel was still there. He looked at me gravely, over
his glasses. 'He's gone,' he said, quite pleasantly – he had a very pleasant
voice, my father – a transatlantic accent that became Canadian while he
was dying, Scots – the accent of his childhood – just before his death.
'He's gone. Mr Burn. I think it's time you went to bed.' This was
certainly the most serious moment of my life until then, the most
shameful – the grave look over the top of his spectacles, the quiet,
pleasant voice, as he sent me to bed – he never sent us to bed, Mummy
always did that, often with a kick towards our behinds if we dallied or
pretended deafness, being sent to bed was a familiar and comic flurry,
safe – my father's doing it was like having a sentence passed that wasn't
a punishment, more disturbing, more adult, and sad – he was sad, on
my account. As if he were banishing me. And next morning's
breakfast was filled by our mother with deliberate silences, dramatic
awkwardnesses, and when Nigel asked what the matter was, 'That
ghastly little man. Your father had to throw him out of the house. But
we're not going to talk about him. Or it.' It. It was left unspecified, even
when it, in the general sense of the word, was discussed years later –
when she talked of Mr Burn it was as if he'd been an impertinent door-
to-door salesman who had nearly duped me into buying something
disgusting, probably would have succeeded if Daddy hadn't turned up
in the nick of time, shown him the door, and as for Mr Brown he was
a brute. Yes. But he hadn't been until Mr Burn turned up.

THOSE WERE THE DAYS

I was nineteen or twenty, and on my way from Halifax, Nova Scotia,
to Clermont-Ferrand, in the Auvergne, where I was going to be Lecteur
Anglais at the Collège-Technique. I'd written to my old English master
and Housemaster, Stephen Lushington, that I was going to be in
London for a few days, and he'd written back, inviting me to tea. I
remember I went into the Abbey and then through the Cloisters and

into Little Dean's Yard – it was early evening, and there were boys of all ages hanging around, scholars in their gowns talking, everything as it always had been on summer evenings, in term time, and there was Stephen Lushington with two boys, senior boys, one of them a scholar, and also a man whom I recognized by the tumult in my stomach, the roll of my heart. Stephen Lushington turned his face towards me, and smiled and gestured me over, but of course I didn't see him, not really, I saw only what my stomach and heart –

Well, let me try and see him now, Stephen Lushington. Mr Lushington. My House Master. My English Master. How bizarre those words look, in those conjunctions, House and Master, English and Master, really quite suggestive, but suggestive of what? Oh yes, *The Story of O*, dead book, utterly dead, whips and chains, blindfolds, gags, hoods and harnesses, the whole kit and caboodle and not an erotic sentence, not one rousing and stirring image – and then there was the film. Poor old Anthony Steel with his crinkly hair, his blue eyes and dimpled, doubling chin playing the, yes, English Master, or possibly Milord, strolling loosely about among the naked ladies in a half-open dressing-gown and silk boots, a hopelessly pretty film from a deadly elegant book, only the French, as the francophonies always say – so what about the *maitre anglais*? Or *maestro inglese*, Englisch Meister, don't know any more versions, except the Scots, Hoose Musturr – what am I doing? Well, whatever I'm doing, I'm not seeing Stephen.

He was very handsome, saturnine, with intense brown eyes, and a sharp, growling voice. His ears stuck out a bit, as most good men's do, in my experience, and he was slightly pigeon-toed, like most athletic and nimble men, again in my experience – I myself am slightly pigeon-toed. He enjoyed tennis, was therefore in charge of school tennis, a neglected and somewhat derided sport at Westminster. He'd once been, or wanted to be, an actor, and was therefore in charge of school plays, which he turned from a lackadaisical ritual into the year's major event. I'd say he was a great House Master, if it's actually possible to be a great House Master, but I suppose the qualities of a House Master are mainly defined by what he doesn't do, by his not making up new rules and not enforcing old and pointless ones, by his suppression of bullying, by his not expressing, or insisting on the expression, of some sinister House spirit –

our House lost in every sport almost as a matter of course, but nobody minded except the actual losers, which is as it should be. He was relaxed, tolerant and incapable of not treating any boy, however imbecilic, as his equal, and to put it simply one was proud to be in his House because he was its master. He was certainly, most certainly, a great English teacher, the first to read a poem aloud and into life, and into my life – the poem was 'Dover Beach', and actually I don't think he read, I think he recited, as I remember it – his eyes didn't move back and forth along the lines of the poem, they rested on us, above the book's cover, as if he were Matthew Arnold and the poem was coming straight out of him, and not off the page. He was the only adult, outside of fiction, that I wanted to be like – even, perhaps especially, when he now and then took me aside in Little Dean's Yard and said a few sentences, brief, firm, sympathetic sentences, about my behaviour – Dr Garten (French) had reported me for unruliness and insolence, Dr Prague (Maths) for sloth and incompetence – he passed these observations on, and then moved on, with his quick, pigeon-toed gait, into the House, leaving me trying to look to all the other boys in Little Dean's Yard as if I'd just exchanged a bit of civilized gossip with Housemaster, or received some privileged communication. Twins. I would have liked to have been his twin, his subtly younger twin.

I'm old enough now to be the father of the Mr Lushington that was then – a useless but scary thought, inducing not just double but multiple vision, a gang of Grays and Lushingtons at different stages of life, all mixed about, so that, for example, eighty-year-old Gray and thirteen-year-old Lushington find themselves once again standing before each other in Little Dean's Yard, generations apart and chronologically the wrong way round, but still fixed in their original roles, pupil and master, hero-worshipper and hero, old Gray with his mottled hands clasped humbly behind his back, his wattles trembling with shame, as adolescent Lushington, kindly, thoughtful, bepimpled, hints delicately at certain indelicacies, no doubt the same old indelicacies, in old Gray's behaviour and habits. So there it is. There is what? I think that what I'm saying is that whatever our current ages and circumstances, my first throb of thought or feeling about him is always from that first perspective – if tomorrow he were to loom up from the gutter as I am stepping out of a limo I'd still fall internally into the same posture of guilt-ridden adoration, although only for a second or so, I hope, before holding out an adult and compassionate hand – not that I can really imagine him in a gutter, broken and old, or even old anywhere – I had a letter from him when he'd just reached eighty, describing his recent scramble around San Francisco to get to a wedding – he'd had to run up and down a hill after a tram or trolley, whichever they are in San Francisco, anyway the sort of thing I could scarcely do in my forties – but then I'd have taken a taxi, in my thirties also, so the situation wouldn't have arisen.

But here's the thing, to get back to that – Stephen Lushington was one of the two born teachers my life has been blessed with, a totally unmixed blessing in his case – the other born teacher was the more than mixed, in fact polluted blessing, with whom he was inexplicably standing when I dropped by that evening on my way to Clermont-Ferrand. He not only recognized me immediately, his face, round, pudgy, ten years older, lit up in a most friendly fashion – 'Oh, I know him, we know each other, I taught him at prep school,' and he gave a quite proud smile. 'One of my favourite boys,' he said. I can't remember how the conversation proceeded, but afterwards, taking tea with Stephen Lushington in his study, talking of Canada and so forth, my mind entirely on Mr Burn, I wondered if I should – well, what? Well, anyway, I didn't, merely saying that it had been a surprise, quite a surprise to see Mr Burn there, in Little Dean's Yard, in the sunlight of an evening (though I don't expect I phrased it like that), a dark and pasty creature from my past there in the sunlight – certainly didn't say that – and so he remained at Westminster, in some teaching capacity or other until a boy or two broke down, their parents investigated and he took his leave, under his cloud. So far this all seems simple and morally straightforward, but – let me try and get this clear – what about the then headmaster, who must have presided over Mr Burn's departure? About him, what? after all, with his noble carriage, and gracious, sideways smile, he really had nothing in common with Mr Burn but the paddling walk, which carried him sedately across Little Dean's Yard to the Abbey for morning service, and tenderly around the boys in their dorms at lights-out – they called him Cute – no, no, not

Cute, Coote, Coote of course, as in 'as queer as a coote' to be precise, and when those sprightly workaholics, Gossip, Rumour and Scandal, were threatening his reputation, he saved it (along with his job) by marrying into a distinguished literary widow, while poor old Stephen Lushington, on the other hand, well, poor young Stephen Lushington at that time, remember, had virtually no chance of rising to a headmastership, at least at a school like Westminster – though he was married, with children, he'd previously been divorced. Divorced! So there were the three careers – old Coote's redeemed by a late marriage, young Lushington's blighted by an early divorce, Mr Burn's – well, who knows how many further classrooms and school yards he found his way into, how many other elderly psyches his ghost still paddles in, with its lemony this and powdered that and hooded etc. but here we go again, here we go, from Mr Burn to *The Story of O* no doubt, and then we'll have old Anthony Steele in a jiffy, well, dressing-gown – so better leave it, yes, just leave it that it really was all simple and morally straightforward back then – at least when you look at it from the point of view of back then, when those were the days.

BROWN-NOSING AND WHERE IT GOT ME

Dinner with Harold and Antonia at Chez Moi, Harold remote for the most part – sunk deep in the effects of the treatment, which he'd had the day before, but there was an encouraging flicker of the old Harold towards the end, when I was describing a letter I'd just received from a troublesome fan, she wanted to let me know that the secret of my wealth and fame is in my ability, not to write plays, they're pretty ordinary stuff, these acclaimed plays of mine, no, my main ability is to 'brown-nose', I brown-nosed my way through Oxford-Cambridge, then brown-nosed my way into the theatre, where I brown-nosed my way to my present distinguished status by brown-nosing critics, producers, etc. – there was a lot of laughter from Antonia and Victoria, some at the thought that anyone should think I had wealth and fame, some at the way I was perceived by the fan to have brown-nosed my way towards them, when 'I think we've had quite enough of this word, brown-nosing. I don't like it.' Thus Harold – not as forcefully as when robust, but effectively, with a sort of spectral authority – it was the authority which was cheering – though he'd made it a bit difficult to think of any subject that didn't seem to lead naturally and inevitably back to brown-nosing.

Still, it's an odd letter to get, it seems to me, even from a fan – although it's true that I have little experience of fans – and going strictly by results she's on pretty shaky ground, in fact I sometimes find myself thinking that if only I'd had a gift for what she calls 'brown-nosing', or even basic diplomacy – that if only I hadn't said that to this one, this to that one, or hadn't drunk so very much through my late forties, throughout my fifties, I might have – well, what? at least have got my plays returned more speedily by Trevor Nunn, for instance, possibly bits of them actually read by his predecessor at the National, Richard Eyre, to whom I never actually sent them, on the grounds that every time I met him he seemed to wince, in a noble and kindly sort of way, and I felt it would be wrong to trouble him with parcels of plays through the post or with phone calls from my agent – and as for the smaller subsidized houses, oh, the Donmar, now I come to think of it, in the form of young Sam Mendes, when he was even younger Sam Mendes, his face as yet unmarked by appearing regularly in the press, once sent a message through my agent that he was eager to do something of mine and so – fatally for me – asked if we could meet, to discuss it. I told him over lunch about the play I was working on, which I intended very shortly to confer on him – it involved an abandoned wife kidnapping her husband's mistress and keeping her chained in an outhouse, it should be a very well-appointed outhouse, I explained, where she would give her captive rival a literary and moral education, and – as is so often the way with teachers and taught – they would fall in love with each other and – and so forth – I said I thought the basic situation was pretty sexy, didn't he think? especially if we got a really pretty girl to chain – I suspect I gave the impression we'd do it together, find the girl, purchase the chain, one of us wind it about her waist, the other snap the padlock – with the prospect of paying customers, too – naturally I didn't say anything along those lines, explicitly, but perhaps he heard things in my voice, lubricious and salacious things, and saw

stuff in my eyes, overfocused and red-rimmed – anyway, he parted
from me no doubt hoping our paths would never cross again, and
they haven't, although since his Oscar I've sent him an idea for a film,
just a few lines, but written out in neat and sober handwriting, to
which he replied courteously, in a loose sort of scrawl, but then why
should he be careful with his handwriting, he has no need to be. And
why rake over these old ranklings, when there are older ranklings that
I still haven't finished raking over like – what? The dawn is upon us.
Let me greet it with a sleeping pill.

SHIFTY WINDOWS

So there was my father and the one beating, the awkward ceremony
of it, but the reason for it – that's the point I don't remember. Was
Nigel involved, were we beaten together? – well, not together,
sequentially of course – no, I don't think so, I don't think he ever
was, it was me solo, but what could I have done that would have
caused our father, of all people, a man whose occasional malevolence
was issued in little asides, or in thoughtful resignation, or – worst –
in deliberately uncomprehending questions – no, there was more
than that, there was the jealousy once or twice – a curious episode
to do with wellington boots – we came out of the house one Sunday
to go for a spin in the car, it was raining, Mummy said, 'Why aren't
you wearing your wellies, you fool! Go and put on your boots!' This
to me, not to her husband – I protested, as I hated wearing my
wellies, they were tight and heavy, impediments – she insisted, my
father also insisted, down I went to the basement, plucked out my
wellies, and discovered a gash in the heel of one of them –
unwearable, as I reported to my parents, showing them the boot.
'How on earth did that happen?' my mother enquired, not
conspicuously perplexed. 'I don't know,' I said, not particularly
curious. 'He did it himself,' said the father, not at all himself. Steely
with anger. 'Did you?' – from the mother. 'No, I didn't,' I said. And
I hadn't. 'No, he wouldn't have,' said the mother. 'He wouldn't be so
bloody silly.' 'He did it himself,' the father repeated. 'He's lying.
Look at his shifty little eyes. His shifty little eyes.' Now this was said

not of the moment – he didn't mean that my eyes at that precise moment, in circumstances to do with my boots, were shifting about, but as a general moral fact about me, my eyes were always shifty, I'd been born with shifty eyes as an indicator of my true nature – eyes-as-windows-of-the-soul-shifty. Mummy, my Mummy, was shocked. 'James!' she cried, cried Mummy mine. 'James, how could you!' He muttered something apologetic – his own eyes suddenly shifty and full of feeling – what feeling? Loathing would be to take it too far, I think, looking judiciously back, but whatever it was it gave me, in all my upset, a little jolt of triumph.

A SIGHTING IN PIMLICO

And so we come, in the most natural way possible, to the matter of my father and his Mrs Rolls. She was a small, blonde, lively widow, who worked as his secretary in his Harley Street consultancy – 'Little Mrs Rolls,' my mother invariably referred to her as, or, in poignant innocence – 'Your Little Mrs Rolls, James, phoned, to say that she's made three appointments for you on Wednesday afternoon' – one of them, possibly two, even all three, being with Little Mrs Rolls herself, it was subsequently discovered. I saw them once, when I was walking back from Westminster – I was about fifteen, I should think, and it was somewhere in Pimlico, mid-afternoon, I was about to cross a street and they went past me in a car, Little Mrs Rolls driving, the father sitting staring straight ahead, a perfectly proper little cameo, really – I'd met Little Mrs Rolls quite often, as for instance when she came to the parents' Christmas party, so I recognized her at the wheel, and him I'd have recognized anywhere, that handsome head (he was said to look like James Mason. James Mason with a pipe – and spectacles), that look of humble, middle-class distinction – but what was there to see? only a small blonde secretary driving her boss to one of his appointments. They weren't laughing, talking, looking at each other, they might almost have been in separate vehicles from the evident lack of connection between them – well, perhaps that was the trouble, that's what I unconsciously grasped, the unlikely stiffness and formality with which they sat – especially him, he gave off the impression of being somehow both lordly and a captive. Or did he? That may be how I see him now, in memory – but what I did notice at the time is that they sat, both of them, as if they were hoping not be observed by someone that they themselves had observed, to wit, myself – well, whether they were or they weren't because they had or they hadn't, the thing is, without actually knowing anything at all, really, about adultery, unfaithfulness, all that, I knew that I'd seen something wrong, that I'd caught him out, and I didn't like it. I didn't mention it, not innocently to Mummy, 'Oh, I saw Daddy this afternoon, it was in Pimlico, he looked quite funny actually, Mummy, sitting there beside Little Mrs Rolls etc.' – or to Nigel – perhaps with him I felt it would be sneaking, even though I didn't understand yet what it was I'd be sneaking about – and I quite consciously resisted the temptation to bring it up two years later, when we'd all moved to Halifax, Nova Scotia –

One afternoon, after lunch, when I should have been trekking back to Dalhousie for a class, she said, 'Si, come and have a drive with me,' and her face had a look, a look that made me at once assume a grown-up posture, manner – we went to the car and sat in it, she didn't start the car, we just sat in the car in front of the house and she told me about Little Mrs Rolls and my father – 'your father' was her term for him on this occasion, instead of the usual Daddy – she cried a bit, and said she'd thought of leaving him – it had been going on for eight years, right up to the day he'd left for Canada – he'd come out ahead of us, to find a house, start his job ('take up his appointment' was the phrase Mummy liked to use) – for eight years James Davidson had been humping Little Mrs Rolls, and she'd never for a moment suspected – not until she'd read her letter – hadn't even suspected when she'd seen the letter, recognized the handwriting, not suspected even as she was opening the letter, why, she'd only opened it because she'd thought it might contain some urgent information that Daddy who was away in Montreal, clearing-up after Grandma's death would want her to pass on when he phoned in the evening. In which case why not wait until he phoned in the evening tell him about the letter, then ask him if he wanted her to open it, or so I would have said, if she were telling me this now – although when it comes to it, it wouldn't have made any difference, if she'd said, 'James, here is a letter from your Little Mrs

Rolls, do you want me to open it and read it out to you in case it contains urgent information you need,' he couldn't have said, 'No, you're on no account to open that letter which can't possibly contain urgent information that I need, above all that you need –'

– she'd been thinking of leaving him, she said, yes, Mummy had been thinking of leaving Daddy, what was my view, Si – we were both smoking her cigarettes – I had all kinds of views, most of all an exalted view of myself as an adult, a confidant, the only person Mummy was going to tell, she told me – and I believed her then as I believe her now because in Halifax, Nova Scotia, she had no close friends, was the 'grande dame', a London society queen in exile to a cold colony, she would have been far too proud to confess her situation, that she was a wronged woman, wronged by her husband's secretary, Little Mrs Rolls – too shameful, too thoroughly humiliating! – so I stood in as an adult friend as best I could, allowing myself to feel, for a moving moment, that my father's fate lay in his son's hands, that with a few words – 'Better let him go, Mummy, there's no coming back from that sort of thing' – and so out of the house he would trudge, gone to – gone to where, in Halifax, Nova Scotia? And could Mummy stay, could I stay? Would we have to go back to London, but I couldn't go back to London, in London I'd have to do my national service, which I certainly wouldn't be doing in London, in fact the prospect of Daddy leaving me – her, Mummy, I mean – the family, that is – and there was Piers – how would he manage, fatherless, and so young, there'd just be Mummy in the house, just Mummy and her three boys, only two of them over eighteen! how could she cope, how would we cope, the prospect filled me with panic, 'But why should I?' she thank God! cried. 'Why should I just give up everything! Everything because of her! Let her ruin my life, destroy my family – give her that satisfaction!' He, I noticed even then, didn't come into it much, he appeared to have been merely a vehicle for transporting trouble from Little Mrs R to big Mrs G – my mother was five feet eight inches, by the way, (an ex gym-mistress who'd long-jumped, high-jumped and broad-jumped for Britain in the Commonwealth and Olympic Games, picked up a medal in one or the other, long legs, long, long legs; broad shoulders, long torso, long chin and nose, blue eyes – a big, handsome, dangerous-looking Olympiad of a woman) – in other words, J.D. was a pretty well absent party to his own infidelities, at least in my mother's account – so it ended, this conversation, with my mother suddenly bursting into tears, as she drove me to the Dalhousie Campus – only a few hundred yards from the house – and then driving off, in her usual harum-scarum way, cigarette dangling, to teach the girls hockey, and I went to my classes with, no doubt, the air of a man who was burdened by secrets and responsibilities for an hour or two, no longer than that, because I had my dash to cut, that of the campus aesthete and intellectual with the effete haircut and effete accent and heterosexual eye – and it was really the end of the matter, at least according to Mummy, who reported crisply that J.D. had replied to Little Mrs Rolls's letter with a letter that required – no, demanded – no reply, there was nothing more to be said, the matter never to be mentioned again, wrong of her to have burdened me, my father was a good man who loved – and almost immediately after that there was laughter again from their bedroom that I sometimes caught when I was up early. I was, well, relieved the father was in his proper place, about his proper business, but I had, there's no getting away from it, a most peculiar mixture of new feelings for him – a respect for his 'otherness' – that to himself he was obviously far more than father, husband, pathologist – he had a secret life, just like me, he had desires and needs, just like me, but unlike me he knew how to satisfy them, he was a grown-up, in other words, who knew how to deceive (eight years!), a betrayer. At the same time I felt a moral superiority because I knew something about him that he didn't know (and was never to know) that I knew – I used to imagine it sometimes – telling him that Mummy and I had talked him over rather as if he'd been a difficult child in our custody – and what about that time in the car in Pimlico? – he'd seen me, I knew he had, no, no, don't lie, Daddy, just look at his shifty little eyes, Mummy – careful!, you said to Mrs Rolls, keep staring straight ahead, poppet, did he call her? there's somebody I might know across the street – could just be one of my sons, the middle one, Simon, can't be sure from where I'm sitting – which was in the passenger seat, it's worth repeating.

THOUGHTS ON DRIVING

He loved driving, he was a manly driver, all pipe and speed, puffing out smoke as he took a corner with an emphatic change of gears, jaw tightening with manly irritation when Mummy cried out, 'James, James, too fast, slow down!', another shift of gears, foot lightening on the accelerator, a mutter to the effect that it was all right, he knew what he was doing, – sometimes she'd tell the story about his driving in India, how she was entertaining his superior officer to tea one afternoon out on the porch, a great honour that he'd dropped in, she was naturally very nervous but they were getting along really quite well, he was being most charming about baby Nigel, who was cradled nearby in the arms of the ayah and so forth, really it was all going delightfully when suddenly there had been a roaring and a screeching and a terrible tooting and a car had shot into the drive and down it straight towards the porch and at the very last second had done a jubilant swerve, brake and skid, sending up clouds of dust and pebbles, causing the superior officer to spring to his feet, 'Who is that bloody fool!' he'd shouted, and the bloody fool that bounded out of the car was your father, wasn't he, James? James chuckled through his pipe, did some stuff with the gears, and admitted that it was, yes.

So he really wasn't one for the passenger seat, even when Mummy was driving – she'd been under his command at the air force base as an ambulance driver, so he knew, in spite of her feckless manner at the wheel and her tendency to lively conversation punctuated by vivid gestures with her cigarette, that he could trust her instincts, her athlete's reflexes – still he made it clear from the way he sat, his hands pressed on his knees and his head slightly back, that he found something unnatural in the arrangement, and would for example say, when I answered one of her questions – they were mostly, it's true, rhetorical – he would say, 'You mustn't speak when your mother's driving. She needs to concentrate.'

'But she asked me, didn't you, Mummy, you asked me –'

'No, your father's quite right, I'm not really talking, just thinking aloud, aren't I, James?'

Who would shortly insist on taking the wheel, allowing her, on our long drives down to Cornwall or Devon in the summer, spells of not much more than half an hour or so. I think that though she loved driving, she loved even more the feeling of wifishness when she sat beside him, his passenger. For her, too, it was the natural order of things.

For me, it's second nature to sit in the front passenger seat, being driven by a woman. I like it, for short periods, at least. I like their hands on the wheel, I like watching their foot moving between accelerator and brake, I like the tops of their knees, the stretched out calf, the tension in the ankle – that is, when they're wearing a skirt or a dress. It is less interesting when they're wearing trousers, which they usually do, these days, and when it comes to it, about twenty minutes of being driven is all I can take, my back begins to hurt, and I become nervous of the traffic, and in London of the pedestrians, who I suspect find the sight of a large smoking man driven around by a woman much younger than himself somewhat obnoxious.

Of course my life would have been completely different if I'd learnt to drive. For one thing I'd have been able to drive away from difficult or hateful situations – it's hard, when things have reached rock bottom at three in the morning to walk out, especially if you're in the country or abroad, there is no public transport, no hotel for many miles, nowhere at all to go really except to a field or some woods, lake, river or sea – you'd get lost, possibly drown, be attacked by bats, or die of hypothermia or from terror of the darkness in an unknown place – then the winds, and with the winds would come rain, hail, sleet – and you, crouched in a ditch, unable to get home and say sorry, I love you, make up – so you pretty well have to do what I've done on the occasions that I've walked out – hang about up the road, smoke a few cigarettes, then walk straight back in, only of course you don't make up with an apology and a declaration of love, you pick up where you left off, your dignity insisting that you're only there again because you've thought of something else to say much better left unsaid. But if you can drive off you can drive off until tomorrow, or the next day, or for ever – or so it seems to a non-driver. The freedom I've missed, in other words – but how can I calculate that against the freedom I'd have lost in jail, for drunken driving, dangerous driving, homicidal driving.

Character is destiny. Mine is the character of a non-driver. And remember the other party knows it too – especially if the other party is a woman, and a driver, which she always is, in my case.

J. Daddy, MD, although a driver, couldn't drive himself away from his Little Mrs Rolls, and out of her life. She ran his office, she sometimes visited his house, she knew his secrets, indeed she was one of them – she had his telephone numbers – indeed she was one of those, too. To drive out of her life he'd have to have driven out of Mummy's life and the lives of his three sons, Nigel, Simon and Piers, then set up as a general practitioner in a faraway country, under an assumed name, a forged passport – well, how did he break it to her then, tell her that after eight years he was off, and thank you?

Well, he could simply have said that he'd decided to end the affair, no hard feelings please, he'd give her the best possible references, find her another pathologist, let's get on with our lives. Which would have required courage.

Or he could have explained that his finances were such (and they were) and his tax burden such (and it was) that he had no alternative, it broke his heart, but to apply for a job in Canada (which he did), where taxes were low, and incomes for pathologists high. Only fair to his family, he could have said. Furthermore he could have pointed out that he was legally still a Canadian. He'd be going home at last. His parents were now very elderly. He should be near them in their twilight. Yes, he could certainly have said that.

And then he might have said that when he'd settled down, sorted it all out, she could come over too! Why not? She could be his secretary again, everything exactly as it had been, except that it would be in Halifax, Nova Scotia, and not in London, England, that would be the only difference when it came down to it. Yes, don't cry, don't cry, join me when I've settled down, we'll write of course. Yes, I bet that's what he said.

WHAT IS THAT MESS?

During the period of my own adultery I frequently hovered on the verge of suicide – no, not suicide, something more violent, more of a sort of self-homicide – what I wanted really was to seize myself by the back of the neck and dash and dash my head, until my brains were out and I was over and done with. On the other hand I didn't want to be dead. One of my plays was previewing in Guildford, a light-footed (I hoped) though melancholy piece about, well, adultery as a matter of fact. I would taxi the forty-odd miles to rehearsals, sitting carefully in the middle of the seat so that I kept an equal distance between the doors, feet pressed against the floor to give myself either leverage or stability, torn between the desire to fling myself out on to the motorway and be mangled under the traffic – the nursery poem throbbing through my head, oh dear mama, what is that mess, that looks like strawberry jam, hush, hush, my dear, 'tis papa, run over by a tram – so an overpowering desire to turn myself into strawberry jam on the one hand, and on the other an obdurate determination to continue existence as I knew it in the here and now of the taxi, i.e., more gulps from the bottle of Glenfiddich in my lap, more puffs on my cigarette, so just one more gulp, one more puff, then a lunge sideways for the door handle, a swift jerk and out with you – but first a last gulp, a last puff, then one more of each and then reach for the door handle, puff gulp jam jam yesterday, jam tomorrow but never jam today gulp puff jam etc. until there was the theatre, all those actors to boss around, and nothing to worry about until it was time to call a taxi for the trip back. Nowadays of course the situation couldn't arise because you a) can't drink in a taxi, b) can't smoke in a taxi, c) can't open the door while the taxi is moving.

THE OTHER WOMEN

Mummy was a middle-aged woman of the middle classes in the middle of the twentieth century, who would certainly, and with complete truthfulness, have described her marriage as a happy one, a very happy one – perhaps the news of Little Mrs R acted as a challenge, put her on her mettle, perhaps her inherited instinct, or her received wisdom, was to believe that it was always the woman's fault, the women's fault, not just Little Mrs R's, but hers, too – after all, if she couldn't keep her man! – so she kept her man, and I'm pretty sure the subsequent pleasures weren't only his, in fact the laughter from the bedroom was mostly hers, even if I sometimes imagined a male purr running under it – well, why not purr, how could he help purring, old J.D., when he had an even more loving wife to show for his eight years of adultery – really, quite worth the effort – a happier man in a happier marriage.

But it wasn't, as it turned out, only Little Mrs Rolls, his secretary, there was also BoBo Carew, his wife's best friend, his best friend's wife – Nigel gave me this news not many years ago, decades after the death of all parties – and of some of their children too – I suppose he'd held it back from me for much the same reasons as I'd held back from him what I'd seen in the car in Pimlico, but now here it was for my consideration, that he'd surprised them when he came home from school early one afternoon, met them on the landing coming out of the bedroom – out of Mummy's bedroom is how I see it – both of them flushed, holding just-lit cigarettes, and Daddy, devious old devil, said, 'Just showing Mrs Carew something in the bedroom.' Yes. 'Mrs Carew.' That's how one's parents referred to their closest friends, when in their company in front of the children – to each other, in front of the children, it was BoBo this, BoBo that, but to the children: 'Just showing Mrs Carew something in the bedroom.' Mrs Carew was almost onomatopoeically a BoBo, a large, round, soft, hoarsey, chuckling sort of woman, as tall as Mummy, but with enormous breasts – boobs, actually – who, as poor old Mummy, flat-chested, used to say proudly, 'worships your father', not knowing to her dying day where and how or with what –

So, to my certain knowledge, J. Daddy was bonking three women, Little Mrs Rolls, BoBo/Mrs Carew, and mother. Or is it more accurate to say he was being bonked by two and bonking one? No, bonking two, because there was also Mummy's cousin, Betty, also always referred to as little Betty, but in lower case, somehow – I'll try to work this out – yes, the Little in Little Mrs Rolls was almost a title, anyway a social distinction, Lady Rolls, as it were, but at the other end of the social ladder, which would go, as we ascend, Rolls (chambermaid, etc.), Little Mrs Rolls (widowed secretary etc.), Mrs Rolls (married, middle-class, unemployed etc.), Lady Rolls (wife of an industrialist, etc.). – Mother,

by the way, would have liked to have been addressed, and referred
to, as Mrs Dr Gray. But if the 'little' in little Betty wasn't a social
categorization, exactly, as the Little in Little Mrs Rolls was, it nevertheless declined her as an inferior family member – she was a widow,
impoverished, with a son to bring up, on top of which she was in fact
physically little, seeming to be roughly half my mother's size when they
entered a room together, but in other respects very like my mother –
especially in her legs, long (in proportion) and shapely, which she
enjoyed exhibiting, stretching them out and flexing the calf muscles
as she sat chattering out family history, interspersed with compliments
to my mother about my father, compliments to my father about
himself, compliments to Nigel and myself for having our father for
a father, all the while stretching and flexing her legs, which the main
subject of her compliments, pulling on his pipe in his armchair in his
corner of the room, glanced at now and then, with a pathologist's, or
perhaps a pathological, eye.

Little Betty knew all the family gossip, all its history – in fact knew
almost every family's gossip and history, able in the course of a single
sentence to make a sequence of connections that reminded one of
those 'begat' stretches in the Old Testament, verse after verse of
who begat whom who begat whom, etc. – so little Betty, 'Oh yes, well
she married a Flyn, Jack Flyn, who was the nephew of one of the
Tomkins, Lionel, the one who married Elsa, who was the daughter of
the son of Lord Dundoodle of the Lancashire Dundoodles, Henry
Dundoodle' – on and on she could go, even to me in my teens,
I would be listless and irritable after the fourth or fifth name, so
that when she came to talk about my own family (hers too), I only
listened here and there, almost accidentally – except of course when
she told how Mummy and Daddy came to be married – 'Your aunt
Deirdre, you've never met her have you, no, of course you wouldn't
how could you, well, you see' – and there would follow an enormous
confusion of coughs, names, irrelevant antecedents, descriptions of
Daddy in the prime of his young manhood ('though being older suits
him even more') with pauses for an exhibition of ankle and calf, out
of which it was possible, after several hearings, to trace the lineaments
of the story:

A LITTLE FAMILY BACKGROUND

Daddy came from Canada to England on spec when he was twenty-five years old, a qualified MD who hadn't yet practised. He answered an ad for a locum in Holloway, North London, at the practice of my maternal grandfather, George Holliday, who was also, of course, little Betty's uncle. The younger daughter, Deirdre, was on the premises, a quick and lively young woman of twenty or so who, little Betty said, was very pretty, though nothing like as attractive as Mummy, and not nearly as athletic. Inevitably and in no time, in a 'mere jiffy' as Betty put it, Daddy and Deirdre were engaged, or 'the next best thing' – little Betty didn't say exactly what the next best thing was, though one has a good idea of what it might have been for Daddy, given subsequent evidence. No doubt – well, let's assume, anyway – that the next best thing would have given way in due course to the best thing, if it hadn't been for Mummy, then a games teacher at a school in Shropshire, who came home for her holiday – what little Betty delivered at this stage of her account was a terrible clutter of hints and innuendoes mainly to do with the instability of Deirdre's behaviour, the trouble she caused – 'she was a bad loser, you see, your aunt' and of course her drinking, 'she got that from your grandfather'. Mummy and Daddy got married in another mere jiffy, and headed straight off to India, where Daddy joined the British army as a medical officer – actually, he probably joined before they left, it would have been more sensible, I think. Deirdre followed them out, but was sent straight back for generally hopeless behaviour – 'flirting and drinking and making a name for herself all over the Punjab' – or wherever. What I know of the rest of Deirdre's story amounts only to this: she married a solicitor from Nottingham, had two children, became a lying-about-in-the-gutter sort of alcoholic, was divorced, prohibited from seeing her children, went into lodgings or perhaps a hostel in Nottingham, was frequently stored for the night in a cell at the local police station, and died of cirrhosis, in her early forties. Nigel and I never met her, but we heard her voice some Christmases if we answered the phone – she was invariably drunk and crying, incomprehensible – Mummy would send us out of the room and she would be, some years, hours on the phone, reappear looking fraught and slightly saintly. 'Poor Deirdre, she really is too, too' – Father would grunt, suck feelingly on his pipe – 'Your aunt gets a little carried away at Christmas, a little the worse for wear.'

So there it is. However little Betty muddled and slanted them and blurred them with coughing fits the facts are clear, my Mummy stole my Daddy from my Auntie and lived happily with him until she died – whereupon little Betty became the second Mrs Dr Gray, a position she'd always coveted, as she admitted on the day of her wedding, 'I was in love with your father from the first moment I saw him in the surgery in Holloway – but as long as your mother was alive – I mean! Good heavens I couldn't compete with your mother, there could only be one winner, with your mother!' as she stood on the tips of the toes of her lovely pins, offering her cheek for cousinly kisses from her three tall stepsons. 'You've got to get me away from that woman,' my father whispered a couple of years later as he lay in bed in their flat in Menton – 'She was always a mistake.' His big toe was gangrenous and stuck out from under the sheets. It looked so dead and so painful that I wanted to cry. 'Yes,' he said, 'she did that.' I knew that he was speaking metaphorically, but I asked him anyway, how she'd done it, how had she poisoned his big toe? She never stops, he said, she never stops. Yakity-yak, yakity-yak. He gestured contemptuously towards the living room where she was on the telephone, talking to the doctor. 'Mon mari, vous savez, je vous dis encore et encore, comprenez-moi, mon mari, il est malade, il est poisonné sur le pied, le pied de mon mari est très malade et poisonné. Vous devez toot sweet visiter mon mari' sort of stuff – on and on she went, on and on, while he smiled at me in ghastly triumph, as if we'd caught her spooning strychnine into his food – but when she came in and said the doctor couldn't come until evening, she'd done her best, she'd tried everything, but it was no good, he wouldn't come, not until the evening, and then began to fiddle despairingly about the bed, tucking him in and so forth, he took her hand and patted it, telling her to calm down, he was going to be all right, after all he was a doctor, wasn't he? – which made her swell up with a mixture of pride and hope, and say yes, of course he was, and more than just a doctor, you know, she said to me, he's a pathologist too, aren't you, James? She sat on the edge of the bed, talking, coughing and exclaiming as she clutched his hand, and he lay there grunting, nodding, dying – well, there was a long history between them, all right. One thing leads to another. That's my point. Perhaps it was his too.

What point? Perhaps our implicit point, Daddy's and mine, is that he was always there for the taking, by the woman of the moment – first Deirdre, then good old Mummy – and good old BoBo, and little Betty here and there, now and then until she became full-time – although here's a thought, where was she, on the afternoon of his death, we were there, his three sons, she was there most of the time on other days, she'd been adhesively at his side when I moved him from Menton to a nursing home in Nice, then from Nice to the Charing Cross Hospital, in fact she caused confusions at every point, especially in Nice, where she drove doctors and nurses to distraction with her disorderly monologues – 'like a flight of starlings, little Betty's conversation,' Daddy used to say to the first Mrs Dr G. – but she loved him, with such utter passion and devotion – and that gold lighter must have come from her, now I think about it, brought to him in Charing Cross, probably just after they took away his cigarettes – yes, well, there you are, that was her sense of timing, at least with him – no doubt she'd gone off to perform some elaborate but useless chore on his behalf, and so missed the moment – or perhaps missed it on purpose, because she couldn't bear to be there at the moment when she became a widow for the second time. Actually it would have been for the third time if the man she was engaged to after her first husband's death had lived to marry her, but he was killed – or so the story went, as told by Mummy – about half an hour after he'd proposed. He'd popped the question while they were motoring through Surrey – why do I write Surrey? I hadn't remembered Surrey until I began to write it down – well, assume Surrey, at least one of the home counties, a busy little town on a busy day, say midday, driving down the high street – well, wherever, whenever, he'd popped the question she'd been waiting for, she gave him the answer he wanted, and then she'd told him to stop the car at a telephone kiosk, she simply had to tell her news to – I don't know, not Mummy, because Mummy would have told it from her point of view, wouldn't she? and described the conversation – whomever. He stopped the car, she got out, crossed the street, entered the kiosk, put in her two pennies, dialled – 'Hello,' she'd said, 'Hello, it's Betty, I've got something to tell you! My dear, he –' etc., etc., and etc., and etc. – and in the car her freshly minted fiancé, driven at last past endurance, or lust, or longing or – just leave it at impatience – as he saw more pennies dropped in the slot, and then more pennies – perhaps a six-pence, or even a shilling, you got an awful lot of talking-time for a shilling, back then when shillings existed – leapt out of the car – and here's the thing, the little Betty part of it, she was so deep in the news of her impending marriage that she didn't take in that not far away the other party to it had been crushed to death under the wheels of a lorry, didn't take in the arrival of the ambulance, the police, the departure of the ambulance, the police – so when at last she headed back to the car, and found it empty, she simply got in and waited – 'Poor little Betty,' as my mother used to say. 'She's had rather a sad life, when you think about it. Of course I know she bores you to death, James, but even so, you're fond of her really, aren't you?'

God knows what he left behind when he came from Canada to England at the age of twenty-five – the same sort of pot-pourri as he left behind when he went back to Canada –

Bound and gagged in Montreal. I'm leaving this as an aide-memoire for tomorrow, when I start again.

A SUNDAY NIGHT AT ORSINO'S

Had dinner with the Waldegraves, William and Caroline, at Orsino's, as we usually do on Sundays. At the far end of the restaurant were Harold and Antonia (as they usually are on Sundays) with a couple of friends, I couldn't make out who. Our conversation was mainly about how a husband should deal with a man who has insulted his wife – some drunk had recently abused Caroline at a dinner party – William, who is an ex Tory minister with progressive views but of ancient lineage, said that in the good old days he would have challenged him, no alternative – or had him horsewhipped, I suggested, because I always like to say the word – horsewhip – generally thinking of a certain theatre critic, who in certain lights does look a bit like a horse, spavined and with dripping, twitching nostrils from his cocaine habit – a horse on horse, in fact – and although for obvious reasons I wouldn't fancy the job of horsewhipping him myself, I wouldn't mind having it done for me – it was a lively conversation, but my attention wasn't fully on it, it was on Harold who several times had to leave the restaurant, walking with a willed step, in an uncertain but straight line, keeping a distance from our table, as if to avoid anxious questions, the first time up the stairs to the lavatory, the next three times out on to the street – and he did look so bravely determined, each time, each time pale, frail, most of his hair gone, his feeble but obstinate tread carrying him out, then back in again, to his far table the length of this long restaurant, it made the heart pucker – so when I got back I wrote him a card, saying that I'd seen he was in distress, hadn't known whether he'd wanted a touch of support or had been trying to escape, what about lunch – I have in fact entirely given up having lunch with friends, and even business lunches (what business lunches?) because a) I find lunch completely fucks up one's day, especially when one's day begins shortly before a normal lunch hour, and b) because I'm never up in time, so can't anyway – but I had a sudden longing to have lunch with Harold, as we'd used to regularly, when we were youngish men, fit and able – able for what? well, lunch in my case . . .

FOR AND AGAINST OBLIVION

I went out. Had just read Ian Hamilton's posthumous book which arrived yesterday, read it last night and then much of it again this morning – it's called *Against Oblivion*, and it's a sort of version of Johnson's *Lives of the Poets*, at least Johnson's *Lives of the Poets* was his model, the point from which he began. It consists of short essays, four or five pages long, on twentieth-century poets, all of whom have to meet two qualifications – one, that they are dead; two, that they either wrote a few, in some cases only two or three poems (in Gregory Corso's case only one) that in Ian's view are good enough to be preserved from oblivion, or represent some fashion in the narrative of the century's poetry that ought to be placed on record. It's upsetting to read, this last book of Ian's, which he worked on almost to the day of his death and which he spoke about often during his illness – his desperation to get it finished, the last thing of that kind – by which he meant prose studies, critical essays, literary journalism, the higher hack work, *that* kind is what he meant when he said the last thing of *that* kind he'd ever do – when he finished it he was going to retire, not give a fuck any more about any of it, read for pleasure, for pleasure only, watch television, football, and hope that poems, or the beginning of poems, might arrive, to grow into all the writing he ever wanted to do ever again –

And I would think, as he spoke like this, that he was running his own race against oblivion, not the oblivion of a neglectful posterity, but his own oblivion, very personal, out of the here and now and into nowhere that makes any sense, viewed at least from the here and now –

Well, of course, Wittgenstein said – what was it precisely – 'Of those things of which we cannot speak, let us be silent' – and I've seen it in another formulation, or is it translation, 'thereof' or was it 'whereof we cannot speak, let us be silent', so let's try it this way, if you want, 'whereof and thereof we must be silent, let us not speak' – there it is, then, finally unravelled, or should it perhaps be ravelled, into perfect meaninglessness because look, look here, if you can't speak of something, whether it's thereof or whereof, then you will be silent, tautologically silent, so to speak, about that something – and if the something whereof or thereof is death, as repute hath it (but how can we know?), then not only will we speak about it, we will in fact insist on speaking about it, because we cannot in fact not speak about it, it does vex us so – well, well, I mean by this, when I think of the manner of Ian's dying, of his having died, and what his absence has done, is doing, to my life, I find myself wishing to speak of it, endlessly, even though I haven't the language for it – there is Tennyson's phrase, it must be from *In Memoriam*, death of Hallam, was it? – when it comes to it I only remember the last few words, it's when he's writing about how to write about death, Hallam's death, and finds he has no language for it, 'no language but a cry', which is really the point, except it's the poet's business to provide a language for the cry, which Tennyson does in those five words – perhaps not in *In Memoriam*, come to think of it, perhaps from somewhere else, but it's certainly Tennyson. In my view.

A LITTLE OUTING

So having read Ian's book again, I went out this afternoon, with nowhere to go, not at all, but with my OAP bus pass to take me there absolutely free. I ended up on Queensway. I always end up on Queensway these days – sometimes I set forth with the intention of travelling far afield, abroad so to speak – well, Queensway is abroad, a heady place to be at my age, like walking along the pavement of eighteen foreign countries, every overheard word a foreign one. I went into the ice-skating palace, sat on a stool watching the skaters for a while, and then went into that enormous shop, Whiteleys, up to their cinema complex. I bought a ticket for one of the films, but I didn't plan to go to it. Instead I bought a hot dog and a coffee and a diet coke (undrinkable, as it came from a tap, not a bottle) and went upstairs to the cinema bar, closed in the afternoons, but the tables are there, and you can sit at them – there are only two proper tables, as a matter of fact, but they were both unoccupied, so I settled at the one that's in front of a large cardboard cut-out of Alfred Hitchcock from where you can peer over the balcony railing down to the ground floor and watch people passing each other with their packages and their prams, but best of all this afternoon, I could watch the children on the trampoline, bouncing higher and higher, really very high they bounced, some with their faces turned up in joy at the height they got to, others keeping their heads down, concentrating on getting higher yet – it was lovely to see them at it, as I ate my hot dog, sipped my coffee, smoked my cigarettes. I stayed there for about an hour, then went back to Queensway, walked to Bayswater, and got the bus home. The conductor didn't bother to glance at my freedom pass when I proffered it to him, my face and baggy figure being enough to tell the story of my age, my right to a free journey, I suppose. It would be nice if they were taught to study the card, check out the photograph with a slight air of suspicion, just to humour us.

VANISHING POETS

But why did I have to go out? Was it too much, too soon, of Ian's voice, as if the book bore the absence down on one more completely – but the book isn't the man, the style isn't the man, otherwise who would need the man when they have a book so completely of Ian's style as this, his last one, possibly his best book in that it goes beyond the usual style, without losing all the usual, the celebrated Ian Hamilton wit, clarity, urbanity, etc. – and each essay, each of the forty-five is a model of coherence without making each life into a coherence in itself. Something is left unexplained, unformulated but suggested – is that true, or do I just want it to be true? We did once spend a whole dinner discussing whether he hadn't always played it a bit safe in his writing, the Hamilton seated at the desk too aware of the Hamilton standing at his shoulder keeping a watch for any hint of vagueness, softness of feeling, looseness of expression, so that rigour, urbanity, wit became the whole bill of goods in itself, that we got Ian's intellectual virtues without actually ever quite getting Ian – well, did we want all of Ian in his biographies, which were after all not about him but about Robert Lowell, Matthew Arnold, J.D. Salinger – though towards the end of the life of Robert Lowell you can feel all Ian's unwritten revulsion working its way through the prose – besides, whose business was it but Ian's to decide how much of himself he should give to the world in his writing, just be grateful that you had so much of the man himself for so many years –

One of the essays is on a poet called – hang on – Weldon Kees, the only poet in the book I've never heard of, but it's not because of that, my lack of acquaintance with his work and even his name that I don't quite believe in him, the story Ian gives us of this Weldon Kees, that one day at the age of forty-one he left his car in a car park near San Francisco's Golden Gate Bridge and vanished, nobody knows whether he killed himself or exchanged his way of life for another way of life or what – but he was, according to Ian, a bitter poet, almost, now and then, but never quite celebrated – my own story exactly, but here I am, not only unvanished but physically, lumpishly available – yes, but then you're not Weldon Kees, are you? But then was Weldon Kees Weldon

Kees, or is he a representative of a certain period in literary history, that it amused Ian to fictionalize for us? Ian gives us no hard information, no personal history at all, or at least nothing sufficiently particular, though there's an appearance of the particular, of detail, in the study, you can't actually find a fact to hang your concentration on, the whole essay slips through without quite sticking, so when you've finished it you find yourself wondering what it is you've read, and even find yourself checking for further information – the man in the small photograph above the essay looks rather like the young Orson Welles, by the way, but we can't see his face clearly as his head is bent over a newspaper, a Citizen Kane hat pushed rakishly to the back of his head – so even the photograph has a bogus look to it, and no source is given for it, while sources seem to be given for all the other poets' photographs.

As for Weldon Kees's poems, the two Ian publishes feature a kind of poetical-functional character called Robinson, a wispy offshoot of Prufrock, and like Ian's essay in that you can't quite grasp him, can't quite grasp the images – I read them several times, then shut my eyes and tried to remember what I'd only just read, and really nothing came back but a rather diluted tone, portentously calm – flat, really – with a pseudo-not-quite-phoney, phoney would be too concrete a word, so yes, pseudo-plangency – I mean, why would a writer try to make a career out of such unvividly expressed life that really only succeeds in suggesting unvividly lived life – or could that be the point of the poetry? – and if so, how could that be a point worth publishing? – unless we're meant to see it as in some way symptomatic of the nature of Ian's activity in the book – look, he might be saying, here are all these real lives, real poems, and here, slipped in amongst them, is an imitation of both, does it really matter if we don't notice the difference because how can such a procedure give us the truth? may be the question Ian is satirically asking of himself, as well as of us, by inventing Weldon Kees. If Weldon Kees is an invention. Suppose he actually existed – might still exist, now in his eighties, alive in some corner of a foreign field – Uxbridge, for instance? – in which case everything I've written down is nonsense except, I suppose, the central point, which is that I don't believe in Ian's Weldon Kees, whether he existed, still exists, or not –

I suppose what I miss from the book, churlishly, is an essay like Dr Johnson's on Savage – of course, Johnson knew Savage, had strong feelings about him, his family – mother, especially – the way he'd been treated, his madness – there is Savage brought before you with vigorous pity and some pain – well, why should Ian have tried the same? and well, why not? He knew Lowell, had met him a number of times over the years, knew many of his friends, wives, mistresses, etc. and once asked me to join Lowell and him for dinner, actually pressed me because he couldn't face doing it on his own – an evening with Lowell could be slightly tricky and somewhat exhausting, Ian said, especially when he was on medication for his psychiatric problems, which he currently was – he (Ian) needed moral support, and what's more I should welcome the chance to pay my respects to a poet I admired, eh? – well, I said, it's true that I admired some of the poems, especially 'Home After Nine Months Away', but I wasn't sure I admired enough of them to spend a tricky and exhausting evening – Oh, come on! he said, I'm paying! It took place at L'Epicure, in Soho, where Ian and I lunched in those days, we had become good friends with the owner, his wife, and the two waiters, and it was probably the place in London we felt most at home in when we weren't at home – in fact Ian's affairs were such at that time that he probably felt more at home there than at home, often when I left late in the afternoon he'd stay on at the table in his leather armchair – luxurious seating was one of the tiny restaurant's many charms – as if intending to elide his post-lunch brandy into a pre-dinner Scotch. We arranged to meet at 7.30, Lowell having told Ian he would turn up at eight. By nine o'clock or so the evening was going well, very well, in the usual way – 'Perhaps he won't turn up,' Ian said hopefully, but an hour later he did, delivered by a middle-aged, plain-looking woman who went away again immediately. What followed was pretty ghastly – well, how could it not be, as he was full of psychiatric drugs, and soon of alcohol – it was distressing to see this ruined poet with his noble, slightly hydrocephalic head lolling, uttering slurred and muddled sentences accompanied by mumbling laughter, even drooling a little – once or twice there was an odd gleam in his otherwise befuddled eyes, that looked very like malice – as when he asked Ian to order up yet another plate of oysters, which he covered with pepper and sauces but didn't eat, and a further bottle of wine when there were still two half-drunk on the table, and Ian, whose financial situation was dire, began to look anxious. I was sure that Lowell took this in, and savoured it, but when the middle-aged woman returned to collect him, he suddenly became alert, told Ian he wanted to pay his share of the bill, studied it carefully, wrote out a cheque, handed it to Ian with the sweetest and most gracious of smiles, shook him by the hand, shook me by the hand, thanked us both for the pleasant evening, put his arm through the lady's, and left. 'Well,' I said, for lack of anything better, 'at least he paid his way.' 'More than paid his way,' Ian said, showing me the cheque, which was made out to a scrawl, and signed by a scrawl, and was for the sum of six million dollars, or thereabouts.

Now I'm not saying that in the essay in *Against Oblivion* Ian should have given us Lowell as he presented himself that evening, but you wouldn't think, from reading it, that he'd ever met him, he's so superbly encompassed by Ian's prose – one of the reasons one always remembers Johnson on Pope is Johnson's own tenderness in reflecting on Pope's love of his parents – and his description of Pope's personal appearance – the description of his getting up in the morning and dressing – the tininess of his body, his little dress sword, his walking in the garden practising his numbers, talking to himself in couplets – Johnson makes us see Pope without Johnson, using a prose that only Johnson could have written, while Ian makes us understand and judge Lowell only as Ian does – no room to manoeuvre, really – you have the feeling that if you don't agree with Ian's understanding and judgement, then likely you're being stupid, phoney or sniffing a whiff of faction that'll lead you to wilful misjudgement – in almost every one of Ian's essays there is a glimpse of the literary pond life, in which there seems to be a ceaseless activity – literary careers, poetic careers, in the making and the breaking – and why should one be surprised and disgusted by it, one only has to read one's Dryden, one's Pope, one's Ben Jonson all the way back to Shakespeare, and Greene, etc. to know that it's always been going on, perhaps right on back to the knowable beginnings, with the juries at the Greek festivals being fixed for Sophocles, Aeschylus, and against Euripides – in with the wrong crowd, weak, no political muscle, poor PR – but those were *real* careers, bringing real fame, a fame that's endured two or three thousand years, but surely Lowell, aiming for the top, could only have expected to remain at the top for what? fifty, sixty, seventy years after his death, and Ian's essay, where he's far less admiring of the poetry than he is in the biography, will shake him a bit from the top, down a branch or two, and maybe he'll only get thirty, forty years of posthumous fame, let's hope he enjoys them.

I'm trying to make my way back out of all this, to when I left the house after reading *Against Oblivion* – I didn't want to think about the book, or Ian, whom I can see now, by the way, whenever I lift my eyes to the window sill, there he is in a photograph not taken by me, when I first knew him in his late twenties his teeth were broken and discoloured, and although he had them fixed at various stages in his life, so that they looked for long stretches rather magnificent really, he kept the habit of smiling in such a way that he never revealed his teeth, which is why it was, in effect, always a toothless grin – but in this photograph he is as I best remember him, the grin has a sound to it if you know the grin, a laugh heaving up from deep inside him, that when it broke through, took hold of the upper body and shook it from side to side and backwards and forwards, he would subside into coughing, momentary exhaustion, some slightly surprised smiling and blinking, and then would often start again –

ON THE INTERNET AT LAST!

Bound and Gagged in Montreal, is where I left myself a long way back, at the age of six or was it seven? The story unfinished and actually unstarted, although it was one of the most significant events in my life. I can't seem to get into it, perhaps because I actually don't seem to know much about it except the event itself – there were the nuns, of course, who have suddenly popped up, but the nuns didn't have anything to do with it, God knows really where they came from or who they belonged to, perhaps they were roving the streets hoping to happen on a small, easily led gang like ourselves – Nigel and I, two other boys, not Carole, this was a boys only sort of business – so four boys being led by the three nuns down Vendôme Avenue, and then along some other streets into a house, down a hall into a room in which there was a table on which there was a dead boy. He was dressed in a suit, his hair was shiny and slicked back, his cheeks were pink and powdery. One of the nuns said he had been killed while riding on his bicycle. He had grabbed the back of a truck, had been pulled along faster and faster and faster, the truck stopped suddenly, he had smashed into the back. Here we saw the consequences of such behaviour. We must look at him properly so that we would remember him whenever we were riding our bicycles, and so wouldn't cling to the backs of trucks, would we? We said we wouldn't. We didn't say we couldn't because we didn't have bicycles. The three nuns led us out of the house, and went back inside. We went home. It was like a dream then, and is like a dream now, and I'm only sure it happened because I've checked with Nigel, who remembers it as clearly as I do – more clearly, as he remembers that one of the nuns wore spectacles. But it was something else in Montreal, not bound and gagged there.

But here's a thing, here's a thing might help. I've just got myself on to the Internet, or rather, as I've been on it for years, I've just discovered how to use it. Some chap that Victoria knows, who does all her computer tasks for her – and for me too, apparently, though I wasn't really aware of it – his name is Steve, and it's true that I've seen him around the house, coming up from the basement or out of her study, and sometimes he's come into my study, fiddled around briefly on the computer and gone out again, I haven't yet seen him coming out of our bedroom, but then why would he go in there, as there's no computer there? – anyway, he's a handsome chap, neatly put together, with astonishing violet eyes, and a quiet, gentle-but-firm-and-clear-minded manner, and a strange little pouch that looks almost like a cache-sexe, except that it hangs outside his trousers – anyway, this chap Steve turned up yesterday at 2 p.m., when I was bound to be up and about, and left half an hour later, having taught me how to use the Internet – half an hour is all it took him to teach me something that I'd never tried to learn before because I was sure I'd never master it, and there I was, another half an hour later, 'browsing the Internet', getting my search system, called Google, up on the screen, and trying out a couple of names, of two playwriting friends of mine, and up came information about both of them. In each case I surfaced in the middle of rather unpleasant reviews of their plays, so I decided there and then, on the spot, that I would under no circumstances ever visit my own name – I haven't learnt how to browse the Internet in order to browse through bad reviews, which I make such a point of avoiding in real life, and so I sat for a while trying to work out in which pasture I really wanted to browse and graze, and it came to me, with a thrill, a thrill at the thought of it, but without much hope, but anyway into the box I tapped the name Hank Janson – and there it was. He was. A whole thingamabob, website, website devoted to Hank Janson, with little rectangles marking history, background, character, books, author, etc. – I placed my little cursor on books, and there they were, on the left-hand side small copies of the covers – all the covers – and on the right-hand side plot summaries and critiques – I went straight for the covers, putting my arrow on a small cover and pressing. I got an enlargement of the first Hank Janson cover I'd ever seen, *Sister, Don't Hate Me* – the title I'd forgotten, the cover unforgettable, a young blonde, gag around her mouth, hands bound behind her back, stocking legs tucked under her, her face turned towards us, the large blue eyes innocent and alarmed, a curl of hair tumbling over a mildly troubled forehead – talk about madeleines – hah! – I really went through the most astonishing tumble of emotions, the confusion of desire and thrilled shame, the twelve-and-a-half-year-old standing at the bookstall beside Leicester Square station, and yet what was I, actually, as I experienced all that, all those years shed, what was I but a man of sixty-five, bent mournfully and salaciously over his computer, or thus I believed I would have appeared to anyone looking through the window, if that anyone had been me – but if it had been somebody else, Victoria, for instance, Victoria, yes, Victoria would have seen her elderly husband toiling at his work as ever, not that she could have seen me through the window anyway, at least without standing on a ladder, as my room is at the top of the house, or where the top of the house was before we added an attic, so forget Victoria standing on a ladder looking in on me through the window, come back to the simple double-image, a twelve-and-a-half-year-old staring, wet-kneed, at the bound and captive blonde on the cover of *Sister, Don't Hate Me* on an open bookstall near Leicester Square station, a sixty-five-year-old sitting in his study under the attic staring at the same cover, etc. – almost the first time since I was an adult that I've been able to short-circuit myself back, back beyond twelve and a half, all the way back to an afternoon in Montreal. I am sitting on a chair facing the class, my hands tied behind my back, my ankles tied to the legs of the chair. I was in my first week or so of school, so I was six years old, and I was crying and making a terrible fuss, obviously, which was why the teacher had tied a handkerchief around my mouth to stop me interrupting the class. Someone came in, an adult, a woman, looked at me with disgust – so it seemed to me, but it might have been shock or anger – and gave the teacher a piece of paper, a message, I suppose, and went out. Now that is all I remember. I know the teacher was a woman, but not how old she was, nor what she looked like – I have an impression of spectacles, large spectacles, but it's only an impression, and I have no idea what led up to this punishment, which I suppose it to have been, though for all I know the teacher might have been acting on an erotic impulse, or may have been anti-English, but I assume there was a motive that led to it – I have a suspicion that I was considered a chatterbox and disruptive, although the truth is that I spent my first year at school in Montreal, for pretty well the whole of it, in a state of terror – the Englishness of me constituting a continuous offence among my peer group. This was, no doubt, the worst period of my childhood, and so probably of my life – they would ambush me on the way to and from school, administer a beating, throw my bag and cap into snow banks in the winter, through the open windows of unknown houses in the summer, lock me in garages, in fact pretty mundane stuff as the world now goes. Now where was Nigel in all this, how did he avoid this daily ghastliness, because I think he did avoid it, I have a sense of him as being at ease in his schooldays – although of course his began a year before mine, he may have gone through it all while I was still a favoured stay-at-home, snug in Grandma's arms or bed, but I don't believe he did. I must ask him the next time we have an evening together. On the other hand, how much do I really want to recall of that time? Perhaps I should go to a shrink, get some of this buried state unburied. I might discover the why of my being tied down by my teacher, but then why bother, the point of living beyond one's childhood is that it all happened back there, whatever good or ill happened happened back there. It's not as if we have to live with the consequences in any way that makes sense. Only psychiatrists who believe in clear logical paths between past and present, unconscious and conscious, can believe that at sixty-five I continue to live with the consequences of what the monstrous woman, whom I only think of as monstrous for this single act, it may have been the monstrous lapse of a mainly kindly soul – and I mustn't forget that I was an exceptionally pretty child, quite gorgeous, in fact, if early photographs are anything to go by (and remained so until my early teens, when my nose suddenly put on a spurt) and possibly I was to her as the girl on the cover of *Sister, Don't Hate Me* was to me only six years later – I mean, on the one hand a succulent little moppet with an English accent, what more delicious than to bind and gag him and put him on public display, on the other a succulent blonde with heaving breasts, what more delicious than to bind and gag her and have her on the cover of a book which you have in your pocket for a mere one shilling and sixpence – but a mere one and six was hard to come by when my pocket money was two shillings a week.

Hence my career in crime.

I've just looked Weldon Kees up on the Internet. He existed. Perhaps still does, somewhere.

A THING AND OTHER THINGS

Here's a thing. A drizzly afternoon. I woke to it shortly after midday, with the house empty – a note from Victoria reporting that she'd be out to lunch, there was no sign of George so assumed she'd gone off with her walker, no sign of Tom, in fact the only living creature to be found was Errol, who in fact evinced few signs of life, he was curled into a thick ball on the sofa, his tail wrapped around him, so at first glance you would have mistaken him for a woollen cushion. I gave him a little poke, said a few words, to make sure he was OK, and he gave one of his mousy little squeaks, otherwise didn't stir, even when I went into the kitchen to make breakfast – usually I can't shake him off my heels when I go to the kitchen, he assumes that he eats when I eat, stands on his hind legs with his front legs whirring until I pop something into his mouth – then I came up here, thinking that I really must get on with a play I'm writing about some English people marooned on a Greek island. I've been stuck for ages in a scene where people keep on talking but I can't make out why I have them saying what they're saying, I don't know what they want, and when I don't know what characters want I don't know who they are, and how they've got onto the page – I sat looking at a line of dialogue – PRYNNE: You would say that, wouldn't you! – which began to incense me, as the line that provokes this, from a character currently called HENRIETTA, is completely inert, idle speaking to fill the silence, idle writing to fill the space – so then I thought I might as well get on with this for a while, but the thought of the last sentence – 'Hence my career in crime' – depressed me, I felt no stirrings of either guilt or joy at the prospect of remembering my career in crime, so I went to the window, stared out at the drizzle, wondering who would want to go out in that who didn't have to, and went out in it, though I didn't have to – or perhaps I did, who knows? I tramped up Holland Park, past the bus stop, aimless but conscious of my hair getting matty from the wet, wishing I still had my Russian-style, waterproof hat that I lost or was stolen from me last year, then heard – no felt – a bus coming up behind me. I got back to the stop and clambered aboard before it could pull away, promising myself that for once I'd ride it all the way to Oxford Circus, but got off at Queensway as usual, went into the ice rink. There was nobody skating. Nobody. Back into Queensway, where there were quite a few people all right, but not milling about as they usually are, coming towards you in groups talking excitedly in foreign tongues, they seemed listless, as if they didn't really have any business or pleasure in mind, like me they were out because they didn't want to be in, but they didn't want to be out either. Much the same feeling in Whiteleys, where I bought a hot dog, a diet coke and a ticket to *Harry Potter*, and went up to the bar. I hoped briefly that I'd go into the film, but I was sure the cinema would be empty, or almost so, and the vision of myself sitting alone in a cinema on a Tuesday afternoon, watching a film about a child with large spectacles doing magic and defeating wizards and battling dragons in a prep school, which is I gather what he does, struck me as so pathetic. When I was at Cambridge, an undergraduate, alone in the

cinema apart from a type like me as I am now, I would try to imagine
his life, the hopelessness and uselessness of it, the squalor and pathos,
etc., and now, of course, I imagined there'd be someone of twenty-two
or so in to see *Harry Potter* who would try to imagine the squalor
and pathos of my life, etc., so really I thought I'd be better at the
bar, looking over the rail and watching the young bouncing on the
trampoline – actually I knew that it would be like the ice rink, nobody
would be on the trampolines, nobody, but at least there'd be the
shoppers, the prams and pushchairs, little packs of Muslims, Japanese –
but when I lit my cigarette, drew my chair over to the rail and looked
down it wasn't just that there was nobody on the trampolines, which
I'd expected, or that there weren't any trampolines, which I'd half-
expected, as they'd obviously been temporary, but – and here's the
thing – below the bar, where I'd remembered trampolines, were
escalators – escalators that had been there since I'd first come to
Whiteleys, on which I'd often ascended and descended, on which,
indeed, I'd just ascended to get to the cinema complex. So what had
happened the other afternoon, when I'd seen the children bouncing?
Had I sat at the table, stared down at the elevators, and hallucinated
trampolines instead, a reasonable enough replacement when you think
about it, after all most of us would far rather trampoline up and down
a shopping mall than trundle through it on escalators – I suppose I'd
seen the trampolines somewhere else in Whiteleys, and when I got
home and wrote it down I conflated the memory of sitting at the table,
looking down, with the memory of the trampolines – after all, the
escalators were so familiar I wouldn't have noticed them in memory.
But supposing there weren't any trampolines in Whiteleys, and never
have been, then I'm dealing with a real hallucination – well, certainly
much better than my usual hallucinations – I'll ask Victoria when
she gets back, I have the distinct impression that I mentioned the
trampolines to her, and that she said she'd seen them too, weren't they
delightful – but what if she says she hadn't seen them, as far as she knew
there had never been trampolines in Whiteleys, what a preposterous
thought, trampolines in Whiteleys – perhaps better not to ask her.
Better to go on with PRYNNE: You would say that, wouldn't you! – or
my career in crime. One or the other. Which?

CRIME

It began with fairly rhapsodic pilfering from Daddy's trouser pocket and Mummy's purse – no skill required for either, I collected money from his trousers every morning for my tube or bus fare, he lay in bed with his tea, papers and post, his trousers lay over the back of a chair, I said from the bedroom door, 'Can I have my fare please,' he gestured to his trousers, and I took out the shilling or whatever and palmed an extra coin or two – and Mummy's purse was always to be found in her handbag which was likely to be found anywhere, and quite often when she wasn't near it. I moved from this rhapsodic pilfering to a more organized and rewarding level entirely by accident, when an aunt chose, for reasons inexplicable, to give me a Georgian penny for a birthday present – inexplicable as I had never shown or had the slightest interest in old coins but of course perfectly explicable if you know that the aunt in question was a pretty mean old bird, who probably turned up the forgotten coin in a drawer, and always one to make do, made it do as a birthday present to her nephew – who carried it around in his pocket for days, hoping that he might find a use for it, and eventually did. I was with my two closest friends at school, one called Quass, and the other Eddis. Quass was short and Jewish, with a terrible sideways grin that he had difficulty removing, especially when he was in trouble; Eddis was a lanky, blond, sardonic boy, who was an exotic in that his parents were divorced, he lived with his mother, and his father now and then turned up at school, an elegant man, soldierly, and drunk. We constituted a small gang of outsiders, really, the three of us in the lowest form in the school, Transitus C, contemptuous of work because we were brighter than the rest of the form. Idle and jeering, we were capable of making each other laugh to the point of physical collapse – really it was the jeering strain that bound us closely, nothing and nobody in the school commanded our respect, especially anything we didn't understand or anyone we suspected of being gifted and intelligent – our conversation reduced the world to our level, or just beneath it, as we had, needless to say, no respect for each other – but that was justified, as we knew each other so well. *Folie à trois.*

Folie à trois. We were at St James's Park tube station, late afternoon, going home, I suppose – Quass lived in Dolphin Square, Eddis in Queen's Elm Gardens, now why should I remember that when I don't recall some of my own addresses, the street that I lived on for nearly a year in Vancouver, for instance, although I remember the desk against the window, through a corner of which I could see the sea, and through which I could also, if I looked down at certain times of the evening, see the parked car in which sat the large, handsome wife of a small handsome colleague. She was in love with me, was the only explanation I could offer myself for her parking there, as I typed steadily away on my second novel, occasionally glancing down at her – I never went down to ask what she was doing or would she like to come in, and she never rang the bell – after a time she'd drive off, and I'd have a sense of mild relief, and absolutely no sense of an opportunity missed, although I liked her very much, as much as I liked her husband – every Saturday night the three of us would meet up, along with several other colleagues of the English Department at the University of British Columbia in Vancouver's China town and have a festive dinner – nothing in her manner on those occasions suggested she was in love with me, but I expect, if she's still alive, she would still remember my address. I don't remember it in an absolutely complete sense, as if I hadn't really known it even while I was living there, and yet for over half a century Eddis's and Quass's addresses have been lodged in me, addresses I visited – well, twice for tea with Eddis and his mother, Mrs Eddis (he spoke to her with the cool contempt of an estranged husband, from whom he'd probably learnt it), and only once to the Quasses, for a legal briefing – but let us suppose then that we were at St James's Park tube for the purposes of going home, Quass to Victoria, Eddis for South Kensington, I for Sloane Square, and while we were sorting through our pockets for money to put in the ticket machine – this is how it happened – I found the aunt's Georgian coin, offered it to Quass and Eddis in exchange for real money, say twopence, was jeeringly rejected, and then one of us, the one of us with the sharpest eye for an improbable chance – not me, more probably Eddis – popped it into the two-shilling slot of the sixpence-halfpenny ticket machine. It fell through the various runners, runners and channels, and landed with a chink and a clump, falling, we realized, into a pile of other coins, accepted coins. This was going to be a familiar sound over the coming weeks, months, a sound deeply satisfying, deeply ominous, the clink and the clump of immediate wealth, impending disaster. I never believed we wouldn't be caught in the end, so the usual criminal's prayer, adapted from St Augustine, not this time, please, God – don't let it be *this* time – anyway, after a moment spent taking in the full meaning of that noise, that clink and that clump, one of us put in a halfpenny, and the machine stuttered, and it trembled and heaved, and out popped the sixpence-halfpenny ticket, and one and sixpence – in the form of three sixpences – change. The machine, in other words, had received the Georgian penny as if it were a modern (1949) florin. So we had sixpence each. The next step, which we took immediately – or so it seems in memory, though there must have been some working out, some research – we found a numismatist around the corner from the Hank Janson bookstall, where we discovered that Georgian pennies were two a penny – well, actually one for twopence. So, we could buy a Georgian penny for twopence, put the Georgian penny in the two-shilling slot of the sixpence-halfpenny ticket machine, a halfpenny in the halfpenny slot, and in return would receive a sixpence-halfpenny ticket, and three sixpences (one shilling and sixpence) in change – along, of course with a sixpence-halfpenny tube ticket, which for some reason we couldn't use, perhaps because we were under sixteen and had to travel on half fares that were actually marked across the ticket (I have a memory of two red stripes?), and travelling on an adult ticket would have raised suspicion – or perhaps we regarded the tickets as evidence that had to be disposed of. But even if we failed to maximize our profits, they rapidly became so vast that we couldn't keep up with them – you have to keep in mind that one, just one, Georgian coin and a halfpenny bought a whole Hank Janson – the London Under-ground was, in fact, financing my masturbation, was also financing as much of the fraudulent cherried cakes, ice creams, etc. as I could eat, and there were still handfuls – by the time we were caught twenty pounds' worth – of sixpences under the floorboard where I kept *Hotsie, You'll be Chilled, Lola Brought Her Wreath*, both genuine titles, I've just checked on Hank's website. Heady days, those were, and full of terror. The accumulation of sixpences became more addictive than the addictions I was feeding them to (buns, cinemas, Jansons) – I say 'I' here because I don't know what Quass and Eddis spent their money on – both bought Hank Jansons, but not as needily as I did, I think, and we didn't really discuss our sexual habits, practices, predilections, whichever word would be appropriate. Eddis maintained a rather aloof attitude to such matters, anyway, kept his council, Quass and I would have possibly a brief, excited but careful conversation about which ones we'd read – but in textual terms – 'You know, the one where he's escaping from the gangsters' – and never really in terms of the true story, which was there, undismissably on the cover and came up in the narrative only as incidents. In fact, our conversations, inasmuch as we had them, were not unlike the careful, thoughtful plods through the texts, as they explicitly call them, on the website – we have the plots of *Hotsie, You'll be Chilled*, etc. with all the 'incidents' ignored, apart from an occasional en passant reference, *regretful* reference to H.J.'s tendency to roughness with women, but the nature, the style, the dash and panache of that 'roughness' is excluded, in the oddly brutish and punitively puritanical, not to say verbally genteel, age we live in – so we have the plots, a meticulous rundown on the main characters, some esoteric snatches of comparative analysis, i.e. 'though *Torment For Trixie* lacks the range and scope of the narrative of the earlier *Frails Can Be So Tough*' etc. – and even pernickety observations on H.J.'s sudden changes of style and tone within the texts, the whole purpose and point of the man and his writing is not so much lost as wilfully and insultingly slighted – but there, lying beside these turgid and earnest critiques lie the heart of the matter in the reproduced covers. I can't say that Quass and I managed to conduct our discourse at the same level as the discourses on the website, but in common with the website we talked around what mattered most to us – at least so I assume, of course for Quass it may have been the plot, characters, narrative style, etc. all along.

A NIGHT OUT

I'd never heard it played straight through before, though I recognized bits and pieces as they came up, the Shepherds' Farewell at the beginning of the second part, for instance, and the later choral passages, especially the last, which seemed to me astounding, and the choir itself – I've never experienced quite such a gorgeous hushing, the noise seeming to fade slowly, so slowly, right inside oneself – but actually, being neither musical nor religious (at the moment) I couldn't make any real sense of the whole – none of these passages of beautiful music seemed to move into the next part or grow out of the last, each passage just happened independently, in spite of programme notes and translations of the songs that suggested that this was a structured telling of the story of Christ's childhood. Actually, it becomes a very peculiar, very sentimental story, if you take God out of it, which is what I think Berlioz did – how else explain the Shepherds' wish that Christ 'grow and prosper/ And be a good father in his turn,' seeming to mean, not a spiritual Father, but a biological father. Had Berlioz thought this through, one wonders, or did he intend a piercing reference to what was missing from Christ's life, or had he merely forgotten the theological facts – but I came out feeling reverential, though possibly it was a reverence for the genius in the music – a genius that expressed itself for an hour and three quarters without a break – I could scarcely believe it, though I checked on Victoria's watch too – an hour and three quarters in the theatre is for me unendurable – physically unendurable, the need for a pee, the need for a cigarette, the need to stand up, walk, stretch etc. would have overpowered my concentration for the last half-hour at least, but not at *L'Enfance du Christ*. We seemed to waft out of the auditorium, at least until our feet hit the bizarre undulating floor of the Barbican – the only floor I've come across that makes you seasick just to walk a few paces on – why did they do it, whoever did it, in fact why did they do the Barbican at all, unless as a challenge to the seriousness of the audience's intentions – the concrete wastes that surround the building, the tunnel that leads to the building, the hideousness of the building itself, make you feel that you've entered a war zone, the final bunker – and then inside, the vast undulating floor, with double and triple sofas arbitrarily arranged by way of seating. On Saturday evening one small area had been roped off, to make a sort of pen in which some elderly people were sitting side by side or at angles to each other, as if they were in quarantine, or petitioners for a stay of execution. They were quite still, not talking, and there was a placard swinging over their heads, on which was written 'Friends of the LSO'.

We went on to dinner in the West End. London was London on a Saturday night, Hogarth or Hieronymus Bosch, take your pick – in the restaurant we bumped into several people we knew, actors and two playwrights, so there was a lot of kissing, the women kissing the women, the men kissing the women, and muddled into all this, the men kissing the men – some of us were heterosexual, but still we ran into each other's arms, rubbed cheeks, kissed, as we made growling sounds of pleasure and love – this male cuddling is a new fashion, probably come over from New York or Russia, and I don't really like it, really rather hate it, especially when they have beards, like both of the playwrights and one of the actors, they're rough on my skin, and probably full of food and insects, and they're smelly, but I see no way of repelling them unless I take to dribbling into them or blowing my nose over them, and word gets round that I'm to be avoided, however soft-skinned, clean and inviting my own cheeks are. I'd had the wit to book a quiet table, so we settled to a good meal and talked about the Berlioz, and then about our writing problems, and over coffee I told Victoria that she looked beautiful, which she did, and how happy she makes me, which she does. She thought about this, and then asked me what was I up to, what was the matter, what had I done? – her usual response when I pay her a compliment, and the reason that I don't pay her more. 'Well,' I said, 'well –' then as if changing the subject, 'Do you remember the trampolines in Whiteleys, a few weeks ago?' 'Oh yes,' she said, 'all those children bouncing, wasn't it lovely?' So that was all right then. When we got home we threw the tennis ball around the front hall for George for a while, and then went to our studies, I to write this, she to work on her stories, though I could hear the ball bouncing, George barking, Victoria laughing.

THE MEANING OF PLOP

Victoria Station was our favourite haunt, a junction into which we could tube from our different places of residence, make a quick killing, then on together to school. It was also special in that its sixpence-halfpenny machine never failed to deliver, accepting warped and wafer-thin Georgian pennies that the machines in other stations rejected with embarrassingly loud groans and grating sounds. It was in the middle of a line of five machines, I think. Yes, five. The backs of five other machines were lined up directly opposite, about a yard away, and there was a machine at the end of the double line, each facing out, thus creating a rectangle of ticket machines, with an inner rectangle of space, which an underground employee could step into by pulling aside one of the machines at the end. He could then open the backs of the machines to collect the coins, put in a new pack of tickets, adjust whatever mechanics needed adjusting – very efficiently organized, I now see, making it easy for a policeman, for instance, to enter the inner rectangle, open the back of the 6d½ machine, crouch down out of sight, cup his hand under the 2s runner and catch the penny as it fell – a legal necessity, because if the coin joined the heap already in the machine, it would be impossible to prove when and by whose hand it had been inserted. The first indication that something was slightly off, therefore, came when the dropping of the coin wasn't followed by chink and clunk, but by a soft plop – it was audible, the plop, like a physical sensation in one's system rather than as a distinct noise – and there was the explanation, in the form of an adult's head rising from behind the machine, and simultaneously hands belonging to a second adult male standing behind us clasping each of us, Quass and myself, by the elbow. We were quite merry, Quass and I, all the way to the police station, as were the two policemen, who were flatteringly full of admiration for our little scheme, forgiving us for their having to spend long periods of time crouching, knees bent, behind the machines, waiting for the wrong penny to drop. I don't think we really worked out what was going to happen when we got to the station, perhaps the conviviality returned us to earlier childhood, the sense that we'd taken part in a game, and lost, with laughter all round, perhaps we were playing being jolly good losers, or perhaps it was minute by minute bravado, the mind refusing to progress even to the immediate consequences – but consequences became real at the station, when statements were taken down – confessions, I suppose they were – and most particularly when we had to give our names and addresses, and a telephone number where our parents could be reached – then the reality, reality of the situation, the pleadings not to call the parents, please, we won't do it again, we promise kind of thing – the Quass parents and the Gray parents turned up, I can't remember in what order, and I can't remember the journey home, or anything much apart from the shame and the fear and the moment when, hearing the mother approaching my room, I fell to my knees and assumed the praying posture, eyes closed. I heard the door open, and then heard the silence, as if the mother were joining me in this act of devotion. Then her voice, 'Oh, get up, you bloody little fool.' A day or so later, when we were walking together somewhere in Chelsea, after an eerie silence that had gone on virtually since she'd summoned me up from my knees, she said, her voice thick with emotion, 'I want you to know that your father and I will always stand by you, whatever you do.' We walked some more. 'Because we know you'd never do anything like this again.' I can't remember whether I made a reply. Even now, I can't think what reply would have been the right one – although the honest one would have been a thank-you for the show of support, but a courteous refusal to guarantee that there wouldn't be a repeat – in fact, there were many repeats, though nothing on the scale of the slot machine swindle, nothing as imaginative, although occasionally, more shaming. At Cambridge I caught myself cheating at a poker game. I belonged to a Trinity poker school, we met twice, sometimes three times a week, played from about 9 p.m. to 3 a.m., and for – given our circumstances – quite high stakes, high enough for a loss to mean desperation, a gain a night out in London. One night, or early morning, on the last hand of the game – it was one of the very complicated games, either baseball or anaconda, with many cards on the table – I nudged, kind of nudged, one of those jerky little movements that I could almost pretend to myself was thoughtless, accidental – nudged a card one way, another card another way, thus giving myself a winning hand. I not only caught myself doing it but also caught myself pretending to myself that I wasn't. And there was a further self in me that took cool note of what the other two of me were up to – as did a Canadian, ten years older than the rest of us and much the best player, he also took note and noted aloud that he'd taken note, although choosing to pretend that what he'd taken note of was an accident – but I could tell from the gleam in his eyes that he saw me for what I was, not just a cheat but a cowardly cheat – I wonder if I could have gone through with it and accepted my winnings, or whether, not that honesty would have prevailed, whether my nerve would have failed, in other words, which was the stronger current in my nature, the cheating or the cowardly. I was never comfortable in that man's presence again, actually I'd never been comfortable in it before then, as I'd always thought there was something cynical and knowing about him, lacking somewhat in respect for his fellow men, particularly me, yes, that was possibly the worst of it, that I'd succeeded in confirming suspicions I knew he held about me.

I've just been out. I got as far as Holland Park Avenue, stepped on to the pavement, two screaming police cars hurtled towards where I was going to put my next step, lurched violently without breaking speed, screamed on in and out of traffic up the avenue – no doubt en route to a crime which will be completed, the perpetrators vanished, long before they've arrived with blood on their fenders and their warning siren still wailing – well, at least there's a good chance that they'll have something to show for their efforts, a broken or a dead body that supplies some of the material of a crime scene, even if they've provided it themselves – every time I read of them in the papers, or accounts of inquiries in which they are invariably acquitted of any offence, frequently saluted if not honoured and promoted for it, I feel ill with anger, in fact one day might come to be counted as one of their victims, though at long range, felled by a heart attack or an apoplexy induced by reading about them, as much their responsibility as if I'd been crushed under their wheels or bounced off their bonnets (hoods? what?) into the gutter. Anyway, I turned around and came home. I was out for about four minutes. It was enough.

PUNISHMENT

Quass wore his 'guilty as charged' grin, appropriately, as we were guilty as charged, but his grin also carried with it a different – entirely unintended, entirely inaccurate – message, not simply of guilt, but of gloating guilt, and I wished, for the first time in our relationship, as I stood with downcast eyes and hands clasped behind my back, that he'd wipe it off his face – whatever happened to him would happen to me, he was grinning and gloating for both of us. There were two men and a woman sitting at the desk before which we stood, one of whom must have been the magistrate – or perhaps they all were. They heard what we'd done from the policemen, and then asked us what we had to say. We said we were very sorry, it wouldn't happen again. Then my father spoke. He said he was very sorry, it wouldn't happen again. He then went on to speak of the career that lay before me, either promisingly or in ruins, depending on the judgement of the court – the terms in which he spoke of me, my achievements, my potential, the high moral regard in which I was held by form-master and housemaster, might have brought a blush to my cheek in other circumstances – but I can't imagine what they would have been, I really can't imagine any circumstances, except the one I was in, that would have prompted the father to have spoken so highly of me. He was usually as modest about me as he was about himself, although for different reasons, his modesty about himself being an acknowledged part of his charm, and doubtless contributing, along with his passivity (and for all I know, enormous cock), to his sexual success – anyway, the father spoke, the mother sat nobly beside him, possibly telling herself that she never thought she'd see the day when she'd see a son of hers, etc. When he sat down, Mr Quass rose, and spoke briefly to introduce his colleague who was sitting next to Mrs Quass. He was a grey-haired gentleman with a silver tongue, a barrister who specialized in criminal law (Mr Quass himself, I suddenly recall, specialized in maritime law), and in a speech of sonorous eloquence, in which he described Quass's and my future in such technicoloured terms that everyone in the court knew he was lying, nearly succeeded in destroying our lives. Well, my life. Well, my immediate future. But then who knows? Being sent to a remand school might have improved my future, if not immediately, at least by now – I could have been among the first of the 'redeemed' writers, a category I have only just invented, but I could have invented it back then, is my point, and would almost certainly have had less trouble getting my books published, my plays put on – a number of critics have long sneered at my typical English middle-class, public school and university educated, literary, so forth, so forth –

a criminal record, reform school, where I would have learnt so much that is useful – robbery, buggery, etc. might have won me a respectful critical attention. Anyway, when Mr Quass's colleague sat down there was a revolted silence from a bench that had been previously disposed to take the policeman's view of the case, that we were decent little chaps who'd been unable to resist – what ordinary boy could have – the temptations that our natural intelligence, combined with an astonishingly unfortunate piece of good luck, had exposed us to. They stopped looking benevolent and scowled at me and most particularly at Quass, who of course gloated grinningly back at them – they put their heads together, muttered briefly, rallied into good humour – I remember being smiled at – and decided that we should be put on probation for six months, sentence suspended for two years, on condition that the parents made restitution to London Underground. This was estimated at twenty pounds each (Eddis excluded, naturally) which the father was able to pay from under the floorboard, and kept the change.

My father's references to the good opinions of me held by form- and housemasters weren't lies or fantasies, or even honest speculation, what he hoped they might have said if they hadn't known that we were up on criminal charges, because in fact they did know, headmaster, housemaster, formmaster – all of them knew exactly what I'd done and had spoken of me exactly as my father said they'd spoken, and this against the evidence not only of the legal facts but their own experience of my moral nature – one of my earliest reports had come right out with it and called me a liar – well, not right out with it, it was one of those whimsical schoolmaster phrases, 'sometimes a stranger to the truth', I think it was – but that was straight out enough for the mother/Mummy. 'That a son of mine –!' the mother said, after waking me with a slap in the face, then throwing the report at it – this was at about seven in the morning, the report had arrived in the first post and Mummy was in her transparent nightie but not her making-breakfast dressing gown, 'that a son of mine,' she drew herself up to her full height, thus revealing bits of herself that Hank Janson wouldn't have wanted on his covers, 'should turn out to be a liar!' 'What about a son of Daddy's?' I might have asked, if I'd known then what I know now –

the scene ended with the father's voice, calling from their bedroom in an unusually peremptory fashion – 'Barbara – Barbara, can you come back in here, please!' – perhaps he thought her reaction excessive, or had suddenly noticed her dressing gown over the chair and realized that she wasn't wearing it therefore, and the thought of her in my bedroom, as good (?) as naked, slapping me about either alarmed the father in him, or excited the husband. Anyway, she went to him with a swivel of the heel, and I lay there, listening to their voices, his low and even, hers tumultuous, dreading breakfast, which I knew would be silent for me, noisy for Nigel – 'Are you playing rugger this afternoon, Nige? Where will you be playing, darling – no, no, I meant in what position, you fool!' with a cough of laughter and a shower of ash, which I no doubt hoped would settle on Nige's fried egg on toast. For me, of course, not a word, and only the sort of looks that communicated that I was too revolting to be looked at. That evening, when he took me through the report, the father concentrated on the academic rather than the moral side of things, worrying that I was bottom in Maths, and very nearly bottom in everything else except English and History. At the end he muttered, almost shyly, that by the way this business of my being 'a stranger to the truth' was a bit upsetting, wasn't it, old chap, perhaps in future I would avoid (he didn't actually say 'for her sake' but it hung there between us) telling even harmless little fibs, let alone large and necessary lies – if this is not the distinction as he actually made it, it's pretty well what he meant. Though what he really and most importantly meant was, would I kindly not get caught doing things that were reported in a report that would be read by my mother. That night, when I was back in bed, the mother made her goodnights by throwing open my door, stepping into the room to show me an icy profile with a cigarette in it, and then stepping out again, slamming the door behind her. I longed, naturally, for the usual cuffs and blows and laughter, longed for Mummy. My Mummy.

Got to stop for a while – it's a bit upsetting to find myself back there without being back there – they're both dead, the cunning child who loved and needed them has evolved or decayed into an elderly creature with a heartless memory – and did I love my father? I don't think –

LOVE, LAW AND ORDER

Distracted from distraction by an hour of television – an old *Law and Order*. Stroke of luck that it was on, and that I came in near the beginning. I love this series – love? Love *Law and Order*? – did I love my father? I don't think – Do I love *Law and Order*? – I know I do. Is it the word that's at fault, or is it my use of the word, or is it my self, my incapacity? Apply the Plato principle that we should love people for their virtues. What were my father's virtues? What are *Law and Order*'s virtues? – That's easy, just consider how it works: each episode has the same structure, three neat little acts. 1) The discovery of the crime (usually a body) and the police investigation. 2) The involvement of the DA's office and the arrest. 3) The trial and conviction – or sometimes the acquittal. Formally very dapper, you see, but flexible within its conventions – even though the official characters are always the same, and played by the same actors, there is a variety of story, of milieu, of incidental characters, played by those marvellous American character actors who give you a glimpse of a whole life in a two-minute scene – a grieving mother, an overworked guy behind a deli counter, a sixteen-year-old Hispanic with a gun under his bed and drugs in his pocket, so the scene-by-scene texture is terrific – as is the dialogue, snappy, authentic, moving the story along – and it's usually a pretty snappy and authentic story that's moved along, with often a twist that really twists – on top of which you get lots of detail about police work, along with lots of detail about the way the law works in New York – and in the one I've just watched, the conflict between the way it works in New York and the way it works, and doesn't work, in Los Angeles, made specially enjoyable by its exhilarating contempt for all things Californian – even to the faces, those round Californian faces, neatly featured, large shiny teeth, smoothly tailored hair, and there among them the New York faces, faces to which I am now addicted, slightly unhygienic, with pocks and other blemishes, slightly more used up, slightly more comically rancorous than the last time I saw them – So there it is, that's what I love about *Law and Order*. As for my father, Daddy, I –

we were swimming one summer afternoon on Hayling Island,

probably the summer that Nigel and I came back from Montreal. The four of us were in the water, all four of us very good swimmers. The sea was calm, light waves, and we moved about in it in a little family pack until I found myself swimming away, heading out to sea as fast as I could until I was out of my depth, and then swam a bit further, and a bit further, the sea got colder, my body weaker, until I couldn't swim any more, the waves seemed to be rolling inside my head, I started to shake, pawing feebly at the water as I slipped under it, and the next thing I was in his arms. He'd kept an eye on me when I'd struck out, noticed the growing feebleness of my stroke, swum after me, gathered me in, carried me to shore. He laid me on a towel, Mummy poured tea from the thermos down my throat – 'Make sure it's got a lot of sugar in it,' he said. 'But what happened?' 'Nothing. He got a little cold, and outswam his strength, didn't you, old chap.' What has remained with me all my life was the feeling I had when I lay in his arms, my head against his chest, I was his child.

ON BEING A GENIUS

So. So. Well, back to the report. Whichever master wrote it would probably have been astonished by the emotional repercussions in 47 Oakley Gardens, he'd obviously used the phrase he'd used because he really didn't mind too much that I told lies, got caught out in telling lies, and in much the same spirit, I suppose, he didn't mind a couple of years later when I was caught thieving from the Underground – although he might have minded more if he'd known about my thefts at school, at the end of term, when I (and Quass and Eddis) would raid the lockers in our common room, extract the Latin primers, Maths textbooks, etc. and sell them in the second-hand shop located in the basement of Foyles – a practice we stopped when we started on the Underground, plenitude making us fastidious. Westminster was morally a wonderfully relaxed school – Quass, Eddis and I would surely have been expelled from any other public school in the country, but we weren't punished except that – well –

Our housemaster, Stephen Lushington, called me into his study and, in the most charming and graceful manner, put it to me that I should do my best to separate myself from Quass (the role of Eddis as partner in crime was unknown to him) as we were clearly bad for each other, and it was evident to him that I was the dominant influence – the Quass parents had said much the same thing to my parents, by the way – which is why he was addressing me on the matter rather than Quass – and perhaps I owed it to Quass, my friendship with Quass, to take the initiative in having less to do with him –

So when he came up to me to ask me, all – as I saw it – winks and leers and smirks, how the talk had gone, what had he said, in other words to share the joke of it, I did a little sidestep away from him, saying, 'Nothing, he didn't say anything really, excuse me, Quass, I've got to go home now.' So I cut him and snubbed him, and mostly felt good about it, even when I saw – as only I, apart from his parents, could – the hurt in the grin, the pain in the gloat. I felt I was cleansing myself of him and everything associated with him in my past, I felt that I was favoured by the authorities, was a special boy to them, to be watched and encouraged and even cherished, and that my disreputable past gave me an aura, a moral charm – yes, though I was known to be a delinquent, the specific nature of the delinquency wasn't known to anybody but the housemaster and the headmaster, as far as I knew, but it was generally understood to be a clean, clear, healthy, unsexual and uncorrupt delinquency, a sort of innocent naughtiness of behaviour that had landed me in a scrape somehow, briefly – and now here I was, a literary figure, winning school prizes for my essays, starting up a house literary magazine, there was a graceful swagger to everything I did, it seemed to me, no, that's not true, it seemed to me that it seemed to everybody else that there was a graceful swagger to everything I did, but really I lived in a chaos, an unchanging chaos, of desires.

And such was still my condition at seventeen and a bit when Daddy made his bacon-saving move to Halifax, Nova Scotia.

Bacon-saving for me, too. For one thing, it meant that I wouldn't have to do national service, for which, with my poet's sensibility and my masturbatory habits, I knew I was temperamentally ill-equipped – I'd got out of school corps after my conversion to the intellectual life by claiming that I was a conscientious objector, which was certainly true as I had the strongest possible moral objection to being ordered around by people I'd decided were inferior to me on the grounds that they weren't me, really, and therefore had no idea what was good for me and were thus post facto, ad hoc, de jure and any other Latin phrase you can think of, inferior to me, QED. Because I actually at the time did feel myself to be a most extraordinary and exceptional creature, a miracle of intelligent life, perhaps the only boy ever who'd travelled from Transitus C to Four B to Five A to the History Sixth (a preserve of the brightest and the best, only about eight of us accommodated) without knowing a single thing outside of myself – it's not that I didn't know, let us say, the dates of the kings and queens of England, it's that I didn't know that Charles I came before Charles II – it's true that given a little thought (but where was that to come from?) I could have worked it out, as I did know that one generally preceded two – really, it was more that my mind and body were hyperactively committed to their own needs, which took the form of self-celebration, self-worship. Well, look, every Friday I went to the cinema on the corner of the King's Road and – and – I can't remember what the other road it's on the corner of is called, but it leads down to Chelsea Bridge, and the cinema was called, I've got it! The Essoldo, yes – every Sunday, from when I became sixteen to the last Sunday before we enshipped to Halifax, Nova Scotia, I went to the first evening showing of the Special Sunday double bill, two old films, and both of them 'B' movies, in the hope that some scene would pop up in which there would be a girl bound and gagged, failing that, bound, failing that, with her skirt hitched to reveal a suspender and a stocking top, failing that, a stocking top. Once the film got going I would fall into the story, captivated even without a captive blonde, but what drove me to the cinema in the first place, whatever the weather, was the primary urge – and when I came out of the Essoldo onto the pavement, exhausted and exhilarated by either hope fulfilled (how could it be fulfilled? In public I was shy even of my own pockets) or hope denied – I say exhausted and exhilarated deliberately, because it was a combination of both, an almost mystical state that came from my reflection, this reflection, that I was by far the most intelligent person to have been in the cinema, by far the most intelligent, by far! I was a genius, I could tell I was, by my searing, scornful searchings of the other faces. I always hurried out, to be among the first through the doors, then cross the road to stand opposite the doors so I could see the other members of the audience leaving – so this was a deliberate and habitual event, every Sunday, this clocking of my inferiors, counting them off – more intelligent, better educated, than him or her or him – inspired, a poet, a genius, a very, very great genius, so established by mine own eyes, those comparing scrutineers as I stood on the pavement opposite the Essoldo Cinema on a Sunday night fifty years ago –

Things look bad for tomorrow, according to a television weather-woman – rather pleasant-looking and young – say forty-eight, or so – but with a nasal and downward-sloping voice – when I first came across that sort of voice I assumed that compassion-politics were at work, high-profile jobs for the vocally challenged sort of thing, but I've since been told that they're trained to speak like that, the idea being that they should sound not just not posh, but positively anti-posh – posh-bashing, I suppose it could be called – so what I was hearing from this pleasant-looking young woman of forty-eight or so was a posh-bashing weather report, promising rain tomorrow. Time to count my blessings, not out loud, though, nor on yellow paper.

PIERS, EARLY AND LATE

I was half his very big brother, who threw him up in the air, caught him, tickled him senseless, half his parent, who wheeled him about in his pram, toddled him to his nursery school, taught him to read and to swim. These were pleasures, although I pretended that I saw them as duties and that they weighed heavily on me. 'Oh, don't be so silly!' Mummy would say. 'You know you adore him.'

In his early drinking days, at Cambridge, he drank to be merry, sociable and free, he drank because he liked the taste, he drank because why not? – in Hong Kong he drank at first for the same reasons, and because that was what they all did in the Senior Common Room, but as the years went by and he went on delivering dazzling lectures on Wallace Stevens, William Carlos Williams, T.S. Eliot, to students who only wanted to master English as a commercial language, and writing long-pondered essays that though they were published were hardly noticed, and plays that didn't achieve productions outside Hong Kong (except once, at the Edinburgh Festival, posthumously) and finally a novel that was rejected with such brutality by a publishing friend that he couldn't bring himself to submit it anywhere else – through all this he drank more and more, from frustration and anger and then despair, more and more, eventually scheduling his day around his bottle. He became claustrophobic, so frightened in lifts that he had to walk up and down the many flights between his office and the common room, and of course, as he could no longer get on an aeroplane, had to give up his cherished vacations in London – in the vacations he kept to pretty much the same routine as in term time, but with the students and teaching omitted, and so with more hours to drink in. Every fresh term time his condition was worse, until finally he was incapable of teaching, became a nuisance in the common room, was banned from the campus, invalided out. He settled down in a flat a short walk from here, spending the hours he used to spend at the university in the Groucho Club, or visiting his old Cambridge friends – those with small children became less welcoming as they became more aware of the dangers – for instance he would suddenly lose control of his balance and topple abruptly to the floor, never actually on top of a child but sometimes close – he also began to lose control of his conversation, joining the same sentences together in an endless circle, and his mouth would suddenly fill with blood, one could see it before he gagged it down or lurched out of the room to throw it up in the lavatory. In his last weeks he would come around and sit silently in a chair in my study, his drink in his hand, his bottle of bourbon at his feet. His stomach was swollen, as were his ankles, which were visible between the turn-ups of his trousers and the espadrilles he wore without socks, even in the coldest weather, even in the rain. His face, though, was unlined, his blue eyes clear and alert – it was a beautiful face, that I had used to gaze at in wonder and joy when it was a baby's, and would now glance at surreptitiously, nearly fifty years on – occasionally he would catch my glance, smile with a serenity that seemed to have a taunt in it, raise his glass to his mouth – and I would turn back to my typewriter, clackety-clackety. From time to time I'd get him into a clinic, but he saw these stays, which he invariably cut short, as courtesies to me, and easily found secret routes to the nearest pub and off-licence – he treated doctors, counsellors, psychiatrists as opponents in a game, to be out-witted, every drink another point on his score card. When he was in his last clinic some friends came in a group to tell him that they could no longer bear witness to his self-destruction, if he didn't stop drinking, at least for a while, they would close their doors to him. He replied that he was sorry, but he couldn't contemplate life without alcohol. There was a long silence, and then one of them said, 'Well, Piers, you've just announced the end of our friendship.' And they left. A few weeks later he collapsed with a burst liver, burst kidneys, burst everything, really. His death caught him by surprise, I think – I certainly don't think he intended it, even though he did it by his own hand – but perhaps he had no choice, who knows? He certainly behaved as if he thought he hadn't, and all in all I'm pretty sure he wanted to go on living, if only to go on drinking. Every month or so I go up to Kensal Green cemetery and sit on the bench that Nigel and I had placed opposite his grave – a pretty spot, and the people who visit his neighbours are always friendly.

FEEDING THE ROT

I've just raked my pen across my yellow page, and jabbed it down and down and ripped it across. An attempt to write a primal scream. After all, I'm a writer and should be able to express everything, but here, once again, I've failed – who, on looking at these marks, would think they represented a primal scream without my having to say so – the need to do something savage was because I'd been sitting with my head in my hands, running my fingers through my hair and thinking how I really couldn't put down another word, I really couldn't, when it came to me that I wasn't running my fingers through my hair any longer because my hair had turned into maggots, long thin wiry and soft, climbing over and through my fingers, and then I realized that the bees were back, settled again into hollows in my body, the gigantic queen bee and her bustling mounds of worker bees, one set in each hollow of my body –

kneecaps, elbows, and behind my forehead – behind my eyes – these hallucinations, if that's what they are, come to me when I'm depressed – a good thing too, one might say, otherwise how would one know one was depressed? Actually, that can't be strictly accurate, I used to have them a long time ago, before a continuous flow of hallucinations set in to do with vegetation and the colour green, that I was sprouting bushes out of my face, etc. – a phenomenon that I thought initially was caused by my alcoholism, then decided wasn't because they stopped coming long before I stopped drinking – but as I say, before that there'd been the bees and the maggots – no, not maggots first, worms first, so bees and worms before vegetation, and now, after quite a few years, bees and maggots – the difference between worms and maggots is not a pedantic one, the worms were fat and brown, the maggots, as well as being soft, are wiry and bright grey – it doesn't last long, this sensation of being a host to bees and maggots, and sometimes I can break the spell almost immediately, with a sudden vicious act – banging the table often works, or, as just now, with the written-down primal scream. I loathe the thought, though, that vegetation might follow, because the vegetation attacks were almost impossible to stop, I simply had to wait until they'd worn themselves out – some of them went on for a long time – I'm looking down at my hand moving across the lined yellow page – 'this warm hand, my scribe' – I don't know what to make of it, actually, I've had it all my life, I couldn't be more familiar with it, know it like the back of my hand, etc., but it suddenly doesn't look like mine at all, with its liver spots, wrinkles over the knuckles, a getting-on-in-life, down-at-heel sort of hand, go to bed.

I did. It's what I tend to do nowadays when confronted by a problem – mortality, for instance. In the old days I'd have taken a drink, and then another drink, possibly eight or ten drinks in a row, enough anyway to take me to a state that resembled tranquillity, but was really passivity – inertia, actually. Going to bed doesn't render me inert, although if I'm lucky I fall asleep. But before I fall asleep I lie on my side, with my knees drawn up as close to my chin as stiff joints, weak muscles and a pendulous stomach permit, the classic foetal position as adopted by a man sixty-five years away from the womb.

Ian's theory was these hallucinatory growths were healthy shoots of self-disgust, bursting out of my sense of my own moral rot, which is why, he said, they so revolted and frightened me. Otherwise, although they were initially alarming, why should I not come to accept them, welcome them even, as exuberant expressions of life and energy, springtime in the soul erupting through my body? This theory struck me as plausible because I did, in fact, feel at that time I was morally a shit-heap. My adultery, probably like so many other men's – I can't speak for women, I only know their side from books and films, not from conversations with women – odd, I almost wrote 'other women' – what would it mean, if I had? What does it mean, that I nearly did – actually, I can't speak for myself either, at least at this moment. 'The French do it better,' Ian would say to me, or I to him, 'That's only because they're French.' 'That's right. If we were French we'd do it just as well as they do it.' 'Absolutely. And if they were English they wouldn't do it half as well as we do it.'

MATTERS OF LIFE AND DEATH

Victoria has just come into the room, accompanied by George. George went to the French windows, out onto the balcony, and began the slightly mystical sniffing and peering through the railings that she does when she thinks, or so we think, that the fox is somewhere about, down in the garden. We talked about this rather as parents might about a daughter with a suspect boyfriend, imagining the possible conversations with George – 'Darling,' one of us might say, 'we don't want to be interfering, or snoopy, you know us, we respect your right to choose your friends, and I don't think anyone could call us – darling, what would be the word?'

'Specist?'

'Specious?'

'No, species. Spee-shees-ist.'

'Yes, nobody could call us spee-shees-ist, I hope, so it doesn't really matter that foxes are, as far as we understand it, rodents and not, like yourself –'

'Well, we don't know that, darling, do we, exactly, in what ways George is like or unlike –'

'Well, we know George sleeps on our bed, in it, sometimes, and sits on our laps. In our laps.'

'Well, we don't know that this chap wouldn't, given half a chance –'

'Yes, but apparently they don't house-train, nobody's ever been able to house-train them.'

'Them?'

'All I'm saying is that we don't know anything about him, George never invites him in. They hang about out there together, in the dark, doing God knows what –'

'Well, perhaps it's up to us to invite him in.'

'What! Like *Guess Who's Coming to Dinner* –'

'Well, why not, if he's anything like Sidney Poitier –'

'But that's just it, we wouldn't want him to be like Sidney Poitier, these days even Sidney Poitier doesn't want to be like Sidney Poitier.'

'Why do you assume he's a he, anyway? He could be a she.'

'Well, now you're opening a whole new can of – of –'

'Where's George?'

'She's there. Out on the porch.'

'No, she isn't. And there goes the cat flap, she's in the garden.'

'Unless George's invited him or her in.'

'Christ, if it knows how to work the cat flap –'

'It'll be in and out all the time. What about Tom and Errol?'

'They say they kill cats, bite off their heads and rip open their stomachs –'

'You know, I heard somewhere that the vermin people – you call them rodents, you see, you say you have a rodent problem, as if you're talking about rats, but it's understood that really you mean – you mean –'

'George's friend.'

'Well, let's get her in now. In and safe. You go down to the garden – I'll call her from here – George – George darling, hey George –'

So there it is. As with children, so with animals – you can't be too careful – oh, yes you can, with children – Ben at eight years old, insisting that he was old enough to walk to school by himself, everybody else did, every other boy and girl, he was the only one, the only one whose father clumped along beside him, he hated it, it made him feel he was just a baby, or that there was something wrong with him – well, I couldn't say that as far as I was concerned he was the only child in the school who was my son, and therefore the only one I wouldn't trust to cross the road sensibly, and as the road in question was the Archway Road, one of the busiest as well as one of the vilest in London, with lorries and those things that are three times, four times as long as lorries – pantechnicons, that's it. So up and down the Archway Road roar the lorries and the pantechnicons, with motorbikes careering on either side of them, it requires nerves of steel to cross the Archway Road with a child at your side, and inordinate patience to wait for the traffic lights to change, and though Ben had nerves of steel when it came to his own safety, he had no patience – so little that there were times that he tugged my hand so abruptly and powerfully that I thought he'd pull us both under the traffic – the short of it is that I refused for as long as possible, offering as a compromise that I would no longer hold his hand (though in fact keeping my hand close to the seat of his trousers), and that we would cross as separate individuals, as far as the world could see, not even related. I got away with two weeks or so of this, but of course he knew the other children knew, he could see that they were looking, laughing, jeering at Ben and his daddy, Ben's daddy and Ben, crossing the Archway Road together not, it was true, hand in hand, but hand by bum, and it was no good my saying that they weren't laughing and jeering (though they weren't, at least as far as I could tell), his view of his humiliation became so ferocious, his spirit and sense of honour, and no doubt his maleness, so diminished – all the girls crossing on their own, Dad, all the little girls, Dad – that eventually after long into the night agonizings we at last agreed to let him go to school by himself. It's actually very easy to follow a child, I discovered, children scarcely ever look around – at least they didn't in those days, comparatively innocent days. Nowadays, of course, children who are allowed to walk alone are probably trained to glance over their shoulders at regular intervals, and if they spot a man of the age I was then, in my late thirties, or indeed a man of any age, ducking and dodging along behind them, would know exactly what to do – and it's perfectly possible that even back then the parents taking the younger children to school would eventually have noticed me, and if they didn't recognize me as Ben's father, or perhaps even if they did,

would have reported me to the police – but I had to stop doing it not
long after I'd started because one morning Ben did behave exactly as I'd
predicted, possibly because I'd predicted it – stood for a few seconds on
the pavement, jouncing with impatience as he waited for the lights to
change, then before they'd changed, when he thought he'd detected a
gap, an alluring gap, in the traffic, darted into the middle of the road.
Whereupon I bellowed BEN! Whereupon he froze. Froze in the middle
of the Archway Road, with pantechnicons, lorries, motorbikes, run-of-
the-mill cars, roaring at him from both directions, there he stood frozen,
then turned, stared at me, I stared back at him briefly, he was obliterated
by traffic for a lifetime of a second and then he turned up, so to speak,
on the pavement beside me. In front of me, to be exact. 'What, Dad?'
'What?' I said. I couldn't say you nearly got yourself killed, as it was
clearly I that had nearly got him killed. 'You nearly got me killed,' he
said, 'shouting like that.' 'Yes, yes, sorry, sorry, I wasn't thinking, just saw
you there, shouted without thinking. I was going to the bank, you see.'
No doubt gesturing towards the bank which wasn't open at that hour,
in those days, and in those days no cashpoints of course. 'But you didn't
wait for the lights, did you?' There followed a brief but unattractive
scene, a 'no, you didn't' 'yes, I did' sort of scene, during which I managed
to conduct him across the Archway Road without his noticing. I decided
never to follow him again, better to spend an hour or so every morning
not knowing whether he'd killed himself, than be the cause of his death.
There's much in this story, now that I've remembered it, that seems like
a foretelling, or would it be a leitmotif, viewed backwards – that my
conscious efforts to help him always contain the elements of his potential
destruction – but on top of all this, this was my point – I think it was
my point – that the deep and frantic and paralysing worry for one's
children extends to one's pets – no, actually it was the other way
around – I got to Ben in the Archway Road thirty years ago, by way of
George and the fox in the garden just now, and there's not just George
to worry about, there are the cats, Errol and Tom, what about them?
Every day they risk being run over. Or stolen. Both are very lovely, in
their different ways – and they have bouts of ill-health, Errol is becoming
so fat he'll soon have to go on a diet, sad for me as well as for him, as I
love him fat, the way he rolls about on the floor, his dainty waddle – and

then at the end, if they survive accidents, illnesses, kidnapping, there's first of all old age, and then that awful bit past old age, when one still can't bring oneself to give them up – for instance, Jeffry, named in honour of Christopher Smart's cat, the first cat of my first marriage. Jeffry wasn't much to look at – although he ate well he always seemed slightly undernourished, with bandy front legs and a small, peaky face – he was black, with short hair, a few white splodges indented on his shanks – he was charmingly affectionate, good, quiet company, but slightly withdrawn and autonomous, in the way that cats are always assumed to be, though in fact not many are, and with a clear sense of what was owing to him – we had a piano in the bedroom, over the keys of which Jeffry would walk every morning, backwards and forwards, seeming to step on the same keys and tinkling out the same notes, until finally forcing one of us to get up to give him his breakfast. He was expert at catching mice and fledglings, the corpses of which he would leave for us as little gifts and surprises, either in armchairs in the sitting room, or on the dining room table. It was hard, of course, not to be disgusted by these offerings, and not to find oneself wishing that Jeffry wasn't so completely a cat in that one respect, but of course something in one was also touched and even grateful. All in all, he brought harmony into the house, and it was therefore a terrible shock when one day he wasn't there. He started his disappearance by not being there on the piano in the morning, and went on to be absent from all his usual places, all over the house, for all that day, and all the next. We asked our neighbours, put up posters, cursed his kidnappers – there were no signs of his having been run over, somebody would have heard, have seen – no, he'd been stolen, no question of it, some swine of an old lady or a besotted child had snaffled him off the pavement, claiming to themselves that he'd looked lost, starved, in need of a home – and at that time there were reports in the newspapers that a gang of cat-stealers went around the city in a van, taking cats and using them in some foul way for profit. It took weeks and weeks for Beryl to reconcile herself to the loss, though of course she didn't really, would still suddenly drop her book or leave the table and go on a wretched prowl up and down the street, or at the back in Highgate woods, calling for Jeffry, Jeffry. One day, when we were coming back with the shopping, a woman who was passing stopped, as if from an afterthought, and said, 'Oh, are you by any chance the people who've lost a cat?' Yes, we said, we were, we were. 'Well,' she said, 'there's a woman up the road in 84, the top-floor flat, who's found a cat.' Around we went immediately to 84, where a very nice woman, and her very nice husband, both ex-teachers, elderly and retired, showed us into the room where Jeffry was now living, in a large, cushioned basket, with soft drapings hanging down the side, and with saucers of water, milk, fish and chicken around it. He greeted us with a pleasant enough purr, though he seemed half-drugged with sloth and luxury. According to the woman Jeffry had followed her into the house one afternoon, accompanied her up the stairs and into the flat and proceeded to make himself so at home that she and her husband – he confirmed it – assumed that he'd been left behind by people who had moved from the neighbourhood. They had, she said, mentioned him to people now and then – no, no, she hadn't seen the posters on the trees – no, no, he hadn't seen the posters on the trees either – but then his eyes – he tended to walk with his head down – and she stepped straight out of the front door into the car when she went out, and she went out very little these days, and so, no, they hadn't seen the posters, but had mentioned to people now and then – all this over a cup of tea, with polite merriment, but that evening I expect there was as much grief in the top flat of number 84 as there was joy in the top flat of number 70 – 'But why can't they get their own bloody cat?' I said to Beryl, who said judiciously, compassionately, something to the effect that they were quite elderly, weren't they, probably didn't think it fair on the cat to take it on and then die, but if a Jeffry just walked in, offering himself, like little what's her name in *Silas Marner* – naturally we kept a bit of an eye on Jeffry after that, although it was comforting that we'd know where to look the next time he absconded – but can you abscond, unless you take something with you, somebody else's money or wife, for instance – but Jeffry had taken our love, our certainty in him, our faith – and his coming back, no, his having to be fetched back, what did it mean, exactly? He never went to number 84 again, as far as we knew – I'd hate to think that he did, and was turned away – and he behaved just as he'd always behaved, straight back to the keyboard for breakfast, etc., but still, there it was, he'd left us for a large basket with drapes and saucers of delicacies, was it a

warning shot across our bows, a lesson in the instabilities of life? It was
a bit of a mystery, an unsettling mystery, but it became an unpondered
one eventually, as the years went by, and life without Jeffry seemed an
impossibility until suddenly it became impossible not to notice that he
was going, and impossible to do anything about it. He was really very
old, the vet said, who was himself very young and called Justin – he
could hang on for another few months, but don't leave it too late. But
we did, we left it far too late, and later than that, we simply could not
bring ourselves to do what we knew should be done, not until he was a
spiky black sack, seeming to grind and creak as he tottered along the
kitchen table, sometimes slipping to his knees but purring, that was the
most piteous part of him, he kept on purring as if purring were a
complete form of life in itself. And he stank; the stink from him was
appalling. I took him to the vet in a taxi. He lay with his shrunken head
on my lap, alternating his purrs with little whimpers of apprehension.
The surgery was just off the Holloway Road, then a Greek-Cypriot
neighbourhood, and standing in front of its door, as if they'd been alerted
and were waiting for me and my pathetic bundle, was a pack of old
ladies, five or possibly six of them, dressed in black – they swarmed
around me as I crossed the pavement, making mewlings of sympathy
and distress at the first sight of Jeffry, which turned into screeches of
outrage and what sounded like ancient curses when they realized his
condition, clearly they believed I had neglected, abused and even
tortured him, which of course I had, in a way. I sat in the waiting room
with Jeffry purring on my lap, stroking him and keeping my eyes
lowered – I remember a couple of dogs, a torpid Labrador and a terrier
with its leg in a sling, and there was a parrot with a bandaged beak – but
I couldn't look at their owners, for fear of angry and reproachful eyes,
and didn't dare look towards the window, sure that the old ladies would
be glaring in, miming vengeance – people came and went, animals came
and went, I longed for a cigarette, Jeffry purred and purred in that low,
passive, haunting way until finally it was my turn and Justin came to
look at what was on my lap. I couldn't meet his eyes either, but I heard
the little noise he made. I followed him into the operating room, where
he put on rubber gloves and got a syringe out of a box. I put Jeffry on
the table. He scarcely stirred, except to stretch out his chin, with its white

patch, but he went on purring. Justin put the syringe in, the purring stopped, and I went back into the waiting room, paid at the desk, keeping my back to the window, then slipped outside. There was just one of the old ladies standing there, a sort of outpost, I suppose, but she didn't notice me, her attention fixed on two small girls coming along the pavement, holding a cage – I couldn't see what was in it, but I hoped it wasn't past its kill-by date.

A LAPSE OF CONCENTRATION

Madame Me's a weed in bloom/ Self goes dogging everywhere is not how it goes, but how it comes out when I think of eight years of dogged, day-by-day, dutiful, not to say onerous adultery that I felt OK about only when I was abroad. Not that I wasn't adulterous abroad, but I didn't mind so much. In fact, I didn't mind at all. I would arrive in New York, for instance, with my wife-to-be, with whom I'd spend the first week, and depart with my wife, with whom I'd spent the second, and during both weeks I would be completely at ease with myself. So he didn't travel, perhaps he had no passport, or was quite simply a stay-at-home, this other, troubled adulterous self. I used to enjoy little glimpses of him in my mind's eye, a doppelgänger, moping in my study, or hanging about in a no-man's-land between two homes which were separated from each other by most of central London. But once I was back, taxi-ing west to north or north to west, breeding maggots, bees and worms in my moral system, with Ovidian translations into shrub, oak or cabbage in the offing – as I write this I try to keep a little of my concentration on the television in the corner there. It is showing *Meet Me In St Louis*. We've just got to Judy Garland singing 'Have yourself a merry little Christmas', but it looks to me – it's very charming, it's always charming, though I haven't seen it for years, but it does, quite truly, look to me as if she's been synched, her lips are doing the movements but not quite matching her voice – yes, it's probably me, these old eyes not matching these old ears rather than her young voice not matching her young lips.

We're past Christmas, now, into spring, we've got over the might-they-move-to-New-York-oh-please-don't! hump, and the whole family is at the fair, all the ladies in white (perfect for a day out) the young men (what else can one call them? although when you look at them closely, some of them are not particularly young, and quite a few of them not at all manly) wearing or holding those hats, the same shape as boaters but not made of straw – yes, there they are now, this marvellous family who've been living the same enchanting life for what, sixty years now, as freshly as ever, not in any way seeming to repeat themselves – that's the great thing about film, if you do it fresh in the first place it remains fresh for ever, on the stage you can be stale by the second night, though you can sometimes freshen up for the last night, it's true . As I write this, the eye aimed at the screen notices for the first time that one of the sisters, the oldest, looks much older than the last time I saw the film, perhaps she was always a bit elderly for the part and I've only just spotted it – I hope so, I'd hate to think that she's ageing away on her own, and that one day I'll find her on the screen looking like her Grandpa's wife – but isn't the Grandpa a marvel of acting, such charm, and effortless, I know him so well from so many films, but I've forgotten his name – I'll catch it on the credits, write it on the top of this page, ah, here it comes, the lights in the great state building are coming on, they stand together in the dusk, close together, admiring their city, their state, their country, happy, happy family, now the theme is swelling, 'Meet me in St Louis, Louis,' lightly it swells, and – fuck, it's over, gone from the screen just like that, the buggers, the shits, they've cut the credits, cut the credits, and something that looks like a roll of lavatory paper is unscrolling on the screen, and a voice too stupid for one to register whether it's American or English, or even what sex it is, is informing us of the programmes ahead, and so, along with the feeling that I've just been party to a brutal amputation, I realize I won't be able to write Grandpa's name on the top of the page. What I'll write instead is the name of the channel responsible, it's Hallmark, the Greeting Cards mob. Here you are, Hallmark. Here's a greeting for you. Two fingers in a V. And the same for my memories of adultery, come to that. Sufficient unto the day. And unto yesterday too.

PART THREE

STRANGERS ON TRAINS

– as I've got older I've developed a claustrophobia, a form of claustrophobia, in cars, more to do with the cars coming towards us or going past us than with the car I'm actually in – perfectly sensible, really, to be frightened in such circumstances, all you have to do is to imagine the guy high up in the pantechnicon that's running nose to nose with you, the big, boozed-up, unshaven, negligent-looking guy, one hand holding a bottle of beer and a bit of the steering wheel, the other hanging out of the window, a cigarette between two fingers jutted upright, and you just know that the eyes in the red pudding of a face are half-shut, the big belly full of turbulence and an ulcer, between the buttocks an abundance of swollen veins that cause constant heavy but sensitive shifts of balance, the whole body, in fact, a mass of disturbances, irritations, congestions, not to speak of a head full of dreams of a lustful and vengeful kind, and who's that old shit staring up at me from the passenger seat in that little what's-it, woman driver, yeah, move over old shit, tell your frosty little wife to move over, come on, nudge nudge, nudge nudge – what you say, a dawg and a cuppler cats? Well, who the fuck gives a fuck, gulp gulp puff puff puff nudge nudge old shit frosty wife two dogs and the fucking cat down the toilet – oh my arse these fuckin piles my ulcer gulp puff shit – is what I imagine going on up there in the cabin of the pantechnicon – which is why I travel by train, First Class smoker on East Anglia Railways.

This afternoon I had a table for four all to myself, on the table a couple of diet cokes, coffee very strong from the espresso bar at Liverpool Street, and Orwell's essay on Billy Bunter versus Miss Blandish for when I wasn't peering out of the grimy window, through the heavy drizzle, at a world that seemed to be all oblongs and squares, it was hard to tell whether streets or fields, town or country – it was all perfect, really, thinking of Victoria, Supervic, my wife, driving along, keeping cheerful company with George, Errol and Tom, listening to an opera on tape or the radio – the only irritation the usual businessmen on their mobile phones, but at least they kept their voices down, not much above the hum of the train, really, until three of them started up a rather loud conversation with each other – it had to be loud as they weren't sitting together, one was at the table for four up from me, the other two at small tables down from him, all of them with their backs to me, which was irritating as once they'd started I wanted to see their faces – it was one of those 'where were you when you heard it?' conversations – one of them had heard it when he was flying to Brussels, he was the nearest of the small-table men, the other small-table man had heard it at the end of a long lunch in Sheffield, while the third man, the four-table man, had heard it pretty well where he was now, only going in the opposite direction, a colleague had phoned him on his mobile at a few minutes after 3 p.m. – so that's when the back of the neck felt a little shiver, because I'd heard the news at the same time on what must have been the same train, in fact we were probably sitting in roughly the same relationship to each other then as now, and we must have been on our mobiles almost simultaneously, in my case I was talking to Victoria – she was driving back to London, with Errol, Tom and George, and I got her just after she'd made a detour to a small kennels from which she'd collected a puppy, a birthday present for my two granddaughters – hi, I'd said, I'm on the train, it left on time, everything was OK apart from the three or four businessmen all of them on their bloody mobiles, all of which had gone off within seconds of each other, bloody mobiles, I said down my mobile, how was she getting on herself, had she got the puppy? 'Listen,' she said, 'I think I've just heard something extraordinary on the radio, well, appalling if I understood it properly –' and she told me what she thought she'd heard if she'd understood it properly, and around me the businessmen were making noises that were probably identical to the noises I was making – and then we were at Liverpool Street, not empty exactly, but spectral, with a long, silent queue for the *Standard,* and its enormous headline, as if the enormity of the print would make the impossible credible. Then the tube, Holland Park and home. In my study, in the empty house, I sat slouched in an armchair and watched thinking that millions were watching with me, including, presumably, the clutch of men who'd organized it – sitting in a faraway cave, enjoying the replays, like a football manager and a spectacular goal – 'The lad did great.' Lads, in this case. The lads did great, dead themselves, six thousand dead others – or so the news reported – to prove how great they did. Victoria, George, Errol and Tom arrived at last. Victoria came straight to the television set. The others dispersed into the garden, eager to relieve themselves after a longish journey, part of which they'd shared with an unfamiliar puppy. Victoria and I sat in front of the television –

Now, on this train, probably the very same train but going the other way, I listened out for what the other chap had done when he'd got off at Liverpool Street, had he gone home to his wife, detoured to his mistress, dropped in on a pub with a television – I felt an odd kinship with him – but he carried the conversation off in a different direction, to do with the effect on the market, share price index or whatever, one of the other men got up to join him, the third man began making phone calls, then sat down with the other two. When I got off at Stowmarket all three were at the same table but on their mobiles – perhaps to each other, a conference call to show they meant business – I wondered which of them was my one, so to speak – I fancied the one with the cigar. Actually, I'm not sure cigars are allowed, even in the smoking section, but I decided to let it go.

I had a twenty-minute wait at Stowmarket. It had stopped raining, but the platform was wet, glimmering in the late sun. I stood on it smoking and blank, happy I think, until there was the little train, more tram than train, on time to the minute, and almost empty. Again I had a table for four to myself, with a discarded *East Anglian Daily News* on the seat opposite, which contained news of local violence, quite a lot of it, really – rapes, burglaries, man shot in a garage, suspected irony in Ipswich – arsony, suspected arsony in Ipswich – no, arson, I mean arson, of course, in Ipswich, and outside Rougham a hit-and-run etc., all quite disturbing, but not quite as disturbing as the chap who suddenly sat down opposite me – I mean where had he come from, we'd left Stowmarket, we were on the move, he hadn't been standing or sitting nearby when I sat down, and furthermore there were lots of empty tables, even tables for four, for him to sit at, why did he want to sit with me, especially when he looked like what he looked like – he was about thirty years younger than me, and big, wearing a raincoat buttoned up to his chin, which meant, really, that when you glanced at him he seemed to be all face, and it was quite 'ugly' as we used to say in the olden days – disabled, do we say now, he had a disabled face? – button nose, small, stumpy teeth, and pop-out blue eyes which were popping out at me, and there was a sort of grin going on, well, anyway, a show of those teeth – his hands were under the table, I could sense them moving about, doing what? I remembered that murder some years ago on the London tube – the middle-aged man knifed to death by a young man who didn't like his smile, it was provoking him, he'd said at the trial (at which he was acquitted), it was personal. I tried not to seem personal, tried not to smile provocatively, and tried to concentrate on the paper, rustling the pages about and folding them emphatically this way and that and occasionally glancing at him casually, noticing his hat, a patch of mackintosh that slid over one ear, with a bit of a bandage sticking out from under it. So some sort of medical hat then, to protect an ear damaged God knows how, perhaps somebody had tried to bite it off – his girlfriend, perhaps, or his father – the eighteen minutes from Stowmarket to Bury seemed to take for ever and ever, I was convinced that he was going to reach under the table and grab me, I decided to get up, stuffing my stuff into my brown bag, but before I moved away, he stood and said something, which I didn't understand, except that want came into it, he wanted something.

'I'm sorry,' I said. 'What?' I waited for him to say my wallet, or my watch, or my brown leather bag, old and battered, or my life, in much the same state, but which I wouldn't give up without a squawk, though I'd virtually done my squawk with my 'what?' We stood with the table between us, staring at each other. Actually, I couldn't move – this was the moment foretold, kind of thing.

He spoke some more sentences, Suffolky sentences, which I completely understood. His newspaper. He'd left it on the seat to mark his place while he went to the toilet. His voice shook and I suddenly realized it was because he was nervous, possibly his eyes were popping for the same reason. It was costing him something, to speak up for what was his.

'Oh, oh I'm so sorry, I thought it was abandoned –' I took it out of my bag and handed it to him. It was a terrible mess, almost in a ball. 'Sorry. I didn't know there was a toilet on these little trains.'

He looked at the paper, made a stab at straightening it and folding it. He had small hands, clean, with neat fingernails. The toilet was down at the end, he said. By the last doors.

'Good to know,' I said. 'In fact, I think I'll –' and went there. I had a pee, did some work on my hair with my comb, and came out again, thinking to move to a different spot, but then remembered my bag and diet coke. I went back to the table.

It was the wife, he said. She expected him to bring it home with him in the evening. Otherwise it wouldn't matter. I had a sudden image of the wife, his ear between her teeth, he shaking his head about, explaining that this man from London had stolen it while he was in the toilet –

He seemed quite keen to continue the conversation, I could see now he was friendly, and potentially even garrulous, but we were coming into Bury and I could get away.

When I got off I looked back, from a sudden sense that there was something I hadn't done, or had forgotten. He was standing at the window, holding out my diet coke and plastic cup. I made a gesture that meant – or I meant to mean – too late, I don't want it, you have it. He smiled and nodded and the little train trundled off – I don't expect he'll drink the diet coke, or want to use my plastic cup, but I think things are OK between us now, which is what matters.

Victoria was waiting for me outside the station. We usually coincide there almost to the minute – while my train is being held up by a person being on the line or whatever, she is being held up by a pile-up on the motorway or whatever – and yet it's somehow always a surprise to see her, George in the front, on her lap, Tom and Errol in their baskets at the back, Tom crying indignantly. Errol, ever the master of his fate, comfortably dozing. It began to rain just after we left the station, and was raining more heavily when we got to the cottage twenty minutes later. As soon as we'd unloaded the car, I came across the garden to my study, and checked it out. The view from my London study is of a small garden, and then the backs of houses. The view from this one is of a small patch of garden, then a fence, and then a field that stretches and stretches – at night, if the moon is up, it is like the sea when it is completely calm. It is so tonight.

HEALTHY APPETITES

Just up the road there are the ruins of a manor house, with a moat and four swans, a mother and father who are a deep black, and two children, who are turning that way but haven't quite got there yet. They're nearly as big as their parents, but still have specks and streaks of grey, the colour they were when cygnets. I suppose they're in late adolescence at the moment, they've got the coarse manners, the greed and the bogus swagger – even in the water it's a sort of swagger – of adolescents, but they still hang about close to the nest, or never more than a foot or two from one parent or another, when they're out and about – a situation which the parents clearly find objectionable, particularly when they're having bread thrown to them. Victoria and I go up every evening to feed them, in all but the very worst weather – we feel guilty when we don't go, so really we should just go up whatever the weather, being wet being better than feeling guilty when it comes to these swans, who honk with pleasure when we appear on the rim of their moat with our carrier bag of crusts, honk out thank-yous when we leave. But in the passage in between, this is what I was aiming to get to – the parent–child relationship – the passage between, the unedifying brawl between the parents and children over the bread, the parents barging the children out of the way, the children barging back – this graceful and extremely well fed, not to say pampered family behaving in a style that would be called dysfunctional by social workers – my heart is always entirely with the parents, of course, partly because they're so devoted to each other – this evening, for instance, the father arrived with the two louts pounding gracefully along behind him, began his butting and barging the moment I began to throw the bread (I do the feeding, Victoria stays a few feet behind with George. Victoria is convinced that George, unless kept closely restrained, would hurl herself into the moat in an attempt to snatch a crust from their beaks) but broke suddenly away, mid-gobble, and swam towards his wife, who'd just decided to climb down from the nest – as ungainly a sight as you'll ever come across, a swan manoeuvring its way down a river bank, its large body pitching and swaying, its paddle feet slipping and skidding under that lushly feathered bum, then the clumsy crash into the water – then lo! the smooth and haughty glide of her – and there was old dad, back turned on the kids and the goodies, gliding towards her, and when they were a few feet from each other they each made a small, loving honk, and dipped their heads at each other, then moved in together, butting and barging the kiddies off the goodies. They had all the zest this evening, of a strong and loving marriage, it made the heart soar, well, made us laugh with pleasure – my, how we did laugh, Victoria and I, as we moved on to the pigs with our carrier bag in which were apples and old lettuce leaves and cabbage stems, potatoes, etc. There are four pigs, to go nicely with the four swans, and their sty is set in a large patch of nettles and bushes, with some cleared terrain so that they can roam about, when not slumbering on top of each other in their sty. Like the swans they've learnt to identify our voices and tread – they have a rather terrifying way of not being there until there they are, surging out of their sty or one of the beds of nettles, groaning and snorting with desire, and although they're not a family – well, they may be related, a brother (a great sack of testicles and an enormous snout) and his three sisters, or perhaps they're cousins, I don't know, must check this out – they're not parents and children is what I mean – they behave as brutally with each other as the swans do, butting and barging, with the brute male of course winning out, or would do if we hadn't learnt to distract him by tossing the first fistful of fruit and veg straight at him, then moving a short distance along the fence and distributing to the other three, who at least fight it out on equal terms, until he's back amongst them, lettuce leaves hanging out of the sides of his mouth, his jaws grinding away at an apple, the juice of which spurts and dribbles and foams around his jaws, which he tries to jam into their share even when he's got no space available in his mouth to snuffle it into – and they of course banging and butting back at him as they gobble down whatever they can pick up. There is no enjoyment here, no pleasure in the appetite, no, it's anarchy, an anarchy of greed, gluttony as a state of war – and yet there is the alternative and incontrovertible fact, that when there is no food on offer they lumber about together in a small, cheerful sort of herd, and as I think I've already noted, sleep, or doze or just lie fully conscious in a pile or heap, on top of each other, higgledy-piggledy.

UNHEALTHY APPETITES

– sad, ironic, and animated may be synonyms but they don't get it, in fact I suspect the truth is that there's no such thing as a synonym, if a synonym will do instead of the word you're using then you're probably not using the right word, so let's leave it that his eyes were full of a wry, lively, melancholy – why am I picking over this so daintily when actually all I want to say is how sweet and loveable he was in his frailty at that time, facing first the prospect that the chemotherapy wouldn't work and the tumour remain inoperable, therefore facing the prospect of a slow and painful death, then the prospect, if the chemotherapy worked, of a long and complicated operation during or after which he might die, and then, at the very best, the prospect of a long and humbling convalescence, when for a time he would be far weaker coming back to health than he'd ever been when he was ill. That was the future he faced, and occasionally talked about. Talked also of course about many other things, seemingly unrelated but all of them somehow stemming from this central fact in his life, that his death was inside him, working busily a-day, busily a-night, busily striving to bring itself to a triumphant negation even as he sat talking about it – and then what does it do, does it move on, does a tumour move on? Is it a separate and individual life form, a sort of galactic immigrant that leaps from host to host – I was going to say indiscriminately, but perhaps not indiscriminately, perhaps discriminatingly, choosing according to its own needs and laws, and from an appetite for more than just survival – perhaps there's a variety of cancer that has an appetite for writers, attracted by their temperaments, then picking out playwrights for the fertile contradictions of their circumstances – that they work in solitude, then expose the work of their solitude in an indecently public, manner, etc., finally homing in on Harold as the perfect example of this playwriting species, and therefore a perfect host, given its own sophisticated and refined tastes –

– actually, the best account of Harold and his tumour is from Harold, in a poem which shows him in intimate, playful, almost doting contact with it – this poem, by the way, which Harold called 'My Cancer', this product of an intensely private communion with what was intent to kill him, was published in newspapers throughout the world, indeed on the front pages of some of them, which leads us to meditate briefly on the nature of fame – who would have heard of Harold's tumour if it hadn't chosen Harold? I must look up in the dictionary the connection between tumour and tumescent, by the way, if there is one. The latter can't be the adjective from the former, surely?

I've just written him a letter – Victoria drove me six miles to Bury, where I posted it so that it would get to him forthwith – well, not forthwith, given the current state of our postal service, perhaps within a week or so. Not that it contained anything particularly interesting, though it might cost him some much-needed strength to find that out, as he has difficulty reading my handwriting – everybody does. I do myself. In fact, I sometimes think that's how I got a decent degree – the examiners taking the easiest route when confronted with page after page of illegible script – just my name readable, and certain key words – 'dichotomy', 'paradoxically', 'Manichean', 'metamorphosis' and one or two suggestive ones – 'uxorious', 'muffins', etc. Nowadays, of course, when students have to be computer literate, which is just a high-tech way of saying they can't read or write – this is nonsense. Stop it.

QUESTIONS OF STYLE AND TASTE

Last night I began revising a paragraph because I was shocked by what I was writing even as I was writing it. So I softened it, sweetened it a little, softening and sweetening myself a little too in the process, and then I thought, but no, this is fraudulent, leave it as it was, so I went back to what it was, ran my eye through it, made a correction to one of the sentences because it looked gauche, and then I was at it, and by at it I mean working at it as if it were a piece of writing, I must have spent hours on a few paragraphs, fretting away at sentences, arrowing them in and out of each other, then doing a fair copy which I then rewrote, and again copied, and so on until the old headache began, the brain felt arid, the sentences on the page were as dead as counters – tiddlywinks, as if I'd been playing tiddlywinks for an eternity, but without a cup to wink the tiddle, tiddle the wink into – it wasn't until I was undressed and about to get into bed that I realized what I'd been up to, so I had to get dressed again, put on boots because it was now raining, clump across the garden, rip the pages out of the pad, tear them into strips, screw them up and bin them, then back across the garden, hating the dawn light, the birds, the rain. 'I thought you'd already come to bed,' Victoria mumbled. 'No. That wasn't me,' I said. 'Who was it then?' she said. 'Bob Monkhouse,' I said. It cheered me up, this exchange, it cheers me up to remember it now, as I put down this resolve, that I will never again rewrite any part of this, on I go and on – feckless, thoughtless, cruel and stupid, it doesn't matter, because in this case you are only what you write, never what you rewrite – there's a football match, a pre-World Cup friendly between England and one of the Koreas. I have to watch it, for professional reasons.

Christ, we were dreadful, especially in the second half. Trevor Sinclair seemed determined to get the ball to South Korean feet, which involved him in perverse displays of skill, as it would sometimes have been easier to get it to English feet – but that's not what really incensed me, what really incensed me was – is – that 'to be fair' has now become a sort of tic with sports commentators, every other sentence, sometimes two in a row, beginning with 'to be fair' – 'to be fair on the lad', which is how one of them began a sentence on Trevor Sinclair, 'to be fair on the lad, he did play very badly,' that's what he actually said. And then there's 'reinvent', you see it and hear it all the time, somebody has 'completely reinvented' herself as a feisty, foxy, tart or fart, whatever – now why do I find this so irritating, no, worse than that, offensive, and tinged with a kind of blasphemy – well, for one thing, in order to reinvent, you have to invent, and who therefore is this self-inventing and self-reinventing self, rather like that definition of God as thought thinking on itself, yes, that's it, I suppose, people who say they have reinvented themselves are thinking of themselves as god-like, and people who describe other people as reinventing themselves are attributing god-like powers to the self, which is a poor, miserable, partly suffocated thing, on the whole – I suppose that really all they mean, the hordes of journalists etc. who are so addicted to the phrase, is 'change', but that's a simple word that contains, when applied to people, some proper element of mystery – 'he changed. He became a good man.' And what about 'majority'? 'He played the majority of the game with a bad leg' – what's wrong with 'most' for most plurals, 'most of the people in the room', etc., saving 'majority' for when it's really useful, as in opposition to the minority, etc. This morning, in the *Independent* I think, though it may have been *The Times*, we were told that Roy Keane is 'flaunting the rules –'

Why do I care? Why does it make me so angry? Is it something that happens to you after a certain age? Ian and I used to paint the picture for ourselves, two old guys sitting in the corner of Chez Moi, full of rancorous pedantry, and of course it was fun when we were being rancorously pedantic together, making a game of it and ourselves into a joke, but I think we always minded, even when we were young, and then began to mind more when we suspected that almost nobody else did, much. Or noticed even.

On the other hand, I've recently heard myself using phrases quite alien to me – borrowed, really, or are they inherited? from my parents' generation. I used to hear them when I was growing up, a play 'was really rather amusing', they used to say and I now say – said just the other evening – and it was of a play that I'd actually disliked – we were at a party, friends of the playwright were present, and the odd thing is that I couldn't for the life of me have said anything good about the play, couldn't have brought myself to tell a clear, direct lie, but said easily, without any sense of a moral tremor, that I thought it was 'really rather amusing', which was accepted all around as a compliment, and I was happy to let pass as one. And at another point at the same party, I told someone I'd never met before that a mutual friend was 'absolutely delightful' – well, I mean she's lots of things, intelligent, obstinate, sometimes stupid, and sometimes sexy, etc. – an endless list of attributes I could have come up with, we could have discussed them and the contradictions implicit in the list, but no, I chose to say that she was 'absolutely delightful', and said it with a kind of drawl, like

George Sanders, or BoBo's husband, Mr Carew, or even Mummy, come to that, she'd have said it with a drawl, too, and a flourish of her cigarette. So one comes at last into one's inheritance – as they spoke in their thirties, so I speak in my sixties.

And by the way, the words 'disgraceful' and 'disgusting' seem to be perpetually on my lips these days – generally applied to some news item about the National Health or education or the prison system or almost any journalist – one columnist, for instance, is 'quite disgraceful', another 'absolutely disgusting', again Mummy's formulations, with her intonation – though not her contexts, which were more personal – her *bête noire*, the man in the little chemist's shop in the King's Road, was 'absolutely disgusting', while the behaviour of Jenkins, who owned the dairy on Chelsea Manor Street and delivered our milk, was 'quite disgraceful' – I don't remember what he did, or kept on doing.

A PRACTISING PLAYWRIGHT

What has happened? Do I remember what has happened? We left Suffolk for London again. That's one thing that's happened. In London I discovered I've got cancer. So that's another thing that's happened. And now we're back in Suffolk again, so that is yet another thing that's happened – ever since we got back here I've been struggling with the play about the people on a Greek island – I've been thinking of moving them to a remote part of Turkey, to make them feel more anxious – me too, as I've never been to Turkey – would I have to do research, even go to Turkey, some remote part of it, so that I could write with authority – write what with authority? Well, the stage directions, I suppose, 'The play is set in a remote part of Turkey,' – write those exact words which I have in fact already written at the top of the play (except I've written Greece, not Turkey) – but with authority this time, because I'd actually been there. Or I could invent some part of Turkey that was so remote nobody would know whether it existed or not, except me – like that friend of Dr Johnson, who claimed he'd been to China and wrote an enormous book about it, describing the country – the landscapes, the people, their customs etc. – all of it completely made up and complete nonsense, but completely believed in by the London literati – I like to think that Dr Johnson himself had doubts, but that they didn't affect their friendship. Of course these days most people have been everywhere, including remote parts of Turkey, either by plane or by television, and the theatre reviewers amongst them would complain that either my local detail is inauthentic, or its absence suspicious, spending the rest of their reviews furnishing authentic local details of their own, under a headline in which the word turkey would figure in its several senses – 'A turkey from Turkey' for example. Better leave the play in Greece, I've been there quite often, after all, though mainly for the swimming – the most beautiful water I've ever been in is around the island of Spetses, though much of the local detail, authentic local detail – the restaurants with their unflushing lavatories located in the middle of the kitchens, the fingernails of the waiters, the condition of the plates and cutlery, not to mention the food itself – you wouldn't expect to see an authentic Greek restaurant on any but a subsidized stage, where they might do it in the style of those Neapolitan plays, but instead of the mouth-watering smells of Mamma's pasta sauces wafting out to the audience there would be the traditional Greek smells of bad fish being fried up in the oil they were using last year too. I still haven't done Mummy's football boots, while I'm on this sort of subject.

STILL NOT MUMMY'S FOOTBALL BOOTS

Antonia's edited a small selection of Harold's poems, twelve of them, and they all seem to me to be – well, poems. Real poems. Which is one of the highest human achievements, in my view. Antonia has chosen with wifely insight – most of the poems are about her, quite rightly, as they are among the best along with the poems about death (one on the death of his old English teacher) and the one about cancer. It makes me wonder whether the rest of Harold's poems are better than I thought – probably not – after all, a dozen decent poems is as much as a man should expect to write in a lifetime, and as Harold's life is quite distinctly not yet over, there may be one – or even two – more. And Hardy wrote his greatest poems when he was about Harold's age. But Hardy had a spirit that nourished itself on pain, most of it inflicted by himself, much of it on himself. One wonders what he felt after he'd written 'After a Journey' – so much yearning, remorse, grief so powerfully and perfectly expressed might have left him with a feeling of placid triumph, yes, done it again, and a special thank-you to the dead wife for serving first as victim, then as subject, and what an alchemist I am, turning the dross of my behaviour into the gold of my verse, and talking of dross, what about that dress of hers, the blue – wasn't it? – dress, yes, there's a poem in that somewhere, do I see it, don't I, that dress? No, gown, gown, air-blue gown and off – 'Woman much missed, how you call to me, call to me . . .' – was his remorse intensified by expressing it, in fact added to by knowing he was going to enhance his reputation by publishing it – he was, after all, a professional. Sometimes, these days, when I've spent hours on the typewriter I feel that I'm a reverse alchemist, no, a negative reverse alchemist, in that I take the dross of my life, of my understanding of life, and turn it into something drossier. The fact that Hardy wrote some of his best stuff at the age that Harold's writing some of his best stuff, doesn't give me the right to think that at my age I can do anything at all except the physical business of battering the shit out of the typewriter, no, battering shit out of the typewriter, about people on a Greek island who can't even go to Turkey – really, I'm only sticking at it as a distraction from my cancer. A little cancer, apparently – like a little pregnant? No, this little cancer is a perfectly self-contained creature, nestled there in my prostate with no plans for growth, as yet anyway, or so say the two urologists I've spoken to. But of course the pattern is unmistakable – from Ian, to Harold, to me, Harold overlapping with Ian, I overlapping with Harold, like a poisoned baton in a relay race – though the simile doesn't work out as Ian is dead, Harold is recovering, and I am merely nursing a little cancer, giving it house room, really, as we did with the cat Errol, who began by straying (quite deliberately, a planned stray) into our kitchen one afternoon, then annexed room after room in the most affable, no, loving manner, and now sleeps on our bed with George, and rolls around the sitting room in George's arms, and otherwise just lounges around the house as if he's paid off the mortgage – but you can't really compare Errol to the little cancer in my prostate, if the cancer annexes organ after organ it won't be in an affable, no, loving manner, and rolling around in whose arms where etc.?

Naturally, I brought it all upon myself by contracting bronchitis when we were in Suffolk the last time – at least, I did if you look at it this way: my smoking brings on my bronchitis: my bronchitis brings on my doctor, who brings on a blood test: the blood test reveals that my PSA (prostate something and something else) is high, twice what it usually is, and it's usually more than twice what it ought to be anyway, which makes my current PSA more than four times what it ought to be; and so on to a physical examination, ultrasound, biopsy – biopsy, absolutely not, I said to my pleasant and intelligent if – in my view – hyperactive doctor, 'you know perfectly well that I don't do biopsies, most particularly in the prostate,' and he did know, having sent me on three previous occasions, from each of which I'd fled, expostulating that I couldn't, just couldn't and what's more wouldn't – I'd concede that it's an irrational response, a phobia, except that it seems to me a rational response, normal. Perhaps what it means is that I'm a rectal virgin, having gone through prep school and public school and all my adult life without having my rectum probed by anyone – and the thought of it, the mere thought of anything not attached to myself touching me there – but all this is no longer true. The truth is I am no longer virgin. I was ravished by a lady doctor who did what the Victorian ravisher did to the little girl in Larkin's 'The Less Deceived' – she doped me with a special, opium-free concoction, and when I passed out, had her way with me – though you wouldn't have thought so if you'd seen her immediately afterwards, her cute little face, mid-forties, I'd guess, possibly fifty, the age at which I now think women are growing towards their most very attractive – she looked neither ashamed nor sexually spent, just cute. She said how good I'd been, brave and obedient, while unconscious.

Victoria took me home in a hired car, and I ate yogurt and honey, and took George and Errol to bed with me, lay there for the rest of the afternoon, and then watched a Steven Seagal film. I am a Steven Seagal fan, loving his retro ponytail, his lushly muscled body with its hints of corpulence to come, his quick-footed, buttock-rolling walk, and above all the softly growling tone in which he issues warnings of death or castration. I would say that in his actions he's a man's man, a man's once-upon-a-time man, but in his style he's a touch womanly – the large, child-bearing hips, and the circle of fat around his stomach that suggest he's in touch with the chocolate and milkshake child within. In one of his films he plays an eco-warrior, shooting holes in different parts of Kris Kristofferson (also terrific) while explaining to him that he isn't going to kill him, he's going to turn him over to one of the prisons, where the convicts would do to him what the cute doctor had done to me, only with unsterilized instruments, I would imagine –

So my hyperactive doctor phoned on Friday afternoon and left a message on my answering machine – the biopsy results had come in, there was something in them that would require some serious discussion, looked forward to talking on Monday. Monday. Monday seemed a long way from Friday, with such a message on the mind. Saturday, Sunday and Monday came and went, Dr Hyperactive being hyperactive in other areas of interest. Most of Tuesday went before I made contact with Hyperactive's partner, who regretted that Hyperactive had been out and about for the past two days, but here, by chance he happened to have my prostate results before him, I had cancer, these were the possible treatments – 1) radiotherapy, his personal favourite for my case, which involved six weeks of daily visits to a hospital near you, only drawback being that it would cause some – perhaps more than some – fatigue, and could bugger up the stomach – in my case further bugger up the stomach; 2) an operation, out of the question in my case, given my allergy to anaesthetics; 3) hormone treatment, painless, easy, convenient, adieu to the sex life however; and 4) something to do with needles thrust up the anus into the prostate, where they would lodge for – I can't remember how long they would lodge for, months, years, until death. And that was it, those were the options, Hyperactive himself would be in tomorrow, to pick up the threads. The next day Hyperactive, full of apologies – 'I won't bore you with the details of my ghastly weekend' – took me through exactly the same list again, named the urologist to whom I was to go, fixed the appointment, and so – and so it's creeping towards five in the morning, the light is changing, birdsong on its way, I've taken a sleeping pill, and my head is full of shapeless stuff –

A SMOKING UROLOGIST

It's half past one in the afternoon, and on television England are playing a test match at Lord's. The sun is strong, this is an English summer's day of the childhood kind, butterflies are tumbling in and out of my study windows – actually a shed in the garden, have I mentioned this, but with mod cons, yes, I have mentioned it, but probably didn't mention that in one of the drawers of my desk I keep a hospital-type plastic bottle in which I pee when it's too cold to open the door. When it's warm I turn right on the step, unzip, hose down the flower bed, good for both of us, I like to think. A very large bee has just rollicked in, rollicked about, rollicked out, more Disney than Suffolk, really – my granddaughters Maddie and Gee-Gee are romping naked in a paddling pool so enormous that I feel it would kill me to do a couple of laps in it – they're naked, these plump and wholesome little girls, pink and white and stark naked, and if I wished I could stare smiling at them through the window – but then of course I imagine myself being observed by a passing social worker or policeman – smiling through the window at two naked little girls plunging about in the paddling pool, and then I imagine the police station, my face, cheeks swollen, small eyes squinting their guilt, etc., and so, reflecting sombrely that it's not only the children that have had their innocence stolen, it's grandpas too, better keep my head bent over my yellow pad and write down my thoughts on urologists – or rather the two urologists I had dealings with, one last week, one the week before. First first. His office was in Wimpole or Harley, one of those, several floors up, reached by a lift. We were greeted by his receptionist, an eager young woman who nevertheless had something troubled about her. She led us into a diminutive reception room, in which a sturdy black man in his early fifties, I'd guess, was sitting with his hands clamped on his knees, staring into a horrifying future. The receptionist, obviously acutely conscious of this chap and the state he was in, sat down at her computer and concentrated on it. Victoria and I went in for strained banter, trying not to look at the black man who almost filled the other side of the room – eventually the receptionist said, 'Here you are,' with a nervous, sideways look towards us, and handed him a sheet of paper. He looked at it with first suspicion, then outrage, 'I'm not paying this!' he shouted. 'I'm not paying, no, no, out of question, out of question!' He had a Spanish or a French accent – a bit of a surprise considering how English his togs, how sturdily English middle-class – old-fashioned middle class the effect of him when silent – 'I better had operation, operation cheaper than this.' 'Oh, but –' the receptionist said, and tried to explain that no, he was getting off comparatively lightly, the operation would have been much more expensive than the treatment he'd had –' (Actually, I might be getting it the wrong way around, he might have had the operation and now wished he'd had the treatment) and so it went on, except it got worse – at one point he flung the paper to the ground. He had a powerful voice, which got more powerful as the receptionist continued, carefully, gently, to defy him with mathematics, further bits of paper, etc., and he was, in fact, demanding to confront Mr X, the consultant himself, when the consultant himself, Mr X, in his pinstripe suit, his Barbados tan, and his deaf smile, entered the room, took the necessary three steps to place himself in front of us, and introduced himself, 'Do come into the office,' he said, 'Do come into the office,' and somehow managed to walk back around the black man, who'd stood up and was flourishing the bill at his averted cheek. We followed him into his office, which was so just around the corner from the waiting room that it might as well have been in it, and as we sat down the row started up again, somehow louder for being invisible. Mr X picked up a sheaf of papers, presumably my notes. He was an uninteresting-looking man, anonymous, a composite of everybody's idea of the professional man, but this may have been achieved by an act of will. He turned over the pages expressionlessly, then folded his arms across his chest, and asked us if we had anything to say. I said we were there to hear what he had to say. All he had to say, he said, half getting out of his chair, was that this wasn't a wait-and-see situation, action had to be taken as soon as I'd had a bone scan which would determine whether the cancer was spreading, all right? his receptionist could fix the appointment for the scan immediately, all right? Well, I said, or Victoria said, could we perhaps discuss how things would go if – no, he said, speaking through the din from around the corner, no point, wait for the results of the bone scan, all right? He touched the seat of the chair with his bum, then stood up, led us out into the hall, gesturing us towards the door as he then proceeded back into the waiting room. I caught a glimpse of him standing sort of side-on to the black man, asking him, in a politely surprised voice, if he wanted to see him, by any chance. Then we were in the lift, and away. I think the reason I never want to see Mr X again isn't that there was a row going on in his waiting room, nor that he'd rushed us through the session from embarrassment, nor that he'd either read my notes for the first time in front of me, or had pretended to – it was his tan that turned the knob on him, as far as I was concerned. His tan. His tan in pinstripes, so to speak. Why? I go to Barbados myself, come back much more tanned than he, and if I don't put on pinstripes when I settle to my work then that's a perk of my profession – consultants wear pinstripes, writers wear whatever they like, pinstripes included, come to that, or bunny clothes, or nothing – so how could I blame him for his pinstripes or his tan, furthermore, he was probably far more entitled to a holiday in Barbados (why did I assume it was a Barbados tan, it might have come from India or Florida) than I, contributing vastly more to the well-being of society by looking after its prostates, than I with my plays, which might, for all I know, contribute to the ill-being of society, the cause of prostates which he in turn treated, thus earning the money that took him to Barbados, or India or Florida or all three annually – but to hell with all that, I wasn't going back to him, nor was Victoria – but then why should she, she doesn't even have a prostate, except by proxy – we'd find someone else.

So to the second urologist. I'd sat next to him at the fiftieth birthday dinner of the friend who recommended him, and inasmuch as I remembered him I remembered liking him because he smoked – a smoking urologist was bound to be my sort of urologist.

Actually, he wasn't my sort of urologist, when it came to it, as he a) was of the view that my liver and stomach were such a shambles that I couldn't expect to live long enough for my prostate to become a serious threat – especially given my smoking habit, b) had himself stopped smoking. What made his verdict on my life expectancy particularly hard to bear was that he repeated it a number of times, as if I were wilfully denying it, which I wasn't, and each time with an apology either at the beginning or the end – 'I'm sorry to have to say this but –' or – 'but there it is, sorry.' I liked one part of his news, though, the no point in treatment part of it – well, not the 'no point' part of it, the 'no treatment' part of it. And at least he didn't have a tan, in fact he had the opposite of a tan – big white face, big white teeth, not much hair, large white hands – and he wasn't anonymous – in fact he was the opposite of anonymous, bags and bags of personality, some of them recently added, I suspect, to compensate for not smoking – so all in all, if he wasn't strictly speaking my sort of urologist, he was the sort of urologist I ought to have. And so I have.

The next day brought the bill, for one hundred and thirty pounds, from urologist number one. We'd seen him for about seven minutes, a few of which he'd spent reading – or pretending to read – my notes, another two of which he'd spent mute, with his arms folded across his chest – so let us concede that these were both urological acts, and justly included in the bill, why then, he was valuing himself at fractionally under twenty pounds sterling a minute. I can't wait to see urologist number two's bill. He gave us more than twenty minutes of his time, all of them filled with speech, which would work out at – let's not work it out. The big question is whether I pay urologist number one's bill. I put it in one of those drawers, and we came down to Suffolk, and here I am now, sitting in my study – see me now, sitting in my study – see him now, sitting in his study, anticipating a smooth run to his eightieth birthday, when he will be found in his favourite armchair, slippered feet resting on his favourite cat, head bowed over his favourite poem, by Hardy, of course, his lips trembling out his of course favourite lines, 'He never expected much/ Just simple-minded slaps and such', and outside the grandchildren dumping in the paddling pool, the butterflies humping in the woodshed, the plumple bees drifting drowsily on little eddies of insecticide, a life spinelessly lived, now supinely closing –

Tomorrow is going to be another lovely day, a woman with a set smile has just said on television. She was talking of the weather. What I liked about her was that she didn't seem to care much, one way or the other.

DIFFERENT SPECIES

Last night, when I'd stopped poking uselessly away at the Greek play,
I took a couple of Co-proxamol – a sort of aspirin for people whose
stomachs can't take aspirin – and a sleeping pill. I then turned on the
television, and looked for something that would soothe or excite
thoughts of my life expectancy out of my mind. I came in in the
middle of a film I've seen a few times before, *Species*, it's called, science-
fiction horror about an alien who's taken up residence in the
exceptionally beautiful body of a young American woman, with the
express object of breeding with a human male, and so peopling (clearly
not the right word) our little planet with her own kind – her own kind,
when it emerges periodically from the body, or rather through it, is a
more than routinely revolting piece of work – stolen, of course, from
Alien, but with some thoughts added, for instance a tongue, softly and
eagerly probing in a French kiss, suddenly transforms itself into a sort
of slithering turd with ridges and spikes, that shoots straight through
the aroused male's mouth and out of the back of his head – this occurs
when the alien, inexperienced as yet in sexual practices, and unused to
desire, loses herself to itself, so to speak, and so foils herself and itself
of what it most needs – no, that's not quite it, itself needs procreation,
herself needs sex. In the end they achieve both, and the expression of
ecstasy on her face as it feels conception beginning as her orgasm
ends! – this alien is a very rapid breeder, by the way, so rapid that
twenty minutes later she's down in a sewer (in flight from her pursuers,
among them Ben Kingsley – class, eh?) having contractions, and a few
seconds later, there among the scampering rats, she delivers herself of
a little flock of aliens, garbed as children, almost Pre-Raphaelite in the
sickliness of their charm and innocence – until one of them flicks out
its tongue and pulls a passing rat into its mouth – and it was exactly at
this moment, a great favourite of mine, that I noticed out of the side
of my bulging eye, a small thing hopping across the floor. My floor. A
small dark thing a hip-hop-hopping. But it was OK, just a baby frog,
come in from the garden, desperate to get outside again. It took skill
and patience to coax it onto a sheet of paper – it kept sliding off,
heading away from the open door into a dark corner where I lost it for

seconds at a time – while keeping attention fixed on the screen – the aliens exterminating Ben Kingsley, Ben Kingsley's resolute team destroying the aliens, Pre-Raphaelite babes and all – but I got it out safely and myself back into the chair for the climax – too much of a climax as usual, fire and water, hangings by the fingertips, hideous mouths agape and screaming (aliens) or pursed with pain and tension (human) – all that – until it's over, or so you think, as our heroes, exiting from the sewer, celebrate their survival, the survival of our world, all that, until the camera has a second thought, nips back to observe a rat eyeing another rat – its tongue shoots out, wraps itself around the other rat, hauls it in. *Vivat!* So really it was in rather an admiring and satisfied condition, the Co-proxamol and the sleeper now pleasantly combining in my system, that I stepped out of my study onto the brick path outside my door, and felt something squelch under my foot.

SOME CONFUSIONS

I'm trying to give up smoking. I'm halfway there, having cut down from sixty to thirty. The unused time I suddenly find myself confronted with, I try to dream away.

Harold phoned us here in Suffolk to say goodbye, he was this day leaving London for Dorset, he will be in Dorset for the next three weeks. Then he will return to London. He is being accompanied both ways by his wife Antonia.

Why did I write the above – he didn't say it at all like that, he said it in a simple, low-voiced, anxious sort of way, fearful of the journey, the uprooting – illness and hospitals do that to you, make you so need to be at home that leaving it, even just for Dorset, seems dangerous, guiding you in imagination back to illness and hospitals.

It is cold and wet tonight, and yet there are mosquitoes. The English tropics is what we have in Suffolk in early August. Cold, wet, and mosquitoes. That is the weather I am under tonight. English weather. Mosquitoes in the cold, the wet. Nevertheless, it is important to affirm that I am sixty-five, not sixty-six. Why then did I begin these pages with an assertion that I am sixty-six? I know I did because I had to burrow through a drawer in which all the past yellow pads – the pads leading up to this pad – have been put. I was looking for a key – the spare key – to this study, thinking I had lost my proper key, and believing there was a spare one somewhere in my desk – a small fit of old man's panic, because I didn't need the key in the first place, as I never lock my door until we go back to London – it was just that I found myself looking for it, even though I didn't need it, and didn't even know that that was what I was going through my pockets looking for until I couldn't find it, and so began my search for the spare one, pulling out the pads to see if it was under them, and so catching the first sentence I wrote, which was an inaccurate statement about my age, which induced further panic, was I sixty-six, and not sixty-five, as I've assumed since my last birthday, except in that brief instant when I wrote the sentence, had I, in fact, written the truth and been living a lie ever since. I went over to Victoria's study, ran stumblingly through the rain to her study, which is exactly like mine but on the other side of the garden, and knocked on her door, pushed it open, and asked her to tell me whether I was sixty-five or sixty-six. 'You are sixty-five,' she said. 'Are you quite sure?' 'Yes. Quite sure.' I was prepared to leave it at that, as she's never wrong on these matters, but she asked me why. 'Why?' she asked, 'why?' 'Well,' I said. 'Well, there's a difference between being sixty-five and sixty-six –' but then I couldn't go on to say that I'd written it down wrong in the first sentence of these writings, because I haven't told her that I'm writing them, I suppose she thinks I'm hammering away at some play or other and as I never talk about what I'm working on – in which case, why do I feel that I'm keeping these writings a secret from her, if I never talk anyway? Well, the answer to that is quite obvious – my not talking about these writings is a very different sort of not talking than not talking about a piece of work, it's a concealment rather than a reticence – so when she asked me why I wanted to know whether I was sixty-five or sixty-six I couldn't really think of an answer, 'Oh nothing, not important, no particular reason, just wanted to clear it up, really.' 'But you're wet, you've got yourself wet.' 'Well, it seemed urgent for a moment – you see, I've lost my key, the key to my study, and then I couldn't find my spare, so I got into a bit of a state, and my age came up, in the course of all this, was I sixty-five or six, for some reason.' 'Well, you're sixty-five,' she said, 'and the spare key is on the counter in the kitchen, with the other spare keys, and I don't know where your other key is, but it's probably somewhere,' and she nodded politely at her computer. The other key was actually on my desk, sort of melded into it from having been there ever since I put it there when we first arrived, so not visible to any but the no-nonsense sort of eye that I now also bring to the first sentence on the first page of the first yellow pad, and now here is the sentence that threw me into such turbulence – 'So here I am, two hours into my sixty-sixth year –' which of course means that I am sixty-five, though it's a bloody stupid way of saying it – but it's a perfectly reasonable way of writing it, I just read it bloody stupidly when in a state about losing one key and not being able to find another when I didn't need either of them, as a matter of fact –

CHEZ MOI

Been back in London for a month now. Harold has returned to the world. First a soft, troubled vacancy he seemed to be – there and not there at our usual table in Chez Moi, occasionally touching a hand or an arm and trembling out a question about the state of one's life; then a week later a fuller creature, by no means vigorous, not completely alert, bloodless but kindly. And now, this evening, the man himself smaller than before the cancer, still frail, most of his hair back though some of it in different places – the eyes beginning to brighten, the voice to strengthen – so in a few weeks, next week even – but probably not at Chez Moi. It closes down next week. Or possibly the week after. Or perhaps next month. Anyway, although it is definitely closing, when it is closing is not yet definite, which gives us quite a number of opportunities for last dinners before we go on holiday. Colin did say, though, that he was sure they'd be closed before we got back in early September, he was pretty confident that the latest date mentioned by his solicitor, or their solicitor, or the estate agent, 26 August would turn out to be the final one, although it might not be, what a pity, he said, we wouldn't be here for it if it was. All this confusion is quite simply explained; the two owners, Colin and Ricky, partners in life as well as in business, decided a few months ago that the time had come to retire – they're both sixty-five – and to travel around the world in boats, stopping off at this country and that as the fancy takes them, and then settling down to do all the things that retired people do, although I suspect they're not yet clear as to what such things would be in their case, as for the last almost forty years or so they've worked in their restaurant, Colin as the most charming maître d' in London, Ricky as the chef, mainly invisible in the kitchen, with very short holidays twice a year, so they've had little chance to practise for retirement, or drum up any hobbies. They're very similar, Colin and Ricky, not only in appearance – short and slim, with roundish, rather bookish faces and large, innocent, slightly troubled eyes – actually like elderly schoolboy brothers, one good at history, the other at geography – or a pair of elves, perhaps, benevolent elves – but vocally too. If one phones up to reserve one's table, one really has no idea whether one is talking to Colin or Ricky, although one naturally presumes it's Colin, taking reservations being more a maître d's function than a chef's (I doubt if you'd ever find Colin in the kitchen, and Ricky ever above stairs during business hours – Ricky is intensely shy (geography) while Colin is extremely sociable (history)) – nevertheless it's often turned out, towards the very end of a conversation, that I've made my reservation with Ricky and not with Colin, the call being put through to the flat in which they live, above the restaurant. This confusion has always pleased me – heterosexual couples may come to resemble each other in all kinds of ways, clothing, gait, political opinions, reading tastes, but while they might also even imitate each other's speech patterns, accents, affectations, etc., they could never sound in pitch, timbre, exactly like each other – sisters can, brothers can, sons and fathers, mothers and daughters, gay partners – but never a man and his woman, a woman and her man – I'm alone, why do I bother to make this completely useless distinction, and what is the distinction between a man and his woman and a woman and her man? Well, clearly, in any specific case, it wouldn't be a useless distinction, might even be making a defining point by going for one instead of another – Elizabeth Taylor springs immediately to mind here, the film star, that is, not the distinguished lady novelist, now I believe dead and therefore irrelevant – irrelevant,

I mean, to the point I'm making about men and their women as opposed to women and their men – one would say Elizabeth Taylor and her man because one would be unlikely to remember his name, at least since post-Burton, post-Todd, post-Burton (if it was that way around) – who remembers who, apart from Todd and Burton and Burton, was married, is currently married, to Elizabeth Taylor, so that's the way one would have to put it if one were considering having them around for a drink and a bite – 'What about Elizabeth Taylor and her man,' or more convincingly, 'What about Liz Taylor and her man, eh?' Now on the male front – who would be the equivalent on the male front? – Well, I suppose Prince Charles, Charles and his woman, although that may be because I can never remember her name, recently confusing it with the name of a woman who got thrown off an island on television, because she wasn't a big enough celebrity – both names double-barrelled, hence my confusion, and hence my readiness to settle for Charles and his woman, let's have Charles around for a drink and a bite, etc., oh, and his woman too, of course, or possibly, and that woman of his too, of course.

Anyway, there are Colin and Ricky, the upstairs and downstairs of Chez Moi, fraternal partners in business and life, not only lookalikes but soundalikes, now having reached the age of sixty-five and deciding to retire themselves onto boats and cruises, with a view to settling down eventually. They can't sell the restaurant as a restaurant, the property being both small and extremely expensive. When they bought it forty years ago it was cheap, Holland Park not being the top address it's since become, and as they lived in the flat above and were prepared not to pay themselves on poor weeks, they could get along, if not always comfortably, then always safely. A restaurateur buying it now would have to fork out more than a million for the property, and given the shortage of table space, couldn't hope to recover his initial outlay – a hopeless business proposition, then, unless a multimillionaire steps forward whose idea of a charitable enterprise is to maintain a small restaurant for the benefit of Victoria and myself, who have come to think of it as our dining room, really, without the inconveniences of clearing up after ourselves –

– in short Colin and Ricky have had to put it on the market as a property destined for conversion into either a family residence or a couple of flats, which is why there have been so many last dinners, as deal after deal has fallen through, some speculators clearly attempting to sell the place before they'd bought it, others going in for reverse gazumping, i.e. lowering their offer once it'd been accepted, and then lowering it again once the lower offer has been accepted – and so one deadline after another has been passed, each new deadline the date for a last dinner at our usual table for four – I can't work out now for how many years Harold, Antonia, Victoria and I have dined at this table, in sickness and in health – and then there's the other table, the table for two, where Victoria and I have spent some of our brightest and certainly our darkest hours, my every birthday since we started together and it was crossing the road on our way to that table that I proposed, and it was also at that table that I sat with Alan Bates, my very last glass of champagne in front of me as I began to slip towards a coma – Alan supporting me past the table at which Antonia and Harold were sitting, my returning their anxious gaze with what was meant to be a cavalier salute, and it was there, at that table, that Harold and I discussed his directing a number of my plays, several of which were to star Alan, and there that Ian Hamilton and I met for dinner every few weeks for years up to the last week of his life and it was at that table –

COURTSHIP AND WEDDING

Chez Moi opened some forty years ago, three years before Victoria moved into this house. Occasionally she would cross the road for dinner, and soon became good friends with the two owners, Colin, the maître d', and Ricky, the chef. Ten years later, when Victoria and I started our affair, we would occasionally have lunch there. I hated it, thinking there to be a cold and protective glitter in the eye of the maître d', as it travelled between his infant neighbour and my middle-aged self, and no doubt it was my sense of his unseemly suspicions that caused me to behave offensively, grunting out my orders for more wine as I shoved my plate away, food untouched, and visibly, coarsely, failed to keep my hands to myself – indeed allowed them to travel all over his infant neighbour – well, not in fact, but every smile and sentence suggested that my hands would shortly close about the softly swelling etc. of my prey, who sat, as was (still is) her wont, with the air of a well-mannered fawn, though in possession of softly swelling etc., and an expression in her own eye that would have startled the maître d' if he'd glimpsed it, or if glimpsed, understood it. I suppose Philippe was around in those days, or perhaps he came shortly after – he's only recently turned thirty, which would mean that he was – Christ, in his late teens, at the most early twenties, when he arrived – my astonishment at working this out comes really from being unable to think of Philippe as ever having been anything but a fully formed assistant maître d', with his grown-up spectacles, his darkish-grey hair slicked back in the manner of my father's generation, and his air of experienced efficiency – his English is agreeably French, almost as if he'd practised to get the right professional accent – how could such a chap be anything but forty-three for the whole of his life? – though he has a tendency to puppyish weight changes, going from trim to portly and back again in a matter of weeks – perhaps he pads and unpads himself, experimenting with his size as he searches for the perfect embodiment of streamlined gravitas – anyway, in his varying shapes and constant effect he was certainly around during all the nights that I now remember, the humdrum nights, the jolly nights, the many nights when Harold raised his voice and silenced the rest of the restaurant with his political passions, the nights when Harold sat silent, humbled by his tumour, picking with feeble purpose at his food – and of course he was there for our wedding reception, over which he and Colin presided with the delicacy and warmth of – well, they looked like a pair of undertakers, actually, in their dark suits at three in the afternoon, such a sunny afternoon, a blessed and sunny afternoon, with all the details quite perfect – the confetti on my shoulders masking the dandruff, my toxic gait easily confused with a bridegroom's airborne strut – besides all attention was naturally focused on the bride, so light and graceful that she really did seem to be floating beside me, though in fact she was both guiding me with her free hand clamped around my elbow – the other clutching a bouquet – and keeping me upright by pressing the side of her body against the side of mine. Harold gave a great speech, which was interrupted only by himself when he shouted at a couple of special-occasion waiters, young and Italian to keep quiet! For God's sake! he was trying to make a bloody speech here! – so there was Harold's speech, it was our wedding, but somehow it lingers in the memory as Philippe's and Colin's event, and Ricky's too, of course, invisible in the kitchen but preparing the dishes to perfection, and sending them up at the perfect moment.

On the other hand, I was very drunk, and can't even remember whether we took George with us. We often take George, who feels perfectly chez elle under the table, asleep, probably dreaming of scraps falling onto her snout – which in fact they often do, from my plate – she seems able to shift them from snout to mouth without fully waking up, a toss of the head, a flutter of the eyelids, a dreamy swallow, a sigh, sleep again – a bit like the lady in Wallace Stevens's great poem, 'Sunday Morning', really, except George doesn't wear a peignoir. What is a peignoir, exactly?

It is midnight. We have to leave the house at 7 a.m. for Gatwick. Economic circumstances dictate Economy – first time since my twenties I've had to fly on the cheap. Perhaps if I'd done it when I could afford not to, but was physically up to it, I wouldn't have to do it now that I can't afford not to, but am physically frail, with a churning stomach and loosening but obdurate bowels. So memory poisons even the pleasures of the past – how I resent that young man strutting behind his porter to the Concorde check-in, resent him sprawling in his First Class armchair, hand wrapped around his glass of pre-flight champagne, most of all I resent him lurching off the plane in New York, so drunk that most of his forward movements carry him backwards, his liver and stomach-lining further eroded by the First Class liquids and solids, which right back then were contributing to the condition in which he finds himself decades on, as he contemplates the hurly-burly of democratic check-in, the cramped knees-up seat from which he will eye the lavatory that some swine will be occupying from the moment the seat-belt sign is off to the moment it flashes on again – enough, enough – at heart I am a merry man, I do believe. I'm taking a lot of books – particularly looking forward to Zola's *L'Assommoir*, which I've never read. The last Zola I read was *Nana*, a few years ago.

Still remember my astonishment at the first chapter, the description of Nana's striptease, the tension in the theatre, the male audience's collective erection – never read anything like it, erotic, pornographic, obscene – a dangerous woman, a dangerous naked woman, a dangerous, naked public woman – I think my eyes popped, the front of my elderly trousers (all my trousers are at least twenty years old) stirred. God knows what would have happened if I'd come across *Nana* when I was sixteen – I'd have hurried myself back to the safe world of Hank Janson, where the women were decorously constrained, in private.

PART FOUR

BACK IN THE SWIM

Yesterday, being the 15th, was the mid-August festival, the day I selected for us to travel on – not, of course, deliberately, but certainly stupidly, as I've been not only in Italy, but in this part of Italy, on the Ligurian coast, many times before, and know somewhere in my system what it's like – in fact, enough drifted into my consciousness for me to say to Victoria, 'Hey, let's go on the 15th, they all go home on the 15th, end of *vacanza* –' but of course the 15th is the day before the day they go home, in fact they turn up in large numbers, those who aren't already here, to celebrate being here for this one day at least – so walking around St Margarita looking for a chemist (I'd forgotten to pack toothbrush, paste, shaving equipment, etc.) in mid-afternoon was on the one hand like trekking around Leicester Square on New Year's Eve, pavements jammed, people shouting, laughing, lurching, and if Anglo-Saxon, vomiting, and on the other hand wasn't, because the sun was beating down. The chemists were closed, of course. Our hotel is on the curve of a steep hill, and looks, as you approach it, like a motel in an American movie – not the Bates Motel, which would have promised peace at last, but a motel in a sweltering and busy Midwest town, though set on the curve of a steep hill. One of my espadrilles, the one I put on my left foot, kept falling off. On the way back from the closed chemist Victoria and I, who scarcely ever quarrel, would have quarrelled, if we'd had the energy. The hotel beach is like the town's pavements, in that it's made of concrete, and almost as public in that, though it belongs to the hotel, it admits anyone who cares to pay a few euros. The sunbeds lie side by side, half an inch separating them, and the Italians are on them, and across them, and around them, and sometimes actually under them, and sometimes actually under each other on top of and underneath them – in other words behaving exactly as you expect Italians to behave on holiday. All this – this Hogarth in the sun, broiling and beating and bloody sun, hot, so hot that it's impossible to be in it, and the sea cold, so cold that it's impossible to be in that either – though, of course, that's where I mainly was, in the sea, or in a small pool of it contained by the slabs of concrete, being bumped and jostled by happy Italians, who really, I suspect, can't imagine being anywhere better – except back on the slabs of concrete, with their mobiles, their girlfriends, their boyfriends, their children, their parents, their grandparents, their grandchildren, their card games, their bottles and bottles of lotions – and of course so many of them look beautiful as well as happy, the sleekness and brownness and litheness of so many of them, from the middle-aged down to the toddlers, yes, sleek, lithe, brown toddlers, many of them completely naked, and the families touch, fondle, caress and stroke each other in a way that in England would bring around the social workers, and land them in courts and prisons – and there amongst them is a sixty-five-year-old Englishman, red of face, puffy and white of body, wearing tatterdemalion swimming trunks, his dead friend Ian's straw hat on his head, on his feet a pair of his dead brother's espadrilles, the left one of which keeps falling off – yes, there he was this afternoon, full of resentment and envy, wishing he was young, wishing he was Italian, and wishing above all that the water wasn't so cold. A cold Mediterranean, in the middle of August! as I kept saying to Victoria, Christ! It's been a bad summer, she said; it's been in all the papers, hurricanes and floods everywhere – and returned to her book, a book apparently so good that nothing, neither the inferno in which she was reading it, nor my stimulating musings, could distract her from it.

It's three in the morning. The noise from the traffic on the road that runs not quite directly beneath us is beginning to thin out a little. There are some pedestrians, though, as I write this – young, Australian and drunk, who are discussing at the tops of their voices some of my early plays. I just checked up on Victoria, in the adjoining room. She is fast asleep. She looks small and forlorn without Errol at the foot, and George curled up against her spine or into her stomach, or spread in the most abandoned way on my side of the bed, on her back with her paws spread wide – another favourite position is on her side, front legs stretched forward, back legs stretched back, her ears flat against her head, as if she's flying – and perhaps she is, in her dreams – flying at speed and with purpose to a destination that will certainly have Victoria in it, and me too, if I'm lucky – but no George for Victoria tonight, no Errol, only me, and me not yet because here I am seated at the table on the small balcony, which to the right offers a view of the sea and the harbour of Santa Margarita, though to see it I have to lean far out over the edge of the balcony at an awkward, possibly fatal angle – 'he died looking for the sea' might be my epitaph, on the other hand they might think that I fell trying to peer through our neighbour's bedroom window. Our neighbour is, in fact, an old gentleman in his late eighties, from the look of him, with a wife a decade or so younger. They sit at the table next to us in the dining room, which, with its bright lighting, its rows of square white tables, and its large, shiny mirrors, resembles a restaurant in an English seaside hotel in the middle of the last century, the only difference being that it's packed, not with middle-class English families, stiff and silent, but with Italians of all ages, from two months to a hundred and two years, who enjoy everything from their own voices to the unusually (for Italy) disgusting food – and there this evening Victoria and I sat in a kind of gloomy wonder that we were here, in this restaurant, in this hotel, and there next to us was our neighbour, our double neighbour in that he's our sleeping neighbour and our eating neighbour. He raised a withered hand in trembling salute every time I caught his eye, emanating goodwill towards even this surly-looking Englishman some twenty or thirty years his junior, and listened with joyful attentiveness to his wife, who talked at him smilingly, but her voice has a rasp in it – perhaps he's deaf, reads her smile but doesn't hear her tone – anyway, charming though the old chap evidently is, and pleasant indeed to have him next door at dinner and next door in bed, tomorrow we start looking for another hotel – failing that a larger room with a direct view onto the sea, and failing that – failing that George will have to fly out to Santa Margarita, with Errol on her back, or between her paws. Or we'll fly back to her, possibly.

The Australians have gone, presumably to check on their texts. Now below there's just the traffic, sporadically, and above, here's me, on holiday.

A NEIGHBOURLY SALUTE

Last night, after dinner, we were sitting in the hotel lobby, trying to decide whether we had the energy to walk down the hill – no, we had the energy for that, but whether we would have enough to walk back up the hill after walking down it. Our fellow guests were playing bridge, or talking in large groups, small groups, lively and absorbed. Suddenly there was the wail of an ambulance, then a group of men and women in medical-type overalls, clutching bags and a stretcher, ran into the lobby, stopped briefly at the desk then ran, two or three of them, up the narrow staircase, while the other two or three of them squeezed into the small lift with the stretcher. Apart from cursory glances and mild exclamations nobody else in the lobby paid much attention. Victoria and I sat, though, as if something of importance depended on the next few minutes. The lift came down again, the two or three got out without the stretcher, waited. The others came down the staircase, manoeuvring with great skill the stretcher on which the old chap, our neighbour, was stretched – really, I don't know how they did it, managed to control the angle of the stretcher, get it around a sharp corner at the bottom without tumbling him off, and into the lobby, through which he was carried gently but with speed. His wife followed, talking at him with the same warm smile, slightly rasping tone. As they went past he raised his hand, as he'd done at the dinner table, in friendly salute, which, as once again nobody else was paying attention, I took for Victoria and myself, and raised my own hand, slightly shyly, to return it. Then they were through the door, we heard the ambulance start up, the whine of the siren. I went to the desk and asked the clerk, whether he was all right, the old gentleman. 'Oh, yes, yes,' he was busy over some papers, bills from the look of them, 'no problema,' which he translated for me as 'No problem.' Victoria and I sat on for a bit, then walked down the hill for coffee. We solved the problem of walking back up it by taking a taxi.

This morning, while we were being shown this room, or rather its large balcony, by the assistant manager, I said, 'The old gentleman, is he all right, then?' 'No,' he said, 'he did.' His English was pretty good, in fact this was about the only word he'd seriously mispronounced, if he'd mispronounced it, which he made clear he had, by confirming our suggested correction, 'Yes, yes, yes!' he said, irritated with himself, 'he die-ed. In the ambulance. Die-ed.' He said that the old chap had come to Santa Margarita every summer since childhood, it was the place he'd loved most in the world, had intended to be buried here, had picked out his spot years before. So that was that, then. Everything had gone to plan, no shipping of his body to Milan, Turin, wherever, just a neat transfer from a local hospital to a local graveyard via a local church. So we admired the view from the balcony, inspected this little area, not really a room when it comes to it, an attic, at the top of the rickety stairs, and agreed the terms, and here I am, writing it down. The old chap's death. The death of the old chap who yesterday evening sat at the next table, and last night – no, the night before – slept in the next room.

WHO WAS THAT YOUNG MAN?

This is the following night. The day was OK really, very hot but we've discovered that we can spend most of the day, from ten in the morning until seven in the evening, at the comfortable little bar just above the beach, which has shaded tables and an exceptionally nice pair of waiters, one, called Emilio, middle-aged, with a wry, melancholy face who speaks no English but seems to interpret our needs from our expressions, and Paolo, much younger, who has a shaven head, is slightly camp, and speaks good English. Paolo and Emilio guard our table whenever we pop down to the beach – I notice that I've taken to calling it a beach rather than a concrete slab – for a swim. We've also taken a beach cabin, where we can keep our swimming stuff, which we dry out on our beach-beds – the only use to which they are put. So there at the table we sit, enjoying the bar life, the intensely intimate physicality of the families, the noisy flirting of the boys and girls, the toddlers toddling from group to group to receive caresses and licks on the cheeks and licks of ice cream, and if we look across from our tables we can see much the same scenes on the beach – oh, and there's no music, no music – so all the natural hurly-burly, laughter, shouting, occasional sobs from the children seem to harmonize with our reading, which we're mostly at, Victoria stuck deep into *Our Mutual Friend*, I in *L'Assommoir*, stuck deep in the winter slums of Paris –

We suddenly remembered that tonight was the last known last night of Chez Moi, surely the final one at last, so we decided to give Colin a ring, to say a final last goodbye, wish we were there (which we certainly did). Colin answered immediately, sounded immensely surprised to hear from Victoria, thought we were in Italy, and then immensely surprised to hear that we were, and then immensely surprised by her farewell speech – 'No, no,' he said, 'We'll be here after you get back. We're closing 9 September. Definitely. Well, almost definitely.' So Victoria booked a table for 9 September. She said Colin sounded cheerful; there were cheerful noises around him.

Then down to dinner. It was difficult. We're still at the same table, and the old chap's wife, now widow, is still at their old table, but in place of the old chap there is his son, daughter-in-law, their child, and a middle-aged man in a darkish suit that we think is probably the family lawyer, and they were doing a lot of rather emotional things, grieving, for instance, and reminiscing, and presumably going over funeral arrangements, some of this on their mobile phones – it was really a very concentrated family table, and we were seated so close that when the head waiter came over I wondered to him in a low voice if it wouldn't be more tactful to move us to another table, so that the bereft family wouldn't feel intruded on – now this head waiter is a rather distinguished-looking man, white hair and spectacles, and a round serious face – he looks like an academic, in fact, and has in fact the limited intelligence of an academic – his English isn't much good, although it sort of looks good – I mean, his face looks as if it speaks good English until you hear what he is saying. He also doesn't like to let on that he can't understand much of what you're saying – another characteristic of academics – the vanity of stupidity, or the stupidity of vanity – and so a real mess of a muttered conversation ensued, in which he kept glancing at the table of bereaved, who kept catching his glances, especially as he interpreted our concern for their privacy as complaints about the intrusiveness of their grief – getting everything the wrong way around, in other words, and attempting to reassure us that we would only have to put up with them for this one meal, they would be leaving in the morning after they'd finished their business, no, no, I said, we're the intruders – but it was hopeless, and we went through our meal (disgusting) with heads lowered in shame, and also to conceal our eruptions of laughter at the thought that we'd been understood to be complaining at having to sit at a table next to a family in grief – anyway, that's the end of that. We've decided we'll forfeit our pensions, and dine in the restaurants in town or up in the hills, so with luck we'll never have to see the head waiter again nor the five widows seated in a row against the wall, trembling soup, gravy and ice cream into their mouths, and out again in a couple of cases – perhaps they've all been coming to Santa Margarita since their girlhoods, have already chosen their last resting places, have children in Turin, Milan, waiting for the summons – but Victoria and I haven't been coming since our childhoods, haven't selected our graves, for us there'd be an awful muddle of coffins on planes, one of us mislaid, or hauled up into the wrong hold, heading for Trieste perhaps, while the other goes home to London. Such thoughts are not to be borne, up here in a little attic of the Hotel Metropole, Santa Margarita di Liguria.

And here's another thought not to be borne, that my present circumstances have turned me into a sort of poor relation to my younger self. A younger and vastly more preposterous – prosperous, I mean, of course, prosperous self, though there does also seem to be something preposterous about the man who first came to this part of Italy – the Ligurian coast – some thirty-five years ago. For one thing this man was comparatively rich. A play of his had just opened in London to considerable acclaim and a busy box office – 'The best thing I've ever done,' the producer informed me a few days after the first night, as we settled down to plan the leading man's replacement five months and three weeks before he would be needed on stage – but that's the way of it in the theatre with a success, you keep your nose to the grindstone (in the form of a trough, of course, Italian, called Luigi's, around the corner from the producer's office) so that your success is still there, playing to good houses, a year or two later – 'The best thing I've ever done,' he said, his eyes hooded – he's got a noble face, like a Roman conspirator's, 'that's what people are telling me. They've been phoning all day, telling me it's the best thing I've ever done.' He really did seem to believe that whoever had written it, directed it, was acting in it, he had not only produced it, he had produced it out of his sole self, in an act of something like parthenogenesis – but then the vanity of producers is far more disconcerting, in my experience, than the vanity of writers, directors, actors, because it's better disguised, manifesting itself only in an hour of extreme triumph, more usually it is cold, serpentine and negative – a matter of 'face' really, now I think about it, in fact it's suddenly perfectly clear to me that 'producer's face' is more accurate than 'producer's vanity', it's as particular to producers as athlete's foot is to athletes – no, the analogy doesn't hold, really, athlete's foot is an affliction that irritates and disgusts only the athlete him or herself, while producer's face is an affliction that irritates and disgusts other people, and most particularly the playwright, the directors, the actors. 'Face' has of course to be taken in the oriental (and old colonial) sense of dignity, self-importance, consciousness of the world's estimation – as in 'He decided that the only way he could save face was by flogging the little scamp in front of the assembled villagers' or 'What Yvonne refused to understand was that every time she visited Jamki in her tent, Gerald lost face with the Turks.' So forth. Face is why, unlike film producers, who dish out huge sums for the rights to novels, short stories, biographies, stage plays, television plays, often for no other purpose than to prevent some other film producer from buying them, theatre producers are reluctant to pay even small sums for the rights to a play, often managing to avoid putting down as much as a penny until the play is actually on the stage – the point being that if they do pay out even as little as a penny they feel that they are publicly committed to producing it, and failure to do so will mean losing 'face' with all the other producers in town, those colleagues and competitors who constitute their peer group. This is all a gross simplification, when I look at it, all I seem to be saying is that producers are pretty normal members of the human race, morally less developed than George, of course, so somewhere down here on a par with the likes of myself and really, I can't waste more time wrestling with their psychological complexities. Why did I get onto them, and where from – oh, yes, my being rich from my writing – no, not me, him, the man who first

came to the Ligurian coast thirty years ago, who not only had a
successful play, etc., he also had a job as a university lecturer for life,
if he wanted it; he owned two houses outright, one in Highgate – well,
just down from Highgate, across the Archway Road, in fact – and
another in Devon; he had a pension plan, through his university job,
and further pension plans from the proceeds of his writings – stage
plays, television plays, film scripts – yes, that's how I see that youngish
man now, in his prime, his pomp and his prime – he'd chosen the
hotel from the Michelin guide, flipping urgently through its pages,
noting only those categorized by two tall red towers, two squat red
towers squashed between them, the grand hotels de luxe in other
words, and pausing only at those right by the sea. Eventually his finger
stopped at a hotel called Gran Hotel de due Castelli in Sestri Levante,
down from Genoa, up from La Spezia. And so he came with his family
to the Ligurian coast and the best hotel in the world, he truly
believed – still believes – two castles, one containing the bedrooms, the
other the restaurant, the two connected by two paths, one open, one
sheltered against the rain – but when did it rain, in all the Sestri
summers? Well, perhaps now and then, for an hour or two, to freshen
up the great, shady lawns that sloped down towards the sea, or the
pine woods that surround the two castles, or the myriads of paths that
lead you by way of views of the town and its harbour to the lift that
took you down through rock to a small bay, a natural swimming pool
where childish swimmers swam, that opened into a larger bay where
ordinary swimmers swam, that opened to the sea where proper
swimmers swam. The tops of the rocks that surrounded these two bays
were as flat as shelves, the gaps between them spanned by narrow
bridges that swayed slightly, but only slightly alarmingly, because you
felt as you crossed them that if they ever collapsed under you they
would drop you into a warm and loving sea, from which benevolent
hands would draw you out and lay you down in the sun to dry, and
eventually you would find yourself settled at your usual table in the
restaurant from which you could gaze out on the ships in the open sea,
and the boats in Sestri harbour, and also watch out for the local train
that spurted out of a tunnel in the mountain at 9.13 precisely every
evening, would pause for a few moments, then with a faint husky roar

shoot off into the tunnel opposite, its little lights, its little noise snuffling into the darkness – it was so friendly and mysterious this little train, so punctual, so clear in its duty, full of passengers we couldn't see going to places we knew, Chiavri, Lavagna, Cinque Terra, perhaps all the way to La Spezia – the pastries at the Due Castelli came from Genoa, by the way –

On our first night here I asked the head waiter whether his pastries too came from Genoa, I had to ask him several times before he understood, and when he did he laughed a proud, contemptuous, stupid laugh, 'We make it ourselves,' he said – of course they do, that's why most of it was still on my plate when we rose from the table –

– but when I think of that self in its prime, guzzling down the pastries from Genoa without adding an ounce or an inch, calling for another bottle of spumante, or French, let's have something French this time round! – watch him padding across the lawns to the lift, or diving off a rock with a cigarette in his mouth, I feel that I'm not just his poor relation, I'm his parent and his child, twice abandoned.

Well, where is he now? Hah! Look at him, look what's become of him! I wish he could see what's become of him – a chain-smoking, teetotal, alcoholic wreck scribbling away in the attic of the Hotel Metropole –

Or did he see me now, now and then, along with alternative visions, and think, well, yes, could be, who knows? but in the meantime back to the spumante, actually it's better than the French, but it's cheaper, so I'll take the French, *che sera, sera* –

Now come on, it's rather pleasant up here in the attic, admit it, it's been a good day, quite a few swims, Victoria looks beautiful, healthy, turning brown, and my stomach is beginning to – well, no, but if I double the swimming, halve the chocolate which I only eat because the pastries are so vile –

Christ! I fell asleep during the above sentence, woke to the yellow pad jammed between my knees, right arm hanging down, pen dangling between my fingers, thank God it wasn't a cigarette. I do that more and more now, fall asleep with a lighted cigarette in my hand, the little sofa I'm sitting on is dry and musty, and the two chairs look like kindling –

I could have burnt myself to a cinder, well then Victoria could have taken me home as hand-luggage, thus resolving the problem of my not having booked a spot in a graveyard in Santa Margarita – I'm not going to write any more in my yellow pad until we're away from this place, the Hotel Metropole in Santa Margarita, which neither of us likes, that I've brought us to, no, not until we're home again in London, and none of my memories has anything to do with my past.

BUNN

Here I am again, tonight, which is the night after last night, when I wrote that I wasn't going to do any more of this until we were back in London, but it occurs to me that if it's the truth I'm after, the truth of my life inasmuch as I understand it at this stage of my life, which of course I don't, because of course when you think about it, as soon as I've written a sentence I've already changed my life, or at least added to it, so that it's impossible ever to catch myself up into a state of completeness, to say here I am, that's all there is, now let's see what we've got – but even so there are certain matters that I've undertaken to face up to, however incompletely, and one of them is the financial side of things – and now is possibly the time to do that, when only ten miles and thirty-odd years separate me from those preposterously prosperous summers in Sestri Levante – how am I fallen! Woe and alack! But better put it as a question, if I'm to get on with it – How am I fallen? How come this woe and alack? Well, naturally, there are the usual reasons – extravagance, self-indulgence, fecklessness, etc., and there is a simple example of all three close to mind – every year after the fourth year of holidaying in Sestri Levante, I could no longer afford to do so, but did so, on the grounds that that's what we did every summer, which therefore made it an entitlement, its cost therefore an irrelevance.

Like Mr Micawber in *David Copperfield* I always assumed something would turn up, and it always did, right up until it didn't, and never did again.

And like David Copperfield, in *David Copperfield*, I was expert at the kind of hallucinatory economics that turned every snake into a ladder – whenever I dined in a fairly expensive restaurant, for instance, I calculated that I'd saved money by not dining in a very expensive one, and the money saved I tacked on to my inner bank account, as if it were money earned. Thus I became richer every time I ate out at my own expense, and twice as much richer when I ate out at someone else's expense. House champagne was a huge earner in the last days of my alcoholism, four bottles a day at a mere twelve quid a bottle, compared to the champagne I'd once drunk, Veuve Clicquot my favourite, at thirty-odd quid a bottle, so every time I put aside an empty bottle of house I was up another twenty-odd quid, courtesy of Veuve – calculations of this sort sustained me psychologically against all the portents, the chief of which were seemingly inexplicable surges of panic that were sometimes accompanied by little visions of humiliation, having my credit cards scissored, my cheques returned with insults, and then of larger visions, of a tramp-like figure roaming the streets, or sleeping in shop doorways – but I refused to read any of these visions literally, taking them as mere metaphors for my most fundamental terror, that I was going broke creatively, would be unable to finish another play. The waiters snipping credit cards and shopkeepers returning cheques were directors and producers rejecting my work. It was my talent that was turned away from theatres and television studios, was homeless, scrounging in doorways – rather like Faith in one of those poems by George Herbert, a personification and a lament, not a prediction.

And so they went on, these various forms of self-delusion, until the end, which came when my accountants drew my attention to an unpaid tax bill that had multiplied itself through fines on fines on fines until it had become almost unpayable, and every week that I failed to pay it because it was virtually unpayable it became more unpayable until it became actually and finally unpayable – 'But how did this happen?' I asked my accountant. 'Well,' he said, 'you see, it's gone on –' now what was the word he used, it made me think of mating, a sinister form of mating – 'accruing', yes, 'accruing', it had gone on 'accruing', my debt to the income tax. My accountant was a slow, thoughtful man – actually I assumed he was thoughtful because he was slow, but the truth might be that he was a slow, thoughtless man, after all he'd failed to notice that I owed the income tax all this money until it had accrued itself beyond the range even of hope, and had brought it to my attention in a letter so pedestrian in its tone and so prolix in its details that it took me two or three accruing weeks to grasp that my situation had passed urgency, had passed emergency, had passed recovery, and that I had no choice but to throw myself on the charity of friends, whom I shall be repaying (gratefully, I need hardly say) with a percentage of my royalties (those that are left to me) for the rest of my life, and probably for a decade or two after it. This accountant, the slow, thoughtless fellow, damaged me by – no, that's not fair, let's try and be fair – let's say that there was collusion between my negligence and his – my drunkenness and his – no, let's not bother to be fair, let's not bother with him at all, really, because the fatal damage was done long before the unpaid income tax debacle, by the senior partners of the firm that he'd left, taking me with him – yes, here's the thing, I went with him when he decided to set up on his own because, precisely because, he was slow and therefore seemed thoughtful, having lost hundreds of thousands of pounds through the agency of his previous partners, who were fast and fearless, full of cunning schemes and nifty devices, whizz-kids, they were known to be, the whizz-kids of the London entertainment industry. Senior whizz-kid was a small, drab man, with pale cheeks and a long nose. His voice on the telephone, which is where I usually met him, if a bit wispy was also wise and kindly, the sort of voice you'd want in your ear if you were suddenly in the dark, on a cliff's edge. Now he – let me call him Guppy, for narrative purposes. Now Guppy's part in my economic downfall – no, start with the other one, the junior whizz-kid – call him Bunn, for narrative purposes – Bunn was a baggy sort of man, his suit seemed to have more than the normal number of pockets and they were always full, bulged, actually, but I never knew with what, and his face – well, it didn't exactly bulge, but it was always a bit swollen, as if he'd been beaten about the cheeks – perhaps by his wife and children? Perhaps by Guppy? But he wasn't at all beaten in his manner, which was actually that of a beater, if not of a world-beater, he had a tendency to shout you down, even if you weren't actually speaking, and oh yes, he had astonishing eyebrows, twice as bushy as mine, which are really quite bushy, and slightly bogus-looking, his I mean, not mine, I was always surprised that they remained in place when he took off his spectacles to wipe his eyes, after he laughed – I had the greatest respect for Bunn, he was my idea of a bully, all right, but then he was bullying for me, and my then agent, who'd introduced me to both Guppy and Bunn, said that while Guppy was canny but conventional Bunn was famous for the flamboyance of his tax-avoiding schemes, he saved people thousands and thousands of pounds with one master-stroke, which in my case was to get me into containers. Containers, yes. The economy urgently needed containers, so that more goods could be moved more rapidly about the country, and between one country and another, from producer to consumer and no doubt back again – the government was prepared to make tax concessions to anyone who bought containers and leased them out – at least this was the situation as I understood it from Bunn, who made the enterprise seem so charmless that I knew it must be profitable.

In almost no time I found myself president or was it chairman? of a company that owned three containers, with Beryl my company secretary, and either Guppy or Bunn, I can't remember which, but probably Bunn, as the scheme was of his devising, the other member of my board. I did occasionally try to visualize them, my containers, packed with medical supplies, or dynamite, or nappies, hauled by trucks across frontiers, headlights in the rain, Yves Montand at the wheel, and there snared in his beams, naked under her raincoat, etc. – but what I could never properly visualize were the containers themselves – obviously they had wheels, but as for their shape, whether they were square, or oblong, or tube-shaped, or octagonal, whether they were decorated, had my name on them even – I really had no idea, and it never, of course, occurred to me to ask to have a look at them. Didn't occur to Bunn either, who was therefore outraged when he discovered that they didn't exist. 'You've been swindled!' he bellowed. 'Taken for a bloody ride!' 'But I've received cheques,' I said, 'made out to my company.' These cheques were for strangely inconsequential sums, twenty-seven pounds and six shillings sort of cheques – totally convincing therefore – 'Yes,' he said, infuriated by my naivety, 'of course they sent you cheques, that's how they pulled the wool over your eyes.' A waste of wool, really – as well as of money, as I wouldn't have noticed an absence of cheques, however consequential. 'And now of course you're in trouble with the income tax. As you didn't pay any tax on the containers, the money you spent on them is liable for tax, which will be backdated to the date of purchase, three and a half years ago.' This is the sort of meaning, if not the precise content, of what he said. 'But if they don't exist –' I said. 'Exactly the point. If your containers don't exist, you didn't spend the money on them, therefore the money you didn't spend is taxable,' etc. 'Plus fines accrued, of course.' Thus it was that I ended up paying tax (eighty-seven per cent) on money I no longer had, because it had been stolen from me. Tens of thousands of pounds stolen, tens of thousands of stolen pounds taxed – and in the days when tens of thousands meant something. Hah! It is raining cats and dogs here in Santa Margarita – I can hear them screaming.

Cats and dogs – dogs and cats – yes, I suspect that Victoria is now seriously, not just wistfully but intensely seriously missing George, Errol and Tom, dog, cat, cat, and would like to go home. Yes, we should go home, this really isn't a place we should have come to, but we flew Apex, and we can't change our tickets, we would have to buy completely new ones, and not even I can Copperfield that into a financial gain. But this has been a bad holiday, the only bad holiday we've ever had, together. Which makes us lucky, really, let's look at it that way – I've just been down to the balcony, stood just inside the sliding glass door, which I pulled open, stared out at sheets of lightning. I've heard the expression, read it often enough, assumed it was a *façon de parler*, but outside now, at rapid and regular intervals, great sheets, great white sheets of lightning blank out the darkness, and the thunder rolls, yes, it actually does, it rolls ahead of each sheet of lightning, like a proclamation. I went into the room, sat on the edge of the bed, looked at Victoria's face, turned upwards in sleep, found her hand under the covers, pressed it to let her know that I was there beside her, she was safe, come what may from the heavens. This is the last sentence I shall ever write in Santa Margarita, I swear it.

SOMETHING LIKE A SWAN

Well, it wasn't, because here's another one. I'm sitting at the beach café, having had my last swim – short and incisive, because the water's very cold again. Victoria's on one of the few beach-beds that haven't been packed away for next season, reading in the sun. Our taxi comes to take us to the airport in an hour, and already I have that odd feeling of regret – something Dr Johnson said about the pain of leaving a place you've become familiar with, even if you haven't been happy there – not that we've been unhappy, really, just ill-at-ease, at odds with it – but it looks calm and peaceful from where I'm sitting, the sea is shiny and I've just had a memory, which I want to write down, of somewhere else, a long time ago – a boy poised on the top of a high rock, the warm and welcoming Mediterranean some thirty feet below. Running past him is a seemingly endless supply of children, many younger than he, bombing and diving into the water, fearless daredevils, free and easy, surging past him on either side, into the water, out, scampering up the rock and then past him again and again, and still he stands there, there he stands, posturing and posing his dive, arms out, feet clamped a little apart, legs slightly bowed – suddenly he drops his arms, scrambles down the rock, slithers and bumps himself into the sea, and takes off with speed and aplomb, becoming in the water strong and graceful, completely at ease, everything he isn't on dry land, where unfortunately he has to spend most of his time. I don't know who he is, or where he comes from in my memory – it can't be me, surely, I always jumped, didn't I? Or dived even, at that sort of age. Perhaps it's a metaphor for me as I am now, but it didn't come as a metaphor, it came as a memory, in an image, clear and distinct, not something lived through but something seen, seen yet also felt and endured, so who and why – here's Victoria, coming up the steps from the beach, her bag over her shoulder, book in hand. I've put Ian's hat on my head, and am now, quite positively, writing the last sentence I shall write in Santa Margarita.

GUPPY

It's 9 October, and we're just back from our last last dinner at Chez Moi, an affair which was dominated by George, who began the evening by barking another dog out of the restaurant – a lanky, greyhound sort of chap, callow and clumsy, virtually still a puppy, no match at all for

George in terms of character, force of character – and ended it rolling about on a chair by the door, as the departing clientele stroked her stomach. I think Colin was relieved to find himself virtually usurped as the host, in fact it was probably his intention, as he'd encouraged George out from under our table and on to the chair, and when the men with their handshakes or the women with their embraces threatened to exceed what he could cope with, socially or emotionally, he swivelled them towards George, a mere foot or so away, as if a rub of her stomach was the final and proper formality. Of course everybody in the restaurant tonight was either from the neighbourhood, or old and faithful customers, and altogether it had a familiar feel to it, not familiar in its own context, London, W11, but familiar in experience, from those great French films of the thirties and forties – *Sous les Toits*, *Le Million*, etc. Victoria, George and I were the last to leave, walking back across the street about half an hour ago, and here I am, not really upset because I know in my heart that Chez Moi will open again tomorrow, and we might well decide to pop over for dinner – no, not tomorrow. Tomorrow's Sunday, and Chez Moi is closed on Sunday, on Sunday we go to Orsino's. Monday then. It'll certainly be open on Monday, whether we pop over or not.

But right now to the story of my finances, which I left unfinished in the little attic room in Santa Margarita di Liguria, on the night of the storm. I'd disposed of Bunn, I believe, but the thunder and lightning got between me and Guppy, who was more of an aristocrat when it came to losing my money – no sordid dabblings in the hurly-burly of the transport business for Guppy, it was a suit and a tie and a taxi to the famous Lloyd's building, where I shook hands with Guppyish sort of men, but more expensively dressed, had words I don't remember spoken at me before witnesses, and then signed at a specially laid table a document giving someone the right to take possession of all my worldly goods in the event of an event that would never come to pass – 'Does that mean that if things go wrong, some catastrophe – I'd be wiped out?' I asked Guppy in the taxi back. 'I'm glad you raised that,' said Guppy, 'because as your sponsor I'm legally obliged to confirm that you could be wiped out, yes. And I suppose I shouldn't add that it won't happen. But it won't, because it can't, thank God.' He laughed from a long way behind his rather long nose, a frail sound, reassuring. 'That's the beauty of it. Can't happen.' Well, just as don't care was made to care, can't happen was made to happen – probably Guppy's mistake was to thank God that it couldn't, thus alerting Him to an overlooked duty. My recollection of how Guppy broke the news is a bit muddled – I remember a voice wispy with grief, my failure to grasp the significance of certain key words in a sentence that went something like this – 'many of the names will be worse hit than you or me, far worse hit – there have been suicides – don't forget I was in the same syndicate as you, we're both names in the same syndicate' – 'hit', 'names', 'syndicate' – the vocabulary of a Mafia movie, really. Still, I grasped the basic fact – that people who'd put their money into Lloyd's were metaphorically in the same boat as the passengers on the *Titanic* – no, doesn't quite work, with the *Titanic* you either sank or were saved, with Lloyd's there was a third category, in which I was to be found – most of me was sunk (the tens of thousands that I hadn't put into containers) but a solid bit of me was saved – the house, which I gave to Beryl when we got divorced, and my copyrights, which I sold when the fatal tax-with-fines-accrued came in a couple of years ago. I have therefore nothing left in the way of worldly goods except my books, five Olympia typewriters, two computers, two television sets plus videos, two desks, two chairs, and my honour – for which so far no takers.

HOW DOES HE DO IT?

Well, I know – I didn't deal with the question of how it is I manage to dine out regularly, far more regularly than I dine in, go to theatres, take holidays even in places like Santa Margarita, let alone in Barbados (again this year, I hope), when I've explained not only that I'm broke, but exactly how it is – fecklessness, self-indulgence, extravagance + Guppy, Bunn, containers, Lloyd's – that I came to be broke. What is my secret? By what alchemy do I turn an overdraft into a Club Class lifestyle? The assumption, of course, made by for instance people who occasionally interview me is that whatever the calamities of the past, I still have a flourishing career as a playwright, with an income to

match – before my last play, *Japes*, opened at the Haymarket, for
instance, three separate interviewers informed me that I was a success.
'As a successful playwright,' one of them began one of his questions,
'don't you feel –' or was it 'think' – 'Don't you feel or think –' 'Think'
what? 'Feel' what? – I can't remember – whereas the other two put it
as a straight proposition, incontrovertible: 'You are a successful playwright and therefore –' and therefore what? Well, so many things would
flow from my being a successful playwright, among them the things
that seem to flow from my not being a successful playwright – i.e.,
restaurants, taxis, holidays, best seats at Covent Garden, etc. – which,
of course, brings us back to the conundrum, because the fact is that I
make almost no money from my plays, not even those from my golden
past that are still sometimes politely referred to as 'classics', which of
course they can't be, since one of the attributes of a classic is that it is
frequently to be found on the stage. My classics exist mainly as
points of reference in the memories of older theatre-goers – occasionally,
I receive programmes of productions in Eastern Europe, Turkey, Japan,
Australia, then briefly I swell with the idea of myself as an international
playwright, and try not to note that the theatres involved are of studio
size, in towns I've never heard of and frequently can't pronounce, gen-
erating royalties that scarcely ever make it to three figures.

I really can't face listing all the areas in which I fail financially, a
doleful business that also requires a head for the arithmetic of minus –
let's look at the pluses – at how many tax-free years I've managed to win
for myself, yes, win for myself, that's how to put it, and furthermore the
fact remains – at least until further notice – that I get by, and in some
comfort, possibly even with an appearance of dash – how do I do it?
The solution is actually quite simple, but – but I can't bring myself to
write it down quite yet. I'd prefer to write it down in darkness. Double
darkness. There is still a greyish tinge to the sky, a sky no longer
autumnal, but wintery, and it's only midday. Some time after midnight
then, though not necessarily tonight, I'll put the words down.

I passed Chez Moi this evening, on my way to and from posting
window announcing that the restaurant has closed, regretting
inconvenience to customers. On the pavement outside there are bags of
rubbish, and an empty open box that was yesterday full of pepper mills,

salt cellars, ashtrays, left there for passers-by to take. In our house, arranged around our kitchen table, are six of the chairs – the most comfortable chairs I've ever sat in in a restaurant; on the wall in our hall hangs a small painting of a young woman reading – the same painting, and therefore the same young woman, I trust, that used to hang above the table for two, our table, Victoria's and mine. A similar painting, of a young lady playing cards, that used to hang over the table for four, the table where the Grays sat with the Pinters and the Pinters with the Grays, hangs on a wall in Antonia's and Harold's house. Within a week or so the builders will start work on converting Chez Moi into two little town houses.

Two forty-five a.m. Nice and dark. I've just been down to the kitchen to give Errol a plate of ham. Ditto Tom, who is getting frail with age. I had to lift her onto the counter. She eats on the counter because Errol steals her food if it's put on the floor. Odd this – Errol can leap onto the counter without much effort, but never does, even if Tom's bowl is full of food and she's out. Tom, on the other hand, will wander about meowing mechanically until she's lifted onto the counter, but will never steal Errol's food, even if his bowl is full and he's out. Both Tom and Errol will steal George's food, however, even if George is in the kitchen and watching them at it. I'm not sure, though, that 'steal' is the right word to use – perhaps the more neutral 'take' or simply 'eat' would be more appropriate, though in the days when Tom's food was put on the floor, Errol did in fact steal it – at least he looked as if he were stealing it, gobbling it down quickly and furtively, seeming somehow to keep his back to all parts of the room on which he nevertheless managed to keep his eye, and he didn't saunter away from the bowl with a lazy contentment, as he does when he's eaten his own or George's food, but scuttled off by a mazy route that took him underneath the chairs and the table to a spot behind the door in the scullery. There's a sentence in between the last one and this one. It explains how I live quite stylishly, without having any money. Now I've written them, the words, in blue on yellow. I can look at them and move on, cross them out and move on, or tear up the page, drop it into the bin, and move on – whatever, I shall be moving on.

PART FIVE

A FIRST CLASS PASSENGER

I've tried explaining to Victoria that I'm ill, possibly very ill. She nods sympathetically, continues with the packing. I point out that George is climbing into the suitcase, hoping to be packed into it and taken with us, isn't it heart-breaking? – 'There, there, darling,' I croon to George, 'don't want us to go, course you don't, and we don't want to leave you, we truly don't' – Victoria packs implacably away, while I toy with the idea of destroying my passport – one of the advantages of being a smoker, you can set fire to things without effort, almost passively, while sitting down – like this: place the passport on the floor, to the side of your chair, light your cigarette, smoke for a while – quite a while, so as not to waste it – then let the arm drop, the eyelids droop, the fingers open, the cigarette fall – and come to think of it, you could actually burn your old passport instead of your new one, who would know the difference from the ashes? and if they turn out to be your ashes, owing to a slight miscalculation, you won't need a passport. There's a high wind, by the way. A very high wind, that means business. Think of bucking about over the Atlantic in a wind like that, darling!

Our flight is cancelled. Naturally, BA being BA we didn't find this out until we were pulling up at the airport, which was when Victoria finally got through to their flight information desk or whatever – we'd checked on the internet regularly throughout the morning. The only flight, I'll write that again, the only flight that didn't show up on the BA website as cancelled was ours – 'We can't be,' I kept saying, 'we can't be passengers on the only plane flying out of Heathrow – if we are we're probably the only passengers on the only plane' – and all through this, the checking on the web, the permanently engaged BA, the anxious conversations, and the drive out to Heathrow, the wind was howling, trees swaying – one cracked and fell against a house at the end of our street – and news bulletins on radio and television were warning people to stay in while reporting maimings and deaths across the country. So, as I say, we got to the airport just as someone in the BA office at last answered Victoria on her mobile, and around we turned, back we came to Holland Park, the winds subsiding.

We are in fact now on the plane, have been airborne for about forty minutes. As BA combined yesterday's passengers with today's, the plane is packed, perhaps overloaded – the take-off was distinctly sluggish, and one has the impression that the plane isn't actually flying, it's dragging itself along, simultaneously airborne and earth-bound. My first event at the Harbourfront Literary Festival, an on-stage interview or colloquy or some such, is scheduled to take place four hours after we land in Toronto, at 9 p.m. their time, 2 a.m. ours. If we'd left punctually we'd have had two hours to get from the airport to the hotel, check in, rest, settle nerves, find the theatre, prepare for the stage – as it left half an hour late, we'll only have an hour and a half in which to do all these things – oh, they've just announced that because of strong headwinds it's going to take forty minutes extra, thus cutting by another forty minutes the time between our arriving at the airport, and my appearing at the theatre.

Well, here I am, let me try and relax. But how can I relax? My seat's at the top end of the cabin, Victoria's is at the bottom end – to get to her I have to go through the galley, turn down into her aisle, not by any means a free and easy little stroll, but a sidling-up, cramped and contorted affair, not too popular with the stewards and stewardesses, whom you have to squeeze between as they stand about snacking and chatting. You also step directly into them when you come out of the lavatory, as it is situated virtually within the galley. The seat itself is high-tech. It has a panel in the armrest with an illuminated diagram on it, and patches on the diagram that you press to make the seat adjust to the diagram's contours – but none of the diagram contours seem to conform to the contours of my body, I either lie with my stomach up and my legs down, or sit with my head thrust forward and knees up. Finally, after wasting half an hour sliding and tilting myself into a sequence of unnatural positions, I've settled for the seat upright, bolt upright, in fact, in the seat belt buckled for take-off and landing position –

I've become acutely conscious that this ghastly and complicated seat is pointed into the top right corner of the cabin, making me feel that I'm sitting in a sort of cupboard, the air in this corner is still, almost lifeless, and full of dust – I can actually see the motes hanging there before I draw them up through my mouth and nostrils and down into my lungs – I've been coughing and wheezing, wheezing and coughing since we left Heathrow. Now I will relax. Now I shall relax. Now I must relax. I picked up a thriller at the airport, to which I will now turn, in the hope that it will take me out of myself, and even better, out of this plane, which I have given up any pretence of piloting. Read.

In the first twenty pages a young woman, Californian, described as 'vibrant' and 'sunny', full of plans for a weekend with her boyfriend in a cabin by the lake, is plucked off the pavement, stuffed into the back of a van, driven to a building site where she is disembowelled, dismembered, etc. – there is a lot of meticulous medical detail, entrails 'shiny', bodily fluids 'viscous' – and then dumped in a dumpster. That's the prologue and it's printed in italics. I'll pass on all the stuff – four hundred and twenty-six pages – in normal print, stick to my yellow pad, where I can make things as safe as I want –

The young man in the seat across the aisle keeps giving me slightly irritable glances, no doubt he's identified me as a smoker, whose continuous coughing and wheezing, which is irritating the shit out of him, is therefore my own fault, I want to say the dust, the dust's to blame, but then he'll point out that he's not coughing or wheezing, is he – do I smoke by any chance? I think he's Canadian, he's scowling but it's rather a bland scowl – he's summoned the steward – small motherly looking chap – they're muttering together – ah! steward asked me in a motherly sort of way if there's anything he could do to help, a glass of water? I've got a glass of water, I coughed at him, but if he could get rid of the dust? Dust, is there dust? he asked, affecting dismay and slight disbelief, can't you see the motes? I asked, suppressing the famous biblical quotation with a wheeze, as it wasn't apt, really, or was too apt, the motes in the Bible being in thine (i.e. mine) eye, after all, and not in his, and therefore I would have to cast out thine (mine) own eye, not he his, which might suit him but wouldn't suit me or thee, anyway he's gone to answer somebody else's ping, and the young Canadian is adjusting his seat so that his head is turned away from me, and really there is nothing I can do about it, so concentrate . . . On what? Oh yes.

How to begin?

On an up note.

MUMMY'S FOOTBALL BOOTS

I was pretty good at sports – very good at cricket, very good at athletics (apparently my Under Fourteen and a Half Long Jump record, seventeen feet nine inches (or was it three – let's split the difference, say seventeen feet six inches) still stands). I was just fifteen when I opened the batting for the First Eleven, fifteen when I played centre forward for the First Eleven – which made me seem a bit of a phenomenon, particularly when you consider that very soon I'd be vying for top-spot as a school intellectual, but in fact at soccer I wasn't a phenomenon so much as a natural – I could do all the basic stuff – I could dribble reasonably, pass reasonably and run fast, very fast actually, which was of course crucial – but I was a natural, a natural centre forward, in that I had a knack for getting into the right place in front of goal at the last possible instant, I could feel where the ball was going to go quite a few kicks before it got there, and I also had an instinct for where the goalkeeper wasn't.

The one practical problem that ran through my soccer life was that I frequently had to wear stolen boots. My own, the ones I started with each term, were gone within a week, either lost or stolen by another boy whose boots had been lost or stolen by another boy, etc., which meant that somewhere in my House changing rooms I had to seek out another pair, which meant that another boy, discovering his boots lost or (as was the case) stolen (by me) would have to seek out another pair, which meant that at certain stages in the sequence I might be, for a game or two, in possession of my own boots again, but I doubt if I would have noticed, or if I had, have made any special effort to hang on to them. Many of these boots fitted comfortably enough to feet for which, when initially purchased, they were the wrong size – if they were too large, an extra pair of those thick woolly socks, or in extreme cases, two extra pairs, would make up the difference, and if too small then the excitement of the game would soon make the pain of crunched-up toes unnoticed until afterwards, when the liberated toes burnt, and the nails were black with congested blood. But by and large the system worked – I played my first match in the First Eleven in boots that weren't mine and scored three goals, and the next in a different pair and scored two goals, and got two in the next in yet another pair of boots, and the next match was to be against Eton, the match of the season, and though I was scared that I wasn't really up to it, I never gave a thought to my boots. Nor of course to Mummy, who, on my sixteenth birthday, a few days before the Eton match, with Eton in mind, gave me for my birthday present a brand-new pair of football boots. I'd never seen a pair like them. I've never seen a pair since, like them. Possibly they were the only pair ever put on the market, especially designed to appeal to a mother with grand ambitions for her soccer-playing son, along with a profound desire to subvert them, and him. It's hard to describe these hated creatures from so long ago, what was so wrong about them from the moment I saw them – they looked, for one thing, enormous, though actually they fitted my feet perfectly. Worse than that, although they fitted my feet perfectly, they felt enormous, as if I were wearing two pairs of boots, my proper boots inside an overall of boots – the visible toes actually curled back on themselves, and the backs went up far beyond the backs of my ankles – in fact, as they take shape in memory they seem like deep-sea diving boots designed for a gigantic pixie. 'Yes, I knew you'd be pleased!' Mummy said, as I gave her a big thank-you kiss and a quick cuddle, Father's eyes upon me (sixteen today, remember, on the brink of manhood). 'They're a special sort,' she said, 'so nobody will take them by mistake!' It would have been a mistake all right, and a pretty stupid one, to want to take those boots anywhere, especially on one's feet – which is where they were, on mine, when the Westminster First Eleven trotted from the changing pavilion to the soccer pitch – First Ten really, as the eleventh was labouring after them, a substantial gap seeming to open up between him and them.

Mummy was at the match, and so was Daddy, and so was most of the school, on an involuntary basis – in fact, almost everybody who was anybody in my life seemed to have turned up except me – not that I couldn't be seen, floundering in a lonely sort of way in roughly the same spot for the first half, and in a different spot for the second half – or anyway, facing the opposite direction – at least I hope I managed to turn around at half time. Well, that's what it felt like. In fact, I did manage to touch the ball, once when I kicked off – i.e. tapped the ball sideways a foot or so – to start the match, and then when I kicked off again, late in the second half, after Eton had scored. The match ended in a draw 1–1. Our goal was scored by a boy called Crook. When I joined my parents briefly after the match, Mummy gave me a smile of angry compassion, no doubt reflecting that she would have played far better herself (but not if she'd been made to wear her boots, *her* boots is how I thought of them), my father drew on his pipe, impassive. Then there were the two friends they'd brought along, a Mr and Mrs Lumsden – her first name was Betty, Betty Lumsden, a red-headed woman who always made me feel shy because she was so pretty, I only remember her name, Betty, because I used to prickle every time my parents bandied it about – well, there I stood, briefly, avoiding all eyes, particularly Mrs Lumsden's, and then off for the team tea with the boys from Eton, again avoiding all eyes. 'Didn't see much of the ball, eh, Gray,' the sports master, a small, sleek man called Lowcock, said while I was changing. 'No, sir,' I said, though he was wrong, and I was lying. I'd seen all of the ball all the time, every second of the game.

I was dropped for the next match, played a few games for the Second Eleven in Mummy's boots, which by now had become much noticed, so there was no chance of suddenly appearing in somebody else's boots without those being noticed – perhaps by the somebody who owned them – played a few games for the House, I think, before I stopped playing altogether. It wasn't difficult to get out of things like football in those days at Westminster – and I'd been an anomaly, anyway, a sporty type who posed as an intellectual. I don't think I was missed by the rest of the First Eleven, who probably suspected me of being an intellectual posing as a centre forward. They probably came to regard my goals in my early games as flukes – which they weren't. I was a natural.

Sometimes I wonder what would have become of me if I'd gone on as a footballer, a cricketer. Three of my best memories now, at sixty-five, come from that period of my life – a late cut off a high-speed ball not that far outside my off stump that went skidding to the boundary, a perfectly executed shot that was entirely reflex, I'd never done one before, not even practised it in the nets, it was a wondrous moment, the sensation of it, it tingles down my arms as I write. Then there was my sweep of a spinning ball delivered by Ian Peebles, who was playing for the Old Westminsters and was, I suppose, in his forties, possibly fifties, when he bowled to me but nevertheless, in his prime, had played for England. It was the impertinence of that sweep that stays with me, rather than the sweep itself – and the look he gave me, of loathing, that can still make me tremble with joy. The third memory is of a goal I scored from outside the penalty box – I can see the players moving towards me, the goalkeeper behind them, and the spot in the corner of the net to which I knew the ball would fly as I was in the very act of kicking it. I had other moments too, that I can sum up by an act of will, but none that are alive in my body as those three, none that bring me such pleasure in myself for having been that self, to which I am still connected. Yes, that's it – that when I remember those moments I'm the same S. Gray then and now – the fifteen-year-old and the sixty-five-year-old fuse into a whole creature unseparated by time or crimes. The only other moments that bring me together in that way are moments of embarrassment and failure, that I struggle to forget when they try (why do they?) to surface. A drab addendum to a happy thought. How typical. How typical, too, to blame Mummy and her boots for funking out of football – you funked out of cricket, too, funkwit, can't claim you were wearing Mummy's boots or gloves or box when you lowered yourself down from opening the batting for the First Eleven to the Second, then a few House matches and into the library, to spend those afternoons you used to spend on the cricket and football pitches. The great thing about posing as an intellectual is that it was safer – that's the crude nub of the matter, safer than exposing yourself to failure on the football and cricket pitches. In other words, let's face it, would I have been any more mobile if I'd worn a proper pair of somebody else's boots for the Eton match? Well, yes, more mobile and as a consequence less visible, I'd have seen to that – I'd have been everywhere the ball wasn't, arriving just too late in front of goal, too late to miss – so in that sense the boots were an appropriate justice, they mired me down, showed me up to everybody, Mummy, Father, Lumsden, Mr Lowcock, Mrs Lumsden, the rest of the Eleven as being never near anywhere that mattered, unwilling, unable, afraid, whereas without them I'd have got away with it, looked willing and able in an if-only sort of way, if only he'd got there a fraction of a second earlier he might have made contact, etc., pity – looking for chances, but not getting them – as opposed to not looking for chances, so as not to miss when getting them – yes, with other boots I'd have hidden successfully, with Mummy's boots I couldn't even try to hide –

It was the same with my brief spell opening the batting, really, although that was more complicated. I was OK against fast bowling, the faster the better, the more dangerous the better, because I had no time to think, merely to react – so in that respect I could again be called a natural, a natural opener, the defensive stroke completed perfectly thoughtlessly, and always the right stroke therefore – but with the first change and the slower ball, especially the slower, spinning ball, the confusions began, the instinctive became the conscious self, hesitating, entangled in choice, seeing the fielders, the spectators, the umpire's expression – all during the flight of the ball, which I would eventually spoon up for a catch – it amounted to suicide really, getting myself caught off a ball that, in the nets, I would have hammered casually and brutally – so I got by at the crease for the early overs, and that might just have been enough to keep me in the team, after all an opener who can see off the fastest bowling is a useful opener, even if he doesn't score many runs, but in the field –

In the field, in unimportant games, House matches etc., I took blinders. Blinders. Once, far out near the boundary, I pedalled backwards at high speed, and then jumped backwards, to take in my left hand a catch that – that – well, frankly, it was an impossible catch that I took, that I nevertheless knew I was going to take as the ball left the bat, a most powerfully struck six all the way until it smacked into my hand just as I knew it would – 'Oh, well caught!' they all shouted, the umpire, the other fielders, the batsman himself – 'Oh, what a catch, well caught – !' said Mr Lowcock, who was walking tidily along the side of the boundary – and it was shortly after that that he watched me score an implacable, not to say interminable thirty-six – again for the

Colts, and entirely against fast bowlers – and so plucked me from the Colts and had me open for the First Eleven and told the captain to make sure I fielded on the boundary, where I was one of the best fielders he'd ever seen, I took blinders.

The first few matches were OK because the ball never came near me. It was holding itself back, it turned out, for the important match, the match after the match with the Old Westminsters, when I'd swept Ian Peebles, the ex-England spinner – now how do I explain this, having explained that I couldn't play spinners here I am sweeping Peebles who spun for England, 'insolently' – isn't that the word I used – swept him 'insolently' for four. Hence his glare. Hence my gloating. What is the point I am making? Oh yes, the point I am making is that I once had it in me to do it, if only once. But why only once – was it because I didn't want a repeat of the embarrassment that accompanied my gloating? Was I embarrassed because I gloated, or was I embarrassed because I swept the old bugger for four in the first place? Was the hubris in the sweep, or in the gloat? Well, whichever, in the next match came nemesis, in the shape of the ball that wouldn't leave me alone – all afternoon it tracked me, even when the batsman presented it with a straight and dignified bat it shot off it with science-defying force, scudded across the turf, underneath my groping hand across the boundary. Wherever I manoeuvred myself, it came at me, failing to reach me only once, when it towered above me, – stopped in mid-air, stopped, just stopped for ten minutes or so, while the bowler shouted, 'Catch it!' and the captain shouted, 'Yours, Gray,' – and I waited for it awhile, my hands cupped, then as it began to drop some yards behind me, I did my back-pedal, the same sizzling back-pedal that Mr Lowcock had observed at close quarters, well, the same as far as the movement of my feet was concerned, but opposite in that it carried me further and further away from the ball, which landed a few yards in front of where I'd started out, and therefore rather more than a few yards from where I ended up. If I had a weakness in my fielding, by the way, it was in my arm: I couldn't throw very far, or accurately, which was why the batsman, instead of being out, bowled Tuffins, caught Gray, added three runs to his score, courtesy of Gray's throw, which went a short distance, and sideways, before it finally made it to the

wicket-keeper, via another fielder. 'What happened to you, Gray?' Mr
Lowcock asked after tea, as I was padding up to bat, a question he
asked again a few minutes later, when I returned from batting – they'd
opened the bowling with a left-arm slow, just for the one over, because
their fast bowler had had to go back to the pavilion to change his boots.
But I've jumped, I've jumped, in fact I've missed my own point – the
point about the catch that I didn't make wasn't that I miscalculated the
ball's trajectory and therefore failed to get near it, it was that my feet
carried me backwards away from it on purpose, if the sudden, intense
operation of a cowardly instinct can be said to be 'on purpose'. In other
words I ran backwards away from the ball in order not to drop the
catch – a dropped catch being when the ball either passes through the
hands, or bounces out of them – a ball that lands many yards away
from one's hands hasn't been dropped, it's merely been missed. Brave
men drop catches. Cowards miss them. That's my point. Yes. So down
to the Second Eleven, a few games for the House, into the library.

And there you are. I've ended the story of Mummy's football
boots somewhere that wasn't at all in my mind when I kept postponing
the writing of it – I don't know what I had in mind, really, except to
blame Mummy for my failure to sustain a career in First Eleven
football – and now I see that I've exonerated her by in effect blaming
myself, pinpointing a basic character flaw – and what a flaw – I do
think certain questions about her intervention need to be asked,
though. Not, actually, how come that she, of all people, so proud of my
sporting achievements, provided me with the means of showing myself
up as unworthy during the Eton match of all matches – and why she
gave me football boots as a birthday present – nobody gives anybody
footwear without having them try them on before purchase (except
carpet slippers perhaps) – and she'd been an athlete at the very highest
level, knew the importance of being at ease in one's footwear – what
would she have done if her mother had handed her a brand-new
pair of spikes on the eve of her Olympic or Commonwealth high jump,
presumably she would have said something sensible yet kindly – e.g.
'Thank you, Mummy, I look forward to wearing them after I've broken
them in a bit,' would have done perfectly – would have done perfectly
for me, too, so why didn't I? – well, from fear of hurting her feelings,

but what were her feelings, what feelings lay behind the giving of this preposterously, not to say fatally, ill-judged gift? Actually, I think I know. I think she'd been energetically lazy, had lazily succumbed to a series of energetic associations – Si's birthday, got to get him something, left it late, late, well, here I am in Peter Jones (she was in Peter Jones every other afternoon, it was her favourite shop for being in, even when she had no money), trying on shoes for herself, shoes, Si, football, Eton, boots, boots yes, boots! – excuse me, I want a pair of football boots for my son, he's playing for his school First Eleven, Westminster, you know, against Eton, needs a new pair of boots, not too expensive, size eight, what would you recommend. Westminster. Against Eton, you see.' 'These, madam, I recommend these! Only pair left in size eight, it's by far and away the best boot of its kind on the market, especially for Westminster against Eton, nothing else like it, and going at a discount.' 'Taken. Taken and done!' cries Mummy. 'And at a discount too!' she would say later to James, because, quite simply, that was her way with presents, first priority – take no trouble; second priority, cheap as possible; third priority, please wrap it for me; and at the bottom of the list, if under consideration at all, actual suitability. And yet, as I've mentioned often enough, she had a generous spirit, our mother – but also a hasty, can't be bothered, slapdash spirit – and the carefulness with money was in fact against that spirit, a matter of necessity, she had so little at that time. If she'd had lots and lots, she'd have spent lots and lots, and the presents would have been lavishly inappropriate, instead of cheaply inappropriate.

That was the kind of rumination I'd had in mind, the treat I'd looked forward to serving up to myself when I'd got through all the unpleasant stuff – prostate and so forth, that kept putting me off putting it down, but now that I've finally put it down it strikes me that it wasn't a treat at all, that the rumination would go on to include the thought that the missed goals, the missed catches – most particularly the missed catches, because they were missed in comfortable boots – were pointers to the future – that throughout my life I have pedalled backwards, so to speak, away from opportunities that might have made the difference, from fear of messing them up – But what opportunities? Do opportunities of that sort happen with a life, hover in the air, waiting for a safe pair of hands to arrive under them, spill them, fail to arrive – are there moments like that with my children when I've failed to arrive? We're about to land in Toronto, Lester Pearson airport. So we've arrived.

No, we haven't. We're on the ground, but the captain's just informed us we can't get to our gate, it's blocked by a plane that should have taken off before we touched down. I'll be too late for the stage, another missed opportunity – but it won't be my fault, not my catch – my spirit is in place, hands cupped, it's the plane that's stationary, no, now actually shifting backwards, away from the gate.

ACCOMMODATING A SMOKER

I'm writing this in our Toronto hotel bedroom at three in the morning, sitting by the fractionally opened balcony door of our bedroom, trembling slightly with cold. Across the room, Victoria is in bed asleep – not a good sleep, she keeps stirring, coughing, because the smoke from my cigarette, which I keep trying to usher out through the crack in the door on to the balcony, is being blown back by the draught towards the bed. But then this has been what Harold would call 'a day and a half' – we had to wait twenty-five minutes to get to our gate, the plane that was blocking it had to unload a passenger who'd died as he was buckling on his safety belt – then it took another forty minutes for our bags to come through, so that we had just under half an hour to get to the theatre, no question of checking into the hotel first, etc. The young man sent by the Harbourfront Festival to pick us up had a slightly reckless appearance – he had sideboards, a jut of black beard, and fiery brown eyes – but was completely Canadian in style, relaxed and affable, as he assured us he'd get me on to the stage with time to spare, and he did, to the wings anyway, where I had a good three minutes in which to greet the Harbourfront director, the small, balding, squat and jovial Greg Gatenby, and the man who was going to do the interview, a man of imposing presence, tall, heavily built, with a short but somehow flowing grey beard and shrewdly twinkling eyes – gravitas, age, weight, dignity, decorum, fashion – he had the lot, and whatever our actual age difference, he was older than me in ways that matter in the world by a generation or two. His name was Michael Bradshaw, would doubtless have been Sir Michael Bradshaw if he'd stayed in his native England, was the director of Canadian Opera, and had especially asked to conduct this interview as he'd been a student of mine, at Queen Mary College, the University of London, and so the actual age difference was about ten years in his favour, when you work it out, which I didn't at the time, Good God, we said, all those years we said, as we shook each other by the hand, cuffed each other on the shoulder, I pretending that I remembered the mere boy out of which this monument to maturity had sprouted, and then I hurried off for a pee, combed my locks, so much darker and more luxuriant, if less dignified than his, then hurried to the wings just as Victoria was leaving them for the auditorium, stood in a kind of trance with my ex-student as we were introduced by someone who spoke around my name for several minutes on the subject of tortured and imprisoned writers, referring frequently to a chair that was kept empty on stage to remind us of the current fate of one particular writer – we were to regard it as his chair, the more his for his not being here to sit on it – and then my ex-student led me on to the stage. My main fear was that I would somehow find myself sitting down on the specially preserved, symbolically charged empty chair, but in fact I didn't manage to locate any empty chair on stage, though I noted through the glare of the lighting, quite a few empty seats in the auditorium.

I remember almost nothing about the interview, what he asked me or how I answered, but there was steady laughter from the audience, though whether I raised it or merely caused it I have no idea. The director, Greg Gatenby, and the interviewer, my ex-student, (Sir) Michael Bradshaw, both seemed to think it had gone OK, and Victoria was impressed by the fact that I was capable of speech, considering the circumstances of our arrival – it was three in the morning our time by the time we'd finished – although adding, 'But of course you're used to being up at this hour, you're just getting going, really.' I pointed out that at this hour I was used to being up on my own, in my study, getting going by myself, I had very little experience of company at such an hour, except when I was so angry I needed two of me, one to expostulate, the other to expostulate back. I then smoked a cigarette in a marked-off smoking cubicle, was led to a chair in the lobby, where a quarter of a dozen people waited with books for me to sign – one of them by the biographer Michael Holroyd, the rest by me. At a table a few yards from mine the novelist David Lodge, who had been simultaneously interviewed in an adjacent theatre, was faced by a queue that seemed to stretch right out of the lobby on to the pavement, and beyond that possibly all the way to the airport, where planes containing David Lodge fans were even now banking, or whatever it is they do when there are too many of them to come down, stacking, yes, in the air, stacking, were plane loads of David Lodge fans. I had the advantage of him, though, in being able to get away within minutes, and within a few more minutes Victoria and I were in the hotel, which is called the Harbour Castle. The name is technically accurate in that it's on the harbour, and like a castle has a tower, two in fact, so that if you drew a diagram it would look exactly like a diagram of the Due Castelli, for instance, in Sestri Levante, but there are no lawns, pine trees, ocean views, and the drive up to it takes you through a vast concrete tunnel into a forecourt which is really a parking lot, at the end of which is a wall of black glass, with revolving doors guarded by men in burgundy uniforms who tip their top hats at you as you get into or out of your cab. The lobby's only distinguishing feature is that you can't smoke in it, nor can you smoke in any of the several public rooms, nor at the very long bar that stretches across half the lobby, and at which nobody was drinking when we went by to our elevator – in fact, it had a generally under-used look to it, the stool tops fresh and shiny, as if buttocks only settle on them long enough for some foul soft drink to be gulped down, nothing about it suggested that authentic bar life flowed and ebbed there – affairs started, marriages ended, births drunk to, dead friends toasted –

STRUTTING IN THE GRAVEYARD

Toronto seems ugly but pleasant – the city ugly, but the people pleasant, which is better than the other way around (Paris) or neither (Athens), but we haven't looked at much of it, yet, and perhaps won't.

Literary festivals are rather strange, really, writers performing – why do people want to see them – us? Actually, I don't think anyone but Greg Gattenby particularly wants to see me, and I suspect he only wants – wanted – to see me because he has a copy of every book I've had published, in every language I've been published in, and wanted me to sign them all. When he brought in his first armful, looking, with his short burly frame, bare and muscular arms, as if he should have been carrying them in a hod, I assumed that that was the lot, but back he came, again and again, armful after armful, into the little smoking hutch in the hospitality suite, and not only did I come across editions in languages I didn't recognize, I also came across a long-playing record of the soundtrack of the film of *Butley*, a Caedmon record, that I didn't know existed. I don't suppose I'm a special favourite of Greg's – in fact, I have no grounds for believing that he's read a single one of my plays, diaries or novels – but he's a compulsive collector, and of course specializes in collecting the work of the writers he invites to the Harbourfront Festival – which actually makes the signing tiresome, because you can't just scrawl your signature, you have to add a special sentence or two – 'For Greg, with thanks and admiration, Simon. Harbourfront, Oct 30th, 2002' but with variations, to show that this isn't a mechanical process, you're keeping him before you, a living and changing human creature – as indeed he is – as you write. Of course it's possible that he actually likes writers. He certainly treats them very well. Honours them, in fact. Although he looks as if he bounces them.

I think the reading went off all right, but of course I don't know what they made of it, really – I did passages from *Enter a Fox*, a sort of ramble around my life – the only other time I've read myself out loud publicly (the same passages) was last year, in New York, at the Jewish Y, where the audience laughed quite a lot. But these Toronto people, probably not many of them Jewish or New Yorkers, seemed uneasy about laughing, as if not sure it was mannerly, or perhaps they didn't find any of it particularly funny, though I now and then heard a guarded, chuckly sound and a few modulated grunts – but the grunts may have come from my brother Nigel, who uses grunts to indicate either interest or a polite lack of it. He and his wife Barbara had chosen

to sit at a table directly under the lectern, which raised my consciousness somewhat during those opening dodgy moments, as did the chap
who'd introduced me at the interview, though he made an identical
speech, with the same references to a significantly unoccupied chair,
which again I couldn't locate. I assumed he'd gone from the scene once
he'd spoken my name and gestured me out of the wings to the lectern
at last, but after I'd got out a few trembly sentences about what I was
going to read I caught him out of the side of my eye, a tall, balding
man with glinting spectacles, standing just below the dais to my right,
staring up at me, and then as I began to read there was his hand,
reaching up and groping towards my book, to pluck it from my grasp,
I assumed. I almost lost my thread, only realizing it was the mike he
was really after when I heard my voice boom and then straighten out –
but I managed to keep my eyes on the page, just as well, as the lectern
was poorly lit and it was quite hard to make out the small Faber print.
Once I got going I could hear my voice developing a bit of a strut,
which was probably OK until I got to the passage about visiting Piers's
grave, when I was almost jaunty, I think, until I suddenly took notice
of what I was reading, and pulled myself down a bit, not all the way
down into a 'palpable design' sort of melancholy, my voice didn't
quaver – at least I hoped it didn't.

GOING HOME

We're staying with Nigel and Barbara for the night, out in Oakville.
Victoria and Barbara went off to bed early. Nigel and I sat talking about
our prospects, now mainly behind us, and our past, which was laid out
stiffly before us in photograph albums – we flicked through them
rapidly, not really seeing them properly, both wanting to talk only a
little about not very much. He was tired, and I couldn't remember any
of the questions about family matters that I'd been saving up for this
meeting. There was a moment though, when we found ourselves
staring down at a photograph taken in the garden in Halifax, in the
mid-fifties of the last century. I just wrote down 'of the last century' for
the sake of it, really, the thought of my having been a very young man
halfway through 'the last century' is oddly exciting, connecting me to

those people who announced, halfway through the last century, that they came from the 'last part of the last century', meaning in their cases the century before the last, or to put it all in basic terms, from the nineteenth century – what am I trying to say - well, I'm tired, Nigel's gone to bed, and I'm sitting in their dining-room, with one of the albums before me opened still at the photograph we looked at together, trying to remember anything about the circumstances – I mean, there we all are, the family Gray in what I suppose was its prime, the mother in a white summer frock, sitting on the grass, the usual cigarette strangely absent; to her right pubescent Piers, hair cut Canada style, his stare oddly intense (myopia, but as yet unrecognized), directly behind the mother there stands the father, arms folded, relaxed and confident, a man in his fifties with a good job, his own house, seeming to grow out of the family around him as if he were a tree in a tub – Nigel to his left, on one knee, arms bent, smiling and urgent, like an American footballer, and to his right, myself, hair long, a lock of it falling over my left eye, Hitler-style – unlike the other males, who are in short-sleeved summer shirts, I am wearing a black blazer that is evidently too large for me – the sleeves of it come over my wrists to my knuckles – and a white scarf that seems at first glance to be attached to the blazer, like an external lining – it's as if I've come into the frame from a different continent in a different season – what on earth was I up to? Can I have been making some sinister statement, winter man among the summer folk, grim and bleak, a harbinger? – then why the sensual smile, lips plump and moist – though moist could be the sunlight. It's a black and white photograph, of course, so the family might have actually been a festival of colours, my jacket not black but purple, my scarf lemon, and – I wonder who took it, there is absolutely no sense of an invisible other behind the camera, as there usually is with old photographs, I can't imagine who would have been there, available – oh, Daddy took it, of course, he arranged us as he wanted us, left a space for himself back row centre, set the camera which was on a tripod, then ran to his space, we would all hold our expressions, until the whirr and click, and there we still are, in black and white on a summer's afternoon in Halifax, Nova Scotia, with expressions held for fifty years or so, so far – and here on the other hand are Nigel and I, the two who are still alive, in Nigel's house in Oakville, outside Toronto – he asleep by now, I hope, and I looking down at this photograph in sudden amazement as I write this and - well, nothing else really.

It's an hour later and I'm still here, smoking in a house that's unused to smokers, there are no ashtrays, I'm using a saucer – jumpy, I feel jumpy. The flight tomorrow – then London again, and here's Piers in another photograph, six months old in a garment that comes down over his toes – he's on my lap, I'm sitting in an armchair, my chin resting lightly on the top of his almost bald head, Nigel is sitting on the arm of the chair, one finger touching Piers's little ear – it's a wonderfully clear photograph, so fresh – perfectly posed, perfectly natural – it must have been taken by a professional –

And here's another of Nigel and me, in the garden in Hayling Island, not long back from Montreal, we've still got the haircuts, I'm eight I should think, Nigel nine therefore and – ah yes, it would be about the time we killed the rat. We came across it late one afternoon on the road by the beach – claws stretching out, head poked forward, belly bloated – it made noises, mutterings and sighs as it pulled itself along to where, did it know – I remember the tail, stuck out from its back like a pink tube. We poked at it from a distance with sticks, threw stones at it, got braver and kicked at it, scraping and scuffing it about so that its head wagged from side to side, and there were the teeth of course – I always think that I find men with rat-teeth sympathetic and kindly, goofy-looking, although I suppose if they also had pink tails – anyway when the rat's teeth are in the mouth of a rat, and you think of the rat scampering up your leg under your trousers (short trousers, I see from the photo), its tail whipping and teeth delving – but when it was stiff and dead at last, and looked so pitiful, and we knew that there was nothing we could do to make it right, we couldn't just let it go, or put it back, we'd finished it, it's life was over with and it was our doing – a few years older and we'd probably have said, 'Well, it was dying anyway, had to put it out of its misery, it would have been cruel not to, etc.' – in fact, we'd have said it before we'd begun to do it, as well as after we'd done it, but we didn't say anything, we went home, I can't remember our ever having talked about it and – well, there we are now in the garden with our ears sticking out, and our Canadian haircuts, and Nigel's front teeth also sticking out – he must have been making a face, he never had trouble with his teeth, never had to wear braces, never sprouted a pink tail – I'll ask him in the morning whether he remembers killing the rat – no, I'll forget in the morning, what with the packing, the goodbyes – and look, here's another one of Nigel and me, Hayling Island again but before Montreal, I'm about three, so he's four and a bit, and we're both sitting on the back of a Great Dane, her name was Sarah – no, Sari – she used to trot us about the garden, sometimes out of the garden and down the road a way, and look – who is this?

Yes, who is this?

From top to bottom: Nigel Gray, Simon Gray (middle)
and Piers Gray in 1946

THE
SMOKING
DIARIES

Volume 2

The Year of the Jouncer

For Ben and Lucy

PART ONE

A PRAYER ANSWERED

Here I am, sitting at my table, pigeons hopping about in the sun, little birds with yellow chests settling on the rim of my fruit punch, in front of me the sea in Caribbean blue and green, and from it the occasional purr and cough of small boats, the roar of a speedboat, brief and violent, and behind me the clatter of waiters laying tables while they talk to each other in incomprehensible Bajan – everything very much as you hope it will be when you're in London during Christmas, longing to be here.

So at least that's another Christmas gone, thank God. For me it has become the worst season, the season when people I love die, beginning with my mother, over thirty years ago, then a long gap, and then almost every other year, sometimes in consecutive years, for the last decade. Two years ago on Boxing Day it was Ian Hamilton, this year on the day after Boxing Day Alan Bates. No, that's wrong. Alan, who died three weeks ago, died in 2003, which is now last year, and Ian, who died two years and three weeks ago, died in 2001, which is now by the calendar three years ago. But on the day after Boxing Day and on Boxing Day respectively, in the Christmas season.

A SELF-PROHIBITION

My plan is to get down some thoughts and memories of Alan, but I don't think I can start today, not on the first day, with the pigeons hopping, and the little birds with yellow chests etc., one of which is now sharing my drink. Best let it happen when it happens, tomorrow perhaps, or later in the week, let it sneak up. Today the thing is just to be here, back here at the usual table, my yellow pad in front of me, free to go wherever – although I think I must make a pact with myself to lay off the subject of my age, and my physical deterioration, it's really time I outgrew all that, it's not becoming in a man nearing seventy, although I must confess that now I see those words actually on the page, 'nearing seventy', I find myself gaping at them. I can't think what it is that's nearing seventy, apart from my body, but the most significant parts of my body, the parts whose ageing have a significant bearing on my life expectancy – the liver (mistreated for nearly fifty years), the lungs (for over sixty years), the heart, the intestines, bladder and bowels – are all concealed from view, their condition reported on a couple of times a year in the form of figures printed out from blood tests. My doctor faxes them through to me and I study them with attentive ignorance, looking for asterisks. If he puts an asterisk by a number it means that the number is either too high or too low. These days the number to do with the prostate is too high, but I'm not to be surprised by this, I'm told, because although I have a tumour nesting or nestling there, it is without territorial ambitions, in fact it might still be nesting or nestling while I die of something else, or a combination of something elses, or in an accident, or unlawfully, at the hands of another. In other words, one way or another, it's here for life. As am I, I suppose. But my point is that while I am decaying within and without, and quite right too – it's nature's way, after all, the way of all flesh – I am most of the time unaware of the decay, though there are the hints, of course – the days when the bladder seems to fill even as I'm emptying it, the wheeze and double whistle in the chest, the faintness that follows climbing stairs, but on the whole, apart from a developing sense of decay and imminent death, nothing much has changed in

THE SELF ITSELF

since the moment in my pram, in the garden of Mallows, in Hayling Island, one afternoon some sixty-seven years ago, when I suddenly shook and bounced within my harness and caused the pram to stir – whereupon something in me sprang awake! might perhaps be the right phrase, sprang awake in the act of understanding the connection between the movement of my body and the movement of the rectile – rectile? What's a rectile? Do I mean reticule? Yes, but vehicle would be the better word – the connection between the movement of the body and the vehicle containing it – how much grasped in that slip of a second – how you could change the shape of the universe, get a move on, hustle, rock and tremble through life, through the garden, anyway, a few feet, it may have only been a few inches, for all I know now, that first time, but that they became feet, and then yards, and then quite a few yards, and then more than that, I know for a fact because I was told about it when I was old enough – from the initial suspicion that somehow the pram with the baby in it wasn't quite where it was when last seen – a large pram of the period, of course, highly sprung, probably brakeless, easily mobile, left with the baby in it for the usual half an hour or so in the afternoon, while Mummy was doing what Mummies did in those days, which precluded keeping an eye on the baby, and Daddy was in his surgery, accepting a chicken for his latest diagnosis, if his patient was one of the impoverished of the parish, or dispensing manly medical sympathy to one of the island's younger matrons, and brother Nigel perhaps toddling about the kitchen where Nanny was having her tea and a gossip with cook – while all those people were doing those sorts of things, the pram with the baby in it, the rocking, bouncing baby, was trundling along the garden path to somewhere quite a long way from where it had been when last seen. It was a complete mystery to the adult intelligences, how had he done it, if it was he who had done it, but if not he, who then and why? So the next afternoon they (Mummy and Nanny?) planted the pram in the usual spot, and stood over it, watching. The baby lay there smiling or snivelling up at them, until it struck them that they should try observing the baby when unobserved by the baby, and they withdrew behind bushes and trees etc. and thus witnessed the swaying of the pram, then the juddering of the pram, then its slow, unsteady progress along the path, the movement accompanied by a low humming and keening sound from within that reminded them more of a dog than of a human, and which they found alarming. On the other hand the mystery was solved, because the simple physical facts were easily understood, although in fact full of the deeper mysteries of self, self-discovery, will, solitude, and the need to make a noise when shaking and bouncing in a pram. Jouncing was the word they used for it. I was a jouncer therefore.

*

MY BATTLE WITH THE WAVES

So. To the left of the hotel, if you are facing the sea, there is a small cove with a shed in it. From this shed a pipe stretches into the sea and pumps water out into something or other behind the shed, a cistern, I think, though I've never seen it. The shed and the pipe and the cistern, if there is a cistern, belong to McGill University, in Montreal, their Marine Science Department. My father went to McGill, which is why I always read the sign carefully, though I know it by heart, when I clamber around the little cove to the public beach next to it – I've taken to swimming there because the hotel beach has developed a high ridge close to shore, when you walk out to sea the ground gives under you, and you have to fling yourself forward and swim before you intend to. I like to have a cigarette as I wade out, smoking and contemplating the various mysteries of life – e.g. where does the sea come from? Why does nature exist? What's that scuttling over my feet? – and it's no fun, plus it's very unsightly, to be caught by a wave with a cigarette between your lips – wasteful too – but the worst part is getting out. It's difficult to get a grip on the ridge, which consists of sand and pebbles, your foot slides down the slope, you topple back into the sea, start again, trying to get out between the incoming waves, which bide their time and then, when you've convinced yourself there isn't one, erupt under you as you place your foot halfway up the ridge again. The year before last a visiting friend of ours, an elderly lady from New York called Bumma, got caught by a brute of a wave – she was virtually alone on the beach, there was no one to help her as she was tumbled and rolled around, sucked back by the undertow, then, before she could regain her footing, rolled and tumbled forward – Bumma was lucky not to have drowned, really, in what would have been a foot or so of water. I kept thinking of her when I was trying to get out the other afternoon, and suddenly hit upon a scheme – a rather daring scheme, basically derived from judo, or ju-jitsu – you use the force opposing you to your advantage – i.e. when a man throws a punch at you, you duck, catch his arm and pull him forward using his own impetus as a lever, then step out of the way as he flows past you and crashes to the ground, where you can kick him at your leisure – I've seen this done often on screen, most notably by a one-armed Spencer Tracy, in *Bad Day at Black Rock*, when he annihilates the brutish two-armed Ernest Borgnine by employing exactly the method I've described, though being Spencer Tracy he doesn't kick him when he's down, he lets him get up to throw another hay-maker. Spencer has to go through the whole process three times, his trilby remaining on his head, by the way, throughout – it's a very exhilarating scene, and now I've got the film recorded I can, and sometimes do, play it over and over again. So. So why Spencer Tracy flinging Ernest Borgnine all over the place? – it's in a diner actually and at the climax through a screen door – Oh yes, conquering the ridge – my plan was to *use* the waves to carry me over the ridge by surfing them – I am actually rather good at surfing, can do it without a board, and lo! there I was on the other side of the ridge, the beach a mere few feet away, all I had to do was scramble to my feet and take a step or two. I'd made it to my knees when the wave I'd surfed in on surged back, taking me with it and peppering my legs and stomach with pebbles, sharp stones and what felt like fragments of broken glass, and then, like poor old Bumma, I was rolled, tumbled, etc., but unlike Bumma I was watched from the shore by a dozen or so guests at the adjoining hotel, lolling on their beach-beds and certainly smiling, in some cases laughing as if I were a floor show – this went on for several minutes. Once or twice I struck out to sea, a dignified, classy crawl, as if I were engaged in a complicated exercise I'd designed for myself, a sort of combat course. I suspect I would still be there, either being rolled around with sand and stone and sea, like a maritime version of Wordsworth's Lucy, or right out in deep water, pretending that that's where I prefer to be, or drowned, if Victoria hadn't come looking for me, sized up the situation in a blink, walked into the water, stretched out her hand – which I took as if intending to shake, but allowed myself to be drawn by it up to safety – extraordinary how much power, I almost wrote brute power, is contained in her slight and graceful form – I've long accepted that she's stronger than me physically as well as morally, but then she's much younger, hasn't got a paunch, doesn't smoke, so she jolly well ought to be able to haul me out of the sea.

SWIMMING WITH A WALRUS

Anyway, the above should make it clear why I now go to the left of the hotel, past the cove with the McGill Marine Science shed in it, and scramble onto the public beach, which has only a small ridge, and furthermore soft pebble-and-shard-free sand – altogether a much better swimming beach, in fact, and much more fun, as the local people swim from it, you see them in large groups, almost like congregations, which they may well be, on outings from the nearby churches, of which there are dozens, of all known, and some (to me) unknown, denominations – portly matrons in one-piece swimming suits with vivid sunsets stamped on them, supple young men, sinuous girls, middle-aged men with angry, Rastafarian locks, families dunking naked babies into the water – and here and there the English, sitting stiffly on boulders and tree stumps if they're middle-aged, or sprawling on the sand with tattoos on their arms and bottles of Banks beer in their hands if they're young, offensive to the eye, let's face it, as offensive as I am in my drooping trunks, pendulous this and puckered that – but I don't have to see myself, do I? And within seconds I'm in the sea, splashing along, ducking through the waves, spouting water out of my mouth something like a whale. This morning, before breakfast, the beach was empty except for a stocky man in his fifties, balding, pink and blotchy, with a small white moustache – he was just wading in as I arrived – he looked so formal and ill-at-ease as in he plodded, up to his knees, up to his waist, scowling blankly – I surged into the water within his sight-line, I hoped, I certainly made enough noise, splashing and whooping, to let him know that there were people for whom the sea is a welcoming place. I dashed and splashed about, dived under, stayed there as long as I could, then surfaced beside a pair of feet sticking straight up out of the water, ankles pressed neatly together, pink soles turned outwards, toes curled. He was doing a handstand. I could see right down to his head between his hands on the seabed – he brought his legs down and somersaulted to the top, not exactly gracefully, but he wasn't ungainly either – his head appeared above the surface, eyes blinking, little white moustache dripping – he looked like a sea creature, a walrus. He stared at me vaguely, scarcely taking me in as he went under again, curling himself into a foetal ball and then rolling on one side, then the other, then a back-somersault, a quick surface, a walrus blink, and down he went again, to celebrate the feel of himself in the sea, this man I had pegged as an office-bound goblin, living behind life's wainscoting.

A GLIMPSE OF A LOST CIVILIZATION

A boat arrived, full of schoolgirls, about thirty of them, between nine and fifteen, I suppose, all wearing traditional brown uniforms, their hair in pigtails, children of a sort I haven't seen in England since my own childhood. They leapt squealing and laughing off the boat into the water, carrying their shoes and socks in their hands, and scampered onto the beach. A young woman, presumably the teacher, got off last, her skirt hiked up. She splashed after them, calling out instructions which she really didn't expect them to follow, but at least reminded them that she was there. They poured up the beach and into the changing rooms in the small park, a sort of compound that also has a café, benches, swings, little shops. A few minutes later they poured out again, into the sea, heads bobbing, screams, shrieks of laughter, splashing each other, ducking each other, an absolute rough house of girls at play, but not a swearword to be heard, nothing bad-tempered, ill-natured, brutish about these children, and it struck me with a pang that such a sight and such sounds would be impossible in the England of today, and will soon be just a folk memory among the elderly, for what authority would dare to allow thirty children to go on a trip to the beach, to plunge into the sea, with only one teacher to supervise them? Indeed, what authority could muster thirty children who would play freely and joyfully, without bawling out obscenities and threats at each other – and at the teacher, probably. When you live in a barbarous country, it's nice, if painful, to spend a little time in a civilized one, to remember what we once were, to think what's become of us.

FROM INFANT GENIUS TO INFANT PERVERT

But what was admired in the Hayling garden in daylight, indeed interpreted as the early manifestation of an original mind, possibly of genius, became regarded as something other, possibly a perversion, when practised at night in an unmoving bed. The bouncing and jouncing and above all the weird canine keening could be heard all over the house, and all through the night, and persisted through my teens and twenties, actually until I got married at the age of twenty-nine – it was worse than snoring because it seemed entirely wilful, even though I was unconscious, or could be assumed to be – my face buried in the pillow, and my body sliding and humping. But if my face was buried in the pillow, how come I was so audible? And how come, at least in my earliest years, I didn't suffocate – I could have been an early example of what used to be called cot death but is now frequently, after confidently delivered though hopelessly flawed medical evidence, misdiagnosed as murder (a number of mothers wrongfully jailed, whole families destroyed, children snatched from their homes and placed with foster parents or in institutions, irretrievably – irretrievably? Well, yes, we know we might have made a mistake, say the social services and government ministers responsible, but it's too late now to correct it, for the children's sake they must stay fostered or institutionalized, besides no smoke without fire, even if we're the ones who lit it you can't expect us to put it out, we're comfortable with what we've done and compassionate and caring with it) – so with the hypothesis that I died in my cot because my face was sunk into my pillow while jouncing, and then with a time-jump of those sixty-seven years, it's easy to see how the course of our lives might have run differently, Mummy's would have run in jail, Daddy would either have remarried or sacrificed himself to clearing Mummy's name, Nigel would have been fostered or institutionalized, and I, well, I would have been dead, of course, officially the victim of infanticide (unless they could pin it on the nanny), but in fact the victim of a jouncing habit that led to pillow suffocation – but what pillow? Surely babies don't have pillows. If they lie flat on their stomachs – a clear impossibility, actually, given that babies' stomachs are round, inflated – I've just been upstairs and tried it on the hotel bed, I lay with my cheek, right cheek as I'm a right-hand-side person, pressed flat against the mattress, it felt so easy and natural that I began to slip away for a moment, the great soft belly of me cushioning the middle of my body, in fact becoming a functional asset instead of the pendulous embarrassment it is when I'm upright and in company – and not only when I'm in company, I'm embarrassed by it when I'm on my own, sometimes I stand still in the middle of my study and try to suck it in – I'll try now, I'm in the bar but nobody's really looking – no, nothing stirred except the ghosts in my chest, the effort has left me short of breath, so let me go back to it as it was when I lay down a few minutes earlier – how did I describe it? As a cushion for the middle of my body – so must a baby's be, when it's not full of wind, so must mine have been whenever I was a windless baby, but just now, when I lay on the bed, I felt no impulse to jounce and bounce and fill the hotel with my keening.

A PEACEFUL AND REASONABLE MAN GOES SLEEPLESS

The thing, though, about jouncing in my bed, post-perambulator, and all through my growing up, is that it brought out the worst in my parents – Daddy, after all, needed his sleep, and when we moved to London, into 47 Oakley Gardens, in Chelsea, he had to be up and off to his pathology lab early in the morning, and also needed energy for his romantic enterprises later in the day, furthermore he liked his sleep, not only was he relaxed and nourished by it, but was addicted to it as a kind of pleasure, or was it vice? He liked to be in bed early, and stay in it until the last possible minute – he took his breakfast in it, along with his post and the newspapers, and he was very uxorious, a very uxorious philanderer, so what with one vice and another, one pleasure and another, you can see that he spent quite a lot of his day, as well as most of his night, in bed, and when he was in bed at night he liked his sleep, drowsy, toasty, in Mummy's arms, she in his, zzzzz – and I disturbed all that, the sound of my bed jumping up and down, my child's voice keening, clattered and sliced into his slumber, their slumber, and drove him quite wild with rage, though he tried, being by nature a reasonable and peaceful man, to bring the rage under control and to devise reasonable and peaceful solutions to my problem, though it wasn't in fact my problem, after all I wasn't waking myself up, in fact I was probably jouncing and keening myself into deeper and deeper layers of the unconscious, into sweet and holy spaces or places – or perhaps not, who knows where you go when you're asleep, whether you're jouncing and keening or as still as a corpse.

ANOTHER USE FOR A HAIRBRUSH

His first solution was to ask me, and then, a few nights later, after I'd evidently though not consciously turned down his request, to command me, to sleep on my back. I remember lying rigidly, eyes closed, trying to lower myself into sleep by an act of will, a kind of reverse levitation. My next introduction to consciousness was when he rolled me back onto my back with whispered imprecations, dark words I couldn't understand that for all their intensity were designed to be inaudible to Mummy in their bedroom next door, and perhaps to me, too. Whatever they were, their meaning was inescapable. He believed, even though reason and peaceableness must have argued against it, that I was doing it on purpose and that I was a deliberate and premeditating jouncer. Well, possibly I was. I certainly came to believe that I was, and fought against the deep, corrupt desire to roll onto my side, then onto my stomach – one turbulent night he ran into my room and unleashed a powerful but soft, because unshod, kick at my ribs. From the next room came Mummy's, my Mummy's alarmed and imploring response – 'James! James, darling!' – to his disowning me, so to speak, with 'Will you shut up, you little bastard!' That he should have come to this! He got his foot out of the blanket, threw it over me, and left the room, a little click, a solicitous little click of the closing door, as if being careful not to wake the sleeping child. I heard their voices murmuring away, mainly hers, consoling – I'd recognize the tone now, though I didn't then – she knew her James, he wasn't a man to kick his sleeping nine-year-old, even with a naked foot, for the mere pleasure of it, this was a James who had been driven to desperate measures, a James beside himself. James, peaceable and reasonable and at one with himself again, devised a practical scheme to prevent me rolling on my stomach in my sleep – a hairbrush tied through one of the buttonholes on my pyjama top.

TROUBLE WITH PYJAMAS

One went to bed in suits, in those days, a thickish jacket and a thickish pair of trousers particularly thick at the waist, because of the thick cord that went through it, the ends of which one tied in a burly bow at the front, navel height. It's a wonder, really, that we didn't wear shoes in bed – oh, and the gap at the front of the trousers that wasn't a gap but folds of cloth that you somehow had to pull apart, a fumbling and desperate business when you were in urgent need – sometimes it was simpler to pull the trousers down and pee over the top, the dangers of this procedure being manifest in smells and stains that mother drew to your attention – 'Really, must you be so lazy!' and one couldn't explain the difficulties to the mother, how in the cold, especially, it was like a tight little knot that tucked itself tightly into somewhere between one's legs, one's numbed fingers needed time to locate it, and then it had to be plucked at and coaxed and stretched like a piece of sensitive elastic, and this after one had fumbled through all the folds of cloth to locate the naked groin, let alone the tightly infolded little knot – so you see, Mummy, so much easier to pull the trousers down so you could actually see where it was, and if one bent one's knees and pushed one's groin – or would that be loins? – forward, one could mainly miss the crotch in one's pyjama bottoms, it would only be the last little bit, the dribble that sometimes, inexplicably, becomes a spurt before becoming a treacherous dribble again, dribbling down into the crotch and causing that stain.

SOUNDS FROM THE NEXT ROOM

So I went to bed with the hairbrush dangling from the buttonhole in the pyjama top, lay rigidly on my back, eyes closed, and woke to Daddy's brawling hands, rolling me back on my back, pulling my pyjama jacket into position – it had become twisted around to the side so that the buttons ran from my armpit down. The hairbush lay away from my body, pointlessly attached. On some occasions, worse occasions, the pyjama jacket was completely discarded, lay on the floor even. These were the signs, were they not, of a deliberate, wilful determination to sleep on my stomach and jounce keening through the night, in complete disregard of the father's need for replenishing sleep? I think that during those nights, many, many nights, I became quite simply the enemy, as a screeching cat or a perpetually barking dog becomes the enemy, first the enemy to sleep, then the enemy to self – in this case to my father's self. I expect he wanted to kill me, from time to time, as he lay beside his wife in the darkness, listening to my private night life expressing itself in what, now I come to think of it, must have sounded like an infant parody of the sexual act, the bouncing bed, the twanging springs, the animal keening, at a consistent, monotonous level of a climax impending but never achieved – an eerie, haunting parody of his own noises after lunch, say, in the bed in the flat of his secretary, little Mrs Rolls, or in the bed next door, where his wife, my mother, lay beside him but around whose body his arms – ah, but that was love, I heard it, not in the dead of night but as I lay awake before breakfast, the hairbrush replaced and resting on my stomach. I listened to the real thing, the noises of love, not keenings but murmurs, grunts, laughs, little cries suppressed but still trembling into screams choked off –

TIME ZONES

1) Today

It's 3.30 in the afternoon here in Barbados, 7.30 in England, specifically in Brighton, where the curtain is going up on *The Holy Terror*, an old play of mine. I say the curtain is going up, perhaps now has gone up, but I know so little about the production that I don't know whether there is a curtain. If there is, though, it won't be going up, now I come to think of it, it will still be down and Simon Callow will part it slightly as he steps onto a bit of forestage, to confront his audience, which is not the audience in the theatre but the audience in the play, composed of members of the Women's Institute in Chichester – it might be Cheltenham – the audience in the theatre is characterized and addressed, in other words, as if it were a small clutch of middle-aged, middle-class provincial women. When it was done in New York, nearly twenty years ago, the preview audiences enjoyed this device, cheerfully assuming the role assigned them, but the critics hated it, which is why there weren't any post-preview audiences.

I suppose I should try and write down the history of *The Holy Terror* – no, actually, I shouldn't, it's all in a preface I've written for a collection of my plays, I'll look it up and stick it in here when I get back –

2) Two Months Later

I'm in London, where it's extremely cold and unpleasant, transferring to this computer the yellow pads, which, I must say, are frequently difficult to read because of illegibility, stains, etc. I've just got to the sentence where I told myself to stick the preface in – quite easy, really, all I have to do is to look through my computer files for my prefaces, find the one for *The Holy Terror*, copy it and paste it

HERE:

I wrote the first version of *The Holy Terror* in 1986. It was called *Melon* and, like *The Holy Terror*, was about a successful publisher who advocates promiscuity for his wife and himself, then has a nervous breakdown when he decides, against all available evidence, that his wife is having an affair with one of his best friends – which best friend being the conundrum that finally drives him mad. *Melon* was produced at the Theatre Royal, Haymarket, and played to good houses, thanks mainly to Alan Bates, whose performance as the brute Englishman with the chaotic soul was so dazzling that it flattered the text, and perhaps it was the discrepancy between the story that the play told and the story that Alan told that made me feel, every time I sat through it, that the play didn't quite work. One day, long after it had closed, I found myself first thinking about it, then fretting about it, then sitting down to rewrite it, and finally, after drafts and drafts and more drafts, I was in possession of a new play that was so different from the original that I changed its title to *The Holy Terror*, which opened at the Promenade theatre in New York, in a production that you would have described as eccentric if you hadn't known that the director was a drunk. He drank quite a bit before each day's rehearsals, and quite a bit after them, and more than quite a bit during them, while never losing the conviction, however many times he stumbled down the aisle and tumbled over the seats, often with a lighted cigarette in his mouth and another, also lighted, in the hand that wasn't holding a glass, that he was in full command of his faculties, and that his genius for cutting through to the heart of the matter had never burned more brightly – thus when he had trouble moving the actors around the furniture, he cut the furniture, and when he had trouble deciding between lighting effects, he cut the lighting – on the press night, the audience found themselves confronted by unnerved actors performing on a mainly empty set, and in the house-lights only – the actors could see from the stage, for almost certainly the first time in their careers, the critics' faces, or more likely their heads, the tops of them anyway, as they bent angrily over their pads in order to avoid the actors' eyes, which were enlarged by panic and loathing. The director himself, frightened, triumphant and drunk, was also fully visible and all over the place, now at the backs of the stalls, now at the head of an aisle, now in the dress circle – if I'd been one of the actors I'd have stepped off the stage and murdered him, the news of which might at least have marginalized the review in the next morning's *New York Times*. Of course the producer, who was devoted to the play, made periodic attempts to fire the director but was thwarted by the director's agent, who pointed out that the playwright had director approval, and as the playwright and the director were one and the same it would be a question of asking him to fire himself, which he was unlikely to do, as he got on so well together. *The Holy Terror* lay dormant until about a year ago, when it was picked up by a London management. There are plans to produce it in the spring of 2004, with Simon Callow in the lead.

3) Two Minutes Later

There. Now I'm back to transcribing from the pad again, with a smear of what looks like bird-dropping coming up – ah, the birds in Barbados, darting onto the table, pecking at my hat, dipping into my drink. What is it, under the bird-shit – the word? Rehearsals is the word.

REHEARSALS

began a few weeks ago, but I decided not to attend them. Alan – with whom I still associated the leading part – had died a few days before, on Boxing Day, and I didn't want to hear his voice echoing in the lines, even though, as most of them had been rewritten, he'd never actually said them. Of course I knew that Simon Callow, an old and dear friend of mine, and an actor of great and distinctive talents, would very quickly make the lines his own. But I thought that even if I didn't bring Alan's ghost with me, I'd be haunting the production myself, the older playwright impersonating the twenty or so years younger one, the consumer of Diet Coke passing himself off as the gulper-down of champagne. I did, however, go, by invitation, to what I assumed was to be a read-through at Sadler's Wells, and found myself on the fringe of a little mob waiting in the reception area outside the rehearsal room – they were the producer and some of his staff, publicity people, make-up people, the wardrobe mistress and so forth along with representatives of the provincial theatres we'd be visiting. Inside the rehearsal room were the director and cast, not about to begin the read-through, the producer, Howard Panter, explained to me, but about to end it. 'I'm sorry you couldn't make it,' he said. 'I could have made it,' I said. 'But I wasn't asked.' 'Ah!' he said. 'The door's open. We can go in.' We went in. The director, a jovial-looking, plumpish, youngish man, whose name I've forgotten, stood at the head of a table and talked to his seated cast of six in a low, excluding voice. He saw us finally, with a little start of delight, and invited us to sit in a semicircle around him and greet and meet, or was it meet and greet the cast, himself and each other. 'I am Simon Callow,' said Simon Callow, 'and I am playing the part of Melon,' etc., a bit like an AA meeting, really. We got to me by way of the wardrobe mistress and several representatives of the provincial theatres – 'I,' I said, 'am the reason we are all here this afternoon.' Yes, I actually said that. There was a ripple of sycophantic laughter from one of the provinces. 'Well, not the only reason surely?' the director said, with a surprised smile. 'Yes, the only reason,' I said. Yes, I actually said that, too, and it was pretty well all I said, apart from a brief discussion with Lydia Fox, who is playing Melon's sexually generous secretary, on the subject of whether her character would be wearing the underclothes that young women wore in the 1970s, when the play is set – what about a girdle, for instance? She'd heard that girdles were very good for showing off your bum. I said I'd heard that too. We said a few more things along those lines to each other, she's very easy to talk to, very pretty, with a laughing, freewheeling conversational style. When she was taken away from me by the costume designer, I went over to Simon Callow. We generally have long and boisterous conversations together, but this time we really had nothing to say, he was for the trenches, as both captain and foot soldier, and I for – well, immediately for Barbados, so I gave him a hug, hoped he'd have fun in the coming month of rehearsals, and that was it, I left.

I MUST UNDERSTAND THAT I AM DEAD

How sour this seems in the remembering, no, in the telling, though I do in fact remember it sourly, and did in fact feel sour at the time – there's something about not wanting to be where you're not wanted or not expected or have not been thought about, especially when the occasion is the read-through of a play, and you're its author – but perhaps they thought I was dead, a dead author, a safely dead author. On the other hand there'd been phone calls, emails, I'd even had a meeting with the director, an hour long, in which he'd told me about his production of *Beauty and the Beast* at Stratford, and his plans for a family holiday in Egypt, so they all knew I was alive at least to that extent, that I could talk on the phone, receive and answer emails, present myself physically to the director, so there it was, I had to face it, I wasn't dead, I was merely negligible, a man for a meet and a greet but not for a read-through – in the old days, I told myself and now tell myself again, it wouldn't have happened, I wouldn't have let it happen, I'd have made them read through the read-through again and again and again, until they collapsed with exhaustion and dehydration, and then I'd have done such things that the earth would tremble at, and then I'd have, I'd have – but what in fact did I do? I stood around looking surly, that's what I did, brightening only when engaged by an attractive young woman in a conversation about attractive young women's underwear, and then tramped off full of grievance and relief, yes, that's the point, relief, and really I didn't think there were intended ill manners on the management's part, just the usual office negligence, and probably there was nothing intentionally unwelcoming in the director's welcome, just the usual director's nerves. I also knew I would have hated the read-through anyway, it would have made me doubt the actors, doubt the director, above all, doubt the play – and beneath all that I knew I just wasn't up to it any more. When it came down to it, what was I but a dead author, at least as far as *The Holy Terror* was concerned?

OR AUTISTIC

I'm in the bar at my table at two in the morning, only Rollocks, the waiter, in the bar with me – he is laying the tables for breakfast, strolling in his measured way from table to table, occasionally looking towards me to check whether I want another Diet Coke – I don't – the truth is I don't really want to be here. Last year and all the previous years I would come every night and write and talk to Rollocks, now I stay on my balcony, reading or writing or looking towards the sea, or sometimes looking down into the bar, where I can see Rollocks moving between the tables, and I feel a yearning to go down, but I don't, I stay up there and watch Rollocks moving between the tables. Is it possible to become autistic, or do you have to start off that way? Well, I believe that all day I've been something that corresponds to my understanding of the word autistic – it's as if I've had no inner context at all, no points of reference, a sort of blankness and not a comfortable one. I'm quite unhappy in this, but don't want to talk to anyone about it, not even Victoria, to whom I tell everything, almost everything, certainly more than she actually needs to know – but this is something that she probably does need to know, that her husband has plodded beside her to bar, restaurant and beach, indeed swum beside her in the sea, sat opposite her at the lunch and dinner table, and internally there's been no flicker of life at all, his mind a *tabula rasa*, slightly soiled.

A GOOD DEED PUNISHED

Can I, in all conscience, keep my table at the bar while I have lunch at a table in the restaurant? Yesterday I decided I couldn't, and surrendered my bar table to a lanky North Country couple – he has buck teeth that fix his mouth in a permanent grin of seeming good nature, she is blonde, with a handsome, beaky face and long legs made longer by high-heeled sandals – both wear sunglasses which don't suit them, they make his face seem all teeth, and to hers they give a hooded effect, like a bird of prey. They accepted the table gratefully, as if with a full knowledge of the ancient tradition that it was mine by right and their tenure was at my convenience. When I returned from lunch they vacated it immediately, with a flourish and some jokes about having been honoured, etc. So that was OK. Today at lunch time when they came to the bar I repeated the offer. When I came back after lunch they were sitting with their heads bowed, stubbornly unaware of my hovering presence. I thought I'd give them a few minutes, but when I came back they were just as they had been, heads bowed. Victoria took me for a walk to calm me down, and I was calm when we came back, until I saw that they were still there, heads bowed. Victoria took me for a swim, and when we got back, there, with heads, etc. – I walked around the table at a slight distance and, though their heads were still, I could see their hands moving and hear little clicking sounds, like false teeth – I moved closer to make absolutely sure, and yes, it was true, they were playing Scrabble, sitting at my table, the buggers, playing Scrabble. So here I am now, looking down at them from our balcony – I notice that she has a long, straight back, and he too sits very upright, both of their postures speak of intense concentration, which is I suppose needed when playing a game for halfwits, you have to keep the other half of your wits at bay, if they joined up you'd surely knock the board and the pieces of the alphabet to the ground – not that I've ever actually played Scrabble, I have no patience with indoor games that involve spelling or knowledge or indeed thought or intelligence of any kind – but the fact is, as I look down at them with scowly eyes, I suspect that they make a more attractive, more elegant spectacle at my table than I do, when I sit there writing, my jaw jutting out, cigarette on the go, a study in ill temper and bad living.

LIKE SON

Actually, I've just realized that it's not true that I've never played games that require thought or knowledge. I used to play chess *en famille*, not with Mummy, of course, she thought it was strictly a man's sport, unlike hockey or cricket, at both of which she'd excelled, along with the standing broad jump and the high jump, but chess, she said, demanded the male mind to grasp its intricacies, she couldn't hope even to set the board, the pieces themselves made her female – or was it feminine? – mind reel, just trying to work out what their shapes meant, but she used to stand, smoking in admiration whenever a combination of the males in the household were bent in archetypal male postures over it – elbows on knees, chins in palms, foreheads furrowed, rather like slightly different versions of Thurber's version of *Le Penseur* – though when Nigel and I played in our pubescent days, our games usually climaxed in our rolling around the floor, with our hands locked around each other's throats, kneeing, punching, kicking, sobbing (me), shouting (him), until she had to come in at the run and separate us with her own more authoritative violence, precisely aimed kicks and clips – 'Can't you two ever play without fighting – and over chess, of all things!' she said. 'Chess!' As we grew older, we played alternately with Daddy, who was, Mummy told us, very good at chess, his natural game, because it required thinking. And he seemed to be very good, beating us within a few moves, again and again. I went from accepting this as quite right and proper, in the natural order of things – I think I'd have been quite fearful if I'd won – if I could beat him what manner of father was he? How could he be trusted to look after us, bring us up? – but soon enough the gorge began to rise, feelings began to stir similar to the ones that had stirred years before when Nigel won – his honest, pleasant, thoughtful face as he mowed me down in game after game, the gentle peer over the rims of his spectacles, the Scots undercurrent underneath the Canadian accent which ran below the English one – 'Mate, I think, old boy.' 'What, you've won again!' came the cry from the passing Mummy, and if I said something primitively spiteful – 'Oh, any fool can beat me' – the triumphant, 'Oh, don't be such a poor loser, the world hates a poor loser.' I tried cheating – nudging a piece into a different position when he was reloading or tamping down his pipe – though I'm not sure I gave myself any real advantage, because I never worked out the consequences properly, probably nudged myself into worse positions – I don't know why I did it, really, perhaps just the thought that cheating gave me a kind of psychological edge, I could do things that would never cross his mind. And then at a certain stage, when I was about fifteen or sixteen I should think, I began to study the board with real concentration, practise moves on my own, in fact began to get a remote glimmering of how to think a move or two ahead, work out what could be predicted, or at least sensibly guessed at. As I got better, our games got longer – he was working through two bowls of a pipe rather than half a bowl – and there came an evening when I had him. I saw as clearly as I've ever seen anything that if I moved my knight, bishop, whatever, he would be check-mated. 'Mate, Daddy, mate, I believe,' I would say, and keep the tremble out of my voice. 'What!' she would cry. 'You've beaten your father!' or with luck, 'You've beaten your own father!' – 'I'm just going to have a pee,' I said. I remember it quite well, the peeing, washing my hands, looking at my face in the mirror, a boy on the threshold, a boy who beat his Daddy, his own Daddy – I went in, sat down, 'Whose move is it?' though I knew perfectly well it was mine. He was relaxed back in his chair, feet crossed at the ankles, eyes miles away. 'Oh, yours, I think.' I bent to the board, made to pick up the assassinating piece, and saw that it was a square or so away from where I had left it. Furthermore, his queen wasn't where I'd last seen her. I lifted mine eyes unto the father. He was still in his trance, lost to the trivialities of the chess board that is life. 'Cheaters never prosper,' I might have said, Mummy-style, but I didn't. I moved my piece, in due course lost the game. 'Well done, Daddy!' I said, losing gracefully for once. 'It was closer than you realized,' he said. 'There was a moment there when you nearly had me.' But I had had him, hadn't I?

THE JOUNCER EXILED

But I wasn't writing about Daddy cheating at chess, I was writing about – the hairbrush, yes, Daddy and the hairbrush, tying it to my pyjama top – well, then, it didn't work. I went on jouncing, keening, until Daddy desperate, Mummy desperate on his behalf, hit on the solution. They transferred me from the top of the house and the room next to theirs, down three flights of stairs, to the bottom of the house – into the dining room, in fact, which therefore ceased to be the dining room, which was moved next door, in the form of the dining table and dresser, to what, until then, had been a sort of sitting room but mainly the father's study, which, in the form of a large roll-top desk with many compartments and drawers, was moved upstairs to the room directly above the new dining room, which remained what it had always been, the main sitting room, but now with certain odd study-ish aspects to it. There was something about this move – it had, I suppose, a whiff of punishment and exile to it – that Mummy found distressing. 'You're quite comfortable down here, aren't you ?' I was perfectly comfortable in that I was comparatively private, and needed to be in that I had discovered Hank Janson and my sex life was becoming tumultuous. 'Well, at least you're not in the basement, darling.'

THE GIRL IN THE BASEMENT

Of course I wasn't in the basement, the basement was damply uninhabitable, though in fact inhabited by a succession of au pairs who were brought in as cheap nannies to look after baby Piers. The first one was Scots, recently out of jail, come to us while on probation. I suppose she was in her early twenties, young certainly, with a pretty face that had something aged about it, her cheeks were full and her lower jaw often moved about as if she was eating when she wasn't – the effect, as she showed us, Nigel and me, of having over-sized false teeth – when she took them out her cheeks sank and her jaw tightened up, and she put on sixty years, just like that, a shocking transformation that we kept asking her to perform for us – the first few times she turned her back, as if to remove an intimate garment, but as she became used to

showing us her new face, old face really, she let us watch the process –
hooking her fingers to the back of her mouth and levering her
dentures forward until they protruded, then a little shake of her head
and they would drop into the palm of her hand, it had the ceremony
of a conjuring trick about it, though it rapidly lost its mystery.
Elizabeth's mystery was her crime. Mummy told us – 'But you're not
to mention it to her. Never. Never.' – that she'd been an accomplice
to a man who was still in jail. 'It wasn't really her fault, he led her into
it, you see. She was just weak, that's all. She's a good girl at heart.' Or
so she had to believe, because in another telling she would be
entrusting her baby son, and the moral welfare of her ten- and eleven-
year-old boys, to an ex-con, still on probation – so of course she was
a good girl, really, though of course she wasn't, at least in Mummy's
terms, because she was seeing men not only on her afternoons off but
her afternoons on, when she was meant to be wheeling Piers about the
Embankment – I would go with her sometimes, and she would turn
the pram over to me, tell me in her soft Scots voice that she'd be back
in half an hour, she'd meet me by the bench, and off she'd hurry – she
was trim and athletic, and walked very quickly, also eagerly, her blonde
hair bobbing – and then more than half an hour later I would see her
coming towards me, while I could see behind her a man going away,
but turning to look – and I think, in spite of the teeth and the slight
deformation on the lower part of her face, she was attractive. I know
that I liked being with her, even when she behaved treacherously, as
when she'd been given money to take us to the cinema to see a
western and we ended up at a film with lots of kissing and crying,
with Lana Turner in it instead of John Wayne or Alan Ladd. Her
explanation that the film we'd been promised had been showing at a
cinema now closed because of the polio epidemic, we knew was a lie.
She put on a lot of make-up for these cinema outings, lashings of
lipstick, as if preparing to meet the characters on the screen, and while
watching them she was quite oblivious to us, and remained oblivious,
in a trance, all the way through our tea at Lyons Corner House, where
she would sit curled on her chair, smoking in a special way, long
inhalations and then the smoke issuing like a secret out of the side of
her mouth. On the other hand she would forfeit her share of the tea

money, so we got an extra bun or two with false cream on top. She also played cricket with us in the basement, along the long damp hall, and if the parents were out in the evening we would go into her small damp room off the long damp hall, and she would give us a cigarette. And of course she doted on Piers, loving to hold him up and show him off to briefly infatuated passers-by on the street.

MY FIRST KILL

We went back to Hayling Island one summer, Mummy and I, because I'd been ill and needed sea air for my convalescence. The father and Nigel stayed on in London, Nigel because he had to go to school and would come down later, the father because he had to go to work. Elizabeth took Piers to stay with an aunt of hers, I think it was an aunt, anyway an older woman who had been approved by her probation officer – 'So she'll be perfectly all right, and she loves babies, Elizabeth says, so Piersy will have the time of his life,' my mother said. We stayed in a boarding house not far from the house we'd lived in, Mallows. The landlord of the boarding house I only remember now from Mummy's subsequent anecdotes – he was small and bald and complacent and common, and used to say – Mummy would repeat it, flourishing her cigarette extravagantly so that, while she didn't become him, she somehow made him become her, a kind of reverse mimicry – 'Be they dukes or navvies, I lets 'em all muck in together.' He made it sound like a policy, she said, often put to the test. I had brought an air rifle with me, a birthday or a Christmas present. One morning after breakfast I took aim from my window and shot dead a little bird with a yellow chest. I went down and picked it up. It was still warm, its yellow chest now scarlet. I attempted a swagger, a huntsman with his first kill. I showed it to Mummy, who admired my marksmanship, then to our host. 'You don't go killing my birds,' he said. 'People come from miles around to stay here especially for my birds.' In fact, I was relieved, but when I explained to Mummy why I was no longer killing birds she was indignant. 'I've never heard of anything so stupid,' she said. 'I mean, what's the point of giving you an air rifle if you're not allowed to shoot things with it?' But really, for her, it was a social thing, that a son of hers should be reprimanded by a common, etc., while for him it was a manly thing, I think, disguising as a commercial objection his revulsion at the little swine's mindless murder of a pretty bird.

A SUICIDE PACT

Towards the end of our stay the seas were very high. People stood on the beach and gaped up at great walls of water that seemed to grow and grow, waves mounting on waves, and then the white combs cascading, one after another. There was nothing for it, Nigel and I decided, but to surge in and ride them, yes, we'd ride them on their white rims right onto the beach, where we would lie broken and dead until we were tugged out to sea, then hurled back on the beach, tugged out, hurled back – this wasn't actually our plan, but would certainly have been its conclusion. We ran back to the house, and caught Mummy in a state, in something of a state, having just put down the telephone. We asked her if we could go for a swim, the waves were enormous, and we tried to describe them – 'Yes, yes,' she cried. 'For goodness' sake don't bother me!', consigning us with a flourish of her cigarette to our death by drowning. We made to dash off for our swimming trunks, hesitated. 'You haven't seen the waves, then?' Nigel asked, whose idea of a future had clearly depended on the request refused. 'No, of course I haven't, I haven't been out, how could I possibly go out!' She gestured at the telephone. 'Why not?' asked Nigel. 'Elizabeth's run away!' It was an exciting thought, like one of the films she took us to – I could see her in the fields, down roads, in her slacks, her brown slacks, down alleys, then in a bar or café, a passport in her hand, eyes veiled, smoke curling. 'Where to?' Nigel asked, as Nigel would. 'How the hell would I know? She's run off, so how would I know where the bloody girl's gone to?' There was another question lurking, an urgent one, that I couldn't put my finger on. 'And did she,' Nigel asked, 'take Piers with her?' Yes, that was the question. 'We don't know. We don't know where Piers is.' So I saw her running with Piers, pushing him in his pram across fields, down alleys – then there was the man, of course, a smallish man, in a shiny suit and scuffed, frequently polished shoes, hair combed back, also shiny, a peaky little face, a Woodbine between his fingers, the whole of him half-turned on the Embankment, looking after Elizabeth as she ran towards me as I waited with Piers in his pram by the bench. 'We don't know,' Mummy said. 'We don't know.' She was almost in tears, her face working and ugly, it was a shock to see her like this, stricken, frightened.

GREEN FLASH

I stopped doing this to go for a little walk on the path that separates the lawn from the beach. I wanted to sort out what I could remember about Elizabeth's vanishing, Piers's whereabouts, there was a whole business to do with telephones, there was a shortage of telephones at this time, whole sections of the community depended on the tall, red telephone boxes, press the 'A' button – if you hear a voice at the other end of the line saying hello and announcing its number – ours was Flaxman 8595 – you are connected, if it rang and rang and you didn't hear a voice, press the 'B' button and get your money back, either two fat pennies, or a neat little sixpence, or a neat but larger shilling –

The memory of the red boxes with their heavy doors, the ponderous contraption with its A and B buttons, fills me with a melancholy yearning for the days when husbands and wives, parents and children were completely absent from each other for long reaches of time. Now of course they travel in each other's pockets and handbags, whole families scattered around the globe can be in touch with each other by pressing a button, and so – what about the adulterers, how do they cope, have they learnt to lie regularly, almost from minute to minute? 'Yes, yes, I'm in the car, just got to pop down to Ealing to fetch some papers, then up to Hampstead to drop them off – yes, I'll phone you as soon as –' and so forth, while proceeding towards the act, or retreating from it, or even – who knows? – during the act itself, while for their ancestors one lie would do, if one was needed at all – and it was probably only half a lie, a lie of omission, in that he had been to Lord's, had seen some cricket, and the act itself so squeezed in between the beginning of one innings and the end of another that it was almost forgotten. Only really stupid people, or exceptionally unlucky people, or people who needed to resolve the problem by getting caught, got caught in adultery back then, but now –

well, I don't know – are moral comparisons possible? Is an adulterer who doesn't really lie because he doesn't really have to superior to an adulterer who is forced by historic circumstance, the invention of the mobile telephone, to lie with almost every other breath?

So I pondered as I walked the path between the lawn and the sea. There were still quite a few people on the beach, about twenty at least, unusual at this late hour. They were standing in clusters or lying on their beach-beds, and there was an odd air of expectancy and tension as they gazed towards the sun, which was at the sea's rim, seeming to hang there, static, as it in fact slid down, diminishing. There was a sudden furnacy glow all around it, and to its left, associated with it in some way, but not attached to it, a bright green dot appeared, a small but complete and brilliant dot. Everyone on the beach cheered, a couple of old chaps threw their straw hats into the air, young people clasped each other in jubilation. I held my own hat aloft and cried out, because they'd seen it, we'd seen it, I'd seen it, the famous green flash, that was already gone while we were still celebrating its arrival, the sun gone with it, and the sea and the sky darkening – you could say it was something, 'quite something' as Harold would say – I mean, there I'd been patrolling along the path, turning my head idly towards the beach and wondering what they were all looking at as I ruminated on red telephone boxes, buttons A and B, with consequent thoughts on contemporary versus old-style adultery, and there it was, the green flash, an inexplicable phenomenon – I felt quite puffed up with the privilege and honour of it. I wonder what Victoria will make of it when I tell her, she looks for it most evenings, has done since she first came to Barbados as a little girl, when she and her mother sat together staring towards the sea, the dropping sun, waiting, hoping, although I expect what they were hoping for was more than a green dot. It may be called a flash, but really, as I say, it's a dot, a speck, a small splodge even, not at all what you imagine from the vocabulary, or from the hat-throwing, the cheering and cuddling which greeted it.

NIGEL'S QUESTIONING MIND

But now back to – let me look – Elizabeth, the day she vanished, with or without Piers is the unanswered question that was ravaging our

Mummy's face, mouth twitching, eyes brimming with tears, perhaps from the smoke, as she was also coughing, perhaps from emotion – where was the father during all this? Yes, where was he, at the height of the drama? And how was it the mother didn't know where Piers was, or at least whether Elizabeth had run off with him or left him with her older friend or relative, who had, after all, phoned up to announce Elizabeth's disappearance – had Elizabeth's older relative or friend simply forgotten to mention Piers's whereabouts, had Mummy indeed forgotten to ask, so full of expostulations over the girl's behaviour, that damned girl's behaviour, that her baby boy had simply slipped out of her mind and it wasn't until she had hung up that she'd suddenly remembered?

Why didn't she ring back and ask her? – this from Nigel, naturally.

Because the bloody woman hadn't got a phone – she'd made the call from a box, she had no idea when she'd next phone, and –

But Nigel had moved on. 'Why don't you phone the police?'

Yes, yes, phone the police, I said, because it seemed to me a terrific idea, terrific and terrifying.

'The police!' she said. 'What do you mean, the police!' The idea of the police, at any time, under any circumstances, except to patronize when asking directions – 'Oh, Constable, Constable, can you tell me, pray, the quickest way to Brompton Cemetery?' 'The quickest way, you bet I can,' said PC Gus/And pushed Mama underneath a bus. – in the middle of one of Mummy's expostulations in response to one of Nigel's lethally simple-minded and sensible questions, the telephone rang, Elizabeth's older friend or relative in a red telephone box to report that, by the way, baby Piers was safe and sound, she was sorry but she couldn't look after him, he would have to be collected tomorrow at the latest. Thus ended our holiday, and our only return to Hayling Island.

MALLOWS REVISITED

Until fifty years later, about ten years ago, when Victoria and I drove there, from Chichester, where I had a play on. It was a lovely afternoon, a childhood afternoon, the sandbanks warm in the sun, the sea slapping, gulls drifting – we walked along the beach and I pointed to this and that, slightly haphazardly, I suspect – the pill-box probably hadn't been exactly there, perhaps a hundred or so yards further along or further back, and perhaps the squares of cement embedded between the thick mats of grass weren't the remains of the American barracks, and I took the wrong track across the dune to Ferry Road, but it brought us out near enough to where I'd guessed it would, a short distance from Mallows, with its well-remembered lawn, and the swampy patch beyond it, which we used to cross on planks to reach the road – and yes, there were actually some planks down, though not the same ones, obviously – and there, behind the trees, would be the lawn, and beyond the lawn would be Mallows. There wasn't a lawn behind the trees, and there wasn't Mallows. There was just a fringe of grass that girdled a little cluster of bungalows. A man came out from the nearest, to see what we wanted, were we lost? No, not really, I said, just looking for a house called Mallows, to show my wife. I must have lost my bearings, it's been nearly half a century after all. Oh no, he said, I had my bearings. This was where Mallows had been all right, until fifteen years ago, when they'd knocked it down and put up – he pointed to his home, and the other little homes that crouched there.

AN EXAMPLE OF LIFE'S UNFAIRNESS

I'm sitting at the table on the balcony of our room, writing this. Victoria is still lying on the sunbed, still reading yesterday's papers – yesterday's were Sunday's, so there are heaps of them. Above us the fan is whirring, and in the nearby trees the cicadas are at it, making their noise, ghastly and mechanical. How could something that sounds so mechanical come from a living creature? In a minute I will take two strong painkillers – co-proxamol, actually – to muffle it, but first I shall tell Victoria – let her finish her article. She's finished. Turned her head to me. Smiled. I told her. She refused to believe it.

'But didn't you hear the cheering from the beach? Over there. Directly in front of you.'

'I heard some shouting.'

'It was cheering. We were cheering ourselves for having seen it.'

'But I've watched every evening, every evening except this evening. And here I was reading a newspaper – and you're saying that just there –'

'Yes. Just there. On the other side of your newspaper.'

'And you've never even looked, have you? Not once.'

'That's probably it,' I said. 'The law of undeserved rewards, something like that. But really, you know, it wasn't a flash. More like a dot. A splodge.'

She brooded for a while and she said, 'Well,' she said. 'Well, well,' and went in to have her shower.

I've just taken two co-proxamol. The music from the restaurant has started up. I can see people walking to the bar, others walking along the path by the sea, all dressed for dinner. Underneath the music, I can hear the cicadas, shrill, mechanical, urgent, purposeless – but why do I think they're purposeless? They may be full of purpose. But if so, for what?

WAS IT DIVINE INTERVENTION?

Who knows what might have happened that afternoon if Elizabeth hadn't run away. Would Mummy have given us permission to swim? Yes, of course she would, she always did, and why not? We were very good swimmers, she would have been pleased on our account – 'What fun!' she'd have said. 'Huge waves! How thrilling! You can do some surfing! I might come down later and do some myself.' So we'd have to have gone the next step, put on our trunks, thrown ourselves against the great falling walls of water, been dashed to death on the beach, or swept out by the powerful undertow and drowned. It's possible that the more sensible of the adults would have tried to prevent us going in, but it's equally possible that they wouldn't – this was in the late 1940s, after all, a time of restraint and politeness, when such people as elderly, middle-class Hayling Islanders might have considered it ill-mannered to interfere with two boys seemingly intent on drowning themselves, and some of them might have found it an enjoyable spectacle. I suppose it's possible that Nigel and I would have had the sense, when it came to it, not to go in, but I doubt it. Once we were in our bathing trunks, and seen to be in them – a matter of a dress code, really. No, what saved us was that call from a red telephone box somewhere in England, made by Elizabeth's older friend or relative, who on her previous call had announced Elizabeth's flight but forgotten to mention that Piers hadn't gone too – and so we didn't change into our bathing trunks, go down to the beach and get drowned, we stayed with Mummy while she talked of Elizabeth's moral character, and how Daddy had always said that there was something about that girl he didn't trust – whether this was part of a plan, God's plan, or fate's, or nature's, that one or both of us were being saved for a great task, still uncompleted, as far as I know –

A PERFECT SHOT

Well then, was the same true for the baby in Battersea Park, about three years later, sitting so stiff and upright in his pram that he must have been harnessed – but why 'his' and 'he'? – it might have been a girl, but I've always assumed a boy, so – *his* pram, therefore, he sitting bolt upright, unattended, about twenty yards from where Nigel and I were playing cricket, just the two of us, but with a proper bat, three stumps with bails, and a hard ball, without a seam, called a 'compos' because it was made of compressed rubber, bouncy and bullet hard, hard enough to kill, certainly hard enough to kill a baby arranged bolt upright in a pram when savagely hooked with a proper bat straight at the baby's skull. It was a terrific shot, pow! shoulders open, right leg stretched forward, left heel rotating as I swivelled my body and opened my shoulders and swung my proper bat across the line of the ball pow! and connected in the centre pow! straight and true towards that thinly membraned head, as if to a target – now I wasn't exactly, not consciously, aiming at the baby's head, but there was definitely a connection between my eye and the ball and the baby's head that had to be completed by the bat in my hand, like an electrical circuit – no, there was intent too, that's the most difficult bit to explain, I, I, the I that I live in, the I that is I, didn't intend to hit the baby's head, would I truly believe have died rather than hit the baby's head, but my eye, my instinct, my reflexes intended the ball to hit the baby's head – or maybe the baby's head was where the ball would go if I hit it perfectly, and that, yes, that was what I intended, the perfect shot to that particular ball, so a born sportsman, you see, Mummy's genes – it seemed to go on and on, the compos, to be speeding through the air without actually progressing until it struck the baby's head, killed the baby, a deep dent in the side of the skull, blood and matter, the ball imbedded –if a thin metal strut, part of the hood, hadn't been raised – that's all, not the hood itself, but a thin strip of metal was what the rifled bullet of red rubber struck, and off which it shot, deflected, past the baby's face, over the pram and on to the grass beyond it rolled, and rolled and rolled –

'Run!' we shouted. 'Run, run!' and we ran, ran, leaving the stumps and bails, though I clung to the bat, all the way to the Albert Bridge. We mingled with the pedestrians, a couple of inconspicuous boys wasting time on their summer holidays. Of course, there was no need to run, no one had seen what happened, not even the baby himself, who was still sitting bolt up while we ran -- well, if he was harnessed he'd little choice, and where was his mother, nanny, au pair? – no question of it being man in those days – was she having a gossipy stroll with a friend, a tryst with a boyfriend or lover, had she forgotten the baby completely? – anyway, nobody had seen what had happened, nothing in fact had happened, I had *nearly* killed a baby, that's all. *Nearly* killed him. So the world was unchanged. We could have gone on playing, but making sure to hit the ball away from the baby, or picked up the stumps and put them down in another part of the park, or even thanked God for our luck and gone safely home, to look for something else to do. But we ran. I suppose we were running from the horror of what had nearly happened, indeed logically should have happened, guilty of killing a baby – instead of nearly guilty of killing a baby, or should that be guilty of nearly killing a baby?

A TROUBLING SIGHT

I saw a woman sitting on the sand under the trees facing the wrong way – i.e. with her back to the sea. She was in her fifties, at a guess, plump, quite short, with frizzy grey hair showing under her straw hat. She was reading. All perfectly normal, really, except that there was something wrong – it could have been to do with the contrast between the parts of her body that were tanned and the white parts, or the unfortunate design of her swimsuit. Anyway, from where I stood it seemed as if her buttocks began directly under her shoulders like one of the freaks in that famous film of Tod Browning, called, well, *Freaks* actually, isn't it? It did occur to me that this might be one of my hallucinations, in which case I'm branching out, I've never hallucinated deformities before. I stood there with the water up to my ankles, hands behind my back, pretending to gaze in a generally vague and benign way on the people lying on their sunbeds, most of them elderly, most of them overweight, but with the light dappling down on them through the high trees they still made quite a pretty sight, sort of French and impressionist, and none of them looked grotesque except the woman with buttocks under her shoulders – or were they breasts on her back? – to whom my eyes kept reverting with more and more revulsion – and then a man came up to her, elderly and scrawny, wearing a baseball cap backwards on his head and an indecent scrap of bright red bikini between his legs, what they call a thong, I suppose. He was carrying a large blue towel which he flung over her. He helped her up, then flourished the towel away, as if finishing off a conjuring trick, and there she stood, a normal woman with normal legs, only a trifle short, with a normal length of back and neck. They walked off towards the bar, she trudging purposefully up the slope of the sand, he skipping friskily behind her, his aged genitals bouncing in their little crimson sac. I must keep an eye out for them in the restaurant, at lunch and dinner, an ear out too – I'd like to catch them in conversation. Now back to baby-killing – why? Yes. Why? Leave it for a while – perhaps tomorrow – go for another swim now, collect Victoria – where's Victoria?

AN ENCOUNTER AND A PHONE CALL

As I was going into the hotel lavatory just now I had a feeling that something older and scalier than myself was going to come out, and it did. It looked down at my feet. 'You're going barefoot,' it cried in astonishment, in American. 'I am,' I said. It pointed down at my feet. 'And you've got five toesies!' 'Ten,' I said. 'I've got ten toesies.' 'So you have!' it shrieked. 'So you have!' and went out. Some form of dementia, senile dementia, I suppose – what can it be like, to live in that sort of consciousness? Or half-consciousness, or whatever it is? – but he seemed merry – does that mean he felt merry? Well, we shall find out as Larkin says in which poem? 'The Old Fools' is it? Now I must go up to our room and phone Harold.

I spent at least fifteen minutes failing to dial correctly – getting the code to England wrong, even getting the number for getting out of the hotel wrong, forgetting to put in the 7 for our bit of London, and then, then when I got all those parts right, misdialling once or twice – 'The weather's lovely here,' I said. 'Good,' he said, as if surprised that I could think he might think it mightn't be. I told him we'd got the table. 'Ah,' he said. 'The same one?' The very same one, I said, that we always sat at. He sounded pleased, pleased and relieved. I also said we'd checked out their accommodation, that it was top-notch in every respect – I did actually use the word top-notch, sometimes when I talk to Harold I find myself using unfamiliar words and phrases. He liked this one, and repeated it. 'Top-notch you say. That's terrific.' 'Well,' I said, 'looking forward to your being here, have a good flight, love to Antonia.' 'Love to Victoria,' he said, and we hung up. I didn't warn him that I'm going to get him to read my new play while he's here, I want him to come light of heart, believing himself on holiday, free of obligations, then wham! I'll shove it at him, 'Mind having a look at this, Harold? No rush of course.' We'd better check out their room – we should have done it before I phoned, but I'm sure I didn't lie, their quarters will be top-notch, all right, all the quarters here are top-notch – top-notch, what a word!

THE BEST MOMENT OF MY LIFE

Twice guilty of nearly killing a baby, the second near victim being baby Piers. Baby Piers, I can't work out the chronology now, but I think he must have been born after I was moved downstairs into the dining room. I can't remember where he started off – perhaps in a cot in the parents' bedroom – but by the time he was crawling he was established next door to them, in my old room, from which every morning he would crawl to the top of the stairs, then manoeuvre himself down them in traditional baby style, bumping from step to step, three flights, on his bottom. He would then crawl to the front door, pick up the morning's post, post it through a gap in the floorboards, where it lay undiscovered until our father, perplexed and possibly even mortified by receiving nothing but medical journals for about a month, launched an investigation. Then he'd crawl into my bedroom, the door of which I left open for him every night when I went to bed, climb onto the bottom of the bed and bounce on my feet until I woke up. I was already half awake, actually, because I always knew he was there and would kick him gently up and down in harmony with his bouncing, gave him a little extra propulsion so that he went a little higher, and a little higher, and I laughing drowsily with his gurgles and cries of joy, higher and higher I kicked and he bounced, until one morning I gave him a little too much extra propulsion and my kick bounced him off the bed – was there intention, was there intention? Well, there was something – malevolent, yes, there was something malevolent working in me through the drowsiness, not an impulse to hurt but to do something unexpected, that would change the mood and rhythm of the game, I wanted to surprise him and shock him, this trusting, devoted two-year-old whom I adored, to make the game suddenly my game and not his. He landed on the wooden floor on his head. It made a sound, soft but distinct, Piers's baby skull. He lay there still, his face a white I'd never seen before, his eyes closed. I picked him up, put him on the bed and begged him to wake up. Nothing happened, no colour in his cheeks, his eyes sealed. I ran around the room crying and pleading with God to bring him back, for Mummy and Daddy to come in and make him all right. I picked him up and clutched him to me. He was soft and dead in my arms. I put him down on the bed – I think that what was going through me was this – that I loved him overwhelmingly, more than I had ever loved anyone, and that I'd killed him and would have to be punished, but that the punishment didn't matter as the world was no longer the place it had been moments before, moments before it had been a glorious and comfortable place and there was nothing I could do that would ever get me back into it, I must now go upstairs with dead Piers in my arms and present him to Daddy and Mummy, and the new world of punishment without

Piers would begin. I remember quite clearly how I bent to pick him up from the bed just as he let out a mewl, and he opened his eyes, blinked, saw me, and gurgled. Oh, the smell of him when I had him in my arms, the sweet soft life in him, it was without doubt the purest flood of emotion, the least complicated, the simplest flood of gratitude and love –

AFTERWARDS

Five or six years later, when we were in Halifax, Nova Scotia, we quarrelled so violently that he seized a carving knife and threw it at me. No, threw it close to me. I can't remember what the quarrel was about, but whatever it was, I was entirely in the wrong – how couldn't I have been, as I was sixteen or seventeen, and he was six or seven, and from my point of view he was mine to control, and from his, he wasn't? 'He threw the carving knife at me!' I said, when the mother came to find out what all the noise was about. 'He could have killed me! Yes, you could have killed me, Piers!' He said he hadn't thrown it at me, he'd thrown it at the floor. 'Well, nearly killed me!' I said triumphantly. 'There! He admits it, Mummy!'

TOMORROW

the Pinters arrive. I shan't give Harold my new play immediately, let him have a day or two of rest and then slip it into his unsuspecting – I was going to write innocent, innocent hand, but what would an innocent hand look like – small, chubby, unmarked, nail-less, useless? – what could Harold possibly do with a hand like that, an innocent hand?

JAMES DAVIDSON SEAGULL

It's a most beautiful day, the small boats are humming across the absolutely still Caribbean, a couple of waterskiers are criss-crossing each other in complicated patterns, oh, one's just come a cropper, a young woman, a second ago all poise and grace as she rode on her skis, arms stretched out, head back, hair flowing, the next a grotesque flurry of upturned legs, the skis sticking out of the water like a compass – she's all right, though, she's waving to the driver, a slim guy in an orange shirt with Rastafarian locks and shades, he's circling around to her – meanwhile a gang of little birds are hopping about my drink, a virgin sea breeze (cranberry and grapefruit), one has hopped onto the rim of the glass, jerking its head now one way and now the other, seeing what's in front of it out of the corner of its eye – I think I have to go on doing what I'm doing, to give it a chance to dip its beak – no, well yes, that is he dipped his beak two or three times without making it to the liquid, gave a couple of panic-stricken twists of its head, flew off – I wonder what sort of bird it is, dun-yellow-chested, dark grey plumage – smaller than a sparrow – a kind of martin, I suppose – it has a blue band around its left leg, just above the claw – strangely large claws, parrot-like, out of proportion to its body – the band looks as if it's made of rubber or plastic, put there by an ornithologist, I suppose, who wants to keep tabs on its movement – yesterday Victoria pointed out a dove with three blue bands, two on one leg, one on the other, making one imagine it'd been specially tagged, like a criminal. I wish I knew more about birds, most of all I'd like to know how much consciousness they have, or is everything they do programmed, I think I once read, like computers. They often look, when they're on the ground, as if they've been wound up, hopping stiltedly this way and that, but in flight they're a different matter, actually not very different with these small birds, martins and sparrows, they zigzag in spasms, as if in response to abrupt electronic impulses, but seagulls now – my father said once, when we were all sitting on the beach in Hayling Island, 'I wish I were a seagull' – what made it surprising was that it was apropos of nothing, a sudden utterance, as if his soul spoke. But why, Mummy asked, why would you want to be a seagull, James? Is it because they fly so beautifully? James said yes, he supposed it was that, the way they swooped and soared, the freedom and majesty of the flying, the ease of it, just cresting on the winds, their wings spread – also they can be quite vicious, attack people, he said, as if it were a continuation of the thought rather than a qualification, so perhaps he was interested in that aspect of them too, he envied them their temperaments as well as their flying skills – I thought of that conversation a few years ago, when we were visiting my brother Nigel and his wife, Barbara, at their summer home in Pictou, Nova Scotia – Victoria and I went most afternoons, and in appalling weather, grey skies, squally rain, an edgy wind, to a very long, dark-sanded beach, on which there were washed-up tree trunks that the gulls squatted on, shrieking angrily – a couple of times when I came out of the sea, cold and frankly rather miserable with it, two or three of them rose from their logs, soared upwards, dropped, or rather lurched, down until they got to face level, just a foot or so in front of me, then up they'd go, soaring, and back they'd come, jolting at me and shrieking their shrieks. The second time it happened I broke into a run, lumbering across the ridges of sand, shouting swearwords at them. We thought they were probably protecting something, their eggs, their nests, but really they gave the impression that they didn't like humans, or more particularly me, as I was the only human going into and out of the sea, their sea, and it was noticeable that Victoria, sitting dry and fully dressed on one of the tree trunks, was never abused or threatened. When we told Nigel about it he said yes, some people had actually been attacked at the beginning of the summer, a man's scalp had been pierced and a woman had had her eye plucked out. Can he have said that? Eye plucked out? Well, Nigel, being Nigel, would never have said it if it weren't true, but on the other hand I'd never have gone back to the beach, possibly gone to a beach in Nova Scotia ever again, if I'd believed that a gull had plucked out a woman's eye – so conceivably I've made it up, but attribute it to Nigel as a way of transforming it into a fact. But I still don't believe it.

WORDS IN MY EAR

I was just about to write my first sentence of the day without any idea of what it would be, when somebody moved behind me, bent into my ear and muttered, 'I think it's wonderful.' I recognized the voice, of course, and the face when I turned to look up into it, and even knew what he was talking about, but still I went into light shock, stomach jumping, brain dead. 'What?' I said. 'What?' 'I think it's wonderful,' Harold said again. 'Oh,' I said. 'Oh, good.' 'We'll talk later,' he said, 'when you've finished –', gesturing down at this my pad, then went to a nearby table at the bar, where I can see him now if I shift my eyes to the right. I've shifted my eyes to the right – Antonia's just joined him. She's wearing a very pretty straw hat, she's smiling as she sits down, he turns towards her with what I can see is one of his loving growls, and no wonder, she looks beautiful. They make a very dramatic pair, the blonde and dark of it, a completion of opposites. Victoria and I adore seeing them dance at the end of the evening, neither of them capable of free movement at the moment, Antonia's knee is bad and Harold is still frail, still recovering from cancer and the treatment for it – so they pick their way carefully from the dinner table to the dancing area, arrange their arms around each other and then, his knees bending and straightening, her feet twitching, they sway together in the gorgeous Barbados night, to the band's quite ghastly music – wonderful. Yes, that was also the word Harold used of my new play, *The Old Masters*, which I gave to him only last night – I didn't think he would get to it so quickly, there being so much dreaming and lolling about to do in Barbados before one settles to a specific chore, if one ever does.

WHAT WAS HE TALKING ABOUT?

I call it 'my new play' but actually what I gave Harold to read was the latest, though I hope to God final, version of a play I've been working on for a long time – how long? I can't work it out, but say at least two years – and a version of which has already been published under the title of *The Pig Trade*, and has nearly been produced on a number of occasions, most notably at Bath, with Peter Hall directing and Corin Redgrave and John Wood playing the two main characters, Berenson and Duveen – but things fell apart for reasons too complicated and depressing to be worth remembering, let alone writing down, especially on a lovely morning in Barbados, with Harold waiting a few tables away to discuss how wonderful the new version is – or perhaps I misunderstood him, he might have meant something entirely different was wonderful, for instance that the view (it is) or the day (it is) or that IT – existence itself – is wonderful ( ) – he might not have read the play yet, might even have forgotten that I gave him the play.

I've just shifted my eyes to his table, Antonia is expounding something to him in a learned manner, he's concentrated on her, nodding, in a way that suggests his mind is completely uncluttered by such debris as a play, read or unread – now he's laughing, and – Now concentrate! And explain why you did a new and final, you hope final, version of the play you now call *The Old Masters* but used to call *The Pig Trade*. The reason that I did a new and I hope final version of the play I now call *The Old Masters* but once called *The Pig Trade* is that some many months ago I sent *The Pig Trade* to a friend of mine, an American director called Nicholas Martin, who last year did a terrific production of a very, very old play of mine called *Butley* in Boston, with Nathan Lane, who is a very old friend of mine, no, perhaps only an old friend, as he's fifteen years younger than me, playing Butley. I hoped to interest Nicholas Martin in doing an American production of *The Pig Trade*, hoped indeed he might do it in the theatre that he'd done *Butley* in, the Huntington, one of the loveliest theatres I've ever been in, and by far and away the most comfortable. Well, there was a silence, one of those silences that playwrights are familiar with (this one is, anyway) and to which the word ominous is usually attached. So a long, ominous silence before he phoned and spoke with characteristic briskness, characteristic politeness, the truth as he saw it – he didn't think *The Pig Trade* would work in Boston, not on his stage, anyway, the stage of the Huntington theatre, it was too character-driven (i.e. no discernible story, at least not enough of one to motor the play along) and as for the epilogue, he said Jesus! in a tone that made it impossible to take for admiring, because he meant of course 'Christ!' – I said I was grateful for his frankness, because I was in fact grateful, or at least there was gratitude mingled in with all the other reactions, such as shame, rage, kill kill kill Nicholas Martin! Once you get to a certain point in your career as a playwright people are reluctant to tell you anything unpleasant and useful, preferring instead to honour your reputation by fobbing you off with compliments, and the truth is that however much you want the compliments you need the truth more, and you always know you're getting it when you feel, along with all the sensations listed above, a cold stab of mortification, right into the heart of your vanity.

FATHERING AN ORPHAN

It took me a few days before I could face reading *The Pig Trade* again. When I did, I sped rapidly along, not allowing myself to become too mired in the character-driven, under-plotted middle, drew a breath when I came to the epilogue, and in I went – 'Jee-zus!! Christ!' – how could this be? How could I possibly conclude a play, after a long, too long, scene between the two main characters – a kind of clash-of-the-Titans scene – with an interminable scene between two minor characters, on whom I actually proposed to bring down the curtain, leaving the two major characters, the leading actors, in the dressing room, no doubt glumly hoping that the audience would remember them when they came on stage to take their bow? Only Shakespeare could get away with such slapdashery, and he wouldn't have spent months labouring over it. Perhaps that's another definition of genius. It doesn't waste time when doing things badly, it does them at the double.

I rewrote *The Pig Trade* with the intention of eliminating the epilogue. In the process I found myself rewriting almost the whole play, and the stretches I didn't rewrite I cut. What I had when I finished was the same story, the same characters, and an entirely different play about which I felt less queasy. The queasiness will certainly return, doubled or trebled, if it ever gets onto the stage, but one mustn't count one's chicken, for the moment I'm queasy-free, and will show myself as such when I talk to Harold – well, at least I shall be able to say that I'm pretty sure it will work on the stage, that whether people like it or not they would have a whole creature, complete in itself, to like or dislike. One can't really hope for better than that if one's a playwright, in my experience – well, yes, one can, there have been a few occasions when I've finished a play – there's been a sort of click that goes right through me, a click of everything, with the last line written, falling into place, of everything being absolutely right, no, perfect is the word, of the play being perfect, and again it's not a question of its therefore being perfect for other people, audiences might in fact hate it when it's put before them in its perfection, but that isn't the point, whether it's liked or not, the point is that there it is, inviolable, intact, unchangeable, quite distinctly itself and quite distinctly apart from me. I've had this clicking experience four times – with all the other plays I've sometimes had the echo of a click, which is really, I suppose, merely the memory of the experience, and which signifies that though it isn't perfect I can no longer make it any better, time to let go before I begin to make it worse, knowing that I'd always be attached to it in an unhappy sort of way, it would have the status and future of a partial orphan. Why am I going into all this? Because I've never tried to think it out before, so much of my thinking about my work has been obscured by a sense of shame. But this might add a dash of understanding – that I feel the sort of shame that a bad parent, or anyway a failed parent, must feel when he realizes he's sent into the world a child not strong enough to make its way.

A ROW OVER MASTURBATION AND OTHER MATTERS

I've just looked up and to my right. Antonia's gone, presumably for her pre-lunch swim. Harold's on his own, and seems to be slightly winking at me. He's at it now, not the real wink of someone trying to pick me up, but a glittering of the eye, and he's smiling. I've just smiled back. He's given a little wave. I've given a little wave back, and now I'm writing this. When I've got to the bottom of the page I'll go over and sit down and we'll talk about *The Old Masters*, if that's what he wants to do, until our wives come. Then we'll go in to lunch, although it's not 'in', of course, as the lunch room, the dining room, is outside, and the bar where Harold and I are sitting is an extension of the dining room, which has a roof but no walls except at the back, and the sea curves around it, all the way around from the end of the restaurant to the bar, and so, whether we're in the bar or the restaurant, we're by the sea, we can stand up, run across the strip of sand and throw ourselves in whenever we get too excited, the conversation too heated, there have been times when we've got too excited, in my view, when explosions in argument have brought one or the other of us to his feet – actually mainly me – but neither of us – I mean me – I've never run away from the table and across the strip of sand and thrown myself into the sea. We haven't had a row of that sort for a while now. In one sense that's a good thing, because I don't enjoy them very much, although I always enjoy the memory of them. In another sense it's a bad thing, because it means Harold's capacity for explosive anger is currently diminished because of his recent poor health.

As I write this I'm trying to remember what the rows were about. There was one here, in this hotel, a few years ago about Hopkins, whether he masturbated, not Anthony Hopkins, the actor, but the poet Gerard Manley, one of us took the view that he did and one took the view that he didn't, but I have no idea which way round it was, if I ask myself now what view I take, did Gerard Manley Hopkins masturbate or did he not, I think I would say something equivocal, to include the psychic side of masturbation and possibly to exclude the physical side, which is perhaps a definition of 'sprung rhythm' now I come to think of it, and even 'inscape', 'outscape' being actual, down-to-earth masturbation, or seed-wasting, but after all this I still don't know whether I argued for or against G. M. Hopkins as a seed-waster or seed-hoarder. There was another row about Coleridge, a few nights after that, but what aspect of Coleridge? And a real humdinger at a restaurant called Tides, down the road from here, about the charlatan and all-round menace of a psychiatrist R. D. Laing. Pretty obvious what side I took on that. It concluded with me leaving the table, yes, but also saying, 'I'm not walking out, I'm going to have a pee, I'll be right back to finish this off, Harold!' Unfortunately I couldn't come right back, I got locked in the lavatory, an outside affair with an unreliable bolt, I had to shout and beat my fists on the door until somebody at last overheard me. When I got back to the table, about twenty minutes later, the three of them, Antonia, Victoria, Harold, were all sitting in exactly the same positions as when I'd left. There was a bit of a kerfuffle therefore. Victoria drove me to a dump called Olive's for coffee. Nice dump, actually, good coffee. Harold and Antonia suddenly came through the door, embraces and handshakes, ambiguous apologies all round, laughter and so forth and off we went again until the next round – which was about what? – no, no, time to go and join Harold, I've gone past the bottom of the page, I'm in fact over onto and into the next page, and if I don't hurry the wives will be down, and our conversation will have to wait, I'm impatient

to have it now, it's only nerves that have kept me at this, so off I'll go –
going –

TABLEAU VIVANT

Back. Not straight back. First I had the talk with Harold. Then, when
the wives came down, I went off for a swim. Now they've gone to
lunch. I've stopped by my table on my way to joining them, to collect
my cigarettes and lighter, and find myself sitting down and writing
this. Isn't it a bit creepy, though, when I should be with them at the
lunch table, to be sitting instead at this my office table, and writing
about them? Well, I'm not writing about them, not yet, and what do
I mean them, them! Them is, are, my wife, Victoria, and two of my
closest and dearest friends, Harold and his wife, Antonia, and there
they'll be, no more than ten yards away, concealed behind the curve
of the bar, though actually, by swivelling my body around, like
this – I can see them. Though they can't see me. At least not without
making an equivalent swivel, and why should they, as they don't
know I'm here to be seen. So I can go on writing while watching
them. Harold is talking to the wine waiter, Sam, who Victoria thinks
looks like Eddie Murphy, slightly finer than Eddie Murphy but, as I
point out, less comedy in his features, in fact rather a grave face, with
the lineaments of Eddie Murphy. Harold's expression is very serious
as he looks up at Sam, his finger stabbing at the wine list. Victoria
and Antonia are bent towards each other, talking, both are laughing,
their straw hats bobbing at each other, Victoria's hat is austere and
classical, Antonia's as always is magnificent around the brim, a floral
tribute – to what? To whom? Life? Love? Harold, perhaps? – They
look very lovely, the two women – the whole tableau is perfect, I'd
like to hold them like that for ever, not in a photograph but in the
flesh, allowing them to pursue their lives as usual – a strange thought,
that we could leave behind in our lives a sequence of tableaux vivants
which we could revisit whenever we wished as we aged away – but
would we want to do that? What would we feel ten years from now
if we were to see us as we are at this very instant? Would it cheer us
up, because it's a cheerful scene, or make us cry? So long ago, we'll

say, so long ago. And yet there we are, not knowing – not knowing what? Not knowing what's going to become of us – Sam's just caught my eye, he'd bent down to where Harold's finger was now resting, straightened and looked in my direction as if he felt an eye upon him. He's given me a radiant if puzzled smile, I'm actually smiling back at him as I write that I'm smiling back at him, my face turned towards his as my hand goes on writing, which means the words will be sloping all over the place when I look at them –

No, they're OK, there's almost no deviation, in fact if anything they're neater and more legible than the writing I write when I'm looking at it. But I'd better go now and sit at the table, though there's no actual rush, they're just getting up to go to the buffet, and really at lunch we all eat at our own pace, it's a stately scramble, with so many dishes to pick and choose from. When I come back after lunch I'll report my conversation with Harold while it's still fresh. I'm looking forward to doing that, as it's one of the most exciting conversations I've had for years – professionally, I mean, of course. I've had various conversations with doctors about the state of my prostate etc. which I suppose could be described as exciting.

WALK OF SHAME

A very jolly lunch, Harold making public – i.e. to Victoria, he's probably already told Antonia – what he feels about the play. I tried not to bridle (is this the word?) and simper (certainly the word), be dignified and yet casual but probably got caught between the two. There was also the problem of lunch itself. It's a buffet affair, which is OK when you're all going up to pile your plates with shrimp and ham and tuna and whatever else you fancy, but it's not so OK when you're the only one who wants a pudding. You have to walk between the tables and past the many waiters, everybody noticing you, you feel, and then at the counter you have to instruct the very charming and pretty girl called Marsha to slice you just a sliver more of the cheesecake, and a little splodge, what is it, actually, Marsha? Oh yes, meringue – yes, yes, that's fine, and a scoop of vanilla ice cream, please, ha ha – for some reason (obvious reason, I suppose) they give you rather a small plate, the pastry and custard and meringue and ice cream lap over its side, or drip or tumble off onto your foot, as you do your walk of shame, past the other guests and the tall, lean, tight-bellied, though in some cases fat, smiling waiters, to your table. My little but loaded plate always attracts comment from the other three. They ask me to itemize the contents – what's that? Antonia asks with keen interest – oh, meringue, and that – that green stuff? from Harold – ah, jelly – and even Victoria finds it necessary to confirm that the cheesecake is in fact cheesecake – none of it malicious, at least I don't think it is, but still I find myself becoming self-conscious and overly bluff, it's difficult to enjoy eating a variety of puddings when three pairs of eyes, however sympathetic, are trained on you – and more difficult when you're eager to present yourself as a distinguished elderly playwright calmly receiving his meed of praise, when there's also a trickle of ice cream on the chin, a crumb of pie at the side of the mouth – 'Oh yes, well – you're quite right, Harold, it's what I was aiming for, wasn't it, darling?' – trying not to gobble down the praise in the same fashion as you gobble down the pudding, you're afraid you'll accompany every spoonful and receive every flattering sentence with an oink and a grunt –

ARE YEARS OF OUR LORD STILL ALLOWED?

The thing about Harold in the conversation before lunch was that he clearly already loves *The Old Masters*, spoke about it as, in my experience, only Harold can, seeming to know it in all its nooks and crannies, citing moments in scenes and reciting lines, actual lines – this on one reading.

'Look,' he said, 'what exactly is the position of the play? I mean, what's happening to it?'

I said that Greg Ripley-Duggan was the producer and that Peter Hall would direct it, if actors and a theatre were available during one of the brief spells when he was free – Harold said he hoped Peter would work it out, he couldn't imagine anyone better than Peter for *The Old Masters*, 'right up his street,' he said, but if it turned out that he couldn't fit it into his schedule – he indicated himself, with a gesture to his chest. So that's how things stand with *The Old Masters* on this day of

January, with Peter Hall to direct it, Harold Pinter on the bench, what day of January? – no, it's February, this day of February, what day of February? Early February – no, still late January, I suspect – that's the loveliest part of being in this lovely hotel on lovely Barbados, with the sun shining, a breeze stirring your greying locks, and the sea, the sea – I've written away enough time after lunch for it to be digestively safe for a swim, so who cares what day this day is, somewhere in late January, in this year of our Lord 2004 – if years of our Lord are still permitted – well, they are on this God-respecting island, and they are by me, and that's what counts.

NEWS

Judy Daish (my agent) phoned to let me know that Greg Ripley-Duggan had just heard from the artistic director of the Birmingham Rep, to whom he had sent *The Old Masters*, that he would like to put it on their stage – a perfect venue for a pre-London try-out, what did I think? I said I didn't know much about Birmingham, but if they wanted to do my play, that's virtually all I needed to know. There are dates, she said. They only had one to offer in the near future, if we found it unacceptable we might have to wait for a year. How near was the near future? May. May! That was – what – three months near. And not a single part cast. I said we'd better find out if Peter Hall would be free in May.

A MEMORY OF *HIDDEN LAUGHTER*

On the beach I can see Michael Rudman and his wife, the actress Felicity Kendall, who turned up at the hotel yesterday evening. Michael is in baggy blue trunks, slight paunch (nothing like mine), pronounced stoop, Felicity is doing supple things with her body, stretching and bending. Michael and I have dinner together every few months, so we're quite friends, and I once directed Felicity in one of my plays, *Hidden Laughter*, in which she was terrific and in her last scene very moving, I thought – sitting on a swing in a country garden at night, reading out to the local vicar a letter she's just written to her husband, reminding him of the happiness of their marriage, their love for each other, she reads it tearfully, and yet with pride in her own grace as a writer, in her confidence in the strength and honesty of her feelings, not knowing, as she reads and swings and sobs just a little, that her husband has already left her, and that the vicar to whom he's entrusted this news he has also charged with the responsibility of breaking it to her, a moment that will come immediately after she's finished reading her letter, just after the curtain falls in fact. I loved the way she did the scene, so fragile and full of hope, loved the way Peter Barkworth as the vicar floundered in an agony on her behalf, and on his own as the bearer of the news, and yet kept making gestures of encouragement and enthusiasm, complimenting her on her prose, half-rising and then remembering he has to remain seated on the tree stump, to conceal the husband's forgotten briefcase, evidence that he'd been and gone, left her life in a hurry and for ever – and frankly I loved the scene itself, one of the few scenes I've written that I liked to sit through, enjoying it and being moved by it as if it had been written and directed by someone better than me.

I DO SOME GOOD

There are four computers in the hotel computer room, all of them next to each other, and if three people are at it when I go in I become nervous and therefore clumsy, conscious of how their fingers ripple over the keyboard, summoning up images and texts and possibly all kinds of pornography in code, while I jab and poke and keep having to go back and start again – it takes me at least twenty minutes to get to my email, I forget my password or get it wrong, it's easy to do both as it has no connection to anything to do with me, in fact it sounds like a breakfast cereal with an 'i' where you'd expect a 'y' or the other way around. I used to tell myself that this is a generational thing, that if I'd been brought up with or by computers my fingers too would flutter and caress and all those mysterious doors would open on fairy lands forlorn – not that I would want to enter them, unless there are some for straights, as there used to be when Keats – but this morning there were two old ladies and an old gent, by old I mean a decade or so older than myself, so coming up to, possibly gone over into, their eighties. They had headgear on, the man a baseball cap, the ladies the usual straw hats, the old guy was wearing an enormous pair of sunglasses that virtually covered the top half of his face, which was quite small, with a neat nose and appley cheeks, so probably American, one of the old ladies also wore sunglasses, normal size, but with a hearing aid attached, the other old lady was frankly fat, mighty fat, but with evidently perfect vision and a ready sense of humour, her plump fingers scampering about the keyboard and bringing up whatever it was that made her so wheeze and chuckle, chuckle and wheeze, it was very distracting if you were me and lowering yourself into the chair of the only free computer, the wheezes and chuckles and chuckles and wheezes coming from immediately to my right, to my immediate left the old guy, his face so close to the screen that it seemed to be growing out of it, and next to him the other old lady – so it took me half an hour to tap out a few sentences to Greg Ripley-Duggan, after I'd spent nearly as long opening his to me, and then opening one from Peter Hall saying that he couldn't rearrange his dates to fit in Birmingham, it was painful as he was very attached to *The Old Masters*, he wished it and me all the best. So Harold is now the official director of *The Old Masters*. And that's that, really, until we get back to London – Harold and Antonia go next week, Victoria and I the week after. There's something else I want to say, whether *The Old Masters* is a good play or not, it's already done good in the world. Until it came his way Harold was rather – not exactly miserable – but for him subdued, rarely exploding into laughter or anger, with a vagueness, almost an absence, about him. Now he's full of energy and purpose, thinking out loud about the set, about casting, etc.

AN IMPORTANT QUESTION ASKED

All the couples here walk on the paths in front of or behind each other, instead of side by side. The paths are wide enough to accommodate them side by side, but they obviously prefer this single-file system, like ducks. I wonder why? Harold and Antonia do it too, and so do Michael and Felicity, who are going up one of the paths now, Felicity leading, lifting and lowering her head in a busy fashion, Michael stooping along behind her, almost hunchbacked – I asked him about it, whether he had a back problem, he said no, not really, just years of bad posture. He's going to do something about it when he's home – posture classes, I suppose. But what about me and my wife, do we walk in single file?

ROLLOCKS BY MOONLIGHT

Two in the morning. I'm in the bar, a bottle of cold Diet Coke in front of me, Rollocks moving about behind me, setting the tables for breakfast. This is only the second late-night visit I've paid to the bar this year. We've had our conversation about how last year was for each of us – his has been good, he says, on the whole, he's thinking of retiring, if not at the end of this summer, then at the end of next, or possibly the one after – fairly soon, anyway – and we've talked about the sandflies, the mosquitoes, the effectiveness of the repellent I've pasted around my wrists, ankles and neck, the steaminess of the night, the partially obscured moon, the absence of stars – then he brought me one of probably a dozen Diet Cokes he's kept on ice for me since he'd heard I arrived, nearly three weeks ago, and we resumed our familiar roles, he to the tables, I to my pad, where I intend to write about – no, it's no good, I have to go up to my room, the anti-insect paste is no longer working, my wrists and ankles have been bitten, my neck is itching – first I must go and say goodnight to Rollocks, he is standing with his tray clasped to his chest, staring towards the sea, as if he can hear the mermaids singing, each to each – I'll leave him be.

A SONG FOR RONNIE

'But for me the light is growing dim,' my mother used to sing in the kitchen of our house in Halifax, Nova Scotia, as she cooked up the stew into which she mainly avoided dropping her cigarette ash. She'd heard it – country and western, I suppose – coming from the radio one morning, and had taken to it at once, not singing along with it, but humming at it, out of tune, every time it came on, and then giving full-throated, tuneless voice to the refrain – 'But for me-e-e-e-e/The light/Is growin'/Dimmmm –'

The only other creature who seemed to love Mummy's singing as much as I did, though probably for different reasons, was the cat we acquired when we moved from Hayling Island to London just before the end of the war. He was a ginger and white full-grown tom called Ronnie. He was hopelessly dissolute, out all night though returning punctually when a Jenkins delivered the milk at seven in the morning. As soon as Mummy heard the rattles of the bottles on the doorstep she would get up and watch from the bedroom window until the operating Jenkins – either the father or one of the sons, it didn't matter, she loathed them all – had trundled off, and then hurry downstairs to pick up the bottles – simultaneously Ronnie would stroll up the path, and on into the kitchen, where he would sit by his saucer, waiting for it to be filled. He arrived in the household already battered from numerous fights – he'd had half an ear bitten off, lost the tip of his tail, and one or the other of his eyes was usually partly closed. I assume there were vets in Chelsea in those days, but Ronnie was never taken to one, whatever his condition – I don't think it ever crossed our parents' minds that they were responsible for anything but letting him out and in and feeding him, though Mummy liked having him on her lap – she would summon him by singing loudly, in her out-of-tune voice, one of her favourite songs from *Oklahoma!*, and Ronnie would lope into the room, spring onto her lap, and stay there purring for as long as she sang – no longer, though, he'd get down as soon as she stopped, and leave the room without a word, so to speak. Mummy treated the pets with the same casual and affectionate violence that she treated her children – though she once knocked Ronnie, who was getting in the way of her cigarette and her ladle, off the kitchen window into the back yard, quite a drop – in mitigation it should be said that it was a tiny kitchen, room for one only standing up, and for once she was appalled, at least momentarily, if only by the shocked reactions of Nigel and myself, who were playing French cricket in the yard, when Ronnie dropped yowelling between us – 'Oh, really!' she said, when she'd had enough of our 'Mummy, how could you!'s etc. 'He's perfectly all right, he's a cat after all, he knows how to land on his feet – look at him!' He'd clambered up the wall and was now staggering along its top as if drunk and about to fall down again –

BETRAYAL

but in fact he was perfectly all right, always – altercations, tumbles, outright and ferocious combat with other toms, ghastly tussles with angry and unwilling sexual partners, whose outraged screams rent the night air – he survived them all, along with the disapproval of neighbours – a Belgian woman who lived in the basement flat three or four doors along and had two female greys called Meenee and Meedee oh, Mini and Midi I realize they must have been now I see them written down. She remonstrated with Mummy whenever they coincided on the pavement. They made a striking pair. The small, angry Belgian woman, who lived in a bundle of shawls and had a sort of pork-pie arrangement of a hat on her head and enormous, globular earrings which shook when she talked, would stop Mummy with a raised hand and a little cry, and Mummy would stand towering over her with arms folded, the head of her fox stole with its bright button eyes fixed over her shoulder on the Belgian woman. 'Yes,' she said, with smiling, middle-class impatience, 'what is it?', knowing perfectly well what it was. 'Would you pliss,' said the Belgian woman, 'pliss ask your kat to ztop visitink my katz.' 'I have asked him, several times,' Mummy said, 'but he pays no attention. Why,' she added, 'don't you ask him yourself, in your own language? He might understand you.' She was always lofty when dealing with neighbours' complaints, the more justified the complaints, the loftier she was, but she was quite right about her inability to control Ronnie, whose romantic exploits she rather admired. Would she have admired them more if she'd realized how closely, in some respects, they resembled those of her husband? – though I like to think that Daddy never made any woman scream in pain and outrage, only with pleasure. Ronnie survived everything – perpetual warfare, public denunciation – he was his own man, fearless and calm though increasingly ravaged – survived everything, except our departure to Halifax, Nova Scotia. We gave him to some friends, who lived not far away, on the Embankment. They'd met Ronnie on a number of occasions, been impressed by his raffish vitality, and took him in with enthusiasm – but he didn't want to be taken in, stood mewing and growling at their front door until he was let out, then made his way back to 47 Oakley Gardens, where he hung about on the doorstep, hurrying forward every time the door opened, to have it closed immediately in his face – he was collected from there and carried back to the Embankment again and again, until one day he wasn't there to be collected. The friends wrote explaining why they couldn't give news of him. They were apologetic, of course, but we understood that it wasn't their fault that he wouldn't become their cat. And I suppose we were philosophical. We told ourselves that it wasn't us Ronnie missed, but his operational base. I don't know what difference the distinction makes, or if there is one, when it comes down to it – it's certainly not one that Ronnie would have bothered to make, I think. All he could have known was that one day his world was there, the next it had gone, and wouldn't come back, however often he hung about waiting for a Jenkins to arrive with the milk, the door to open –

AN IMPORTANT QUESTION ANSWERED

Yes, we walk in single file, Victoria and I, just like the others, sometimes she leads, sometimes I do.

IN MEMORIAM

We began our days in Halifax, Nova Scotia, with a succession of kittens that died very quickly, one from eating something poisonous in the surrounding woods, another, who liked to sleep tucked under the wheel of our car, was run over by my father when backing out of the garage, two or even three others from natural deaths – it became really quite depressing, as if there were a curse on us for betraying Ronnie, anyway it seemed a good idea to switch to dogs, to change our luck – some neighbours offered us a beagle from their new litter, and so Sam came to us when he was still a small puppy, though he never really behaved like a puppy, he was slow, thoughtful, food-directed from the beginning, and just grew larger, without any perceptible maturing, into a dog. I used to practise my bullfighting with him, attaching chocolates to the corner of a tea towel, then swivelling it around my body, Sam lumbered after it, trying to catch one of the corners as I shouted, *Olé, Olé, perro!, Olé*, with a stamp of my feet. Eventually he twigged that he'd never catch a chocolate, but that he'd always be rewarded with one if he kept stumbling around after it – humiliating, perhaps, but I think when it came to food Sam lived below the humiliation line – and anyway, it was better than a sword between the shoulder blades. When he was about three he took to leaving the house after his breakfast and not returning until dusk, keeping strictly to this schedule like a civil servant – one could almost see him with a briefcase, especially on his return, when he had the air of bearing a heavy load, a day's load, which indeed he was. We discovered that between breakfast and dusk he kept appointments around the neighbourhood and quite deep into the centre of town, receiving at every house he visited a substantial meal. He was a commercial traveller of a pet, really, giving in return – what? Well, just the pleasure of a visit, I suppose, from a friendly dog, a friendly and hungry dog. When my parents moved back to London they took Sam with them. He was quite old by then, older in dog's terms than my mother was in human terms, but he survived her by a couple of years. My father kept him when he went to live in Lyme Regis, but saw him not as a companion but as a burdensome leftover from the days before he was a widower, and solitary. He overfed him from laziness and walked him reluctantly, letting him crap on the pavement and even on doorsteps, and when I remonstrated – 'You know Sam,' he said, 'he goes his own way, as your mother always said.' Sam died shortly after my father married Betty, my mother's cousin. Piers and I carried his corpse on a winter evening through the back streets of Lyme to the Cobb, from which we flung him into the sea, and said a few ceremonial words. Piers had been five or six when Sam came to us, was in his early twenties – an undergraduate at Cambridge – when Sam died, so he'd known him for most of his life. Daddy and Betty went off to the South of France, fulfilling at a stroke Betty's, little Betty's, double dream of living on the Mediterranean, of being married to Daddy. But dreams can be like prayers if too many years lapse before they're fulfilled. Living by the Mediterranean with her husband, Dr James Davidson Gray, the distinguished pathologist, my dear!, became living in a poky little flat in a hideous block on a hill above Menton with a dying man who'd never enjoyed her company – except for short periods in bed, of course, on occasional afternoons many years ago. After his death I invited her to stay with us one summer in the Hotel de dui Castelli, in Sestri Levante, on the Ligurian coast, where I went with my family and usually Piers, every year for about a decade. When she arrived, she was in the middle of a spluttering and coughing monologue that she seemed to have begun on the train from Menton. She was carrying her suitcase. A cardboard label was attached to its handle and on it she'd written in red ink in bold capital letters MRS ELIZABETH GREY. Gray was the name she'd known since she'd first met her cousin's fiancé fifty years before, it was now legally her own, and yet there it was, misspelt, significantly misspelt, because it turned my father from a Scot into an Englishman. Piers and I saw the label simultaneously, and we turned to Betty to say – what? Whatever it was, we couldn't say it – what would have been the point, after all? She never listened, as her husband complained to me when I went to Menton to take him to his last bed, in the Charing Cross Hospital, never listened. But then he never really listened to her either, hearing in her voice, seeing in her gestures, a first cousin's approximation to his dead wife. The fact of the matter is that there was something neither understood about the other – probably Mummy, whose hold on them both was unbreakable – Mummy was the wife of his heart, Betty merely little Betty. So poor little Betty. And poor old Daddy too, for marrying his little Betty, and of course poor Mummy too, for dying before her time and leaving them to each other. Perhaps they separately heard her voice, as they lay sleepless beside each other in their Menton bed saying to her husband, 'Oh, James! Really! That a husband of mine! And with little Betty of all people! How could you, James! What were you thinking of!' and to his new wife, 'Really, Betty! That a cousin of mine! My own cousin! With my own husband too! And after I was dead! What were you thinking of!' It's all right, Mummy, they were thinking of you – that was their trouble.

SPIES?

Now this couple, Americans I think, though they're young and fit-looking they don't seem quite right in the open air, in the sunlight, there's something depressed and rodenty about them, as if they belong in the lofts and cellars of New York, possibly they're theatre critics or in publishing, she's very skinny, black hair drawn back and down her neck, a long nose that goes up in a point at the last minute, quite a pretty nose, really, quite a pretty face, but urban-feral – they're speaking in low voices, almost as if they think I'm trying to overhear their conversation, which I am, so I must busy myself over my pad, keep my head down, my pen flying – voices muttering, hers slightly squeakily, his – Minnie Mouse, that's who she reminds me of, Minnie Mouse, the dark, lovely eyes and the chin falling away in little folds – can that be right, that Minnie Mouse had a folding chin? I don't know any longer what Minnie Mouse's chin was like, not having seen any of her films for years and years, in fact all I really remember are her high heels and her lipstick, and her artificial eyelashes – and as the American woman over there isn't wearing high heels or lipstick and her eyelashes are normal I can't in fact claim that she resembles Minnie Mouse – nevertheless she reminds me of Minnie Mouse – the reason I'm delaying getting around to the man is that he's got his back to me, a round head, thick black hair so neatly packed on it that it looks like a lid, a strong white neck and then a medium-sized man's back, quite sturdy, he's wearing a shiny blue shirt, obviously new, probably only just unwrapped, an impression of shiny blue swimming trunks, could he be wearing a twinset? Matching trunks and shirt? A glimpse of solid thighs, then under the table his feet, in black Speedos – I know they're Speedos, it's written on them – are turned out like a duck's – he says almost nothing, soft little grunts in response to Minnie's squeaky paragraphs. God, I wish I could hear what they're saying, I have the feeling now that they may be academics – he's turned around, Minnie dropped her voice from a squeak to a whisper and around he turned, I can feel his eyes on me, can they know that I'm writing about them? She's staring at me too, I can feel their eyes –

What they were looking at was a pigeon on my table, a few inches away from me, dipping its beak into my hat and attempting to extract a strand of straw – I made a gesture, a fuck-off-off-my-hat kind of gesture – it snatched out the strand, flew off into the rafters of the bar –

'That's nice,' the man said to me, 'helping her build her nest.'

'Him,' the woman said, less squeaky now she was speaking at a normal level. 'The males build the nests.'

'Is that how it works?' said the man. 'Or how you think it ought to work?'

'Both,' she said. They laughed together, and I laughed with them.

'Looks like you've provided for a lot of pigeons,' he said, nodding at my hat, which, it's true, is very tattered, but then it's inherited from my dead friend Ian Hamilton, who wore it to cover the effects of chemotherapy – I brought it with me to Barbados last year, just a few days after his funeral, and I wore it in Italy last summer, and I shall keep on wearing it whenever we're in sunny spots until only the rim is left, and then I might try to have it thatched, or whatever you do to keep straw hats going.

'Yes, it's getting on a bit, this hat. Worn down.'

His eyes were now on my yellow pad, and so were hers. There was a question shaping itself, but she said, 'Well, I guess you don't want to be disturbed.' And he said, 'Yeah, you look kind of busy,' and they both gave me a nice smile, and left me to get on with writing about them, and trying to overhear their conversation, which I will now make myself stop doing. It would be wrong, I think. Still, I wish I knew what they did. Definitely New Yorkers, publishing possibly, or in television – yes, television – they've got up, nodded pleasant farewells, are walking across the lawn towards the beach – she's got a rather loping walk, loose-limbed but not athletic – he's taller than I thought, stiff little strides, almost military – CIA?

PAN, AT THE NEXT TABLE

Anyway, now I'm alone again, the bar is empty again – I'd just written that – the bar is empty again – when lo! an elderly man, by which I mean older than myself, with a nose so bulbous and knotted and veined that if he's not an alcoholic he should sue it – there he is at the table next to mine, he has chosen it out of all the empty tables, there are ten of them, I've counted, just to sit beside me, attracted by the long shapelessness of my own nose, perhaps, or just by a muddled desire to be a nuisance – he's carrying an object the size and shape of a large book that I didn't at first notice which he fiddled with for a few moments and then, just as I turned away, he pressed a knob and a man's voice, plus music, both cackly, burst forth, yes, a radio, the old bugger's got a radio, and he's sitting there, holding the radio to his mouth, like a sandwich, he's got very bushy eyebrows, by the way, thickets, actually, and a beard, also thickety, but just sticking out from the base of his chin – it's the head of a Pan, and he's holding the radio to his mouth no longer like a sandwich, like a flute, with hideous, unflutish noises emanating from it – he's conversing with Sam, the very neat and handsome young waiter, the one with the Eddie Murphy face, which he is bending to Pan's lips, so that he can hear him behind the music, no need – Pan's voice is loud, boisterous, slurred, he's requesting tea – 'Lots of good, strong tea, to wash the alcohol out,' he says, following his words with a coarse chuckle. Sam gives him a polite, blank look. 'I drink lots and lots of alcohol, that's why I drink tea, always a pot or two at this time of the morning. Sluices it out. The alcohol.' Sam nods gravely, goes off. Probably, like most of the waiters in this hotel, he's teetotal. Pan goes on chuckling to himself, changes the channel on the station, is trying to catch my eye, which I keep resolutely fixed on the page as I write this sentence, which will be my last until he's gone, or his radio's off –

The radio is off. He is drinking his tea, and smoking a large cigar. Clouds of his smoke are drifting over me, making me feel queasy. Nevertheless I've picked up my pen, feeling it important to get this down – that there is a very coarse-looking man in his swimming trunks and straw hat sitting smoking a cigar, trying to catch the eye of an elderly, not particularly refined-looking man in his swimming trunks and a straw hat who is, in fact, smoking a cigarette and writing about him, and one day when the elderly writing man is back in London he might take out this pad from his drawer in his desk, leaf through it, come across this account, ponder it, and wonder if the old roué of a Pan with his stinking cigar and nose like a rotting fig is dead – he's

blowing the smoke in my direction, quite deliberately, he's picked up
the radio, he's turning it on again and he's leering at me, I can feel it –
Christ! Ah, he's been joined by a middle-aged man with a boyish
haircut. The radio goes off. They are talking in loud voices, blurred
laughter from Pan, and the younger man, who is the type – what
type? – yes, could be something to do with the *Daily Mail*, for instance,
morally seedy, down-at-heel, but lots of money, ill-gained, and a dreary
cynicism about the eye – they're talking about his boat, he's got a boat
that's passing through, or rather not passing through customs, he's been
waiting for days now, ten phone calls a day but still they're keeping it
from him, him from it, so perhaps he's in drugs, more likely to appear
in a photograph in the *Daily Mail* than work for it, one of those inner-
page sort of men, with inset a photograph of his girlfriend, or 3rd ex-
wife, he's got up, he's coming my way, coming straight at my table, at
me, I'll keep my head bowed, keep scribbl—

FIRST ONE

He's gone. He stopped at my table and said, 'Hello, Simon.' That's
what he said. My name. I said, 'Hello,' in a mumble, keeping my
head down. 'I admire your discipline.' He sounded faintly lascivious.
'Yes. The way you keep at it.' This too sounded lascivious, more than
faintly. 'I couldn't do that,' he said. 'Here you are in the sun, and
there's the sea, and you're sitting at a table writing away. I admire
that.' I thanked him. 'What are you writing?' I remembered recent
phrases – *Daily Mail*, seedy, down-at-heel, 3rd ex-wife, etc. 'A novel?'
'No, not exactly a novel, not really anything really.' 'Well, Simon,'
he said, saying 'Simon' with a particular relish, almost satirically, 'you
keep at it.' I said I would, or anyhow would try to, and he went off.
He was wearing shoes, long brown flannel trousers and a blue shirt,
proper shirt, as for an office, looking as if it needed a tie – what is
he doing in this hotel, in Barbados? Could he be a policeman, or
some combination of journalist and policeman that seems to be the
new form, chaps who mobile the *Mail* even as they're slapping the
cuffs on, at 6 a.m., the television cameras in place, but he can't be
here for me, surely, his conversation a sinister introduction to the

main event – my arrest tomorrow at just two hours after I've gone to bed, but I can't think of anything I've done recently, and would he get the money to fly out from London to arrest a man of sixty-seven who hasn't recently committed a criminal act?

THEN THE OTHER

And now here is Pan, for God's sake –

He had the cigar in one hand, the radio neither off nor on, but spitting and humming slightly, in the other hand. And his chin, his beard resting almost on my shoulder, which put his nose almost in my ear – he spoke pleasantly through his nose into my ear – this hotel, he said, was one of the nicest he'd ever been to, the staff were so charming, he said, and the guests, the great thing about them, he said, was that they were all friendly, but never intrusive, never intrusive, he said pleasantly into my ear, his beard scraping my shoulder, as the fumes from his cigar drifted across my face and the radio hummed and spat almost in my armpit. 'Don't you find that?' – a young lady turned up, attractive, with curly dark hair, bangles on her wrists, a silver chain around each ankle. 'Ah, there you are,' she said. 'I knew I'd find you in the bar,' and gave me a smile, as if she'd known she'd find me in it too. 'I've been having tea,' he said. 'And talking to my friend. And waiting for you.' He clamped the cigar in his mouth, put the radio into one of her hands, looped his arm around her waist, lurched her off towards the swimming pool, or perhaps its shrubbery.

AT LAST

Now he's gone it's the most beautiful morning again, and I would be tranquil, I really think I would be, if I weren't convinced, beginning to be convinced, that I'm the victim of a conspiracy. Is it that people can't bear the sight of an elderly etc., sixty-seven etc. sitting at a shady table at the sea's edge on a sunny morning in Barbados, working – or not even working, just writing, and not even writing to any particular purpose, merely moving his hand, which happens to be holding his pen, across a yellow pad with long pages with lots and lots of lines on it with lots and lots of spaces between that have, naturally, to be filled. What else can I do in life but fill these spaces?

But does the sight of me doing it provoke people into feeling that they've got a duty to stop me? I've been doing this very thing, on this date, at this table, for eleven years now, every year on 20 Jan at this hour, this very minute, in fact, I could be seen at this very table, in this very chair – nonsense, not this very chair, every couple of years they change the chairs for chairs of a different style, progressively more uncomfortable. When I started out the chair was a miracle of comfort, a firm, weather-proof armchair, more elevated than you'd expect in an armchair, that seemed to settle you over the table into a natural writing position, but also allowed you to collapse backwards for thought, vacancy, erotic meditation, then a slight adjustment, almost unconscious, and one was at it again, the shifts between inertia and activity unnoticed by myself – recumbent, erect, active, a full page, recumbent, erect, active, a full page. This year we still have last year's chairs, wrought-iron, gardeny sort of chairs, with thin white cushions that keep you in a stiff, upright position, oddly unsupported, and you can't help seeing your hand, the pen, the movement across the page, every single word you write as you're writing it – Alan. Yes, there it is at last. Alan.

HIS DEPENDABILITY

We were here at this time last year, when he phoned to say he'd been diagnosed with cancer of the pancreas and the liver. His voice was robust, cheerful, just as it was when he was talking about the usual sort of stuff we talk about, a new role, a new film, a new illness – he'd had a lot of unexplained illnesses recently – he'd had a hip operation, his stomach had been bad, his knee hurt, sometimes shortness of breath – but he'd taken them in his stride, little spells in hospital, a long one for the hip because the operation had gone slightly wrong (botched, he wondered), but he had been unremittingly robust, cheerful, the sense of the comedy of it all pervading – the comedy of getting older, of people's reactions to his illnesses, the expressions they adopted, the tones they assumed – so was his tone when he was talking now – then –

a year ago, about his cancer of the pancreas and liver. The trouble was, he said, that he'd known from all the other illnesses that there was something more, something more wrong with him than a dodgy stomach, a difficult knee, occasional shortness of breath, something else had been going on all the time, and actually he'd thought so all the time, but he'd been in New York, playing in *Fortune's Fool*, a complete triumph, he'd been the toast of Manhattan – funny, if you change that only slightly to in Manhattan he'd been toast, a phrase I loved when it first turned up in the sort of movies I used to love – 'Make a move and you're toast!' – well, he wasn't toast in Manhattan, he was the toast of Manhattan, winning all the acting awards – and the thing was, it was his show in more than the star's normal sense, as he'd done the play first in Chichester, where it really hadn't been much good, a plodding and ponderous fable, badly lit and erratically acted by the supporting cast, although he himself, at the ebullient centre, had been Alan enough to give the evening a charge – but really, it had floundered along, and he'd been depressed by the impoverished lighting, the helter-skelter staging – but on the other hand his son Ben had been in it, for Alan a great thing, perhaps the greatest thing, to be on the stage with his son, it justified the enterprise, it justified going on with the enterprise, it justified the long struggle to take it to New York, to play it in first for a long period outside New York – I got gloomy reports from people who saw it in its early days, in one town or another – things were changed and then changed again, the staging was still all over the place, but his co-star, Frank Langella, was sympathetic and great fun, his director was old but sympathetic and great fun, and Ben was having a great time, learning more and more as he got better and better, and Alan knew, he just knew, that by the time they got to New York it would be a triumph, and so it was, a triumph, he was the toast etc., and yet the things that were wrong with him got worse, the knee, the stomach, the fatigue, whenever he went on stage he was exhausted, couldn't understand, went to a New York doctor who did a series of tests, gave him some pills that settled his stomach, but said, 'When you get back to London you've got to have all this checked out. Don't leave it.' So when he got back to London he left it, didn't have anything checked out but his hip, and even with all the complications of that,

he didn't have himself checked for anything serious. 'But why not?' I
asked, after a dinner, as we went to his car, a large and ridiculous car,
built for cross-country driving, that sort of thing. 'You keep saying you
feel awful, you think there's something really wrong with you, so why
the hell don't you!' He said he would. We had the conversation several
times, with the same firm conclusion – he would, yes, he really would.
Well, of course he was a diabetic, had been for nearly twenty years or
so, and partly assumed that his diabetes might be behind it all. He was
used to being very insouciant about his diabetes, rolling up his shirt in
a restaurant, crouching slightly so the syringe couldn't be seen as he
plunged it into the side of his midriff, pulling it out, slipping it back
into his pocket – the whole business completed in a matter of seconds –
but really behind the diabetes he now knew there was another illness,
showing itself in different guises and glimpses – but he was in all
respects such a sturdy man, his body sturdy, the will and spirit within
it sturdy, the whole of him rooted in a sure sense of himself and his
place in the world – it was this that made him so complete a presence
on the stage and screen, and yet gave him freedom and brio in his
acting – though he was so quick from one thing to another, from
tenderness to savagery, from contemptuous wit to unfathomable pain,
the centre always held, Alan was always there, however dangerous or
defeated his mood, the final dot of him was intact, so that audiences,
thrilled and sometimes nearly unnerved, felt finally safe in his
company. I suppose that's what they loved about him, really, that he
could take them into anarchy or despair without loosening them from
their trust in his kindness, it was visible in his eyes, even at their iciest
you could feel it there, and you knew that you could depend on it, an
essential part of his kindness was its dependability.

HOW HE DEALT WITH THE LIGHTS

Also his dependability was practical, you could count on him in a
tricky situation, on the stage as in life. I remember him making his
entrance as Butley, hungover, a wreck, lurching to his desk to turn on
the lamp that was scripted not to come on, had never come on before,
not in the dress rehearsals, not in the two weeks of performances in

Oxford, not in the four or five previews, but at the Criterion, on the night of 14 July 1971, the official opening night with a full house and all the critics in, it came on. Harold and I, director and writer, standing at the back of the stalls, looked at each other, aghast, then looked towards Alan, who, we supposed, would be looking aghast at the lamp. He scarcely gave it a glance as he Butleyed to the other desk, and the lamp which was scripted to come on and therefore, I assumed, now wouldn't, not only came on, it came on while Alan was still reaching for its switch, but went off again the instant he touched it. I'm no longer clear about what Alan did next, actually I don't think I was clear at the time, whatever it was it couldn't have made any logical sense, but it made complete emotional sense and sense therefore to the audience, who laughed in sympathy with Butley's evident frustrations, even though they seemed to be mysteriously, even magically, created. But my real memory of the incident is not what Alan did, nor my momentary panic, but my underlying confidence, shared I believe with Harold, that whatever he did it would be the right, the perfect, thing, because he was so right and perfect in the part, so founded and centred in it that his any action became the right action by virtue of its being his, and because he was Alan, in whom one had a perfect and complete trust, on and off the stage.

HIS LAUGHTER, ETC.

There was a scene in rehearsals that he was unsure of – he hadn't got the feel of it, his tone was wrong, something he couldn't quite catch in the meaning of the lines – each time he got through the scene he would turn enquiringly to the director, who looked at him with a blank, though friendly, smile, then turned his attention to something else. Finally Alan asked him – could he please have a comment straight out, whatever struck the director would be welcomed, however trivial, he just needed a note, any note, he badly needed a note on how he was doing this scene. The next time he did the scene, he turned eagerly towards the director, who almost succeeded in failing to catch Alan's eye, but couldn't avoid his eyebrows, fiercely raised in interrogation. He stood for a minute, broodingly, as if sorting through note after note in his head, then swiftly raised his right thumb then turned away, to the other actors. Alan, telling this story, one of his favourites for illustrating the general uselessness of directors, would bend so far forward with laughter that his forehead would actually touch his knees, and he would actually have to mop the tears of laughter out of his eyes 'Oh dear!' he would say. 'Oh, God,' and as like as not he'd jerk his thumb up again, and the laughter would start again – any meal with Alan would contain as much laughter as speech. But when I think about it, what could the director say that would have been more eloquent than a raised thumb – obviously what he meant by it was that Alan's acting of the scene was true and honest and right, words which would also apply to the way he tried to live his life, and why not a raised thumb to that too, especially if it would have caused him to laugh so much that his forehead met his knee? It was his merriness, I think, that marked him out from anybody else I've known – his laughter made you feel instantly better. A generous, forthcoming laugh that demanded company, so that sometimes you laughed not because you found it, whatever it was, particularly funny, but because Alan's laugh had somehow got into you, yours fed on his and his on yours so you ended up like children, clutching at each other, the initiating cause often forgotten – 'But why did we, what were we –? Oh – oh yes!' and like as not, off again. It's terrible to think I shall never hear it again, and that it's nowhere to be heard – his laughter on screen is not the same thing at all, of course, being an organized and probably in some cases frequently rehearsed laugh, although what you do get on screen, in his eyes, is the mischief and the appetite, the exuberance –

HIS CLAUDIUS

in Zeffirelli's *Hamlet* is the most sensual, the most appetitive, the most louchely endearing – during an early scene when he's trying to lecture and cajole Hamlet out of his woe etc. a servant on the other side of the room brings in a tray with a flask of wine and some goblets on it, Alan's Claudius, attempting to be doleful, measured, earnest, catches sight of the tray, scampers across the room, fills the goblets to the brim, turns to Gertrude with lascivious delight – his wine in his fist, his woman before him, his crown on his head, what more could a man want? Except to be rid of the spoilsport, killjoy nephew – you can see too, for once, what's in it for her, what fun she has with him in bed, what a rollicking place he's turned the court into, a playground – it's as if Falstaff had come to Elsinore, where he'd been tracked down by a poisoned Hal – Alan would have been a great Falstaff, the wit, the relish in life, the sexiness that would have embraced Hal as well as Mistress Quickly, I used to nag him to do it, and he would pretend to ponder it, but really his vanity got in the way – the problem was the fat, he couldn't bear to play a fat man, however nimble-tongued and quick of wit, however gorgeous in his pomp, broken in his fall – really, he still saw himself, until quite late in his career, too late in his career, as a leading man, romantic – to his inner eye lean and svelte and dashing when in truth he was big-boned, stocky, a heavy mover, though his energy also made him quick when he wanted to be – but his natural tempo was slow, his natural walk an amble – his energy distracted the attention from his shape, as did the marvellous eyes, the handsome mouth, the line of the cheeks, and the exuberant head of hair – but it grew on a round head, set on a bullish neck, and physically he was a peasant, a Derbyshire peasant, and his hands were agricultural. His consciousness of his body made him shy of exposing it professionally, though he famously exposed all of it in the film of *Women in Love*, but that was when he was young, and besides the camera and the editor could redefine, above all select – later, and especially on the stage, he was careful – in *Melon*, for instance, he hid behind the furniture when stripping down to his underwear, and pretty well stayed there, almost crouching, until the end of the scene – his no-nonsense, let's-get-on-with-it exchanges with the girl he was about to fuck seeming more like bombardo – bombardo? Is there such a word? I must have meant bravado, or did I mean bombast? Well, both of them combined give my meaning – his bombardo perversely made him more attractive, it created a tension between his desire and an innate modesty, possibly prudishness, that made him irresistible, so the girl, instead of being swept along by the force of his brute male assertiveness, succumbed to his sweetly boyish bombardo. I tried once or twice, out of a sense of duty to my own text, to get him out into the open, but he invariably said it was no good, wherever he went he seemed to end up behind the desk or the chair, and added that he wasn't a young man any more, there was too much of him, he was bloody well going to keep most of it to himself, they were already seeing more of him than was good for them – or him. But, as I say, the truth of it is that though he was in fact bulky, he never seemed it – his intelligence transformed him, gave the illusion of his being light-footed, mercurial – sometimes you scarcely noticed the movements that carried him from one side of the stage to the other, as if his mind and the meaning of his lines had taken him there without help from his body, but in repose he was a massive presence, nothing to do with his height or weight, but of density, really, the bulk of him somehow compacted, concentrated in the audience's concentration – Alan alone on stage at the end of a play, motionless, was volcanic. He was also beautiful, I think, in the way that no artefact can be beautiful, because he was breathing, dying.

HIS INADEQUACIES AS A HATER

He was a great mimic, a great creative mimic – in the course of an evening he could give you a whole novel full of characters, waiters in restaurants, agents, publicists, the nurses and doctors during his last weeks in the hospital, and earlier, in his palmy days, his mother-in-law, whom he adored, and not simply for the comedy she provided him with – and that was it, every character was suffused with his own delight in their being, so that they were always presented in all their vivid absurdity without malice, with a kind of love, and a gratitude for giving him so much pleasure in their creation. Correspondingly, he was not much of a hater, although capable of explosions of anger and contempt, mostly against directors, but he would usually append a coda of forgiveness and the suggestion that it was probably his own fault really. Once, though, when he was coming to the end of his chemotherapy, he went abruptly, without warning, into a low, muttering but precisely articulated monologue of loathing for a famous director. He went on for quite a long time, and when he finished he sat in silence, his head lowered. I waited for a burst of laughter or the fabulous smile, but neither came. 'There,' he said eventually, 'there.

I've said it at last. And I don't feel any better for it.' I think he was in part speaking about his illness, about which he scarcely said a bad word, seeming to accept it as a mysterious visitation that probably made sense if one understood the real order of things, rather than as a betrayal of his body, or as an outrage against perfectly reasonable expectations. Shortly after he'd been moved back into the London Clinic for the last time, he said that if he was going to die soon, it was all right – 'I've had a very good life. I've done everything I want, really. Yes, it would be all right.'

WAS HIS A GOOD LIFE?

For Alan, the birth of his twin sons, Benedick and Tristan, was life's greatest gift, its blessing. Tristan died in a freak accident in Tokyo at the age of seventeen. At his funeral Alan spoke of his memories of the twins' growing up, of the differences and similarities in their natures, of the promises for both the future had seemed to offer, he spoke calmly and gently, seeming almost at ease, until suddenly, mid-sentence, he stopped, his face seemed to fall apart, his mouth hung open, his eyes started, as he gaped into the horror of where he was and why he was speaking. He blinked, looked towards Benedick, gathered himself and went on. I've always thought that giving that address was the bravest and noblest thing I've seen a man do. Two years later his wife, Victoria, wasted to the bone with grief and bewilderment, drifted to Italy, to a hotel where she, Alan and the twins had gone one summer. For her it was a place of special memories, memories of herself as a young mother in her prime, of a dashing film-star husband, of two beautiful sons who were also *enfants sauvages*. She arrived at the front desk so enfeebled that the receptionist immediately phoned for an ambulance, she was taken off to hospital, where she died the next day, of malnutrition, dehydration, extreme self-neglect, in fact – but how had she managed the journey? How had she found the strength even to contemplate it, let alone complete it? In his funeral address Alan spoke of her with such tenderness and understanding that he sounded at moments almost parental – the truth is, I think, that he was born to be a father, not a husband, and his marriage was really a sort of flawed adoption. He was honest and sad about the ways in which he'd failed her, but then she was always, in a friend's phrase, a reluctant incarnation, and I doubt if anyone could have given her what she needed in life, or even known what it was. His own death – his own death –

BOTH ALIVE AND DEAD

I've been trying to remember the film of *Women in Love*, whether I like it. I know I wrote down its title the other day, presumably in some context to do with Alan – well, I haven't seen it for ages, doubt if I'll ever see it again, or any film with Alan in it – such a disturbing part of modern life, you can find yourself watching an old film with great pleasure, a film you saw and loved in your childhood, take one of my favourite films of all time, *Shane*, with Alan Ladd as a gunslinger who rides away from his death-dealing past into a valley where circumstances compel him, against his will and for the sake of peace for people he has come to love, to deal out death again, and then ride on to oblivion. I have watched certain scenes from the film probably more than thirty times over the last fifty years, I was seventeen, in my last year at school, when it came out in London, so yes, fifty years – nobody in the film is over forty except perhaps the villainous rancher, and the old chap, played by Buchanan, is it? Edgar Buchanan – who wants to give up and go away until they burn down his ranch although now I think about it, nobody apart from Brandon De Wilde, who plays the son, he's about ten, I should think, of Van Heflin and Jean Arthur – nobody is much under forty, which is surely unusual for a film, even of that period – but you see them there still, is my point, Brandon De Wilde, Jean Arthur, Van Heflin, Elisha Cook Jr, Ben Johnson, and of course Jack Palance creaking about in black, his every movement measured and unnaturally, almost mechanically, paced, even when he goes for his gun – and of course Alan Ladd, blond in blond, or light-brown, buckskin – and there's the great scene, the open-air party, the settlers celebrating what can it have been? Thanksgiving, I suppose, Shane asking Van Heflin's wife – Jean Arthur – to dance – 'We're leaving Cheyenne-eh oh, eh-eh –

We're leaving Cheyenne' – of course I've forgotten the rest of the words, though I remember the tune, I can't carry a tune to sing, but I carry this one in my heart, soul – and Van Heflin leaning on a fence, watching Shane dance with his wife, seeing the attractiveness, the almost rightness of them as a couple, Shane's tenderness and delicacy, his wife's dignified submissiveness. And of course later, when Van Heflin prepares to go to his almost certain death to protect his homestead, his family, he tells his wife that he knows she will be well looked after, as will their son, who idolizes Shane, Shane will be a better protector than himself – well, think of all that now, from now, in these days of cinematic trash, where the foul and vacuous *Lord of the Rings*, with its interminable set pieces, one set piece after another, of hideous mass slaughter, is voted by the nation as the nation's favourite film, and you find yourself asking yourself, what kind of nation is this? What kind of nation? *Shane* seems not only immensely dignified – indeed noble – in its conception, but also immensely innocent in its assumption that there are good people who struggle to live honourably, that a man who has lived badly, like the professional gunfighter Shane, can acknowledge what he has been, and sacrifice himself so that people he has come to love will have what he yearns for, that their future counts for more than his – even Wilson, the dead-souled killer, sticks to a code, or the appearance of a code – he doesn't draw his gun until the helpless Elisha Cook Jr, provoked by Jack Palance's smiling, jeering contempt for his Southern sense of honour, reaches for his gun – to my mind the most terrible moment in cinema – the rain beats down, Palance stands sheltered from it on the porch of the saloon, Elisha Cook Jr stands not many yards from him, drenched, his boots mired in mud, his gun only just out of its holster, still pointing down – Palance's gun drawn so quickly one can hardly see the movement, pointing directly at his chest – the long pause is the rest of Elisha Cook Jr's life, Palance smiling, Cook's eyes bulging – then the shot, Cook hurled backwards from the impact, spread out dead in the mud. This is awful violence, violence with meaning, it makes us know and feel what an act of murder is – in fact, there are only two killings in the film, that one and Wilson's, caused by Shane in the saloon in almost identical fashion, but this time it's Shane who does the taunting, and Wilson's guns which are incompletely drawn – Wilson hurtling backwards, his guns a quarter up, one I think firing uselessly, his thin limbs sticking out in all directions, a skeleton in black clothes, and of course the child watching from underneath the saloon's swing doors, his arm around his dog, sees the two ranchers concealed, one on the landing above the bar, his rifle aiming, warns Shane. A brief fusillade, the ranchers dead – so four killings not two. Shane stands wounded but impassive, then the sudden, completely unexpected, flashy and arrogant twirl of the gun before he drops it in its holster – 'You got him, didn't you, Shane? You shot Wilson!' 'Yes. That was Wilson. He was fast. Fast on the draw', this said almost in a trance, before riding off into the darkness, hunched sideways from the pain of his wound, the child crying out for him to come back, music swelling, child's voice echoing – and so forth. Well, not so forth. Credits, and The End naturally. But what I was thinking about, what I started all this from, was not *Shane*, its plot and its people, but the fact that they're all dead, all the actors, including Brandon De Wilde, who must have been about seven years younger than me, killed in a car crash in his twenties, early thirties, perhaps, and yet there they all are again, and the contradiction that never existed before the invention of movies, of people who are long dead being visibly alive, you can see them breathe, there they are, the characters and the actors, both with futures of life and death unknown to them in the two stories they're in. I'll go on watching *Shane* until nature prevents me, but I think I shall always avoid seeing Alan on the screen, or at least avoid watching him, I've already seen him a few times when channel-hopping, a glimpse of him in a bowler hat, an eyebrow raised, smiling quizzically –

HE IS SPOON-FED

He looked like Galileo, have I said this before? The rim of white beard, his hair growing back to a thick white stubble on his skull, his marvellous blue eyes as clear as they were in his youth, all his natural exuberance distilled into a different sort of energy, to be released after a few moments of rest, but the range of expressions as great as ever, with a new one, sweet and sly as he lay on the bed, his head propped up, studying you, or from his favourite position, a small armchair facing the bed, where he sat in his hospital gown, his feet planted, with the air of a benevolent emperor. He was, in fact, imperial in his dying, deeply happy with what had come to him at the end, his Tony Award on Broadway, his knighthood, all that was his due had come at last. He received his friends until nearly the end, sitting in a chair by the bed, a rug over his lap, full of delight and above all attention. He wanted to hear everything that was going on in our lives, gave sympathy and advice where things were bad, and shared in any pleasures and successes. He was Alan as I'd always known him, the very best of best friends, the one you phoned up immediately when you were in need, the one you hoped would phone you up when he was. Ben came from New York to lodge with him in his room for the final few weeks, sleeping on a camp bed so that he was available at night, tending him like a nurse and son, spooning food into his mouth when he resisted eating, getting him to swallow by cajoling and teasing. Alan adored this reversal of roles, describing how he'd used similar tactics when spoon-feeding Ben and Tristan, and then going into imitations of his father, at the end of his life, assuming a quavering and tetchy tone – 'Take it away, it's disgusting, disgusting, I can't eat it, who are these people anyway, call themselves nurses, call themselves doctors!' – and then spluttering with laughter, Ben laughing too as he slipped another spoonful down. They touched each other a lot, Ben patting Alan's head, Alan stroking Ben's cheek, as if they were the same age. Mates.

HIS LAST DAYS

I used to have the taxi stop on the Marylebone Road, at the top of Marylebone High Street, and walk the hundred yards or so to Harley Street and the London Clinic. I'd do it slowly, spinning it out, smoking two cigarettes, and then often have one more on the steps of the Clinic, where there would usually be someone smoking, either one of the hospital porters, or a relative or, like me, friend of a patient, and once or twice a patient, I think – we all had pretty well the same manner of smoking, it was a cigarette that mattered, that we couldn't get enough of, but couldn't linger over, short, greedy puffs, then a decisive step onto the pavement, drop the butt, a quick stamp, a decisive step back and into the clinic, then the lift up to the third floor, or was it the second? Anyway, the cancer floor – along the corridor, not bothering to stop at the reception desk because the nurses know you by now, or seem to, and there's his door – the first thing I did on returning to the pavement was to light up, putting myself in touch with the man I'd left on the pavement smoking, as if the visit itself were in parenthesis, that linked up to the parentheses of the previous visits, so that the visits now seem to be a continuum, a main sentence all of its own – I would smoke my way through to Marylebone High Street by the back route, and sit at a pub that had chairs and tables outside, even though we were in December, and Christmas nearer with every visit – I would sit at a table with a Diet Coke and concentrate on anything but Alan, or find a blankness sometimes so successfully that I'd forget what I was doing there, smoking, with a Diet Coke, outside a pub in the cold, and I'd get the next taxi that came along, hailing it from my table. The truth is that, whatever joy there was in seeing Alan, it was also unbearable. That stretch from the top of Marylebone High Street to the top of Harley Street – whenever we pass it in a taxi I look out of the window and measure it with my eye, but even as I register how short it is, I feel the lurch of dread in my stomach and hope I never have to walk it again, never have to stand on those steps again – and there's another thing that comes back to me, that as I approached the clinic I used to look up to the window of Alan's room, imagine him sitting in his chair or lying on his bed, and then imagine myself as I would be in a few moments, in that room that seemed to me from the outside, looking up at its window, so self-contained and far away that I could never be in it.

HE AND TOTO FIND PEACE

So that's how it was all the days in December, leading up to Christmas – Alan dying in the London Clinic, and Toto going mad in Holland Park – I could hear her screams as I came down the street towards the house – not, I suppose, technically screams, but shrill, joined-up yaps that had the effect of screams in that they shredded the nerves and made one think of cruelty, pain and ambulances – such a small dog, and in repose such a pretty one, with alert, intelligent eyes, and affectionate. We'd originally given her as a birthday present to my granddaughters, Maddie and Gee-Gee. Victoria had picked her up at the kennels on her way to London from Suffolk at 3 p.m. on 11 September – in fact, she was drawing up outside the kennel doors as the news about the twin towers came through on her car radio – so in a sense Toto is a 9/11 baby, about whom songs could be written therefore, but her condition that Christmas was actually the result of something far more momentous in her world, an hysterical pregnancy which coincided with her having come to live with us – she gave birth to a small stuffed bear, which she protected with extraordinary savagery from predators like Victoria and myself. When she wasn't crouched snarling over it, she was drooling over it and cuddling it, and then would suddenly rampage around the house screaming the screams I used to hear on coming home from the London Clinic. So the two experiences are intermingled – no, they're not – as I've said, Alan's dying is a long, separate event, and Toto's madness is a long, separate event that happened at the same time, parallel with it, one home and one away – the worst was Christmas, Alan in his coma, Toto in a frenzy because somehow her stuffed bear of a baby had vanished and she decided that she had delivered herself of all the presents under the Christmas tree and crouched, snarling, among them – this meant that no one could approach the tree without being threatened – a mad dog is a mad dog, however charming to look at and sweet her nature, and her shows of teeth, saliva dripping from her muzzle, were terrifying among the pink and gold and silver and scarlet packages – when she went on one of her looping, screaming runs, we tried to gather up the presents, but either she would be back before we'd done or, if we shut her out, she would patrol the hall screaming – so when it came down to it there was nothing we could do but leave them under the tree and let her embed herself. Eventually the stuffed bear was found on a high shelf in the kitchen, and was placed on the floor some way from the presents, Toto ran to it, buried her face in it, licked it, stroked it and rolled it about, then carried it gently down to the basement and put it to bed – and so, apart from sudden rushes upstairs to check briefly on her other family, under the tree, and other rushes through the flap and screaming circuits of the garden – which led to a petition from some of the neighbours asking us to confine her to the house, her garden screams were too distressing, and set their own dogs off – the situation held through to Boxing Day – we saw him a few hours before he died, when we took Ben some food, as the visitors' cafeteria was closed over the festive season, indeed the Clinic gave off the feeling that it had closed down, the only occupants the ill and the dying – he was still, his arms lying straight outside the blankets, his eyes closed, his chest moving irregularly – we could hear his breathing, shallow suckings in and expulsions after long intervals – he was obviously near the end, and looked ready for it, neat and noble, only the breathing disorderly. Ben white and staring, looked as close to death as Alan – but then he hadn't eaten for a long time, nothing was open in the neighbourhood, not even the pubs. We stayed until Ben had eaten, said goodbye to Alan with a kiss on his forehead, and came home to Toto, running this way and that, screaming. In the New Year we got canine Prozac from the vet. It calmed her down somewhat, and she began to treat the bear as a toy rather than as a baby, knocking it about, throwing it into the air and catching it, until she discarded it altogether – it still lies in her basket in the basement, but she scarcely ever goes down there, now that she sleeps in different spots all over the house in the daytime, and on our bed at night.

DEPARTURES

Oh, I saw Pan this afternoon, sitting in the reception with his suitcases, waiting for the taxi for the airport. He looked subdued, no cigar, his hands folded in his lap. He was dressed in a blue blazer, cream-coloured slacks and sturdy brown shoes, for London or Manchester, wherever. His nose seemed to fit in better when he was wearing his usual togs, it could go almost unnoticed in the Garrick Club or the MCC. The young woman with bangles and chains was attending him, but not departing with him. She was wearing beach clothes and hotel slippers, and kept going to the desk to ask about his taxi – 'Mr Prynne's got to be at the airport by three, at the latest' – there's something solemn and poignant about these departures in the lobby, the piled-up luggage, the cold-weather clothes, somebody at the desk worrying about the taxi and the flight – flamboyant Pan with a cigar becomes passive Mr Prynne staring down at his mottled hands. I wonder if Pan and the young woman are lovers, and Mr Prynne is going home to the wife and children, grandchildren? Well, the day after tomorrow it will be our turn, Victoria's and mine, to sit beside our luggage in the lobby, waiting to be returned to the fitful fever, all that, and people who are staying on will observe us and try not to think that one day soon –

PART TWO

IT TOLLS FOR SIMON

The Holy Terror in Brighton, then. How did it go? Be honest. Well, I registered only two things – that the audience was having a good time, and there was something about the play that didn't ring a bell, or rang the wrong bell – I can probably put this down to jet lag, and the intense yearning for Barbados, the sun and the sea, that always immediately follows on leaving them, I really was scarcely able to listen and watch, understanding only that the sets were very complicated and seemed to rattle on and off stage like bumper cars, which I found exhilarating, and that I loved the sheer exuberance of Simon Callow's performance, his conspiratorial relationship with the audience, who liked him even when he was abusing them – oh, yes, that was one more thing, the audience – the theatre manager told me when I came in that the audiences are terrific, he's getting lots of feedback, telephone calls, letters, the box office is jumping, nothing like it for a long time, people are really excited by it, he said, best of all they're passing on the excitement so that the houses are not only full, they're full of people who expect to enjoy themselves, and consequently do – so that was all right, though it was before I'd actually seen the show, and so before it rang – or tolled – the wrong bell. Simon and I had supper, I talked enthusiastically, while admitting that I had nothing useful to say – after all, it would hardly have been useful to say it was all fine except that it rang, or tolled, the wrong bell, and I don't know which or what bell, still don't, would it? I'll go and see Victoria, chatting about it out loud may stir up some thoughts or memories.

She was asleep, with George on one side of her, Toto on the other side, my side. I rolled Toto onto the chest at the foot of the bed, lay down and set about whispering stuff into Victoria's ear – 'There's something wrong with the play. I don't mean the lines, none of them sounded as if they weren't by me, I vaguely remembered all of them' – whispered stuff like that, which she seemed to find rather soothing, anyway she didn't spring awake as she usually does when I interrupt her sleep with a sentence, and when I finally realized 'It's the wrong play. They're doing the wrong play!' she murmured something that sounded approving or grateful. I rolled Toto back beside her, and now I'm here at my pad trying to work it out. Actually, they're not exactly doing the wrong play, they're doing the wrong version. There are two published texts, and they're delivering the earlier one, which was six or seven drafts away from the later one, the one I'd assumed they were doing.

I don't quite know what to do. After all, they've learnt the lines, have already performed for ten days in Brighton, can I simply phone Simon up in the morning and ask him to start rehearsing a different text, which would certainly involve changes in the actors' moves, and might involve changes to the set, adding new bits to bump in, while bumping existing bits out altogether? Does it matter that they're using the wrong text? If the Brighton audiences are happy with the wrong text why not leave it alone? Of course this wouldn't have happened if I'd been invited to the read-through on the first day of rehearsal, can I take satisfaction from that?

I've just phoned Simon and told him the situation. He took it with astonishing resilience, seeing it, not as a calamity, but as an opportunity to do interesting work on tour. I've sent him the authorized, let's call it that, the authorized version, and during the coming weeks, in places like Woking and Milton Keynes, charming ones like Bath, he and the other actors will, without benefit of the director – he left after the opening in Brighton to do a seventeenth-century Spanish play in Stratford – put in scenes from the authorized, cutting roughly equivalent stretches from the version they've spent weeks rehearsing and are now performing – an epic task, really, involving long hours and no doubt embarrassments on stage, when actors will suddenly find themselves living in one text with an actor who is living in the other text. I'll have to go and see it, not at Brighton again, too soon, and not at Woking, I went to Woking once, no need to go again – Milton Keynes, then, I've never been to

MILTON KEYNES

with its wide desolate boulevards, its noisy ghastly mall, a town designed for a future that it's somehow missed, so it's both aggressively modern and hopelessly out of date. The theatre, naturally, is vast and ugly, inside and out. I forgot to ask how many seats but I'd guess, at a minimum, twelve hundred, it probably does lots of pop shows, that sort of thing, anyway the audience was there like a rash, splotches of them sitting together, then an acre of space, more splotches, although if you'd joined the splotches they might have made up a decent little house. The show looked small too, as the stage was big, the surroundings cavernous, but I concentrated as keenly on the play as if I'd written it myself, admired the work that had been done, noticed the differences in the text and came out feeling that I'd had exactly the same experience as at Brighton, which I can now remember more clearly than immediately after Brighton. When I had dinner with Simon I told him confidently that he was growing in command – as he was – as the other actors were – worried a little about the set, but had nothing to say about the play at all. And Simon –

THE PLURAL OF PIERS?

Simon. It's odd to be writing my own name when referring to somebody else. I remember having dinner with Simon at a restaurant a year or so ago, and introducing him to the *maître d'*, also called Simon, so there were the three of us, Simon and Simon and Simon. When I was growing up my name was an agony to me, in fact I didn't meet anyone called Simon until I was at Cambridge. It was the same for Nigel and Piers, we all blamed Mummy for our names, we were victims of her affectation, we believed, Piers especially, who had to go to schools in Canada with a name that to infant Canadians was precious and effeminate and couldn't even be abbreviated. Now of course they're all very common names, there are probably whole nurseries of Simons, Nigels and – I don't know how to write the plural of Piers – is it the only Christian name to end in an 's'? I can't think of another one – Thomas, you fool. There are bound to be others – all right, is it the only monosyllabic Christian name that ends in 's'? Bess. Tess. But they're abbreviations, and a double 's' isn't the same as an 's', but still, to be safe – is Piers the only monosyllabic *male* Christian name that ends in 's'? Charles and James, you fool. Safe from what?

UNLEARNING EXPERIENCES

Tomorrow is the first night of *The Holy Terror*, at the Duke of York's. I've been to four consecutive previews, including tonight's, which is the last apart from a matinée tomorrow, which I shan't go to – I've never heard of having a matinée before a first night, can it be a good idea? If it goes badly they'll be depressed, subdued, come on stage in the evening, for the crucial performance, and act without conviction. On the other hand, I suppose if it goes well they'll be confident – too confident?

But what can I say about the four previews? Only that although all four were well received by the audience I came away from each one with the feeling that I'd had exactly the same experience as at Milton Keynes, which had been like the first experience in Brighton. Half a dozen identical experiences then, three in completely different places, all with different texts, lighting, sound cues. I can't make out what this means, it may just mean that the play hasn't got into my system, in the way that my plays do when I worry and fret through each rehearsal. It may also mean that I'm still going through an autistic phase, I've got an idea that I've already described this, when nothing seems to make much impression, or matter much – although I want the play to be a success, quite positively want that, and just as positively want Simon to be a success in it – I've always admired his gifts, as an actor and as a writer, and I consider myself lucky in our friendship. I can't bear to think of him coming a cropper on my behalf, and also – and also – well, it seems to me that his talents, his relish for life, his love of his friends all come from the same source – of course they do, how could they possibly come from different sources? What am I trying to say? First-night nerves, I'd assume, if I were nervous.

MY NEW SHOES

I was wearing a pair of new shoes, black and soft, a bit like moccasins, that would have been comfortable if there hadn't been an odd sensation, that they were full of water – it was air, I suppose, but every step I took made a whooshing sound inside my shoe, I couldn't actually hear it, but I felt it, whoosh, whoosh, whoosh, whoosh, as I walked along St Martin's Lane to the Duke of York's, for a quick visit to the actors, about an hour before the curtain went up. Whoosh, whoosh, as I went down the stairs backstage, into the dressing rooms. I decided that these shoes, never before worn, would never be worn again, they seemed to be whooshing even when I was sitting down, talking to the actors with chuckling optimism about the night that lay before us, and were going whoosh as I walked to Sheekey's, around the corner from the theatre, and met Victoria in the bar. I told her about the shoes. She looked down at them, and said yes, there was something odd about them, they didn't look quite like shoes, didn't quite go with my trousers, so perhaps my trousers were odd. My trousers were at least comfortable, I said, inasmuch as I wasn't consciously wearing any, whereas I couldn't keep my mind off my shoes, even when I was attempting to raise the morale of the actors, which was worryingly high, perhaps it would have been wiser to lower their morale a bit, blessed is he that expecteth nothing – I went on to talk about the play, telling her that it was an old play, nothing to do with me any more, really, apart from the fact that my name was on it, and on the posters outside the theatre, and probably up in lights above the title.

We sidled back to the Duke of York's, acknowledging but not recognizing people on the pavement, then into a private room where there were about eight people standing right in the middle of the room, holding glasses of wine and champagne. I sat down on a sofa that was in a corner, and Victoria stood in front of me, as if to guard me, not a gallant arrangement, but these occasions bring out both my defenceless side and her protective nature. A man and a woman detached themselves, came over to us, the man someone I know but my mind blanked out, I couldn't remember his name or a thing about him, but it didn't matter because his intention was to introduce me to the woman, whom he ushered around Victoria and arranged in front of me with a sweeping gesture – 'Behold!' his gesture seemed to say, 'Behold this woman!' And I did behold her, and lo! she was passing comely, and passing compliments too, although they weren't compliments about any of my theatrical works, they were about other

290 THE COMPLETE SMOKING DIARIES

things I do, in another life, – but you can't be choosy with compliments,
I've discovered, you have to take them while you can get them. 'But
you don't want to talk to me on an occasion like this,' she said, with a
pretty smile, wished me luck, and returned herself to the centre of
attention in the centre of the room. 'She does a quiz show,' Victoria
said, 'she's famous for being clever and rude.' I said that I was glad she
hadn't been rude to me, it would be a bit much to have someone being
rude to you before the curtain went up on a play that virtually nobody
in London had yet seen – or at least that virtually nobody had yet seen
in London, well, that a few people had seen in previews in London,
but if she'd been one of them she'd hardly come back for a second
helping on the off-chance of a chance to be rude to the playwright –
Victoria explained that she hadn't been in the slightest bit rude,
evidently hadn't seen the play as she'd said she was looking forward to
it – I agreed that if she'd already seen it, she'd know better than to
look forward to it. Victoria terminated the exchange by pointing out
that we now had the room to ourselves. 'Why?' I said. 'Where have
they gone?' She said that as the final bell had rung, she imagined
they'd gone to their seats. We should go to ours. We sat down at the
back of the dress circle of what must be the prettiest theatre in
London. There was a strange fretfulness in the atmosphere – there
wasn't a buzz of anticipation but of impatience, fidgeting and sighing,
noisy mutterings and angry sniggers – when Simon started the play
by stepping between the curtains and addressing the audience as if
it were composed of the ladies of the Chichester Women's Institute,
a silence descended, not a silence of concentration but heavy, inert
and rancorous – it really was most peculiar, and deeply troubling for
a playwright who has always longed to be taken to the bosom of
first-nighters, as they are mostly critics and determine the future of
the work in question. Now it's true that there were spots of attention
and even laughter, and even appreciative laughter, so somewhere
down there in the stalls was a small alternative audience. I reminded
myself that we've opened in an almost empty city, half-deserted streets,
muttering retreats, etc., possibly everybody in town was now in the
Duke of York's – all the critics and theatre journalists summoned
back from their Easter rituals, egg hunts with the children, maypole

and fertility dances, to cover a play that they could detect from its title, or had been told by relatives in Brighton, Woking or Milton Keynes, was a bad play, which it may be, and anti-life, which in fact it isn't, although I admit it's not a play that is 100 per cent unequivocally pro-life, rather it's a play that advises you to be careful where you tread, there can be an empty space where you're aiming to put your foot next, it's that sort of play, equivalent to a health warning on a packet of cigarettes – well then, consider my own reactions to health warnings on cigarettes, yes, consider your own reactions to health warnings of any kind, they're very similar to the reactions of last night's audience to your play, perhaps that's the explanation then –

At the interval we went back to Sheekey's, sat in the bar, at the table where we'd sat earlier, when we'd discussed my shoes – now it was the play, but the vocabulary was very similar – whoosh, whoosh, flop, splat. A couple burst into the bar – it's the only word for it – burst in, walked to the end of the counter, hopped angrily onto high stools, and slapped their programmes down – no, she didn't, he did, but it was in its emotional content a simultaneous gesture, her hand was on his knee as he slapped the programme onto the counter, not once but three times, punishing it, was what he was doing to it – now Sheekey's is close to a number of other theatres, so I hoped this couple had come from one of those, we couldn't actually see the front of the programme, at least not until he raised it, and showed it, with a contemptuous gesture, to a sympathetically enquiring barman, and then we knew that they hadn't come from one of those but from ours, which wouldn't be ours, we were already surmising, for very long.

I BECOME CHILDISH

We left Sheekey's, heads again bowed for anonymity, discovered that though we were a couple of minutes late we were in fact early, inasmuch as the pavement was crowded with people who clearly felt no need to get back inside the theatre – from what I could see of them as I peeked past, they were having a better time – i.e. animated and gesticulating – where they were than where they'd been, and would have to be again about three minutes ago. I imagine they were critics, comparing notes, as I've oft heard tell that now and then, when they really all agree that they're on to a bummer, they cluster together instead of keeping a fastidious and ethical distance from each other. I suppose it's a kind of herd instinct, really, perhaps a celebration, demonstrating to the world that whatever their individual differences, they tap in, at the profounder aesthetic levels, to a collective consciousness – well, whatever they were up to, I didn't like the look of them, there's one in particular that I seem to have known all my life, I mean as far back as the day I was born there was this face, that tone – reviewing my emergence from the womb with a lumbering melancholy, a shake of the ponderous head, he always makes me think of a nappy, a full nappy, as if he's just over-eaten, and is pausing briefly on the way to the potty – this is just childishness, I'm being childish, he's merely doing his job – his big jobs – ha ha – stop, stop – though it's grotesque to think that he's already written his review, that in a few hours it will be steaming away on people's doormats –

AN ADULT AGAIN

well, back to getting off the pavement into the lobby of the theatre, through that, down some stairs to the private room, which was stuffed with people, so many that it was difficult to get the door open, all of them with glasses in their hands, all of them throbbing with a noisy, ill-judged optimism – these were the producer's friends, backers and so forth, people with something to lose, including their wives if they'd invested her money in the play – we hung about there in a corner for a few seconds, the sofa being heavily occupied, then went up to our seats. It's a general rule that however badly a first night goes in the first act, the second is always a bit better – the actors have got used to the house, the house has got used to not liking the play, everyone is halfway towards going home, or somewhere else where the evening will pick up – a bad evening at the theatre guarantees a good evening in the restaurant, so much to laugh at and be apoplectic about – 'I couldn't believe it, couldn't actually believe it when he began –' 'And that ghastly bit when she –' 'And that line, did you hear that line? and so forth. I've had many happy dinners of that sort, pausing only sometimes to wonder about all the dinners I haven't been at, when my own play has provided the merriment and apoplexy.

AN ENCOUNTER WITH A RABID WOMAN, PROBABLY A CRITIC

The second act didn't go any better than the first, it went a little worse, the ill-feeling was slightly intensified, the spots of laughter more subdued. Perhaps some of the laughers had left, or had been brought around to the majority view during the interval. I actually can't remember the curtain call, so it was probably polite, merely lacking enthusiasm and honesty, like some of my school reports, but I do remember that we were the first out of our seats and through the doors, into the corridor – there was a small woman coming towards us, she must have come up from the stalls, and was probably a critic. I'd arrange to have only a very small photograph of myself, passport size, in the programme in the hope of preventing identification, but this small woman gave me the impression that she'd not only identified me, she knew me well, that she'd hated the play and was enjoying letting me have a glimpse, by baring her teeth, of her review – in all my years in the theatre, years and years in the theatre, in all those many, many years, with no time off for good behaviour, I have never seen a more chilling sight than those bared teeth – although I suppose it's possible that they were false, and a bad fit, that she wasn't a critic and that her intentions were entirely friendly, or that she was on her way to a heart attack, and her teeth were bared in a grimace of agony – but no, there were the eyes too, the sort of eyes that went with bared teeth and a bad review. In seconds we were safely by ourselves, in the private room, and astonishingly, seconds later, we were in the company of a multitude, they seemed to come in from all sides though there was only the one door, and they already had glasses in their hands. The producer bundled himself in, holding bottles of champagne, and talking at speed, loudly – have I mentioned him yet? Howard Panter. I can't be bothered to describe him but he's balding, about fifty, medium height, not portly but looks as if he has been and will be again. When I first knew him he was subject to seizures and so

forth, but he is currently robust, last night extra-robust, his voice as
I've said loud and jerky and all over the place, as if he were a
hyperactive ventriloquist. His movements were jerky too. I can't
remember seeing him in the private room before the curtain went up,
so he must have braved the bar, presumably because he preferred to
mingle with strangers rather than his backers and accountants, shortly
perhaps to become strangers too. The reason I ought to have
mentioned him, if I haven't, is that he's been a devoted and intelligent
producer, attending the play regularly when it was out of town and
present at every preview, his comments have always seemed to me
shrewd and constructive, and he has faith, and shows his faith – this
should probably be written in one of the past tenses – he showed, has
shown, had shown his faith – the coming week might sap it out of
him – or do I mean zap, zap it out of him? – I suddenly see the little
woman-critic with those teeth fixed in Howard Panter's throat,
economic throat, as well as in my writer's throat, Simon's actor's throat,
all our throats, and Howard's faith, ripped out of him by that
Rottweiling little – teeth could be false, remember, incipient heart
attack, remember, sad little lady with her dentures on the bedside
table, sad little lady on a slab in the hospital – I mean bed in the
hospital, slabs are in the mortuary – though these days a bed in one
soon becomes a slab in the other, why don't they merge?

We hung about until the audience had left the building, then went
up to the lobby, where there was to be a party for the actors, backers,
etc. As we came through the door a little group of tightly knit stragglers
were heading for the pavement, among them the famously cruel and
clever quiz lady. She saw me, her step faltered, she smiled, she raised a
thumb so courteously and compassionately that it seemed to jab
straight into my kidneys, then the faltering step quickened and she was
gone. Victoria and I were alone in the lobby, though we could see
people standing on the pavement outside, lighting cigarettes, moving
towards taxis. I longed to go out there and light a cigarette, but it was
safer, wiser, in the lobby where there would be allies from the company,
the producer's family and friends – I wondered whether the director
had sent family and friends along in lieu of himself, I gather he'd been
seen once at a preview, at a matinée performance when, exhausted by

his labours on the Spanish play in Stratford, and the exhausting trip
from there to the Duke of York's, he had come into one of the dressing
rooms, lain down on a sofa and requested a kiss – 'Isn't somebody
going to give me a kiss, don't I deserve a kiss?' When he'd got one – at
least I suppose he'd got one, but from whom? – he gave his blessing to
the work Simon, the other actors and Howard Panter had done since
he'd last seen the play on the first night in Brighton, talked awhile
about his life and times in Stratford, departed with soft hugs and
squeezes, and was glimpsed no more. The social responsibility for this
celebration thus devolved in part on me, but I reckoned that after a few
handshakes, kisses and cuddles, whatever was mandatory, we could
leave for a restaurant near home, where we'd arranged to meet up with
friends. Once we were with them we would be carefree until the
morning brought the reviews. Well, not carefree exactly, but we could
allow ourselves to relax into gloom among close friends who were more
like relatives, without the attendant problems – none of us looked like
each other, talked like each other, reminded us of ourselves and our
lineages.

A LAUGH SEEN THROUGH GLASS

The actors came in a group, minus Simon. They were flushed with
the triumph of getting through the evening without mishap, no
fluffed lines, no false moves, no stalled scene changes, a full house,
and the adrenalin still up but the panic that caused it leaking away.
They said the house had been a bit sticky, but then first nights,
London audiences, critics, what do you expect, they'd known worse,
though several of them couldn't have, as this was their first West End
experience. Simon came into the lobby through the main doors of the
theatre – I was having a stilted conversation with a fellow playwright
and a titled actor, who were both working hard on their bedside
manner, finding ways of reassuring me that the rope was secure
around my neck, the trapdoor ready under my feet – the compliments
that told the true story were 'brave' and 'bold', as in 'It's such a bold
piece of writing and Simon is so very very bold in it' and 'How good
that the West End still has brave producers, willing to take risks' –

they and Simon embraced *à la mode*, then Simon and I went to a quiet spot and spoke about the audience. There was a fat man in the front row, he said, who stared fixedly at him during the curtain call, and gave him a very personal slow handclap, which he continued after everyone else had stopped clapping – the worst audience, he said, the worst audience he'd ever – absolutely the worst, I agreed, absolutely – and then, for want of a howl or a scream, we burst out laughing – no big deal with me, as my laugh is really a wheeze with cackles in it, but a very big deal with Simon, he has a laugh that could fill, or perhaps empty, a cathedral, it is a cheering noise, it comes from a deep relish of the awfulness of life as well as of its pleasures – with an adjustment of the shoulders, he advanced into the lobby. I extracted Victoria from a quaint young Indian who was dressed in the style far beyond his years and now completely out of fashion, a grey suit, white collar and dark tie, and a large pair of spectacles. He had a pad in one hand, a pen in the other, and held them out to me as if for an autograph. When I made to take them he pulled them back quickly and said, 'No, could you just tell me how you feel?' 'How I feel?' 'Yes, please, how you feel after such a successful night.' 'He's from the *Telegraph*,' Victoria said, smiling pleasantly at him. 'Ah!' I said. 'Ah! Well, we'd better be off, better be off, eh?' and went out onto the pavement. Through the doors we saw him stepping quickly towards Simon, whose head was thrown back in a laugh we couldn't hear, reminding me of the Munch – visually there's sometimes little to choose between a soundless laugh and a soundless scream – the interesting question is what would Simon have seen, if he'd seen but not heard himself laughing that laugh.

HOW DID WE GET THERE?

I don't remember how we got to Kensington Place, the restaurant in Notting Hill, I might ask Victoria tomorrow, when we're both fully awake, or perhaps ask her when I go to bed, which will be some time around 6 a.m., from the feel of me. One of her many accomplishments, and one that is crucial to the smooth working of our marriage, is that she is willing to have, seems even to enjoy, conversations, some of them quite complicated, at whatever hour I come to bed, however deeply asleep she might have been the second before I ask a question, frequently factual – e.g. When exactly did we go to Spetses for the first time, was it in August, you can't remember the actual date can you, was it a Monday? I seem to have got it into my head it was a Tuesday or Monday? etc. – and she will provide answers one after the other, most of them correct. Or I make a statement, an emphatic statement – e.g. – I can't think of an example of any of these emphatic statements right now, but they're usually to do with the state of the world, education, literacy, that sort of thing, and involve the usual adjectives – loathsome, disgraceful, revolting, so forth – but when I get in beside her tonight, I shan't ask her how we got from the Duke of York's to the restaurant, because by then I will have forgotten that I want to know, and will need to know something else entirely, or will make an emphatic statement about first-night audiences and theatre critics, she won't even have to wake up to deal with that, her response will be automatic, having been given so many times before. Anyway the only reason I found myself wondering how we got to Kensington Place is because I can't remember, and the reason I can't remember is because it isn't important – but the thing is, the thing is, it's now become important because I can't remember it – if I worked it out logically I'd say we took a taxi, how else? I'd certainly remember if we walked, or went by tube or bus, because it would be difficult to believe, in fact I wouldn't believe it, I'd think I was the victim of false memory syndrome, that someone had artificially implanted in me the idea that we'd walked or tubed or bussed from the Duke of York's to Notting Hill –

HOW WE GOT THERE

Hah! Got it! We had a hired car, of course we did, Philip drove us, as he always does on such occasions, he was wearing his semi-official chauffeur's uniform, a very natty dark suit and black tie, but no cap – the suit and tie establishing to the world at large that he is a professional driver, the absence of a cap signifying that he is also a friend to the occupants of the magnificently upholstered back seat – it has an armrest with a hole in it for your glass, or in my case a can of

Diet Coke, it has an ashtray that is grand enough for cigar stubs, and it has tinted windows so that not only can the world at large not look in at you, you can't look out on the world at large, which is frankly very irritating, but it's a beautiful car, so spacious that it must have been designed for celebrities who, in the way of celebrities, don't want to see – what is there for them to look at? – or be seen – no, that can't be right, celebrities surely want to be seen, that's why they become celebrities, so it must be that they don't want to be seen when they're doing certain things in the back of a car. I'll ask Philip if there are in fact two windows, a removable tinted window over a transparent window, so that when the celebrities have finished doing their certain things they can show themselves off – wait a minute – why then are the tinted windows in place whenever I'm in the car? Could it be that he's ashamed of me? It's true that I often look quite scruffy and I chainsmoke – so he doesn't want an elderly, scruffy chain-smoking man to be visible in his car – but then that wouldn't apply when Victoria's in the car, she's always elegant, he would be proud to have her in his car – that's unfortunately put, he'd be glad to show her off, yes, that's better, to show her off in his car – silver, sleek, expensive-looking car – what make is it, I wonder? Yes, that's the question I'll put to Victoria when I go to bed, what make is Philip's car, and she'll say, 'But you've been in it lots of times,' and I'll say, yes, I know what it looks like, both on the outside and the inside, but I've never noticed the make, and she'll say, 'Oh, it's a Mercedes,' and she'll be right, because I've just realized that it is in fact a Mercedes, Philip's referred to it as such – 'Yes, I can take you,' he'll say. 'I've just got my Mercedes back from the garage' – so now I know, no point in asking her – Philip, by the way, is not ashamed of me, he's not trying to prevent people from seeing me in the back of his car, he just assumes I don't like being looked at, especially when I'm smoking, and he doesn't think I want to look out of the window because I'm either bending my head towards Victoria, or, if I'm alone, I'm reading or thinking or fidgeting, and of course, of course, I always lower the window – I nearly said wind down the window, but these days you press a button – so it doesn't matter if it's a single tinted window, it's only closed when you're very cold – Get to Kensington Place, for God's sake, why not?

BREAKDOWN

Why not? Well, not because I can't remember it, but because I prefer
not to. It wasn't unpleasant in itself, how could it be with such
company, Judy Daish, my agent for twenty-five years or so, a great
beauty with many sympathetic features – kind, generous, thoughtful
and I would say caring, if I could bear the word; and then there was her
new chap, Gordon, just come into her life, actually almost the first
chap I can remember with husband status, he's charming, with flowing
brown locks and a toothsome smile, and says intelligent things in a
murmuring voice – and then there were William and Caroline
Waldegrave, Victoria's oldest friends, now old friends of mine, William
was a politician, an MP and minister in Thatcher's government, he
seemed destined for great things until his party killed its queen bee, and
the hive went to hell, is perhaps a lazy way of putting it – anyway
William left politics, or the other way around, and he is now in
banking, his formidable and kindly intellect engaged on matters that
can't be as destructive to the public good as what goes on in Parliament,
especially in these days, when governments pretend to believe that they
have an obligation to protect the citizen from himself (and herself,
needless to say, needless to say) – nanny state is a term frequently used
to convey its moralistic, dependence-making, interfering nature, but it's
an inadequate one, as nannies also make you feel safe, or should do,
and the government of today is determined to do the opposite – the
terrorists are coming, the attack is inevitable, London, Huddersfield,
Sheffield, Little Sodsbury, who knows where or when, but come it will,
we can't prevent it, but we can make your life complicated, anxious and
miserable by implementing regulation after regulation that will help to
guard you from the terrorists and their attacks, from which no one can
protect you, which are coming because they're inevitable – here is a list
of things you may not do, tomorrow will bring a list of other things
that you may not do, eventually you'll have forgotten how to do them
and even why you wanted to do them, and in the end, by the time
we've finished regulating you, you should come not to mind the
terrorists and their attacks, which are coming, from which no one,
especially us, can protect you, because your lives will be so cabined,

cribbed and confined that you might as well give them up to people who think it a duty and a pleasure to take them, so be supine in the name of Western civilization, our values are that we don't have any, our future is to pay for our past by surrendering – surrendering – actually the thing about William, which is what I was talking about – writing about –

A GOOD TIME IN NOTTING HILL

There is also his wife, Caroline, who is beautiful, kind and good, what more need I say? Why am I saying it, anyway? The point is that with such company, in a familiar restaurant where the food is fine, better than fine, it should have been a good and fine evening, especially as the other four, the Daishes and the Waldegraves, were in excellent spirits, had enjoyed the play, were convinced that the audience had enjoyed the play and that we could anticipate nothing but good news in tomorrow's (today's) papers – Victoria and I tried to explain the real facts of the matter, that the audience had hated the play, the reviews would stink. This disagreement sustained itself for about ten minutes in a low-key kind of way, subsided, bobbed up, subsided, other matters were discussed, food was eaten, wine was drunk, one bottle of Diet Coke followed another, the mood became jolly, vibrant, Judy and Victoria climbed onto the table and danced a samba to stamping feet and handclaps – five Russians – four girls and an elderly woman – joined in. Gordon grappled with a waiter who tried to prevent Judy and Victoria from taking off their skirts, William stood on his chair and called for UN intervention, Caroline made friendly gestures through the window to passers-by on the pavement, coarsely misinterpreted – so inevitably, in the jolly hubbub of an evening in Notting Hill, the agony of the Duke of York's became a thin and inconsequential memory – and here I am at seven in the morning, with nothing much on my mind but the reviews that the producer and most members of the cast will have read, and Victoria and I have no intention of reading. Time for bed, dozy-dead, head I mean, dozy-head, time for bed, hozy-dead.

CONGRATULATIONS ARE IN ORDER

I've just about got up, and am shortly going back to bed. Judy phoned at some hour or other, not long after I'd gone to sleep. I heard the ringing in Victoria's study, then Victoria's voice, a long pause, then in she came. She said that Judy said that our policy of not reading the reviews has again been completely vindicated. So a triumph, really, for practical wisdom, is one way of looking at it.

SIMON INTRODUCES SIMON TO TWO-BEERS

Home from dinner with Simon. We went to a dining club I'd never heard of, down an alley off St Martin's Lane. It really seemed to consist of a steep, narrow stairway, with several landings off which there were rooms of different sizes. We ate by ourselves at the top, in a medium-sized room, deliberately underlit. There was an attractive waiter, an attractive waitress, both attentive without being much present, who brought us food – but from where? I have no idea where the food came from, but it was OK, or would have been if I'd had an appetite. Simon, hungry after a performance that had been doubly draining because the house had been so small – he could have counted it, he said – was shell-shocked, was the phrase he used, shell-shocked. The laugh, though, was miraculously there, and we had some fun even when he quoted from the reviews. He tactfully refrained from quoting anything about the play, confining himself to himself. They were so wounding that I once or twice suspected that he was making them up, or was engaged in some weird auto-therapy, or like a medieval monk thrashing his naked self for the good of his soul. But they were all true, he assured me, and I suppose it was his actor's gift – or curse – that had enabled him to commit them to memory verbatim. There were a couple of sentences from a woman in one of the heavies, with a name like a beer – no, like two beers – that were so vile that he gaped at me after saying them, as if not quite believing what he'd just heard from himself. I gaped back at him, equally incredulous, then we both burst out laughing, it really did seem inconceivable that anybody would want to have their name attached to such words. Actually I pointed out, possibly correctly, that if Simon had been Simone and the critic a man, she could probably have sued him for libel, or had him prosecuted under some recent legislation – there was bound to have been some – for sexual abuse, harassment, stirring up sexual hatred, whatever. But Simone was Simon and two-beers was a woman, so all he could do was to quote her, gape, laugh and – no getting away from it – suffer. How could he not suffer, having to go on stage with those words boiling in his consciousness, feeling sure that everybody in the audience had read the review and had also committed it to memory, in fact were only there because of the review, were savouring it as they watched him perform. One of the advantages of being a playwright is that not only can I stay away from the theatre, I don't have to leave the house even, or I can go about in taxis or walk quickly with my head lowered, deny my name if questioned, claim that there are, in fact, two Simon Grays at work, one of whom wrote flops (him), the other of whom churned out turkeys (him), and that neither of them was me –but actors can't, or won't, at least not 99.9999 recurring per cent of them, jump the sinking ship, it's not in an actor's soul, while a playwright – well, that the playwright is the sinking ship, is perhaps to put it too solipsistically – but I had the feeling that while Simon would stand on the prow, hand to forehead in final salute, he would be relieved when the waters closed over his head.

IS SIMON AN ASSASSIN OR A HOMEBODY?

We sat on quite late, then went down the narrow steep staircase out into the alley, and walked down St Martin's Lane to a minicab rank opposite the Arts Theatre. London had that eerie, empty feeling it always has at the tail end of a long public holiday, almost seeming to be at peace with itself, though there were little packs of drunks wheeling about, shouting menacing words into the night sky and half-trying to collide with us on the pavement. They were quite easy to avoid, as their movements were uncoordinated and they were too full of booze to be more than blustering, unfocused belligerence. I assumed that they were English, this being nowadays characteristically English behaviour, home and away, but some were Slavic or Russian, Simon thought. I noticed that as usual he was carrying various briefcases and packages – it's an odd thing that whenever I meet Simon, in whatever circumstances, he is always thus loaded down, and the contents of the packages are impossible to identify with the naked eye, they are shapeless and cumbersome, perhaps laundry, and little packages of luxury foods, treats for his two handsome boxers, Biff and Roxie, a new tablecloth and napkins, or fresh socks for his partner – as well as scripts – and almost certainly the manuscript of his current work in progress, a further volume on the life of Orson Welles. I could always ask him, I suppose, I don't think it would be impertinent, but it would ruin the mystery, if it is indeed a mystery, which it probably isn't – my own guess is completely against mystery – napkins, socks, Orson Welles. Of course, the truth might be more glamorous, a gun – a length of rope with a noose at the end, a bottle of poison, parts of a chainsaw and dossiers on the London theatre critics containing detailed studies of their day-to-day movements and photographs of their loved ones.

HE HAS IT COMING

The odd thing is that, apart from Simon and its effect on him, I don't find myself caring very much. I really don't believe this is hard-won maturity, or a lack of imagination about the content of the reviews I haven't read. Mine were obviously as bad as Simon's, or worse, so what really is going on here? Is it another manifestation of the autism I sometimes suspect is taking me over, a diminishing capacity to respond adequately to situations to which I know the adequate response – play opens, bad reviews, failing box office, play closes, career on the ropes again = deep depression, acute self-loathing, fear of others, possibly hallucinations again. I think, though, the truth is that it doesn't matter because it doesn't matter, that's the truth. Or isolate the bit that does matter, Simon's distress, and abstract it – consider it – it matters, his distress, because you care for him and you're sorry that your play's the cause – but you don't care about the play because you don't care about the man who wrote it, he was twenty years ago and is now a stranger to you – the work's his work, the reviews are for him, let him suffer them, after all he's still quite young, in his late forties, he can take the knocks, pull himself together, go back to the old Olympia portable, begin writing something else – what did he write next? – oh yes, *Hidden Laughter*, that went OK, a good run – eight, nine months – so he's got that to look forward to, along with alcoholism, stomach operations (well deserved), three weeks on nil by mouth (do him good), insolvency (that'll teach him!), Victoria, a happy marriage – all that he's got to look forward to – so let him get on with it, take the rough with the smooth, dream, fret, have fun, etc., back there twenty years ago. I'm here, at home in my study, writing this, Victoria's in bed with George and Toto beside her, all three asleep, Errol's asleep under the table in the hall, and Tom – where's Tom? In the kitchen, on the counter, where I've just put her, her nose in a bowl of those nutritional nuggets that look like mouse droppings, which later she'll probably drop onto the carpet outside the bedroom, where it will look like cat crap. So, all present and correct. All present and therefore correct.

A PENULTIMATE PHONE CALL

The producer, Howard Panter phoned this afternoon to apologize for the reviews. I said I couldn't see how they were his fault. He said what he really meant was that he was sorry people had written such things about me. I said it was OK, thanks, because I didn't know exactly what they'd written and had no intention of finding out. He sounded surprised, slightly disbelieving, also grateful as he wouldn't have to waste pity he needed for Simon and himself, his wife and his backers. He then told me in a reasonably clear, firm voice about the advance. None and falling. The size of the audiences. Almost none and falling. Then we talked for a while about how unfair it all was, how foul for Simon, who had worked so hard, so devotedly. Occasionally he laughed, not entirely hysterically – one of the other nice things about Howard is his sense of the preposterousness of life, and particularly of the business he's in – it sometimes occurs to me that he's in the right business but the wrong branch – he was apparently a superlative stage manager in his youth, has once or twice lit shows when something happened (the sack?) to the lighting designer, no doubt there are many things he could do, most ably, why then suffer the agonies and calamities of a producer? Not a sensible question, really, it's like asking why someone likes being a boss, or goes gambling. Actually, I suspect he was really making a penultimate phone call. In a few days he'll make the ultimate one, announcing the closing of *The Holy Terror*.

SIMON UNBOUND

I went in tonight, and was surprised to see a number of reviews and quotes up. I didn't read them but assume they were favourable – they wouldn't display unfavourable ones outside the theatre, after all – at least I hope they wouldn't – unless of course Simon has ordered them there, as *aides-mémoire*. I thought his performance was extraordinary, as if all the critical hostility had liberated him from inhibitions – no, that can't be the right word, his performance was always uninhibited, but previously it had had an element of strained-for uninhibitedness and therefore an element of disorganization about it. Last night it was completely free, yes, that's the word, and it was also completely under control. A real man, not a magnificent performer, was going through all these self-inflicted ordeals. The house was small, of course, but it too was both free and under control, and made it clear that it was having a good time. A charming and attractive novelist introduced herself to me at the interval, said how much she and her husband – a publisher – were enjoying it, couldn't believe it was closing tomorrow, then said a few words of the sort one likes to hear on these occasions about reviewers. I shook my head sorrowfully, not saying much, but adoring her, of course. I must try and get hold of one of her novels. At supper afterwards Simon was serene, really, like a man who has just realized that he has not only survived but been strengthened by a brutal operation. He mentioned that nobody from the management had been to see him since the first night. But then, we agreed, that's life in the theatre. Perhaps it's life in life, too.

WHEREABOUTS?

I went out. I'm just back. I don't have any sensation of having been out, in fact the only evidence that I've been out is that I'm still wearing my raincoat, which might of course mean, not that I've been out and come back, but that I've put on my raincoat, saw this pad on my desk, sat down and started writing. Well, the evidence for having been out would be in my memory, that's the only place I could hope to find evidence – check my shoes, they're dry, check outside, it's not raining, check my pulse, it's still pulsing, so not dead then, check my . . . what next?

Reconstruct. If I concentrate I'll remember a) whether I went out and b) if I did, where I went to.

What I normally do at about this time, five in the afternoon, is walk up Holland Park Avenue to the Renaissance café, sit at a table on the pavement, order a small espresso in a large cup with hot water on the side, so I can adjust the strength to my pleasing. I smoke a few cigarettes, sometimes read a newspaper or the *Spectator*. Then I order another espresso in a large cup with hot water on the side – in fact, this has become such a routine that it's not surprising that I don't remember it – a routine not only for me but for the young waiters and waitresses at the Renaissance, I just show myself at the door, when I see that one of them has seen me I sit down, and a few minutes later he or she puts my order, that I no longer have to order, on my table. The clammy truth is, though, that I simply do not remember doing any of that just now – can't remember walking up Holland Park Avenue, or back down it, leaving the house or entering it, walking down the stairs to the front door, up the stairs from the front door, I only remember standing in my raincoat, looking down at the pad on the desk, and sitting down to write this. Concentrate. Concentrate. I know. I'll see if I can pick up a clue from the animals. Will they show by their reactions that I've already been out, therefore why am I doing it again?

Toto is asleep on the sofa in the sitting room, lying on her side, her paws tucked in. She is completely absent in sleep, nothing of her stirs at all, no sign even of breathing, her eyes are open but seem completely sightless. I whispered her name, very softly, 'Toto, Toto,' and I thought her muzzle twitched slightly, but I wasn't sure, if it did it was more a wrinkling than a twitch. George is asleep on the sofa in the sitting room – that's confusing, but only because of the words, we have two sitting rooms that open into each other but don't make up one large room, the double doors between them, although wide open, still divide them – so Toto in the back sitting room, by the garden, George in the front room, by the street, both of them in exactly the same sleeping position, but George with her eyes shut and her upper side, the side she isn't lying on, heaving gently – I didn't say her name, because I thought it might wake her, and why should she be woken when she's asleep, possibly happily? There was no sign of Tom – there's usually very little sign of her, as she likes to hide away from the other three, who get on so well together – but she's old now, a little old lady, probably up in the attic room, her favourite spot, sitting neatly, her paws in front of her and nearly crossed, they're so close together. She's become very demanding, I should note, after nightfall, when only the two of us are up and she feels it's safe to roam – then she comes calling on me, if my study door is shut she scratches at it and then makes soft thumping sounds, as if she's butting it with her head – as soon as I let her in she makes a noise, somewhere between a growl and meow, and turns and walks out of the room, and down the stairs, stopping, looking over her shoulder to make sure I'm following her – then into the kitchen – she stands waiting for me to pick her up and put her on the counter, then she walks in a wobbly but eager fashion to her saucer, which, if it's empty, I fill with those nutritional nuggets – I leave her there, go back to my study, and about half an hour later she's at my door, scratching and butting, and down we go again. Sometimes we do this six or seven times, until five or six in the morning, when I go to bed, and I do sometimes get very fed up with it, seeing it as mainly an exercise in power on her part. I mean, there she is, elderly, indeed quite a bit older than I am in her terms, and frail, and refusing to go outside in London – though she does in the country, stays out all night, slaughtering away – but still she commands this younger, more robust and higher – no, better say taller, to eliminate any hint of evolutionary vanity – creature to do her bidding, up and down, up and down I trek, grumbling at her and complaining but nevertheless onto the counter she goes, upstairs I go, then scratch scratch, butt butt, and downstairs we go –

ON THE SCENT

Errol was sitting by the front door, looking important, and as if he wanted to go out, but when I opened the door for him, he turned around, walked past me into the kitchen and waited pointedly by his bowl on the floor, but I wasn't having any of it, because something had clicked that promised to sort it out, whether I had been out for a walk or not – first what clicked was a deduction – or is it induction? – that Errol wasn't waiting by the door because he wanted to go out, but because he'd only recently come in, and being Errol, and somewhat lazy and comfort-seeking, hadn't come very far in and furthermore was warming himself up from being out by sitting by the nearest radiator in the hall, and this deduction or induction having clicked into place cerebrally, what further and positively clicked was the actual memory of Errol coming out with me when I left the house, and Errol coming in with me when I re-entered the house, they weren't visual memories, and not specific, but I felt both experiences in my body, I remembered in my body, my nervous system, the very recent sensations of going out and in with Errol, and so I've established I've been out all right. Which means, for a start, that I can take my raincoat off, as I don't need to go out again, I've had my walk and my two coffees at the Renaissance – and now that I know this I find I can taste the coffee down there in my stomach, taste the memory of it in my mouth, and furthermore, from the sudden rawness in my stomach, I'm sure I had not two, but three, as I sometimes do when I'm trying to think about something, or just feeling relaxed and enjoying the pavement life – and then comes the reminder, in the form of stomach rawness and a sudden burp of coffee-flavoured air, a touch acidic, up the various tubes of my stomach into my mouth, that three is one too many, one and a half too many I suspect – anyway, the fact is that I am now receiving positive information from various sources that I have actually been out, and if only I could remember being out, the stages of it, some incident during it, I could put the matter to rest – why should I care, anyway? the important thing for me is that I have to go out every day, preferably when it's still light, breathe in the fumes and pollution of Holland Park Avenue as an alternative to the fumes and pollution of my study, have two or three coffees to upset my stomach, and then come home again. As long as I know I've done it, why really does it matter whether I can remember having done it? I never remember posting a letter, haven't for years, I only know that I've posted it because it's no longer in my hand or my pocket, and come to that why does it matter whether I've posted it, as these days it has only a limited chance of arriving, at least at the address I wrote down on the envelope, and then when and if it gets to the postmen – no, they're not that any more – then when and if it gets to the people who carry the post bags, no, they don't carry them any more and they're not bags, either, the post is wheeled about the pavements in little wagons, from which, one gathers from a recent newspaper report, passers-by help themselves – and why not, as they're left unattended while the postman is at somebody's door, his back turned as he puts somebody's post through somebody else's letterbox.

A SHORT STATEMENT ABOUT THE NATURE OF THE UNIVERSE

The thing to take in is that there are billions upon billions of subjectivities, which represent themselves to you as objectivities and which, when I'm alone in my study, as I am now, can be thought of as one massive objectivity, which we call the world. Sometimes the world is only me, at other times everything except me.

GIVEN THE ABOVE

Yes, it does matter that I don't know for certain whether I went out or not. It's not something I should guess at, or have to work out from clues deduced or induced from the demeanours of our animals. Not knowing might mean that there's something going wrong with me, or my memory – not *or* my memory, I am my memory, therefore –

Here's what I'll do. I'll go out again, clock what's going on on the pavements between here and the Renaissance, note which waiter or waitress sees me at the door, which one brings my coffee, study every passer-by, keep on full alert as I walk home, and I'll – what? Yes, I'll check on the animals, their position and state of consciousness when I leave and register any changes when I come back, then straight up here and put it all down immediately.

I'm off now.

THE ABDUCTION OF TRIXY

And now I'm back and I'm buggered if I'm going to put down anything about being out. I remember it all quite clearly, every moment of it, it was all quite usual in the usual boring way, which is to say that it was all quite interesting in the usual interesting way – there was, for instance – oh, the bag lady, for instance. She stands outside Tesco's, holding out her tin cup in which she hopes you will put either money or cigarettes – I generally put in cigarettes, as I fear that she might spend the money on something that could harm her – when I put the cigarettes in her cup she says, 'Thank you very much, I'm really grateful for that,' and she says it in a dead little mutter, so that it in no way sticks to you, it's as if she doesn't see you, only the cigarettes going into her tin – the fingers around the tin, showing through half-gloves, are darkly stained with nicotine, the fingernails filthy – her whole outfit is a shamble of layers of clothing, but you can't tell which is on top of what, cardigans, sweaters, scarves going in and out of each other like wrapping cloths. She has a face that has sharp life in it, the dark eyes under the half-lowered lids move watchfully, you can see that she makes identifications, categorizes you in ways which aren't only commercial. We sometimes have conversations, it used to be about her dog, which I liked a lot, it was scrawny but not ill-fed, obviously devoted to her, and turned its face up and seemed to be listening to the conversation. We would talk for a while, she quite animatedly about her comings and goings, the dog looking up and listening, and I mainly asking questions – then I'd give her the cigarettes and her voice would change completely, and out would come the dead little mutter about gratitude, as if the moment we moved into the transaction we ceased to be two people who'd been talking, I became an unobserved giver, she a mechanical beggar, receiving. The little moment was quite unpleasant, really, the point of course being to remove embarrassment from the exchange, but actually importing something sullied and dishonourable into it – though I have no idea how either of us could have handled it any better, and it's preferable to her more intimate moments, as when she mutters out of the side of her mouth, as I pass her by, 'You look lovely with your hair like that' – this, I should say, when I've just had it cut, not styled or fashioned or *au bouffant* or whatever the phrase is, I get it cut twice a year, once in December or so, for Christmas, and once in July or August, the effect of it being traumatic both for me, because I feel vulnerable around the back of my neck and at the tops of my ears, and for those who are fond of me, who tend to rear back when they first see me, and to say things like, 'It's taken ten years off you', though what they really mean is that there's much, much more face than we're used to, possibly too much much more – but Annabelle, let me call the bag lady Annabelle, so that I don't keep calling her the bag lady, when she says, 'I like your hair that way', it makes her sound like something from the olden days, when ladies of the night spoke similar words under the street lamps, though of course the effect is unintentional, because Annabelle's a perfectly respectable bag lady, though more ambiguously so now than when she had the dog in her arms or at her feet – the dog, a terrier-like bitch, I can't remember her name, let's call her Trixy, was stolen from her by a smartly dressed middle-aged woman with a foreign accent. She approached Annabelle one morning and praised her for having such a loving and beautiful dog, and then the dog for being so loving and beautiful. She asked to be allowed to hold her and then asked whether Annabelle had had her spayed. Annabelle replied that she'd often thought about it, but really she never seemed to find the time, and probably didn't have enough money. 'Oh,' said the lady. 'How sad. How sad for you and for Trixy. Would you like me to arrange it for you? I know a vet who will do it cheaply – it will cost you nothing, I will pay whatever small sum – and Trixy will be back with you this afternoon, shall we say three, no, we shall say four o'clock, to make sure Trixy is fully recovered from the anaesthetic, so I will see you, we will see you at four o'clock here, on this spot, on the pavement', and away she went, bearing Trixy to her home, perhaps by way of the vet and perhaps not, depending on whether she wanted Trixy to have puppies or not. Her motives were probably clear to herself, she was saving the dog from Annabelle's seemingly louche and feckless lifestyle, and the question as to whether Trixy was content to live in Annabelle's lifestyle probably never occurred to her – or it may have, she may have considered all the moral pros and cons and come to her decision regretfully, as God is sometimes said to come to His. Annabelle put little posters up on the trees along Holland Park Avenue – 'Missing! Trixy was last seen in the company of a well-dressed lady with a foreign accent' sort of thing, and added at the bottom of the poster that she and her granddaughter were missing the dog very much. The granddaughter came as a great surprise to me, I had never thought of Annabelle as a likely mother, let alone grandmother, though once you accept the former, the latter is a perfectly reasonable proposition – and she does seem to have a partner – could he be a husband? – a man of the same indeterminate age as herself, with lanky legs, a narrow face, and long flaxen hair which he sometimes wears tied back in a pigtail –

IS THE GRANDDAUGHTER A BORE?

He has a touch of the dandy about him in a tattered sort of way, and likes to stride urgently along Holland Park Avenue, or lie on his side on the pavement, in front of what was once Harts and is now Tesco's, holding out a tin cup that you have to bend quite low down to, to put money in. He's an artist, when he's at work he sits cross-legged, doing light, lyrical but – to my eye – slightly insipid watercolours of beach scenes and woodland glades. He and Annabelle meet up from time to time and talk to each other. Sometimes they exchange coins, and one or other of them will go into the telephone kiosk opposite the Renaissance and behave mysteriously with the telephone and the coins, squatting with the telephone in hand, but not talking into it. I avert my eyes if they do it while I'm having coffee at my table, I feel that whatever they're doing, though highly visible through the windows, is also private and probably illegal. On the other hand they may simply be calling the granddaughter, squatting to get down to her size as a way of feeling closer to her – in which case, why not talk to her? Could it be that she's talking to them and they find her too boring – as children often are – to listen to, and so they squat there, holding the telephone away from themselves, until the money runs out. No, I'm sure the kinder explanation, that they're doing something illegal, is the likely one – I just can't work out what it is. But why am I on the subject of

Annabelle and her partner? – oh yes, to prove to myself that I went out – I shouldn't call her Annabelle and him 'her partner', he should be dignified with a name too, something Jamesian and floral to go with the aesthete in him – in summer he likes to wear shirts with roses and daisies on them, I seem to recall – rather than a name that represents the grubbier side of his personality, as represented by his appearance. I'm referring here to the nails on the fingers that clasp the cup, the texture of the ponytailed hair – so what about Hyacinth, as in Hyacinth Robinson, in *The Princess Casamassima*?- Hyacinth and Annabelle, yes, that makes for a pleasant-sounding couple.

MIDNIGHT

A feeling of inertia – a lump of flotsam, or is it jetsam I feel like, what is the difference? There is a difference – is flotsam what floats on the surface, and jetsam what's been tossed away, tossed into the waves to be washed this way and that? 'Flot' Old English for float, possibly, while 'jet' from the French *jeter*, to throw – well, that's me, that's what it feels like to be me, something thrown on the waters, a floater and a bobber – but thrown by whom? Fate? Circumstances? The ambition of others? My own ambition, which is what? Well, nothing more, really, than to sit here, doing this.

2 A.M.

I've just dropped my cigarette onto my shirt. I do this more and more, most of my shirts have brown streaks on them, or neat little holes – neat because I rub away the charred edges, in the hope that the neat little holes will appear deliberate, a fashion statement, but really I know, without Victoria having to tell me, that they look as if they've been made by dropped lighted cigarettes. Most of my trousers are similarly marked. Smoking is such a complicatedly dirty habit, staining and soiling and altogether ruining one's garments as well as one's body, and causing so many expenses in such a variety of ways that if I were sensible I would welcome its being banned, but I've only to read a letter in the papers from an anti-smoker or see a couple of them on television to feel that I should regard all stains and holes as wounds won in a fight to the death, though I admit that I'm frightened that one night I'll doze off, well, not exactly frightened, worried, merely worried, that one night I'll wake up in flames.

DAWN

Well, say I could go back, where then, and when? I suppose to Halifax, Nova Scotia, when I was eighteen. I'd stay there for a while, in fact for a decade or two, anyway long enough to learn that I didn't want to leave – but then it would have left me, wouldn't it? Gone on to become what it is today, a pleasant-looking town but where women (men too, I imagine) are forbidden to wear perfume in public places because, like cigarette smoke, it may cause offence to others, and with a beautiful harbour so polluted that you aren't allowed to swim in it. When I was eighteen I used to swim in the harbour every day in summer – the beach was only a hundred yards away, you opened the front door, crossed the road into the woods and followed one of the paths down to the sea – there was a deep shelf, so you could dive straight into the water, which was never warm but always so clean and fresh. Now humans endanger their lives by going into it, fish die in it.

PART THREE

MY PROJECT

Various things are going on that I ought to try writing about, but I always forget – not forget that they're happening or have just happened, but forget to move on to them. So now's the time, why not? Put down a sentence that will get you going – put down two sentences would be even better, because there are two distinct things – a) my book, *The Smoking Diaries*, is about to be published and b) my play, *The Old Masters*, is in rehearsal. So get down to it. Start with b).

HABIT BREAKING

The rehearsal room is in a church hall off Kensington Church Street and is actually within walking distance of here – not that I've actually walked it, Victoria drives me, or I take a taxi. It's a large, handsome room on the first floor and I can smoke in it. I sit on a chair beside another chair with an ashtray on it, and watch the actors, watch Harold at a long table directing the actors, watch and watch, sometimes saying something, but not often. I've grown out of the habit of attending rehearsals. When Harold and I first started together, on *Butley* in whenever it was, the summer of 1969 I think, he would encourage me to speak freely, which I began to do, and continued to do through the next five or six productions, more and more freely, in fact, even though I noticed that he would occasionally engage in a brief, dark-cheeked and scowling tussle with his patience, but always hearing me out, thinking about what I had said, then agreeing or disagreeing, and on we'd go – but when we got to the seventh, think, think – *Butley*, *Otherwise Engaged*, *The Rear Column*, *Close of Play*, *Quartermaine's Terms*, *The Common Pursuit* – that's six, the seventh – yes, it was the seventh, *Life Support*, I was in hospital while he was in rehearsal, and when I got out I was too ill to see the play until late in its tour, at Bath, I seem to remember. The next play we did was about three or four – no, I must check this, for the moment just say several, several years later – *The Late Middle Classes*, when I was almost but not quite well, but found myself not going into rehearsal much. A few times I started out for rehearsals, which were in Watford, but turned back quite early in the journey, though if I actually got as far as Watford Station I usually went on to the rehearsal room, where I sat awkward and tongue-tied, and left as soon as I could. So what started as an enforced abstinence through illness turned into a habit, really, and now emotionally I'm in the habit of not going to rehearsals of *The Old Masters*. This habit I force myself to break every single day. I cajole and bully myself out of the front door and into the car or taxi, and usually I ask Victoria or the taxi driver to drop me off a little way from the church hall, so that I can pretend to myself I'm not going to go in. I do now and then walk past the entrance to the driveway, walk around and around and up and down for a while – the weather has been lovely since the first day – smoking and thinking that I'm thinking, but really what I'm doing is not going in yet. In the end I never get in before three or four in the afternoon, and so only have to sit there through a couple of hours or so, which is still too long, by a couple of hours or so. It's not that it's boring, or that I'm inactive – I have to do cuts, some of them quite large, and a few small rewrites, there's always something going on to watch and think about and I do my best to do all that's required of me, but the difficulty is that – that – the truth is that I'm not really very interested. Not interested enough. Although there are many passing pleasures to be found in

HAROLD AND CO.

observing Harold's powers of concentration, for instance, and the clarity of his intelligence, his quick sympathy with the actors as well as the command of his presence. He says he's exhausted the moment he leaves, and quite tired in the morning when he gets up, but the moment he's there, in the rehearsal room, he feels galvanized, enjoys every minute – 'every bloody minute' – scarcely notices the time passing. The day's work over, the adrenalin drains away, and he feels tired and elderly again. Then of course it can never be dull watching actors like these at work, the cunning and expertise of Peter Bowles, the complete originality of Edward Fox – he is, in a sense, perfectly miscast, Berenson being a man of great mental agility with a tongue to match – 'If a panther could speak, he would speak like Berenson,' someone who knew him well said of him – emotionally mercurial, in all his aspects vain as well as arrogant – Edward is temperamentally the opposite, well, he has, like all of us, his own vanity and arrogance, but his thought processes as revealed in rehearsal are eccentric and seemingly spasmodic, his speech made up of half-sentences, strange, almost goofy smiles, uneasy gestures and brooding silences. Probably the only thing he has in common with Berenson is his size and his neatness of presence – what he is creating isn't in accord with historical reality, inasmuch as we have it, but a character unique to Edward and yet of absolute integrity within the terms of the play – unlike Berenson in almost all his aspects, he will give us the equivocal moral being that Berenson was – well, that my Berenson is – and a bafflingly perverse opponent for Duveen, as unlike Berenson as a character as Peter Bowles is unlike Edward as a rehearsing actor, Peter being methodical, detailed, openly fretful, his eye alert to contradictions in the text, his manner apparently easy and generous but also dogged, in fact positively stubborn – a question once raised is a question that he will make sure is returned to and returned to, however eager Harold and the other actors are to press on, until it has been solved to his satisfaction – which is when he has more than a sniff of how he will say the lines in performance weeks from now.

Peter and Edward treat each other with great respect, equal beasts of a different species, but have in common a care for outward appearances, even in rehearsals. Most actors in rehearsal turn up in loose-fitting old clothes, comfortable shoes. Peter and Edward, tall and dark, small and blond, are always immaculately dressed, formally dressed, in much the same style – tailored jackets, creased trousers, dapper shoes, shirt and tie, frequently waistcoats. Yesterday afternoon they both had neatly folded handkerchiefs protruding from their top pockets, like a pair of period philanderers – you expect them to be joined by Terry-Thomas, and Leslie Phillips in his heyday. I find the effect very charming, as I sit, slumped, pot-bellied, in my chair, wearing an open shirt over a half-open shirt, baggy trousers, espadrilles, cigarette hanging from my fingers, mouth half-open in a half-yawn, my proper companions Annabelle and Hyacinth, hanging about on a pavement outside Tesco's, is where I probably looked as if I should have been.

I've just remembered that Peter, Edward and I are all the same age, sixty-seven, Barbara Jefford is thereabouts or more so, Harold is more so – three actors, the writer and the director all between sixty-seven and seventy-five. The other two actors, Sally Dexter and Steven Pacey are three decades our junior. Is this desirable? And if so, to whom? And why?

These two, Sally Dexter and Steven Pacey, are young and therefore desirable – no, young and also desirable is what I intended to write. They are also talented actors, which makes them doubly desirable and are already playing their scenes together with great charm, and sexily – or, more interestingly, flirtatiously. What is lovely about Sally in the part is how versatile she is as a woman – girlish, maternal, sisterly, a mistress, a daughter, a wife, depending on the immediate needs of the men (and the woman) she's with, almost a perfect female in Goethe's accounting, plus the gift for deception and a weakness for jewellery, which make her in fact more perfect than Goethe's perfect woman – a woman without a weakness being too frightening to contemplate, a monster, inevitably – what would sex with such a woman be like, I wonder? How could you make love to a woman without a weakness? Probably she'd have to make love to you, perfectly? Would this mean, with infinite variety? But she'd have to desire you surely, and if she desired you she couldn't be perfect, you would be her weakness – well, that might work.

ON A HIGHER LEVEL

The German professor of German at Dalhousie University fifty years ago was Frau Doktor Richter, the widow of the original professor of German, who had been knocked down and killed while cycling towards his classes one spring morning some, oh, let's say sixty years ago – very few people bicycled in Halifax, Nova Scotia, in those days, so I suppose the driver was taken by surprise, as was the good Doktor.

Frau Doktor Richter was almost certainly the only person in the whole
of Nova Scotia, possibly the whole of Canada, qualified to take over his
position. She was in her late sixties when I attended her seminars, stout
and serious and handsome, with twinkling blue eyes and a quick smile
and no sense of humour – though this is probably unfair, as I only
understood her when she spoke English, and her English, though
accurate, was slow and pains-taking – pains-giving too, when returning
one of my completely bogus essays composed in a language that was
mainly guesswork – I used to put an *ich* and *er* at the end of English
words, and sometimes I spoke English with a thick German accent
taken from American movies about the Gestapo – the only written
phrase in which I had any confidence, and so employed repeatedly, was
'*Aber das kann ich nicht*' which means, or I hope it means, 'But that I
do not know.' Her passion in life was for the literature of her country,
and her passion in that literature was for Goethe, whose poetry and
novels I found it difficult to understand, as my reading German wasn't
much of an advance on my writing and speaking German, and Frau
Doktor Richter insisted that we read everything in the original.
Fortunately she conducted the most interesting parts – the biographical
parts – of her seminars in translation, first a long paragraph in German,
then a few short sentences of paraphrase in English, which is how I
came to discover that Goethe at seventy had some kind of relationship
with a girl of seventeen, whose name I can't remember but might come
back to me. What kind of relationship? I asked Frau Doktor. 'It vos a
ferry luffink relationship,' she said, twinkling at me solemnly through
her glasses. 'Very loving?' 'Ferry luffink, yess.' Everyone in the seminar
waited for the next question, which I felt obliged to ask. 'Was it a sexual
relationship?' 'Yess,' she said, 'yess, it voss. But only on ze higher leffel!'
At that age – I was eighteen – I had only had sex on one level, and it
was a pretty low one, since it was with myself, but I knew instinctively
that Frau Doktor Richter was making the best of a bad job, or a good
job if you were Goethe, who was the first old man I ever envied. I wish
I could remember the girl's name – it was oddly ugly, even when
spoken by the soft-voiced Frau Doktor.

Her name was Vulpius. Kristina Vulpius. I'm pretty sure that was it,
although probably not how it is spelt.

TOOTHACHE

If I'd been told then, at the end of the seminar, that one day I'd be sitting in rehearsals of my own play with a famous writer directing in it a clutch of highly regarded actors, would I have been envious? – well, that's absurd, how can one envy the self that is fifty years away, and that one's going to end up with or as anyway? What I really mean I suppose, is the other way round, how I envy that eighteen-year-old, and wish he hadn't ended up as me, sitting in rehearsals etc. in the afternoons of the spring of 2004 – or indeed sitting in my study, writing this. I'd like everything else to be the same, my context, my environment, my world – Victoria, George, Toto, Errol and Tom, Harold, Antonia, all my friends – but at the centre of it a different, kinder, more intelligent, more energetic – that above all – more energetic me, who had behind him a different lifetime, a lifetime of usefulness, of practical goodness – not that there's been much theoretical goodness either – and large-spiritedness, so much of me feels ungrown, so much of me unkind – but it's never too late, it is always said, never too late to change. Oh yes, it is. But that doesn't mean that it's too late to do good, find out where help is wanted and give it. No, it isn't, but given what I know of me, of my inertia and feebleness of will, any excuse will do, even my vices – yes, I would certainly go forth and do good in the world, if only my vices would let me. Alas, I am what I am, alas. Know what I mean?

I'm writing down these thoughts because they tend to intrude more and more often, and not in searingly painful stabs like flashes of guilt, but in a dull and aching, almost boring way, like an old toothache that has returned without your noticing it really – and then it is sapping away at you, you pat it and stroke it with your tongue, it subsides, but still throbbing, and suddenly there it is again – this is what goes on in me morally, if it is moral, during rehearsals, so that though I take in all the pleasant things, like the actors and the director going about their work, enjoy the jokes, the rides back in Harold's taxi when we discuss the text, for instance – through it all the moral toothache is throbbing away until it is all I really think about, why am I not a good man, why have I not done better, why am I sitting here chain-smoking in a rehearsal of my play, lazily surveying all the excuses for not having done good in my life – oh yes, because of my vices etc. I suppose the soft war between the entertainment of the rehearsals and the discomfort of the moral tooth settles into a truce, which is really indifference, when it comes down to it.

AND A GLIMPSE OF THE UNIQUE REAL THING

at least until Barbara Jefford has a scene, then I become riveted, even at this stage of rehearsals, I can't remember seeing anything like it in a rehearsal room – I don't mean that she's doing anything astounding, in fact I suspect that I'm the only one who sees it so clearly, not because I've any special gifts, or am more finely attuned to acting than the others, but because I wrote the part, I know Mary for what she is as a character, and Barbara Jefford isn't impersonating her, acting her – when she's fluffing her lines, fumbling for a word, she is emotionally so straight and direct that she already seems to be Mary Berenson, it's Mary Berenson that can't find the word, has lost the line –

So that's b) done with, on to a).

TRUE COMPLIMENTS?

It's hard to tell with books, because no curtain goes up, no lights go down, reviews start to appear before you're actually on the shelves (or shelf), and the publishing party, launch, launch it's called, can take place before or after the official publication date, which therefore seems quite arbitrary, and has to be remembered as a date, which I can never do – but there was a party, launch, and it took place this evening, in a room at the top of the Groucho Club. It wasn't a small room, but it seemed so because there were so many people in it, all of them friendly and shouting quite loudly. At a certain point, quite early on, my editor, Ian Jack, made a muttering speech in Scotty – it was very flattering, from what I could make out of it, too flattering to put down here, and he looked sincere – I suppose he had to, I mean it would have been a poor show to have one's editor speaking well of you in a manner that was noticeably insincere, of course the great thing about Scotty is that it's a language in which it appears impossible to tell lies, which is why so many of our most successful current politicians speak it, whether they're from Scotland or not – would Blair be an interesting exception, I don't know whether he's Scotty in the sense that I am (in the blood but not the bones) but I do know that he was educated there, even so there isn't a trace of it in his speech, which is why he produces the opposite of the usual effect, his every sentence sounding like a lie even when he's telling the truth, although I don't know how we'd know he was telling the truth – how do you distinguish between sentences that are actual lies and sentences that merely sound like lies? – he has the liar's trick, too, of widening his eyes when delivering his real as well as his bogus lies, so you get no help in that direction, whereas if he'd taken advantage of his education to learn Scotty he'd probably also have learnt to shift his eyes about when speaking it, thus reinforcing the appearance of truth – Ian Jack, for instance, in his little speech about me, seemed to manage the almost impossible feat, in a room jam-packed with people, of not looking a single person in the eye, his eyes shifted about at stomach level, or perhaps a jot lower – of course I may have got it all wrong, perhaps almost nobody in the room believed what he was saying about me but me. Anyway when he finished he gestured to me, and I said a few words – very few. Enough to make up three short sentences, in which I complimented myself on having Granta for a publisher, Ian Jack for an editor and Victoria for a wife. I don't know whether my eyes shifted and my accent had a burr in it, but I was telling the truth on all counts. Nobody else spoke. The party went on. We came home. That's all I'm going to put down about *The Smoking Diaries*, for one thing there is a far more pressing matter to consider –

HIS CHARMS

Now in my view he is perfect – fat, round, black, long-haired, his eyes are little saucers and his walk a dainty waddle. He started life with us as a stray, his first appearance, via the dog flap in the kitchen door, was under the kitchen table, his next was on the kitchen table – he wasn't chased to either of these positions, in fact George, our only dog at this time, accepted his presence from the start, seeming almost to usher him in through the flap, and would often be sitting at his side when Victoria or I, or both together, came into the kitchen, and though Tom, our elderly but dapper – now very old, and still dapper – short-haired female cat with white splodges on her chin, and on her sides and her ankles, hated him, she kept out of his way, as if he were the landlord and she the sitting tenant. At first we shooed him out, thinking that such a portly, indeed pampered-looking, creature must have a substantial residence close by, and that he was merely slumming in our kitchen, or had taken a barrier-breaking fancy to George, but our shooings never flustered him, he seemed to be exiting through the flap by choice, as if remembering an appointment, and sometimes the flap would still be swinging from his departure when he re-entered, and settled comfortably under a chair. Eventually we found him in other rooms, the sitting room, the bedroom, nestled in one of George's beds, or if he was in the kitchen he would be polishing off one of Tom's meals, or eating with George from George's bowl. I knew from the very first encounter that he was here to stay, and I admit that I wanted him to stay. I admired him for his insouciance, his implacable will, his evident sweetness of disposition, and his good looks, and though I agreed with Victoria that his habit of spraying in the areas which he thought Tom had laid claim to was disgusting and unhygienic, I persuaded her that with certain amendments of a surgical kind –. So it was settled. But before we took him to the vet, which we looked on as a sort of adoption process, we put up posters on trees and lamp-posts in the neighbourhood, describing him and advising where he could be found. They stayed up for two weeks, and when no one came forward, we took him across the road to the vet and made him ours. Now he sleeps on our bed with George and Toto, allows George to hump him before meal-times, allows Tom a fairly free passage and was among the first to welcome Toto into the house – when he's not lying nose to nose with George, he's likely to be lying nose to nose with Toto, or sitting at my feet in the study. He would like to sit on my lap, I know, but I'm allergic to his long hair – when I stroke him, which I can't resist doing, my hand comes up in welts, and my eyes run, but apart from that he is, as I say, perfect, and I adore him.

Nevertheless, nevertheless – I am not going to say that I've stopped loving him, but I find his behaviour harder and harder to accept, it's beginning to affect my feelings, to tinge them with a certain amount of revulsion. He's just come into the room, has gone under the desk, is brushing against my ankles – so I can't possibly go on with this.

A STAR IS BORN

I'm currently – even as I write this – being filmed. There's a camera on me, being held and pointed by a tall, pleasant, smiling young man called Patrick. Crouched beside him Margy, the director, holds a metal box with a screen in it which shows her what Patrick the cameraman is filming. Behind Patrick stands Andy, a shortish young man, also generally smiling, who is recording the sounds of my typewriter, the keys of which are clogged from months of disuse. I am in my study, at my desk, at my typewriter, pretending to be me, doing something I always do, although I haven't actually done it for a while – I wonder how long they'll want me to go on doing it, I find it slightly umiliating – what does it mean to feel umiliated? – to umiliate yourself? – I'm writing umiliate because the 'h' on this machine, one of my old Olympia portables, is beginning to stick – now I'm getting te old rytm back, te singalong of te typewriter, the trut is tat it's suc a long time since I sat at one, aving mainly worked by long and on yellow pages for my recent plays and diaries, and so te abit, wic I tougt would be te abit of a lifetime as, it would appear, would it not, become lost to me, but ten again ere it is growing and saping sentences wit every downward stomp of my two fingers. O, I've certainly lost my old ligtness of touc, well, it wasn't particularly ligt, certainly not dainty, but a great deal less stompy tan tis – I ave the feeling, toug, that now the 'h' is beginning to sort itself out – my insistent beating down on it is getting it used to stamping its mark on the paper and then releasing itself, if slightly sluggishly, back into its slot – here we go, look at thathhhhhere we go, I'm off with a flouris of hhhhhhhhhs. Well, I'm off camera now, they've gone, Margy the director, and Andy the sound man, and Patrick, the cameraman, gone to their world of light, and I alone sit lingering here, a private man again, in sole possession of his study, his pad and pen, his 'h' and his life.

ERECT IN THE GARRICK CLUB

It all began in the Wolseley, when I joined Victoria and some friends for dinner – she'd come from the theatre, I forget what she'd seen, and I'd come from home where I'd been doing I forget what. I pushed through the doors, as they used to say in the sort of books I once loved, I pushed through the doors of the restaurant, stood gaping around, and had just spotted in a far corner the bushy hair above the beautiful and beloved face when Alan Yentob sprang in front of me, seized my hand and stroked it, saying that this very evening, a mere few hours ago, in fact, he'd finished reading *The Smoking Diaries*. 'I'm sure we can do something with it,' he said, speaking from under the hat of the Head of Culture – I forget his exact title at the BBC – 'What do you think, would you like us to do something with it?' I said yes, I'd love them to do something with it, as long as it didn't consist of my appearing on one of those panel discussions with the sort of people who use words like 'comfortable', 'uncomfortable' – 'I don't feel comfortable with this' – 'It makes me uncomfortable' – 'this' or 'it' not being a chair, or a hat or a thumb, but someone else's attitude, behaviour, piece of writing – 'I just', yes, there's usually a 'just', functionally strange but effective – it manages to intensify without in any way defining the moral power of not being 'comfortable', the implication being, I suppose, that these people possess a balance so delicately moral that it can only express itself in that softly self-centred way – a bit like Lady Bertram in *Mansfield Park* when talking about her physical well-being, but at least we know what it is (her sofa) Lady Bertram is making herself comfortable on, while these people, yes, let me call them 'these people!' are making themselves comfortable on their vanity and your good manners – we never say back to them, 'Well, if you're not comfortable with it, why don't you adjust your position?' because we know that in fact they're saying to us, 'I'm not comfortable with it, so kindly adjust your position' – of course, I didn't go on to Alan Yentob about 'these people' and 'comfortable' and so forth, I merely said I didn't want to be on a book panel, or have *The Smoking Diaries* touched in any way by a book panel. 'No, no,' he said, 'a proper programme. I know there's a programme in it somewhere.'

He took down my telephone number on the sort of slip of paper you find in a corner of your jacket pocket three months later and put it in his jacket pocket. 'I'll call you,' he said, 'in the next few days.'

Victoria asked me what I'd been talking to Alan Yentob about. I said, oh, something about wanting to do a programme on *The Smoking Diaries*, he says he's going to phone again in the next few days to discuss it, but he won't – I was pretty sure of this, as I've dished out my telephone number to many people over the last few years, some of whom wrote it down in impressive-looking Filofaxes, others punched it impressively into their mobiles, both lots passing it straight on to various commercial enterprises, judging by the number of unsolicited phone calls I've received from double-glazing people, for instance, which I suppose is better than the sort of stuff I've started getting through the email – offers of penis-expanding drugs, vastly superior to Viagra, they claim, delivering an erection within minutes and sustaining it for four days. But how would one cope with a four-day erection? One would have to get a whole new wardrobe of loose garments, or stay in one's home, probably confine oneself to one's study, though perhaps I could go to the Garrick. Could they black-ball you for strutting about with an erection. But why strut? Why not saunter? – saunter about with an erection for four whole days at the Garrick Club, cut some ice at last, though not necessarily. On one of the few occasions I've had lunch there I sat at the long table next to a famously elegant, in clothes and prose, novelist, who got up in the middle of someone else's sentence, announced that he needed a piss, unzipped his fly as if he were going to take it there, over his, or possibly my, *crème brûlée*, then headed towards the door, half-cocked. He returned a few minutes later, zip still down, fly gaping, I noticed that both his shoes were wet, so I wondered, I wondered – well, we shall find out, as Larkin says in . . . 'The Old Fools' i'm pretty sure.

THE IMPORTANCE OF PEEING IN THE RIGHT PLACE, AT THE RIGHT TIME

Alan Yentob, who I knew wasn't going to phone me in the next day or so, phoned me in the next day or so, and we arranged to have dinner, plus wives, at an Italian restaurant above a pub somewhere off Notting Hill Gate. A good choice for food, a lousy one for conversation. It was crowded, and the acoustics, as is the fashion in London these days, were dreadful – you had to strain to hear a sentence from the person next to you, and had to shout to make yours heard it was nevertheless a relaxed and pleasant dinner, Alan's wife, Philippa, charming to look at, charming to try to hear – the play of her features etc. when she said how much she'd enjoyed *The Smoking Diaries*, if it was *The Smoking Diaries* she'd enjoyed. Alan outlined his idea for a programme, which would consist of conversations with me, intermingled with lots of readings aloud by me of passages by me, and perhaps visits to some of the locations – the book starts in Barbados, I pointed out, in one of the world's most charming hotels – no, he said, the BBC couldn't run to that, besides we didn't have the time, he already had the dates for the programme, it would be transmitted in the first week of June, so we'd have to start making it straight away, he'd introduce me to the director he had in mind, a talented and intelligent young woman he was sure I'd like, we'd work out a schedule, could I be free from next week on? I said I would clear my diary of its empty spaces immediately. From then on we bellowed and mimed our way through other matters, mutual friends, past experiences, among them a film he'd commissioned me to write, called *Unnatural Pursuits*, in which Alan Bates played me, right down to my chain-smoking, my pigeon-toed gait and my wheezy laugh, as I followed the fortunes of one of my plays from London to New York by way of Los Angeles and Dallas. There is a scene in a hotel in Dallas when I'm slumped in my bedroom at seven in the morning trying to drink away my hangover with a bottle of champagne. A piano strikes up, discordantly and as if in my skull. I totter out to the landing, stare down into the lobby. A group of Texans in stetsons, dinner jackets and long dresses are gathered around the piano, about to sing. I raise my glass to fling it down at them, open my mouth to shout an obscenity just as they launch into 'The Yellow Rose of Texas' and I find myself, to my astonishment, joining in – yes, Alan, hungover, bawling 'The Yellow Rose of Texas' down into the lobby of the Hyatt Hotel in Dallas at seven in the morning, is one of my favourite moments in both our careers, and it came about because Alan Yentob and I had happened to be standing in adjacent urinals at a BAFTA function, and as conversation is mandatory in these circumstances, he asked me if there was anything I'd like to write for the BBC. So if you want to see yourself on the television screen, either as yourself or as impersonated by an actor of great wit, charm and style, get a stall next to Alan Yentob in a BAFTA lavatory, or stand gaping in a restaurant until he springs in front of you.

I JUSTIFY MY DRIVING HABITS

It's a sunny afternoon, and I've just come back from the churchyard at the end of our street, where I sat on my favourite bench and answered questions put to me by Alan Yentob, who was very relaxed and gentle except for a small patch when he probed away at my driving arrangements – my arrangements being that Victoria drives me when I need to be driven. He pointed out how in my book I describe Victoria driving herself and all the animals down to our cottage in Suffolk, while I travelled down by train, first-class smoker. He seemed to find this in some way unfair on Victoria, a lot of people do, but should they bother to ask Victoria herself, she would explain that the last person she wants on a long car journey is me – well, perhaps not the last person, she wouldn't want a car-jacker, for example, but I'm the last person among the people she knows well. I'm impatient, irritable, and fill the car with my smoke, so obviously she prefers driving along listening to an opera and talking to her companions of choice, the animals. As for driving me about London, that's an entirely different matter, a source of pride to her, as if, really, I were a large dog, a bloodhound or a beagle, perhaps, apart of course from the cigarette, though, come to think of it, beagles have an infamous connection with the tobacco industry, involuntary chain-smokers used to establish a link between smoking and cancer. I'm against banning smoking, but I'm for banning scientists who force dogs to smoke, I'm for jailing them, actually.

I can't remember whether the interview/conversation with Alan Yentob followed the lines of the paragraph above, from Victoria's driving me, the rights and wrongs of it, to smoking beagles, but it was rhapsodic in that sort of way, but given – I hope – a sense of purpose by Alan Yentob's, well, rather bloodhoundy or beagly manner, tracking a scent of a thought or an argument even if it looped in haphazard circles and brought us back to the side of where we began.

HOIST BY MY OWN PETARD

The most difficult thing about my reading aloud to the camera is that I have to smoke, and to smoke all the time, a matter of continuity, as I always light a cigarette at the beginning of a passage – it's called *The Smoking Diaries*, after all, and as the publishers, Granta, have with great enterprise issued books of matches with the title and my name on it, I'm anxious to get them on camera as often as possible, striking the matches sideways for maximum exposure, then holding the match-book casually towards the camera as I lift the lighted match to the cigarette between my lips, a manoeuvre which, having used a lighter for the last thirty years, I'm not very expert at. I often blow the match flame out before I've lit the cigarette and have to do it over again – but once I've started to smoke, this is the point, I'm committed, I can't be seen to be smoking at the beginning of a sentence and then, when the filming stops suddenly because, for instance, I can't think of a way to end the sentence, be without a cigarette when the filming begins again we would have a brief but bewildering passage in which I'd be smoking, then not smoking, then smoking – viewers will wonder what is going on, then think the conversation is completely phoney, which it is, at least in the pretence of flowing seamlessly along – so, so, so having always to have a cigarette on the go is beginning to have the effect of aversion therapy, really, eyes smarting, throat dry and raw, head aching, stomach acidy – hoist by my own petard is one of the phrases that springs to mind – I had a cigarette between my lips even when I walked up the street to have my usual coffee at the Renaissance, Patrick the cameraman running backwards in front of me, Margy running backwards beside me out of frame. Normally I find it difficult to walk far without wheezing to a stop, but for some reason, when a slow, stately gait, with pauses, would have been the most convenient style, I found myself pattering along in my espadrilles at three times my normal speed, and all the time puff-puff on the cigarette – then back twenty yards because I'd zipped past the camera without realizing, so another cigarette, more puffing and pattering – during one of the botched attempts to keep the camera and Margy in front of me, a man who was standing by the bus stop, vaguely taking me in, then noticing the camera, then connecting me to the camera, spat at me – he was rather seedy-looking, it's true, with some wispy blond stuff on his chin that wasn't quite a beard and wearing battle fatigues, are they called? – khaki trousers with what looked like camouflage patches on them – a lumber-jacket sort of shirt, altogether seedy-looking, military-style aggressive and spitting at me. I felt that I had nothing in common with him at all, and yet understood completely why he wanted to spit at a figure who looked as louche as himself but went around with a camera trained on him, from the belief that not a minute of his life should go unrecorded for posterity, and furthermore must have had the funds to ensure that it wouldn't be, who did I think I was, who do I think I am? On top of which the waiters at the Renaissance didn't like the camera either, perhaps they thought I was an investigative reporter who had been undercover and was now emerging to expose them as – as what? I finally persuaded them that the camera was for me, not them, and was allowed to sit down. They then brought me the wrong coffee, the 'they' here being the indignant pronoun, because the waiter concerned who had brought me the right coffee – a small espresso in a large cup, a jug of hot water on the side – day after day for months, now brought me a revoltingly thick-foamed cappuccino. Instead of sipping my usual sophisticated coffee in my usual relaxed and sophisticated manner, I sat stirring what looked like a child's pudding while gazing in an appalled way at what would be for the audience nothing in particular. How would they know that in fact it was at Patrick the cameraman standing in the middle of the road with his camera aimed at me, and seemingly on the verge of taking a step forward under a bus coming down the avenue, or backward under a bus coming up the avenue. Let's hope they decide not to use that bit of film. And also the bit of film they shot of me in the study, when I thought they'd finished. I was slumped in the armchair, and patting my stomach, which felt and looked rather bloated, when from some instinct I turned my face and, yes, there he was, with his beard and his camera and his pleasant smile, filming. Tomorrow – something's happening tomorrow, fortunately I can't remember what it is. I'll take a sleeping pill and see if there's some cricket on television, there's bound to be cricket somewhere in the world where it's not three in the morning, our time.

EXKIEWS MY VUSE

A taxi arrived this afternoon to take me to rehearsals. I was surprised to see it, as I hadn't consciously ordered it, but I suppose I shouldn't have been further surprised to find Margy already in it, along with Andy the sound man and Patrick the cameraman and his camera. They had a newspaper for me to pretend to be reading – the *Guardian*, of course – and had got permission from the driver for me to smoke. I wanted only to pretend to read the *Guardian*, but inevitably found myself reading the sort of article that is precisely the reason I never read the *Guardian*. When we got to the rehearsal room, I had to wait in the taxi while they arranged themselves so that they could shoot me getting out, then they shot me going up the stairs, then pushing the door open, then they went away and I went in – there was Harold at the table, staring down at a script which he was tapping with his finger like a schoolmaster, and Peter Bowles and Edward Fox standing in front of him, like schoolboys who had been caught cheating. 'What have you been up to?' he asked, as he always does – an exciting formulation, I find, suggesting activities he couldn't conceivably expect me to confess to. 'Nothing much,' I said, 'just doing this BBC thing –' 'BBC thing? What BBC thing?' – he has an extraordinary memory, able to recall passages of poetry, Shakespeare, not passages, merely, but pages, I envy him the gift enormously, thinking how useful it would be if ever I were taken hostage – all I've got to keep me sane in captivity are fragments, most of which have only stuck because I hate them so much – 'Sir, no man's enemy forgiving all, but will his negative inversion be prodigal' – think of that running through your head time after time, as you struggle to recall the first line of a poem you love – and if at last you manage to get going with 'Busy old fool, unruly Sun,/Why dost thou thus' and you romp along to 'Nor hours, days, months, which are the rags of time' something sidles in, and you go – 'Which are the rags of time, that with this strange exkiews? Pardoned Kipling and his views/And will pardon Paul Caud-elle- uh/Pardons him for writing welle-uh' and you check yourself and go back, 'Time that with this strange ex-cuse –/Pardoned Kipling and his vuse –/And will pardon Paul Claudel/Pardons him for writing wel'. It's hopeless, you realize, you can't get it to rhyme properly without mangling the last words of each line, whichever way you go at it, but on at it you'll go and on, writhing in your captivity, struggling to make rhyme and reason – consider the meaning of those two lines, see a classical statue, TIME holding out a PARDON to three figures bending in supplication at her feet, Kipling, Yeats and Paul Claudel, each carrying a basket of VIEWS, peeping out like malformed babes – it's called personification, I think – EARTH, receive an honoured GUEST – best room, long stay – William YEATS laid to rest de dum de dum de dum de dah! The lines usurp all the lines by other poets you cherish, entangle you in frustration and ugly thoughts, better hope that you succumb quickly to Stockholm syndrome, come to share your captors' literary favourites, might be educational if they're Muslims, they'll pack your head with all those beautiful passages from the Koran that Mr Blair reads to himself every night, and then they'll saw it off in front of a camera. Perhaps Margy and Alan Yentob have something like that in mind for me, Alan says that the end of the programme is going to be unusual, and I've become very obedient, so if they ordered me, now Simon, time to kneel down, we'll put something over your eyes and around your wrists, now push your head forward a little, there's a good Simon, and Alan will –

AND SEATED AT THE END OF AN AISLE

Oh yes, Harold's extraordinary memory for lines – he has the gift, actor's gift, no, it's more than an actor's gift, it's no doubt not unique to Harold, but he's the only person I know who has it to the extent that he has it, and it may be a condition of his capacious, long-range memory that he has trouble remembering the answers you gave to questions he asked only yesterday – 'What BBC thing?' is a good example – I'd been into the BBC thing with him quite a few times, because I knew that at some point Alan Yentob and Margy will want to involve Harold himself or get his permission to involve the production – how could they not? After all, at the centre of the film of *The Smoking Diaries* is a wretch who's just put a turkey called *The Holy Terror*, on a West End stage and might shortly be putting on another West End stage another turkey, called *The Old Masters*, whose first night falls on the last day of filming – so for one thing they need to persuade Harold to let them into the theatre, to capture the audience's response at the curtain call, to follow us about beforehand and afterwards – It's unpleasant to write this, it brings the event nearer, the lights going down, the audience rustling and heaving like a small sea, and there are the reviewers, sitting on the aisles, like school prefects and rodents – I can't think of any rodents that sit on aisles, so let's leave it at school prefects.

DIFFERENT MOODS, DIFFERENT TENSES

Victoria's going to bed, and I'm doing this. Let's put it in the present tense, to help me remember.

So here we are, Victoria and Antonia and I, walking down Panton Street, having come into it from around the corner and down the street, whatever it's called, where there's a wine bar. It's a loathly wine bar, everyone seems to enter it shouting and already drunk and sitting solitary and dark in its unsavoury hurly-burly is Harold, at a table in a corner, with an opened bottle of white wine and some glasses, waiting for us. I went to the bar and ordered a Diet Coke, which they served from a tap into a tankard-sized glass, and then threw into it ice and plastic lemon-rind in order to kill off the effervescence without cooling the liquid, I suppose – it was warm and fetid and looked as if something frog-like might stick its head above the surface. I left it on the counter with an emphatic gesture of disgust and went to the table, where Harold spoke calmly through the din about the actors, he said that they were in 'excellent nick, really looking forward to the evening' etc., swallowed a few times as he always does when he's nervous – you actually see his Adam's apple bob up and down – drained off his glass, and said that we'd better go. Yes, we agreed, we'd better go. So up the road we went, around the corner into Panton Street. Suddenly, in Panton Street, running backwards in front of us were the now, to me, familiar figures of Margy the director, Patrick the cameraman and Andy the sound man – I wore on my face, for the camera's sake, the most unlikely first-night smile of my life, my mouth stretching, it would have been from ear to ear, in the old phrase, if my ears weren't so far from my lips. Waiting outside the theatre was a pack of newspaper photographers etc. They spotted the playwright, and therefore star of the evening, Simon Gray with his lady-wife, Victoria, on his arm, ran towards them, then accelerated past them to the Pinters, who obliged in their respective styles, Harold by turning his head away, Antonia by smiling absent-mindedly. The autograph hounds followed the photographers to the Pinters, not so much pushing past the playwright and his lady-wife as shoving them sideways, into the gutter.

Margy and Patrick the cameraman stuck to their drab task, which was to follow us into the lobby, and then down the little hall into a private room, where they left us. Harold and Antonia arrived a few minutes later, most of their clothes intact. We sat not saying very much, although there was some coughing, because I filled the room with smoke at astonishing speed, almost as soon as I lit up, in fact. The stage manageress, whose name is Pea – 'What's your real name?' I asked her once. 'I'm not telling you,' she said. 'Why do you think I changed it?' – so in her past is a name to which she prefers the name Pea – came in to announce that the show was about to begin. Harold had secured the box that was directly off the private room, so he and Antonia had only to move a few steps. I had secured a couple of seats at the back of the dress circle, rodents', no, prefects' seats on an aisle, close to an exit, which took some getting to, we just made it as the house lights were going down. I picked out Barbara Jefford making her way to her on-stage chair, sitting down, stage lights up, and there she was, in the sunshine in the garden of I Tatti, as settled as if she'd been there for at least an hour. She clutched at her stomach, she groaned, and we were off.

In the interval we sat in the private room with our drinks and told each other that it seemed to be going OK, that the actors were on song but Edward not actually singing, as is his tendency when tired or under stress, that the lights were on cue, etc., and so forth. Realizing that the room was entirely without any form of ventilation, which explained the speed at which I was filling it with smoke again, I went outside, pushing my way deafly through the crowd in the lobby onto the pavement, and then along to a pub nearby where I discovered a television set showing a European Cup match, a small set on a high shelf – one had to stand with one's head at an awkward angle to see the screen. I can't remember which sides were playing, but one was dashing, the other stubborn, which suggests that it might have been the Czechs (dashing) against almost any other team. I made it back just after the second act had started. It was beginning to rain lightly but with purpose as I went into the theatre –

LIGHTS DOWN

We folded the actors into our arms, thanking, congratulating, kissing, fondling, fawning – these little ceremonies of mutual devotion are often sneered at – luvvies at their luvvying – but really if you observe them with an anthropological or zoological eye, they would be seen to be no different in kind from the rituals practised by George and Toto and Errol when they're gathered together in the kitchen for their dinner, for instance – they rub noses and dance under the table and at a certain point, as tins are being opened and packages shaken, George (spayed bitch) will mount Errol (neutered tom) and simulate fornication – they both simulate it, actually – Errol throbbing, heaving and squealing under George bucking, heaving, eyes rolling – well, I don't mean anything like this actually happens backstage, after a first night, at least not that I've witnessed, nor even its equivalent, my point is only that there are moments in the lives of humans, as in the lives of animals, when something of consequence – the arrival or non-arrival of bowls of food for the latter, bad or glowing reviews for the former – is nervously but keenly anticipated, and physical contact with one's colleagues is needed – George fucking Errol, Harold hugging Barbara Jefford, Toto nuzzling George, Edward Fox rocking in Sally Dexter's arms, I taking Peter Bowles by the shoulders – the instincts of the herd, really, however gruesome. I wonder if we could make gruesome into a collective noun, a gruesome of producers, for instance, was fondling a coven of critics –

WHAT BECAME OF A TRANSITUS 'C' SCHOOLBOY

Most of the audience were gone, but Stephen Lushington, my old housemaster, not in the true sense 'old' – though well over eighty, he's many steps to take before getting anywhere near his chronological age – stood with his wife, Beatrice, who is blind, sheltering in the doorway, wondering how to get to the party, to which, not having foreseen rain, they'd intended to walk – as they were my guests, and I'd already put them through two hours of my writing, I urged them to have first use of our car, which would come back and collect Victoria and me when it had dropped them. Now there's a period of confusion here I can't work out how we finally made it to the party, but we went with Harold and Antonia, so I imagine they must have seen us sheltering in the doorway, picked us up, and taken us with them to the church of St Martin-in-the-Field, in St Martin's Lane, to the crypt of the church, an odd venue for a theatrical party, which seemed even odder when we stepped out of the car, and Antonia led the way through the drizzle down a short path that was littered with winos, beggars, the defeated – cheerfully defeated inasmuch as they raised themselves up, in biblical fashion, and advised Antonia not to go in there – 'No, don't go in there, me darlin'' – what used to be called a crone cried out – much laughter and raisings of bottles, cans, skirts and trouser legs – it could have been from a Buñuel film, *The Discreet Charm of the Bourgeoisie* – except the merriment wasn't sinister or even satirical, it was affectionate, as if we were four rather endearing outcasts, simple-minded, to be protected from a world of which we knew nothing, and sent back to our own world, of chandeliers and champagne –– we retreated to the car, and were driven seven yards or so to the next path, then passed through a door that looked exactly like the door we'd been warned against. We had some difficulty making the entrance that we would have liked, playwright and director and wives, come in out of the rain to celebrate much-deserved whatever it was going to be, because we were blocked by a powerful young West Indian – possibly, from his accent, Barbadian – who demanded to see our invitations. We didn't have invitations – why would we require invitations, we were the author, we were the director, Harold explained in short, stabbing sentences. 'Be that as it may,' the young man said, he had been ordered not to let anyone in without an invitation, he was perfectly polite and perfectly adamant, but he was beginning to fall into a bouncer's posture, hunched, arms swinging free – 'To hell with that!' Harold said, and with an unbounceable strut went past him, the rest of us sidling quickly after him before he vanished into the shadows of this low-ceilinged, ill-lit vault where once, from the feel of it, they must have stored bodies before burial – Alan Yentob and Margy and the cameraman and the sound man were already there, and followed me as I shook hands, kissed proffered cheeks, proffered my own – the ones on my face – for kisses, generally luvvied about, in other words. There was a nice moment when Stephen Lushington and I were arranged with our arms around each other's shoulders, smiling into each other's faces, like a couple in a newspaper article – 'Found after a fifty-year search, missing housemaster' or 'Found after fifty years' search, missing Transitus C schoolboy'.

THREE OUT OF SEVEN

I had a few sharp words, unfilmed, I hope, with a producer figure who jumped straight, without a word about *The Old Masters*, into an account of a production he hoped to launch of one of my old plays, *Otherwise Engaged*, with Kelsey Grammer in the lead. I'd directed Kelsey Grammer in a play of mine in New York long before he turned into Frasier, of the world-famous television series, in fact in the days when I'd known him I'd occasionally had to lecture him on his unpunctuality and, well, some other problems, which were almost as serious as mine, along with his habit of falling asleep when I gave notes, all of which, I told him, pointed to a lack of a future. The producer-figure said that Kelsey Grammer had told him that the main character in *Otherwise Engaged* was the only part in the whole world that might lure him back to the stage. 'He did Macbeth last year in New York,' I said, 'so he's already been back on stage.' 'That's Shakespeare,' he said rather foamingly. 'You're the only living writer –' 'What did you think of *The Old Masters*?' 'Oh, very good, very good, but if we can get Kelsey Grammer we can go ahead with *Otherwise Engaged*. Subject to dates, of course.' I felt an odd, blurring sensation. In the original production of *Otherwise Engaged*, which Harold had directed, Alan Bates had played the lead, Nigel Hawthorne had played his brother, Ian Charleson had played his lodger – it had opened at the Queen's Theatre, then, after six months, moved to the Comedy, where *The Old Masters* is now playing. Of the original cast of seven, Alan was dead, Ian Charleson was dead, Nigel Hawthorne was dead, and here were Harold and I, back at the Comedy in the same capacities, though with different wives, both of us now older than the three when they'd died, Ian Charleson hadn't got much beyond thirty, an early victim of Aids. 'Really,' I said, 'this is a first-night party for *The Old Masters*, it's here and now. *Otherwise Engaged* was in the long-ago on the one hand – and in the might-be, subject-to-dates-of-course on the other' – actually I rather snarled it at him, quite unreasonably, I imagine, from his point of view, turned on my heel, Harold-style, and left him there – Well, I mean! And Really! I found Victoria. She was talking to Lucy, who was looking both glamorous and kindly, an unbeatable combination in a young woman. She gave me a kiss and a cuddle, and told me the evening had gone well, thus completely fulfilling her daughterly duties. Victoria said that Harold and Antonia had just left for Sheekey's, in the bar of which only a few weeks ago we'd seen the man slam down his programme of *The Holy Terror* in a pantomime of rage and disgust – 'Let's go,' I said, and explained to Alan Yentob and Margy that we were off, and where to – I could see flares of interest in their eyes, so I said I didn't think we wanted the camera on us as we ate and talked about the evening, it really was a private business, old tradition, the four of us reliving the immediate past, and pasts beyond that.

THE TURKEY QUESTION

We could see Harold and Antonia moving slowly ahead of us, picking their way past the Duke of York's, which only a few weeks ago had housed *The Holy Terror* and was now lying in wait for the next show,

Dirty Blonde about the life and times of Mae West, which a close friend of ours, Dena Hammerstein, was producing – not a lucky theatre, I'd warned her grimly, as the show before *The Holy Terror* – it was called *Calico* – about Joyce's relationship with his daughter, had closed in a couple of weeks. On the first night of *The Holy Terror* a man who looked as if he'd run all the way from Heathrow or even Gatwick to the box office, his chest was heaving, his face was sweaty, urgently demanded three tickets for *Calico*. He refused at first to believe that it wasn't there to be seen – 'But it's only just opened! I read about it in the plane, just a few hours ago, in the plane! – how can it have closed?' Overhearing this in the lobby, I had one of those feelings, shameful and smirky, that I suspect the gods take note of. 'There's *The Holy Terror*,' the man in the box office said valiantly, 'it opens tonight. There are still a few tickets left –' '*The Holy Terror*! *The Holy Terror*! Why should I want to see *The Holy Terror* when I've come to see *Calico*?' I wondered if there might be a similar exchange on the first night of *Dirty Blonde*, some desperate creature exhausted from the airport, demanding tickets for *The Holy Terror* and being offered tickets instead for *Dirty Blonde*.

I pointed out a tattered poster for *The Holy Terror* – it must have gone up tattered, I said, it hadn't been there long enough to have been tattered by the elements – and look! Victoria said, gazing up from the edge of the pavement, and yes, there it was, announced not only in the down-at-heel poster but actually in lights, like a tawdry tombstone – Simon Callow in *The Holy Terror*, by me.

Harold and Antonia turned down the lane that Sheekey's is in and we trailed behind them, contemplating the swings of fate, at least we hoped they were swings, from *The Holy Terror* to *The Old Masters*, there may well be no swing at all, *The Old Masters* may turn out to be another turkey – but why 'turkey' by the way, why do we also call a flop a 'turkey'?

END OF AN EVENING

Over dinner the director and his wife assured the author and his wife, and vice versa, that the evening had gone as well as can be expected on a first night with a new play, the cast had hit their stride early and never faltered, the audience had been benevolently disposed, and as for the critics, one of the nice things about the evening, we all agreed, is that we hadn't seen a single one, not that we could identify anyway, although we were assured by the management that they had all been there, on their aisle seats, pads in hand, opinions at the ready. One of us recalled the life of the composer Warlock – I forget his first name, if he had one – who was also a music critic, writing under a name I must also look up – and although he was well-known in each capacity, nobody knew he was the same man – in fact he reviewed himself increasingly viciously, and was eventually found dead with his head in a gas oven, suicide therefore, or perhaps self-murder would be the more accurate term – the question of course is, which murdered which, the critic the composer, or the composer the critic? Each clearly had a strong motive – although it might conceivably have been death by misadventure, the composer turning on the gas, the critic putting his head in the oven to see what was up – and then we enjoyed the memory of a recent production of a play generally and rightly regarded as a modern classic, in which the leading actor had mangled virtually every single line, causing all the other actors to come in at the wrong places with lines they had to get wrong so that they connected to the leading actor's wrong lines – it was a textual slaughterhouse, the night we saw it. Outside the theatre, on a placard jammed with quotes, there was one that proclaimed, with Olympian authority, 'Every line spot on' – 'Every fucking line spot off,' said the defeated director, who'd been in love with the text since his schooldays. One evening an elderly lady, perhaps mother to the playwright, or the director, or one of the actors, sat in the stalls reciting the correct lines of the play, quite loudly, as if she were doing a simultaneous translation –

So the talk went, vindictive, malignant, vengeful, agreeable, until a selectively shaven chap, one cheek and half his chin gleaming, the other cheek and other half of his chin stubbled, got up from a nearby table and came over. 'How's it going?' he asked. 'How's what going?' Harold growled, jaw jutting. The chap, youngish and a director of some distinction, looked yearningly towards the chair he'd just left – he'd had experience of Harold in this mode, obviously, and was now recalling it – 'The play,' he said. 'What play?' Harold asked him. 'Well, your play. His play,' nodding at me. '*The Old Masters*,' I said, quite anxious to avoid what was already happening. 'That's the one. *The Old Masters*.' 'What about it?' Harold was staring straight up at him, his eyes had turned milky with a dark glitter in them. 'What about it?' he said. 'Well, it's in previews, isn't it? How are they going, the previews?' 'We've just,' Harold said crisply, 'had a first night.' 'Oh,' said the youngish director, 'I hope it went well.' 'What do you mean, went well! Went well!' 'Anyway, good luck,' said the youngish director, as he backed away, not to his table, but into the next room, and from there doubtless to the street, and away, away. 'Went well,' Harold repeated several times. 'Went well! What did he think he meant?' We tried to explain to him what we thought he thought he meant, but were really too tired to do a proper job of it – probably the half-shaven director had inadvertently reminded Harold that however much he believed in the play, however fine he knew his production to be, *The Old Masters* would only survive if other people allowed it to – oddly, Harold looked the least tired of the four of us, though in fact he was probably the most tired, certainly far more tired than me. He'd had a month of intense rehearsals, three weeks in Birmingham, then putting the play into the Comedy for previews and now a first night, and he'd had almost a year's illness behind him, was in fact still frail from it when he'd taken the play on back there in Barbados, whereas I had gone in to rehearsals at my convenience, and I'd only stayed long enough in Birmingham to see what a terrific job he'd done and to make a few small cuts. Why stay longer when you were staying at the Hilton and couldn't open the window, the air-conditioning not working, during a heat wave? Most of the time, right up to and including the first night, I'd been cavorting for the camera with Alan Yentob, Margy the director, Patrick the cameraman and sometimes Andy the sound man, a business I'd only found tiring because of the non-stop smoking. I looked at Harold, alert in his exhaustion, and suddenly realized that our long professional association was now ending as one would have prayed for it to end when we'd begun it. It had survived some blizzardy spells, rows, froideurs, etc., but still, here we were, in Sheekey's, half our lifetimes on from our first first night together, celebrating what would certainly be our last.

We went back in the hired car, I sitting in the front, Harold between Antonia and Victoria in the back – they got out first, in their bit of Holland Park, we drove on the few minutes to our bit, took George and Toto for a walk, they saw off the usual foxes and other shadows under a bright moon, Victoria went to bed, I came in here, and here I am, doing this, and Brendel doing Mozart behind me. Now I shall sit for a while, and listen to him properly, while I smoke.

THE TURKEY QUESTION ANSWERED

All the main reviews are now in. Judy says they're OK – the advance is high and rising, we look set for a decent run, there's been foreign interest – in fact it looks as if it might be a success. I must be careful. The last time I told myself I had a successful play in the West End was on the evening before one of the two stars, and therefore half the reason for the success, departed for foreign parts, the resulting headlines closed it in three weeks. Oh, I see why 'turkey'! – because a turkey can be said to have no future, you look at a turkey gobbling its way across the farmyard, and you're looking at a dinner, Christmas or Thanksgiving, though in fact you're unlikely to find a turkey to look at in a farmyard these days, you're most likely to find him in a factory, in a coop just slightly larger than himself, immobile therefore and stuffed with chemicals, a creature not only without a future but without a present, thus making it an even closer analogy to a stage turkey, in that the cast, if it has any sense, will also be stuffed with chemicals. But let us say for the purposes of this discussion and for sanity's sake that my new play is not going to be a turkey but a golden, well, silver goose – well, then what? What then? So what? Some money perhaps.

And now to bed. Oh, Christ! Before I go there's something I must do – I've written and written about *The Old Masters* and haven't once

mentioned the two men without whom I'd never have written it, Roger
Jenkins and Simon Langton, to whom therefore I must pay

AN OVERDUE TRIBUTE

Very different in demeanour, personality and physique – Roger
Jenkins is small and scampering, Simon Langton tall and relaxed,
but I always see them as a unit, like a couple on a bicycle, sometimes
Langton on the handlebars, Jenkins pedalling, sometimes the other
way around – I think it was Jenkins who approached me with the
idea of doing a filmscript about Berenson and Duveen, and when
I found myself unable to do it, it was Langton who phoned to
ask whether I might consider trying it again as a stage play – and
when I'd done it as a stage play together they purchased the rights
forthwith, then refused the control over the play that the rights
gave them, asking only that they should be colleagues, fellow
adventurers, fellow sufferers in the process of getting it on. Over a
number of years – years! – we had regular dinners to discuss casting,
directors, ways of finding other producers who could raise money –
and if there was an undercurrent of hopelessness as dinner followed
dinner, with only rejections and humiliations to report or conceal –
for example, they sent the play to the artistic director of an Irish
theatre, I bumped into him at a party, he was drunk and disorderly,
with wandering hands, not sexually wandering, but Irishly wandering,
he liked to place them on your shoulders or around your waist – he'd
read the first act on the plane over from Dublin, he said, he'd enjoyed
it, yes, yes, honestly enjoyed it, looked forward to reading the second
act on the way back, was shore he'd enjoy tat too – no, no, don't bother,
I said, please don't bother – the disgusting truth, and he knew it, was
that really I was beseeching him to put the play on his stage – how
could such a man, I nevertheless thought, or rather how could I stand
there having my shoulders groped by such a man! but no, I said, no,
no, don't bother – take your time, read it when you can, there could
be no better place to start the play than in a theatre under your
management, but really don't feel you have to read it. He twinkled
at me in a fiery sort of way, patted my elbows, then lurched off to

fondle other writers, who, I hoped, treated him with more – more – dignity. In due course I heard that the Irish rascal wouldn't dream of having my play on his stage at all, at all – no doubt Roger Jenkins and Simon Langton had similar encounters too shameful to pass on to me, but it was understood between us that we'd been through things, not to be talked about – as if there were priests, choirmasters, scout masters in our backgrounds. The only problem with people who behave as well as Langton and Jenkins is that they tend to get treated badly, if only by neglect – naturally modest men who didn't like to intrude even in matters that affected them directly, they were frequently forgotten when it came to making decisions – the casting, for instance, went ahead without their being consulted, though I think, I hope, I kept them abreast *post facto*, when it was too late for them to object or to register reservations – they dealt with this by being, or pretending to be, delighted with each decision, although conversations with Roger Jenkins can be slightly confusing, as he has the kind of deafness that sometimes allows him to hear exactly the opposite of what you've said, it either obliterates a negative or supplies one, so that he exclaims joyfully when grief is in order, and vice versa.

THE PROSPECT OF AN EVENING WATCHING THE TELLY

In about half an hour we're going around to Margy's flat to watch ourselves as we will be seen in approximately two million homes. I would like to say, in a dignified sort of way, that thus our privacy is being invaded, but in fact you could look at it the other way around, and consider that Victoria and I are about to invade the privacy of a couple of a million homes, or perhaps more accurately are about to inflict our privacy on a couple of a million homes. I may also, of course, have got the numbers wrong – it may, when it comes to it, be a couple of hundred homes, or even a couple of homes, one of which will be Margy's, whose home we will thus be invading twice, simultaneously. When I come back I shall almost certainly avoid writing about the experience, and try to return to a subject still much on my mind, which is of course

ERROL, HIS DEFECT

I've never attempted to conceal from myself that he is very greedy, the consequences of his greed are immediately apparent in his bulk, but his bulk has always, for me, been part of his charm – he carries it on short, skipping legs not exactly lightly but easily, in comfort and with style – 'a dainty waddle' I believe I've described his walk as, but that only captures his routine, unhurried movement from a) (sofa) to b) (armchair) – it doesn't encompass his movement towards the kitchen when he hears me in it, or sees me going towards it – then the short legs move so rapidly they're almost invisible, he looks like a large black fur hat skimming across the floor, although you can hear the pitter-patter of his feet as he comes along the hall, or quite loud thumps, so close together it's almost a continuous noise, if he's coming down the stairs – once in the kitchen he stalks me, treading on my heels as I move from table to sink to fridge to cupboard to table, generally silently and therefore at risk to himself – if I were to step back suddenly I'd hurt his head – no, more likely I'd trip over him and hurt myself – badly, too, given my weight, size and age. At first I tried to ignore him, thinking that rules are rules and mealtimes are mealtimes, but as soon as I'd sit down to eat he'd stand on his hind legs and, using his paws like clubs, batter away at my calves and knees – if I ignored him or knocked him away he'd get onto one of the chairs, clamber onto the table and advance on my plate, head lowered, butting at it. My solitary lunches, which I've always enjoyed so much, calmly eating while calmly reading, degenerated into dreadful scuffles, punctuated by shouts, swearwords, until I gave up and popped some food into his mouth, but it was

NEVER ENOUGH!

He'd be back at my plate while he was still swallowing and the thing about Errol, who is a stray, don't forget, and took over the house in methodical stages, is that he doesn't take no for an answer, and never takes offence – if you sweep him onto the floor he gets straight back onto the chair and sprawls his way onto the table and butts his way to your plate, which he also reaches for with outstretched paws. This situation is entirely my own fault, as Victoria explains to me, for having fed him scraps in the days when he merely stood on his hind legs and pummelled my legs. If I'd refused him then he would have accepted the situation in the end and left me alone, as no cat likes to stand bolt upright whirring his paws for no gain – after all, it's an unnatural act that drains the energy, and probably strains the back – but once he grasped that I was weak, a giver, he decided to become strong, a taker – yes, he's turned himself from a beggar into a mugger, and I'm his permanent victim. I would like to say that we've reached accommodation, but it's the kind of accommodation that Brits of yore achieved with the Vikings – before I sit down to eat, I put some of my food onto a saucer, which I place outside the kitchen and as soon as he's bent over it I shut the door. What depresses me most about this is that he is massively overweight, more so and more so, you can tell by the way his head seems to have grown smaller every time you look at him, and though I acknowledge that gluttony is part of his character, part of the charm of his character, it is inexcusable of me to gratify it and so hasten him to an early grave, simply because I lack the strength of will to refuse him. I wish the dogs would do the job for me, and chase him off every time he comes mugging, but really they're just as weak, just as devoted, allowing him access to their own dishes, and cleaning him up when he's too indolent to do it for himself. At least I don't have to do that, go down on my hands and knees and lick away at him, I hope it never occurs to him –

FRIENDS AND BROKEN PROMISES

A friend phoned this afternoon to say that there was a piece in the *Guardian* about the television programme, had I seen it? I said I hadn't, and didn't want to, I no longer read reviews. She said I really ought to make an exception of this one, which anyway wasn't really a review, was more a meditation, and was quite delightful, was the word she used, delightful. On my way up to the Renaissance I bought the *Guardian*, and when I got there, having signalled for my coffee and settled into my chair on the pavement, I opened it and found the piece – the words that immediately caught my eye were 'obese' and 'slob' – there was a photograph in illustration – so I closed the *Guardian*, thinking that perhaps in context the words meant something different, but better not find out, and then indulged in a little meditation of my own, on the contradictory nature of friendship, and on the inevitable and deserved consequences of breaking promises one has made to oneself –

Well, tomorrow we go to Suffolk, where we'll stay for most of the summer. Let's hope this chaotic spirit finds some peace, or at least placidity. And why not? There will be long walks around the fields with the dogs, the pigs to feed, and the black swans, serene in their pomp –

PART FOUR

TROUBLE WITH THE BLACK SWANS

There are three of them this summer, old Mum and old Dad, and one offspring, as black as they are, but slighter, almost but not quite grown up. They make a magnificent trio, gliding in a compact triangle through the murky water, sweeping around the moat's bends, sometimes drifting lazily and nobly around each other – we love watching them, and love their grateful honks when they see the bread, their ceremonial dips of the head before they surge towards it – and then the comedy of their scuffles with each other, the brutality with which Mum and Dad barge their only child off the crusts, and then when it's over off they swan around again, a tight-knit and royal little family – so it was when we got down here last week, but in the last few days they've taken to not being on the water, at least when we arrive to feed them – they're generally out of sight, behind a tree on the bank, or a tree in the field quite some way from the moat, and when they see us, and always before we've seen them, they lumber out, as if they've been waiting in ambush. Victoria retreats with George and Toto. I briefly stand my ground, casting my bread towards them. Mother and child stop to feed, but not Dad, he keeps on coming, trampling on the lumps of bread, crashing through the long grass, towards me – he has a strange gleam in his eye, not hostile, in fact eager and friendly but greedy too, as if he's anxious to get to the source, or perhaps he harbours dreams of taking it from my hand, the whole family gathered around the great provider – well, whatever his intentions I lose my nerve, tear the remaining bread into lumps as I back-pedal, hurl them at him, and then turn and run, slowly, ponderously, wheezingly, and only fractionally faster than Dad, whose implacable waddle has staying power, which I haven't – as long as he doesn't use his wings, I keep thinking, dreading the sound of his great wings beating, the rush through the air, and I a wrinkled male Leda, taken from behind –

So far he's stopped in his pursuit, as if realizing that he's missed the point, which is to get himself fed – when I turn to look he's swaying his great, black, feathery body towards wife and child, who are getting the bread down as fast as they can while they have the chance. This has happened three afternoons in a row, and I'm sitting here now, in my study in the garden, noting that the hour is approaching, and yes, Victoria and the dogs are getting ready for a walk, she's putting them on their leads, and I should be heading for the kitchen, to get the bread which we buy especially for them – they're very fussy, they don't like brown bread, or organic or home-baked crusty expensive breads, they like doughy white bread, the sort that comes factory-sliced and factory-wrapped, looks and smells as if it's made out of chemicals, at twice the size and half the price of edible bread – well, *chacun à son gout*, but I don't think I can give them their *gout* this afternoon, what I'll do is – we'll walk to a safe distance from the moat, I'll command Victoria and the dogs to stay – 'Stay, ladies!' I'll say – then I'll take a few steps forward, honking, and if they return my honks from the water, which they always do if they're in the water, we'll all go forward and I'll feed them, but if they meet my honks with silence, I'll know they're lurking on dry ground, out of sight, and we'll hurry on.

I'm back. They were on the water, so that was OK. What wasn't OK was

THE PIGS!

I went to say hello to them and give them their scraps, while Victoria went on with the dogs. There are five of them, just as there were last year, but they're not the same ones, they're new, replacements, so to speak, for reasons I don't want to go into but could be guessed at from the contents of our fridge a few months ago, packages of pork sausages etc. – gifts reluctantly accepted and mournfully consumed. These five are smaller and leaner than their five predecessors, with a quick, scuttling run that turns into a gallop when they get into their stride – they appear from different parts of their vast sty, a couple of them bursting through the undergrowth to your right, another out of the ditch to your left, and the third from out of the nettles right in front of you – they stand in a line and look up at you pleadingly, and with almost dog-like devotion – you think they're going to beg prettily, like George and Toto – well, this is all quite charming, their little ways are usually quite seductive, and indeed were just now, until I'd emptied the carrier bag of its swinish titbits and turned to catch Victoria up. There was a hideous noise behind me, of snouts smashing against wire fencing – they were hurling themselves at it, their tiny eyes gleaming with what looked suspiciously like lust, but was probably just rage. Either way they really did look as if they were out to get me, and when I hurried off, walking along the road that runs beside the sty to catch Victoria up, they continued to hurl themselves at the fence, butting and kicking at it and then, realizing that I was almost gone, raced after me with a thunder of hooves, passed me and began their assault on the fence further up, obviously planning to cut me off. Then what? Gobble me down as a prime titbit, or maul me to death in revenge for what? I give them tasty scraps, after all, I am a patron, trustworthy and punctual – perhaps they picture me going to the fridge a year from now, reaching in for a package of fresh sausages – anyway, instead of trusting to the fence to hold, I swung away briskly into the orchard, and caught up with Victoria on the edge of a cornfield, very high corn, into which Toto vanished, so we spent an hour calling 'Toto, Toto, come on, come, Toto' – once we saw her about twenty yards away, her head and her front paws showing briefly and desperately above the stalks, but looking the wrong way, and that was it, she'd obviously lost her bearings, too many bewildering scents of mice, rat, rabbit and hare to find her own scent and get back to us. She'd be sniffing and running in circles, getting more and more exhausted, frightened, finally collapsing, tongue lolling, eyes staring hopelessly – or so we imagined as we went back to get the car, drove to the field, up and down the side of it, at least Victoria did, while I hung out of the window, watching out for her, willing her to hear the familiar motor. We stopped at last and got out. The sun was going down, the endless East Anglian sky darkening, the cornfield darkening, our hearts doing much the same, and George standing with a melancholy stoop, her favourite posture when Toto's gone awry, and then we all heard it, a heavy breathing at our feet, and there was Toto, her golden muzzle pitch black from burrowing into the earth, burrs and twigs and clots of dirt in her fur. We might have suspected her of not having been lost at all, but simply of having had a high old time down there among the stalks, if she hadn't keeled over on her side, from what was evidently a combination of fatigue and relief.

So what's going on down here in Suffolk? Not with Toto, that's routine behaviour, made exceptional by the corn, but with the swans and the pigs – their behaviour has been bizarre, though I don't know whether out of character – species character, that is – because the only pigs and swans I've been close to are the ones down here in Suffolk, in this little piece of Suffolk, where the swans used to take their food on water and the pigs battered and buffeted only each other for theirs, and my role was to stand on moat bank and at sty fence and cast bread to one and vegetable matter to the other – obedient, not to say obsequious, swans and pigs who once knew their place and mine, but who now pursue and harass me, forcing me into unseemly jogs and ponderous, cowardly sprints –

I think I know what's going on, actually, actually I think it's because the surrounding farm has turned organic, everything grown here is now organic, the corn, the wheat, the apples, the pears, the potatoes, and with them come more wasps and hornets than have ever been seen before, invasive, aggressive wasps and hornets as big as my thumb. How can the pigs and swans not be affected? They're becoming, perhaps have already become, organic too, and so are behaving organically. Eventually, I suppose, the people will become organic, Victoria and I will start to behave organically, as will George, Toto, Errol and Tom – this is what happens when you stop interfering with nature, nature starts to interfere with you. God knows where we'll end up, especially if He's turning organic too.

A CORPSE IN THE MOONLIGHT

It's late, but that's not it. I'm not tired. I'm anxious. I'll write about what Errol's just done because I don't want to think about what I'm anxious about, there being no point to it, the thinking leads to no solutions, in fact only intensifies the anxiety, but once it starts there's no stopping it, except chemically, so I'll take a couple of sleeping pills and – the thing about Errol being a cat, in spite of his extraordinary gift for relationships, his kindness, his warmth, and indeed his sloth and love of good living –

Tomorrow.

It is tomorrow, and here's what he did yesterday. I was sitting in my study in the garden at about two in the morning, the window wide open for the breeze – generally all you get at that hour are moths and mosquitoes – the black beetles and spiders that are quite active on my desk (the spiders) and the floor (the beetles) don't come through the window, they're residents, and I'm so used to them that I scarcely notice them – but anyway there I was, at my desk, not writing, inert really, with Errol slumbering in the armchair beside me, when something quite large hurtled through the window almost into my face, banged into the wall behind, slid to the ground, then flapped up to the ceiling and fell onto the top bookshelf. It was the size of a small crow, but not a crow because it had a grey chest. It began to stir on the bookshelf, then to flutter, then to flap, rising to the ceiling, falling to the bookshelf, then rising again to the ceiling. I did the only thing I could think to do, which was to open the door and hope that it would make for the garden. Errol meanwhile had woken, stretched, and was taking up a thoughtful position under the bookcase. I went across to pick him up and carry him out, just as the bird launched itself across the room, bounced off the wall and dropped behind the television set. I can't say that Errol sprang, it was more a rapid mince between my bent legs and my down-reaching hands, and then he too was behind the television set where I couldn't get to him, so I left the room, trying to make myself deaf to the scuffling noises.

I stood outside, waiting. Beautiful night, moonlit, soundless – wherever you are in London, at whatever the hour, there is always the sound of the city, but in Suffolk there is, or appears to be, complete stillness and silence, at least in the hours after midnight, when you feel you can hear it, palpable – and there was old Errol coming out into the garden, his jaws stretched, something dark throbbing between them.

Well, what then? I went into the kitchen and sat with a Diet Coke, smoking. George came from the bedroom, licked my hand – in

London she does this almost every night, a little ritual of affection, before she goes on down into the garden for a pee. Here, as my study isn't on her route, she only does it if we coincide, as we did now, in the kitchen. She went out through the flap. A few minutes later she came back in, nodded at me, went through to the bedroom. I could hear her hind legs scraping on the floor, and her grunts, as she heaved herself onto the bed, no doubt stretched herself out between Victoria and Toto. Then the assassin Errol came in, brushed against my leg, purring, then minced off to the bedroom, no doubt to squeeze himself between Toto and Victoria or George and Victoria. I looked in the sitting room – Tom asleep in an armchair. So everyone safely to bed, I thought. I went into the garden to check on the little red and black heap, its feathers shining in the moonlight. I decided it could wait until tomorrow, and then, deciding it couldn't, got some kitchen roll for a glove, picked the heap up, carried it to the end of the garden and lobbed it over the fence, into the field of organic corn.

THREE ANECDOTES, WITH AN IMMORAL FLAVOUR

A man, young, from the sound of him, has just phoned on behalf of BBC 3 or 4, to ask if I would contribute to a debate on smoking, whether it should be banned in restaurants, bars, etc. I said thank you for thinking of me, but I'm in Suffolk, furthermore, etc. – as I talked to him I realized I was wheezing. I also coughed once or twice – not a voice you would want to hear defending smoking, unless you were against it. What you want is a firm, clear voice, rather like his, in which to tell point-making anecdotes – that time in Athens, for instance, springs to mind, when the old American guy and the receptionist – no, try for a dignified tone, worthy of the subject matter –

Well then:

1)

At the front desk of one of Athens's most distinguished hotels – grand, seedy and unaccommodating – a little old American chap with a feeble voice but excellent manners was presenting his case to the receptionist, who was like his hotel in its seedy and unaccommodating aspects, while lacking its grandeur –

'Well, sir,' the old American said, 'you see, we in the United States prefer to eat in restaurants where there's no smoking. We feel that smoking is an unhealthy and unpleasant habit, you see, so my wife and I were wondering, would it be possible for you to make part of the restaurant suitable for non-smokers?'

The receptionist looked at him with puzzled contempt.

'It would be a great help to us Americans –'

'In our restaurants there is smoking.'

'Yes, sir, but couldn't you oblige us Americans who don't like to sit in a smoky atmosphere?'

'No,' said the receptionist, and turned his back on him to answer an unringing phone.

The old American waited a few minutes, then trudged back to his wife, who looked like his twin, in a skirt and a blue rinse.

'What did he say, dear?'

'They said – they said they would see what they could do, dear.'

'Oh, that's good,' she said. 'That's really good.'

The receptionist was now talking to a colleague, both laughing in the direction of the ancient Yankee-Doodles, who were tottering arm in arm towards the heat, grime and nastiness of outdoor Athens, a heart-wrenching sight.

I imagine they're dead now, possibly the receptionist and his colleague are dead too, why not? Or retired on their tips and credit-card scams. The thing is, though, I can't recall my attitude at the time, or even work out my attitude now. On the one hand it was a neo-colonialist impertinence of the Americans to make the request, which, on the other hand, I saw, and can still see, was perfectly reasonable. The receptionist was a shit, whose main pleasure in his work was in expressing his contempt for the guests – furthermore I believe that he stole one of my credit cards – I'd put two or three on the counter while searching for a third or a fourth, and I'd only put two or one back into my shirt pocket and didn't discover a card was missing until I answered the phone that usually didn't work in the small house in the middle of the island of Spetses, at an address which was unknown, so we thought, to everybody in the world except, as it turned out, to the lady from the Diner's Club, who reached us from where? – somewhere in Cincinnati, possibly. She wanted to ask me whether I'd recently bought half a dozen shirts, many gallons of gas, a television set, etc., etc., in Athens. When I said I hadn't, she said, 'Then your card's been stolen, sir.' My mind went straight to the receptionist, I saw him quite vividly, settled in front of his new television set in one of his new shirts, a silk affair with orange and black dots – and yet, such are the paradoxes of the human heart, I find my sympathies mostly with the thieving, ill-mannered receptionist rather than with the enfeebled, dignified old Yankee-Doodles. Is this really a point-making anecdote? If it is, what's its point, because I clearly haven't found it, but then the moral of any story involving Greeks is likely to be obscure.

2)

Consider the catamaran that takes you from Athens to Spetses, a marvellous outfit in blue and white, with a luxurious upper compartment in which you could buy a seat for a small supplement. The counter used to be covered by plates of caviare, bottles of champagne, cheeses, cakes, and you were invited to help yourselves – the seats were armchairs, most of them unoccupied, and ashtrays were everywhere. But the last time we were on it, the line had a new owner, the caviare, champagnes, wines, cheeses, cakes all replaced by saucers of crisps and pretzels, the only drinks were soft drinks and beer, locked in a large glass safe, to which the steward, who used to be jovial, had a key – a key! – and of course the ashtrays had gone, smoking wasn't permitted anywhere in the boat except by the crew, all of whom appeared to chain-smoke, including the one-time jovial steward, who had a cigarette between his lips when he told me to put mine out – but I suppose he was Greek and unionized, and I wasn't – I remember noticing the supplement had gone up too – but to extrapolate from the xenophobic particular a universal moral law, as Kant advises us to do, it would be this, or something like it: most campaigning non-smokers are at heart criminals and bullies –

3)

for example, at an airport check-in, I remember it as being in Holland, possibly Amsterdam, which is confusing because I haven't been to Amsterdam, or anywhere else in Holland in the last forty years – anyway, to revert to the xenophobic particular, she was American of course, and she'd just joined the queue – inserted herself into it, and not in the middle, at the head, pushing in front of me just as it became my turn to step up to the desk. I rose to my full height, about six foot by the old reckoning, 'Excuse me,' I said, 'excuse me but actually I believe that I –' 'Hey, you! Hey, get that thing out of my face, you wanna kill me or what?' So instead of arguing about her right to jump ahead of me in the queue, we argued about my right to smoke in a place where the right to smoke had never yet, in my experience, been questioned, and were still arguing as she received her boarding card. No, this didn't happen to me, it happened to my brother Piers, so it might well have happened to him at Amsterdam airport, at the time in his life when he was a great traveller and a heavy smoker – later he gave up travelling because he was frightened of going in an aeroplane, and smoking because he thought it was killing him, though there he was wrong, it was drink that was killing him, just as it was drink that made him frightened of flying, induced his claustrophobia, convinced him that Hell was a geographical as well as a theological fact and that he was predestined to a place in it, and it was drink that destroyed his career, endangered his friendships. In my own case I gave up drink because it was threatening to do to me what it had done to Piers, although there were variations – I wasn't afraid of flying though I had difficulties getting to the airport, I didn't believe in Hell except as a metaphor, most of my friendships were perfectly safe as I was too inert to do them serious damage – but I can't give up cigarettes, which are helping to kill me, that's the phrase that's most commonly used – 'If they're not actually killing you, they're certainly helping' – but helping what, helping whom?

DOES IT MATTER?

Ironically, now I'm writing about smoking – no, I mustn't go on with a sentence that begins with 'ironically' – there was that very nice young man at Alan's funeral who spoke of how he'd been present in the same church for the funeral of Alan's son Tristan, then for the funeral of Alan's wife, Victoria, and now, 'ironically', for the funeral of Alan himself. Not only, what did he mean? What did he think he meant? Or think the word meant? Surely he must have realized that when Alan died his funeral would, as a matter of course, be held in the same church as his wife's, his son's and both his parents', so he can't have meant coincidentally, a common and slovenly modern usage, as it was quite the reverse of a coincidence, and he can't have meant an utterance that said something different from what it seemed to be saying, which is the old usage – in fact, the natural adverb in the context would have been 'naturally' – though I suppose he might have begun, 'So here we are again!' which could have had a touch of irony in it, as it certainly had when another young man said it at the beginning of his speech at his father's fourth wedding.

CONVICTED

I visualize it often, this mute, passive, helpless creature pushed and prodded by creatures rendered semi-human by their uniforms and power – and my fellow inmates, some of them at least semi-human in their attitude to violence, myself gradually assimilated into their world, a freak because of my age, my accent, my feebleness, my lack of survival knowledge – I see no hope for myself at all, not even in my passivity, and then the noise, the noise of clashing stereos, of voices shouting above them, the foul language, every noun and verb preceded and followed by an obscenity, no, by the same dreary obscenity, more a verbal tic than a word that has meaning. And then there'd be the food, of course, and then meeting my visitors. But would anybody come, would I want them to come, because this is what visiting me would entail – demeaning and lengthy ceremonies – searches, palm-stamping, etc., on arrival; demeaning and lengthy ceremonies – searches, palm-unstamping, etc., on departure, both ceremonies designed as deliberate side-effects to the punishment, really. You know this prisoner you're visiting, do you? In what capacity? Write it down. Empty your pockets. This is for him, is it? Put it there. Give me your hand. Put it there.

What's that behind your eyes? Humiliation? Whose fault is that? His fault for being in here. Your fault for visiting him. Most of the packages they'd bring for me, books, cigarettes, money, would be forbidden on different grounds, although there would be free and easy access for drugs, alcohol and pornography – would that thought cheer me up as I sat in a chair in a costume with the name of the prison on it, an orange, or a yellow, or a green costume, sharing a joke with my visitors?

But why should I have to go to jail? I haven't done anything illegal, to my knowledge, nor immoral – at least not for years. I haven't lived, am still not living, a good life, a life of active virtue, I concede that, but whatever harm I do is unintentional, the consequence of humdrum selfishness or thoughtlessness, all my malice I keep penned in, except in the occasional remark to Victoria or a close friend, someone I can trust – but really my fear has nothing to do with what I've done, or even haven't done, it's to do with who and what I am, the world of this who and what is filled with – no, that's not true, not filled with, infiltrated by, my world has been infiltrated by police people, social workers, judges, recorders, prison wardens and jailbirds – I carry them with me through life, my just deserts. And they like to walk about in my skull at all the dead hours, the alternative to death, and which, I must say, never strikes me as a favourable alternative.

Of course I'll never end up in prison, why should I? Well, why did he and he and he and she? And don't forget those like poor

BUGALL

I don't. In fact, I think about him ridiculously often, really, considering how inconsequential in the large scheme of injustice his story is, and how long ago it was, back there in the 1980s or 1990s. He was a barrister in Edinburgh who loved his work, was highly sociable in his instincts and clearly fancied himself a lady's man, something of a goer, an optimistic goer, though friends and colleagues, who chattered happily about him to the newspapers after the trial, suggested that he cut a slightly preposterous figure – foolishly self-regarding and off-kilter, a bit of a nincompoop, really –

There was a legal ball, an end-of-the-sessions sort of thing, with kilts and bagpipes and Highland flings – in the thick of it Bugall, having the time of his life with the young lady of his choice – though she said afterwards she found him a bit of an embarrassment, didn't really know him, just enough to accept his invitation –

They'd arranged to spend the night at the flat of friends of the young lady, because the ball ended late, and they had no transport. She retired to one bedroom, he to another. He undressed down to his shirt-cuffs, which were elaborate and separate from the shirt, then bounded into the young lady's bedroom, making a loud whooping noise, and flung himself onto the young lady, who tipped him straight onto the floor, where he fell asleep, or into a stupor, and was still in one or the other when the police arrived to carry him off to the cells. He chose to conduct his own defence – and why not? He was a practising barrister, after all, and this was a marvellous chance to hone and display his skills – that's why not.

His defence was this: if a young man took a young lady to an expensive ball, he was entitled to hope for a sexual reward. Of course he would never force himself on her, a rejection was a rejection, he was not a rapist, no, he was merely a normal man – come on, chaps! I mean! was his defence. Before he was sentenced he wrote a letter to the Recorder, begging him not to send him to prison. He got three years. The young lady, who'd been anonymous throughout the case, told the newspapers afterwards that she'd never wanted him to go to prison, had never wanted to ruin his life, she didn't quite know how it had happened. The newspapers had great fun with the story – particularly with the detail of the detachable but undetached cuffs, and the absurdity of his name, which wasn't actually Bugall, but something like that. One or two columnists took a more serious view, however, and congratulated the Recorder for sending out the right message, which oddly enough failed to reach Bugall, whose application for early release was turned down on the grounds that he was still transmitting the wrong social and sexual signals.

Well, if Bugall, why not you? I've certainly behaved as badly, if not worse, when drunk. On the other hand I no longer drink and anyway don't have the energy, on top of which I don't live in Edinburgh – my Scottish side comes from Glasgow, which must be a very different sort of place, at least if my grandmother was anything to go by – in fact, now I think about her, I realize that she had certain Bugall tendencies, in that she drank and she loved to romp on the bed – with me, actually – perhaps she's responsible for my lax moral attitudes, perhaps Bugall too had a grandma from Glasgow – could he have pleaded that in mitigation?

I hope he's all right, Bugall, and has good health and a good woman – and hope that his anonymous ladyfriend, and the friends who persuaded her to phone the police, and the police, and the jury, and the journalists who had such fun and copy at his expense, and above all the Recorder, are all in the place that they deserve to be in. Now that's the sort of thought which could lead to an orange uniform – pushed and prodded –

AT THE OVAL

The television is on, we're playing the West Indies at the Oval – so far we've beaten them six times in a row, three times in the West Indies, three times here, and we have at the crease now the England captain, Michael Vaughan, and a young Warwickshire batsman I've read and heard about, but not seen before – his name is Ian Bell, this is his first test match, and he has so far scored seventy. He looks very good. Michael Vaughan also looks very good, but then he usually does. I'm glad to see England playing well, of course, and with style, but I wish it weren't at the expense of the West Indies – oh, Bell is just out, caught behind, still on seventy – not long ago, not long ago in terms of my lifetime, anyway, the West Indians were the best in the world, brutally efficient fast bowlers, the best batsmen in the world and probably one of the two or three best ever in Viv Richards – they were relentless and dominating, not to say domineering, and one saw no end to their triumphs, especially over England, who often looked like schoolboys against them. But cricket teams, empires, theatre companies have their seasons, and in no time it seems their time has gone, their triumphs bewildering memories – well, that's OK for South Africans, New Zealanders, Indians, Pakistanis, and especially Australians, but it's not really

OK when it comes to the West Indies – I hate to see the arrogant saunter of yesterday's teams parodied in the lazy and demoralized slouch of the present lot – I hate to see them losing, I hate to see us losing as well, what I would really like is for us to beat them by one close-fought and exciting match at the end of the series, a clincher that leaves everyone full of hope, looking forward to the next – Vaughan has just gone for sixty-six, driving when he shouldn't have and nicking to slip, and here comes Flintoff, who always reminds me of the cheerful half of a Housman poem, hale and hearty, a peerless youth, before Housman snuffs him out at the end of a rope. The camera's doing a pan around the ground, the Oval in the early evening, shadows and sunshine, ground pretty full, England, yes, England – still recognizably the same ground that Mummy brought us to, Nigel and me, when we were eleven and ten. She wanted to show us, to make us understand and feel –

I took a break, walked around the garden, sat smoking – here there hasn't been sunshine, here there's been rain, thunder, lightning and sunshine all mixed up, get a patch of sunshine while you can, so I sat smoking in a sudden patch of sunshine, George and Toto and Errol settled around me, Victoria in her study, I was gone for not much more than half an hour, I should think, with the video working to record Flintoff's innings, and came back in as he was saluting the crowd who were saluting his half-century. He stood with his bat raised, massive and young, blond hair curling out from under his helmet, his eyes clear and joyful – fodder for the slaughter in 1917, in Ypres or the Somme, body deep in the mud and entangled in barbed wire, hand outstretched, palm mysteriously clean, turned upward, doomed youth from the anthem, but here he is instead, the glorious young man of the moment, this moment in the evening of 19 August, in the year 2004, standing in the London sunlight in the centre of the television screen, his bat held up as if he'll be there for ever –

MORAL GEOGRAPHY

I'd thought I'd got rid of Bugall, at least temporarily, by writing it all down a few days ago, but he's obviously still much on my mind, in fact

I found myself talking about him this afternoon, on the telephone with Ian Jack, editor of *Granta* and of *The Smoking Diaries*. He seemed to know rather more about the case than I did, probably because he'd thought of doing an article about it in the days when he was still a journalist. He said I was quite right, Bugall wasn't Bugall's real name, then told me what Bugall's real name was – is, I hope – but I've already forgotten it, infuriating because it's so like Bugall that it almost rhymes. He also said that I'd got a few of the details wrong – that the ball didn't take place in Edinburgh, for instance, but in London, that the sexual assault manqué also took place in London, for instance, and that the trial, for instance, also took place in London. I asked him to consider the possibility that Edinburgh might have had him extradited on the grounds that they could guarantee him an unfair and prejudiced trial, with a vicious sentence at the end of it, but he said that as far as he knew there was, as yet (as yet!), no extradition treaty between London and Edinburgh. Well then, I said, well then, the Recorder must have come from Edinburgh, because that's where everyone who has any power to do harm in England seems to come from, so it was in its moral essence an Edinburgh affair, whatever the geographical incidentals. He said he'd check the Recorder's biography for me, find out where he was born and educated, I said no need, facts were merely facts, mistakes merely mistakes, we didn't want either of them getting in the way of my long-held convictions, besides we might conceivably have been thinking of two completely different but coincidental cases, involving men whose names almost rhymed. Convictions, now there's a word – the Recorder was, like me, a man with convictions, and when he'd finished with a.k.a. Bugall, a.k.a. Bugall was also a man with convictions, or with at least one conviction, a man convicted, a convict in an orange uniform, poked and prodded –

Enough, enough, I want a Bugall-free, a prison-free evening, here in Suffolk. But I must remember to think carefully before speaking to Ian Jack about issues that have left scars on my soul, take into account that he himself is from Scottyland, has a retentive and accurate memory, and is generally in the right – on the other hand he smokes, and is from Glasgow, I believe, which makes him what Harold would call 'a completely different kettle of fish'. A sympathetic kettle of fish.

HOME

Well, we came back from Montreal with our jug ears and our crew-cuts, our Canadian accents and absolutely no manners, and she saw at once that something had to be done, and quickly – first, then, to the girls' school in Hayling Island, where Nigel and I and two others, the Puke twins, one of whom actually did verb his name all over my father, at Nigel's tenth birthday party, were the only boys. We were sent to it partly because it was the only school on the island, and partly because the mother hoped we would be introduced to more delicate ways of behaving and speaking, a course of feminization, really, of the sort now popular, I understand, with the police force, large businesses, etc. I suspect that Mr Blair put himself through something like it when training to be Prime Minister, which would explain why he speaks and gesticulates as he does, and why women don't like him –

A couple of terms at the girls' school was followed by two years as boarders at Portsmouth Grammar School, where we were reprocessed from Canadian louts with a few girlish manners into basic English males – we added 'sir' and 'miss' to our vocabulary in short order, were very well taught at the school in Portsmouth, and rigorously overseen in the boarding house – I remember having to stand in the corridor outside my dorm, holding up my wet pyjama bottoms for the interest and amusement of passing boys. Mr Poole, the headmaster of the boarding school, was of medium height with spectacles and thinning grey hair pasted to his scalp – his particular gift was for dressings-down. He would have you stand in front of him, with your head lowered and your hands behind your back, and tell you about yourself in a thin, staccato voice for what seemed like hours, and he enjoyed an audience, summoning other boys to gather around and listen to what he had to say to Gray Minor, some of it might apply to them too, etc. He would finish abruptly, wheeling off and out of the room, leaving you standing, head still lowered, before a semicircle of your peers – lifting your eyes to them, trying not to see their expressions, was the worst moment of the experience, and made you wish that Mr Poole was still in front of you, protecting you from them by telling you how disgusting you were – 'disgusting' was one of his favourite words, also one of my mother's, and is now one of mine, by the way. At the school itself there was Miss Foster, a pretty young woman, soft and round – I fell in love with her because she reminded me of Grandma, and furthermore took trouble over me, helping me to catch up to where I would have been if I'd started my education there – and Mr Watson, a cockney with a foul temper who must have been on the verge of retirement, or even beyond it – he read *Great Expectations* to us with gestures, growls, a vast range of facial expressions. I remember particularly how he turned the whole class upside down in the graveyard and dangled us by our ankles, every one of us, by the sheer power of his reading personality – he was a magnificent Magwitch, of course, but he was also Miss Havisham, Estella, Joe and Jaggers – for all his sudden and inexplicable savageries – a thump across the back of the head, the blackboard duster hurled at your face – he was a great teacher, of the sort now jailable, or would be if he weren't extinct.

FROM 0 TO 12

Three years jouncing in a pram or toddling in Hayling Island, five years smoking on the streets of Montreal or romping on the bed with Grandma, two terms in a girls' school on Hayling Island, and two years with Mr Poole in a boarding school in Southsea, the same two years with Mr Watson and Miss Foster in Portsmouth, and then another two years in London at a prep school in Putney, where my life was controlled by the perfumed, prowling Mr Burn and the gym-shoe-wielding, bottom-beating Mr Brown, is how I went from nought to twelve – the early years, neatly accounted for in the terms that mattered most, or matter most now, when I remember them – our Canadian accents didn't last long, not only were they feminized and nuanced out at the girls' school, but at home Mummy made us repeat after her 'the brown cow went round the white house' – can that be right, white house? – and 'how now, brown cow?' and so forth, until we were on our way to being plummy, our ears grew smaller as our hair grew out to a length where Brylcreem could be applied – no, the Brylcreem came later, in adolescence, but there was a sort of oil, paraffin oil – can it really have been paraffin oil? – for special occasions. But some of our Canadian attitudes were difficult to reform – in England boys of our class and age had had food rationing and proper teaching, in Montreal we'd had cream, butter, eggs, meat, poultry, fish, cakes, biscuits, chocolates, candy and cigarettes – and for education Captain Marvel, Batman (and Robin, the Boy Wonder), Superman, Superboy, Supergirl, Spiderman, the Green Hornet, and it was from American comics that we learnt that America had won the war, both wars, all wars – so we had a sturdy contempt for the perceived namby-pambiness of English life, at least in its social aspects –

JOHNNY, FROM THE CLOUDS

But then there was cricket. Mummy believed in cricket, her father had loved it, she herself had played it, it was at the heart of England, of being English, it was through cricket we would learn how to be gentlemen and, best of all, we would learn it out of doors. One afternoon she took us on the ferry from Hayling Island to Gosport, and then on the train to Waterloo, and then on the bus to the Oval – it was a weekday, sunny, and the ground was full – for a few years after the war the cricket grounds of England were almost always full, whatever the day of the week, whatever the weather. Surrey were playing Glamorgan – I'm sure it was Glamorgan because this was the first I'd heard of it, Glamorgan – and Mummy explained, or tried to, the rudiments of the game, i.e. that the jerk who couldn't seem to throw the ball properly, in fact didn't seem to know how to bend his arm, was called the bowler, and what he was doing he was doing on purpose, in conformity with regulations, and the two men who kept running past each other with lumps of wood, long handles attached, were the batsmen, who seemed feebly incapable of doing what any American would do – smash, thrash, belt and beat every ball out of sight – instead they sometimes actually missed it completely, at other times patted it along the ground, even when it was thrown up so slowly that a blind man could have had enough swipes at it to make contact, and then there were the cowardly protections around the legs, the comical little man with enormous gloves behind the three sticks of wood with tops on, and also there was the lack of noise, excitement, adventure – all those people, and all they did was clap, for reasons incomprehensible, though it's true that there were occasional exclamations, 'Good shot, sir!' 'Oh, well caught, well caught!' and 'Bowled, sir!' and 'Well played, jolly well played!' from Mummy, sitting on the grass behind the boundary, near the pavilion, dressed for the occasion in a floral summer frock, a large summer hat on her head, legs tucked athletically under her, a hamper containing boiled eggs, unwieldy chunks of bread and marge, and a thermos of sweet tea at her side, a perfect picture of an English mother at the Oval on a summer's day, but in memory with a whiff of something else about her, perhaps it was her cigarette smoke, and the red lips, that suggested another life, another history, of the wartime air base and waiting at dusk for Johnny or Jim or Jack to come plunging down through the darkening clouds, or limping back low over the trees, over the hedgerows, the fuselage leaking a black plume or billow – Jack or Jimmy or John – Johnny, it was Johnny, the lover I gave her in my play *The Late Middle Classes*, written when I was older than she was when she died – it was almost a paternal gift, you might say, from her ageing son to the ghost of his still-young mother. Anyway, back or rather forward to the Oval in the summer of, probably, 1945, Mummy clapping, smoking, crying out, 'Oh, well played, sir' – but it was no use, it didn't take, the game was obviously for very old people – and actually they were quite old, most of them, older than they should have been, because of the war – some of them balding, and some with spectacles, and some quite slow and fat, how could this be a game for boys who lived their internal lives as Superman, Captain Marvel, and in my case above all as the Boy Robin? – so we scuffled off and messed about in some corner of the ground, fought too, I expect, as we couldn't get through twenty minutes alone together without fighting, and viciously, thumbs in eyes, knuckles in nostrils, elbows, heels and toes, giving and receiving, then back to Mummy and the hamper for our picnic lunch, Mummy pouring out the tea from the thermos, taking the lumps of bread and margarine from the hamper, cracking an egg with a flourish, and out ran the yolk and the white, into her lap and over her frock, because she'd forgotten to boil it.

WHERE I WAS WHEN –

Now this was before I'd seen Denis Compton, I know precisely when this was, well, not to the day, the week or even the month, but to the year – I'm rotten at calendar chronology, I can never remember where I was or what I was doing in any given decade, I can't retain the numbers, can't see them in my mind, I'm only confident of the date of my birthday because I can recite it, and I have to say it to myself out loud before I write it down on forms etc. – so to myself my chronology is really a sequence of 'and then's – and then I went to Canada, then to Hayling Island, then – then-then – right up to where I am now, now I am in our garden in Suffolk, writing this – in the same way I couldn't tell you the date of J. F. Kennedy's assassination, even if you pointed a gun at me. Like everybody else, I can tell you where I was when I heard the news – in the University of British Columbia, getting out of the lift as a North Country Englishman, an expert on D. H. Lawrence, was getting into it. 'Kennedy's been shot,' he said, glowing. 'Good thing. Johnson will do much more for the poor.' I remember trying to get back into the lift for more information, but the doors slid between us. He might even have said, or tried to say "ta poor,' because regional English took you a long way in the English Department of British Columbia – so did a Canadian accent, but I'd given mine up before I was nine and it was too late to get it back, even with tenure and a rise in salary at stake – so I can remember that, and his accent, and his expression, but I couldn't tell you the day, the month, the year of John F. Kennedy's assassination, and here is the ghastly truth, I couldn't even tell you the decade without working it out, like this: lecturing at the University of British Columbia when I was twenty-six, born in 1936, 26 plus 36 equals 62, Kennedy shot in 1962. Or in 1963 if it was after my birthday on 21 October (Trafalgar Day). Of course I could find out by looking it up on Google, but why bother, as I don't really want to know, and will forget it immediately after I've written it down. By the way, it was raining in Vancouver that day. I think I remember that. But then it was always raining in Vancouver every day of the eight or so months I was there, or so it seems to me now.

But here is the point – the one year I remember, that I shall always remember, is 1948, because it was in the summer of that year that I first saw Denis Compton, and it was at the Oval, and I was eleven, and within minutes of watching him I understood everything about the game that I needed to know – and also what it was to be in love – Boy Robin had transferred his affections from Batman to batsman, did I really write that? Christ! Hello, batsman, goodbye, Batman – well, I don't think I can take it any further, although I admit that I find it difficult to imagine how Boy Robin would fit into Denis's life, Denis liked the good things, most especially women, so that would cut that aspect out from both our points of view, inasmuch as I like women too.

WELL, AM I GAY OR NOT?

Although a woman who interviewed me recently concluded, or pretended to conclude the interview – she was putting various things that were on the table, most of them belonging to her, I assumed, into a capacious handbag, was in fact bending down into it, as a preliminary to picking it up and departing with it from the premises – with a last question: 'Are you by any chance,' she asked into the capacious handbag, 'gay?' These days perhaps one is obliged to take it as a compliment – 'How kind, how very kind, I am flattered, but actually I'm afraid I'm actually quite the opposite, sorry to say –' But what is exactly the opposite of gay? And what is gay anyway? All my gay friends are quite different from each other, with quite different sexual tastes, and I can't imagine what exactly the opposite of any of them would be, except perhaps in one case, his exact opposite would be Virginia Mayo, or close enough for me not to know the difference. They say that everybody in the world has a doppelgänger –

AN OUTLINE FOR THE FUTURE

If so, isn't it equally possible that everyone in the world has an exact opposite, that to meet up with him or her would result in a double death, as a single death is said to be the case when doppelgängers meet? But what I actually said to this woman, who asked me via her capacious handbag whether I was gay, was 'Why do you ask?' to which she replied that I seemed to have close relationships with my men friends, which is certainly true, yes, but where does sex come into it? The thought of having sex with any of my men friends is actually revolting – to me, anyway, and I'm pretty sure to them too, even, perhaps especially, the gay ones – the confusion was really hers, not mine – or are many of what seem to us the most natural and easy of relationships really a subject of baffled speculation to others, even to our other friends? Well, how can I say, all I can say is that there is nothing about sex that is comprehensible except the primordial purpose of orgasm, which will surely be removed when genetic engineering gets into its stride – babies produced without sex, so a procreative drive with no creation needed, soon to become a vestigial instinct, but there nevertheless, poignantly – why is it such a poignant thought? No couples ever fucking for a purpose, although no doubt they'll all have a sense of purpose, from simple pleasure through the range we read and hear about, revenge fucks, grudge fucks, vanity fucks, comfort fucks, equality fucks, but no life fucks, new life fucks – well, if they find out how to prolong and prolong life, perhaps they'll eliminate the birth element altogether, no new life, just the old lives renewed, the process of rejuvenation starting at an officially designated age – when you get to forty you go back physically to twenty, but go on emotionally and intellectually towards sixty, eighty, a hundred, a thousand, for ever. Why should it be assumed that death is inevitable? There may be men and women now who don't assume it, who are starting their work in chemistry, biophysics, mathematics, from the premise that death is not inevitable, merely another natural process that can be circumvented as so many already have been – you can't put your foot in the same river twice. No, said the clever student, you can't put the same foot in the same river twice, and no, said the one sitting at the back, you can't put the same foot in the river even once, because there never is a same foot – so imagine molecular change being looped into a circle, and instead of growth or decay you get a foot that endlessly repeats itself – could the brain be made to repeat itself endlessly? If so, it would have one of the main characteristics of Alzheimer's – there's already more than a premonition, expressed in the government's increasing desire to eliminate our past. The quickest and most successful way of eliminating the past is to eliminate the memory, which gives us the perfected citizen of the future, a zombie.

A LOVE STORY: PART ONE

Errol got another one this morning. Don't know what it was except that it had a tail and it was twitching – when I rose to my feet with an oath, he hurried into the shrubbery and stayed there a while, then came mincing out, portly and abstracted – which brings me back to whether or not I'm gay. The reason I'm coming back to that is this – that it's been on my mind that I didn't quite tell the truth when I told the woman interviewer that I wasn't gay. I believe I went on to write a few more sentences about the implausibility of my being thought gay, even by myself – but the truth is that I'd forgotten that for a brief period of my life, well, two years – how brief is that in the romantic chronology of a man coming up to sixty-eight in a month's time? – I was in love with someone of my own sex – what an odd phrase, my own sex – his name was Robert Symonds. Queen's Scholar at Westminster School. We were in the History Sixth together. He was as tall as me, with a deep voice, deeper than most boys of sixteen anyway, and he could make it boom when he wanted, boom quietly in a normal conversation for comic effect, and he had a deep laugh, deep and frenzied, his eyes would roll and he would throw his arms up and make shapes with his hands and it would almost seem that his hair stood up with laughter – it was a complete cartoon of a laughing boy, it wasn't exactly false, but it was deliberate, stagy, and intended to convey more than you could understand by the laugh itself – he was amused, but he was complicatedly amused, there were references that were entirely his that this performance hinted at. He was much cleverer than me, I think, and introduced me to all kinds of mysterious names – Man Ray, Manolete, Modigliani, just to choose one letter out of the alphabet, Charlie Parker, Cervantes, Camus, to choose another, and the Surrealists. He admired Jean Cocteau, his poetry and the photographs of him as well as *Les*

Enfants Terribles, he could quote patches of the dialogue, in French, and he was very good at Latin, Greek, and English, of course. He was also a very good actor, a hypnotic Antonio in *The Merchant* – at least I couldn't take my eyes off him, and can see him now, standing alone in a self-created space on the stage – the other actors around him only there to make him the centre – dark, melancholy, brooding, opaque, lots of words like that, lots of stuff like that. Actually I don't really know if that's how he was in *The Merchant*, I think I'm really describing the effect he had on me as he stood in Little Dean's Yard in the mornings, in the place he used to stand when he was waiting for me – my eyes went straight to him, I could see no one else as I came through the arch from Dean's Yard into Little Dean's Yard, the end of my journey from 47 Oakley Gardens, the beginning of my day – and those things happened – my heart jumped, the back of my neck tingled, there was a dizziness in the brain – those things happened as they were never to happen again, at least not with that intensity –

A LOVE STORY: PART TWO

and sometimes I couldn't see him, I would step through the arch, my eyes going to where he wasn't, and the lurch of disappointment, close to despair. I would check the faces, knowing that the one I hadn't seen immediately couldn't possibly be there, and then he'd be suddenly revealed in a group of other boys, or talking side-on to a master, looking indeed like a master himself, and he was so easy and adult in his manner with adults, as well as charming and intense and singular in his manner with other boys, that seeing him with one or the other instead of with me – I could scarcely bear to look at him as I lurched from disappointment through despair to an almost suicidal desperation, now identifiable, in my late maturity, here in my Suffolk study, at the tail end of a glorious August afternoon, as jealousy – easily identifiable, actually, because frequently experienced subsequently, but never experienced so bewilderingly – subsequently, I knew it for what it was, and behaved accordingly, in two ways simultaneously: internally, I was down on my hands and knees, 'Oh, you do love me, please, you must love me, look what you're doing to me, help me, deliver me with vows of undying love and comforting cuddles and before that sex – yes, yes, why don't we talk about my sexual jealousy after we've had some sex, when it won't matter so much because our minds will be clear and our hearts pure?' etc., but externally, to the naked eye, I was up on two feet and proud with it, indeed blustering and self-righteous – 'Jealous! Jealous of what? Him? Hah! I was fed up, slightly, slightly fed up because you two went off without any explanation, leaving the rest of us, including your aunt – who's come all the way down from Dorset – all the way down from Dorset!' etc. – just like Fanny Price in *Mansfield Park*, really, when she sees Edmund giving Mary Crawford the riding lesson that she's expecting for herself, and declares that her emotional tumult is out of concern for the horse – 'She thought it rather hard on the poor horse to have to do such double duty' is, I think, Jane Austen's sentence, and if it's not, hers will be better – actually, the horse doesn't get to do double duty, Edmund finding his own moral justification for weaselling after Mary instead of plonking away with Fanny – well, that's Edmund for you. And that's Fanny for you. And that's me for you. No, it isn't. At least it wasn't with Robert, fifty years ago. There was no blustering and self-righteousness, there was just –

I'll come back to this if I want to, at some other time. No, what I'll do is look up my novel *Little Portia*, where I give a version of those events, as one might say in an old-fashioned detective novel, a version of the events leading up to the death of Robert Symonds, my first true love – perhaps it was spelt with two 'm's – Robert Symmonds, yes, that looks right – a version of the events leading up to the death of my first true love, Robert Symmonds – I haven't got a copy of *Little Portia* here in Suffolk, so it'll have to wait until I'm back in London – I have a suspicion, though, that I was too careful, kept myself as a writer too fastidiously at a distance from what had actually gone on, by which I mean what I'd actually felt, to have been quite honest in the version – version of the events – and how can I hope to do it now, half a century on? – at least the novel was only a decade on. But a decade on I wanted to keep it under control, in perspective, somehow not too personal, while half a century on I'd love to go half a century back, back to when Robert Symmonds and I sat hand in hand in some obscure nook in the Abbey cloisters.

A LOVE STORY: PART THREE

Hand in hand? Yes. How quaint it seems when I write it down, how quaint the image, two full-grown boys, tall and well built, in their school suits that weren't quite uniforms, a liberal school prescribing only the colours but not the shades or the textures of the trousers and jackets, and allowing some slight varieties in the cut, but then there were the stiff white collars, big black shoes – so if not uniforms then a general sense of uniformity, and of uniform clumsiness, yes, that was it, so clumsily dressed we were, or dressed to make us seem clumsy, as we sat on a stone bench or the lid of a tomb, generally in the late afternoon, our hands intertwined as we spoke of our feelings not for but about each other – now what is this distinction? I suppose I mean that our conversation, sometimes tremulous, sometimes savage, nevertheless moved in speculations and observations, 'The thing about you, Simon,' and 'I often wonder, Robert, why you –', rather than 'When I see you in the yard, waiting for me, my heart dips with apprehension and longing – it's because I love you.' 'Love me, what do you love about me?' 'I love – I love –' What did I love about him? That he was mysterious, unpredictable, would suddenly snatch his hand from mine, get up and walk away, standing with his head bowed, as if in despair at the company he was keeping, while I would sit staring at him hopelessly. I could never go to him and touch him and say, 'What's the matter?' or the question asked truthfully, 'What have I done? How can I put it right? Please forgive me.' It would have been a breach of something I couldn't formulate then and still can't quite understand, so let me think – well, perhaps going to him and touching him would have had too many possible meanings – and to touch him where? On the shoulder, like a policeman – or made everything too explicit, and above all it would have been a trespass, in the sense of entering dangerous and forbidden ground – on the other hand it might have been cowardice, a fear that any gesture I made would be met with contempt, or a complete departure – perhaps he wanted me to go to him and touch him, the more meanings in the touch the better – at least he was still there, averted but present, and would return, I prayed that he would return. Usually he did, would come back and sit down and say in his loud offhand voice something that amused him, and he would follow it with his loud, forced laugh, and our hands would touch, enfold, fingers intertwining – how odd it seems now, the intensity of those meetings, how odd that I remember the feelings so strongly but can't recall a single conversation, a single sentence from any of our conversations, although I remember the content, which he mainly provided – Sartre, Man Ray, Cocteau, etc. – and of course my sporting life, how incomprehensible he found it that I should spend afternoons playing football or cricket, it was a joke to him, though not one that he much enjoyed because it was also treason, all those hours when I could have been doing something intelligent, by which he meant being with him in the cloisters, where we could hold hands, or in the Wren Library, where we could sit together in one of the rooms off, in the armchairs, and of course we talked about his impending death – he would be lucky to live until he was twenty, he said, would certainly be dead before he was twenty-five. He said it loudly and comfortably, or matter-of-factly or dramatically, and of course I didn't believe him, although I wanted to, death being a great and romantic adventure that seemed almost an aspiration – yes, I thought it was a boast, really, and admired him for its extravagance, because death was also something that didn't actually happen, at least to anybody one knew, apart from elderly relatives, who had been alive one month and then were dead by post the next.

A LOVE STORY: PART FOUR

It was true that on some of the days when I came to the yard and found him absent he was in the infirmary, his stomach bad again, but generally he would be back the following morning, or the morning after, his large pale cheeks slightly sunken as he hadn't eaten during the attacks – his stomach was rotting, he said, so yes, there's a fragment of a sentence I remember, his stomach was rotting and killing him – the rot had started at his prep school. He had been served a meal with little shards of glass in it, one of the cooks had broken a glass in the school kitchen, some of it had got onto his plate, he had swallowed it and – peritonitis, yes, he'd had peritonitis, which had become recurrent. I don't know how feasible this is medically – nowadays I imagine that you wouldn't die of recurrent peritonitis because they wouldn't allow it to become recurrent, if you survived the initial swallowing they could probably repair the stomach lining – or is it wall? Anyway, the infected area – yes, they'd solve the peritonitis problem, and you would merely die of something you'd caught in the hospital, from a dirty instrument or a pair of unwashed hands or because of language handicaps in the surgical team – in those primitive days you died, as Robert did, of your illness, not because of the people who were treating you – so half a dozen of one, six of the other, I suppose, given that the outcome is the same.

He was at Oxford, in his second or third year, I think that's right, and I think I'd just come back from Halifax, Nova Scotia, and was on my way through to France – no, back from Vancouver, where I'd been teaching at the University of British Columbia – back from somewhere, from somewhere, perhaps from France – no, this is irrelevant, I can't remember the chronology, all I really remember is the phone call to his house, his mother's voice on the line telling me that Robert wasn't there, he was in hospital, it was his stomach – his stomach again. Oh well, I said, when do you think he'll be out? She said she wasn't sure – she wasn't really sure he would be out, he was very, very ill. Then she told me which hospital he was in and asked me to go and see him. He'd love to see you, she said, he was seeing all his friends, and he'd mentioned me, that he'd had a letter saying I would be in England and that I'd phone – and here I was, having phoned, she was so glad that I had, before it was too late, so that I could go and see him. Well, I said, well, I'd love to go, I hoped very much I'd be able to go, I'd find some way of fitting it in, if I possibly could, before I went on to wherever it was I was going on to, Halifax, Nova Scotia, Clermont-Ferrand, France, Vancouver, British Columbia, wherever the hell it was I was going on to –

A LOVE STORY: PART FIVE

The thought of Robert, in a hospital, dying – it was too complicated, dark and grown-up a thought, I couldn't allow it in properly. I talked to several friends from school who had been with Robert at Oxford and who visited him in hospital – prepare yourself for a shock, they said, he's very thin, his voice is thin, you almost won't recognize him – but there's still something about him that's Robert, the smile of course, and the way his eyes light up when he sees you, he doesn't seem to mind that he's dying, that's the most Robert part of him, so exactly Robert – he'll be so glad to see you, you and he were always so close, everybody knew that it was a special friendship, he loved getting your letters – he used to read bits of them aloud and laugh, laugh – be so glad to see you –

I set out one day, in fear and trembling. I can't remember how far I got, but it was nothing like far enough – I think I knew before I set out that I wasn't going to arrive. Nor after that did I phone the hospital, or his mother, or his friends, to find out how he was doing, whether there was any chance – a reversal of fortune, it had all been a bit exaggerated, panicky – but suppose he recovered, how would I be able to meet his eye, explain my failure to see him when he was supposed to be dying? I could imagine him telling me that really, it had been a test, and I'd failed it.

If it did, in fact, feel like a test, it was because I knew I'd failed – I was ashamed, but the shame wasn't as strong as my fear, I could live with my shame if it meant not having to see him, it was a price willingly paid. I was in that respect in complete sympathy with myself – the truth is I'd rather have died than seen Robert when he was dying, it would have been far less taxing, I could coast through my own death, which was after all an impossibility, and besides both events were unimaginable, though his came to pass whether I'd imagined it or not –

I'm at an age now when I should be able to forgive my young self – I could claim that I'd had too little experience of life to be expected to deal with death, the death of a friend – it was precisely because I'd had such a tangled and intimate relationship with him, because I'd held hands with him and longed to please him, had in my imagination saved his life on numerous occasions, had loved him more freshly and intensely than I'd loved any human being before, etc. – I wish I could say all those exonerating things, but the truth is that the shame has not only persisted but grown, I see that first failure as the most abject, because it seemed to mark my way in life – all my failures to come, including my present failures, were somehow licensed by that one – when you've been cowardly once you can be cowardly twice, indeed come to expect it of yourself, and then accept it in yourself – I am what I am, not my fault, childhood or genes to blame, and so forth –

A LOVE STORY CONCLUDED

I made it to the funeral. I remember absolutely nothing about it. Surprising, really, as it was my first.

AT HEART I AM A MERRY MAN

A playwright friend says he doesn't 'do' funerals. I point out to him that there's one he'll have to do, willy-nilly. He says that that one doesn't count, as he'll have no choice. But the other thing about him is that he loves memorial services, or 'celebrations of a life' as they're called these days, which I find baffling – I mean, how can you celebrate a life when it's no longer there? I can quite see that you can't celebrate a death, at least publicly, though there are quite a few deaths coming up during my lifetime, I hope, which I won't allow to slip by without a grateful thought – 'Yes, I admit I hated him/her,' suspects frequently say in thrillers, 'but I never wanted her/him dead!' But why not? I could reel off, right now, a list of people I want dead, and I don't think I hate them, I just don't like the thought of them, and if they were dead I'd stop thinking about them, and the point really is this – that so many people are going to die today, how much grief and suffering there's going to be, much of it anticipated, some of it not – in a film once a woman dying between putting on the kettle and the kettle coming to the boil – the shot of the kettle whistling as the steam flowed out – do kettles whistle any more? – but all those deaths bringing all that grief, why not hope that one or two from your list will be among them, bringing a little spasm of pleasure to at least your sad self?

A RESOLUTION

Enough of this. This must stop. You have to cultivate a new ambition, which is to continue writing this without again mentioning death or dying, friends dead or dying, and it really should be quite easy, as most of your closest friends are dead, none of the few left are dying, as far as you know, except in that they're living and therefore, etc., so enough of this. At your heart, you are a merry man, I am a merry man – so on to some merry thoughts, memories –

LAST DAY IN SUFFOLK

Suffolk, at two in the morning, after a warm and beautiful September day, with a large section of the moon, cold and beautiful, visible through my window when I push my chair forward and then tilt it backward – no, I've just done that and it's no longer visible, it must now be behind my study – I'll go out and look. No, not behind, at right angles to it, it's a three-quarter moon, the fourth quarter not gone but shaded down, so the eye fills it in and gives you the impression of a full moon that isn't properly round, slightly deformed, that fills the garden with light, and there is Tom. I left the door open and I can see her standing in the middle of the garden, her legs bent with age but her face lifted attentively, so there's a mouse about, or a vole – oh, I hope not, Errol did one this afternoon in front of me, a vole, held it in his paws and juggled with it before gouging it to death with his claws, he did it in a very detached manner, as if he had more important things on his mind – I don't, really don't, want Tom doing the same thing in the moonlight. Her body may be old but her eye and teeth are sharp, and she's more businesslike than Errol, no posturing and playing, a quick but ghastly dispatch, and all to show for it a speck of blood on her neat, white little chin, and a little red heap, there in the moonlight – solution, my favourite solution to a problem – shut the door, shut the door and the problem or corpse is no longer there. At least until you go out. Which you have to, in the end, even if the end doesn't come until dawn – but in the dawn there it'll be, a claim on your attention, and there I'll be, scooping it up in kitchen roll, carrying it to the fence, hurling it into the field – an elderly man at dawn, disposing of the remains, and Tom will be in the kitchen, waiting for my step and a saucerful of dry nodules, which is what we give our two cats for food these days, as dry nodules are said to be good for their health, makes them springier and more active, according to the package, which means that they're bad for the health of birds, mice, moles and voles – perhaps it would be an act of mercy to put Tom and Errol back on their previous diet, tins of compressed rabbit, chicken, etc., which they much preferred, I think, even if it made them bloated and ponderous – almost everything I eat makes me bloated and ponderous, I hope it doesn't occur to Victoria to serve me up saucers of dried nodules, if she does she might find me in the garden one night, with something between my jaws that she won't care to identify –

This is all because I am waiting for the telephone to ring. Dreading its ring. You can't shut the door on a mobile telephone, which is why I sometimes wish I could see its inventor between the paws or jaws of Errol or Tom.

PART FIVE

A BIRTHDAY CHECK-UP

Trafalgar Day – I am now officially sixty-eight, having from time to time during the year thought I was already sixty-eight. I suppose in a month or so I shall be claiming that I'm sixty-nine. But then my father used to say that I have a tendency to get ahead of myself, hence the troubles that befall me – but let us, today of all days, not get ahead of ourselves, let us look in the mirror in the cupboard in the hall outside our bedroom and study what there is here, in the present, on the first day of his sixty-ninth year. I've looked, I've studied, and what did I see but a man of my sort of age, with swollen cheeks, uneasy eyes, a lot of blackish hair sticking out in tufts, eyebrows that do much the same, plump lips, no visible teeth, general impression of paunchy slackness, of low self-esteem comfortably lived with – nothing, in fact, to surprise, all quite as expected.

We're talking of sixty-seven years ago, after all – just think of that, a man who, in 1936, was the age I am now would have been born into a world in which Dickens was alive, Tennyson, Browning, Matthew Arnold, Carlyle, Thackeray – Thackeray, not sure about Thackeray – so how the world changed between 1867 and my real birthday in the summer of 1937, when I was self-perambulating around the garden in my pram, with Mummy smoking away somewhere in the distance, Nigel in the kitchen with the Nanny, Daddy in his surgery behaving well or badly with a patient – and changed since then to now, when here I am sitting in my study, brooding on what I found in the mirror of the cupboard outside our bedroom – what will I find next year? Well, you can't look in the same mirror twice, that's for sure.

A VICTIM OF HIS APPETITES

I've just come back from an unsavoury walk. I always intend to settle for a quarter of an hour plodding away from home, and then quarter of an hour plodding back, thus giving me a full half-hour of walking – when I'm stopped by traffic lights I jog on the pavement until they change, keeping to the same pace and rhythm as when I'm actually on the move, but the sad fact is that I'm not getting past the Renaissance these days, I make it to there, and have two or sometimes three cups of espresso with hot water on the side, read whichever newspaper or a magazine I've brought with me, and then a quick bit of shopping, as if to explain to myself that that's really why I've come out, not to walk meaninglessly around and home again, but to perform certain necessary duties – today, after I'd finished my espressos and read most of the book reviews in the *Spectator* I ransacked my mind and became convinced that I had run out of chocolate – in this desk, in the first drawer to the right, level with my knee, I keep envelopes and postcards and bars of Green & Black's organic white chocolate, which I guzzle down – it really is a sort of guzzling, if I understand the word properly, in that I cram it into my mouth in lumps, sucking at it until it turns into a kind of custard, gulp it down even as I cram more lumps into my mouth, and I think I also make snorting and gulping noises – this is not a pleasurable exercise, I assume it's connected in some way to my alcoholism, some time after I stopped drinking I began to crave sweet things, all the things I used to loathe, biscuits, cakes, ice cream and so forth. Usually at dinner I'm the only one eating a pudding – in Barbados Harold and Antonia are always very keen to watch me eating my pudding, there I sit while the band plays on, usually out of tune, a girl with a raspy voice strangles a beloved ballad, elderly couples reel about in the moonlight, there I sit, under the benevolent gaze of wife and friends, with their glasses of wine in front of them or uptilting down their throats, yes, there I sit on display, a prize pig at his trough is what I feel I look like, but, trying to maintain a degree of dignity, I don't lower my snout into the bowl, I wield a spoon in a leisurely fashion, make between swallows interesting observations on this or that aspect of life and literature – but I believe I've already described my pudding behaviour in Barbados, probably described it when we were in Barbados, and anyway there it's a social matter –

GREEN & BLACK, RED-HANDED

But here, alone in my study at this sort of hour, when an awful gnawing begins in the pit of my stomach as if rats were at me there, and I begin to double up with hunger cramps, hunger-for-sugar cramps, I jerk the drawer open, scrabble a bar of Green & Black organic white onto my lap, tear off the wrapping and proceed as described above, grunting and snorting, custarding or should it be custardizing – guzzling. Yes, guzzling. So inevitably I need to be sure that there are lots of bars in the drawers, I dread running out of them as I dread running out of cigarettes, and even if I buy more when I've already got a drawer full it doesn't matter, I'll get to them in the end, I like to eat in sequence, as I like to smoke in sequence, pushing the new bars to the bottom, piling the old cartons of cigarettes on top of the new ones. In other words, it was perfectly reasonable to justify my outing, during which I happened to have consumed a couple of coffees, by bustling on up to Tesco's and emptying the shelves of Green & White's black organic chocolate, or whichever way around it is, Green & Black's white organic – I didn't actually empty the shelves, I took two handfuls and dropped them into my wire shopping basket, on top of the *Spectator*, and, trying to give the impression that I was shopping for a children's party, joined the queue in an orderly fashion. The service is very quick at Tesco's, they have a long counter with five or six cashiers, one minute there are a dozen people in front of you and you get irritable at the prospect of a long wait, the next you are at the counter, and a smiling young man is greeting you, and asking you if you have a club card or something – I don't know what a club card is, perhaps I should find out as it may entitle you to certain Tesco privileges, or reduced rates – anyway I said no, I didn't have a club card, and he said would I like one? And I said not immediately, perhaps the next time I come in – 'Ten bars,' he said, picking them up and counting them. 'Yes,' I said, 'ten bars,' and smiled an unembarrassed smile. 'And the magazine,' he said. 'No,' I said, 'no, I came in with the magazine. The *Spectator*,' and picked it up, and for some reason held it aloft, and out from between the pages slipped another bar, the eleventh bar, of Green & Black's white organic chocolate. There was no doubt about it – it had the look of something that someone had tried to hide – and probably no doubt either that I looked – the expression on my face, my eyes shifting about, the Welshness of me – as if I'd been the one who'd tried to hide it. I made no attempt to explain it, anyway, what could I say but that I didn't know, I really didn't, how it got between the pages of the *Spectator*, because in fact I didn't know, and saying it would make me sound as if I did know, know perfectly well, as mothers and wives are in the habit of saying – 'You know perfectly well that you, how you, why you – how could you!' etc. I lowered my head and stood with it bowed, so that I didn't have to see his face as we completed our transaction. I gave him a twenty-pound note that I keep in my back trouser pocket, instead of my credit card, which I'd planned to give him – I had some idea that tendering cash might make me seem more honest, although it probably has the reverse effect these days, that I get by on cash gleaned from other people's pockets, or from begging. I took my change, and the carrier bag with the eleven bars of white and black and green in it, and also the wire basket – this was entirely a matter of nerves, false guilt, false shame, etc., and I have to admit that he didn't behave as if he thought I were trying to make off with the wire basket, in fact he was quite gentle, reached over the counter and took it from me, and I left. Annabelle was on the pavement in her usual spot, but facing the road, so I could pass her without her seeing me, I didn't feel in the mood really, for giving her cigarettes or receiving a compliment, but something made me stop and touch her on the shoulder. She turned around, and I took all my change out of my pocket and put it into her hand. It was quite a lot, because there was a fiver included, at least I hope it was a fiver, it might have been a tenner, or even a twenty – no, couldn't have been a twenty, it was change for a twenty, so all she got, really, was what was left of a twenty-pound note after the price of eleven black and green whites had been extracted from it. 'Thank you,' she said, in her usual dead-when-receiving voice, 'much appreciated, I really appreciate it, thank you very much.' Thus I atoned for a crime I hadn't committed, and didn't feel any the better for it – I suppose I wanted the young cashier to have witnessed it, to know that I wasn't the sort of man who, at sixty-eight years old, stole bars of chocolate, in fact that I was the sort of man who – what? The sort of man who is, I think, getting a bit absent-minded.

COMPLICATIONS AND MUDDLES

From one point of view it's perfectly reasonable for me to hate my work, lots of other people, all of them probably perfectly reasonable, also hate it. I like to think they hate it for obvious reasons, that they're bored by it because it's slow and undramatic, they find the dialogue irritating and predictable, etc., but it's possible that they dislike it for more complicated and personal reasons – they can actually hear my voice, feel my personality, running under the scenes, or possibly on top of them, and they recoil. Well, the personal and complicated is what I feel when I go to one of my own plays, although I'm not too sure about the complicated – my feelings, it's true, are a terrible muddle, dark muddle, but muddle isn't necessarily complicated, complicated suggests all kinds of subtle interconnections that you might be able to work out – as in the Shakespeare sonnet, for instance, 'Those that have power to hurt, and will do none' – whereas muddle is what you get when you buy a theatre ticket on one credit card and take along another one to collect it, or sign a bill in a restaurant where you think you have an account and don't, as I did the other evening. I signed with a flourish and left, and only wondered in the taxi going home whether I actually had an account, became increasingly convinced that I had or why would I have signed – 'Oh, by the way,' I said to Victoria when I got in, 'we do have an account there, don't we?' 'No,' she said, 'we don't.' 'Well,' I said, 'I think we may have now.' On the other hand we may not, what we may have is a criminal prosecution and/or a civil action, either of which could end in my ruination – what's the difference between ruin and ruination? But

WHY AM I HERE?

Oh yes, I've just looked back, I'm attempting to describe my feelings when I go to one of my plays, they're not complicated, as in a

Shakespeare sonnet, but muddled, as in realizing you've signed for a bill at a restaurant where you haven't arranged an account – so furtive comes into it, a sense of having committed a criminal act – that's it, the public aspect, I feel like a criminal forced to sit with the jury and witness my own crime, witness myself committing it, and then showing it off. One of the things that might strike other people as odd, but doesn't strike me as odd, which is probably the oddest part of it, is that my sympathies, no, more than my sympathies, my whole digestive system and nervous tract, are with the jury, at least its hostile members. I remember at the Huntington theatre in Boston last year, with Nathan Lane as Butley, a middle-aged and distinguished-looking man, almost certainly a Harvard professor, was actually slumped sideways as the play began – I was sitting on the aisle seat in the row behind him, he was about three along to my left, his spectacles dangled like mine from a cord – I couldn't keep my eyes off him, for the whole of the act I watched him, my fervent hope being that he was dead – but he started awake the moment the lights came up, turned to an equally distinguished-looking woman beside him, and spoke quite animatedly and warmly about something – and then they got up, laughing, and went off to the foyer and out, I presumed, into the muggy Boston night, mugging Boston night I hoped. They came back during the interval, sat close together as he expounded something erudite to her, down went the lights, and out he went, a few seconds into the second act, slumped in the same position, spectacles dangling, but this time he was less inert, I could see his shoulders twitching occasionally, as if something was interfering with his sleep, but – though here, in the early-morning calm of my study, I feel in retrospect a certain loathing for this man – then, as I watched him sleeping through both acts, the person I really loathed was myself. I always loathe myself when I see a member of the audience bored or made irritable by my work, it seems to me manifestly my fault that they're having a terrible evening, which they might even have paid for – sometimes, I suppose I should admit, I also blame the actors for having agreed to do the parts, the director for having chosen to do the play, the producer for making it all possible, but there is no getting away from the fact that the responsibility is mine – those hours and hours and hours spent toiling away, the long periods of worry, fret, sleeplessness, struggling to get a scene right, an exchange of dialogue telling and natural, I see myself there, at the typewriter, as a combination of fool and criminal, as if all those hours of worry, fret, sleeplessness were actually spent on planning a hopelessly unworkable robbery, for instance, or a vile sex crime which furthermore I intended to commit in public. So shame, really, is what I'm writing about, shame at seeing my work produced on the stage – or is it mortification? I think there's a difference, well, there must be inasmuch as I've sometimes felt both simultaneously – shame being a kind of hot washing down of oneself, a sort of sluicing, and mortification, a violent bitterness of the self against the self, when you're in shame you want to hide, when you're mortified you want to give yourself a hiding. Can these two states coexist? Well, that's what I meant by muddle as opposed to complicated.

FOR PURPOSES OF GRAMMAR

Let's treat shame and mortification as singular and ask – where does it come from, and why? Or is that the same question, the whence and the why? – I've not met any other playwright who experiences anything like this, in fact I know several who take an immense pride in the public performance of their plays, and not only consider that they're entitled to money from them, but get angry when it seems insufficient, talk about prosecuting the producer for fiddling the box-office returns, or suing him for not spending enough on advertising, I know of one or two who even blame the critics and the audiences when their plays fail – and there is one in particular who is fearless, one might almost say shameless, in his pride in his work – when years ago I went to see one of his plays, a well-written autobiographical piece in which he traced the roots of his present flowering back to his childhood – he'd been a misunderstood boy of quick feeling and powerful, original and, by his immediate family, discouraged talent – at one point, I glanced away from the stage and spied the author leaning so far out of a box that he was in danger of falling into the stalls, on his face an expression of sublime joy as he looked down on the boy on the stage impersonating the creative genius that was to become the figure in the box gloating down on him – I really don't think I have envied a fellow playwright as I envied him, with his proper and healthy pride in himself and his works, in contrast with my own cringing, cowardly dog of a spirit that would rather be skulking in a dark alley with a goat – goat? What do I mean? What do I imagine myself doing in a dark alley with a goat? Get to the question, which is: is *The Old Masters* a good play, or even an OK play? Now I've put it down, I gaze at it with dread, because I can see that it contains an implicit injunction: 'Go and see *The Old Masters*, then come back and tell us in all honesty whether you think it's an OK play, let alone a good play. Go and see for yourself.'

I SEE FOR MYSELF

I didn't think I could do it, actually, get myself to the theatre. I haven't been near the play since its opening night five months ago, though I was constantly proposing plans to Victoria – 'I'll go next Thursday, if I'm up to it.' 'Why shouldn't you be up to it?' 'Well, you know, the West End at night –' 'You can take a taxi to the theatre, have one waiting when you come out, taxi straight home again.' 'I'd rather go by tube.' 'But you hate the tube.' 'Yes, that's the problem –' I refrained from ordering a taxi until the last possible minute, and didn't phone the stage management to say I was coming until I was in the taxi and past Notting Hill Gate, and even then I made it contingent – 'The traffic's very bad,' I said into my mobile as we sped along Bayswater Road, hitting a succession of green lights, 'so I may be late, and if I'm very late I won't come in, don't want to disrupt proceedings.' As I got out of the taxi, at the corner of Panton Street, I could see the hoarding for *The Old Masters*, and I thought of walking on and away, down the Haymarket, but my feet carried me to the doors, and then I was in the foyer, head down, shovelling my way through the crowd – crowd? Well, there was a definite cluster of people at the bar, almost enough to block my way to the little corridor that led to the private room. In the private room the stage manager who calls herself Pea had set out two Diet Cokes, a glass, a saucer for an ashtray, and from behind the door to the box came the peculiar hum and rustle of an invisible audience close by. I sat on the sofa, lit a cigarette and poured a Diet Coke in a kind of this-is-the-life manner, elderly and experienced playwright looking in on his successful play. Pea put her head around the door, and I told her not to tell the cast I was in, thinking that if they knew, I couldn't leave at the interval. I went into the box, which was long and narrow and could seat six, sat in the chair at the very end, adjusted it so I could get a proper view of the stage, crossed my legs, glanced down into the stalls, briefly took in the people moving along the aisle to their seats, the tops of the heads of the people already seated, got up, hurried back into the private room, and on into the lavatory, had a pee, flushed the lavatory, lowered its lid, sat on it and lit another cigarette. I was shaking. I wondered if I could get out onto the street without being noticed, wondered if I could leave a note for Pea saying I'd been taken ill, had had to go home, realized I hadn't got a pen, thought that perhaps I could go backstage and find Pea to ask her if I could borrow her pen so that I could write her a note telling her that I'd gone home because I was ill – flushed the cigarette down the lavatory, wondering if the flush could be heard in the auditorium, went back into the box and sat on the chair in the furthest corner just as the lights were going down to signal that they were about to come up. And they did, on Barbara Jefford in the garden of I Tatti, reading a letter, clutching suddenly at her stomach and moaning in pain, then forcing an appearance of ease on herself as Edward Fox and Sally Dexter – Bernard Berenson and his mistress, Nicky Mariano – entered, Edward quacking like a duck – this is not a criticism of Edward's vocal delivery or acting, he is in fact imitating a duck.

I hoped that the actors couldn't see me – or, what would be worse, couldn't just make out an unidentifiable and ominous bulge deep in the shadows of the box, and imagine perhaps an armed psychopath seeking care in the community, or a theatre critic – but they went on playing the play as if I weren't there, and almost as if the rest of the audience weren't there – they hadn't quite achieved the perfect arrogance that separates the world of the play from the world in the auditorium, there were moments when they paused slightly too long to accommodate a response they'd become used to but last night didn't come, then suggested by other pauses or a break in a line that they had become used to laughter there and there, but that didn't come either – so, assuming a slowness in the audience, they developed a thoughtful, expositional tone, to help it follow the line of the story, but the crucial thing was that even when they did their pauses for one reason or another, and fell into expositional mode, they were still listening to each other, keeping their concentration on each other's lines, and so the play moved naturally if a bit ponderously through the exchanges. Altogether, the production was as solid as it had been on the first night –

Which only leaves the play to be all right to make it an all-round all-right evening. Well, here goes. The play, *The Old Masters*, seemed to me, it seemed to me that *The Old Masters*, my play – what's on? Let's have a look –

IN DENIAL

bowls on the sports channel, bowls – well, I always think that if I forced myself to watch bowls often enough, for long stretches at a time, I could get hooked on it, but then it's not, for me, a very interesting game, so why would I want to get hooked on it? I don't think that, even if I got hooked on it, I'd find it interesting, although there's no reason to believe that I would feel guiltier watching something I'd made myself become addicted to, that wasn't interesting, than I feel watching all those other things I'm addicted to, cricket, soccer, tennis, rugby union, and now even rugby league, and sometimes even golf, that I do find interesting. The guilt has to do with what I'm not doing instead – writing – rather than with what I'm actually doing, so it doesn't matter what it is I'm doing if it isn't what I think I ought to be doing – let's change the channel. Oh, here's

CARY GRANT

in black and white – God, he's beautiful, extraordinary, I've never seen a modern face, a young face – how old is he in this film? Early forties? – I've not seen a face like that on any man in his forties in these days, not that it's an old-fashioned face, his haircut doesn't look particularly old-fashioned, although the film was probably made in – what? At a guess early 1950s, let's have a look at the title. It's a marvellous thing about Sky Plus, you press the blue-coloured crescent-shaped button on your remote control and the name of the film you're watching, *People Will Talk* in this case, comes up on the screen, but you have to be careful, if you hold the button down too long it tells you what's on the next channel, and then the next, and you get confused, not remembering which title belongs to the film you're actually watching – ah, he's a doctor, putting on a white coat, lighting up a cigarette – in a bit of an old film I saw recently there was old James Coburn, well, a very young James Coburn – I came in on it when he was lighting a young woman's cigarette, in close-up, and then he lit his own cigarette, they spoke intensely to each other as the camera moved back, and you saw that they were both wearing surgical gowns, the scene went on for a bit, they talked movingly to each other and it was about then that we discovered, no, everyone who'd been watching the picture already knew, it was I, coming in late, who discovered that this conversation between a smoking surgeon and a smoking nurse was taking place over the operating table on which the patient, full of the usual tubes etc., with the anaesthetic mask over his face, was laid out – otherwise he or she would have been smoking too, I hope – now those really were the days, and in Technicolor. So Cary Grant as Dr – she's just said his name, Preorious was it, Pythagoras, no, obviously not, well someone will say it again soon, the girl is obviously the other star of the film, I know her face well from a memory of all the films I saw when I was in my early teens, but I can't remember her name, if I ever bothered to take it in, a neat little face, pretty, I suppose, but slightly foxy and knowing, not quite right for the part, which is a mess of a part, as far as I can make it out, she's pregnant by a man she's not married to, and who is probably going to remain off-screen because here she is, falling in love with Dr Pergorious, whatever, anyway Cary Grant – and furthermore she's just tried to commit suicide by shooting herself in the hospital corridor having left Cary, who first of all told her, his face and voice full of cheer, a good-news doctor, that she was pregnant, and when she told him that being pregnant was in fact bad news, given her circumstances, he told her to look on the bright side, though I don't think Cary was quite sure what the bright side was – she leaves his office, we stay with him while he lights a cigarette, there is the sound of a shot and we go to her lying in the corridor –

(BUT WHY SHOOT HERSELF?)

It seems a bit odd, to me, to be visiting a doctor with a gun in your handbag, and using it on yourself when you find out that you're pregnant, which you didn't even realize was on the cards – the reason she'd wanted an examination from Cary was because she'd fainted suddenly while attending a sort of post-mortem Cary was giving, no, that he took over because the old doctor who was meant to be giving it was in somebody or other's office, snooping about for information on Cary, of whose success with patients he has become jealous, leaving his first-year medical students idle – so Cary, who popped his head into the lecture room, immediately grasps that the students have been abandoned, and starts to discuss the corpse of the young woman spread out on the table in front of him, discusses it with relaxed authority, elegance, charm, wit, etc. – absolutely pure Cary, as self-possessed with a corpse as when dodging bullets from the nozzle of a crop-spraying plane. Is all this clear? Why do I want it to be clear? Why am I writing it down? Oh yes, it began with turning on the television in order to avoid doing something distasteful – oh yes, thinking about *The Old Masters* – and seeing Cary, Dr Cary, smoking a cigarette – and realizing yet again what a beautiful man he was,

CARY GRANT AGAIN

with something secret about him, all the merriness, the sparkle in the dark eyes – what colour were they when he was in Technicolor? – but in black and white they're dark – the voice with its odd, engaging accent, neither English nor American, not transatlantic either, entirely his own accent, it's merry too, a merry, intimate, crisp voice, but it also has something secret about it, it's almost the most important thing about Cary's charm, the feeling that he's withholding, will always withhold the self that is the source of all this sparkle and merriment, so he's also a bit dangerous, in a way that has nothing to do with his slightly studied unpredictability – an odd, out-of-place gesture or an over-extended vowel that is nearly a mispronunciation, those are gimmicks, actor's personality gimmicks – now what was it he said about himself? 'Everybody wants to be Cary Grant. Even I want to be Cary Grant.' And then there were all those rumours, even before his death, about him and Randolph Scott, the rock-solid hero of lots and lots of B-movie westerns, he was really an off-the-peg version of

GARY COOPER

– no, that's not fair to either of them, there could never be an off-the-peg version of Gary Cooper, he was unique, inimitable, impossible to follow the contours of his smile even if you had it in a photograph in front of you, impossible to capture the shifting shyness in the eyes, the odd, wayward furrows of his brow – the face of a poet, really, that a poet never has, the most beautiful poets' faces have never expressed the poetry of Gary Cooper's face, and very few of them could express it in their poetry, either. Now there's a question for an old-style examination paper, which poet has come closest to expressing the poetry of Gary Cooper's face? I suppose we ought to try and think of an American one, but actually I'd go for Andrew Marvell myself – but you wouldn't look to Marvell for Randolph Scott's face, which wasn't poetry anyway, it was prose, sturdy, workmanlike prose, almost inexpressive apart from the rather rugged smirk he always wore, as inexpressive as his voice, which was rugged too, of course, almost without inflection, robotic, but he had presence, no getting away from that, he looked right in cowboy clothes, deer-skin type, and usually a hat – so let's give up the intended comparison between Randolph Scott and Gary Cooper, and get back to the question – which was whether Randolph Scott used to tie Cary Grant up in his gym and whip him? And to the next question, which is why I'm asking this question, as I'm not keen to know the answer, especially if it might be yes, yes, Randolph did hang Cary up in his gym and whip him – but why should I mind, there's nothing particularly wrong in wanting to be tied up and whipped, I suppose, unless it's the thought of Randolph Scott doing, and of Cary Grant receiving, the whipping – it offends not as an act in itself, people who get pleasure from whipping should whip whom their whipping pleases and so forth, but there's something about Cary Grant –

LET SCOTT WHIP SCOTT

well, what it comes down to is that I can't bear to think of Randolph Scott even lighting Cary's cigarette, let alone whipping him, they shouldn't ever have been in the same room together, Randolph Scott should be whipping Lizabeth Scott (no relation, as far as I know), who was a regular villainess, femme fatale, etc., in B movies of the 1950s, she had a husky, lisping voice, and a boldly androgynous face, and a sheaf of hair that fell down one side of her profile, masking it almost, and she made me uncomfortable every time I saw her on the screen, not in the way that Virginia Mayo made me uncomfortable, aroused, quite the opposite, she made me feel that she was – was – well, now I can identify her, I think, as a lesbian, at least my memory transforms her into a lesbian because it brings knowledge and experience gleaned over a number of decades, not that I believe for an instant that I can identify lesbians by their expressions, voices, mannerisms, unless they're wearing earrings, nose-rings, tattoos, have spikily cropped hair, purple lips, growling, angry voices and biceps – in other words are actually presenting themselves to me and the world as bull-dykes – but Lizabeth Scott was sleek and silky and, as I say, lisping, and used to like to stand with her hand on an out-thrust hip, or her arms around a man's neck, smiling intimately into his eyes, and all the time she was letting you know, making you feel, that she wasn't feminine, not in relation to men anyway, that she was a snake, poisonous, that her kiss would be a bite and you'd sicken from it, become corrupt, die – in fact, she scared me when I was eleven or so, and I hated her being in films with men I loved, like Glenn Ford – I don't think she was classy enough ever to get into a film with Gary Cooper and certainly not Cary Grant, but she'd have been perfectly right in any frame of a Randolph Scott film, they could whip each other in scene after scene, as far as I'm concerned.

CARY GRANT: PART THREE

I still haven't got Cary's name in this film, irritating, as people keep saying it perfectly clearly but it slips straight through my consciousness – it's moved on quite a bit since I started writing about it, the rodenty girl has introduced us to her family, a grisly, pipe-smoking father who tells us that he's a failure in everything he does, which we're meant to find lovable, but as far as I'm concerned he's failed in that too, in fact I vastly prefer his completely unlovable brother, off whom he sponges, a mean-spirited, small-minded bigot of a farmer – the sponging, lovable brother, by the way, lets us know that in the heart of himself he's a bit of a poet – horrible to see Cary having to pretend to lap all this up, having to pretend to love this phoney old father, as well as be in love with his rodenty, pregnant, suicidal daughter – it's a ghastly film, really, Cary is far too good for it, and so is the dialogue. That's strange, but it's the case, the dialogue flows along, some of it smart, some of it witty, always eloquent, with long sentences that are not only grammatical but elegantly constructed and yet sound natural when spoken – now those really were the days, cigarettes and proper dialogue properly and easily spoken – everybody in the film, minor roles included, gets to speak it – in a silly, psychologically nonsensical film there is proper dialogue, while nowadays we get – oh, don't bother, don't bother to go into what we get nowadays, instead get on to

LOOK AT ME

which is the idiotic English title for the French film *Comme une image*, we saw at the Gate last week – a freak of a film, full of intelligent and civilized people behaving to each other as such people frequently behave to each other, egocentrically, thoughtlessly, narcissistically, with mainly accidental but sometimes deliberate cruelty, all of them perfectly observed in their smallest reactions, all of them intensely sympathetic even when they go against the grain of one's own good manners and kindness, which are always at their most evident to oneself when one is witness to the bad behaviour of people rather like oneself – there is a marvellously painful moment when the novelist father goes to a concert in a church at which his daughter, a fat girl with a great deal of prickliness in her, to do with her consciousness of her fatness, and the ways she is constantly slighted, or feels she is – though at moments the film catches her in an expression which makes her the most beautiful – I mean physically beautiful – creature in it, and one sees how one could fall in love even with her ill-temper and her swiftness to take offence – anyway, it is one of the most important moments in her life, her singing solo at this concert, and we watch her, and then her friends, her boyfriend, her music teacher, and then and above all her father, in the back of the church. As his daughter sings, he gropes in his pocket – for what? We don't know, but whatever it is he can't find is something he needs urgently. He turns to a faithful acolyte beside him, makes a gesture, the acolyte fumbles through his pockets, until further down the row someone produces a pen, it is passed from hand to hand to the father, who nods thanks, gets up and slips out of the church, his daughter in full, haunting flow – we see shots of him from a distance, slightly hunched, walking with a purpose, the music from the church following him as he recedes, and then we go back to the church, to the daughter unaware of his departure – such an everyday sort of treachery, which should nevertheless have robust consequences, and in fact the daughter minds, the father is embarrassed, when they sit alone and discuss it later, on the doorstep of their country house, the moon out, a few guests inside, he manages a hint of an apology, she accepts with a daughterly laugh of incredulity, and the moment is gone, an amusing moment because it's true, and a sad moment for the same reason – so here is a film, a film worth going out for, looking for, travelling across London and the Channel for too, if it's stopped showing in London, a film that makes you ask –

WHY CAN'T WE MAKE SOMETHING LIKE THAT?

And how can the French do it? How do they get the funds to do it? Of course it's elitist, one imagines the British whatever, lottery, I suppose, is what you go to when you want to make a film – they say, what's it about? And you say, it's about this rather fat girl who wants to sing professionally – not pop and crap but proper music, cantatas and so forth – and is the daughter of a talented but selfish (unusual combination) novelist who thinks his creative balls are shrivelling, and about another younger but rising novelist whose wife teaches the rather fat girl singing, about these sorts of people and how they get involved with each other, take advantage of each other, fail with each other etc. Now, can one seriously imagine anybody from the lottery, anyone from our film industry, putting up money for a film with a story like that, with people like that in it? What they put their money into, our money into, is

GUNS AND BUMS

vile gangsters films in which disgusting people mangle and shoot each other and every next word, and sometimes the word in between, is an obscenity – or into a lumpish comedy in which much the same people, using much the same language, expose their bums etc. It's true that there's an occasional classy product, once every few years or so, in which a mixture of English and American stars fall in love with Hugh Grant, who frowns and frets and stammers and tumbles his hair about in that charmingly old-fashioned way, and shows his teeth a lot – they're probably very good, the fact that I can't stand them myself is not really the point, they make money without being on the one hand violent or on the other infantilely lavatorial – but I don't want to give the impression that the vile and violent gangster films we make, or the infantilely lavatorial films we make, also make money – they lose it, as they certainly should in a just world, but in a just world they wouldn't get made, in a just world the English, British, whatever name we go by these days, director would be forced to sit through *Comme une image* – and then he would be given a gun, as from one of his vile gangster films, and then locked in a lavatory, as in one of his infantile lavatorial comedies, no, not locked in it, bricked up in it, and he there can mess about with his favourite prop in his favourite location until shame, hunger, madness and so forth compel him to raise it to his mouth.

   None of the above speaks well for the civilizing influence of *Comme une image*, at least on me – in fact, thinking about it with affection and admiration seems to have driven me into a frenzy of disgust – but sometimes the contemptible awfulness of this culture of ours – but what about your own play, eh? Which is what started you off on all this. Well, at least you can claim that a) there are no guns in it, b) there are no lavatory jokes in it, c) there is no nudity in it, d) nobody swears in it, not once, and e) everybody speaks in complicated and mostly intelligent sentences, and they do it as if it were natural to them – which makes them freaks in our world, and the play a freak in London's West End. How amazing that anyone comes to see it, regardless of whether it's any good or not, which is a completely other consideration, and one that I'm trying to avoid addressing – so, so how come Cary Grant and the disgusting British film industry have between them led me

OUT OF DENIAL?

Because you can never walk in a straight line away from a thought you want to avoid, the thought is controlling your escape route, making your straight line into a circular one, back into the mouth of the thought – the thought being in this case that though the director and the actors had given the evening a rich and polished shape, and found a way of engaging the audience's attention, the playwright, the playwright, well, let's put it out there in its most unavoidable form, no, what I'll do is wait until I go in again, which will be three Saturdays hence, the last night, and I'll sit through it without flinching, no, I can't promise that, let's just commit myself to sitting through it, and concentrating on it with the intention of – well, just sitting through it. The good thing about this promise is that I can now abandon the subject for at least three weeks. So out with you, out and about with you. No, actually what is worrying me about *The Old Masters* is whether the scenes grow out of each other organically – Christ! Or Jee-zus! – 'grow out of each other organically' – the sort of horticultural vocabulary I used when I lectured on English literature at Queen Mary College, University of London, 'organically' was a particular favourite, long before it marked all those packages of everything from pork pies to yoghurt on the supermarket shelves, everything in *Hamlet*, for instance, was organically related to everything else, plot to character, character to theme, theme to structure, structure to symbol, symbol to image, image to plot, plot to character and here we go again – when of course the truth about any play – well, take *Hamlet*, as we've already taken it, take *Hamlet*, for example, particularly appropriate, as we're going to it soon – I must ask Victoria when – 'Hey!' I called out, 'when are we going to *Hamlet*?'

WHEN DO YOU THINK?

No reply from her study, so I went into the bedroom. George was on the bed, looking depressed, which suggested that she knew Victoria was going out. I could hear noises from the bathroom, the shower running and what might have been singing. 'When are we going to *Hamlet*?' I bellowed. She came out with a towel draped around her, hair damp, cheeks pink, charming to look at, obviously preparing for a night out. 'Where are you going? I didn't know you were out tonight.' 'So are you,' she said. 'What? Where? Where are we going?' which was almost a rhetorical question really, answered by the lurch in my stomach. On the other hand Toby Stephens is Hamlet, he's a friend and a terrific actor, so two excellent reasons for going, and really, when it comes down to it, the only slight thing against going is the play itself, which is bound to run well over three hours, it always does, and furthermore I can't bear – But I'd better go and get ready, ready for going out to *Hamlet*, which means popping a couple of co-praxamol against the anticipated longueurs, packing chocolate in my pocket against the inevitable hunger, and changing my shoes twice for no particular reason, that's what I do these days before going out, change my shoes twice, sometimes three times, usually ending up in the ones I started with – I expect Victoria would prefer it if I changed my shirt once, but I never promised her a rose-bush.

AND ONE JAUNDICED EYE

We had a smashing dinner, with Toby and his wife, Annie-Lou, who is very tall, with a stalk of a neck and a face like a sunflower, beautiful, in other words, and a very good actress. Toby, of course, is also beautiful, both on and off stage, has a glow about him – aura, is it? – that makes me think sometimes of Rik Mayall, who sometimes made me think of the Sun King, *Le Roi Soleil*, because of the glow or aura, as in those icons, Toby has that as Hamlet, and it's a fine thing, a royal body containing a royal mind – a quick, sarcastic, sometimes desperate royal mind, so there was that going for the production, and that, really, was all there was. The set was a circular grey wall, with sliding doors to keep the action flowing along, but the action that flowed along flowed along for far longer than registered by my watch – it was colourless, that was the thing, perversely colourless, when Claudius and Gertrude are reprimanding Hamlet for his mourning attire they themselves are kitted out in dun-coloured costumes, as was everybody in the court, so that Toby, with his starkly contrasting white and dark outfit, and his paley-pinky handsome face and luxuriously abundant golden hair, was by far the most striking figure, as of course he should be, but not in reverse, his bleakness should contrast with their opulence, he the funeral, they the wedding, etc. – but then it seemed unlikely that this couple, Gertrude and Claudius, had ever spent a moment together in bed, he was a bristly bureaucrat, meaninglessly emphatic, who'd knocked off Hamlet Senior because he thought he could do a better job as king, anyway would put in more hours at the office, and she was so agonized and bereft, so much the widow and so little a wife – what rank and enseamed bed, one kept wondering, or who's been sleeping in it, to make it rank and enseamed? Nobody in this court, not even Laertes and Ophelia – when they have the routine grope, the grope that most directors get them into these days while lecturing each other on the need for sexual discipline, pretty disgusting stuff actually, they behaved like two strap-hangers on the tube accidentally and irritatingly entwined, and they did their exchanges in much the same manner, their sentences meaninglessly but irritably entwined – now this Laertes wears funny white make-up when we first see him, and walks and postures in a manner usually described as camp, not that he has an interesting interest in Hamlet, either, or in anyone but himself and what shampoo to use – while Ophelia, who struck me as possibly a good actress unsuited, by temperament and, it has to be said, physique, to be Ophelia, comes into her own when madness descends, stalking everyone on stage with fingers pointing at their eyes or crotches, voice rasping, so that really you want her to get to the pond as quickly as possible – but on the other hand you can't imagine her sinking passively to the bottom after lying on top with flowers, you imagine her entering the pond with something of a splash, then realizing where she is, striking out for the bank with a powerful crawl. Osric, who requires plumage in dress and speech, is dun-coloured in both, Rosencrantz and Guildenstern not only indistinguishable from each other but from Osric – this court has neither life nor echoes, no distinguishing characteristics of any kind, although Polonius tries his hand at comedy, developing a self-important but lunatic laugh as the evening progresses. Bernardo, by the way, is inaudible in Welsh – you know he's Welsh, or is assuming a Welsh accent, because you half-catch a sort of lilting noise when he speaks, and his body has a lilt to it too, though it makes no more sense than his speech – he doesn't help himself or us by mainly addressing the back of the stage or the wings, which at least makes him different from most of the other actors in the production, who speak out front, to the audience, even when purportedly speaking to each other. This is the famous RSC house style, entrenched through decades – I first noticed it during the famous Henry IVs about thirty, could even be forty years ago, and what's more, no, nothing more, think positively, think – ENTER Fortinbras, thank God, surveying in stately fashion the proliferation of bodies generated by poisoned onions in the wine, mishaps, cunning, false slaughter, etc. He rolls his eye from corpse to corpse, pauses, hunches a shoulder, as if about to make an absolute corker of a joke, yes, please, then speaks in the rolling tones of an actor whose only scene is the last scene, only speech the last speech, announcing that Sheekey's is just around the corner, thank you.

AN ENDANGERED GHOST

But it strikes you, if you allow the thought to enter, that it's a narrative for an audience with lots of other things to do – drink, brawl, fornicate, eat oranges, urinate, etc. – it lollops all over the place, and to so many places, some of them unreachable even by academics and theatre critics – the two have a lot in common when it comes to Shakespeare, above all received opinion, which they send out in their turn to be received by others in their turn, so the view rolls on, through the generations, from generation unto generation, that Hamlet is one of the greatest masterworks of the human spirit etc. the completest expression of Western man's consciousness etc. – which speech by speech it possibly is – and that seeming anomalies and idiocies can be explained by intelligent (i.e. academic or theatre critics') analyses. The truth is that Shakespeare, although indisputably the greatest genius of moment-to-moment drama etc., and the greatest poetic intelligence in the history of the world etc. was in the making of plays – well, you get the feeling that his left hand is holding down the pages of his source, Plutarch, Holinshed, whatever, while his right hand is investing a character with character and translating his reported speech into iambic pentameters that pulse in the here and now of the stage. The trouble is, he follows the stories almost sentence by sentence it sometimes seems, and while it's OK to be haphazard in a chronicle, discursive, anecdotal, so forth, it's not OK with polite modern audiences, who can't skip the longueurs, unless they're lucky enough to have nodding-off tendencies. The undeviating nature of his transcriptions accounts for the oft-pondered mysteries – the ghost in *Hamlet*, the witches in *Macbeth*, etc., on which so many articles, theses, no doubt published books have been written – 'What function do they serve, these supernatural influences that Shakespeare insists on bodying forth and on which directors devote so much ingenuity? How do they connect symbolically, thematically, above all ORGANICALLY, etc., to the poetic dramatic unity, so forth?' – In the current production of *Hamlet* we have the ghost as a star turn, he has a ghastly and chalky glamour, and drags an immense sword that is both a weapon and an anchor to the underworld. He also has a slow, creaky agility – he leaves the stage by clambering up into a box, an interminable process which involves him in heart-stopping feats of balance and concentrated muscular strength, as well as nerves of steel – there was a moment when he hovered and trembled, one leg stretched forward to the rim of the box, another straining back to keep him upright, when we were in a sort of catatonic circus, the audience gripped by the intensity of the physical danger to the actor. But how can a ghost be in physical danger? – Well, that's the problem created by this production's ghost, that however spectacular a spectre, he belongs to a different order of underworld mythology from any suggested by his environment. But it doesn't really matter, because the problem created by Shakespeare is one that no production can solve, whatever sort of voice the actor gives him, booming, husky or hollow, it only works when it's issuing injunctions – 'Swear!' and so forth – it won't carry him convincingly through his bits of narrative. When he describes how he was murdered, there is too much detail – you can't go into narrative and detail in a cavernous, husky or hollow voice, you are working against yourself, losing your ghostly dignity with every sentence, turning yourself into a grievance – bore with a chest problem – the play would be vastly more interesting if Hamlet had to deal with the naturally perceivable facts, his father dead from a snake-bite while dozing in the garden, his mother remarried within a month, a little month, to his father's brother, and thrilled to be so – why not? A satyr is a satyr, after all, and knows a thing or two, while Hyperion isn't going to do the business where it counts – a sequence of thoughts along these lines might lead Hamlet to bleak speculations about what really happened in the garden, the snake crawling into his father's ear – now there's an image to jumble a son's emotions – and with the fangs striking and squirting into the dark whorl everything changes, Hyperion's court becomes the satyr's playground, funeral cold meats become a wedding feast, incest in the corridors of power, carnality and festivity throughout the kingdom, riot in Mummy's bed, Daddy's bed, Uncle's bed, whose bed? Shakespeare didn't need the ghost, but in it goes, because there it was in his source, and besides they always like a ghost or some such, and isn't old Bundlebap in town, he specializes in comic gravediggers, ghosts – so on with the story, what comes next, let's have a look, scribble, scribble, scribble, Mr Shakespeare –

Same with the witches in *Macbeth*. They're in the source, they're in the play therefore, therefore on the stage, and therefore they're a nonsense that has given rise to a steady stream of nonsense in the academies – that is, they used to, I don't know if Shakespeare is taught in schools and universities any more, though I think he must be, going by the number of teenagers in the theatre last night, why would they be there unless they were doing him in exams? If they have exams any more – anyway, exams or not, I must admit that they sounded as if they were having a good time whenever Toby was on stage, screamed with joy when he took his many curtain calls – which, by God, he deserved, because after all he'd given us Hamlet and the Prince, even though the director had left out Denmark, and there wasn't a state to rule over, or die in. Or for, therefore.

A GLUM PROSPECT

And oh Christ! there's another Shakespeare tragedy coming up in a few months, with a friend in it, so another night like this one in the offing –

WORDS OR INSECTS?

Offing? What on earth is the etymology of offing? But is etymology the right word, or does it mean the study of insects and such, and is the word I want entymology – I've just looked entymology up on Google, and the first item that caught my eye was An Entymology of the word FUCK, with FUCK in bold letters, like that, and the entry directly underneath it was (still is, I suppose) Entymology for Utah Fly Fishers, so I think I'll leave the question open for the moment, though I'd guess that my initial instinct was correct, and the word I wanted was the word I used, etymology, which brings me back to the etymology of Offing. In the offing – an extraordinary phrase, it almost ceases to mean what you know it to mean the moment you look at it, it becomes particular, as if it were a place – if it's in the offing, who put it there? Could you imagine saying, 'He left it in the offing,' and if you could, what would you imagine he'd left there? Stockings, he left his stockings in the offing. What would be the opposite of offing, onning? Yes, yes, they got tired of her perpetual offing and onning, people would know what you meant by that, especially if they spoke English – it would mean that she kept saying that she would, and also that she kept saying that she wouldn't. I must try it out on someone when they least expect it, to see if they look bewildered, or if they take it in their conversational stride – Harold would be a good person for this little experiment, as soon as the right context comes up – there's the problem of Peter Bowles, for instance, who has said several times that he'll do a tour of *The Old Masters*, but then again has said several times that he won't, so I'll raise the subject with Harold, and it'll be easy at some point to slip in, no, not slip in, I'll make it emphatic – 'I wish to God Peter Bowles would stop offing and onning' – and Harold will either say, 'Quite. I quite agree with you, we need to know one way or the other,' or he will look puzzled, he'll start up slightly, he'll say, 'What exactly do you mean by offing – and thing – what was that other word –?' 'Onning.' 'Yes, well, what exactly do you mean by that? That word onning?' To which I'll have to say, 'Well, you know – now on, now off, now off, now on, onning and offing, offing and onning,' and then he'll probably say, 'Oh. Prevaricating, in other words,' and 'Yes,' I'll say, 'prevaricating, in other words,' and the conversation will move to a different subject – though I doubt if it will be as important as finding an actor to do the tour, because the tour will bring in some money, which I will need when the London run ends next Saturday.

BUGGINS'S TURN

Judy Daish phoned this morning to say that a letter had just arrived at her office, it was from the Office of the Prime Minister, 10 Downing Street, it was marked on the envelope as urgent and private, so she had opened it, to make sure it contained nothing abusive, should she send it around, as it was in fact an enquiry as to whether I would be prepared to accept an honour in the New Year's list? Yes, I said, do send it around, let's have a look at it. It arrived half an hour later, inside a large brown envelope which was in the grip of a helmet-headed, leather-jacketed delivery man – we did a scuffly business on the doorstep, with him giving me the envelope while he sorted out his clipboard and pen, me returning the envelope to him as he gave me the clipboard and pen, and then us both fending off Toto and George, who were scampering around our feet trying to gnaw his boots and the bottom of my dressing gown, a tattered blue-towelling affair that looks more stained than it is – I signed my name twice, once as a signature and then with a scrawl to identify my signature, handed him back his clipboard and pen, ushered the dogs back into the house, climbed the stairs back to my study, climbed down them again when the doorbell rang again, opened the door to see the same man, in his helmet and leather, holding a brown envelope out to me exactly as he'd done a few minutes before. It was, of course, the same brown envelope, which he'd taken away with him, along with his clipboard and pen. We had a little laugh about it, each blaming ourselves – a pleasant alternative to the common human practice – I got the dogs in again, got up to my study, sat down at my desk, not this one, the other one, with the typewriter on it, this one has the computer, lit a cigarette, put on my spectacles, opened the brown envelope, took out the white envelope, slim, elegant, official, and, as Judy had said, with the words From the Office of the Prime Minister at the bottom left, and Urgent and Private, top left. Inside were a couple of sheets of extremely white paper, one of which, couched in courteous but impersonal language, asked if I would consider accepting a jumble of letters with a B in it, the other resembled the sort of form you have to fill out when going through Customs, with little empty boxes that had to be ticked or written in. I wondered if I oughtn't to shower, shave and get dressed, there was something a little indecent about this companion and almost colleague of Annabelle and – and her partner, what name did I give him, can't be bothered to thumb back through all the pages, think, think, James, Annabelle and James, no, that's not right. Henry? Annabelle and Henry – Henry James, yes, of course, dreary little Robinson from *The Awkward Age*, *Tragic* – no, *The Princess Casamassima*, Hyacinth, Hyacinth Robinson, Hyacinth and Annabelle! Yes, so this companion and almost colleague of Hyacinth and Annabelle is sitting half naked, belly hanging, cigarette between his fingers, spectacles halfway down his plump and shapeless nose, stubble grey and growing, studying a letter in which he is being asked if he would like to have his name submitted to Her Majesty for consideration etc.

IMAGINED DELIVERY BY ROYAL MALE

On the other hand there is a distinct possibility that I am the victim of
a joke, nobody in this country who was serious about communicating
with someone else would send a letter through the post, especially if it
involved the Prime Minister, the Queen and so forth, they would send
it by a special messenger, who would run with it through the streets on
naked feet, or thonged sandals, in a tunic and carrying the message
slung over his shoulder in a special satchel with an insignia on it, and
in his right hand an official stick which would possess such authority
that it would work like a magic wand, traffic would gather to the
side of the roads down which he ran, as would pedestrians when he
ran along the pavements, traffic lights would change from red to green
as he approached, the citizens would lower their heads in respect as he
passed them, and on the door behind which the recipient waited, he
would give three knocks with the knob of his wand, and when the door
opened there would be a brief exchange – 'I have an Urgent and Private
message from the Office of the Prime Minister, 10 Downing Street, for
the playwright and man of letters Simon Gray.' 'I am Simon Gray, the
author of the play *The Old Masters*, and of many letters to newspapers
and to my son.' He would fall to one knee, the message extended. I
would take the message, and have the messenger escorted to the kitchen,
there to be treated with the courtesy due to, etc. – this is how, it seems
to me, a serious man in 10 Downing Street, the Office of the Prime
Minister, would send a letter to a man who might be seriously interested
in acquiring an honour from Her Majesty the Queen. Needless to
say, the same process would be repeated with the response, the refreshed
messenger again on his knee, the letter placed in his hand, then through
the door, the streets, back to the office in 10 Downing Street. It
would be difficult, of course, to send an equivocal answer in such
circumstances – 'I need a few days to talk it over with my wife, Victoria –'

A HUMBLE ACCEPTANCE

I woke at midday, got up for a pee, ate two sour plums, brushed my
teeth, went back to bed, thought for a while, then called out for my

wife, Victoria. I'd like to report that she came running from her study, which is next to the bedroom, but she merely answered my call, and only at the third or fourth time of calling, with a brisk noise that meant 'Wait.' When she came in she had the letter and the form in her hand. She sat on the edge of the bed, and I asked her if I were honoured what form would it take. A medal, presumably, she said, what other form could it take? Well, a garter, or a belt, or a combination of both, so a garter-belt, but how would I, albeit modestly, manage to show it off – wear a kilt? I'm entitled to a kilt of some sort, being half-Scottidge, a descendant of the Macdonald-slaughtering Campbells – my wife, Victoria, is descended on her mother's side from the slaughtered Macdonalds, which perhaps explains why I feel we were destined for each other, a happy variation on the Romeo and Juliet theme, although it's taken a few centuries to work itself out –

My wife, Victoria, filled out the form – she's practised from filling out medical forms on my behalf, though this was less complicated, just date of birth and some ethnic stuff when it came down to it. She said there was no point in going into all the quarter-English, quarter-Welsh, half-Scottidge, I'll put down British and have done with it, she said, and she did, then she handed me the form to sign, and I did, then she put it in the envelope and said she'd post it when she went out later, which she did. Everyone in the Prime Minister's Office, 10 Downing Street, now knows that they have an unambiguous 'Yes' on their hands, but from them I shall only have an ambiguous silence, I won't know if I'm in fact honoured until it's announced, or not announced, in the papers on New Year's Day.

LAST NIGHT AT THE COMEDY

I saw it pretty clearly, sitting at the back of the dress circle with Victoria, only missing a few minutes at the beginning of the second act because I couldn't tear myself away from the little private room in which we spent the interval. I wanted to have a cigarette on my own and savour the moment – although I don't quite know what the moment was that I was savouring, the run was coming to its end, the characters who'd walked the stage of the Comedy would walk it no more, the actors would go back to their homes, some of them start new jobs, they might never meet again except fleetingly, at those events where actors bump into each other, and, perhaps most movingly, my cheques for the week's royalties would stop arriving at my agent's office – so I doubt if I really wanted to savour the moment, I just wanted to savour a cigarette where a cigarette is best savoured, on one's own, in a room where you're not really allowed to smoke – so I missed that much of the second act, a cigarette's length, furthermore I only missed the sight of it, Edward Fox and Peter Bowles were perfectly audible in the little room, I could even hear the silences, one of which went on for so long that I thought Edward, whose turn it was to speak, had either dried or died – but then it came, Edward's voice, floating into the little private room like a phrase from a Gregorian chant, he gets into the mode sometimes, not exactly singing but not exactly speaking either, which I suppose is why I think it sounds like Gregorian chant, perhaps plainsong would be better, or the way we used to intone psalms at school, anyway definitely ecclesiastical, starting the sentence very high, dipping down a notch or note or two, rising again, then a pause, which you assume is an invitation to the other actor to speak but is actually ended eventually by Edward, so it's rather as if he is plain-singing back and forth with himself – this is the experience you get, or rather I got last night, listening to him through thin walls in the little private room before I dropped my cigarette into the lavatory bowl in the rather large private lavatory, peed over it and then flushed it away. This time it occurred to me that the flushing noise might be audible not only in the auditorium but also on stage, so I slunk out, down the little corridor, through the curtains into the dress circle, and sat at the end of the back row, next to Victoria – there was a thin pillar in front of us, whenever the action moved from one side of the stage to the other one had to reincline one's body and shift one's head – that's the thing about the theatre, it always keeps you engaged, active, even when nothing much of interest is going on on the stage.

THE JURY RETURNS A VERDICT

Nevertheless and – I wasn't shamed/mortified by what was going on, on the stage. The acting was very fine. Edward, as I've already hinted, slow, but so rooted in his Berenson that he was utterly convincing, not one of his pauses seemed phoney or willed, but an integral part of his sense of the character, so that my eagerness for him to hurry along there, please, went really against the other grain in me, which relished the sheer Edwardness of what he was doing. Peter Bowles was – everybody knows, of course, that he's technically one of the most accomplished actors of our time, and he brought all his accomplishment to Duveen, but there was also a world revolving within the razzmatazz, geniality, panache that made you feel that the more he exposed the less you knew – the moment in the second act when he becomes befuddled, then absent, then seems about to lapse into unconsciousness, one grasps that it has a physical cause, something has jammed in his brain, but one also feels that he has actually been somewhere else, seen and experienced something at the dark heart of things, and the effect of it lingers through the rest of his performance, giving a poignancy to his apparently triumphant exit. Sally Dexter as Nicky was as she had been from her first performance, sexy, graceful, loving and alive in every moment, I adore watching her just walk across stage, she flows, head held high, the line of her so delicate – and so unlike her off-stage movements, which are boisterous, not exactly clumsy, but jolly and impetuous – in her scene with Fowles, when she sits neatly, somewhat primly, in fact, on the bench, she suggests layers of humour, sensuality and reserve, not only available to Fowles, but you feel almost a mistress to the world at large, she could have conversations of this equivocating intimacy with any man she met, and possibly any woman – yet we also feel her complete faithfulness to Berenson, the love of her life – and her loyalty to her lover's wife – a good woman, she seems to me, whose little treacheries and deceits do her credit. So that's the cast, apart from Barbara Jefford, who plays Mary Berenson and Steven Pacey who plays Fowles, Duveen's intermediary. Now I'll make no bones about this, why should I? – I think Barbara Jefford is a great actress, have thought so from the first moment I saw her in rehearsals – and yet I can still only define this greatness by negatives that I've already used, the simplest of which is that she doesn't appear to act – there is not a tremble, a drained, angry look, a sudden playful smile, a stricken laugh that isn't Mary's, and it's extraordinary to me, extraordinary that – stop here. Getting overwrought. Still, I'll just add – I don't know who'll get the various awards this year for best actress, but I'll bet it won't be Barbara Jefford. Their eye will fix with their usual sightlessness on the unique real thing, move sightlessly on to the sort of acting that happens all over the place, and light blindly up when it finds it happening at one of the subsidized theatres, in a part that appeals to heterophobes, which quite a few current theatre critics are, or feel obliged to make themselves into – some, of course, have arrived there by a direct route, a consequence of genes, hormones and ill-nurture – I wonder if what I've just written is against the law, and whether my computer is tapped in to by a government agency – I must be careful when transcribing it onto the computer – although it's possibly within the reach of modern technology to tap in to the yellow pads themselves, in which case my goose is cooked, goodbye to the future, certainly goodbye to the honour – to be stripped of it before getting it, the characteristic feat, no, I mean fate, of a Libran, or a homophobe, some people would call me, I suspect. They can call me homophobe, and it's thumbs down for me and my future, but if I call them heterophobes, it's also thumbs down for me and my future – well, I've addressed elsewhere the question of whether I'm homosexual a.k.a. gay, I can't remember what my findings were, but whatever they were let's put them aside and address the question of whether I'm a homophobe –

WELL, AM I A HOMOPHOBE?

Start by examining what it means. *Phobia* is Greek for 'fear', right? And *homo* is either the Latin for 'man', or the Greek for 'the same'. Assume it's not the Latin-for-man meaning – after all, lesbians are also considered to be homosexual – so it must mean the same – a homosexual is someone who has sex with a person of the same sex, simple really, and therefore a homophobe is someone who is frightened of someone of the same sex, which in my case is male. Am I frightened of other males? Well, it depends entirely on who they are, I don't think I'm frightened of them because they're males, only if they're dangerous, angry, violent males – but on the whole I'm not as frightened of dangerous, angry, violent males as I am of dangerous, angry, violent females, so really – on the grounds of semantic logic – I can't properly be called a homophobe, can I? But I'm being disingenuous, I know perfectly well that a homophobe is someone who is frightened of homos in the demotic sense of the word, so down to the knuckles at last, am I frightened of homosexuals, of either or both sexes?

I've been sitting here, trying to think it through, with no result, just a whirl of images, memories, experiences best left forgotten – so I shall try thinking it through as I write it down, and when I've finished I'll read it back, and then I'll know where I am on the question of whether I'm frightened of homosexuals – no, no, this will never do, as somebody said of *The Lyrical Ballads*. It'll never do to go on pretending that *phobia* means 'fear', which is actually what it means, when it's come to mean – through years and years of the usual sloppiness and misuse – hatred. So the genuine question I have to think through as I write is, do I hate homosexuals of either or both sexes?

Here I go, writing blind, so to speak. The reason I'm having difficulty is that I really don't know what a homosexual is, other than that he or she prefers to have sex with someone of the same sex, and I can't really imagine what the sexual act would be like – no, what it would be, when it comes down to it. I suppose if I work on it I can visualize the acts of buggery and sodomy, though at the moment I wouldn't do it very clearly because I've forgotten what the difference between the two acts is, do men sodomize other men as well as buggering them, or are they synonyms? That's hard to grasp, because they're such different words, so let me begin by pursuing –

BUGGERY

How can I? For one thing I haven't the slightest idea where the word comes from, its root, but it has an Anglo-Saxon feel to it, dense, clotted. But no, one can say it quite lightly, so that it trips off the tongue, I've just tried it with a French accent, *la bogarie*, it sounded pleasant, rather vague – and the verb, *Je me bogue, tu te bogue, il, elle se bogue, nous nous boguons*, no, no, hang on, it can't possibly be reflexive, *so vous boguez, ils, elles boguent* – but the act itself, one assumes, isn't at all vague, though it may well be pleasant, depending on which one you are – perhaps it's pleasant for both parties – and that's as far as I can go with buggery, so on to

SODOMY

I know where the word comes from, of course, from the Old Testament, the town of Sodom, but what did the residents of Sodom call it when they did it to each other? They can hardly have been conceited enough to name the act after their town, as if no one in any other town had thought of it before – or perhaps the people in all the towns in the Old Testament named the act after the name of their own town – ah, but not Gomorrah, there is no verb derived from Gomorrah, as far as I know, merely the noun for the ailment. No, that's another word entirely, gonnoreah, not sure of the spelling – pity, really, the sentence 'She gomorrahed him' is full of interest, as long as you refuse to let the Irish aspect seduce you – I'm sure there's a joke about that, there must be, I can't have got to the age of sixty-eight without hearing some joke made out of the confusion between Gomorrah and Begorrah, if that's how it's spelt. Now, that's about as far as I can go on the sodomite aspect of homosexuality, though I still haven't worked out whether it's a different act, and the only friend to whom I could put the question – what is the difference between sodomy and buggery? – is no longer available, although I could presumably simply look it all up in a dictionary, or even on the Internet, but I feel embarrassed at the thought of doing that. Nonsense, I mean I'm too lazy, especially as I know that the moment I stop writing this down I will lose interest in the subject, and the last thing I'll want to do is to write down all the definitions of sodomy and buggery, especially as one thing is bound to lead to another, it always does in dictionaries and on the Internet – my departed friend once confided to me – he didn't confide it, he told me in an open and above-board manner – that the best sexual experience of his life came when he was twelve, he would go into town – he was a Shropshire lad – on market day and hang about the pig and sheep pens asking the farmers and shepherds there to give him a treat, which several of them invariably did, being simple and kindly country folk. What made it so perfect, he said, was that they had no teeth, just these old gums masticating away – bliss, he said, bliss, and he was a man who'd had a great variety of sexual experiences, with men and women, from early boyhood right up to his death in a windsurfing accident off Nmeth Island – I've never understood why he wanted to take up windsurfing, as he wasn't really much of a swimmer, in his soul he was a landlubber. None of this has brought me any closer to finding out whether I'm a homophobe, in the current meaning of the word. So

WHAT WOULD MUMMY HAVE WANTED?

She'd have wanted me to be a homophobe, an anti-Semitic, racist homophobe, as would have befitted her idea of the complete, middle-class public-school all-rounder – actually, it probably doesn't work like that, that's what she would have wanted me to have been then, because it's what she thought was mainstream, patriotic, Churchillian, but if she were alive now she would want me to be mainstream now, which means she would have wanted me to be a homophiliac, heterophobic, anti-racist and – no, not pro-Semitic, in fact politically anti-Semitic, I assume, and pro-Palestinian, but no talk of noses and avarice, no Fagin and Shylock – my cousin Betty, who became my stepmother, once told Nigel, when I was out of the room, that she thought I had Jewish blood, 'Not you, Nigel, no, no!' she said. 'But Simon – I mean –' and she made a gesture, a hook-shaped gesture, over her nose, which was pert and neat. 'And some of his ways!' Though there she might have been muddling my seeming Jewishness with my seeming homosexuality – in her view, which Mummy half-shared, they, both 'theys', Jews and homosexuals, liked the same things – art, music, books – and natural, healthy gentiles preferred manly things, like rugby and war in Nigel's case, and bonking little Betty, along with other friends and relations of my mother's, in my father's case. If little Betty really believed I had Jewish blood, and saw my nose as a literal statement – a sort of involuntary confession – rather than a symbol, then who did she believe was my biological father? Where was the Jew who had entered mine father's spouse, and made me, and my nose? It was an attractive thought at the time, explaining why I always felt uneasy in my father's company, and why I often wished, dreamed indeed, that I would turn out to have been Jewish and adopted – being only half-parented, and through my anti-Semitic mother, was the closest I could hope to get –

POOR OLD THINGS

But facts are facts. DNA tests would doubtless resolve the conundrum, but really there is no conundrum to resolve – I know that I am my father's son, know it more with each passing year, as I find developing in myself all the attitudes and some of the mannerisms that so irritated me when I observed them in him – I am more my father's son at sixty-eight than I was at eight, eighteen, twenty-eight, fifty-eight . . . It's not that I understand him better or that I love him more – in fact, I despise myself in the way that I used to despise him, the younger creatures that I once was somehow unify into a still-present self who catches me in some elderly, inherited movement or gesture, and sneers, 'There he is, there you are, one and the same, poor old thing.' I probably have inherited characteristics from my mother, but I've never recognized them, never recognized them in either of my brothers – though I recognized him in them all right, he was strongly present in Piers's face, his features, his expressions, but they never irritated me in Piers, nothing about Piers irritated me, though at the end his drinking infuriated me until I realized, half-realized, it was terminal. On the other hand his presence in Nigel irritated me when I first consciously noticed it, when he was twelve or so, and I eleven or so, about then, until we were both in our forties, when I began to find it reassuring – grown-up, sensible and kindly – paternal, actually.

THE FAMILY TREE

We sit when we're tired with our lower jaws thrust out, shoulders hunched, our right hand clamped into our left armpit – simian. I remember writing about this once, somewhere, describing looking around the room one Christmas about forty years ago, I suppose, and seeing my father, Nigel and Piers sitting in that posture, and realizing that I was sitting watching them with my shoulders hunched, hand in armpit, jaw thrust out – my grandfather did it too, I think I remember, but I may be imposing it on him, wanting to see him as part of a procession that goes back to the crack of time, the gang of us sitting in a tree, lower jaws thrust far out, shoulders hunched up to our ears, but there'd be women too, or females, perhaps the more tactful word in these times of ours, you can't really talk of women apes, can you, without giving offence, whereas I suppose ape women could be merely descriptive, neutral therefore, but better not try it out, may not sound exactly neutral, not neutral at all to say, for instance, that there was this ape woman, apish woman, ape of a woman, in the Renaissance this afternoon, buying carrot cake – better visualize this tree from time's early light as cluttered with entirely male apes, with senior ape – Grandad, mine on the lowest branch, about to fall off, Daddy in the middle, keeping one eye on his dad below and one eye on his own son on the branch above, while at the top of the tree, his own son's one furry hand at work in his armpit, the other reaching for a banana in the sky, and more likely, in his confusion of appetites and yearnings, to topple to his doom than his great-grandad, who clings to his low bough with the intensity of senility. I wonder if apes get Alzheimer's. Are humans the only creatures to get Alzheimer's? Probably only humans are intelligent enough to prolong consciousness into imbecility, and only humans are imbecile enough to want to continue life – this comes of taking two sleeping pills. I'd like to think I took two by mistake, but I know better, I took two because I was afraid that one wasn't enough.

A WILLINGNESS TO MOURN THE DEATH, BY ANY MEANS, OF A BLACKBIRD IN LONDON

There is a bird that sings through the night, from about 11 p.m. on it warbles away until – I don't know, it's still warbling when I go to bed at 5 or 6 a.m. It seems to live in the little alley between our house and the house next door, at least that's where the warbling sounds as if it comes from, but I suspect that the bird is actually on one of the streetlamps on the pavement, and that it sings because it mistakes the artificial light for natural light, which means it lives in a perpetual day, and gives up its song without a break, from dawn to dawn, dusk to dusk, dusk to dawn and dusk. It sings and sings away – its warble is charming for the first moments, but it never changes, it's the same warble, with little fractures of silence that become as offensive to the ear as the sound it is interrupting, but have I heard it in the daytime? I think not. The traffic might cover it, though. What sort of bird is it, anyway? One or two people I have consulted say it must be a blackbird, my imitations have a blackbirdy sound, they say, and blackbirds are notoriously stupid – for instance, they build their nests in hedges at cat level – anyway, I have come to hate it, and believe it is mainly responsible for my taking two – and I'm afraid that one night it will be three or four or five – each one shortening my memory span, so that I ask after the fifth or sixth whether I've already had one of these. And I'm afraid, in short – I am afraid.

A SUNDAY MORNING IN SPRING FIFTY-SEVEN YEARS AGO

I can still remember the feeling, as I crouched in an alley off the King's Road and a man walked towards me carrying a large piece of wood which I'd seen him take out of his truck, he had gone back to fetch it, after seeing where I was hidden, and sized up what was necessary for what he wanted to do – had walked quite slowly back to his truck, and searched out the piece of wood, knowing that I couldn't possibly get out past him without his catching me, and possibly bundling me into his truck and driving off to murder me slowly, in a private place he knew about, where he'd done it before – of course it was my own fault, as these things often are, with me anyway, also the fault of a beautiful morning, which gave rise to an enormous sense of exhilaration, a devil-may-care exuberance, and a conviction of complete lovability. I had come up Manresa Road from Oakley Gardens, mid-morning on this beautiful Sunday, going nowhere in particular, out and about on my own – I have an idea that I must have had some money in my pocket, but I don't think I had any actual plans to spend it, there really wasn't very much to spend money on in London 1946, especially if you'd already used up your sweet ration and if your sexuality was a year or so away from being on the rampage, and dictating the course of most of your thinking and planning – there was nothing but the day itself, and me in it, and precious little traffic, very few pedestrians, the King's Road on a Sunday, immediately post-war, springtime, and I bouncing and jumping and darting along and forking two fingers at a trundling rubbish truck as I bounced, jumped and darted across its path, two fingers raised in defiant *joie de vivre*, something I'd never done in my life before, but it felt terrific, what did I care if he cared –

It didn't occur to me that he cared until I realized he was driving steadily behind me, when I picked up speed he picked up speed, and when I looked at his face for the first time, the face that I had insulted with my gesture was a blob of fury with a cap on top, I had never before seen such fury on a face that didn't belong to my family, from which I at least knew that it would pass, and it was a fury that also expressed an overriding purpose – to hurt me, really, to do more than that – I ran, I ran very fast in those golden, pre-pubescent days, when my energy was unspent in idle, hard-working devotions – ran very fast along the pavement of the King's Road, turning into squares that inevitably led back to the King's Road, he trundling implacably just behind me – twice I stopped in doorways, hoping that having hunted me down he'd go on his way, game over – but he stopped too, and got out, a large but squat man, I now see him as, in overalls and thick boots – the overalls and thick boots are accurate, I'm sure, but about the size, really all I saw was that he was a full-grown man, the size of my father. He got out, and off I ran again, back along the pavement of the King's Road, and when he stopped at a traffic light I ran behind him, crossed the road into Dovehouse Street, a street of small houses, for the poor, in those days, that led to another street that brought me down into the King's Road, although this was by choice, my intention of course being to get home, please get home, and there he was, parked at the kerb, engine running. I crossed the road again, ran towards Manresa Road, then, as he was making his turn, ran back, then completely outwitted myself by running down the alley, which had a wall at its end, and nothing but a doorway to crouch in – so he parked, got out, went back to fetch the piece of wood, walked steadily down the alley until he was a few yards away, and I crouched with my hands around my ears, please, please, please. It seemed like a minute that he stood there – as I didn't look at him I'd no idea what he was doing, frowning, scowling, grinning, thinking, deciding – then I heard him walk away, and when I looked up he was getting into the truck and it trundled across the top of the alley, and out of sight.

I went up the alley, saw the truck going down the King's Road towards World's End, then walked to Oakley Street, down it to Phene Street, into Oakley Gardens. I could see Mummy's face at the upstairs window, the living-room window, the cigarette in her mouth, behind her, Daddy, his hand on her shoulder, the sight that made me feel as protected and safe as I've ever felt, the immortal parents, guarantors of my immortality, though I was still trembling, the fear still hadn't left my body. She appeared at the top of the stairs, again looking down, pointing her cigarette at me.

'You bloody little fool!' she said. 'How could you be so shaming!'

I couldn't think what I'd done while I'd been out, except running for my life.

'Why?' I said. 'Mummy.'

'James, you tell him. Your father will tell you.'

'Come on up,' he said. He was wearing his troubled, stern expression, usually summoned up by his wife.

I went into the living room. They sat down, he in his usual chair in the corner, next to the table on top of which, some years later, the television set would be. He picked up his dead pipe, pulled on it, eyes over his spectacles. She sat on the sofa, coiled, seeming to chain-smoke her cigarette – in and out of her mouth, puff, puff, she was furious, furious! And humiliated, she said, humiliated! I'd humiliated her. Them. The family.

Nigel came into the room.

'Leave us alone for a few minutes, old boy,' my father said.

'Unless you've done something bloody stupid too, Nige,' she said, with extra dollops of affection.

'I've been upstairs in my room.' He spoke with mournful dignity, as he went back up there. I'd seen from his expression, though, that he knew what I'd done, he'd been listening upstairs in his room, or outside the living-room door, and what I'd done was so bad that it was outside his experience, outside his imaginative experience of bad behaviour, his expression had let me know as much –

'Sit down,' my father suggested.

'Yes, sit down.' She wouldn't look at me, just the profile, and the puffing.

'Where have you been?' asked the father.

'Just out. Up to the King's Road.'

'Running about on the King's Road.' From the mother.

'Well, and up Sidney Street – and by the church.'

'What were you doing?' He held the pipe away from his mouth, brow furrowed and wise.

'Nothing. Just – well running . . . about.'

'Hah!' Puff cough cough. The coughs were explosive, because she was trying to suppress them. 'Jenkins saw you. The younger brother.'

The Jenkins family, the milkmen, on a rota system.

What the younger Jenkins had seen me doing, my father explained with that grave kindness that was worse than a beating, was their boy Simon running up and down the King's Road, making obscene gestures at people, people like him, the younger Jenkins.

'I didn't,' I said. 'I didn't even see him.'

The point was that he'd seen me, running about, with two fingers up, and then running all over the place, not looking where I was going, bumping into people without so much as an apology – it was a wonder somebody hadn't given me a good thrashing, it was no more than I deserved, and how could I expect to get in to Westminster if I went running around with two fingers up, and worst of all –

'To hear this from little Jenkins!' She'd opened the door to him, had expected the usual respectful but insolent conversation about the bill, which was always delivered too early, from her point of view, or paid too late, if you were a Jenkins. 'I've never been so mortified – mortified! That a son of mine! From a Jenkins!'

'I'm sure he won't do it again. Will you, old boy?'

I said I wouldn't, under any circumstances.

Puff cough, went my mother, puff cough cough, and then the coughs exploded, and revealed themselves to have been suppressed laughs. Daddy laughed too, splutteringly, jamming his pipe into his mouth to help stop himself.

'It's all very well,' she said, struggling to change her mood, by aiming a blow in my direction, 'but what were you thinking of, you fool?'

'Yes –' Daddy, no longer peering over the rims, but packing tobacco into the bowl, in a spirit of real enquiry – 'why did you do it?'

'What on earth's the matter with you? It's not worth snivelling over. Really, really, Si!'

And 'Really, old boy!' too, from him. But he got up quickly, put his hand on my forehead. 'He's very hot,' he said, 'and damp.' It was his professional voice, James Davidson Gray, MD.

She put her hand on my forehead, probably but not necessarily the one without the cigarette. 'Yes, hot and damp. Feverish.'

So, crying and shaking, I was put to bed, she put the thermometer in my mouth, he took my pulse, it was agreed that I was running a light temperature, I was given a something – aspirin? – from her a kiss on the forehead, from him a pat on the head, they had a brief conversation about whether it would be all right to go to the Phene Arms, where they went every Sunday before lunch, for a drink with their friends the Lumsdens. They decided it would be, I seemed calm enough now – 'Aren't you, Si?' – cooling down by the second, anyway they would only be half an hour, and there was Nigel to keep an eye on me – won't you, Nige? – and off they went.

Nigel loitered briefly, with a knowing smile, he knew me better than anyone else in the world, after all. He asked me what I'd been up to, really up to? I told him. 'Well, you got away,' he said, 'so what were you crying about?' I couldn't tell him, because I didn't know – but it was probably to do with being safe, that would likely be it, safe in their anger, then safe in their laughter, then safe in their worry – and it was also a bit to do, perhaps, with the discovery that a small, impulsive gesture to celebrate the bounce in your blood could lead almost immediately to your running in terror from a man who could trap you in an alley, with a piece of wood in his hand, walk slowly towards you, and next time not change his mind about killing you – though perhaps he hadn't intended to kill me, perhaps he'd intended to do precisely what he'd done, which was to teach me a lesson – a lesson well taught, I've never since forked my fingers at an approaching vehicle, never forked my fingers at anyone unless I loved them, and felt pretty sure that they loved me –

I've just remembered a sentence I wrote, and checked on it – yes, there it is, 'I think Nigel came into the room about then, yes, the whole family present, as I started to cry –' The whole family? But where was Piers? Let me think, work this out. If I was ten when it happened, Piers was either just born or just about to be – but I don't remember Mummy pregnant then, nor his presence in the house – but one or the other was the case. Nowadays, of course, her smoking and going out for a drink would suggest that she was no longer pregnant, but back then, in 1946, a pregnant woman wasn't pregnant with moral complications – nowadays a pregnant woman can have her unborn baby killed off virtually at her convenience, but let her try smoking and drinking in a public place. 'It was a nightmare,' a very nice woman who came to interview me last month told me – she was in her early thirties, with a baby, now about six months old, that she hadn't really wanted, but now that she had it, had her, I seem to remember, now that she had her, she couldn't imagine not having wanted her – during her pregnancy, after a long day's work, she liked to go to her local wine bar, as she'd been doing for years, and people she'd never seen before, complete strangers, would come up to her and admonish her – wag their fingers and sometimes almost spit at her, for having a drink – she only ever had one drink, at the most two – and as for smoking! Smoking and drinking and pregnant! How dare she! Perhaps if she'd said it's OK, not to worry, I'm getting rid of it some time next week, so no harm done, at least none that would make a difference to its future –

I think Mummy must have been pregnant. It was a cool sunny morning, which suggests spring, so she would have been, well, at least seven months – but I don't remember it, can't see it, just the smoke, anger, laughter, worry and love – still, I'd better cross the sentence out – there it is: 'I think Nigel came into the room about then, yes, the whole family present, as I started to cry –' crossed out.

PART SIX

A PRAYER OFFERED

Christmas is over, thank God, and we're into the New Year, without anyone close to me ill, or dying, except inasmuch as we're all, etc., and with luck, God willing, DV, etc., next week – or is it the week after? – we'll be in the hotel in Barbados. The Pinters are going before us this time, so it'll be their job to nab the table, check the room – no, they won't have to check the room, we'll have the same room that we always have.

Harold phoned this evening from the hotel. 'It's pissing down!' he barked, quite cheerfully. 'Been pissing down ever since we arrived – four days of it.' 'Oh,' I said. 'How bloody awful.' 'Yes,' he said. 'I just thought you should know.' Well, yes, perhaps, perhaps I should. But then things change in Barbados, in a blink there's sunshine, and after an hour or so you can't remember the rain. It's four days before we go, four days to blink.

It's still pissing down, it hasn't stopped since he last phoned, he said, they've had a week of it, and it shows no sign of letting up. 'Be of good cheer,' I said, 'be of good heart. We will bring sunshine, and there'll be sunshine thereafter.' He didn't sound convinced. 'All shall be well, and all manner of things shall be well,' I almost crooned at him. 'Not a wink of sun!' he said, 'not a wink of it, all the time we've been here.'

The threatening-looking baby in the seats behind us remained comatose for the whole journey. It had been raining almost up to the moment we touched down, we were the first off the plane, first through Customs and Immigration, first out of the airport into the sunshine, then into the waiting car, half an hour to the hotel, and half an hour after that into the sea, which was warm and clear, unruffled. Now we're on our balcony, a balmy night, the torches are flickering around the restaurant, the band's in place, and the music sounds OK, it really does, a bit bland, but soft and jazzy – it won't last, though, because it's Thursday, and Thursday night is limbo night, the band will get boisterous and drown out the sea. If I stand up and look down into the bar, I can see Harold's profile, and beside him Antonia's face, partly obscured by one of her majestic hats. At their table are two elderly ladies, whom I can't identify – I think they're playing bridge – yes, Harold made a movement, an emphatic putting-down-a-card-take-that! kind of movement. In half an hour or so we'll join them, and then, minus the two elderly ladies, we'll go in to dinner, sit at our usual table, and all, all manner of things –

THE
SMOKING
DIARIES

Volume 3

The Last Cigarette

For my beloved Victoria

PART ONE

A RESOLUTE MAN

2005

I'm still in Suffolk, where it's a typical August afternoon, cold and damp, with England losing a test match in Birmingham, and things can't go on like this. I say that, but how can they change? Well, I can make them change by stating categorically –
                    That intend to give up smoking.
I've left out the 'I'. Do it again, with the 'I' in it.
                    I intend to give up smoking.
There. I've put it down. It's legible, in firm, blue ballpoint. There's no getting away from it because it's plonk in the middle of the page, and to tear it out would be cheating.

This diary is going to be about my attempt to give up smoking. It is also going to be my main help in giving up smoking. By the time I've finished it I will be a free man, able to leave the house without my two packets of cigarettes, and my two lighters, able to sit down and read without compulsively checking that I've got these four articles in place on the desk in front of me or on the little table beside me. I shall never again have to grope for a cigarette while watching television, fly into a panic when I can't put my hand straight on the package – is that an unintended double entendre, 'put my hand straight on the package'? I have an idea that 'package' has a salacious meaning, or am I thinking of 'parcel'?

   Nor worry that I might fall asleep with a cigarette burning on the brink of the ashtray, or while hanging from my lips.

   There will be no cigarette burns – at least of my making – on my trousers and my shirt fronts.

   The cuffs of my cardigans will no longer be singed. No, that's not right. I am devoted to my two cardigans, which are identical in every respect, including the location and the extent of the singes, so to put it accurately, there will be no further singes on my two cardigans. In the unlikely event that I ever have a new cardigan, and that I wear it, it will never be singed at the cuffs. At least not by me.

Socially
I will no longer need to check whether smoking is permitted at any unfamiliar restaurant at which I want to book a table.

And when smoking is banned in all restaurants, cafés, pubs and bars, as it surely will be, I shall no longer contemplate having to spend my last years in my two clubs solely because smoking will be permitted on their premises. If it is permitted. It's entirely possible that, as in Scotland, smoking will be banned even in private clubs. It makes my blood boil even to think of it. Banning smoking in private clubs! In all restaurants, bars and cafés, come to think of it! What a nonsense! What an impertinence! What an infraction of the fundamental liberties of an Englishman, let alone his human rights!

Hold on, though. Hold on to this. You are going to give up smoking voluntarily. The bans are irrelevant. It is your choice.

I read in one of the papers the other day that they're going to ban smoking in California prisons, including in the cells on death row. As all things Californian, except its weather, eventually spread around the world, there's more than a good chance that smoking will also be banned in prisons near home, the ones in which, if I am sent to prison, I'm likely to be housed. I once spent almost a month in Los Angeles, but apart from a misunderstanding with an attractive Jewish lesbian stand-up comic whose breasts seemed, from a drunken male heterosexual point of view, more Jewish than lesbian, I don't believe I did anything in California for which I could still be extradited, although you never know, with new sex laws being introduced every day, no doubt all of them to be retroactive, I might conceivably end up in a prison there, perhaps even on death row. On the other hand, as I'm trying to give up smoking, that could be the sort of extreme solution I'm looking for. Turn myself over to the electric chair and that would be the end of it – though given the American system, I could end up on death row with years and years of no-smoking appeals all the way up to the Supreme Court ahead of me, and then be put down without a last cigarette. Surely this would approach the 'cruel and unusual' treatment that their constitution forbids? How can anyone decide what is 'cruel and unusual' for someone else? Only I know how unusual it is for me not to have a cigarette, how cruel it is for me to be deprived of one. The judges in the various American courts who would decide against me, as they doubtless would, what sort of men and women would they be? If they were told that if they allowed me a last cigarette their lives would be blessed with peace and joy, as would their children's, and their children's children's, even unto etc. would they say, 'Hey, it does seem a little tough to send the old English guy to the chair without letting him have one last cigarette'? Or would they remain true to – what? What would they be true to? Is it just or decent or humane, no, it is unusual and cruel! It is American! Is any of this helping me to give up smoking? How am I going to do it?

Perhaps the solution is to throw away all my packets and my lighters – Yes, I might do that. Tomorrow we go back to London. Perhaps it would be more sensible to start stopping then. I'm not sure that I can do it entirely by willpower – there are various aids – patches, lozenges, gum.

But I've tried nicotine gum – about twenty years ago, when you needed a prescription, which made it more appealing by making it seem almost illicit. In no time, it seemed to me, I'd swapped clouds of nicotine in the lungs for pools of it in the stomach. Just as I'd never been without something between my lips, I was now never without something between my jaws – I kept this up for six months, six months of worse than the usual indigestion, a drain-like smell around my mouth, the grinding of teeth upon teeth, and I might still be doing it, or more likely be dead from it, if I hadn't undertaken to direct one of my plays in New York, and had to deal with a very difficult actor, an eye-rolling, shoulder-shrugging, gesticulatory young ham of an actor. One night, in the interval of a preview, I found myself at the bar nearest the theatre, trembling with rage at a new on-stage walk he'd developed, as if he had two wooden legs or had soiled himself. I ordered a double whisky, then plodded to the cigarette machine, put in the right number of quarters, pulled out a packet of Marlboros and a book of matches – it wasn't until I was on my third or fourth cigarette that I realized I was smoking again, and knew that from then on there was no going forward – well, until now, of course – but my point is that gum, lozenges, patches won't do the trick, it really does have to be by a sustained act of will, by resolution.

Give myself a date. If the purpose of this diary is to accompany me on my journey as I struggle not to have a cigarette, day after day, hour by hour, minute on minute, struggle to go without a cigarette – then why, as I write this, have I just put out a cigarette, why am I now lighting another one? I should put it out. Why not put it out? NOW. Start stopping smoking NOW.

IS TOTO, TOO, A CHILD OF HER TIME?

I was sitting in the kitchen reading about the snug little world of Moscow's elite in the early 1930s, all the prominent families living near each other in their apartments in the Kremlin, with neighbouring dachas by the sea, all the droppings-in, the children playing together, the drunken evenings, the gossiping, flirtations, adulteries, all the men chummy and drinking together while vying for the boss's ear and promotion. And then this tight and sociable group, almost an extended family, began to poison itself. Lifelong friends, husbands and wives, brothers and sisters betrayed each other, all at the behest of the avuncular psychopath who connected them each to each –

It made for miserable reading, but I kept at it, miserably, until Toto, who'd been sitting under the table by my feet, suddenly growled, reared up, ran through the dog flap into the garden, and began to make a screeching noise. When I went out she was standing over what I took to be one of the mounds of earth that the moles throw up – they are all over the lawn, like little prehistoric citadels. She was butting at it with her head, then lifting her head and screeching, then butting, and I realized it wasn't a mound of earth it was a pheasant, about half her own size, and more than half dead, but shuddering. I couldn't think of any way of getting her away from it, short of kicking her.

I went out again just now. The corpse, at least I hope it's now a corpse, was sodden and still. Toto was crouched over it, also sodden, her haunches quivering, licking at it. She sensed me watching her, crouched lower, and snarled. So here I am, back in my study, writing about it. And there is Victoria, in her study, writing about something else, probably.

It's stopped raining, the sun is out, and I'm back from the kitchen, into which I tried to lure Toto with leathery-looking strips which come in a cellophane bag and are called Doggie Treats, something like that. The first few times I held them out she ran towards me, then wheeled around and whipped back to the pheasant. This happened four or five times, though each time she got less far from the pheasant, until finally she didn't come at all – she adjusted her position so that she couldn't see me, and resumed her snarling, licking and butting. So I'm back in my study. It's raining again.

Toto has at last left the premises. Victoria effected this by putting the lead on George at the garden gate, then holding up Toto's lead and summoning her in a soft, coaxing voice. I waited for a while after they'd gone, then scooped up the wretched mess and heaved it into the organic field at the end of our garden, right out into the stubble. This field has received many corpses over the years, mice, moles, voles, birds, all victims of our two cats, Tom and Errol. I don't know whether the pheasant was in the first instance a victim of Toto's, it might have dropped into the garden from the sky, from a stroke or a heart attack. We can assume, surely, that animals in the wild sometimes die from natural causes, perhaps even from their vices. The phone is ringing – Victoria on her mobile to ask whether I'd disposed of the remains. I said I had. She said, well the walk's impossible, Toto's lying down and refusing to move. I said that I'd go and meet her, which I'm just about to do, after I've tied my shoelaces and lit a cigarette, which I've just put out after a very few puffs.

*

It was a gorgeous walk, with the sun setting, the fields and woods so green and fresh, George trotting along obediently, Toto skipping in front of me, pulling a bit but quite content to be doing what we do every evening in the country. Now and then she ran to a fence and looked for a horse. She likes to lick their faces and they seem to enjoy it, cantering over to her and lowering their muzzles so her tongue can reach them, but this evening they were too far off, standing together in little clusters, their coats shiny in the light. When we got back to the garden Toto ran immediately to where the pheasant had been, sniffed around forlornly, eventually gave up, came into the kitchen. In a minute I suppose I shall pick up the book about Stalin, reluctantly but with purpose – many of the things described in it happened in my time, after all, and I am a child of my time, as are we all, or so they say.

I, SOLIPSIST

It's still cold and wet in Suffolk and we've just won by two runs the test match that I said yesterday we were losing. This proves that I am a pessimist; also that I'm bad at predicting the outcome of sporting events; also, and most importantly, why I am right to go on watching cricket. The best thing about international sporting events is that the team I passionately hope will win is called England, not Britain, or the UK, but England. My team. From my country. Well, they're not all from my country. Our best batsman is from South Africa, our wicketkeeper grew up and learnt his trade in Australia, and is called Jones, one of our fast bowlers is also called Jones, but wherever they come from, or learnt the game, they all represent England, and therefore me.

I wasn't always so insular, so solipsistic. In fact, in my early years I was a citizen of the universe. I wore a cape that carried me from pole to pole, where evil resides. As I grew into my maturity I became a Continentalist, though not a European. What's the distinction between a Continentalist and a European? Well, I suppose a Continentalist likes to be in Paris, or Rome or Madrid, or dabbing himself in the Mediterranean, he likes to sit at a pavement café with a bottle of wine on the table, a book in his hand, a cigarette between his lips, and have at his command not so much a command of the language as an appearance of fluency in the demotic, an ability to slur vowels and consonants into a seamless flow, accompanied by a flurry of gestures with hands, shoulders and eyebrows, so that his speech both sounds and looks like the native tongue, though incomprehensible to any native.

The other trick was to pass oneself off in Italy as a Frenchman, in France as a Spaniard, and in Spain as an Italian etc. One only wanted to be taken for an Englishman when there was a danger that one would be taken instead for Dutch, Scandinavian or, above all, German. The Continentalist has of course passed into history, if he's remembered it's only with tender embarrassment by people of my age and background. Besides nowadays we have our own seedy version of the Continent here at home. Many people on the streets or in shops speak English as I once spoke Italian and French, and there are cafés and restaurants on the pavement, though it has to be said that they're mostly uncomfortable and unhygienic because our pavements are narrow – your moules marinières, however wholesome when brought out of the kitchen, are swiftly layered and peppered by grime and whatever else comes out in the fumes of passing exhaust pipes – not necessarily passing, either. The other day a rubbish truck was parked belching and farting alongside the Renaissance café for the whole half-hour that I was drinking my coffee, and the men, who seemed to be stuffing rubbish into the back and shovelling it out again before scooping it back in, were hawking, spitting, banging up against the table, bellowing in tongues – what in other words you'd expect from London when it goes Continental, alien and disgusting but also, in an unanalysable way, Anglo-Saxon, and endurable –

The Europeanization of England begins with the enfolding of this little country into a larger organization called the UK, which isn't so much a geographical place as a dead thought in a bureaucratic head. Nobody with a decent sense of self would say, 'I live in the UK', unless you were a desperado dealing with a customs or immigration official in, say, Libya. Where do you live? London, England. And where were you born? Hayling Island, England. And that's it, really it stops there, in the particular. You can't be a European without becoming yourself simply an idea, and not your own idea at that.

There is rumoured to be a law pending, or perhaps it is already secretly passed, that will make it a criminal offence – treason, I suppose – to slander or to libel the European Union. I suppose that by making it into a potential victim of a crime – the victim of a crime of utterance; the next step the victim of a crime of thought – they hope to convince us that it actually and specifically exists, as a person exists, and that we can feel its pain when unkind and disbelieving things are said and thought about it.

When I ponder such matters, I consider it astonishing that I have decided to attempt to give up smoking.

THE FACE IN THE OMELETTE

Let me resist lighting a cigarette by thinking about Mao, Stalin and Hitler. The other day, on a radio phone-in, I heard the old argument repeated – Hitler was the most wicked because he murdered millions in the name of fascism and racial superiority. Mao and Stalin were less wicked because they murdered millions in the name of communism, a noble if possibly imbecilic ideal. Therefore people who supported fascism and Hitler are much more wicked than people who supported communism – in fact, people who supported the USSR, those of them in this country who are still alive, are to be considered rather endearing, to be cherished and even honoured. Their hearts were in the right place when they argued, with decent regret, that you can't make an omelette without breaking eggs – which actually is only a pleasantly domestic way of saying that Lenin and Stalin couldn't make a communist state without breaking heads, legs, lives, families, spirits – without maiming, torturing, starving, killing – all the things that Hitler did but in one respect more terrifyingly because more arbitrarily. If you were Aryan and an indifferent servant of Hitler's state you were safe, and knew what to do to remain safe, at least until the war came. If you were a good servant in Mao's or Stalin's state you were in danger every minute of your life, and if it decided to extinguish you because, say, of a joke you were rumoured to have told, or to have laughed at, you went to your end knowing that your legacy to your parents and your children, your friends, colleagues, even your neighbours, was likely to be torture or death, or a labour camp, certainly ostracism and penury – their crime, of course, being you, knowing you and perhaps loving you.

So what was Osip Mandelstam thinking when he recited the famous but unpublished, indeed vanished, poem that evening in Moscow? Supposing you were there, pleased to be numbered among his friends and colleagues, your excitement as he takes the paper out of his pocket, unfolds it, begins to declaim it – you relish his mischievous smile, the sparkle of his eye, the familiar, expressive voice, old Osip with a new poem! And then you hear the words 'Stalin', 'murderer' – but for a second or two you don't grasp their meaning, and you hope that you're not going to, but when you look away from Osip's face in all its merriness and mischief you see in the other faces what they're probably now seeing in yours, and you know that you all know what you've just heard – a suicide note, a collective suicide note because all your names are on it, you signed it with your ears – so if you value your life, and the lives of your loved ones, you'd better hurry to the authorities, describe the poem, provide a list of everybody in the room, and hope that you are the first to inform, because if you aren't it will seem that you've only informed because you're afraid that you've already been informed on. But whether you're first or last it is unlikely that you will survive, in fact not even the officials to whom you've informed will survive, the time will come when they will be swept away with all the muck and eggshells from 'those days', that's how the historical process works, after all, these days become 'those days', the subjective becomes the objective, the executors the executed, more and more and more eggs get broken, the omelette gets bigger and bigger and bigger, it has a face with a moustache and a pipe, and Joe's your uncle! Yes, dear old Uncle Joe, the human omelette.

AN EGG FOR THE OMELETTE

Really it doesn't matter whether a state becomes an omelette for reasons that sound virtuous, if imbecilic, or for reasons that sound nasty, the sounds are irrelevant, the intentions are identical – to control all its members through terror. The state of terror is the state itself. And the state itself is the man himself. Hitler, Mao, Stalin were the state and the terror, and in the end you can only decide morally between them in quantitative terms – Which of them killed most? The one who had most to kill. And after him, Stalin. Or the other way around. And after them, Hitler. Once the debate takes this form, it isn't worth having, even on a radio phone-in. They were foul states, created by foul people by foul means for a foul purpose, they spoke different languages, used a different vocabulary, but the experience of living in them would have been pretty well identical – unless, as I said, you were an Aryan in Hitler's Germany, but that's scarcely a moral distinction.

It's now three in the afternoon, my lights are on, the rain is drizzling down, and I'm cold. I'm cold in mid-August, but I'm not smoking – he's not smoking! – so supposing you while away the rest of this non-smoking August day by deciding which, among your literary contemporaries, would have survived if they'd lived in, say, Moscow through the 20s and 30s. I would like to say none of them, but I suspect there would be several. Of the playwrights – let's think: well, let's begin with yourself. Would you have gone under? I don't think I'd have lasted long, but not because I'd have been full of defiance, I know that I'm a coward in almost every respect, that is, morally, emotionally and physically. I can't bear to be hurt, and I can't bear to hurt people, but the two are intertwined, aren't they, the fear of hurting people seems to have within it an element of virtue, or at least sensitivity to others, but it hasn't, in my case – it's not really that I can't bear hurting people, it's that I can't bear the consequences – no, let's be scrupulous and precise – I can't bear the consequences for myself of hurting people. I think if my actions had only bad consequences for others, and not for me, and I didn't have actually to witness their suffering, I wouldn't at all mind committing bad actions. How true is this? I don't know. What is true is that I would want to survive. I'd try to keep my poems and my jokes to myself, but I have a loose and wayward tongue which might shorten my life under a malign regime, just as it's shortened a few evenings under a comparatively benign one – and what is also true is, look, without your noticing he's lit up and, yes, smoking, he's smoking again. Perhaps the sensible thing is to put off giving up until we get to Spetses.

SHARKS V. RATS

We go to Athens tomorrow morning and we should be on Spetses by the early evening, in time for a swim. I've sent instructions to the mayor, to ban smoking everywhere on the island, including in private houses. That should settle my hash, this long disease my hash.

I wonder, though, what sort of accommodation we'll find ourselves in when we get to Spetses. We've put ourselves, orphan-style, in the hands of an old friend who lives there, an intelligent and practical woman in whom we have an absolute trust. She has found a house that she describes in terms that doom us to disappointment. No place could conceivably match our desires and needs as, according to her email, this one does. It would have been better if she'd found us somewhere Greek and hopeless, so that we could draw on our limitless resources of stoicism and declare it 'Not as bad as all that! Good heavens, we'll make do! Besides we're out most of the day! And much of the night! And it's only for three weeks!' – that sort of house.

The house we used to stay in, that we had come to love, changed its aspect and its atmosphere as I either reached the end of my drinking years or began the days of my abstention, depending on which way around you look at it. It was my habit to sit on the stone steps leading down from the house to the heavily scented garden late at night, reading under a dim lamp – this was my habit for five summers running, but in the last of these summers, when I was either at the end of my drunk period or at the very beginning of my sober period, I began to hallucinate enormous rats coming and going up and down the stairs past me, vanishing into the darkness in the corner of the wall at the top or into the bushes at the bottom. They should have been pink, of course, to qualify as the alcoholic's perfect rats, but they were the usual grubby grey, long pale tail, prominent teeth – common or garden rats, much more terrifying as hallucinations than surreal rats. I couldn't give up reading outside at night because, as I say, it was my habit, and I'm very bad at giving up habits, so I bent over my book and tried to concentrate on not being aware of the comings and goings of the rats, though I could hear them and sense them, and if I looked, see them, coming and going.

And then one night there was a massive sort of presence at the door, a lurking, unmoving, antediluvian rat, and I bent deeper into my book. 'Christ!' he said. It was Piers's voice. 'Christ! Look! There's a rat.' Now it's true that Piers was as drunk as I was during my drunk period, and as prone to hallucinations as I was during both my drunk and my early sober periods, so one way and another we might both now and then have hallucinated rats, but not at precisely the same time surely? Which meant that there were real rats coming out of the house, rats to be faced up to, that couldn't be dodged by concentrating on a book.

Piers, as a matter of interest, wasn't terrified of rats, real or hallucinated. He was terrified of not getting another drink, but nothing much else frightened him – oh, apart from the sea, but that was with just cause, he'd nearly drowned years before, off Bondi Beach, and since then had virtually given up swimming, going in perhaps two or three times during his weeks in Spetses, and they weren't really swims, they were grim-jawed, fist-clenched wades out to just below his chest, a dozen turbulent strokes back towards the beach, then to his feet and a lunging, splashing, panic-stricken run to dry land and a drink.

Also, of course, he had spent years in Hong Kong, with its actual and rumoured shark attacks, about which he nevertheless affected, when we went out to visit him, to be blasé.

I have a horror of sharks that is quite different from my horror of rats. Rats come out of the unknown, yet seem to be in some foul way secreted in oneself. Sharks, on the other hand, come upon you, drag you down, bite you to death. Any man swimming in shark-infested seas who is not afraid of sharks is, in that one respect at least, an imbecile – I don't really expect to be eaten to death by a rat that comes across me, though it could happen of course, especially if he has a pack with him (rats are always male, in my grasp of them). I would expect to be eaten to death by a shark that wouldn't have just come across me, he would have sought me out, perhaps not specifically me, but one of my kind which might well turn out to be me. Almost the first thing I asked Piers when Victoria and I arrived in Hong Kong was, 'What's the shark situation?' 'Look,' he said, in a calm, mature voice, thus turning himself from younger into older brother, 'I know what you feel about sharks, Simon, and yes, there are sharks in these waters, naturally there are sharks, of all kinds, but the last shark attack was fifteen years ago, Simon.'

The next was a week away. We heard about it on the news, from the radio of the car we'd hired, a magnificently upholstered, air-conditioned affair. A man had been 'taken' at Clear Water Beach that morning, his leg had been ripped off, he'd died on his way to hospital. This was the first of four fatal attacks, and the most startling in that the victim, a hairdresser, had been witness to the fifteen-years-ago attack Piers had mentioned, when a woman standing at waist-height had been 'taken'. The hairdresser, who went to Clear Water every morning for a swim and had been standing near her, virtually beside her, was so horrified by the experience – he would never forget, he said in an interview in the papers, the sight of her standing there, her hands on her hips, and then, on an instant, her being upturned, her bewildered screams as she was dragged out to sea, the kerfuffle of her dismember-ment, her torso bobbing to the surface – these weren't his exact words, but the gist of his account as Piers remembered it from fifteen years back.

Piers also remembered that the hairdresser had sworn that he would never swim in the sea again, certainly never ever in Clear Water Bay, and for fifteen years he had stuck to it, this simple and most sensible of promises to himself. But the years went by, no attacks, he began to be tempted, the weather so sultry, the wonderfully clear water of Clear Water Bay so close, just a short drive – so he went one morning, and stood in the water not even waist-high, knee-high, and the shark came and took him. It was thought to be the same shark. So what does this tell us about sharks, fate, will, broken promises made to themselves by Hong Kong hairdressers?

Well, about sharks, or this one anyway, it might mean that it had been gone a long time, snacking off faraway shores until eventually his travels had brought him back. Was there some palpable memory of a place he'd come across where a good meal was to be had? And unlike the rest of us, who return for that fondly remembered meal in that now-vanished little restaurant, his restaurant was still there – as indeed was the meal himself, standing waiting, legs spread, hands on hips, exactly as he remembered him. Is it possible that the shark had sized him up on his previous visit, and tucked him away in the recesses of his extraordinarily complicated yet simple brain. Or perhaps he didn't wait for fifteen years, he came back frequently and impatiently, desperate to find his meal in place, prepared and on the table, so to speak, *la specialité de la maison*.

But the hairdresser, what was tucked away in the recesses of his far more complicated brain? In the forefront it was simple enough: 'Do not swim again in the sea. Do not swim again in the sea. Particularly do not swim again in Clear Water Bay.' The physical shock of what he'd seen must have lingered in his body, would linger there for the rest of his life, surely, so why, why on earth? After all, this wasn't an idle promise, of the sort he made and broke every day of his professional life – 'Madam, let me cut this little bit, lop off this, shorten that, and you will look twenty years younger, that's a promise, madam!' His promise to himself about the shark wasn't really even a self-injunction along the lines of 'Never again allow a play of yours to be done at Milton Keynes!' It was a statement of fact. Nothing could be more certain than that he would never again go to Clear Water Bay, let alone stand in the water. But he went. He stood. Did his will insist that he follow the diktat of reason: 'Nothing has happened for fifteen years, it's probably long dead, the odds on your being taken must be one in trillions, you're being a silly-billy, a cowardy-custard.' And all the while something in him demanded a date with destiny: 'Go and be taken, go and be taken, you know it's you. Think of the splash you'll make. People will remember and wonder. The very man who witnessed! Who swore he'd never! Yes, the very he, the very same he! Go. Go and be taken!' Or perhaps he sleepwalked, programmed from birth. Or accepted into his unconsciousness a direct command from the shark's appetite. 'Be back here in fifteen years. Fifteen years. On the dot.'

What is incontrovertible is that sharks have their ways. They know things that we don't. Perhaps they know things about us that we don't. There's the story of the two sailors who survived a capsized ship far out in deep water. They swam for hours and hours and hours, until exhausted, all hope gone. 'Look!' one of them suddenly cried, standing up, 'I can stand up!' but the land turned under him, opened its mouth. I don't know what happened to the other sailor but he must have survived. How else would we know the story?

I don't know any equivalent stories about rats, but then rats don't move to the profound, impersonal laws that sharks move to, if indeed sharks move to profound, impersonal laws. The sharks featured above may merely have been lucky – 'Could you believe it, my dear! In the exact same spot! Like he was waiting for me!' and 'Stood right on me, all I had to do was roll over and open wide!' – but I don't think so, I think destiny comes into it somewhere, even if it's the victim's destiny, the shark only the instrument.

The rat's way of being seems much more haphazard, secret and dark. He doesn't 'take' his food in public off a sunny liquid snack bar in front of lots of people, he snuffles through holes and crouches in corners, waiting his chance on a dead body or a dying one, otherwise it's crumbs and larder raids, although I seem to remember a film called *Herbert* or *Hubert*, which told the story of a super-intelligent rat that made himself, Hitler-like, the leader of an enormous pack with which he planned to take over the world, but then something happened to thwart him, I don't know what as I didn't see it, nothing could get me to see a film about rats –

But the thing about the hallucinatory rat that passed me as it went down the stairs that turned out to be a real rat that passed me as it went down the stairs, and was confirmed as such by my brother Piers, is that from then on I moved about the house in a suppressed state of terror, even in broad and sunny daylight, and even in the enchanting and sweetly scented garden – sometimes a little too sweetly scented for my taste, especially at night, it made you long for a blast of wintry Suffolk air – but until the rat it was a safe place, is my point, and after the rat its thick perfumes suggested putrefaction, and I stepped carefully through it, eyes darting into shady crannies during the day, all over the place at night –

I phoned up the owner, a most kind and intelligent woman who had made us a present of this house every August for five years running, phoned her up and said, 'There are rats in your house.' Not as baldly as that, I hope, I hope I asked her about her health and so forth, but I got to the point very smartly, my eyes no doubt hopping around the floor. There was a pause as she waited for me to go on, and when I didn't she said, 'There are rats all over the island, in every house, why should mine be exempt?' 'Of course,' I said. 'Of course. Just thought you'd like to know – and was wondering if there's anything I can do about them. Anything you'd like me to do about them.' 'Oh, ignore them,' she said. 'That's what I do. It's probably why I never see them.' 'Hard to ignore if they keep brushing against you.' 'Well, if they upset you, you have my permission to do anything you can think of to get rid of them.' I thought immediately of setting the house on fire, then thought beyond that to the eventual solution, which was to take rooms the following year in a house with a majestic terrace overlooking the sea that I persuaded myself was too high up, too light and airy and breeze-swept, to attract the attention of rats. The landlady was a middle-aged Greek/German woman, kind, thoughtful, practical and sometimes playful, called Alex. From her house a steep path, with steps, leads to the beach, an arduous climb down and up. This year Alex is not letting out her rooms, but she has found us the house that we go to tomorrow, the house that she is sure we'll love, and sounds so perfect for our needs that we must prepare for disappointment. Come to think of it, Alex said that this most perfect of houses is only a few yards on from her own, so there will be the steep path, the steps, the arduous climb down and up – I hope that's our disappointment taken care of.

MY TRAVELLING COMPANIONS

I think that the loud woman across the aisle from me on my left is probably very pleasant, everything she says is certainly pleasant enough, to do with adjusting her watch to Athens time, helping her husband, whose face I can't see but whose hands were quite prominent during the watch-adjusting business – odd hands, foreshortened, without fingernails, in fact I think their tips are missing, but he uses them with authority, stubbing a knucklish stump into her lap, where the watch is again because she's started the whole business again, having set it two hours behind instead of two hours ahead, and is now having, starting from there, as he points out in a slow, emphatic, German-accented voice, to put it four hours ahead – all this would be all right except that she shouts, really shouts, as if he were deaf and in a different room, a distant room – no, in a different aeroplane almost, furthermore she repeats everything he says in this shout, as if she were deaf, too, deaf to her own voice as well as to his. She's a sensible-looking woman of about fifty, I suppose, long feet in flat shoes planted on the floor, a floral skirt of the kind that women of what I take to be her disposition have worn all my life, I remember them from when I was knee-high to such ladies. Though they are evidently women, they look as if they're cross-dressing. Not like men cross-dressing as women, but women cross-dressing as women, de-sexing themselves. Her voice is like that, too, not a man's voice but a woman's voice, loud and de-sexed – ah, she's got some magazines from the stewardess or whatever they're called these days, hostesses, anyway quite evidently not chosen for their looks or their appealing little ways – the particular one who is serving us dumped a pile of magazines in the woman's lap, the woman spread her floral skirt to receive them, plucked out a gourmet magazine, then shovelled the remainder into her husband's lap – 'Jolly good, have these, *Newsweek*, you like *Newsweek*, it's American.' So he's got three *Newsweek*s, same issue, to read from. He's now got his foreshortened fingers around a magnifying glass, is studying an article in *Newsweek* through the magnifying glass as if it were a specimen in a lab. I still haven't seen his face, only his fingers, and the sleeve of a grey suit – and heard his voice, of course, like something from a 1940s espionage film with Conrad Veidt in it.

There was one Conrad Veidt made with Valerie Hobson – a beautiful woman – so stylish and playful – she's tied to a chair for a good ten minutes, a very good ten minutes, black stockings (pre-tights after all), high heels, arms raised, *Contraband*, that's it, the name of the film, *Contraband*, now the thing about Conrad Veidt, whose name nobody remembers when they're talking about *Casablanca*, is that he was the highest-paid actor in the film, which also featured Marcel

Dalio, the Jewish count in *La Règle du Jeu*. In *Casablanca* Dalio plays the part of the croupier, a very small part, though he does get to say, '*Faites vos jeux, mesdames, messieurs, faites vos jeux*', and wears tails, I think, though perhaps only a dinner jacket. There was something poignant, unbearable really, in coming across Dalio in a bit part, his great years, the pre-war years of French cinema, behind him. I suppose he got out before the Germans came, he wouldn't have lasted long as he was so patently both Jewish and homosexual, a small, portly man, he had the saddest eyes, a natural aristocrat, but one always feared for his feelings – he was also one of the escaping prisoners in *La Grande Illusion*, I think, at least I see him in my memory in conversation with Erich von Stroheim, who has his cigarette in a long holder, a monocle in place, or is it an eye-patch, a lost eye and a lost arm too – he and Dalio, the Prussian nobleman and the French aristocrat, at one in spirit, divided by war, preserving the civilities. Can you imagine a film like *La Grande Illusion* being made these days? – but oh, don't start, don't start on your 'these days those days', and I don't really remember *La Grande Illusion* clearly, I'm only going on like this because we're on the verge of taking off, we've been on the verge for half an hour, revving up, jolting forward, fading down again, the cabin full of fumes and suppressed ill-temper, along with the usual dose of fear, not all from me – false starts on aeroplanes are worse than false starts in sex really, because on an aeroplane you're anticipating relief from the anxiety of being on the ground just before you go up in the air where you don't want to be, while in sex you're anticipating relief and pleasure, pleasure through relief – I'm not sure the analogy can be pursued any further, I shouldn't have embarked on it, it doesn't hold – we're now rocking down the runway, the barking woman in the floral dress has seized one of her elderly Germanic husband's deformed hands – he reminds me of Isaiah Berlin, I realize, though his voice doesn't, I could never understand a word Sir I.B. said, I know it was in English because he talked to me as if he assumed it was in my language, and also friends assured me he spoke in English, it was obvious, therefore, that I lacked some part of the brain that could decipher his accent, we're in the air.

Now we're flying. We're in business class, BA, horribly cramped, the man in front of me has just put his seat back so that it's pressing into my knees, and I can see, with very little adjustment to my position, the fine, thick grey hair across the top of his scalp, with a whorl right in the centre – an astonishingly healthy scalp, marvellously lustrous hair, nothing moving about in it or flaking off from it, it would be a pleasure to damage it in some way, to make up for my being able to see it so clearly because the selfish sod has his seat back. The young woman beside me keeps blowing her nose into a scrap of tissue, the non-cross-dresser on the other side of the aisle has a cough like a horse, an explosive whinny, I can now see her elderly husband, his deformed hands are part of a deformed package, his face, which might once have been an Isaiah Berlin-like face, is peeled and scabbed, his eyes are naked, no eyelashes or lids, must be the victim of a fire or bombing, his lips are loose, pendulous, but they could be undamaged, loose and pendulous by nature.

The only good thing about the flight is that no food is served on it. Owing to an altercation the catering staff are on strike – Gourmet-Gate I believe the managing company is called, and it seems that BA is incapable of providing food except through the services of Gourmet-Gate – but where, in these cramped, claustrophobic conditions, could you put a tray of food without getting most of it over yourself? I daren't ask Victoria how much we paid for this flight, how much extra to go business. Economy can't conceivably be more cramped and uncomfortable without breaching all kinds of human rights laws. I'm going to have a look, if I can get up.

Well, yes, economy is worse. The rows on either side of the aisle have three seats, the rows here in business have three seats on one side, my side, and two seats on the other side. Victoria is in a two-seater, on the aisle, further down the plane. So what it comes to is that people sitting in the three-seat blocks in business, like me, have exactly the same deal, in terms of space, as people sitting in economy, while the people seated in the two-seat blocks in business would seem to have a better deal. I tested this by trying out Victoria's seat. It had the same leg-space as mine, i.e. almost none, but she has a much more charming companion – mine is now blowing her nose on little shreds of Kleenex about twice a minute, long, thick, wet blows, then she screws up the Kleenex and places it in a paper cup, already bulging, in the rack on the back of the seat in front of her. There is an already full paper cup beside the one she has now nearly filled. She is frankly a very disgusting person to find yourself sitting next to on a flight. The third person on our row, on the window seat, I can't see properly. He's a middle-aged man, I think, and I imagine he's inclining himself as close to the window as he can, to escape the nose-blowing girl who separates us. Victoria's only companion, on the other hand, is a wiry old Australian woman with a twin in San Francisco and she would, I think, be a fizzing conversationalist if she weren't crumpled and drained from exhaustion and hunger. She's flown BA and therefore foodless from Sydney to Heathrow, had to transfer to the Athens flight so hurriedly that she didn't have time to pick up anything to eat between planes, and here she is now, not having eaten for a day or so, not even in possession of one of the clumsy blue cardboard boxes that those of us who arrived, fully breakfasted, were issued with in the business-class lounge. These boxes contain smatterings of this and that, a little roll of ham that looks like a boiled thumb, a smudge of cheese, two lumps of bread, a chocolatey lump of dough, and a plastic container of small shreds of fruit – altogether like scraps left over from a reception, really, and repulsive to look at. I offered my box, and virtually all its contents – I'd taken a bite out of the chocolate dough – to the Australian lady, who refused it for reasons I didn't want to enquire into, perhaps I look unhygienic, and she suspected that my fingers had poked and delved into each item, or perhaps she was too proud to accept charity, or perhaps, driven by fatigue and hunger, she is in a delusional state and thinks that by not eating any food not provided by BA she is punishing BA for not providing any food. But wait a minute! This box of soiled tapas was provided by BA, so perhaps her plan is to be so enfeebled by malnutrition that she will have to be carried off the plane, put into an ambulance and driven to a hospital, from there to initiate successful lawsuits, the proceeds of which I hope she'll share with her Frisco twin – anyway, she managed a short but sprightly conversation with Victoria, Victoria told me, in which she said that Australian boys are having immense sexual successs when they visit England by telling the girls that they are writers, although they aren't and don't want to be. I am surprised and proud to learn that our girls still care enough about literature to go to bed with its practitioners.

The girl beside me is starting on her third paper cup. I don't think I can go on doing this without describing her in detail, and I'm anxious these days not to write from hatred, so I'll take out a book. All the books for serious reading are packed into a capacious leather bag that's been checked in, but in my floppy briefcase there is a last-minute chuck-in for the plane, I'm not sure what it is, but think it's an old Penguin, yes, I remember choosing it exactly because it's an old Penguin, yes, an orange Penguin.

The Light and the Dark – how can a novel with a title like that conceivably be any good? It's almost a parody, *The Light and the Dark*, by C. P. Snow, Charles Percival Snow. Percival? You're just guessing, why not Philip? Or Patrick? Why not Clive, come to that? Clive Patrick (or Paddy) Snow's *The Light and the Dark, The Wet and the Dry, The Hot and the Cold, The Pie and the Sky* – are you sure that retitling the novel and fiddling about with the author's name is more interesting than actually reading?

– actually, actually, her last one took about thirty seconds, longer than you would have thought possible to blow a nose, and where does it come from that she keeps having to blow it out? Open, turn the pages, read – She's taken a fourth paper cup out of her carrier bag – perhaps she's collecting it for a scientific experiment, or on doctor's orders, we'll see what she does with the cups when the plane lands, if she repacks them it's germ warfare – against whom? The Greeks? But bringing germs to Greece would be like bringing coals to Newcastle, every sandwich is like Russian roulette. Surely she's just being thoughtful, what can she do with her germ-laden tissues but put them in a receptacle, and it's not her fault that we're squeezed so closely together – the tip of her nose is very red, her eyes watery, she has an annoying habit of thrashing over the pages of the newspaper (*The Times*) with maximum noise and fuss – she has long, elegant legs – if there were some way of getting her upright, hands bound behind her back, would she suddenly become a bold, proud, defiant beauty? Or would the consequences of her not being able to get at her tissues make her even more disgusting? Better leave her as she is, making her way through her fourth paper mug – give myself over to Carlos Pepe Snow.

More like fog, really, but an odd sort of fog, everything described so clearly, and yet everything important obscured, obscured by clarity, in fact – he describes his world without seeing it, almost as if he thinks adjectives are in themselves full of detail and content – a girl is 'passionate, generous, capable and free' – and that's it, it's no good you wanting this passion, generosity, freedom and capability in action because there's no girl to act. I've read fifty pages so far, in that old, small Penguin print, and I still have no idea what the story is about, or who the characters are, apart from their names and their positions in life, or rather their positions in a Cambridge college in the mid-30s of the last century. I know, in a vague sort of way, what it purports to be about – a brilliant young linguist who is subject to bouts of depression, bouts of manic behaviour, so a manic-depressive therefore, and old Snow describes and analyses these bouts with responsible lucidity, grave, deliberate, well informed, hollow, lifeless – so that the hero, Roy Calvert by name – dashing sort of name – really becomes very irritating. He's a character without a pulse. The narrator, who of course has a name like two surnames, let me check – yes, yes, of course, Lewis Eliot – Lewis Eliot, doesn't have much of a pulse either. He's a ponderous and bulky man, one feels, but as a character weighs nothing. I suppose he's a front for old C.P. himself. One of his tricks is to bring himself to our attention by having himself complimented. A character will say, usually apropos of nothing, something like 'There is no doubt, Lewis, that you are one of the most intelligent/compassionate/understanding of men' or 'You, above all men, Eliot, know what suffering is' – but the tone of the novel is that of a man who really doesn't know what suffering is, though he certainly ought to, as he has a mad wife that so far – as far as I've read – he keeps buried in London, I suppose she might turn up, but I'm not too worried about meeting her because however mad she is she won't be mad where it matters, in my imagination – a moment ago the pilot said we would be landing and the plane has just done two big downwards hops, stomach-jumping hops – here is a sentence: 'Once I saw them in a party, when she thought herself unobserved: she looked at him with a glance that was heavy, brooding, possessive, consumed with the need to be sure of him.' All his adjectives come in threes and fours as if he has to fill a quota, it's like reading P. G. Wodehouse without the jokes.

We're coming in now, coming into Athens, hoppity-hop, I don't know whether we have an old plane or an ungifted pilot, but this is not the way you want to land in a place where you haven't been for five years – oh, how I could do with a cigarette, thank God I'm not giving them up until we're settled into Spetses.

GREEK WELCOMES

Here we are, in our magnificent little house, a few yards further along the path I was describing back in London. I'm sitting on its narrow terrace, it's 11 p.m., and when I look up from writing this I can see the moving dots of the sea-taxis taking people at high speed from one part of the island to the other, from one bar or café to another. In daytime they remind me of little dogs, they scamper across the water, their bows like little snouts, but at night they become mysterious and urgent dots of light, travelling through dark space because you can't separate the sea from the sky – there's a great field of dark punctuated in its lower half by the skimming dots, in its top by the stars.

So we're in Greece again, Spetses again, home after five years away. As soon as we were out of Athens airport, walking towards the car our friend Alex had arranged for us, we could feel the difference in the air, the dry lightness of it, and the feet correspondingly light as we zipped along after our driver, a jolly well-dressed man called Soros, whose only discernible flaw at this stage was that he'd been waiting at the wrong exit – there was an interminable business, with mobile phones, Victoria phoning Alex in Spetses to say her man wasn't there, Alex phoning her man to find out where he was, then phoning us and saying her man was at the bureau de change carrying a placard with the name SIMON on it, then when we went to the bureau de change Victoria phoning Alex to say that there were lots of drivers holding up placards with names on them, none of them SIMON, so Alex phoned the driver again and I spotted a man holding up a placard that had no name on it because it was the wrong way around because he was hurrying away from us, so I ran around to the front of him, saw SIMON on the placard, led him back to Victoria and our bags and then we were out of the airport, sucking in the air and thinking we'd made it, actually made it to Greece, and we smiled triumphantly at each other, smiled forgivingly at the driver, this jolly, eager, roly-poly man whose name was Soros and who was smartly dressed, a picture of respectability, unlike the furry, slovenly, dark-aspected (I mean in temperament, not race) drivers on the rank that we passed on the way to our car. We could see that Soros was a very careful and steady driver, even in the hundred yards or so he drove us before we were stopped by the police –

A young man in a slick brown and green uniform stepped out on to the street and waved us down, then came to the window and ordered Soros to get out. A police car drove up behind us, and another, older policeman got out, dressed exactly like his partner but unlike him in that he looked ill-tempered and authoritarian. The younger one, who was merely passive and low-voiced, could speak English, quite reasonable English, as transpired when he began to speak quite reasonable English about our situation, which was complicated and possibly dire – we were being driven illegally, our driver, Soros, was a bandit, he had infringed the law by the mere fact of having us in the back of his taxi, he and his taxi would shortly be taken away, the one to be placed in custody, the other to be impounded. He said all this, or what amounted to all this, in his pleasantly broken English through the window in the back of the taxi where we sat stiffly, as if under arrest ourselves. I got out, having noticed that there were no ashtrays in Soros's taxi, and that it was probably a non-smoker therefore, and lit a cigarette, grateful really – in these oppressive days you have to snatch your opportunities as they present themselves, which means that most bad situations can be transformed into good ones if, while they're going on, you can take your cigarettes and lighter out of your pocket and enjoy a good smoke under pressure – a better smoke for its being under pressure. In fact, here's an interesting thing – if I had been able to smoke in Soros's taxi, I would have been much more worried by the sudden intervention of the police, I would have sat in the taxi smoking, but not noticing that I was smoking, and concentrating on our situation. As I couldn't smoke in the taxi, I was mainly thinking about wanting a cigarette, and then delighted when I saw I could have one by getting out of the taxi – without the police I wouldn't have been able to get out of the taxi. For this small but intense pleasure I had to thank a) the Athens police and b) the anti-smoking laws.

So there I was smoking on the pavement – no, it wasn't a pavement, it was the edge of the wide road that leads out of Athens airport – presumably nobody walks, or is allowed to walk, out of an international airport. Victoria got out to join me. The superior, or anyway older, policeman was listening with a grim, unkind face to the explanations of Soros, who kept laughing in disbelief. The young speaker of reasonable if broken English, who was clearly beginning to suspect that he was taking part in a mistake, began to question us as to how we had come by the services of Soros. We explained slowly, calmly, a touch loudly, however, to penetrate the foreign layer of his understanding, that Soros was a perfectly legitimate taxi driver who hadn't been cowboying for tourists outside the official ranks, but had been commissioned by our friend in Spetses. He asked if he could speak to our friend in Spetses. Alex was no longer answering her phone, she was on the answering machine – Victoria held her mobile to the young policeman's ear and he listened to Alex's rather gruffly important voice announcing that she wasn't there, and then he went to his superior, to convey whatever information he had to convey. The superior and Soros were now standing facing each other in silence. I lit another cigarette and put an arm protectively around Victoria's shoulder, a proud gesture, also defiant and noble, except that there was nothing she needed protection from except my smoke. Soros and the two policemen fell into quiet discourse, the whole tenor of the engagement seemed to have changed, they shook hands, the two policemen went to their car, Soros got into the taxi, gestured us in with a boisterous, angry laugh, and off we went, I hanging on to my cigarette, on the grounds that a legitimately lit cigarette can stay lit until it comes to its natural end. I used the open window as my ashtray and half hoped I missed the open window of a parallel car when I finally flicked it away. Victoria can sometimes speak Greek, and even sometimes understand it, so she bent forward and she and Soros had a cheek-to-cheek about what had happened. The senior policeman had been implacable, was going to impound, fine etc., because he refused to believe that Soros wasn't a bandit and a cowboy, a stealer of other men's fares, until Soros decided to tell him that his brother-in-law was a policeman, and that was that, we were on our way. I asked Victoria to ask him whether his brother-in-law was really a policeman. Yes, he was, of course he was, Soros said, and gave his rank, where he was stationed, so forth. Although he continued to smile and laugh a little, he was evidently hurt and a little indignant that his integrity had been questioned – Soros was an honourable man, and expected to be treated as such, was what his demeanour conveyed. He also drove very well, through the foul and dusty suburbs of Athens to the port of Piraeus.

It took about an hour, and when we got there it was foul too, as foul as I remembered it from five years ago, and all the years before that, the afternoon sun beating down, no bars or cafés, and the only shade from a long strip of tarpaulin some distance from the quay, so that when your boat comes in you have to walk fifty yards or so through the naked heat, with all your luggage, and dragging children and great-grandparents and whatever other burdens you have, how is it, how is it, that one of the most famous ports in the world, that receives so many of the country's eager guests and dispatches them to all its lovely islands, can be allowed to be so unwelcoming, so positively and aggressively hostile? It's as if it's set out to show that an ancient seaport can be as nasty as a modern airport, and the fact is, to come to the very heart of the matter, we had four exceptionally heavy bags, two of which could be rolled along on their attached wheels, but two of which had no wheels attached and had to be carried. Victoria spoke to Soros, asking if he could help, he said he would be glad to stay – it would be half an hour before the boat to Spetses came in – and get our bags on board. He accompanied Victoria to the ticket office and helped her to collect the tickets, while I stood by the taxi, guarding our bags and admiring the shapely young men in smart white sailor suits and peaked caps that were strutting about – two of them were quite close, and getting closer, they were both handsome, no, sharply and darkly pretty, and in those crisp outfits and rakishly angled caps reminded me of a film – now what film can it have been that they reminded me of? Who were the actors? Two sharp and darkly pretty men, crisp white uniforms, caps – oh yes, Tom Cruise and Demi Moore in *A Few Good*

Men. Demi Moore is a woman, of course, but throughout the film she seemed to be the same sex as Tom Cruise, so really you could equally well think of them as a pair of crisp, dark, pretty women or a pair of men, crisp, dark and pretty. Of the two of them I think Tom was the more fanciable, had more sex appeal whether you took him for man or woman, while poor little Demi was really his sidekick of either sex – what kind of name is Demi anyway? It's a size, surely, half of semi, as in demi-tasse, but what would a demi-attached house be like, or a semi-mondaine, on the other hand, or a semi-Moore, would that be twice as much Moore as Demi, who though small and tightly built would never move you to call her petite? But could you call Tom Cruise petite, by any chance, if you came across him in something frilly, suspenders glimpsed – he has very showy teeth, slightly rat-like but too white and unused for a rat, and he doesn't actually bare them, he flashes them, 'mine eyes dazzle' teeth. But back to the film itself. Although Tom and Demi rattle their way through it, crisp, dark and equivalently gendered, it belongs to Jack Nicholson as a psychotic admiral (no, not perhaps an admiral, but high in the chain of command), rather like Humphrey Bogart in *The Caine Mutiny* but up a notch or two, or down a notch or two, depending on whether you're talking of the power or the subtlety of the performances. Bogart was hateful but poignant, Nicholson merely, but swaggeringly, hateful. We saw Nicholson in Spetses one year, sitting in the wagon of a motorized tricycle, the wagon really rather flimsy, made of canvas and wood, just about wide enough, long enough and strong enough to hold three suitcases, or two Al Pacinos or one Jack Nicholson. It had tiny wheels, so that Jack was also very close to the ground, and looked rather as if he were being hauled around in his container like a trophy in one of those big old movies about the ancient Romans. You expected, say, Charlton Heston or Susan Hayward to be his captor and driver, but it was only your usual Spetsiot, seedy and out of sorts. I suppose they were going off to a yacht, or to the island owned by the Niarchos family – anyway, Jack didn't look as if he enjoyed being in transit in Spetses, in the wagon of a motorized tricycle, he lacked his crazed, mischievous grin, in fact he looked downright sullen, possibly hung-over.

In the film, made when Jack was in his prime, he is a spruce and gleaming monster of the liberal imagination, who believes in discipline, order, punishment, cleanliness, wholesomeness, death, and here were his creatures in front of me, Tom and Demi, one of them was holding in his hand a flapping booklet of pink forms that reminded me, for some reason, of the kind of booklet carried by London traffic wardens. Well, of course these weren't London traffic wardens, these were Greek maritime traffic wardens, Piraeus was their beat, and they were writing out a ticket for Soros, who was standing, incredulous, incredulous once more, on the step of the ticket office, staring at them, Victoria beside him. He came over, expostulating. They shrugged. Tom wrote while Demi took off his sunglasses and put them on again, they were completely impassive. One of them had an eye-catching golden buckle on his belt. Soros phoned Alex in Spetses. This time she was in and, being of a forthright and frequently furious disposition, demanded to speak to Tom and Demi. She stayed on the line as Soros held the phone out, they waved it away, Tom going on with her writing, Demi taking his glasses off, etc., I with one arm hung over Victoria's shoulder as I smoked my cigarette, until the ticket was completed, a fine for seventy euros, then they gestured Soros towards the car park, a few hundred yards further into the heat. We got in and he drove us there, we got out the bags, and between us dragged them all the way to the quay. The Dolphin arrived, in unexpected colours, reds and greens. The last time we'd been in a Dolphin, and during all the years we travelled between Piraeus and Spetses and back again, they were yellow and always reminded me of a torpedo, because they looked as if they could travel under water, indeed had been built to do so in spite of the lofty skis on which they rode, but this new Dolphin, probably redecorated for the Olympics, had VODAPHONE written on it in large black letters, just as the cricket pitches for the recent test matches have VODAPHONE written on them, at least on the screen – it seems actually to be written on the pitch, as if the bowler is going to run through the letters, but it's a digital trick, I suppose, because it can't actually be carved and painted into the grass, surely? Anyway, here's my point, not much of a point really – the name of the thing that gets into one's life by ringing in one's pocket, or more irritatingly in other people's pockets, bags or purses, and then shears itself across one of my favourite television pictures, the pitch of a test match, is now smeared on the side of the familiar and beloved – no, that's crap, Dolphins aren't beloved, not by me anyway, they're uncomfortable, usually very crowded, and you can't see the passing islands when you're seated, because the windowed hole – the porthole, I suppose it technically is – is too small. In fact it's rather like being on the London tube if it went just under the sea rather than under the ground. Still, a Dolphin is a familiar, if unloved creature, and I hate to find it transformed and abused in this way by Vodaphone, just as I hate to see the sacred turf of our cricket grounds turned into a Vodaphone advertising hoarding.

Also familiar and unloved is the business of getting on a Dolphin. All the tickets are numbered, your seat is your seat, whether you get on first or last, so why is there always a desperate scramble to be first up the gangplank, people shoving each other, stepping on each other's feet, swinging their enormous knapsacks or bum-packs or whatever they're called from side to side in the hope of buffeting the people behind them or to either side of them. My own instinct, being an elderly and in some quarters highly regarded playwright, is to get in among them and barge and shunt and kick my way to the seat that is reserved for me and which I could therefore get to in peace if I only waited, as Victoria advises, for everybody else to be settled. Why do I do it? Perhaps it goes back to prep school days, when the amount of cake you got depended on your rough-housing skills, or to nursery school, when one had to jostle for a turn on the pottie. But I didn't go to nursery school. Well, back to Mummy's teat then. But who would have been my rival, Nigel, sixteen months older than me? Would he still have been on the breast? And did Mummy breast-feed anyway? I don't think so, I can't remember, although sometimes when I light a cigarette and suck in, I have a soothing, backwards-rolling feeling that I'm on the end of something life-sustaining, no, life-enhancing, almost as if it were unfiltered. Of course Mummy was a heavy smoker, so perhaps I was suckled on nicotine milk. And now a word from his sponsor. He smokes Silk Cut. He is now smoking a Silk Cut. He is not feeling bilious. He has not just coughed. He is by no means on the verge of throwing up. He is as happy as a babe on the teat, and why not, as he cannot distinguish between mother's milk and nicotine, as long as he sucks, sucks. You too can be suckled by Silk Cut. Five pounds a packet. Five pounds × three times a day = £15 × 7 = £105 per week × 52 = somewhere under £6,000 a year, wow! Is that all? All those headaches, phlegm-driven coughing fits and rancid stomachs for only £6,000. And just think of all the things you can't get for £6,000!

I threw myself into the hurly-burly, determined to be the first person to my reserved seat, but fell back almost immediately, having been caught in the stomach by a particularly knobbly bum-pack, or perhaps just a knobbly bum – anyway, I was winded and slipped out of the ruck, reached for Victoria's hand, and left it to Soros to do the man's work. He got the bags on board, got the only porter, a large, stocky man with a viciously curling moustache above a snarling mouth, to put the bags in the rack. Soros then, always smiling and sometimes laughing, cleared a way through the mob and settled us into our seats, and then settled beside me to sort out our account. He scribbled some sums on a piece of paper and handed it to me. The sum of sixty euros was underlined. Preposterous, clearly preposterous, he'd incurred a seventy-euro fine, been bullied and threatened by first the land police and then the maritime police, hauled four heavy pieces of baggage aboard when surrounded by a tumult of Greek and tourist desperados, on top of which he'd performed his basic professional task of driving us for an hour from the air- to the seaport, on top of which, through all the stress and injustice, he'd remained unfailingly good-humoured and courteous. I gave him forty-euros extra, 100 euros, not as much as he deserved but seemingly, from his expression and gestures and from the words Victoria understood, more than he expected. It strikes me now that there is a rich paradox in all this. Out of the worst possible, and completely characteristic, welcome from the Greeks had come the best possible, and also completely characteristic, welcome from a Greek.

THE WHOLE WORLD'S A HOSPITAL

I phone Harold every evening. We're each on a mobile. I think Harold has learnt how to use his since he became ill the first time around. His voice is stronger than it was when we last saw him in London a week or so ago, but then it was little more than a whisper, the husk of the barking, powerful voice it used to be. We have little to say to each other. Well, what is there to say, really? He's over there in London, in a hospital, quite possibly dying, and I'm here in Spetses, swimming, eating, reading, writing, and though I'm also dying, it's only in the *sub specie aeternitatis* kind of way, as people are, everywhere. I feel abundantly, even boisterously, healthy. I would write obscenely healthy because it would make me seem less callous, more aware of the contrast in our two states, but I know that whatever's on his mind he can't share with me properly, and it would be – yes, obscene, actually – to share with him what's on my mind, although in fact very little is on my mind except the thought of him, the image of him so ill. I can hardly tell him how I spend my days – 'Well, over here, Harold, all is well, the sun shines, the sea shimmers. We walk down the path that leads to the beach several times a day, plunge in, drift around for as long as we feel inclined, climb out, dry ourselves, drift along to one of the cafés on the front, read the English papers, drift back for another swim, then up the steep but dappled path to the little house perched above the bay, and loiter there, reading, writing, living.' Or I could complain about the insects – 'Bitten by mosquitoes, Harold, I'm taking vitamin B because Victoria says that mosquitoes hate vitamin B, also I have little pencils of repellent I dab over myself, Harold, and if they fail to repel I have little pencils of after-bite, so you see there are serious irritants and inconveniences to the otherwise blissful days, and to be quite truthful about the dappled path to and from the beach, it's actually very steep, very steep indeed, it may only take three minutes, I timed it, to go up, but it feels like three hours, I find myself dragging myself up the last steps, and going down isn't easy either, I stumble sometimes, and overbalance, and what's more the food in Spetses is mostly pretty foul, and what's more, and more and more –'

So what happens during our conversations at the moment is that I ask him how he is, he tells me how he is, clearly and concisely, but with an exhausted fatalism in his voice. He says a little about his eating, whether he's managed to get anything down and keep it there, and then his voice comes to a halt, then falters into news of the test match, which we discuss with fraudulent animation. Fraudulent for him because the effort of seeming to care is enormous, I think. And fraudulent for me because I already know the news, having picked it up from someone else a little earlier. Still, it gives us a subject, for which we're both grateful, keeping us in touch with all the conversations we've had over the years about cricket, test matches, so forth. Then we say to each other, 'Let's see how tomorrow goes, fingers crossed for tomorrow,' and we hang up, and I try not to keep the thought of him sitting upright, absolutely drained by the effort of our conversation with his mobile in his hand. Does he fiddle with it first, looking for the little red switch-off symbol, pressing it with a feeble and unpractised finger, then put it carefully by the bed? In what state of mind does he watch the cricket? I wonder where the television set is in relation to his bed? Does he have to look at it at an angle, or is it above the foot of the bed? I can't imagine the layout of his room. I've been in the hospital he's in quite a few times for this and that, but I have no sense of its rooms, or of its exterior even. I have an idea that its nurses are pleasant. I wonder if he loses his temper with them, whether he has the strength to lose his temper, and then the further strength to apologize. I hope that if he can do the first, he can also do the second – it's not safe, really, to be on bad terms with your nurses. Anyway, there he is, in a place I can't visualize even though I've been to it, and here am I, in a place he certainly can't visualize as he's never been to it, with the moon above and the sea below, and the cicadas clicking their knees.

Actually, Harold is very good at apologies, an outburst over the dinner table will be followed the next morning, or sometimes very late the same night, with a self-denunciation on the telephone, and the manly hope – and I mean manly, I don't know if this word is much used now, it may have passed out of the modern vocabulary, an archaism as unusual as the creature himself – forthright, unadorned, full of strong and delicate feeling, manly. His voice seems to have peeled off layers of bark, as in both tree and dog. In the ordinary currency of life it always has a bark to it, even when – as often, in rehearsals – he was being gentle with an actor in trouble, there would be the rough, brusque coating that went with the out-thrust jaw and the glittering eyes. When he becomes angry the eyes go milky, the voice a brutal weapon that is virtually without content. What I mean by this is that he speaks violently, really violently. His voice is like a fist driving into you, but he uses almost no words, three or four at the most – 'shit', 'fuck', 'I' are the ones you hear – recognize anyway, the other words aren't words, they aren't even inexactly uttered expletives, they're dark and ugly sounds, incomprehensible because not intended to be comprehended except as dark and ugly sounds, and full of eloquence therefore. You may not have understood what he was saying but you knew what he meant. Thus he will preface his subsequent apology with 'I don't know exactly what I said last night, I went off the rails a bit, I drank too much and – well, I hope you'll forgive me.'

It's the drink, of course, but it isn't only the drink, of course. The primitive, I really wanted to write the primeval, savagery of Harold's rages comes from somewhere or something drink may have opened the way to, but isn't itself created by drink. It is a chaos of self. 'Seething with rage' is an often used phrase, but I've never felt its truth except with Harold, he 'seethes' as things in nature seethe or he 'erupts' as things in nature erupt – volcanoes, naturally – a volcanic temper, but if you could see into the depth of the volcano what would you see there? Certainly nothing to explain it, you would see only molten substance, and if you could peer into Harold's depths when he seethes and when he erupts, I don't think you'd find the explanation – friends invariably use phrases like 'I think what set Harold off –' and out will come some plausible motive, based on biography. I can't remember any of the explanations now, but they're always perfectly reasonable, with due acceptance of the irrational influence of drink – 'all that, you see, and then he was slightly drunk of course' – but hopelessly inadequate because they omit their own often physical responses to the rages, the assaults, in fact we're struck dumb by them, sit white-faced and in shock as expletive follows expletive. Women cry, mostly. I can't remember anyone standing up to him. Well, how could you? He's like a man having a fit, if he was having it in the appropriate context, a psychiatric ward, for instance, he would be restrained physically, a strait-jacket and then chemically. Then you think about the plays and you wonder if the genius of them is that they both contain and express the dark turbulence they come out of, in some ways they are more like people than works, you feel you might bump into them in a pub or in a dream, you see them living from moment to moment, impulse to impulse, but you don't quite understand how the moments and the impulses connect, which is why you're never sure, even if you've seen one many times, how it's going to end, or whether you're safe in your seat while it's happening, it might come down from the stage and beat you up.

On the other hand, there is his gentleness. What makes him seem so very gentle is the contrast with what we remember and dread. The eyes that go milky when he is in a fit are luminous with concern, the voice becomes soft but – more importantly – tentative, almost shy. Unlike most people he is actually more exposed, more simply and directly himself, when he is concerned and touched than when he is angry, beside himself. Harold tender and gentle is Harold in himself, gathered together and at your service, which has the specific effect of liberating you, so that you become intimate and uninhibited in your confidences and confessions, and in that respect he is oddly priest-like, and gives you a sense of being protected. If I try to distinguish this Harold, the perfect Harold, from my other close friends in similar circumstances, I would say that there is a sense of almost religious seriousness in the exchanges with him, and of absolute concentration – the subject is the subject, not to be deviated from until it has been explored in all its possibilities for help, whereas with my other friends there is always, however desperate the subject, an element of rough and tumble, unrelated complaints and confessions intervene, they offer examples from their own experience that make you equal confidants, and sometimes, by the end, you have forgotten which one of you has come to talk about what problem. This is never so with Harold, if he has something to discuss he will place it before you and you will begin, quietly and gravely, to discuss it, you'll bring to it the sort of attention he brings to you, there are no byways or turnings off, no bursts of hilarity. These are rather moving experiences, the dominating image, for me, always being Harold's eyes, wide and full of soft feeling.

*

I've just phoned Harold. He sounded exhausted, but his voice was again clear and stronger. He gave me the test score, which isn't too good, the Australian openers still batting with 101 on the board, I said that both sides had a habit of collapsing when apparently set, and then reviving when all seemed lost, perhaps we'll take lots of wickets tomorrow, he said, 'Yes, well, we'll see.' And then said he was being taken to the hospital on Monday for another look to make sure that the cancer hasn't come back. I said, 'Oh.' I couldn't think what to say really. There was a pause, just like the one that had followed our conversation about the cricket. 'Well, we'll see,' he said, and we hung up. I don't think I was of much use. His going into the hospital seems to me distinctly ominous, how can they not know, after all these months, during which he has seen specialist after specialist, whether he's in remission or whether the cancer has come back? And yet a mere few days ago we were celebrating the news that they had identified his illness. It was a dental problem, all they had to do was to fatten him up and give him the appropriate drugs.

In remission. It's such a hopeful word, but when you think what it means, you realize that we're all, always, in remission, even the healthiest of us. In fact from the day we're born. Does that make it a less hopeful word? I keep remembering how, when Alan was, according to the doctors, a day or so away from death, and there was nothing more to be done but to wait for the end, they'd make the process as painless, as peaceful as possible – at least that is what they said to Alan's son Ben. They nevertheless subjected him to a last dose of chemotherapy, the chemo being some chemical not available in England, that had had to be shipped over especially from Switzerland. Ben couldn't understand why they insisted on doing this, it was completely useless and upset the equilibrium of Alan's last days, and upset Ben, who had to encourage his father through needless discomfort and to pretend that it might be a dramatic step towards recovery. Alan was really past taking in what they were doing, all he registered was the physical unpleasantness, and as I say, it made no sense at all to Ben, no sense until he saw the bill, which arrived with cruel punctuality on his father's death and included a vast charge for the last dose of chemotherapy.

*

How can one trust doctors? They seem to know more and more about their own specialities, less and less about their patients. If they are ear, nose and throat people, then they know the ear, nose and throat of you, but not what these are attached to, you're not present as a living and ailing organism, you're there in the bits and pieces he knows about, and he's unlikely? unwilling? unable? to speculate about alternative explanations for your illness, there's nothing wrong with your ear, nose and throat, so you'd better go to someone who specializes in something else and if you're lucky you might eventually hit on a man who happens to specialize in whatever is killing you.

I'm not ready to give up smoking yet. Insufficiently settled. I tried yesterday, managed until dinner, but then sitting in the café, a coffee in front of me, the sea lapping softly a few yards away, and such a moon! It was the moon that did it, the moon's fault.

THIS ISLAND NOW

The beach we swim from is a couple of minutes away from here, down some steps between grand houses at the top, fairly humble new ones at the bottom. When you've gone down the steps you turn right into another little alley with a wall on one side, behind the wall is a dry river bed, and small apartments on the other side. Each apartment has a poky terrace on which a man or a woman is sitting, serenely reading a paper or smoking a cigarette. They're all and always very polite, and utter a greeting (at least I hope it's that) in Greek, and I doff my straw hat, in the manner of an English gentleman of the old school. It's pleasant going down these two alleys, as there are great trees and dappled shade in the first alley, and the sides of the apartment and the wall create shade in the second. When you emerge, though, you are on a shadeless main street along which motorbikes and the motorized tricycles roar and whine, emitting exhaust fumes that you have to close your mouth and screw your eyes against. The tourist brochure about Spetses tells you that no cars are allowed on the island, which is almost true – there are three officially sanctioned taxis and some delivery trucks – it also says that you can travel about the island in a horse-drawn carriage, which is completely true, you can indeed travel that way if you can afford it, and it's undeniably lovely, late at night, when most of the other traffic has stopped, to come clip-clopping home in a rocking, swaying carriage. The horses are remarkably strong and gifted. They know the intricacies of the island roads so well that the drivers scarcely have to use the reins, just saying a few words now and then to indicate left or right. They do complicated manoeuvres, U-turns and so forth, with economy and skill.

What the tourist brochure doesn't tell you, though, is that the no-cars, horse-drawn-carriages stuff is strictly for the tourist brochure, and leaves out of account the fact that any other form of motorized transport is allowed – tricycles, Vespas, and motorbikes from the frailest to the most powerful, some of them so large that with a burly man on them, his elbows and knees sticking out, they virtually fill the narrower roads. All the drivers go very fast, and very noisily, and if you come in July and August, as Victoria and I used to do, the island is a bedlam, and dangerous. On our first year we saw so many people, from children to ancients, in plaster casts – ankles, thighs, whole legs up to the hip, wrists, whole arms up to the armpit – we thought that there must have been a seismic catastrophe. In fact, they were only the season's regular harvest, either the drivers themselves or their victims.

So you cross this road in your swimming trunks and your loosely buttoned short-sleeved shirt, with your espadrilles under rather than on your feet, your towel over your arm, taking great care to look both ways, and when you arrive on the opposite pavement, you take three steps down through a gap in a low wall and you are on the beach, a long slab of concrete with cracks and holes in it, and uncomfortable sun-beds on it, and on the sun-beds a selection of bodies, all heavily oiled and unnaturally gleaming, and for the most part it's a pretty disgusting sight which would be rendered more disgusting if you added your own body to it, but you don't, you shed your shirt, drop it on the wall along with your towel and hat, and totter to one of the ladders down which you climb in a burdened – burdened? Burdened by what? Worry? Responsibility? Years? Wrinkles and fat? Well, all those, but just let's just say that you climb down the ladder in an ungainly fashion and lower yourself into – and this is the point – the soft Aegean Sea. Once you're in it you can lie there for hours, or do as the Greeks do and form impromptu little parties – you see them in groups of four, five, six, seven, their heads form a loose and bobbing circle as they gossip, laugh, quarrel, their voices rising to shrieks, dropping to conspiratorial whispers. It's really very charming to watch them at it from the shore, in fact watching them at it is about the only charming aspect of being on the shore, where the sun beats right through the umbrella which you can hire, along with a beach-bed, for a quite outrageous price – I hate it, and even Victoria, who loves the sun, finds it uncomfortable, but the Greeks sit and sprawl in it, many of them without hats, and they seem not only comfortable, but happy and grateful – I don't understand it, why don't they feel ill and angry, as I do after two minutes, what is it in their pigmentation or their souls that makes it possible for them – and many of them don't even swim. There's a certain type of middle-aged woman, hair dyed yellow or reddish, with freckled, almost ginger breasts on full display – she struts up and down this strip of cement, promenading, so to speak, with her mobile to her ear, her voice piercing, she never swims, but occasionally lowers herself down the ladder to a rung where the water is knee-high, she stays like that, still on her mobile, for a couple of minutes, then climbs back up, shakes her legs irritably as if something slimy has got on to them, then goes to her bed, lies down, still on her mobile – something about her reminds me of bacon.

You can't spend much time on the cement beach, even if the Greeks can. Or rather you shouldn't. Get into the marvellous welcoming water as quickly as you can, stay in it until you feel yourself going cold even in the warmth, and the skin on your hands begins to pucker and whiten, then get out, jostle your way to your clothes and towel, dry yourself, go away. You don't, of course. You stay for a cigarette or two, to watch the people on the beach, observe them with the detachment of a writer on the make, is how you like to see it, but in no time you're loathing them, and the ones chatterboxing in the sea, with their bobbing heads and their rasping laughter, seem suddenly to be a coven.

And then there's bound to be a blonde, there is one now and I'm looking at her as I write this – leggy, with a little strip of material between her legs and nothing over her breasts. The stocky, bullet-headed brute lying indifferently at her side, sucking from a can of beer, is almost certainly English, and possibly she is too. They seem to have no physical interest in each other even when they rub oil into each other, the man, so unappealing, is as narcissistic as his appealing girlfriend – if she is his girlfriend, she might be his sister, or his probation officer, he might be on one of those therapeutic outings that the British prison or social services offer, on some bizarre but carefully worked-out system, as an alternative to a prison sentence – The general policy, as we all know, is to bung as many people as possible into prison – all political parties seem to agree that the British public likes to have the most overcrowded, educationally depriving prison system in Europe, but every so often, and equally incomprehensibly, they like to single out a sociopath with a particularly obnoxious criminal history, and send him on an experimental holiday, so why not include in his package a leggy, bare-breasted prison officer with a voice you could grate cheese on, she's now on her mobile, talking to Lav – a nickname, I assume, short for Lavinia, or a joke name for a man whose behaviour it sums up, or who knows? Who cares? I seem to care as I rest briefly on a white plastic bed, the sun pouring through my straw hat like a molten headache, my cigarette jammed into my mouth, as I scrawl down that suddenly I loathe her pert breasts, her long legs, her pretty, unsensual face, her voice above all, and Lav above all that, to whom her voice could reach without benefit of mobile. She's talking about Tone's hangover, Tone being, I suppose, the inert lump basting himself at her side, an absolute catch, and already half prepared, for an enterprising cannibal who could take him off in the back of a motorized tricycle and deliver him to one of those old-fashioned butchers who specializes in human flesh, there's always one in an out-of-the-way quarter, you'll find him if you look.

I say it was the heat beating down on the cement strip without affecting anyone but me that made me hateful, so the sun, the sun's to blame, but the fact is that now that I'm back on my terrace, with the fan whirring above my head, the cool sea gleaming in the darkness, when all appears to be right with the world as far as the eye can reach, I am still hateful, by which I mean full of hate, and it's nothing to do with the memories of the beach, because between being down on the beach at midday and being here at midnight on the terrace there should be other memories – let them find me, the memories of some other day, let them be good and unchoke me from this hatred that comes on me like a sickness more and more.

THE MAN IN THE WHITE PLASTIC CHAIR

We still haven't been to Zogheria, though it's only a short water-taxi ride, fifteen minutes if the sea is rough, from the harbour. On still days the water is so clear that you can see to the bottom when you are out of your depth, and you can stay out of your depth without thinking about it, lazily, dreamily stirring a few yards on your back or rolling on to your side, and if you look out to sea there will be the outline of the mainland, and if you look to shore there will be the beach sloping up to the taverna, set in pine trees, the pine trees cover the slopes around the beach, and at evening the light –

The last time we went, five years ago, I sat at a table in the taverna. It was evening, about six I should think. I watched Victoria sitting on the sun-bed by the edge of the sea, she was bent over a small pad, doing a watercolour, and the light – It really felt like the last time, the light so soft and closing down gently, the end of the day, the end of the season, love in September, the end of a great deal in our lives –

In the first year we came the family that ran the taverna consisted of a father (Taki), a mother (Elena) and two sons (Yannis and Bright-eyes) and a Labrador puppy, bouncing and playful, called Kim. There was also a very pretty, dark young woman who was Yannis's fiancée, and the next year she was his wife and pregnant, the year after the mother of a baby girl – we dropped in on these lives for eight consecutive years, saw the baby become a little girl, saw the young wife pregnant again, then Bright-eyes absent, doing his national service – and there was the grandfather, a retired fisherman who sat in a small wicker armchair, his hands on his knees, not talking much, and an uncle with a trim grey moustache and furrowed grey hair who was still an active fisherman with a small blue boat – now the odd thing, the odd thing about either these people or my memory of them, is that, in spite of the dramatically changing circumstances, the pregnancy, the baby, the absence of Bright-eyes, nothing seemed to change, it was as if a tableau sprang to familiar life every time we re-entered it, and one memory could serve for all memories – for example, on one of our earliest visits there was the most perfect young woman, Scandinavian, surely, lying alone on the beach as the afternoon sun became twilight, she wore bikini bottoms only, her bra spread along the handle of her basket by her head – short blonde hair, long, long legs, her face turned, impassive and lovely, the inevitable sunglasses, she really was a delight and a mortification to the aged eye I kept trained on her from my table in the taverna, I hoped she would get to her feet and I could take in the full-breasted length of her, but she showed no sign of moving, and I could hear the distant hum of the taxi, Michaelis or Martina, growing louder behind the promontory – then lo! the puppy Kim tumbled down the terrace of the taverna on to the beach and bounded up to the girl, who reached out a leisurely hand to stroke him – he darted away, skipped back, plucked up her bra, scampered around her, and lo! there she was, up and frantically about, an arm across her breasts as she tried to catch Kim, who was one moment at her feet – so over she bent – the next jumping away from her – so she darted and pirouetted this way and that, reaching for him with both arms at last, in an abandoned and despairing fashion, and her breasts, elegant and shapely, like two upside-down puddings – I don't think puddings is quite right, doesn't give the sense of contour and grace, though it does catch the mingling of desires – the nicest thing about it, though, was that in spite of the indignity, the necessary immodesty of her movements, she was convulsed with laughter, she clearly adored Kim for the puppy he was, even when she was caught in the hurly-burly of a tug-of-war. She'd managed to snatch back one of the straps and was trying to jerk it free with both hands, and Kim, settled back on his haunches, was determined to keep hold. I don't know how it worked out, the memory stops there, on that image. I wonder if she ever remembers it, wherever she is now, perhaps married, with children, and with a dog or two, I bet.

So that was Kim, in subsequent years a proper-sized dog, and then a lame one, and then he was gone, he died quite young, at six, possibly seven, anyway between one summer when he was there and the next, when there was a puppy instead, another Labrador.

And so, having been in Spetses a week, we've still hadn't done the thing we always used to do the day after we arrived, go down to the new harbour to find Michaelis or his daughter Martina to take us in their water-taxi to what is probably our favourite spot in the whole world. Each evening we say, 'Tomorrow we'll go to Zogheria. Or perhaps Wednesday, we'll go on Wednesday.' I suppose we're afraid that something might have changed for ever, a death most likely, the uncle or the grandfather – after five years they won't remember how things were the last time we saw them – if, say, the grandfather died two years ago it won't be on their minds when they see us, so that when we look around, look towards his small wicker chair, say, and they follow the look, and realize that we don't know, they'll shake their heads sorrowfully, etc., so forth – that's the sort of thing we're afraid of, or worse because it might be one of the children, God help us all – I am beginning to doubt that we will go at all to Zogheria this year.

We used to have five Spetses friends, Athenians who spent the whole of the summer on the island and who were more than holiday friends. We kept in touch one way or another throughout the rest of the year. Now three of them are dead, they died during the winter months, of course, one of them no longer comes to the island, and only Nata is left. She's become more and more a year-round friend, coming to stay with us in London, or in a nearby hotel. We have in our sitting room in Holland Park a bull she cast in metal. It stands on the table by my armchair. It's about a foot long and six inches high, its head is lowered to a butting position, and its shoulders are gathered together, all compact, muscular force, its front legs bent, its back legs lunging forward, so in shape, if you follow its line down from the top of its head to the tip of its tail, it's a model of noble and powerful aggression, but on its bent face there is the most curiously shy and timid expression, a sweetness, and its testicles are small and delicately shaped bells that tinkle slightly if you shift its body about – not easily done, as it's very heavy, I can only just lift it, and if I do I need to put it down again immediately. When Nata arrived from Athens she was carrying it under her arm. She'd carried it under her arm on to and off the plane, and while at the airport waiting for a taxi. It's true that this was some years ago, seven I should think, when she was – if I deduct seven from eighty-three, which she now is – so when she was seventy-six. Yesterday she joined us on the beach, she had a cheroot hanging out of the side of her mouth and hanging from her hand her elegant little basket, decorated with flowers and leaves – well, there she is, Nata – on the one hand, the cheroot, her eyes squinting through the smoke, a tough, almost manly image – on the other hand the charming and feminine basket – she is very like, in that way, in the contradictions of her nature and her appearance, the bull that I love so much. She's quick to denunciation and shows of anger, banging her fist on the table or shaking it in the air, the cause of these outbursts never personal, but general, generous, political – the state of the world, the moral and mental health of President Bush, the ancient and future quarrels with the Turks, the iniquities of the Northern Barbarians. Once she denounced us – Victoria and me – it was only the second or third time we'd met her, we were having dinner with her and a number of her friends – she was talking passionately in Greek at one end of the table, we were talking calmly in English at the other end, and suddenly Nata was on her feet, her dress flowing around her like a toga, she pointed a finger at us, and said, in a tumultuous voice, 'Yes, it is the fault of you – your fault – you Northern Barbarians!' I can't remember now what was our fault, but it was historical, and went back a long way, something en route, no doubt, to the Elgin Marbles. And then, of course, being Nata, she laughed, though adding, 'But still, it is true. I am sorry to have to say it, but it is true.' Her English is upper-class *circa* 1930s, as she was brought up, as were so many Greeks of her generation and class, by an English nanny. She makes grammatical mistakes and her vocabulary is sometimes faulty, but the accent is impeccable even though she invests it with so much un-English feeling, not only passionate feeling but tender and concerned. In repose she has the face of an owl, and she walks like an owl, too – her feet paddle along, her body swaying from side to side – but when she's swimming, the water flattens her hair so that it is sleek against her scalp and neck, and she has the head of a seal. This morning she came down to the concrete beach and sat beside us smoking a cheroot and talking about her work, her family, her plans for her grandchildren's careers – she admits to being, no, boasts of being an oppressively ambitious grand-mother, and she entangled her conversation about her grandson, a brilliant mathematician now teaching in London, at Imperial College, with a consideration of the problems she's having with a statue she's working on of Poseidon, King of the Fishes. Poseidon will be carrying in one hand his three-pronged fishing spear, and in his other hand a fish he has just caught – it is going to be larger than human-sized and is designed to be placed in the sea by the Spetses lighthouse. I asked her if this King of the Fishes planned to eat the caught fish, and she said, 'Yes, of course.' I started to debate this with her – I mean, what kind of king would eat his own subjects? A king was a god, she said, who could do what he liked with his subjects, and I suppose that makes sense, in that every god that man has created seems in some way or another to consume his children, who are also his parents – this idea is running out of meaning, I can't pursue it here, prefer rather to dwell on Nata, in her leather espadrilles and her voluminous dress flowing to the metal ladder that people like me clamber down, rung by rung, and that Nata dives over, her arms stretched out, unbending, the sides of the hands and the sides of the feet pressed together in a straight and true dive, classical, but with her dress billowing around her as she hits the water. She remains under it for quite a while, and then surges up and settles into a steady crawl, her cheroot drifting in her wake. She likes to fill her mouth with the sea and then, lying on her back, jet it out in an enormous arc. It's much more difficult than it looks, neither Victoria nor I can manage half the distance that she manages, then she swims out quite a long way and there remains, her seal's head turning this way and that as she engages other swimmers in conversation –

'The fact is that I am diseased,' he said on the phone this evening. 'I am a diseased man.' He said it huskily and in wonder, as if to be diseased against one's will is an almost ungraspable concept. Everything I said to him seemed to be completely inadequate. Perhaps the time has passed in myself when I can be of much good to anyone in need of support of a moral kind. The truth is that the moment I begin to consider it, I can't think of any reason, moral or otherwise, why Harold shouldn't be dying, everybody else is, after all, though not many of my acquaintance are as consciously close to death, but unconsciously – I mean by that unawares – who knows? Perhaps I myself, or Victoria or my children. This thought I cannot pursue, on no account can I pursue this thought, which nevertheless remains the case – 'remains the case', there's a Harold phrase for you.

*

This evening, on a sudden impulse, we went to the harbour, in search of Michaelis. We found him sitting at a table outside the bar, where all the sea-taxi drivers sit. He is a short man with splay feet and only one good eye, and you can't be sure that his one good eye is actually any good, at least as far as seeing goes, but it's good to look at, as it sparkles with life, friendliness, ironic malice. He damaged the other eye in a motor accident here on Spetses, went to England to have it treated privately – this was about thirty years ago – and came back without it, having spent a year of his life and all his savings trying to save it. It had been extracted for reasons that I don't understand, and replaced with a dull, false one that remains fixed and staring, while the other glints and swivels expressively – but he can't see even with the good eye at night, he becomes a blind man when the sun goes down, as Victoria and I discovered one summer, when he took us across the gulf to the mainland. We set out just as twilight was becoming darkness, Michaelis standing upright at the wheel, his face blank with apprehension that became more than that as we approached the shore, a bulky black mass pierced here and there with little dots of light – his wife, a handsome woman – a hairdresser by profession who once cut my hair so brutally – no, she didn't cut it brutally, she cut it easily and pleasantly, patting my head as she closed in on the skull – it was the final effect that was brutal, I looked like an elderly version of the beer-swigging lout on the beach this morning – anyway, this practical and pleasant-looking woman was seated in the small cabin of the boat, the whole boat being not that much larger or more capacious than a London cab, knitting. She'd come along for the ride, she'd said, for the pleasure of a jaunt across the strait, the night air – she really did communicate this in gestures and half-phrases that Victoria and I could understand. As we approached the lump of blackness in the darkness that was the shore, I noticed that Michaelis was standing sentinel-like sideways on to it, that his face was frozen and that the glitter in the eye was the glitter of panic. His wife came out of the cabin quite casually, stood beside him, chatting in low, wifely fashion and smiling warmly at us, as we sat there on the low wooden seats in the prow, Victoria on one side, I on the other, Michaelis and now his wife between, he physically and she morally at the wheel – so the wife guided through the calm, impenetrable dark the clearly completely night-blind Michaelis, who steered, slowed, reversed, lurched forward, according to her directions – but though she spoke calmly and gently, smiled warmly, a picture of wifely companionability, she had a gesture – plucking at tufts of her hair over her ears – which became like a neurotic tic at what were key moments, in fact one knew they were key because of the tic – but why am I going into all this? We didn't hit anything, we didn't sink, nobody fell into the water, nothing really happened at all. We got to the jetty belonging to the man who'd asked us to dinner, he was waiting with a torch to guide us in, we disembarked, we walked along the path to his home, had dinner – actually I remember nothing at all about the dinner apart from the dread of the return journey, which was exactly like the journey there, in reverse. Getting away from shore was the nightmare but once we were out at sea, and safe, the wife went back to her knitting.

And there he was this evening, Michaelis, at the sea-taxi drivers' bar, facing us as we approached but not really recognizing us until he caught us out of the corner of his functioning eye. He adjusted his head so he could get a view of us, then he exclaimed, encircled us with his arms, kissed me on both cheeks, took Victoria's hand with formal gallantry, and held it but didn't kiss her, was in fact shy, I think. Martina came gliding along the side of the harbour in her taxi, saw us, moored the taxi and was up the quay steps and on us like an enormous and friendly dog. Now we were with them there was no turning back. We established we'd be there tomorrow at 1 p.m., and that one or the other, Martina or Michaelis, would take us to Zogheria.

Midnight. I am sitting on the terrace in a white plastic chair, the sort of white plastic chair you see in bars and cafés across the world, and staring at this yellow pad with a kind of angry listlessness – I long to want to pull it towards me and write about the lovely afternoon we had in Zogheria, but instead I find myself writing a sentence about the white plastic chair that I'm sitting in and – and in short –
in short
and in short
I am afraid.

*

2 a.m. We go home tomorrow. Home. London in autumn, and the light fading earlier and earlier, day by day – and I'm sitting here on the terrace for the last time this year – and who knows, perhaps for the last time ever. It's balmy, with the gentlest of breezes, the lights of the sea-taxis zipping through the darkness below, and I feel that I should be able to draw on a rich vein of melancholy, write an elegy, valedictory, Greece, Greece, oh my Greece, when shall I—? But really all I want to do is sit here in the white plastic chair on the terrace, as blankly as possible, smoking. Smoking. Yes, well, perhaps when we get back to London – remove all the ashtrays. That might be a start.

4 a.m. It's beginning to get misty and there are only two lights down there on the water, they're doing zigzags, rather sinuous zigzags, one behind the other – the one in front has stopped, the other has caught up, they're moving again, so close that they make just one light in all that dark sea.

Dawn soon, so no longer home tomorrow, home today.
  Home today.
  God help me.

OLD MAN DROWNING, BUMPITY BUMP

We're on the tarmac at Athens airport. Waiting to take off. There's a slight delay, owing to something or other – a late passenger, a pregnant stewardess, a terrorist trying to get an upgrade – I didn't really take it in, it is enough that the pilot had the usual soothing voice, that Victoria a few rows behind me is looking quite relaxed from a mild overdose of Temazipan. Why are we going backwards for take-off? Pay no attention. Concentrate instead on this and that. Think of a word

racist

Is a reasonable definition of a racist someone who thinks anyone of a different race inferior, simply by virtue of being of a different race? Or is that simply another definition of stupidity? What about attributing someone's bad behaviour to their racial origin – as in 'Well, of course, he would say/do that, wouldn't he, given that he's Aryan/Jewish/Welsh/ Asian?' But what if you attribute their good behaviour to their racial origin? 'Naturally he did the honourable thing, how could he not, he's Arab/Scots/African/Oriental' – which should be, logically, as insulting as its reverse – the notion that, for racial reasons, a man can no more help his virtues than his vices, he is his race, etc. – 'What do you expect from a Czech/a Pole/an Englishman, except cowardice/ courage?' Let's make it personal, if someone said to me, after I'd rescued an old man from drowning –

– which, actually, I did once,

on a beach in Liguria, an old Italian – heaved him on to the shore after his legs buckled under him in about three feet of water, there was no danger to myself actually, as I was standing almost next to him, I only had to scoop him up by his armpits and hold him steady as he tottered back to land, but there was danger to him because he had fallen face down, so my virtue, if it was a virtue, was in my alertness, I'd had on my eye on him because he'd looked out of his depth in water just above his knees. His wife said to me, 'Oh, thank you, thank you, you are an Englishman, are you not, so naturally you are brave and strong, noble and true' – would it have been reasonable of me to take offence, and to reply curtly that my bravery, strength, nobility and truthfulness had been acquired by hard work, constant self-scrutiny and self-discipline, as I had decided at a very early age, in my sole self and independently of parental influence, social background, and above all my racial inheritance, that my task in life was to look out for the good of other people, take minute- by-minute note of who might require help of any kind – myself I did it, madam, I, I, I, not some Englishman, but I, Simon Gray, rescued your husband from the broiling sea – or would I have swelled up with pride at having my race identified as brave, strong, noble and true? I think I would, yes, I would like to be thought a credit to my tribe. As I say, this is reduced to the personal – if I were a *Guardian* reader I might well have replied, 'Madam, I acted not as an Englishman, but as a member of the human race, from impulses that know no frontiers' –

But supposing I'd been observed swimming away from the old man drowning, and he'd drowned, and his wife had said to me, 'Oh, you cowardly Englishman, you are all alike' – would I have felt more ashamed? Personally, yes, for having brought discredit to my tribe, though I suppose I could have said, as a *Telegraph*-reading person, 'Madam, I behaved as any sensible, risk-assessing, self-interested member of the human race would have behaved – I realized that there was a good chance that if I went to his aid he would have taken me down with him, I have a wife, children, grandchildren, two dogs, two cats to consider, I had no reason to suppose on the evidence available that your husband contributes more to the general good than I do, in fact, now that I see him properly, laid out on the towels and turning blue, I suspect that both justice and nature have been properly served etc. in that he is evidently very old (thus nature's claim) and (justice's claim) corrupt, if not corrupt, venal – after all, he's a Greek, isn't he? Furthermore show me a Greek, madam, or a Jap, come to that, or an Afro-Caribbean that you can swear would have behaved differently – I can certainly show you quite a few Englishmen, several of them friends of mine, who would have behaved exactly as I behaved, equally I can show you quite a few Englishmen, even better friends of mine, who would have given an assist to your husband in the form of a downwards shove, before duck-paddling rapidly away, not out of malice, but out of an apprehension that your husband's desperate last thrashings and gropings might pose a danger to their own continued existence.' So in my imagination, the squabble between me and the freshly minted widow rages on over the purpling corpse of her husband, carrying me further and further from my discussion of the meaning of the word 'racist'.

Have we established anything at all? Apart from my inability to think sequentially or coherently.

Well, this at least.

Anyone who calls anyone a racist in an argument has lost the argument. Unless, of course, the person he's calling a racist is a racist.

I've just woken up. Must therefore have fallen asleep. What was I writing?

we're touching down,
bumpity-bump
bumpity bumpity bumpity
bump
bump

ANDREW AND LILIANNE

It takes an act of will, now that we're back in London, to put on my shoes, my scarf and coat, and get down the stairs on to the pavement, where often I do a lumbering pirouette and within a few minutes find myself back where I started, taking off my coat and shoes – or I make it up Holland Park Avenue as far as the Renaissance, drink down two coffees at a table on the pavement, and then labour home, take off my coat. This is no life for a sentient man, or at least sentient enough to know that this is no life for him. The question arises, therefore: what can I do? To what end should I eke out my remaining days? Furthermore, a question that excited me in my adolescence, when I first came across it in *The Myth of Sisyphus*: why bother to eke out my remaining days, why not just kill myself, and so put an end to the eking? Now how do you answer that question, which Camus, if I remember correctly, says is the first question we should put to ourselves – actually I don't think that's quite how he formulates it, I think he begins by saying that the question 'Why do men kill themselves?' should be replaced by the question 'Why do men not kill themselves?' and of course he puts it in French, and I read it, at the age of sixteen, in English, and haven't looked at it since, so really I'm not guessing, exactly, because it's very clear in my memory, but hoping, let's think of it that way, hoping that my very clear memory of the opening sentences of *The Myth of Sisyphus* is correct. It certainly makes perfect sense to me now, is in fact the question I might have put to myself without reference to Camus if the memory of Camus hadn't intruded – what I'm doing here is stalling, because in fact I don't want to answer the question 'Why don't I commit suicide?' After all, the best I can hope for is another day like this, of which the best that can be said is that I don't believe I've caused anyone any harm, or done any damage in the world. As far as I know. I may have done incidental harm and damage quite unawares.

I might, for example, have reminded somebody of somebody they had loved and lost, and stirred long and hitherto successfully repressed feelings which then engulfed them. Well, suppose a woman, suppose she was driving by in a car, had glanced out of the window and my face, my body posture, the dreary drum of my feet heading up Holland Park Avenue had brought to her mind a husband or a dog, yes, more likely a dog, that she buried a year ago, the dog that had been a mere pup when she had – had what? Her first child? Got married? Got arrested? Got her driving licence? Does one remember dogs as pups anyway? I don't think so. I think one remembers them, carries them about in one's heart, as full-grown dogs, with their characters firmly established. Besides, if it was the sight of me plodding up Holland Park Avenue that reminded her of her dog, it would scarcely be of a puppy, would it, that I reminded her? It would be of an elderly dog, the equivalent of a seventy-year-old man, which would be a 420-year-old dog if you multiply by six to translate dog years to human years – which can't be right, is clearly nonsensical in fact, a 420-year-old dog would be a dead dog, surely, even in dog years, so have I got the multiplication factor wrong? But let's get back to the point I started from, which was whether I might have done unintended harm today by reminding a woman driving past me on Holland Park Avenue of a beloved husband or dog, now dead. There. That puts it all very clearly. She saw me, into her head surged a memory of her dead husband going about a particularly beloved piece of business, what? My imagination fails me, I can't make up a beloved piece of husbandly business, I seem to picture him coming out of the lavatory, shuffling out, doing up his belt – not much hope that she'll remember that as a beloved bit of business, but possibly its very characteristicness will have something lovable about it, perhaps just its regularity – 'Every morning, on the stroke of eight, I'd see him coming out of the lavatory. He had a way of fumbling with his belt, such a way of fumbling with his belt! It was so him!' She may, of course, remember it, particularly the regularity, with revulsion, in which case he would be likely to be in all his aspects unbeloved by her – surely there are other bits of business you can give him that don't have lavatorial associations and that she might remember with, well, a degree of affection at least –

*

'He is remembered with a degree of affection' might be a decent enough epitaph, come to that, it's certainly more precise and therefore more convincing, than 'Beloved', which is what I put on my brother Piers's tombstone. Now, when I sit on the bench opposite his grave and look at the word, it no longer seems simple and eloquent, but brutal and pretentious. I used to distract myself from it by getting up and walking around for a while, and then pausing in front of one of the graves eight down from Piers, on the right, as you face him. Actually I've described it somewhere else –

The headstone is rather jaunty, yellowy-grey in colour, with a photograph of a young man embedded in a little glass dome at the top. He is bare-headed, dark hair cut short, round, handsome face with slightly child-like features, unformed anyway, as if he hasn't grown into them yet. He is dressed in shiny black leather, mounted on a powerful motorbike, a helmet under one arm, the other resting on the handlebars. Underneath this is inscribed 'In Loving Memory Of Andrew Crabb' and underneath that 'A Dear Son, Brother And Friend' and underneath that 'Born 12th February 1963 Died 10th April 1996' and underneath that is written in curling, flourishy letters the following poem:

> He rode through life
> Fast and Free
> His candle burning bright
> And through the smoke that we still pass
> He left us with his light

Once, when I worked out from his dates that he was just two days short of thirty-three years and two months old when he smashed himself up on his motorbike, I suddenly became interested in this question of ages, how long the dead in Piers's vicinity had spent in the world. I suppose I must have checked on about fifteen gravestones, and found two, both men, on which the arithmetic worked out at forty-nine – the age Piers was when he died. Altogether three out of sixteen, if one included Piers – must be unusual, surely, a freak clustering – 'clustering', isn't that the right word, the word they use when compiling statistics of this sort?

Now a new grave has come between Andrew Crabb and Piers, of a woman who, like Andrew Crabb, died in her thirties, and on the tombstone which marks it there is a poem in italic letters:

> Do not stand at my grave and weep
> I am not here. I do not sleep
> I am a thousand winds that blow
> I am the softly falling snow

and above it, etched into the stone, is the figure of a woman who could be an angel or could be a nurse, it's so vaguely, rather than delicately, executed. I suppose the statement of the poem could be described as pantheistic, sentimental-pantheistic, anyway it's certainly not Christian and it's self-evidently untrue, you might even say that it's a lie, just as the nurse/angel etching is a lie, she wasn't like that in life and she isn't that in death. I wish I could remember her name, her Christian name was Lilianne, I'm sure of that, but why I mention her, or rather her tombstone, is that it always gives me comfort, because it speaks well of the feelings of the people – parents I think – who buried her, and makes me feel less well about the people who buried my brother Piers and if I exonerate my brother Nigel, who was in shock and not well, I am left with me, as the family member I feel less well about, the unexonerated. I always slide some of the feeling on Lilianne's tombstone on to Piers's, although he would never have thought of himself as softly falling snow, or as a thousand winds that blow, furthermore he might well have wanted me to stand at his grave and weep, but to what avail as he is to be found, if he is to be found anywhere, At The Still Point Of The Turning World, which is where I plonked him, according to the line I had inscribed on the bench. Furthermore I atrributed the line, as if to give it added value, to T. S. Eliot. 'Piers Gray, At The Still Point Of The Turning World. T. S. Eliot.' Lilianne's lines, unattributed, seem simply to have drifted down and settled on her tombstone – when I say them aloud I don't say them directly to Piers, of course, as that would be a sort of thieving. I say them almost directly towards Lilianne but keep Piers in the corners of my eyes.

CAN WRITING FICTION REPLACE SMOKING?

But what was I doing up at the graveyard? What chain of thought, if it can be called thought – ?

Oh yes, my wondering whether I did unintended harm today by being mistaken by a passing woman driver for a beloved husband or dog. Well, how would that develop? I'm shambling up the street, heavy-limbed and flu-ridden, she glances in my direction just as she approaches the traffic lights, her heart leaps or her mind drifts, either way coordination disintegrates, the car bounds through the red light or stalls at a green one, then either runs over a pedestrian or is run into by the car behind, she either faces criminal charges or is seriously injured – in one way or the other her life is ruined. Or is it? Who knows how she would emerge from either catastrophe, seeming catastrophe? Take seeming catastrophe one: she runs over a child. She – Adele, let's call her, after her French grandmother – Adele has had a heavy lunch with Miriam, an old friend from schooldays. The school was St Muphet's, a boarding school in Shropshire which has long since been converted first into a hotel and more recently into a halfway house for sex offenders who are being returned to the community. It was that sort of school, the seeds of its future already in it. It was also the sort of school that girls like Adele and Miriam found themselves being sent to by parents who wouldn't contemplate state education and couldn't afford the best or even the better private schools.

Adele's father was a doctor with a long history of migraines, insomnia and adultery, her mother was consequently, or so a rationalist would argue, a bit of a dipsomaniac, who grew fat and developed a heart condition, and was subject to asthma attacks, some of them wilful – cats brought them on, but whenever she saw one she picked it up and buried her face in its fur. She had a small but genuine gift for painting, and did surreal landscapes from her sofa, which one of her husband's rich patients would sometimes buy when Adele's school fees were in the offing, but were otherwise stacked in various rooms around their house in Barnet, in those days a cheap and inconvenient London suburb. Adele was still living there at the time of the accident on Holland Park Avenue, which happened when? I must look back – Oh, today, this morning, when I went up to the Renaissance – so she's still living in it as I write this, along with one of her daughters, Wendy, who is a single parent and an unsuccessful freelance photographer – her one exhibition, in a small studio in Whitechapel, consisting of shots of her two children, three-year-old Seraphina and seven-year-old Jacques (different fathers) playing on the beach, in the bath, in the garden, all in the nude, was closed by the police and almost led to Seraphina and Jacques being taken into care by Social Services. This crisis brought out the sleeping tigress in Adele. She adored her grandchildren with a passion she'd felt for no one and nothing else in her life. She hired lawyers and wrote letters to her MP and went from door to door collecting signatures for a petition and got interviewed on afternoon television and finally managed to gain custody, which Wendy resents far more than she would have resented losing them to the state – other than when she was photographing them she found them 'a fucking nuisance' were her actual words to Klaus, the seventy-five-year-old father of Seraphina, a Swiss violinist whose concert career came to an end when he lost the use of his left hand in a beer-house brawl in Stuttgart in '83 with some English football fans from West Ham. Where is Wendy now, then? Is she with Seraphina's father, Klaus, the one-handed violinist? No, she's gone to join Jacques's father in Morocco, a faith-healing drug dealer, or a drug-dealing faith healer, depending which way round you look at him, and gay – his name is Willard and he comes from Texas. This is surely all the background I need on Adele. The key points I should try to keep in mind are that she is in her early sixties, she's the world's best grandmother, a well-intentioned but spurned mother, a conscientious if little-loved daughter, a dutiful if undervalued friend, and this is what she looks like –

ADELE RAPED IN PRISON! IS THIS JUSTICE?

Adele has curly grey hair, a round, gentle, thoughtless sort of face with a snub nose and large grey eyes that don't see much or well – her spectacles have an odd effect, they make her eyes seem small and crafty, which won't help her cause at her upcoming trial, although the real problem is going to be the amount of alcohol I've had her consume – two vodka turganovs before the meal, a bottle of red wine and a bottle of white wine during it, more than she'd drunk altogether in the

previous six months, and certainly enough to see her sent to prison –
and how can she not be, given that she badly maimed a mother, her
child and their dog – a dog? Yes, yes, the child was carrying the dog
when the mother scooped her up and bam! Adele got the lot of them.
I can't bring myself to decide who lives and who dies. The sentimental
side of me is inclining towards the dog as the sole survivor, but is it wise
to introduce another dog? The whole business only arose, the accident
and so forth, because Adele mistook you for a dog, surely this other dog
just gets in the way, so kill off the dog, no, not kill off, eliminate it from
the child's arms, also take the child out of the mother's arms and put
her in a pram – so Adele smashed into a pram. Christ! – let's leave that
for a moment, toy briefly with the idea of making Adele herself her
only victim, paralyse her from the waist down or up or both – no, no,
just leave it that she hurt her knee slightly, the point is the drunken
driving and jail time, that's what we want to get to, that's where all this
is tending, redemption, a Tolstoyan redemption in jail, a bit like
Resurrection but without all the mystical stuff, or a Dostoyevskian
redemption, like *Crime and Punishment* but again without all the
mystical stuff, just a straightforward, no-holds-barred Anglo-Saxon
account of a middle-class, middle-aged soul discovering herself through
rough Anglo-Saxon justice and sexual humiliation, in jail she was the
particular favourite of brawny inmates with child-like dispositions, but
eventually her innate dignity, her gentle manners, her generous and
unreproachful acceptance of the needs and desires of the socially
deprived and less fortunate whose sexual appetites –

All this coming about because she a) drank too much at a lunch with
her old friend Miriam and then b) glimpsed through her car window
an elderly man (me) who reminded her of a beloved dog. Now all that
really remains for me to work out is the nature of her conversation
with Miriam, and what it was about the man (me) she glimpsed that
reminded her of the dog, and then what it was about the memory of
the dog that caused her to lose control of her car – what sort of car, by
the way? Oh what does it matter what sort of car, a car is a car – well,
it is to you, because you can't drive and have therefore never owned a
car, so it's hard for you to visualize Adele driving past you up Holland
Park Avenue, glancing out of the window – no, actually it's not hard,

I see her quite clearly, her round face purplish-tinted from all that alcohol, her spectacles slightly askew, her mouth half agape and her jaw slack, like something seen through the window of an aquarium, I see her in fact from what would have been my point of view if I'd turned my head as she drove past – but I didn't turn my head, I kept plodding listlessly on, thinking little angry thoughts about not wanting the coffee I was forcing myself towards, not wanting the cigarette I was about to smoke that would make me feel worse and thinking I really wanted to be back in my study, or, better still, back in bed –

What did Adele and her friend Miriam talk about? What did they drink about? I don't think I've said yet that Adele didn't really like her friend Miriam. In fact she thought of her as a responsibility she'd been saddled with at the ghastly little school whose name I've forgotten and can't be bothered to look back for – actually I think it was St Moppet's, an unlikely name for a school, it might have been Mupphet, St Mupphet – in the narrow, damp and underlit dormitory in their first term Adele had had the misfortune to be bedded next to Miriam, but 'next to' doesn't give the sense of the closeness, it was almost as if the ten girls in the dorm shared a vast mattress with gaps in it, Adele had only to reach out over the blankets, an instinctive and uncontrolled maternal gesture, and the sobbing child was in her arms, and there she remained. It was as if some strange adoption contract had been drawn up, in which Adele had had no say and the terms of which were absolute: it was Adele's task in life to look after Miriam, Miriam had assumed it when she had lain, snivelling, with her head against Adele's soft young bosoms, her long lean legs locked around Adele's short sturdy ones, and her thumb in her mouth – her own mouth, that is, though so complete had been the act of possession that it might easily have been Adele's, the image would have perfectly represented what Adele sometimes felt about the relationship.

At St Moppet's it was rumoured from time to time
but really nobody believed it.
I don't believe it, I can't even imagine it.
Just because I can't imagine it doesn't mean it didn't happen.
Well, possibly once. Just the once. In the library.

WHAT HAPPENED IN THE LIBRARY

On a fine spring afternoon. The 2.30 cooking class that had been cancelled because its teacher, Miss Sally Twark, had had to rush to the sanatorium with gastroenteritis, so Adele and Miriam went to the school library, a small room, not much bigger than, say, a room in the Hilton, that contained a free-standing bookcase, a low understuffed armchair and a wooden three-legged stool. There was also a wrinkled brown leather sofa – courtesy of a governor and parent, the distinguished psychiatrist R. de Witt Witt, who at the time being written about (1969) championed hallucinatory drugs, spontaneous violence, chaotic sex and was a crusading enemy of the family ('only psychically healthy when engaged in incest') – but at the time of writing this (Nov 2006) he is a vegetable resident of what would have been called, at the time being written about, an asylum for the criminally insane –

Look, what happened in the library?

I don't know. I'll have to come back to that tomorrow. The important thing is that I've been writing steadily through the story of Adele and what's-her-name without smoking a cigarette. It must be the longest sustained piece of writing in my whole lifetime written without a cigarette, and I suddenly notice how dry my lips are, and that my lungs and my blood are pleading – no, no cigarette! Back to the library. Find out what happened there. Bondage? Rape? Murder!?!?

Miriam is as we left her.

She is lying on the sofa, one leg dangling over the side, so that the heel of her squat brown shoe (regulation school issue) is on the floor. The hem of her pleated grey skirt has slipped under her buttocks. Her long and shapely legs are thus exposed up to her thighs – her left one, stretched to the floor, is straight and true, almost no sign of a kneecap, just a small inverted pouch, while the line of her sinewy calf is tautly curved. Her head is flung back over the end of the sofa, her fine blonde hair cascades to either side of her narrow head. Her small beaky nose and tight, almost lipless mouth seem both sharpened and softened by the light that falls through the latticed window – it may be her abandoned posture, or her almost translucent skin, or the general impression she gives of having been drowned in a lily pond and then dried out in a linen cupboard – hush, she's speaking:

'I wish I was Ted.'

Adele, doing her best to ignore the drip sliding down the runway from Miriam's nostrils, responds with her customary warm-hearted curiosity.

'Ted? Who's Ted, dear?'

'Dead, I said. I said dead. I wish I was dead.'

'Oh.' She tries to think of something new to say. 'I think you have a cold coming on.'

'That's why I wish I was dead, is it?'

'It's why I thought I heard you say Ted instead of dead. The "d" sounded like a "t" – Ted. Instead of dead.'

Adele is sitting on the stool, which has a shiny top off which her bottom skidded when she first sat on it. She has hitched up her pleated grey skirt so that her buttocks can have a purchase – actually there is only enough surface for one buttock to purchase, and she is aware of how unseemly she looks, as if lopsided on a lavatory, but feels, more sadly than bitterly, that this is appropriate for her relationship with Miriam –

'But why would you want to commit suicide?' Her eyes are on the base of Miriam's nostrils, where another drop, so shiny, like the morning dew, so shiny –

'I didn't say I want to commit suicide.'

'Oh. Why don't you?' She was surprised to feel a throb of pleasure. She smiled.

'Why don't I? What do you mean?'

'Well, you haven't got anything to live for, have you, from what you tell me, and from what I can see for myself. You say your parents never wanted you, your father says you're not his and your mother wishes you weren't hers, your father likes boys, that's why he went into the navy, and your mother drinks all night and sleeps all day –'

'I never said any of that.'

'Yes you did. You say it all the time. In your sleep. That's why you cry and I have to put my arms around you.'

'Daddy's an admiral, and Mummy's ill, she can't help it –'

'That's what you say when you're not asleep.'

Miriam wipes her sleeve across her nose, as if just waking up. 'You're trying to hurt me.' It's a whisper, child-like. 'Why are you trying to hurt me?'

'Because I'm just like everybody else who knows you. I can't bear you.' Without seeming to herself to move she has shifted her bottom from the stool and is grinding it into Miriam's face.

You can see them there, if you concentrate. Adele is suffocating Miriam to death with her bum, and she is grinning while she's doing it, no, actually she's more than grinning, she's making noises through her grin that might sound sexual, but come from deeper in her, and are in fact homicidal. She wonders vaguely why Miriam isn't trying to bite her – but ah! How can she bite, given that her mouth, whether opened or closed, is being crushed by mounds of flesh and wads of cloth, and that's why her legs aren't threshing, her fists have fallen away, why she has become still, quite still.

The sigh that Adele sighed as she rolled her bottom off Miriam was one of regret. She wished she'd done what she wanted to do, but it was too late to clamber back and finish the job, there were voices that at first she thought were outside the library, faint but clear from a distance, and then were inside the library, and then inside her head –

She slid her buttocks into their previous uneasy position on the stool, and sat watching Miriam's return to consciousness with a cool, unworried eye.

Miriam twitched and gobbled, the white began to return to her nose and cheeks, which had gone puce under pressure, and foam gathered at the corners of her mouth. Her legs and arms trembled and her bony chest sucked in and out, raspingly. She reminded Adele of an ungainly young bird, say a gosling, just rescued from the jaws of a cat, except, except for her lips – Adele felt a stirring of desire, and such was her state might well have – might well have – if Miriam hadn't – but Miriam did. She pulled herself up, and she looked at Adele with such a vague, puzzled look of terror –

'We must never do that again,' Adele said firmly. 'We don't know what came over us.'

'No' Miriam's voice was feeble but eager – 'I don't know what came over us.' She winced as she spoke, and touched her lips, which were swollen and bruised, like the plums of August, and had provided Adele with the thought – they looked, those lips, as if they'd been kissed and kissed, which in a way they had been.

'It was wrong of us,' Adele said huskily. 'I blame myself most.'

'No, no, it was my fault, I know it was.' Miriam was pleading, yes, but was she pleading for her life? Or pleading to be forgiven for being such a temptress? Or did she merely sound pleading, because she had her whiniest voice on? And did Adele care? She felt such a surge of freedom, such a surge of lust and power combined –

'Well, yes, it was your fault because you looked so pretty – but I shouldn't have done it, and I promise I won't, ever again.'

'Do you promise, honestly, honestly?'

'Only if you promise never again to look so sweet.'

'I shan't, ever again, I promise.'

'Then I shan't, ever again. So we're safe, aren't we?'

'Yes, safe!' But she squealed when Adele got off the stool and went to her and bent over her. She drew her knees up and she hunched her shoulders.

'But we must kiss a little kiss, to seal our promises. Mustn't we?' Adele put her finger under Miriam's chin, and turned the thin, sharp strip of a face towards her, and pursed her lips. Miriam squeezed her eyes shut, and tried to purse her lips –

If Adele had known what rape was, she'd have raped Miriam on the spot. She'd have thrown her on the floor, bound her hands behind her back with her own flaxen tresses, ripped off her blouse and bra – whoops, whoops, whoops! Forward. Forward to
a cigarette.

Alas, alas, now two.

PART TWO

JERRY ORBACH AND LENNIE BRISCOE
ARE SORRY FOR YOUR LOSS

I've spent most of the day looking at the chaos on my study bookshelves and wondering what I can do about it. Just now I noticed, half hidden on a top shelf, Ian MacKillop's biography of F. R. Leavis. I took it down to put it somewhere more visible, somewhere more honourable, found myself dipping into it and then thinking not so much about Leavis as about Ian. We met when we were in our early twenties, in our second year at Cambridge, both taking the English tripos and both teaching in the same language school for foreigners in the vacations. At that age he was tall and thin, like a comically doleful but good-hearted cleric as conjured up by Boz and illustrated by Phiz, with spiky hair and the confused, sometimes desperate expression natural to an undergraduate with a wife and baby to support – and yet there was this oddly ecclesiastical aspect to him, partly a matter of his dark clothes and his pallor, but also the timbre of his voice and particularly in the carefulness with which he chose his words –

But there was never, at any time, anything ecclesiastical about his thinking, or the things he was willing to talk about. He seemed to have a completely uninhibited mind, I can't remember him being shocked by any subject or event. His curiosity was limitless, willing to go through endless byways for the pleasure of the journey.

Actually, the Leavis biography was a brave undertaking, given that Ian had been a pupil of both the Leavises. His critical impartiality was bound to offend their acolytes, his even-toned sympathy to irritate their enemies, but it succeeded in its main aim, which was to make us aware of what at his best Leavis represented, and what the personal cost had been in broken friendships, lost trust, isolation. The last stretch of the book, on Queenie Leavis's attempts to usurp her husband's reputation by laying claim to his work, make for pretty desolating reading, but Ian tells it scrupulously, unflinchingly, with a deliberated kindness all his own. I think he was a man of great tolerance and geniality but no softness – in his writing, with his friends, or in his living.

He knew so much about so many unexpected things – horror films, pulp fiction, westerns as well as thrillers, early Agatha Christie, every poet alive writing in the English language, dozens and dozens of poets that one, this one anyway, had never heard of, and he enjoyed reading them even when he didn't understand them – in fact not understanding them was part of his pleasure, it made him puzzle, worry and think, and he had a plan, not altogether a fantasy, to travel in a caravan around the British Isles and the States, park outside their homes, observe them in their habits, quiz them about their poetry.

He made a calm comedy out of the worst events in his life, out of even his last illness. I don't know anyone else who could make a dispassionate tone so droll – he was never ungenerous, except about himself in abrupt little asides, mutterings really. On our last meeting he remarked that there was something, I forget what, that he was really determined to do, really was obliged to do, then he chucked in, in a low voice, as an afterthought, 'Unless I'm dead, of course. And then I won't have to.'

When he came to stay he would bring a gift, anthologies of seventeenth- and eighteenth-century verse, or a little bundle of mid-twentieth-century detective stories – we have a charming wooden angel, hand-painted, from Guatemala on our mantelpiece. On his last visit he brought half a dozen eggs laid by his recently acquired hens. He'd carried them with him all day, while he'd gone about his London tasks – a visit to the British Library, meetings with colleagues and with publishers – before coming to us late in the evening. It made the eggs more delightfully and specially a gift, the thought that he'd had to keep them in mind all day, carry them carefully –

'I'm sorry for your loss' is what television detectives say when interviewing the victim's widow, widower or children, the phrase has become so inert that you no longer listen to it, if the actor changed it slightly, to 'Thank you for your loss' or 'We're happy for your loss' or 'Have a nice loss now', none of the characters, or the actors, or the audience would notice – but an actor who managed to give it unexpected poignancy was the late Jerry Orbach, who played the late Lennie Briscoe in *Law and Order*. In his last episodes one kept noticing his make-up, presumably he wore so much because without it he would have been visibly ill, visibly dying – when he said, 'I am sorry for your loss' his old, cynical roué's face, though powdered and covered in rouge, with eyeshadow, and even lipstick, seemed suddenly to get so much older, more cynical, and he would switch his eyes sideways as if he were sending a message to those in mourning on the other side of the screen, and how could there not have been quite a few of us, given the size of the audiences, though very few of us would subsequently be charged with murder – it's a fair bet that one out of every three of the characters to whom Lennie Briscoe says, 'I'm sorry for your loss' will end up in prison gabardine – the effect is really double, on the one hand the actor Jerry Orbach intimately consoling the grieving multitude with 'Hey, me too, I know what it's like, furthermore I'm on the way out myself' and on the other hand Detective Lennie Briscoe saying to a character, 'We'll continue this conversation down at the station, we're going to have to ask you for a DNA sample, and oh, hey, sorry for your loss.'

I wonder if Americans actually do say it to each other, and if they do whether they say it in an attempt to nullify the fact that gives rise to it. 'I am sorry' has the primary meaning of 'I feel sorrow', but still trails a slight suggestion of apology, perhaps for the inadequacy of the phrase, while 'loss', well, it means at its simplest that you don't have it any more – loss of money, loss of time, loss of patience and of temper, loss of a child – your son, your daughter, your mother, father, best friend, but what exactly is lost? This gesture, that expression, the early morning cuddle, the endearing laugh and endearing smile, her uniquely irritating laugh and his noisy way of gulping down his coffee, his way of not leaving the table when blowing his nose, 'Sorry for your loss.'

The trouble with the dead is not that they are lost, and therefore might be found, but that they are beyond finding and are not therefore lost, they are absent to this world, in all the places that they were accustomed to be present in, and that you were accustomed to their being present in, the space at your side, the opposite seat at your usual table, the other half of the bed, the neighbouring pillow – nothing can be more finally absent than a dead person, and yet the dead persist in being almost present in traces and glimpses, whisking around the corner of your memory to drive you mad, like the incompletely forgotten name of a film star from many years ago – there was one I was trying to remember the other evening, a man in the restaurant reminded me of him, a slim, middle-aged man eating by himself, not out in the open part of the restaurant but in a cramped bit by the bar – he reminds me, I said to Victoria, of that actor, in that film – I could see the actor's face quite clearly, though in the film it was usually half in shadow, a neat little moustache, opaque eyes, and he had a cleft in his chin, more dimple than cleft, shiny black hair pasted back, and there was the voice, drawling but toneless, I knew him so well in my teens, but who was he? In what film, *Zorro, Mask of Zorro*? No, no, Peter Lorre was in it, *Dimitrios*, *The Mask of Dimitrios*, and he was Z, Z certainly comes into it – in the film I'm trying to remember he generally lurked in alleys and hallways, or in a seedy hotel with large, bogus-looking rooms and cluttered corners you couldn't see into – I can't remember a particular scene, or a line of dialogue, or the plot, or even the climax, just Peter Lorre and Zachary Scott – Good Lord, there it is, Zachary Scott, what a name! And now I've got it written down I'll have it here to tell Victoria – Zachary Scott, I'll say, in *The Mask of Dimitrios*. He died not too long ago, there was something anomalous in the obituary, he went to Harvard to study Classics, or he played chess at international level, or fenced in the Olympics, something like one of those things but not actually any of those things. The next time the film turns up on television I must watch it to the end and at the end of it, when the credits roll and there is his name, I'll try to remember to feel sorry for the loss. Our loss. Our losses.

I've been sitting here for half an hour, still thinking or thinking yet again about the word 'loss' and wondering why I can't leave it alone, a bit of grit in my inner eye.

As my life has emptied of friends over these last years, I shouldn't find it strange that I frequently feel lonely –

LOVE BEFORE THE TIME OF
THE ANSWERING MACHINE

I think I miss the voices most, on the telephone. What was friendship like before the invention of the telephone? We know of its intensity for Tennyson, say, or Pope, for Milton or Matthew Arnold, all of whom wrote about their friendships, about the deaths of their friends, and all their poems, so different in form and vocabulary, strike the same note of grief and yearning, they make the same attempts to catch and hold the lives that have gone, we know the nature of the friendships from the manner in which they are missed – but it's hard for us now to grasp the developing of friendship before the telephone, when it depended on physical presence and letters – and before that, before the invention of the railway and the penny post – you can convert an impulse into a disaster within seconds now, and from pretty well anywhere in the world – why, merely by taking my mobile out of my pocket while strolling down Holland Park Avenue I could ruin friendships with people in New York, Rome and London in five minutes. It would have taken weeks in 1907, months, many months, in 1807 –

But for decades now most friendships have developed partly through the voice, disembodied but full of character, though not exactly the same character as the embodied one – does this mean that in those days, before the telephone, the physical meetings of friends were more intense – we know, but are still surprised, that Victorian men publicly kissed, embraced, touched each other in a way that modern men don't, except, I suppose, for theatricals and homosexual men in love with each other, who presumably touch and fondle like heterosexual couples in love with each other – well, not entirely like, as they don't do it in public that I've seen, though come to think of it young hetero-sexual couples today don't fondle and caress, or even hold hands very much, in public, although some of them don't mind being seen fornicating on beaches in the Mediterranean or in Greece, in Spetses actually, during the high season they hump away, all the night long, all the short night long –

As for the changing nature of friendship – when once a friendship was sustained by correspondence interrupted by intense physical presence, it's now sustained by telephone and more and more by email – I suspect email is most often used by friends when a) they don't want to waste the time and b) they can't face the emotional complications of a conversation – or, embedded in this proposition, that they want to present their side of the case without contradiction or diversion. I've noticed that people don't really enjoy receiving chatty emails, it's something like getting tightly written postcards – such stuff is for letters, in envelopes, that you open when you're ready – I was going to say that there are letters you open at breakfast, others you keep until lunch, others you face up to after midnight, after a few drinks if you're lucky enough to be a drinker, or after a few cigarettes if you're unlucky enough to be a smoker – but where we live, in Holland Park, we don't get letters at breakfast, or by lunch, we get them, when we get them at all, in the early evening, or later, when our neighbours return from work and redistribute the post according to the addresses on the envelopes –

When I talk of letters I mean, of course, personal communications, written by hand or on a typewriter, or if on a computer with an accompanying apology – i.e. my handwriting has degenerated so much from under-use that nobody can read it, therefore I have to write this on the computer, therefore if you don't understand it, it will be because of a failure of clarity on my part or of intelligence on yours – although I admit that I've never actually written an apology of that order in one of my computer letters, but – but – but to get back to telephones, or rather the era of the telephone, before the invention of the mobile, right back to the old telephone, lying in its sturdy cradle, when it used to ring just as you opened the front door, went on ringing while you pounded up the stairs, went on ringing as you hurtled along the hall, flung open the sitting-room door, lunged across the room, ring-ring, ring-ring, ring-ring it went, until you closed your hand around the receiver, ring-ring, ring-ring until the instant before you lifted it off its cradle, and you knew even as you lifted it that you were too late, you'd get the low, impassive buzzing sound that was the dialling tone – then you could do a number of things, depending on who you suspected or hoped had made the call – I'm going back, note, past the telephone answering machine, when there was nothing from the telephone except the ring-ring when it rang, and *zzzzz* when you lifted it a fraction of a second too late to your ear, so there was absolutely no way of knowing whose call you'd missed – it could have been a wrong number, why not? But you hoped not, you hoped it was a real call, an important call, so you did one of two things – you either sat by it, lifting it now and then to make sure it was working, and zzzzz, it was, or you phoned up everybody you knew who was 'on the phone' to ask if they had just called you – that was the telephone fifty years ago, you were its prisoner if you were in love, it gave you enormous freedom if you were out of love – if the phone rang, nobody could prove you were actually there, listening to it ring, waiting it out – however often and pleadingly it called you, you could never be proved to have heard it – you would think of the person at the other end giving up at last, or going out for a walk, a half an hour walk, before allowing herself to call again – and then another half an hour – but don't forget that you never knew, when the phone rang, who was calling you – you might have thought you were waiting her out, and then discovered weeks later that it was in fact somebody who would have changed your life if you'd answered – 'I did phone you a couple of times, when I was passing through London, to see if you still wanted to take me to bed, but you were always out, and so I assumed', 'I did wonder if you'd be interested in the job, but I could never catch you in and then somebody mentioned somebody not quite as well qualified as you but –' But it was most probably the one you knew it was, that you didn't want it to be, sometimes it took a lot of icy-hearted cowardice not to answer the phone in those days –

Most of my time – eight years of time – at Cambridge I didn't have a telephone – the nearest one to my lodgings was a public telephone booth in the nearby park. Many hours of my life were spent in its vicinity, either making calls at an appointed time or waiting at an appointed time for it to ring. I would arrive half an hour early, and take possession of the booth, with the directory opened in front of me, the telephone to my ear, acting out an intense conversation – when the precise moment came for the arranged call, I would hang up with a little pantomime of exasperation, fumble open the directory as if I had to make an urgent call as the consequence of the last one – this for the benefit of the queue of four or five waiting with heads bowed, which in those days was the usual position for people waiting their turn – only in films did you see people pantomiming impatiently, beating on the little square windows etc. – in life they stood there, however desperate, in calm despondency, with their heads, as I've said, lowered, never meeting your eyes, or mine, especially mine as they glued themselves to the pages of the directory until the phone rang – or didn't ring. On one occasion it was, in a sense, the other way around – in all senses the other way around, actually, in that the booth was occupied by a man with parcels around his feet, and he was reporting into the phone very slowly from a notebook, a thick notebook, perhaps he was a journalist – and the reason I needed to be in the booth was that I needed to phone the girl I had been in love with, to tell her not to come for the weekend, actually it was essential that she didn't come, because – because – I can't remember what reason I was going to give, probably not the truth, that I'd fallen out of love with her. I'd put off making the call and suspected I'd left it too late, certainly too late if this man went on and on – I was still standing outside the booth when I saw her in the distance, walking across Parker's Piece towards my rooms, with her overnight bag swinging from her hand, she'd caught an earlier train than usual so that we could have more than usual of the weekend together –

There had been so many times before then when I would be at the booth, inside it, at the precise moment of her call, and we'd discuss which train she'd take, and we'd talk about whether I'd meet her at the station or not, I adored seeing her get off the train, she was an exceptionally pretty girl, only just seventeen – I was twenty-five – and I would feel such a thrill of ownership – 'See that lovely young creature you can't help looking at and thinking about, she is going to be in my bed in about twenty minutes, yes, that pretty young girl with the breasts you can't find the nerve to look at, mine, me, belongs to me.' She, on the other hand, preferred to make her own way from the station, walking across Parker's Piece with her overnight bag swinging from her hand, thinking, she would tell me, of all the things she would be doing to me in twenty minutes or so – So in our happy days we had a lot in common, we both had my best sexual interests at heart –

I've just re-read the above paragraph. It is disgusting. What am I doing, what do I think I'm doing? Well, trying to recall my feelings when twenty-five, in sexual experience a very young twenty-five – no, trying to recall my inner voice when I was twenty-five but the language above isn't the language of a sexually callow, possessive twenty-five-year-old, it's the language of me, as I am now, which makes me, given that Topsy was seventeen and I'm seventy, a near-paedophile. I'm not sure what the legal age of consent is, these days – going by what I see in ads on television and the newspapers I'd say it's about five years old, but from reports of court cases I come across it could be somewhere in the forties –

Christ, look at the rest of the vocabulary, you can hear the cackle running through it – so Volpone gloating over his gold, or Goethe (also at seventy) fondling Christiane Vulpius (also seventeen) – so I with my Tipsy. No, Topsy, well then, let's try for a more mature note, thus:

Of course I found the idea of arranging myself on or in the bed, waiting for her, very stimulating, although one had to take into account the fact that the British Rail service between Cambridge and London (Liverpool Street or King's Cross) was chaotic, and it could be that having arranged oneself for the early afternoon, one would be still so arranged when she arrived after tea – but patience is a great stimulator, at least it is if one can control oneself – Harold's powers of concentration, for example, are the product of a tightly controlled impatience –

The more often she came down the less complicated the arrangements had to be – during our period of high sexual activity I didn't have to go to the Parker's Piece telephone booth at all, the excitement of it would be that she would turn up when she turned up – it became a routine, one of the happiest of my early adult life, or should I say one of the happiest of one's early adult life, until I and one and all of them, aye, fell out of love with her. In my experience –

In my experience there really is only one thing worse than falling out of love, and that is being fallen out of love with – being fallen out of love with fills you with all the horrors of abandonment, you are contemptible to yourself and therefore, you assume, contemptible to others and consequently even more contemptible to yourself, and really you have no choice but to go away and commit some form of temporary suicide. Well, falling out of love is an altogether grubbier affair, there are no blinding rages or weeping breakdowns to obliterate what is really one long act of procrastination – you look at the only recently adored face, so sweet, so trusting, so vulnerable, and you think to yourself, how could I bring pain to that? And what you also think is, why can't I hurry up and get it over with, get her over with? The longer she's around the more you hate the sight of her – actually, it's worse than that, what you feel above all else is nausea – you are nauseated by her for having fallen in love with you, and by yourself for having fallen in love with her, and terrified of the pain you're going to cause her – how many men have murdered a woman because they couldn't bear to hurt her?

Do women feel the same way? All the women who fell out of love with me seemed to find the pain they were causing quite bearable, though they did say, now and then, that they hated, really hated, seeing me so unhappy, though that didn't stop them seeing me.

A GLIMPSE OF THE FUTURE, A GLARE AT THE PAST

Two odd things happened today. First – when we were crossing the road this morning to post a letter Victoria said, out of nothing, really, as if the thought had suddenly opened itself in her head – 'I think Harold's going to get the Nobel Prize.' This came as a complete surprise to me, because I hadn't realized one was on offer, so to speak – I mean, hadn't realized that it's that time of year, and it is a seasonal thing, I suppose, that Victoria is particularly aware of because a few years ago she went over to Stockholm to see her brother-in-law collect one. 'Well,' I said, 'why not? And he's had such a wretched year . . .' And yes, he's had such a wretched year, the other night at the Belvedere he sat unspeaking, unable to eat or to drink – his only connection to life when he raised his wine glass to his lips and took a kind of phantom sip, although he didn't let the wine into his mouth, it was as if the movement of an old habit stated a fact, however feebly founded – 'Look, I am here, I can do this as I've always done this, now I've put the glass down but perhaps shortly I'll raise it again –' One longs for one of his old rages, one would probably cry from joy at seeing the

cheeks turning dark and red, the snarl back in his voice, his eyes
glittering with venomous life. It never seems remotely possible that he
can make his way into and out of the restaurants, one somehow forgets
noticing how he does it, but Antonia I suppose guides him within a
loving ambit, he creeps along within it, little steps, resting on his stick,
a few more little steps – you assume every dinner will be the last you
will have with them, arrangements made a few days or so in advance
seem quite fantastical – but there he is, his presence seeming to be
beyond a miracle, what can that be but his will and his wife? And his
wife is quite simply a marvel – the most lovable, as C.P. Snow would
have put it, of women – and on top of that a wonderfully readable
historian, and now it turns out an elixir – she deserves to be married
to a Nobel winner, just as he deserves to be married to a Nobel winner's
wife, furthermore it might be good for his health – So we spake unto
each other before we popped the letter through the slot – I can't
remember who it was to, or even which of us was sending it – and then
we separated, Victoria going back home and I heading up the Avenue
for a cup of coffee. On my way I passed a man who reminded me of
someone.

   He was wearing a trilby with a plastic bag over it, had a spiky grey
beard, a yellow mackintosh, baggy blue trousers, white socks and
sandals – there was an element of contradiction in his get-up, it was
raining, which made sense of the mackintosh and the trilby, but
nonsense of the white socks and the sandals. He looked very eccentric,
but not poor, all these garments looked as if they'd been selected
from a wardrobe, rather than assembled by chance from the tips and
dumps that fall in the way of a tramp. He was about my age, I should
think, perhaps a tad older, in his early to middle seventies. As we
passed each other he turned his face towards me, and gave me a smile,
and it was this, the smile, that sent a shiver of recognition through
me, and made me stop and look after him. I half expected him to
stop, too, I was sure he'd seen something in my face that had given
him a momentary glimpse backwards, about forty years backwards,
actually, to Cambridge, to a large red-brick house on Station Road
where he – or the man I took him to be – and I had taught English
to foreigners. The name of the man I took him to be was Manfred

Hendow, and he had then exactly the same sort of beard, and – as I've said – the same sort of smile as the elderly man on Holland Park Avenue – a mystical smile, with a hint of a sneer in it. Yes, he was full of contempt, he told me, but most of it was for himself – he'd had a breakdown when an undergraduate at Oxford, an emotional and intellectual breakdown, as a result of which he'd got an inferior degree, but more crucially, had lost his ambition, his will to act in life. He'd read Russian, his family was Russian, and perhaps his fatalism, his depressive taint, that made life in all its manifestations seem futile, was in his genes. On the other hand, he'd been to India for a while, and had learnt there the value of detachment, the withdrawal of the spirit from the ordinary clamours of life. He spoke in a measured, slightly rhythmical voice, and his eyes, dark brown, were usually lifeless, as if willed to be so. Although he was only a few years older than me, he seemed to me vastly more experienced, vastly more complex than I was. It was his loneliness, his calm acceptance of failure, his inert postures – when he wasn't teaching, he would lie on the common room's only sofa, his sandalled feet crossed on the arm at one end, his head resting on the arm at the other, his hands folded across his chest, corpse-like. There were several middle-aged women teachers, and two or three old men on the staff, when they came into the common room for their breaks he would turn his head slightly, and wonder if they wanted the use of the sofa – they invariably declined, as if acknowledging that it belonged in some way to him, he had an unchallengeable claim on it – of course it's quite hard to say to a man who hasn't actually shifted his body an inch that yes, you'd like him to shift it completely, you'd like to sit where he was lying, so make way please, and hurry up about it – but the truth is that I don't think anybody resented his occupancy, several members of the staff were both forthright and simmeringly disappointed by life, and quarrelsome with each other, but Manfred on the sofa, elongated in a melancholy glow, was in some way out of their reach, like a saint, or half the Arundel tomb. Occasionally, in the evening, when everyone else had gone, he and I would go to the students' common room and play a game of ping-pong. I was naturally quite good at it, and intensely competitive, as I was at any sport, but it was Manfred's trick to drain any element of tension or conflict out of the game. He played in a leisurely and absent fashion, his eye only partially on the ball, and it was difficult to work out exactly how he managed to beat me on most occasions – although he did explain to me that he didn't really beat me, rather he let me beat myself. Well, that can't have been quite true, because in order to beat myself I had to get the ball to come back at me, which I couldn't have done without some skilful play by the seemingly lackadaisical figure on the other side of the net. On the other hand, I do believe that he didn't care whether he won or not, although he was mildly amused by my losing. It seemed to satisfy an abstract sort of malice in him. We didn't exactly develop a relationship – anyway, not a friendship. We talked quite a lot about books. He was interested in Buddhism, particularly Zen, and he was impressively scathing about Christmas Humphreys's Penguin introduction. I suppose I talked a lot, in my florid manner of the time, about all the novels and poetry I considered to be overrated. I'd come to Cambridge to be a Leavisite. In fact, I was already a fully fledged Leavisite in the sense that I was in possession of all the works of English literature that were hostile to life, 'against life' was the phrase I tended to use of almost anything in, say, the twentieth century that hadn't been written by D.H. Lawrence. So I'd practise my Leavis positions on him, and he would meditate in a weary sort of way, and sometimes in a dreary sort of way, on the uselessness of being, the transcendence of indifference, and so forth. One evening he invited me back to supper, in a cottage he was renting in Little Shelford, a few miles outside Cambridge. We cycled there together, left our bikes at a gate, and walked across the field towards a dimly lit kitchen where I could see, through the window, a young woman doing cooking-like things, with a baby at her hip. He'd never mentioned the existence of a woman in his life, let alone a baby. It had never occurred to me that anyone of roughly my generation could be in possession of either – I was still a virgin, after all, and though I believed that sex would be immediately punished by offspring, I yearned for it, but feared that however long I lived, I'd never be old enough or mature enough to earn it. The woman, small and neat and lively, with a slight but sturdy figure and a squawking but not unattractive voice, was about his age, a few years older than me. He introduced us to each other with a gesture that was like a dismissal, not just for me, but for the other two. 'This is Simon Gray. And that's

Donna. The baby's name is Tertius.' And he sat down at the table, folded his hands and closed his eyes, looking as he so often did in the common room, self-excluded. I didn't know what to say, but nevertheless said it. 'Oh. I didn't know you were married.' Donna squawked a laugh, Manfred opened his eyes in amusement.

I wish I could remember the evening, the dinner, the conversation over it, but I don't really, beyond the fact that apart from eating with us Manfred wasn't really there – he behaved as if he'd effected a substitution, as if he'd brought me along to fill in for him, and I suppose I must have done because I do recall I watched as Tertius was bathed, and then as he was breast-fed, which I took to be an immense privilege from which I mainly averted my eyes, it was such an open and natural act from which I should have been kept away because I brought to it a prurience, I was conscious of the pull on her breasts, the full nipples, the busy, greedy mouth – and Donna's face, her expression calm, her eyes radiant as she rested them on me, and asked me questions in her squawking, abrasive voice but about what I no longer know – she had a direct, uncomplicated way of asking, and I liked it because I could answer her reasonably directly, and didn't feel I had to make the best of myself. Now and then Manfred drawled in and offered her a fact about me that was also for me – 'Simon likes teaching foreigners English. And they seem to like him, the pretty ones. But I don't know whether he likes them. He doesn't do anything about them. He thinks it would be wrong.' He made me feel like one of the students, with too feeble a grasp of English to understand what he was saying about me, but suspecting that it was contemptuous. Yes, I was suspicious. Nothing was right about all this –

I can no longer follow the stages that led to my being ensconced in a flat in Harley Street, on the run from St John's College, Cambridge, which had given me a writing fellowship the main condition of which was that I had to go abroad – but I wasn't abroad, I was in Harley Street and not writing anything, not even replies to sent-on letters from St John's College, Cambridge, asking where I was – the only bits I can remember are the bits I don't want to remember – our first fuck, for instance. Actually, it wasn't her first fuck, obviously, as she had a baby by what was also evidently not her first fuck – she had a long and turbulent history with men, she used to entertain me with it – I think I've put down that she had a slightly quacking voice, but did I mention that she laughed in husky yelps that were almost like screeches – her voice sometimes made me grit my teeth, and yet I fell in love with it, I came to find it attractive and exciting, no young woman I'd met before had a voice like it, so uninhibitedly dissonant, but then I'd never met a young woman who talked about the kind of things she talked about, and in a voice like that. Before Harley Street, before she'd left Manfred, long before our first fuck, so back in Cambridge therefore –

Back in Cambridge she would sit on my one chair in my room in Jesus Lane, and I would sit on the edge of the bed, a double bed oddly enough, as only Trinity students – young, single males – ever occupied this lodging house –

LEN TO THE RESCUE

This lodging house, which was owned by a large, bald Pole with a loud voice. His plump younger wife, sweet-voiced and English, cleaned our rooms and made our breakfast – they were a very kind couple, considerate and helpful, though a bit mean with bathwater unless you took your bath cold, but then gas heating was expensive – and the breakfasts were ample, lots of toast and butter and jam and tea, bacon and eggs – actually the eggs were a problem during my first year, there was sometimes quite a lot of hair underneath and around them, like a rather scanty nest – when I came back for my second year she had taken to wearing a rubber shower cap, so obviously she had a scalp condition, possibly alopecia. One of my co-lodgers was a research student who was writing a history of mathematics, a ten-year project, he would say frequently, not counting the three he'd already spent on it. He was from the north, so much from the north that he really did think that southerners were effete, lazy, corrupt – not far wrong in my case, I suppose, although I was also miserable – yes, effete, lazy, corrupt and miserable is a reasonable thumbnail of my spiritual and/or moral state at the age of twenty, in my first year at Cambridge, while a reasonable if external thumbnail of Len – is Len his real name or do I just think that basically all northerners of that period were called Len,

THE COMPLETE SMOKING DIARIES

after Len Hutton? – would be dour, hard-working, moralizing and miserable – so really there we were, the pair of us conforming exactly to each other's stereotypes as we bantered miserably away across the breakfast table fifty years ago. Like me he spent every evening at the cinema but, unlike me, he went actively, with an alert eye and a sharp ear and an encyclopaedic knowledge of actors, directors, screenwriters, even editors and cameramen, and yet he seemed to despise every film he saw, or perhaps he only talked about the films he despised, unwilling to contaminate the films he liked, loved even, by discussing them with me – we had many breakfasts together, three years of term-time breakfasts, in fact, and our conversations would go something like this – 'Saw a film you'd like last night,' he'd say, 'yes, you'd like it.' 'Really, which one?' ' The John Ford at the Regent.' 'Oh,' I said, ' *The Searchers*. Yes. I've seen it. I liked it very much.' 'There,' he said. 'Knew you would. Knew you would. Said to myself, that's the film for you.' I got his drift, of course. 'And what did you hate about it?' 'Everything,' he said triumphantly. 'Great big phoney bloated artistic –' artistic was one of his most scathing words, he somehow slipped the hint of an 's' in before the first 't', making it sound almost lavatorial, Arse-Tist-Tuck. 'Absolutely not,' I said. 'Epic, poetic, humane –' etc. – I saw *The Searchers* again, about five years ago, and about halfway through I found myself recalling Len and his judgement, and from then on it was as if I had double vision, one eye mine and the other Len's, completely at odds with each other but both of them true, because actually *The Searchers* did seem simultaneously epic and bloated, humane and phoney, poetic and Arse-Tist-Tuck –

Well, Len got into this because I can't bear, when it comes to it, to struggle my time with Donna back into my life, but having started on it, I can't seem to find a way of not going on with it, either – stalled is what I am, stalled. Try Q & A –

MORE Q THAN A

There's a film called *Q & A*, I came across it on Film Four the other night – no, a year or two ago – about a homicide detective who is also a homicidal detective in that the suspect he is interrogating he ends up killing, he was played by an actor with an odd voice that didn't go with his face, which was saturnine, a beaky nose and dark liquid eyes, altogether an impressive and glamorous figure of the Hispanic-American type until he spoke, or piped rather – he's been in quite a few David Mamet films, all convoluted plot and rhythmic, demotic dialogue, you almost nod your head to it, your poor old head which is befuddled by all the twists and turns and surprises of a plot so complicated –

Did you love her?
I remember anger, bitterness, hopelessness, despair, so yes.
Did she love you?
Yes. Until –
Until?
We had sex.
Bad sex then?
No, worse than that.
Can you be more precise?
Well, actually it was no sex – a lot of physical activity but no actual sex.
Can you be more precise?
It was in a room in Harley Street.
Oh, it was some sort of medical thing then, was it?
No. I was living there. This was after I'd left Cambridge. A flat at the top of the house. It belonged to a surgeon, a very nice man. Donna was working as his receptionist. He let me have this flat for a very small rent. For Donna's sake, I suppose. As I was thought to be her boyfriend.
But you weren't?
I was until –
You had no sex with her?
That's it. Yes.
What form did this no sex take?
When I'd peeled my trousers down to my knees, and rolled my underpants down to my trousers' crotch, I lay on top of her and bucked about, yelping.
Why?

I didn't know what else to do, obviously. I was a virgin.

A twenty-five-year-old virgin?

Right.

Unusual, possibly?

Don't know. This was 1961, remember, before the Beatles' first LP and so forth.

And so you were anatomically ignorant?

Yes.

But you're a doctor's son.

Yes.

Couldn't you have consulted a book?

I did, but it didn't make much sense. I suppose I could have copied a diagram but I could scarcely have held it in my hand when I got on top of her, like a road map.

Was she naked?

Yes. She took all her clothes off, and let down her hair, talking all the while in her slightly quacking voice, brightly and eagerly, how we'd waited long enough, and now Manfred was out of the picture, and as little Tertius – at this stage quite a big Tertius, at four years old – was so happily settled with her parents – and we had the use of this flat and this nice double bed – I wanted her to undress for ever and quack for ever, to put off the moment of reckoning –

She didn't know you were a virgin?

No.

Would it have been better if you'd told her?

I expect so, because the next time she showed me what I was expected to do, and how and where to do it, and after that it got easier and easier, and by the end I would really have enjoyed it if she hadn't hated it so much.

Why did she hate it?

Probably never got over our first time, my first time, to be exact, she never got over my first time. She liked older men, really, older than herself and much older than me – men who took charge and ran the show. Even when I got used to it, I never ran the show, I got into the habit of waiting for instructions.

Why didn't you warn her that you were a virgin?

Too embarrassed, obviously. And also before I met her there was another girl, an undergraduate, who was famous for having slept with a man who was famous for getting sent down for smoking pot. She came around regularly in the afternoon for tea and conversation. One afternoon, before I'd begun to make the tea on the little gas ring beside the gas fire, she said, 'I keep wondering when you're going to ask me to go to bed with you.' I was very calm, though parts of me stirred. 'Yes,' I said, 'I was wondering that too.' She was a very shapely, round girl, Jewish, sexy and yet maternal, with russet hair and pouty lips – a firm chin withal. Her father was a doctor, with a practice in London, Goldhawk Road, and she was reading History. She had been very much in love, she'd told me, with the chap who'd got sent down for pot smoking – I should point out that pot smoking was at that time very unusual in Cambridge, a truly exotic offence, so he was a legendary figure – undergraduates of both sexes who didn't smoke pot themselves because they didn't want to get sent down liked to have their names linked with his – as did Esther. That was her name. Esther. I think there was something in front of it – Emma Esther – sounds wrong, Anne – or Anesta – yes, Anesta, not sure, though, if that's how it was spelt, but I'll stick with it. Anesta was very proud of having been Pot-boy's lover, she liked to say the word 'lover' in confessional sentences – 'My mother would never have accepted my having . . .' – she always said his name in full, not Ned or Japes or whatever, but Michael Stumpfield, let's say, 'Everybody knew that Michael Stumpfield was my lover,' 'My mother never accepted that I was Michael Stumpfield's lover.' So we had tea and conversations about her being the lover of Michael Stumpfield, of whom of course I was not only jealous for sexual reasons, but envious for life reasons. My body was full of hope but my mind, or wherever the will is lodged, was full of confusion and despair, because it knew that the 'I' of me – what Kant calls 'the synthetic unity of apperception' – was too timid to make even a shy move towards getting what my body wanted – on top of which there was the not completely suppressed suspicion that when it came down to it I didn't really like her very much, not only because there was too much Michael Stumpfield, but also too much breasts, which were prominently covered and gave me a headache until that afternoon when she said, 'I keep wondering when you're going to ask me to go to bed with you.' And I said, 'I was wondering that too' – but what I was really wondering was whether this was a variation on Michael Stumpfield's opening gambit, had he perhaps said, 'I expect you're wondering when I'm going to ask you to go to bed with me' – or more casually, more confidently, more pot-headedly, 'I expect you're wondering when I'm going to take you to bed' – anyway, the way she said it didn't sound right to me, even to me, who'd never heard words like these spoken before, except in films with subtitles – nevertheless she took off her clothes in a modest and stately fashion, as far as I could see, I partly averted my eyes, which I believed to be the polite response, and at some point, before she was completely naked, I explained my – our – situation. I hope I didn't actually say, 'So be gentle with me', but I suppose that was the implication – anyway, as soon as I broke the news she got dressed again.

Didn't she say anything?

Well, she laughed. As I've said, she was quite a big girl, soft and curvy, and when she laughed her breasts seemed to laugh too, bouncing and bobbing to her laughter. She liked my jokes, which I now see was the best thing about her.

Did she think this was one of them?

No, it wasn't that sort of laugh. When she was dressed and having a cup of tea, she explained that she just didn't want the responsibility.

The responsibility of taking your virginity?

Presumably. From then on she let me nuzzle her whoppers.

Which is to say?

That she used to let me sit on her lap like a very large baby and suck her nipples and when I got excited and wanted more she would stroke my head and murmur, 'No, no, I'm still not ready, still not ready, Mr Jumblenose.'

Mr Jumblenose?

A private joke.

Sometimes you wanted to kill her. By the end you were sick to death of her breasts, you associated them with pain, hunger, torment – they were a form of torture, really. Lust aroused and unsatisfied.

That's not a question.

No. It's the answer you might not have given. Tell me –

Mmm?

What aroused your lust in the years of your adolescence and early manhood, before you suckled at Michael Stumpfield's lover's whoppers?

Oh, the usual stuff – a flash of thigh, stocking tops, the curve of a medium-sized breast in profile, a nipple erect in a diaphanous bra, the slope of stomach into a tangle of hair, handcuffs, Hank Janson covers, *The Collected Works of Immanuel Kant*.

Pornographic clichés, you mean?

Absolutely.

Women as objects and pornography?

Ideally. I'm only talking ideally here. Hence Kant.

Are you ready to go back to Donna?

No.

The double bed – you were sitting on the edge of it, as you did with Anesta, and like Anesta, she was sitting on your desk chair –

– and like Anesta she told me about her past, about which I remember nothing except that she'd been at art school for a short time and had been promiscuous. For me, at that time in my life, promiscuous was undoubtedly one of the most exciting words in the language. I was only twenty-one, after all, and so ignorant of sex that its vast vocabulary, of which I had some command, had no proper – i.e. 'lived', as we Leavisites, worshippers of D. H. Lawrence and the dark Gods of the Unconsciousness, used to say – no proper 'lived' content. In the following months, many, many months, about forty-eight of them, in fact, our relationship developed, matured, ripened until it imploded in my first fuck, as reported somewhere above. This was Cambridge just past the middle of the last century – we did things differently there. At least I did.

BILLY AND THE GOLDEN BITCH

Donna, as I've also reported somewhere above, Donna didn't love me. As she was the first person apart from myself with whom I had sex, I was passionately and hopelessly, the more hopelessly the more passionately, in love with her. If that's the right phrase – 'in love'. I've always had a jealous disposition, I think, as well as an envious one – I know that there's a distinction, people are constantly making it over dinner tables, but my feelings for Donna combined them both, I was jealous in the way that Othello is jealous, and could easily imagine writhing about on the floor and jabbering nonsensical obscenities about her friendships with other men, but also I was envious, envious of her, I'm not quite sure that I can get to the core of this, how to explain it, though even as I write this I know exactly what I mean – I mean that I wanted to be her, and envied her for being her when I couldn't be, because I had to be me, instead – I don't believe she was a particularly mysterious or contradictory person, she seemed always to know what she wanted – a proper husband with a proper job, a proper house with a proper garden, another child, possibly two, and eventually an artistic sort of job of her own. She also liked neat clothes, good food, a bottle of wine. The only contradictory fact in her life was Manfred, that she should have become embroiled with him and found herself living for a time in isolation with an illegitimate child in a village outside Cambridge, but that was in the past, Manfred was gone abroad, I forget where to, and she was in London, in Harley Street, working as a receptionist to a successful surgeon with whom I became friends – he once invited me to watch him at work, he was so confident and calm and full of distinguished stoops and gestures until, dealing with an old woman whose artery burst, he had to hold it down in her stomach to stop the blood spurting but it kept coming up in plumes, and he was suddenly all brute strength and angry exclamations, like a plumber dealing with a burst lavatory pipe. He was a New Zealander, successful and handsome. I wasn't jealous of him, he so clearly wasn't a lover or an ex-lover of Donna's, but fond of her in a paternal kind of way, so as far as I was concerned she was in the right sort of element during the working day. The evenings were more complicated because she had to spend either an unwanted few hours in bed with me, or a few hours thinking up and then defending excuses for not spending them in bed with me, and then had to go home to Wimbledon, to her parents, who were looking after Tertius, and they were both completely mad, she used to say, and not as a figure of speech. She took me there for high tea a few times, at weekends. Her father was a small, middle-aged man with a grey moustache and he had a way of sitting with his ankles neatly crossed and his arms folded – and stood like that, too, although not with crossed ankles – as if he were being photographed. He had a vision of the country crashing and mentioned it often, with irritated satisfaction, in brisk, dark sentences, which he addressed mainly to the television set, even when it wasn't switched on. He made it clear that he didn't like me, or the thought of me, probably placing me among the pinkos and pansies who were conspiring with the unions in the nation's downfall. He had a managerial position in a mowing-machine firm, I think it was, and had a lot of trouble with office dissidents. On one occasion, a sunny evening, and the french windows open, he suddenly left the room, returned with an airgun, shot a pigeon that was plodding aimlessly about on the lawn, then ran to the corpse and booted it into the bushes. It was all so horrible and so unexpected that it made me laugh, and little Tertius laughed with me, in one of our few moments of togetherness, and I think Donna laughed too, pleased perhaps that there was a little fun in the room at last. The mother paid no attention, she was bowed over her knitting, her elbows out to her sides, her needles clicking away, humming lightly. So from that limited experience of them, I would say that she was right, they were slightly mad. And before she went home to her slightly mad parents, she would have to spend a few hours with me, who was also, and not slightly, mad – there were times when I was a fucking loony, actually, from the reasons given above, a combination of sexual jealousy and sexual envy and frequently sexual frustration.

One evening I was waiting for her in the kitchen of the flat at the top of the house, waiting and waiting, until long past the hour she usually finished work, and then going down at last to find her – to find out what she was doing – who she was doing it with – as I say, I didn't suspect the surgeon, I knew that he wasn't particularly attracted to her, in fact I knew that he found my company much more interesting than hers because he liked to talk about literature, and all of Donna's reading had been done under Manfred's auspices, to help her understand him – books about Buddhism and so forth, which she hadn't understood – anyway, the surgeon wasn't interested in Buddhism, he was interested in T. S. Eliot and so forth, which is where I came in. So down I went, pretty certain that I wouldn't find her with the surgeon, or if I did it would be innocently – just as I got to the top of the last flight of stairs I saw a heavily set man wearing a trilby strutting down the hall, then letting himself out. He was framed for a moment in the doorway, as if in a film, his back to me so I couldn't see his face, but I had the impression that something was sticking out of the side of it, a pipe presumably. Well, people were always coming and going, it was a house full of medical specialists, there was nothing particularly surprising or ominous – nevertheless, I knew by the boiling in my blood and the tumult in my brain who this was, he was Donna's – he was hers – hence the strut and the pipe, the trilby, the bulky, confident maleness of him, framed in the doorway. I didn't think it odd then, back there in the spring of 1961, that a man with a trilby, smoking a pipe, was standing on the doorstep, leaving a house full of doctors, though logically he must have put his trilby on his head, lit up his pipe, while still in the house – of course people smoked much more back then, many men smoked pipes – the other day, looking out of a taxi window in Holland Park, I saw a middle-aged man in a sensible suit walking along the pavement, smoking a pipe. It gave me quite a shock, he must have been the first man I'd seen for years smoking a pipe, my instinct was to shout out to him through the window to be careful, there might be a policeman about, then it struck me that he might be the victim of a time accident, he'd walked into his next century without knowing it, go home, go back to where you came from, 1980s, 1970s, whenever, get back there! – and then we were past him, and when I looked through the rear window, to check that he wasn't a hallucination, he was strolling along as real as life, it was the people around him, the young men in ghastly sawn-off trousers, the tops of their knickers showing, tufts of hair on their faces, swilling from cans and bottles, slouching towards Bethlehem etc., that seemed hallucinatory, the chap with the pipe and I were from the same world that wasn't this one, how is it then that he looked so at ease, and I was so anxious on his behalf, and on mine? It must have been the pipe that gave him a sense of solidity and confidence, made him feel at home in any century until he ventured too far forward, when he'd find himself surrounded by men with guns, who'd pick him up on their technological intelligence networks because of his strange costume and the incendiary device in his mouth, a new breed of terrorist, obviously, and so pow! pow! pow! but not so that you could hear it, more like little kisses, and holes right through him that you could see through, no blood because the discharged little missiles somehow absorbed the blood as they passed though the body, cleaned up after themselves, so to speak – well, I would have put holes through my man, Donna's man, exiting the house in Harley Street in the spring of 1961, wouldn't have minded seeing his blood spurt out all over the floor of the hall, to punish him for the pain he caused me, for the panic and bewilderment –

If he'd been facing the other way, about to come down the hall, what would I have felt? He stepped into the sunshine, closing the door behind him, and, I would like to write, out of my life for ever, but I can't be sure of that, because if it was Billy, in insurance, he didn't step out of my life for ever, he probably stepped down the road to a pub, to wait for Donna, with whom candlelit dinner and sex. A trilby hat? The one time I met Billy he had a hat in his hand, but I can't be sure it was a trilby. I was too busy trying to meet his powerful blue gaze to notice the details of his clothing etc., but he had a hat in his hand all right, my money's still on a trilby. The question I have to ask myself, though, is about the man on the doorstep: was my eye inventing the trilby for the man on the doorstep, or is my memory inventing it now? Has my memory taken it out of Billy's hand and placed it on the man's head? Did Billy smoke a pipe, or is my memory shifting it from the man's mouth to Billy's?

The next bit I remember pretty accurately I think, I went to Donna in her little office, more like a cubicle, at the end of the hall. She was curled intimately over the typewriter, taking dictation from a tape-recorder through earphones attached to it – I often caught her like this, sealed off in a private world of the surgeon's voice speaking into her ears, and into hers alone, of his patients and their forth-coming operations. She would type at great speed, with a little frown, occasionally breaking into an inward version of her quacking laugh as the New Zealand surgeon's voice shared a joke with her. Of course she didn't acknowledge me as I loomed ominously away at her desk, although it seemed to me quite impossible that all my boil and tumult should fail to make its presence felt – and I am quite tall and she's quite small, with her neat, strong little legs crossed at the knees, her neat, round little breasts bobbing under her blouse, those hands playing like a pianist's across the keyboard, the frown, the smile, another little quack –

She felt my presence at last, took off her earphones, and gave me too much of a smile, as if I were one of the surgeon's sadder cases. I explained that I had been getting worried, had been waiting for her upstairs in our flat until long after she'd said she'd be finished for the day, normally I wouldn't have dreamt of coming down to interrupt her, just wanted to make sure she was all right, in fact had intended just to listen from the top of the stairs, if I'd caught her voice on the telephone or the sound of her typing, I'd have gone back up again – in fact I'd been about to go back up again and resume my waiting but I'd caught a glimpse of a sinister-looking bloke in the hall – I don't know if I talked trilby and pipe, but at some point early on in this heated exposure of my jealousy and fear cleverly disguised as a farrago of nonsense, she exploded into her quacking laugh, and said something, made a gesture, something, something – I think what I felt most of all was her weary exasperation, an unloving adult to a boring and unlovable child – how it went on from there, the step by step of it that led to my raising my fist – I remember hanging there above her, fist raised, bellowing phrases that I'd never thought of and heard with a kind of bewilderment – where had they come from, these phrases, was it really I who was shouting them in a tone I'd never heard before at a volume I didn't know I had in me, and if so who was this I that spoke so strangely, so exotically, so violently, it certainly wasn't me as I knew him. The words, the three words that astonished me most, and still do, and astonished her most, but no longer do, because she's dead, came at the climax of a sentence the beginning of which I don't remember – 'you golden bitch!' 'YOU GOLDEN BITCH!' What? I look at them now, on the page, and hear myself shouting them, and see her face, her incredulous expression. Neither of us had the slightest idea of what I meant, she was in no understandable respect golden, she was, if anything, a sort of dun colour in her general effect, she wore brownish clothes, had brownish hair, had on her best days a pink complexion – she had a negligible income – golden simply didn't come into it – into any aspect of her –

*

I am sitting here, it's the dawn following the dawn when I wrote the above, which I've just read through. I am almost in tears, not because of the content of the passage, but because I now remember that while I was in the middle of writing it something very important struck me, a memory of something that happened, that I thought could wait until I'd finished writing what I was writing, and then I'd go back to it and write that down too, but I didn't go back to it, I got to the image of myself threatening her with my raised fist, shouting the incomparable – incomprehensible, I mean of course, words about her being 'a golden bitch', laid down my pen, took a couple of sleeping pills, remembered I hadn't gone back to that other memory and then decided no, it can wait until tomorrow, it's too important to tackle when I'm beginning to feel drowsy, wait until fresh and vigorous, vigorous? Hah! Well, until fresh, fresh? Also hah! Well, until tomorrow, then, and here I am, in the tomorrow, and I can't remember, haven't a clue as to what it was, that important memory, and so my almost tears are of frustration with myself, and contempt for myself, my anger at my stupidity about my memory, that I don't even remember that my memory keeps failing, and always when I most need it – why then does it tantalize me with tit-bits so vivid that they are both unforgettable and forgotten, it's almost as if they have a life of their own, like fish, say, they swim towards the forefront of our consciousness like fish and just before they get there you blink and they're gone – sometimes as you blink you see them going, their tails flicking them into the muzzy waters they came out of –

Well, perhaps if I go back to 'you golden bitch', trembling above her with my fist raised, her incredulous expression – the moment when we both knew that the affair, such as it was, was over. Well, of course, not quite like that over – I didn't turn on my heel, stride down the corridor that Billy in his trilby and pipe had sauntered down just a few minutes before, I went back up to the flat, and she – in her own good time possibly, or possibly as soon as I'd left – either went home or, more likely, went to the pub, where Billy was waiting for her, calm, on a stool by the bar, at their usual table by the window, or in the corner on the phone to his wife – he was married, Billy, at least he had some children – but that wasn't the important thing I was trying to remember. Everyone involved – Billy, the surgeon, Donna, Manfred – had children – except me, of course.

It seems, in fact, that affairs are never over, or I wouldn't be writing about my affair with Donna, which was in its hopeless prime more than forty-five years ago, two marriages ago, two children and four grandchildren ago, and yet here it is, long after her death, vexing me again this mid-October midnight.

I positively made the decision to leave her that night. I would go abroad, to a cheap country, and write a novel. Spain seemed a likely place, a dictatorship, a depressed economy, cheap food and lodgings, I could be a subversive, Republican spirit, with a blighted heart – who knows what damage I could do to the ageing tyrant in the Prado, or is the Prado where they hang the pictures? – well, then, in Madrid, or wherever Franco hung out.

A SALUTARY TALE

We went to dinner with the Dashwoods last night, Jonnie and Sylvia, it was one of those cheerful and funny evenings spent discussing the sheer awfulness of this country, from the condition of its children – educationally, morally, socially the most backward and neglected among the advanced countries – and the lethal nature of our hospitals, where people die of illnesses they didn't bring in with them –

And so forth. And so forth

And then we talked of murder, albeit unrelated.

A couple of friends of theirs, sophisticated, they enjoyed theatre, concerts, exhibitions, all the cultural life of this great city – they went to absolutely everything, though not necessarily together – he was a businessman, a stripper of assets, as far as I could make out – anyway, there they were, a much-liked and distinguished couple who didn't perhaps quite get on – she had something of a temper, could be – our hostess witnessed it on occasions – a bit of what we used to call a nag, or a shrew, but he dealt with any little exhibitions, in public anyway, with dignity and forbearance – he was known as a calm and collected soul, unruffled and kindly in manner, and always impeccably dressed, formally dressed, for his business engagements as for his cultural nights out –

One morning he turned up for his first meeting looking slightly dishevelled, no tie, his collar undone, not serious lapses, but noticeable because uncharacteristic. Nevertheless he went about the day's business in his usual mode, nothing else awry that subsequently anyone remembered, and when he'd worked through all his day's appointments he went to the local police station, and told the officer on duty that last night he'd murdered his wife when she was in bed. She'd told him he was mean, and by way of a response he'd suffocated her with a pillow. 'Mean.' It was the way she said it, I suppose.

The police went to the house and found the body in the bath. He explained he'd put it there because he understood that bodies, after death, sometimes made a mess. He'd also enveloped her in a blanket, presumably for seemliness, or perhaps from an idea that she would be more comfortable. On examination, she was found to be wearing earplugs, which, I was told, was odd – would she be wearing earplugs, it was asked, if they were in the middle of a row? My guess, for what it's worth, is that she put them in immediately after telling him he was 'mean' for punctuation – 'No good your answering back, I can't hear you! Conversation closed! Silence, thank you!' It meant, of course, that she didn't hear herself being murdered, the pillow over her face, her ears blocked – blind, deaf and mute, completely full of herself as she died. Apparently it takes quite a few minutes, four or five, to suffocate someone with a pillow – I wonder how he did it, did he stand over her, pressing his full weight down on it with his hands? Or did he perhaps sit on it? Either way it had to be a prolonged act, with only one conclusion – although you could argue that backwards, and say that given the conclusion it must have been a prolonged act, and it's possible that he was appalled to find her actually dead when he lifted the pillow – but then if he hadn't intended to kill her he would have pleaded manslaughter at his trial, surely, and he didn't.

Although the police charged him with murder, they released him on police bail, thus enabling him to attend her funeral. As the widower his was the privileged position, seated directly in front of the coffin, and only a few feet from it. He sat through the bleak and rapid service with his head bowed very low, his hands clasped in his lap, and remained sitting so when the service was over. People stood, hesitated, began to leave, then a man went over to him, took his hand and shook it. Other men did the same, women came and stooped down to kiss him on the cheek. He received each shake of the hand and kiss with a muttered 'Thank you', his head still bent.

He represented himself at his trial. He was methodical, businesslike and clear-minded in his presentation of his defence, which was that he suffered from a mental defect that had a physiological cause – when he became angry a sort of shutter came down in his brain that separated him from his actions, and he therefore couldn't be held responsible for them. It's possible that if he'd pleaded provocation, or had it pleaded for him professionally, he might have got away with a lesser charge, a lesser sentence – anyway, something less than life imprisonment, although of course these days 'life imprisonment' is a *façon de parler* – having served some seven years, and now nearly eighty years old, he is in the process of being returned to society – on the grounds, presumably, that prison cells, like hospital beds, mustn't be blocked by the elderly.

Did he love her?

If he'd loved her, wouldn't he have pleaded guilty? Wouldn't he have wanted a punishment, if he'd loved her?

But perhaps I'm missing the point. The point is that this murder was a very private business, as intimate and as contradictory as, well, as intimate and contradictory as sex, or as Othello's suffocating of Desdemona, come to think of it –

Only he would know those moments of killing for what they were, knew whether he expected a corpse as their conclusion, or whether the intensity of the explosion, the release of his righteousness and rage, was the complete experience – perhaps he thought that once he'd done it, and at last cleansed their marriage with a sort of giant orgasm, they could then both get on with their lives with a better understanding between them – and if that was impossible because, as it turned out, she was dead, if he'd sat or pressed a minute or two too long, if it turned out that some sort of expiation was needed, well, then that too was a private matter, he'd see to it himself, or in communion with the spirit of his departed – external processes like the police, the courts, the law shouldn't be allowed to interfere in the happenings between a widower and his wife – or perhaps he should have done what Othello did and spared himself as well as us the embarrassment of a trial, of hearing his explanation of how especially funny things happen in a brain like his, etc.

The bit I completely understand is his going to work the next day, going through with all his meetings as normal, because if you can make today normal, then possibly tomorrow will be normal too, more meetings in the morning, lunch with a colleague or to clinch a deal, an opera in the evening, then home to – home to – ?

But just a minute. After he'd killed her, and wrapped her in a blanket, then put her into the bath, he still had that night to get through. What in God's name did he do for the rest of that night? Doesn't bear thinking about –

I suppose he tried to find ways of waiting for the dawn, then for the day to begin, then for his day to begin – went once or twice to the bathroom to make sure he'd actually done what he'd done, apologized – 'I'm sorry, so sorry. Oh darling, darling' – or explained – 'If you'd seen your face when you put the earplugs in, the purse of your mouth, you'd have understood, darling – I know you couldn't help it, but nor could I, you see' – or he might have blamed her – 'You made me do it, damn you, damn you – see what you've done, your fault, your own fault, your own bloody' – very possibly a jumble of all three.

As he was a rich man, and lived at a good address, I assume he had another bathroom at his disposal. But if there was only one, and he had to share it with his dead wife – peeing and crapping, shaving and brushing his teeth, his eyes averted from the bath and its shrouded contents – and of course he couldn't have had a bath or a shower –

Let's assume he had another bathroom, that they each had their own bathroom. His and hers. And that he put her in hers.

So he got through the night, and started the next day, neither the last day of his old life, he'd already had that, nor the first day of his new life, he hadn't got to it yet, so really a hiatus, a pseudo-day, in which he mimicked himself as he had been twenty-four hours earlier, a cultivated asset stripper going about his business with his familiar aplomb, apart from those two details, the unbuttoned shirt collar, the absent tie. No one noticed anything amiss, apart from the collar and tie, which they might well have interpreted as welcome signs of a relaxing of the spirit, a touch carefree and, who knows, a mite sexier.

How did his lunch go? Was it a working lunch, a sandwich grabbed amid the hustle and bustle of some asset-stripping, or did he slip off somewhere, a solitary, meditative meal, or he went without, kept his nose to the grindstone, telephoning, emailing, faxing, strip, strip, strip –

But at the end of the day – at the end of the day he went home – let himself in through the front door, went to the bathroom with the bath with the corpse of his wife in it, and yes, it was there, yes. Perhaps for a short while he tried to think of alternatives – all those scenes from films when a man with a long burden over his shoulder stumbles down the stairs into a garage, gets it into a car, then drives through the night – but where would he go?

There was a story in the papers recently of a man who drove from somewhere in Surrey, I think it was, all the way to somewhere in France with his wife's body in the boot. He stopped eventually at a motel, and found himself phoning one of their children. 'Hi, Dad, where are you? We've been trying to reach Mum. Where is she?' He told them where Mum was, and where he was, and then phoned the local police. He too had killed in a rage, no forward planning, he'd had to make it up as he went along – think of all the luck he'd had, getting through customs and immigration on either side of the Channel with a corpse in his car – But then the more luck he'd had, the more he'd had to keep going, and where to? In the end the luck had worn him out – really, he just wanted to go home.

It was sensible of our own wife-murderer to go to the police and set in motion the next part of his life. I wonder, did he button up his collar and put on his tie before he went? And what did the police think when they saw him come through their door – almost certainly not that this elderly and respectable-looking man had come to confess murder, more likely that he had come as a victim of a crime, which he was, or as a man who had lost something valuable, which he had.

AND A PREDICTION FULFILLED

They're usually among the first to arrive, but on this occasion everybody was there – there were about sixteen of us – at the Ivy before them, the dinner having been arranged as a birthday dinner by Faber, his publisher, some time ago. The day before Harold had been in Dublin, where they've been having a festival of his plays, a week-long festival – at the airport coming back he'd stepped out of his car, slipped, and gashed his head. Antonia had had to get him to a hospital, an emergency ward, to have the wound dressed – fortunately it wasn't a deep wound but all their travel plans had gone awry. I'd last seen him a couple of weeks before, when he had been much as he'd been that night at the Belvedere – that he'd actually made it to Ireland seemed to me beyond belief. I'd heard from our mutual agent, Judy Daish, who'd seen him there, that he'd been very frail, but enjoying himself – had even managed to do some readings, sometimes thin-voiced and husky, but always audible – it had gone well, and he'd seemed to have flourished – and then the calamity at the airport. It struck me that it wouldn't just be the damage to the head but to the whole system, when you fall down after a certain age it's a long, long fall, we are our own precipices etc., so while we all busied ourselves with talking we were also all keeping an eye on the entrance.

They weren't really very late, perhaps twenty minutes or so. It was an almost surreptitious entrance, nobody in the Ivy except those sitting at the table looking out for him seemed to notice him, he looked quite small, actually, slip-slopping softly along in special shoes because his feet hurt, with something oddly nautical about him – a matter of the blue jacket and particularly the cap, pulled rakishly down over one eye to conceal the bandage – he also looked very continental, from the South of France or Sicily, and distinctly roguish, like a Resistance fighter in an old Hollywood movie, and though you couldn't say he looked robust he looked as if he were back on this side of life's frontier. We stood up and clapped as he took his place at the head of the table, and would have liked to have done more – thrown our caps into the air, raised our voices in song, chaired him around the Ivy – to further honour the man whose birthday we were celebrating, and who only a few hours before had been awarded the Nobel Prize. Antonia came and sat at our end of the table. She was almost solemn with relief and happiness. 'Who would have thought?' she asked. 'Who could have thought?' looking down the length of the table to her husband, who raised a glass to her with a pirate's wink –

PART THREE

A TABLE IN BARBADOS

One of the reasons I was particularly looking forward to Barbados this year is that I thought it would be the perfect place, sun, sea, no stress or strain, just swimming, reading, lolling, sleeping, the perfect place to give up smoking, but now of course –

Consider this: there we were, stepping into our hotel, the hotel we've been coming to for the last fifteen years or so, and in spite of uneasiness during the flight, a sense of being ill-fated, something momentously wrong in the offing, I felt, we both felt, a flood of relief akin to joy to be here again, to see the familiar buildings in the familiar sunshine, the turquoise sea shifting to a nice, gentle rhythm, the staff pleased to see us, as if they shared in our sense of a shared past – and then to be back in the old room, standing on the terrace and looking down at the lawn, the beach-chairs, the bit of the bar where in the evenings Harold and Antonia used to play bridge with two old ladies, when suddenly behind me Victoria's voice – 'What's this!' – she was holding a sort of card, or a sheet of what looked like laminated paper, shiny to bring out the force of the print – SMOKING IS NOT PERMITTED IN THE RESTAURANT.

The hotel is owned by two brothers, both personable young men, one more attractive, the other more intelligent, but hard to tell apart when they're not together. The one who visited our table to welcome us back seemed to be as attractive as he was intelligent, his public school manners in good working order during the annual exchange – how had our year been? Oh good, good – and theirs, how had theirs been? Oh good, oh very good, oh excellent! back and forth for a few minutes, and it would have been quite delightful except that I kept remembering the laminated card on the bedroom table which made me extra-fidgety for a cigarette, and I was about to terminate the conversation and take the several steps to this table at the bar when Victoria with her sweetest smile asked him quite suddenly, it was a non-sequitur really, the reason for the ban. 'Oh well, it's bound to happen, sooner or later,' he said, smiling warmly back at her. 'Like death, you mean,' I said, 'but surely there's no need to grab at it before your time,' and added, 'Presumption is sometimes presumptuous, in my view', which I thought interestingly enigmatic. 'But what about pregnant women?' he said. 'We have to think about the pregnant women, don't we?' 'Praise the Lord for pregnant women, where would we be without them?' I replied, I hope not snarlingly, got up, raised my wife from her chair, and conducted her here, where awaited us our puddings and coffee, over which we had a brief discussion about whether he was the less attractive or the less intelligent brother, and agreed that there was no way of knowing, as his brother wasn't there to help distinguish them. I smoked irritably, stubbing out many cigarettes before I was halfway through.

Nevertheless, having betrayed my intentions and myself in so many ways, I must address the smoking issue four-square on.

Well, not tonight. Tomorrow perhaps, when I am feeling fresh, and without rancour. Tonight it is enough to be sitting scantily dressed by the sea, a cigarette between my fingers and nothing to distract me except Rollicks, the waiter, who like me is a year older, probably to the day, since we last met. Rollicks is laying the tables for breakfast, moving about with brisk, soldierly movements, coming over every now and then to see how I'm doing with my Diet Coke – if I look up to my left, as I've just done, I can see Victoria on the terrace, standing quite still, looking out towards the sea.

A low wall separates this bar from the sea. All the people on the beach have their backs to me, quite naturally, as they are facing the sea, apart from one small, elderly woman who has her back to the sea and is facing me, and 'facing' really is the right verb here, every time I glance up from my yellow pad and from habit expect my eye to meet the sea, I find it meets instead the face of this woman staring over the wall straight at me, the wall cuts off her body from the waist down, it's quite unsettling, really, she has a turban on her head, swollen cheeks, her mouth is open in a sort of leer, in fact she reminds me of those old seaside postcards, a sinister version of them, instead of a large, disorganized woman's bottom there is a large, disorganized woman's face. She may, of course, merely be trying to get into my writing – everybody in the hotel now knows that I write, and what is more that I write about the people in the hotel. In previous years when they've seen me at this table, they've assumed that I'm engaged on an epic novel, perhaps, or a legal brief, or that I suffer from a compulsive deficit disorder – I'm not sure that that's the correct term, 'compulsive deficit disorder' seems more appropriate to my bank account – anyway, I mean a psychological disorder that compels me to write on and on meaninglessly, or seemingly meaninglessly, but eventually there might emerge a meaningless, or seemingly meaningless masterwork, of the order of *Finnegans Wake*. In previous years I was ignored, being a familiar part of the scenery, nodded to now and then by this and that guest, but always treated with respect by the waiters and other members of the staff, who have an innate reverence for a writing person who is also reputed to be a heavy tipper. Now, though, a lot of what I have scribbled at this table has been published, and what is worse, a case of really bad planning, the last book was published during the week that we arrived here, and my face has appeared in the newspapers that they read, a day late, over their breakfasts – not just my face but much of the rest of me, in some cases complete with a cigarette and one of the dogs – usually George, as she's developed a nose for photographers and flings herself on to my lap whenever she notices a man pointing a camera at me – it occurs to me that in the photographs I am almost completely clad, whereas at this table I am almost completely unclad – so their eyes can go from the elderly man in their newspaper, posing in distinguished writerly fashion, a dog in his lap and possibly a cat at his feet, his hand resting on the lower shelf of an overflowing bookcase, cardigan hanging loosely and cloakingly over a stomach that expresses itself in a dignified and graceful slope – their eyes can go from that photograph to the actual elderly man in flesh and blood and swimming trunks, the dignified and graceful slope exposed as a shapeless and pendulous sack, with scary brown nodules growing on his arms and chest – when I asked my doctor why I had these nodules that seem to have multiplied every time I count them, he said they were nothing to worry about, they come with age – my fear is that they will join up, so that they will eventually cover the whole of my body like a sort of suit – anyway, these nodules are part of the package that the people in the hotel, looking up from the photograph on the table in front of them, take in with a little gulp of disgust, I expect –

But the point is, as I've said, that not only do they know what I am doing, but they suspect – with good reason – that I'm doing it about them. In fact, I'm beginning to get the feeling, confused and I hope merely the symptom of a short-term mental disorder, that some of them are posing for my writing, are expanding their characters, or assuming new ones, in order to be caught and recorded on my yellow pages. They gesture to me, wave and wink, some actually come over and ask me how it's going, and spindle off into anecdotes about writing relatives, or how they themselves once thought of reporting in a book on their strange and dangerous holiday in Kenya, also how an aunt once met Noël Coward, but I don't get the impression that any of them has actually read one of my books, or seen one of my plays – I'm known to them entirely through appearances, my recent photograph in the newspapers, my posture as I write. My situation is therefore hopeless on two counts – not only can I not spend any more hours this holiday sitting at this table doing this, but we can't come back next year, or ever again – I look at those words 'can't come back' appalled – we've been coming for year after year for more than a dozen years, arriving on the same day and roughly at the same time – at this very table I've written one complete book, and large parts of two others, rewritten and further rewritten scenes from two of my plays, I've had a great deal of happiness at this table, at which I've also mourned, writing about the loss of my closest friends, dreamed of sex and my childhood, remembered my schooldays, loved my mother and failed to love my father all over again, it really should be a sacred place for me, but in the course of the last few minutes it has simply become a table at which I used to write, I notice how uncomfortable the chair is, and that the table itself has an irritating tendency to sway unless a little pack of paper is inserted under one of its feet, and of course I also notice the many people who are seated at nearby tables – quite a few of whom go out of their way to pass close to me, and say, for instance, 'Still smoking, I see! Good for you!' so that I feel I'm putting on an exhibition – the hotel writer at his smoking or the hotel smoker at his writing – a lively blonde lady of some sixty summers, I'd guess, who has a frolicky, friendly manner just came up to me and told me she'd heard my book being read aloud on the radio the day before she left, she'd had such fun identifying the characters, was she right in assuming the one I described as a 'drunken Pan' was – and she pointed her finger across the bar to where the man I had described as a drunken Pan was sprawled across the counter, his arm around the waist of a slender young woman in a bikini so neat and sexless that it looked like a uniform – and what I described as his 'rotting fig of a nose' was where I described seeing it, deep in a glass of something that looked as if it had come out of his nostrils – the last five words are freshly minted, so probably more a mark of my deterioration than his. 'No, no,' I said, 'no, that man over there Pan! No, of course not, I can't remember ever having seen him before.' She said he came here most years, at the same time that she and I did. 'Really,' I said, 'well, last year was the first time I've seen him.' I don't think she took in the implications of this completely reflexive giveaway remark, although I might have helped her by hurrying into 'Not that I saw him last year, as far as I can remember.' I fixed indifferent eyes on Pan, who had dismounted from his bar stool and was rolling unsteadily towards me – the neat girl in the bikini was still at the counter, so perhaps she isn't connected to him except accidentally, perhaps he'd wrapped his arm around her waist as if it were a pillar, for support only – he arrived in front of me and punched me in the stomach. It was by no means a powerful blow, it might have passed for an over-weighted friendly cuff, and his speech was friendly enough. 'Hello, old writer!' he said, in a gust of alcoholic foulness. 'Good to see you back, how's it going, you've been busy, seen you in the papers' – but his small brown eyes had a gleam that gave the punch, which I can still feel, a vindictive or possibly vengeful meaning – 'And you're here too,' he said, his arm curling out and around the lively lady's torso, and drawing her into him, 'come and have a drink, come and have a drink,' and back to the bar he went, she with him, clicking along in her high heels, and throwing me a glance over her shoulder, as if to say, 'What can I do? Here is a man!' Or even,

'Here is a Pan!' And there they are at the bar, he bellowing slurred laughter, she screeching with merriment, she sounds rather like our dog Toto in one of her frenzies. So I'll have to go. That's it. I'll have to go –

It's odd to think that these are the last words I'll ever write at this table – well, it's my own fault, as are most of the things that I don't like about my life.

PART FOUR

ON NOT BEING SIMON CALLOW

We're in Suffolk and I'm just back from our local bookshop, where there was an unpleasant scene that I'm trying not to dwell on. Let me dwell instead on what I've been mainly doing since we came down here, two weeks ago.

Well, I sits and reads, I sits and smokes, and sometimes I just sits, my only physical activity the tonguing of my recently acquired false teeth, lifting them up and resetting them on my gums. They're quite uncomfortable when I leave them alone, twice as uncomfortable when I toy with them, as I am now doing –

Which reminds me, I've got to send Simon Callow an email. Something's been troubling me about my last meeting with him. We had dinner where was it? Oh yes, the Wolseley. And I have a feeling, have had it ever since we parted on the pavement, that I'd been mildly unpleasant in some way. Not unpleasant to him, I hope, he's one of the people I couldn't bear to be unpleasant to – though I realize that not being unpleasant in intent doesn't mean I'm not being unpleasant in effect – but there was an incident involving a clutch of actors, friendly actors, friends almost. One or two came over to our table and offered hugs and cheek-scraping and so forth, which I responded to as best I could, actually managing to clutch them fiercely, if not affectionately, and rub my cheek up and down against their stubbles and beards – one of them was an elderly man, older than me, who I hope will do a tour of one of my plays later in the year, and the other was an actor who was once, years ago, in a play of mine. We stood there talking of old times and new, then went with them to their table, where there were three or so women, wives, mistresses, whatever, whom we hugged and kissed, we sat down for a very few minutes, a very few, before the huggings and kissings, the scrapings and gruntings of our farewells – all well and good so far, all well and good, I'd got intact through one of those little social skirmishes I hate so much without giving anyone offence, as far as I

knew, but when we were on the pavement, just as we were about to step
into our respective taxis, I heard myself saying: 'A lot of false teeth in
there.' 'What?' said Simon, bewildered. 'You know,' I said. 'False teeth.'
'No,' he said, 'I don't know.' I named the two actors, the older and the
slightly less old, who'd first come over to our table. 'Oh,' he said, and
looked faintly shocked, not at the thought of their having false teeth, but
at my having noticed and commented on them. And yes, it is an odd
thing to have commented on, I can see that, though not odd to have
noticed. One notices what one notices, and the fact is that I'd been
intensely aware of their teeth, and had studied them to see whether they
were false, and now I suspect that perhaps Simon was upset on their
behalf – they'd been so innocently and boisterously friendly and
affectionate, and there I was, on the pavement, a few seconds later,
making comments about their teeth as if I were talking really about their
morals – so I feel I must explain to Simon that what was really on my
mind was not their false teeth but mine, which I was either wearing that
night for the first time or was going to be wearing the next night – I
can't remember whether I had them in my mouth or merely had the
thought of them in my mouth. I'll send him an email. I'll compose it
here and then transcribe it. I don't want to put a foot wrong:

Dear Simon – I've had some false teeth installed, and have been
sitting here (in Suffolk) shifting them with my tongue up and
down on my gums, and then suddenly remembered the last
time we met, at the Wolseley, when I became acutely conscious
of the false teeth in others, who actually may not have false
teeth, but as my own were either recently arrived or
impending, I was determined to find them in every face.
Which made me think of what they mean to someone of my
generation. They mean grandpas and other ancients, whose
teeth you could note in a glass if you should happen to find
yourself in their bedroom, or moving about in their mouths
while they were eating – sometimes they would do something,
a sort of clicking, with their jaws and the contraption would
hang free and then jut forward, giving one a ghastly glimpse
into the mechanics of old age. My own are uncomfortable, but

at least invisible to others, I think, as they're silicon (can that be right?) molars, right at the back of either side of the jaw, and artificially yellowed to match the nicotine originals in the front of my mouth.

Why am I telling you all this? Not on a need to know basis, surely.

LIBRARIES, BOOKSHOPS, BROTHELS

Why in God's name did I write all that down here, and not on the email, and then zip it off to him? I'm not seriously going to type all that out on the computer, am I? Actually, to tell me the truth, I think I'm in serious trouble, and I'd better start facing up to it, before it's too late and I slip under the waves. Let's try and get it straight.

Start with what's been upsetting you. The scene in the bookshop. So trivial, really, and really not worth –

– to begin with, I hate going into bookshops these days, not a book that isn't whoring after you, slashes of paper across their middle and between their legs like lewd costumes, three of us for the price of one, the publisher their pimp – 'Three of my best girls! Or boys! For the price of one!!'

– and a lot of the novels gave the impression that they were written by the same woman under a variety of similar-sounding pseudonyms, and the faces of these women looked strangely misogynist. I imagine them at parties, praising each other's work with moues and grimaces, or in the literary pages describing each other's plots in coils of deadening prose but with adjectives 'engrossing, enthralling, delicious, delightful' – that the publishers can trowel out and paste all over the paperback edition –

– and there's a new look that the middle-aged male authors have, or the ones conscious of entering middle age (their 'maturity'), their mouths go up in a grin of spiky, or disdainful, imbecility, the dandy as village idiot –

– but to come back to this afternoon –

– the reason I went to the bookshop this afternoon was to buy *Arthur & George*. It's a novel by Julian Barnes about Conan Doyle and the half-Indian, half-Scottish solicitor whose name Conan Doyle cleared of a particularly disgusting offence – slitting open the bellies of horses, as far as I can make out from the reviews, etc. – I have a feeling that I'll enjoy it, not the slitting-horse's-bellies part, needless to say, though I'm sure it's done very engagingly, but the Conan Doyle-on-the-case part, as written by the man who'd written *Flaubert's Parrot*. Furthermore I've taken a fancy to the cover – an olivey-green mottled hard-board cover, with two figures etched into it – Arthur, bulky, and George, schoolboy size, both with hats, seen from behind, in silhouette. It's very beguiling, with a flavour of an old-fashioned book, a turn of the century – whoops! turn of the last century – sort of book. In fact it looks almost as if it belongs in the Chelsea Public Library from sixty-five or so years ago, when I was ten or so, that I would pick from the shelves marked 'Mystery' possibly, or 'Historical', and I would tumble through the pages, looking for a paragraph that would suggest that this was the book for me.

You were allowed to borrow books for two weeks, if you were late you got a fine, and if you were later than that a portly man, middle-aged and jocular, a friendly bailiff figure, would come to your door and collect both the book and a larger fine for the trouble he'd been put to – Mummy would be embarrassed, apologizing again and again for the trouble her dolt of son had put him to, and directed a few lazily aimed cuffs at me after he'd gone – 'Why can't you remember, you little fool, it's so humiliating having him at the door like a debt collector, and you should think about him, he has to trek around Chelsea because of noodles like you!' – I never thought to say, because I didn't know enough, that if noodles like me remembered to return their books he'd have been out of a job –

I've been in many libraries since, though not as many as I should have, but none that gave me as much pleasure as the Chelsea Public Library, where every spine of every book carried the promise of adventure, or laughter, or an erection – the 'Romantic Historical' section, with pulsing titles – *Desert Maiden* might have been one of them. I wish I could remember the title of the fictionalized biography of Katherine the Great. In the first part of the book, when she was the young Katerina, she was tempestuous, rebellious, untameable, consequently frequently half-naked and bound. In the second half her sensual and voluptuous rival, the soft-skinned blonde with the cascading hair, Anna Mons, was stripped naked, fastened in chains at the neck, wrists, waist and ankles, and sent sprawling at the feet of her former lover, Peter the Great – I must have borrowed and returned the book about thirty times in the year 1947, and could hop from passage to passage without checking the page numbers, as if I were blind and working in Braille, a skill I would have needed if our forefathers' predictions about the consequences of filthy practices had turned out to be true. That was the thing about books then, not just the ones that aroused you but also the ones that made you laugh or frightened you – it didn't matter how many times you'd read them they were still incompletely experienced, in fact the recollection of them seemed to freshen and sharpen them, while making you feel secure –

The best stories were the favourite stories, beginning them again made your toes tingle, and your eyes still popped with surprise at revelations that you knew by heart – now, half a century later, I read some books again and again, most particularly Jane Austen, but I don't re-read even *Mansfield Park* as I re-read books I loved when I was twelve – it's that I want to hear Jane Austen's voice, so personal and confidential, that has run through all my adult life, and makes me believe that I have a continuous self – though not one's normal sexual self, because she speaks to you as if you were a woman – her sister, an equal, her confidante.

THE GREAT DICTATOR

Is one ever aware of one's sex when reading fiction that isn't erotic or pornographic? I have an idea that I feel more manly when reading Tolstoy, but what about Henry James? What sex does one feel – do I feel – when reading Henry James? I haven't read him for years, I don't believe I have the powers of concentration any more, at least for the late ones, *The Golden Bowl, The Wings of the Dove, The Ambassadors*, with their endlessly unwinding and rewinding sentences – but of course they were dictated, the late novels, they were dictated to a lady with the name of a spin bowler, Rhodes, no, no, Bosanquet. I can't be making this up, surely?

Assume you aren't. Think it's all true. Then think of Miss Bosanquet sitting there with her pad on her knee – no, Miss Bosanquet took the dictation on a typewriter, the Master liked to hear the noise of the typewriter, the steady clackety-clackety-clackety of Miss Bosanquet's typewriter as she loaded his sentences on to it as if it were a cargo train, chugging and clacking his sentences from the sofa where he lay to the generations beyond, clackety-clackety went Miss Bosanquet's faithful but mortal fingers at the typewriter, clackety-clackety – did his sentences keep time to her fingers, or did her fingers keep time to his sentences? – that's the question that comes to me, as I consider those works of his dictatorship – at the end he thought he was Napoleon, actually signed off one of his deathbed letters with Napoleon's name – but there was something else about Miss Bosanquet. something extraordinary. I'll Google her, what was her Christian name? I've an idea it was Tabitha, Tabitha Bosanquet? No, here it is, Theodora, Theodora Bosanquet, literary editor of *Time and Tide*, etc. etc., and here on Google is the extraordinary thing – she was psychic and a medium. James came back to her in a seance and asked her to take down dictation. Other writers, Galsworthy, Hardy, Meredith also dictated to her from beyond the grave. They explained that they had a great deal of unfinished work and that it was her duty to transcribe it and pass it on to the world. After her death they found notebooks full of their mint-fresh but posthumous work, so really she was a ghostwriter to ghosts –

And here's his Napoleonic letter, quoted in a little article by Leon Edel, with all kinds of copyright warnings underneath. It consists of instructions for the improvement of 'certain apartments' in the palaces of the Louvre and the Tuileries, and though it doesn't actually make much sense, it concludes with an imperial flourish:

> Please understand I regard these plans as fully developed and as having had my last consideration and look forward to no patchings nor perversions, and with no question of modifications either economic or aesthetic. This will be the case with all further projects of your affectionate NAPOLEONE.

Napoleone seems odd to me, as if he were a pasta – ravioli, macaroni, napoleone – but still, one can imagine the Master on the sofa, slipping in and out of consciousness, his mouth moving soundlessly or to inane purpose, Miss Theodora Bosanquet at her typewriter, her fingers following their impulses as if on a ouija board, clackety-clackety-clack –

I've just sent another email to Simon Callow suggesting that I'd like to take over his life – he wrote to me that he was just finishing a television series in which he travels to glamorous European cities and sits in the rooms, sometimes in the chairs and on the beds, of great composers, Sibelius, Haydn, Mozart, the various Strausses, in his capacious briefcase an already well-received script he's written on the relationship between Noël Coward and Gertrude Stein, no, that can't be right, surely Noël Coward and Gertrude Stein couldn't have – oh, Gertrude Lawrence, of course, Gertie, a script on Noël and Gertie, and in a few days' time he begins rehearsing the part of Fatsco, I think it is, in *Women in Whites*, I'm getting all these things wrong deliberately, out of envy, because, yes, there's nothing I'd rather do than take over Simon Callow's life at the moment, well, for the next year or so, and possibly his bank account, too, perhaps not his bank account, nor his body either, come to think of it, it's a body that suits Simon but wouldn't suit me unless I also took over his eating and drinking habits, in which case I'd certainly need his gastric system, I'm not allowed to drink alcohol and I have no appetite for proper food, only savage cravings for disgusting things, cakes, chocolate, cigarettes, Diet Cokes – so my gastric habits wouldn't go with his digestive tract – there'd have to be modifications here and there, in fact I'm beginning to see that the whole thing is impossible unless I take over complete occupancy of Simon Callow and his life, his body, his lover, his appetites, his vices as well as his virtues, tasks, rewards, consciousness, dreams and nightmares, relatives and friends – in which case I would just be Simon Callow, and what would be the point of that, when he's already Simon Callow and there certainly wouldn't be room for two of us – now then, now then, what happened in the bookshop was this, I plucked a copy of Julian Barnes's *Arthur & George* from a table mainly devoted to this one book and took it to the counter, where a girl, more a girl than a young woman, with red hair and businesslike spectacles and a noticeably pretty smile was dealing with another customer and while I was waiting two portly and respectable local matrons came and stood beside me, facing the counter and talking animatedly about something that I enjoyed overhearing at the time but of course have forgotten in the light of – this: the girl finished with the customer, wished her a very good day in a soft Suffolk accent, turned to me, to take the copy of *Arthur & George* along with my held-out credit card, checked herself, looked at the two women who were still chatting and not aware, really, that they were in a sort of queue, then said to me, 'No, I think these ladies came first' and to them, 'Good afternoon, can I help you please?' They glanced with vague reproach in my direction, really I think noticing me for the first time but nevertheless assuming that I'd been justly reprimanded – so I sort of spanked *Arthur & George* with my hand, slap, slap, slap against its cover, threw it back on the table and left. I've an idea that nobody noticed me, particularly.

How sad, though, that I couldn't have said, simply said, 'Well, actually I was here first, I think. Not that it matters, I'm in no rush, after all', because after all I wasn't. I wasn't in any sort of rush. I wasn't feeling impatient, even.

A HOT DOG AND OTHER MEMORIES

Peter Hall rang just now to discuss the future of my new but rapidly ageing play *Little Nell*. He says that he definitely wants it to open his new theatre at Kingston, and then take it to Bath and Birmingham, and then into London. Or he might open it in Bath or Birmingham, then move it to Birmingham or Bath, then on to open his new theatre at Kingston, and so to London. The thing is, though, that he's not sure that he'll have a new theatre in Kingston to open it with or move it to, because he's not sure when, or even whether, he'll have a new theatre in Kingston to be opened by anything. The theatre itself is there already, everything physical is in place apart from the money – I had to stop to dab my eyes, which were running slightly – not from grief over this latest lack of firm news about poor *Little Nell*, I hope – perhaps my eyes are just rheumy, as elderly eyes often are. So – now dabbed, vision clear, back to – well, nothing, really, because actually I'm struggling to fend off a sudden yearning for a hot dog. I really don't understand this at all, because hot dogs are shiny pink and brown rubbery sort of sausages enclosed between two halves of an elongated synthetic bun, with runny red and green sauces over the sausage that leak through the bun into the palm of your hand and when I write it out like this I cannot understand how I could conceivably be yearning for one, and indeed I no longer am – what I must have been yearning for was the sight and the smell of a hot dog as I experienced it when I was six or seven years old in Montreal – certain Sundays were hot-dog Sundays, Grandpa and our aunt Gert would take us to the park, Grandpa would buy hot dogs from a cart attached to a horse, Gert would supervise the putting on of tomato ketchup, French mustard and that green stuff, and then present us with exactly what I've described above, which would make us, my brother Nigel and me, almost swoon with pleasure –

We were sent back to England a year before the war ended, when I was eight, and I remember being haunted by the memory of Montreal hot dogs through the long London years of rationing, when the main feature of food was its absence, especially noticeable to boys who were in the Canadian habit of too much of it, until eventually we fell into the English habit of too little of it. It took a French boy, staying with us 'on exchange' to bring the too little of it back to our attention – his appetite hadn't been reduced by the war and rationing, so he had expectations that Mummy couldn't meet. When she put his first dish in front of him, slivers of cold meat, he consumed it in seconds, almost before we'd picked up our knives and forks, waited for his next course with visible signs of impatience, and when he grasped that there wasn't one, only more of the bread and marge he'd disdained while swallowing his meat, his indignation broke through his limited English – he was fourteen, I think, anyway his voice had broken, unlike mine, and I was very impressed by his gruff aplomb, that he should dare to speak to Mummy like that! Her initial impulse must have been to give him a swipe across the chops, in fact she got to her feet and for an instant she drew herself to her full height, chin in the air, cigarette smouldering, no, she probably wasn't smoking, it's that I always see her smoking whenever I think of her, and then explained in her slapdash French that we English were still, through rationing and other deprivations, fighting the war from which you French had withdrawn before it had scarcely begun, and although *vous français* had had the Germans occupying *votre pays*, you *français* had continued to eat very well – Pierre, I actually do think his name was Pierre, we had two Pierres in successive years – failed to understand much of what she was saying, but he got the essential drift, enough of it anyway to find it worth reporting in a letter to his father, who reported his reporting of it in a letter to my father, which Mummy had translated by someone or other, to her further mortification, because not only did Pierre Numéro Un find the food inadequate, but he also found the house in which he was served it, from which he'd departed a day or so before his papa's letter arrived, to be little better than a slum. A slum! 47 Oakley Gardens, SW3! A slum! Just because there were a few bombed-outs living at the bottom of the street and pre-fabs around the corner in Manresa Road, because of the war, the war that they hadn't even joined in –

And yet she loved all things French, loved being in France. When we went there *en famille* after the war she exclaimed continuously on its marvellous Frenchness, everything was just as French as she remembered it – 'Look,' she said, as we drove away from the boat through Calais, 'the very streets – the cars, a Citroën, James! – oh, a *gendarme*, and there, the little outside lavatory, they're called *pissoires*, and you see the wine shops – James, see the windows! all that wine – and the pavement cafés and there's a *pâtisserie*' – she said the word with such a French flourish – 'you boys have never tasted a real French *pâtisserie* – do stop, James, and we'll all have a *pâtisserie*, the boys can have their first *tarte au pommes*!' James stopped, and she led us to the little shop, its open counter just off the pavement laden with cakes, fruit tarts, etc., the smell of their recent baking hanging in the warm air, and it's certainly true that Nigel and I had never seen such a display, not even in Montreal, nor smelt such smells – 'peach, pear, apple,' she said, 'apricot, *fraises*, *framboises* – and that's the one I'll have' – she gestured at it, one of her grand gestures – 'the blackberry!' and a swarm of flies rose up from it, leaving not a blackberry but a plain custard tart – we hurried back to the car, and Nigel and I experienced our first real *pâtisseries* further down the road, deep inside a café off the pavement, where the *pâtisserie* counter had a net over it. 'Of course you have to understand,' she said, 'that the French have never cared much about hygiene. But you get used to it, it's part of the charm.' 'On the other hand,' said our father, still a doctor though on holiday, 'there's dysentery you know, my dear. You don't want them to get dysentery.' Our mother agreed that she didn't want us to get dysentery. 'So do try to be careful what you eat! Make sure it's fresh, if it isn't, send it back!' Easier for her to say than for us to do, as we were being dispatched to our different exchanges, Nigel to one outside Paris, as I remember, and I to one in Valandre-sur-Mer – I can't remember anything about the boy I was exchanging with, or his family, but the sea was full of jellyfish for a whole week, I remember that, and we couldn't swim.

The only exchange I really remember was the second Pierre. He was theoretically Nigel's responsibility, being the same age as Nigel – fifteen and somewhat – but Nigel had gone to spend the summer with an aunt in Ireland, so I was appointed to the position of English boy in his place, and was sent to meet him at Victoria Station. I waited at what I was sure was the right platform, the train arrived at the announced time, disgorged its passengers, there were lots of them, French and English – think of it, Victoria Station in 1950, all those people in drab clothes and hats, so many of them smoking – and all of them gone at last, no one left at all except a man, the very image of middle-aged oddness, wearing not just a hat, but a deer-stalker, like Sherlock Holmes, and like Sherlock Holmes, smoking a pipe – he stood there serenely puffing, waiting for someone that couldn't possibly be me – well, that was the second Pierre, eccentric and charming and with me quite paternal, an older brother without the complications. Mummy adored him and even Daddy, also then a pipe-smoker, quite took to him – they'd sit together in the sitting room, in their armchairs, puffing away but not saying much – well, they didn't need to, Mummy with two maley males in the room could converse with both of them simultaneously and with me lolling beside her on the sofa, in the comfort of her scent and cigarette smoke, for squeezes and cuddles. Pierre's English was serviceable enough to express his admiration for Mummy's cuisine, especially for her versatility with Spam – he thought Spam completely delicious, however it turned up on the plate, covered in batter probably his favourite – I don't know what he and I did together in the daytime, but he always seemed to enjoy himself, and not to mind my being almost two years younger.

I wish I could remember what he looked like. I wished we'd taken photographs. I've always been a lazy and reluctant photographer. The trouble is that the present never seems worth photographing, only the past, when it's too late, which is why I suppose I've so few photographs –

Now of course I wish I'd taken lots and lots, especially of my parents, especially of my mother, my mother in her prime, to block out the memory of her skeletal hand clinging to mine, and I determined not to look at my watch until I did, a swift, casual glance down at my wrist. 'Oh,' she said, in an anxious whisper, 'don't go yet, Si, stay a little while longer.' 'I can't,' I said, 'I have to pick Ben up from his nursery school.' She held her hand out to retain me. I held it to my lips, kissed her quickly on the forehead and left. I had enough time, more than enough time to get to the nursery school, so I walked along Putney towpath, and thought about the kind of son I was, who would deprive his dying mother of a few more minutes, that's all she'd claimed, a few more minutes of his company. I still don't know why I wouldn't stay. It wasn't coldness of the heart or fear of seeing her so extremely ill and dying. There had just been an undeniable impulse to remove myself. Inexplicable that it comes back to me now, as it did one afternoon last summer on Spetses when, drying after a swim, I watched a tiny old lady sitting in the rim of the sea, picking stones out of the water, looking at them, putting them back, not childishly but like a child, and my eyes filled with tears of shame. I am now nearly ten years older than she was when she died, I've had all those years more than she had, and I hadn't given her a few minutes of those years, on an impulse –

HOW TO KILL THE QUEEN

We're in a heatwave, so hot that it's a real effort to cross the garden from my study, which is a slightly dangerous place as it's full of winged insect life, including horseflies and blowflies, which means there's a corpse somewhere about, I suppose. Let's hope it's in the bushes outside, not actually in here, a dead mouse or vole rotting underneath my desk, by my feet, or the corpse of my most recently uncompleted masterpiece rotting away in a drawer. There are also bees, wasps and hornets, not swarms of them, of course, they come in singles, twos and threes, then drift about in the corners of this small room, or become suddenly animated, and beat against the wire mesh I have over the windows, before drifting off again. I try sporadically to usher them out through the door, which I have to have open, in the hope of catching a bit of breeze, any whiff of living air in this inert weight of heat, but even if I succeed they come straight back in, as if their understanding is that they belong here, that my study is really a kind of public nest, like a bus shelter, say, where they can hang out until inclined to return to their private quarters. I wouldn't mind, really, if I didn't hate the thought of blowflies, and weren't nervous of being stung by wasps. The last time I was stung by a wasp, on a small boat in Greek waters about ten years ago, I went into shock, and had to be carried, on the point of death I was subsequently told, in a slow, unresponsive ambulance over mountains and through flocks of goats and herds of wild horses to a hospital which was in its hygienic arrangement more lethal than a wasp sting. Actually, it may not have been the wasp sting that caused me to pass out, simultaneously vomiting and squittering on the deck of the small boat, but the sea urchin I was eating while I was being stung, it had an odd taste. And actually it may not have been the sea urchin or the wasp sting, it may have been alcohol poisoning, which is what one of the doctors claimed in the hospital – gathering his students around him he stabbed his forefinger at me with ill-humoured contempt and gave a lecture, a brief, scathing lecture. I only understood those words we share with them, alcohol being one of them. His students nodded and laughed mutteringly at the old English guy between the tattered and grubby sheets who was dehydrated from being poisoned by let's say the lot, insect and crustacean and alcohol.

Victoria thought she could see a nest in the roof above my door, another of wasps or hornets around the side, and a nest of bees at the back. 'You mean that they all, wasps, hornets and bees, get on with each other!' I exclaimed, sniffing a moral in it, to do with possibly the present situation in the Middle East. 'If wasps, hornets and bees can live in harmony so close to each other – Where are you going?' She said she was going into the house, to telephone pest control. 'What do they do?' I asked. 'Get rid of them, I hope,' she said. So any moral to do with politics and the Middle East would have to find a role for the pest controller.

The pest controller was a very pleasing man, we thought, short, balding and neat, with an academical, almost professorial manner. He spoke in long, easy sentences, rather like an accomplished television expert. He walked quickly around my study, identifying the nests pretty well where Victoria had identified them, then he donned his uniform, a sort of loose helmet with a transparent mask over his face, so that he could see through the cloud of chemical he was about to squirt through a hose attached to a canister. He explained what he was about to do, and sent us, for our own protection, to the kitchen. He joined us there in under five minutes, having destroyed the nests of bees, hornets, wasps. This is how he did it, as far as I could glean, and anything I didn't glean was my failure, because he spoke in the relaxed, confidential manner I've described above, eloquently and informatively – the chemicals he squirted into the wasps' nest would be picked up by the feet of the worker wasps as they went into the nest to groom the queen, so of course when they groomed the queen they'd be grooming her with poisonous feet, she would die, then without a queen they would die partly from the poison partly from redundancy, loss of purpose, I suppose, or grief. He was quite clear about it, but I got a bit confused taking it in, as it involved possibilities that had never occurred to me before. I remember another fragment – he told us that the slow, sluggish wasps we see at the end of summer that we call lazy and think – most of us, anyway – are that way because they've come to the end of their natural time and are dying out with the season, are in fact pregnant wasps, looking for somewhere to lie during the winter, a spot under a tile on the roof of my study, for instance. Come the spring they give birth to the worker wasps who will construct the nest in which they will dwell the summer long – at least until he comes along with his hose and canister and poisons their feet. He also said that one of the extraordinary things about the nests is that they always, every nest ever investigated, contain exactly forty-eight – I think it was forty-eight – anyway, always exactly the same number of chambers, maybe it was forty-nine because the central chamber was the queen's, and an even number of forty-eight chambers would encompass the royal chamber. And he said that the size of the royal chamber was in proportion to the size of the queen, so that every queen, large or small, had precisely the same amount of space at her disposal. He stood there, in the kitchen, drinking water, a hand on the counter sort of propping him, his feet crossed at the ankles, his eyes shiny with the pleasure of imparting information that we both wanted and didn't want – I think I can speak for Victoria here. She looked spellbound but stricken, making polite little sounds of distress because the fact was, and still is, that we had called in this pleasant, well-spoken and balding man to put an end to a complicated scheme of life. Had we the right? Now I think about it, I realize that he didn't describe the fate of the hornets and the bees, would they have been approximately the same as that of the wasps?

'Now,' he said, 'if you want to keep insects out of the kitchen' – all sorts of them were all over the place as he spoke, masses of flies. Flies in kitchens are disgusting, there's no getting away from it. They defecate, urinate, salivate, vomit and probably masturbate over any bit of food they alight on, sometimes as you're raising it to your mouth. So yes, we said, we wanted to keep them out of the kitchen and out of my study, their two favourite places. He said that there were very good systems we should consider, but the one that he advocated, he had one himself at home and it worked perfectly and he went on to describe it – it seemed rather complicated and technological to me. I'm not sure that Victoria grasped it properly either, but we were so completely persuaded by him, he was so meticulous in his manner and so authoritative, that we agreed to have it, two of it, whatever it was, expensive though it was. He said he would arrange to have them delivered in a couple of days, accepted a cheque – included in the amount was a sum for his work on the nests – gathered his equipment and drove off in his van. I had an idea that he would be singing as he drove back through the country lanes, 'Bee-loud glades, loud-bee glades, here I come, here come I.'

The fly-killing contraptions were delivered this morning and are now in place, one on the windowsill by the fridge in the kitchen, the other on a bookshelf in my study. They look somewhat like birdcages, but instead of containing a bird they contain a circular tube, and behind the tube is a sheet of metal. A cable goes from a plug in a socket at the top of the cage to a plug in the wall. When you switch it on the tube turns a luminous blue and the metal sheet behind it is electrified. Insects of all types are attracted by the luminous blue light, fly to it between the bars of the cage, circle around it, settle on the sheet of metal behind it, and are promptly electrocuted. It's quite unsettling, really, because the electrocution makes a sharp, sizzling noise, as of a strip of bacon tossed into a hot frying pan, and is sometimes quite prolonged – So far we've been unable to watch the final moment, averting our eyes as we see a wasp, say, winging its way eagerly towards the cage, and keeping them averted until a little while after the sizzling's stopped, but the animals have been distinctly uneasy, the cats sitting with their backs to the cage, Toto lying curled under the table, growling, and George, the most sensitive of creatures, hurrying about the kitchen, darting in and out through the flap, making whimpering noises. We wondered, in fact, whether she could hear within the sizzling other sounds, screams for instance. Do insects scream? A question for a Moral Sciences paper: 'Do insects scream? Discuss.'

At the bottom of the cage is a tray on to which their corpses drop. When the tray is piled high you slip it out and shake the corpses into the rubbish bag in the kitchen, or cross the garden and shake them over the fence into the field. You can glance down before you do so and take note of the astonishing uniformity of the dead. Moths, mosquitoes, blowflies, wasps, hornets, bees, horseflies, greenfly, grasshoppers, ladybugs, butterflies, almost indistinguishable from each other, dried and frazzled as they are, like toast crumbs.

It's 3.15 a.m. and I've just come back into my study from having a pee. A moth came in behind me, a very large moth, almost the size of a small bird, and with powerfully beating wings. It flapped and flapped around the lamp on my desk while I tried to usher it back out into the garden without touching it, because I have an idea that touching moths, or anyway their wings, kills them – so I waved my hands at it and blew at its arse, then fanned at it with a newspaper – it was pale grey, so pale that it was almost colourless, in fact it would have been ghost-like if it hadn't been in such a tumult, blundering around the light until I fanned it off course towards the door, it actually went out and then banged back in before I could shut the door, it just missed my face, sort of helicoptered over my head and when I turned around it was squeezing its large body through the rails of the electric cage – I got hold of the cage and tried to shake it out, but in fact succeeded in shaking it right into the cage, it went around the blue tube several times, and then it made for the electric plate, there was a small flash, more like a spark, and I turned my head away from the noise that went on and on and on – like Harold's poem of that title, and its content too, come to think of it – on and on and on and on –

Now it's a few minutes later, and I'm sitting at my desk writing this, and as I write I realize that all I had to do to save the moth was to switch the cage off – instead of tipping and tilting the cage to shake it loose, just switch the bloody cage off – Well, I've done that now, I've switched it off, and tried not to see the husk, no longer grey but brown, lying on top of a heap of flies, wasps, other moths and so forth, so forth in the tray – I think I'll keep the cage switched off until I go to bed, and meanwhile let me remind myself that the natural life-span of a moth is very short, possibly only a matter of hours, but then a matter of hours may be a long time if you're a moth – the equivalent for me of, say, seventy years come next October –

I was watching Agassi beating a big chap called Pavel, who looked much older than Agassi – but almost everybody looks older than Agassi, who has the eyes and smile of a very sweet child, or one's best idea of a very sweet child, and is as bald as a baby, shaven bald, one assumes, not alopecia – anyway Pavel, heavily built and lumbering, but with a powerful backhand and marvellous powers of retrieval, is in fact a couple of years younger than Agassi, and was giving him a very hard game, but Agassi, swept along on waves of love from his New York fans, triumphed and blew kisses at us, bowed straight into the camera and blew kisses at me, personally it almost seemed, with McEnroe's voice, over, telling me how much I loved him.

A moth blundered on to the screen, on to Agassi's mouth, then blundered off, towards the insect-killing machine, which I turned off just before it could get through the bars. I tried to usher it out through the door, but it vanished, probably behind the curtains. I left the door open so it could get out, and in came Errol. He went around my feet to the curtains, fished behind them, stuffed the moth in his mouth, then it was down his throat. Bits of the wings hung out. Then down they went.

THOUGHTS, USELESS AND STRAY, AFTER A BOMBING AND A SHOOTING IN LONDON

A policeman who in quieter times likes to discuss his sexuality with the public has just appeared on television and said that the words 'Islam' and 'terrorist' don't belong in the same sentence. But any word can belong with any other word in any sentence – 'It would be wrong to say that every follower of Islam is a terrorist' is an example of a sentence in which the two words belong. 'The words Islam and terrorist do not belong in the same sentence' is another example, as is the sentence 'The words Islam and terrorist occasionally belong in the same sentence.' But of course what he was really saying, and what he intended us to hear, was, 'Do not dare to engage in a discussion in which you associate Islam with acts of terrorism'. He went on to instruct us not to think ill of Islam, these murders are merely criminal acts, to be viewed as non-racist, non-ethnically discriminatory unreligious acts and so forth, as if his first thought was that the population is so imbecilically homicidal that we'll rush out and stone the first Muslim, or approximate Muslim, we see, and then burn down mosques, etc. and so forth. Or does he hope that a man who's packing himself with explosives will hear his words, rip off his psychic camouflage and identify himself to himself as a mere criminal, and defuse himself, resolving henceforth to lead a civically blameless life?

Saying that murderous acts can't by definition be acts of faith only makes sense if you are referring to a specific faith, a clear and basic tenet of which is that murderous acts must not be committed in its name – but there are different faiths, and different gods – I suspect if our cop has any idea of God it's as a mush-headed, compassionate, sexually open cop, just like himself, if marginally outranking him, with whom he can have conversations about their love for each other as they share a joint. OK, it seems less harmful than a view of God as a patriarchal pimp, running a Paradise brothel you can blow yourself up and into, with a portion of girlies for every infidel you take with you –

A god who's lodged himself in someone's psychological and moral system by whatever means – pre-natal trauma, psychosis, hypnosis, divine manifestation, sexual frustration – and who says I Am in You, Through Your Bombs Shall My Will Be Done, is a god in occupation and it's no good thinking you can evict him by denouncing as 'criminal' the works committed in his name and for his sake.

Islam is a beautiful faith, I read or heard somewhere or other just yesterday, possibly from Blair the politician but it might have been from Blair the policeman, but there's no such thing as a 'beautiful' faith – there can be beautiful churches, mosques, synagogues, temples, paintings, icons, prayers, music, all artefacts that can be judged aesthetically, but there can't be a beautiful faith because faith can only be judged morally and logically – and with a faith the logic tends to work backwards, from a deeply held belief to the arguments that confirm it. The only proofs of God's existence I've ever studied are from Thomas Aquinas, and made perfect sense in the way that any perfectly worked out construct is likely to make perfect sense, but I could find nothing in the arguments that would persuade me to believe in the existence of God – inasmuch as God's existence can be proved by logic, He will only exist in logic, man-made –

Almost piecework, really, so many corpses bringing in so many virgins – are these virgins live virgins or dead virgins? Inasmuch as the murderous martyr receives them after his death how can they be alive? But if they're dead too, how can they get to it, carnally speaking? This is fatuous and literal thinking, the point is that they're heavenly virgins, enjoyed in heaven, which is a transcendent but physical place, actually made visible in Hollywood films *circa* 1950, with Tony Curtis in baggy pantaloons and Janet Leigh in diaphanous ones, Paradise as a Hollywood harem, or an adolescent's wet dream, and all you have to do to get there is blow yourself out of where you are now – a poky flat in Birmingham, for instance, with its dismal, seedy, rowdy streets, or – who knows? – a pleasant maisonette in leafy Muswell Hill.

What reward if you take a few co-religionists on the side? It's a scatter-bomb approach, after all. Say that though you get ten infidels you also get four Muslims, two of whom had planned to back-pack themselves to Paradise next week. Well, from one point of view it doesn't matter, they were Paradise-bound anyway, from another point of view they might feel aggrieved that they will now miss out on the virgins. Well, they'll just have to put it down to the disadvantages of a multicultural society, in which you're unlikely to get a bus- or tube-load that is 100 per cent infidel –

As I light yet another cigarette I swore not to smoke, I find myself wondering about the Muslim fundamentalist attitude to smoking. Is it OK for them to smoke as they back-pack lethally along crowded Oxford Street? Could they be encouraged to use cigarettes as their next weapons, dishing out packets for free, seeing them as long-term weapons of mass destruction? They have endless patience, centuries of patience, they bore their ancient grudge secretly, in silence, until everybody forgot that they had one, and then here they are, looking almost exactly as they looked when the West last thought about them, in flowing garments, bushy beards, bundles on their heads, and something in their hands, a book, a hook, a bomb, a throat –

A man who saw him in the tube said he was crouched on the floor, quivering with terror, then a man in jeans ran to him, pushed him down flat and shot him through the mouth and through the head, eight times – finally, when there were no alternatives, the truth – terribly sorry, not a Muslim terrorist on his way to Paradise but a Brazilian electrician on his way to work – yes, terribly sorry, but still, aren't we lucky to have such brave and highly trained policemen who will run up to a man crouched quivering with terror on the floor of a tube and push him down flat, and shoot him eight times through the mouth and head –

A few days after the bombings a friend of mine was on a London bus, on the very crowded top deck, sitting beside a man who from his complexion was possibly from the Middle East, and was wearing baggy trousers, a baggy shirt, and holding on his lap a lumpy carrier bag. His face was very tense, and he made little noises, like mutterings, that could have been prayers. He suddenly shouted out something that sounded like a name, whereupon a man several rows up turned around and shouted something back. Then the man sitting next to him shouted the word 'Basri'. The man in front repeated it, 'Basri', and held up two fingers. My friend rose, went down the stairs, got off at the next stop, walked rapidly around the nearest corner and lit a cigarette, and then – actually I don't know what he did next – but what he didn't do was phone the police, from fear of having to explain the stereotyping nature of his thought processes – dusky hue, loose garments, carrier bags, sudden exclamations to a friend in an unrecognized tongue, etc. Now let me ask myself what I would have done in his place. Would I have done as he did? Or would I have alerted the police? Or would I have risen to my feet and shouted, 'Listen, everyone! There's a possibility that this bus is going to be blown up! I might be wrong. It's up to you. I'm leaving. Goodbye and good luck!' I hope so, but I doubt it.

PART FIVE

TURBULENCE IN THE AIR

The captain has just informed us that there is no impediment to our taking off, we're running a mere ten minutes late, for which he wanted to offer his personal apologies, he hoped we would enjoy our flight as much as he would enjoy flying us.

He's just spoken again to explain that we're about to experience a bit of a delay, a passenger has failed to turn up and claim his seat, therefore they're going to remove his baggage from the hold 'because we can't be too careful in the present environment', as he is sure we will understand. He said that if we look out of our portholes, those of us on the appropriate side will be able to watch the missing passenger's baggage being taken off. I don't know whether I'm on the appropriate side, but I haven't looked through the porthole, being unable to imagine a less interesting spectacle than baggage being taken out of a hold and driven off – though I do wonder a bit about the person the baggage belongs to – how come he's checked in both his luggage and himself, but hasn't taken up his seat? Has he been blocked at security and carried off for interrogation, or is he asleep in one of the departure bars, or too involved in purchasing duty-free to notice his flight being called, or suddenly decided to call it off, go home to the wife and kiddies? Is he a terrorist or a loser? Or both – after all, what could be more of a loser than a terrorist who is nabbed going through security, it would be a first, even the shoe-bomber who couldn't ignite his shoe managed to get on the plane, Christ, he's an irritating bugger, whoever he is, delaying the flight by not turning up to be on it, irritating of BA too, etc. –

We're in the air, an hour late. I have on the tray in front of me the third volume of Mahfouz's Cairo trilogy, which I've been keeping especially for the plane, having read the first two volumes last week, but I don't think I can concentrate on it – the fact is that I have a bit of a stomach problem, a euphemism for irritable bowel syndrome, itself a euphemism for, among other things, feeling a need to go to the lavatory, itself a euphemism for something I can't think of another euphemism for, and can't bear to be forthright about, I find the word when written even more offensive than when I hear it spoken, put this down to the hyper-sensitivity of an over-educated but not especially well-taught man who has been embroiled in many of the unsavoury aspects of gastric life – thus it was that I was on my feet as soon as the fasten seat belts sign was off – on my feet and patrolling the aisles between the two sets of lavatories, keeping an angry eye on who went in and out, occasionally slipping in myself to no avail. I hung around for a good half-hour outside the economy lavatories at the bottom of the plane. It's a very full plane, not an empty seat in business or economy, and it strikes me – firstly, so where is the empty seat of the passenger who failed to come aboard? Secondly, that all the passengers, several hundred of them, have good strong bladders and bowels, as the only one to show any interest in the lavatories is me.

I stayed there, down by the economy lavatories, too long, when I wanted to return to my seat at the top of the plane I found both aisles blocked by stewards and stewardesses with trolleys of beverages, and the only place I could stand and wait for them to pass through was, of course, outside the lavatories – I'm beginning to worry that I'll be suspected of having an agenda, a sexual one, that I'm trying to pick up a fellow passenger, perhaps squeeze into the lavatory with him or her.

There was an interval between the passing of the drinks trolley and the arrival of the lunch trolley, and so I got back to my seat in time for a tray of food, which I'd been dreading because I knew I would eat it, whatever it was, and that as soon as I'd eaten it I'd be back on my feet, up the aisle, hovering outside the now familiar doors – It was lamb curry, they'd run out of chicken curry, the malignantly beaming stewardess explained, as if guessing at the explosive effect a curry of whatever animal would have on my stomach – I got it down in no time, followed it with a bread roll that I stuffed with cheese, then sent down a thick-textured pudding and two cups of black coffee, thus placing myself by mine own hand in an emergency situation. I tried to clamber to my feet but lost my balance and tipped sideways into the aisle. I had a glimpse as I fell of an elderly i.e. my sort of age woman in a green blouse who is seated a row up from me on the other aisle getting to her feet, obviously lavatory-bound. I raced ahead along my parallel aisle, but she must have spotted me, her mind working to the same pattern of competitive urgency as mine – her seemingly heavy trudge was in fact quite speedy, and she kept her lead, a bulky figure whose mauve trousers contrasted uneasily with the green blouse, there was something about the bunch of her shoulders, the bundle of ginger and grey hair that hung down her neck. I could sense her satisfaction as she closed the lavatory door, having noticed, as I had, that the facing lavatory was occupied – so down the further aisle to the depths of economy I bustled, assuming a scholarly air because I couldn't bear to think that these people should know where I was going. How come this atavistic modesty in an age in which you can see on your television the frankest, not to say grossest, ads for diarrhoea cures, irritable bowel syndrome, constipation, as well as lavatory paper. The other night, racing on my Sky+ through the commercials between the overs of a test match I'd recorded, I glimpsed a young woman holding up something I couldn't believe she was holding up while sitting on something I couldn't believe she was sitting on, so I tracked backwards and froze on it. Yes, she was sitting on the lavatory (toilet) holding up a toilet (lavatory) roll, and she was smiling, no, almost laughing, with joy. I wondered whether anyone else looked at her with the same outraged disgust that I did – certainly not the green-bloused, mauve-trousered bulky woman with gingerish hair who made it to the lavatory before me. She might be of my generation, but she was open and matter-of-fact about her mission, triumphant in her victory, while I tried to persuade interested spectators – what spectators? – that nothing was further from my intentions, that I am a man of strange impulses and sudden distractions, who could guess what business he has outside any door, let alone a lavatory door?

Then at last we were rolling down the runway of Athens airport, and then we were slickly and efficiently through immigration and on to the baggage collection. Baggage was already rolling smoothly through the flaps and around the track. While we waited Victoria confirmed on her mobile that our driver was in the correct place in the arrivals lounge, waiting to drive us to Porto Heli, where we'd take a little water-taxi over the sea to Spetses.

AND TURBULENCE ON THE GROUND

There were only half a dozen people waiting, increasingly restlessly, when our black suitcase came through, and the conveyor belt stopped for a few minutes. When it started again we began to recognize a few pieces of unclaimed luggage because they'd already passed before us several times. Then they too were seized by grateful hands and the little cluster of us saw it in each other's eyes – the dull recognition that now we knew whose luggage they'd taken off at Heathrow. The black bag, the one they hadn't taken off, contains almost everything we don't need. The other bag, beige and missing, contained almost everything that we do need – all Victoria's clothes, my sponge bag in which I'd put the only nail clippers – they're toenail clippers actually – that work on my fingernails, and a carrier bag full of my pills, a load of books, and finally, most crucially, Victoria's Filofax, which she'd been forced to transfer to the now missing bag at Heathrow check-in, and which is probably her most cherished possession, apart from me.

A very polite and therefore appropriately gloomy chap in an official uniform came up and said, with great clarity and force, as if they were the only words of English he knew, 'Is finished the baggid. No more. Is happen often in BA! Go there!' and pointed us to the counter which dealt with lost luggage. We went there, and engaged in a miserable jostling and hustling to get to the head of the queue – the trouble was that there were several attendants behind the counter, several queues, therefore several choices. When we joined a queue the one beside it shortened dramatically, but when we shifted across to join it several people came out of nowhere discernible and added themselves to the front, then when we turned back to our original queue a couple of couples had got into our previous places, so by the time we reached a very pleasant young woman with fetchingly sympathetic eyes and fluent English, had filled out forms etc., given our address and mobile numbers, we were the last at the counter, the last off the plane, so to speak, and over two hours late.

The driver who met us was Soros, the charming but ill-fated driver who picked us up last year, and was arrested twice in the half-hour trip from the airport to Piraeus. This time we had a four-hour drive ahead of us, so the opportunity for calamity was increased eightfold. There was only one calamity, though, and it was me, my stomach, swollen and inflamed by BA's incompetence.

Sometimes it's as if my bowels are carrying a weight of guilt – load of guilt – I can't work it out. Try again. A moral man's conscience must feel like this, heavy with undischarged guilt – enough. Leave it alone. Let's just say that it heaved and groaned through the darkness, around the hairpin bends, up and down the mountains. I sat at times almost bent double with the pain, the dread. Whenever we passed a remote outpost, a taverna or a garage, I wanted to cry out, 'Stop! Here there must be a lavatory! Stop, I say!' but I didn't cry out because Soros wouldn't have understood, as he has no English at all, relying on a natural sympathy to interpret our wishes, and very few people are in sympathy with other people's bowels and bladders. And I was too shy to find an alternative means of communicating, for example tapping him on the shoulder and miming. What would I have mimed? I could have asked Victoria, who knows a little Greek, but I thought that would be unfair. I don't understand it at all, really, why I should revert to childhood timidity on such a matter when I pride myself on my forthrightness in most of my life-dealings.

So on and on and on and on through the darkness except for one stop at a large bar in a car park, just after we'd got outside Athens, where I managed a dribbling pee, and then, dare-devil that I am, poured a Diet Coke and a large espresso diluted by hot water into a bladder that already felt more like a boil. Then on and on and on and on through the darkness. At one point I asked Victoria how much longer, did she think? She said she thought about half an hour, and when half an hour later by my bladder I saw a signpost which said Porto Heli 48km I did actually let out a throbbing kind of moan that must have made the hair stand on the back of Soros's neck, but still he drove, steadily, imperturbably, implacably through the darkness, on and on, on and on, on and on and on. Yes, there had definitely been car journeys like it in childhood, 'Why didn't you go before you left?' 'Because I didn't need to go before I left.' 'Well, then, it serves you right, you little fool.' 'But it's not my fault I didn't want to go.' 'But it happens every time, every time!' 'But I can't help it!' 'Well, try and hold on a bit longer, just a bit longer, there's a good boy!' 'How long, how much longer!?' I yearned for a conversation like that, one in which the responsibility was shared with an impatient but loving adult who knew everything worth knowing about all one's physical states, and was sure to get you to where you needed to go in good time, if only just in time, which was the best time of all.

We got to Porto Heli at about 11 p.m., and as is the body's way it immediately ceased making its demands. Relaxed and easy, I lounged casually on the quay, one arm supporting itself on the roof of the car, the other wrapped around the wife's waist, the bowels and bladder lapsed into genial passivity, all of me in harmony with the smooth, unruffled sea as I played out the familiar and comfortable role of your run-of-the mill BA passenger, angry, contemptuous, despairing, etc., no hint in the voice and gestures of the recent physical agonies that could also, of course, be attributed to BA.

And so we crossed the sea to Spetses, where Alex was waiting for us with her motorized tricycle, which had a small cart attached for our bags, and within five minutes we were at the house. I am now in its garden, writing these last words before I go to bed.

PETALS, MICE, CATS

Again in the garden and again at night, our second night in Spetses. I'd planned to read the third volume of Mahfouz's Cairo trilogy, but can't because there's nowhere in this maddeningly disagreeable house with enough light to read by. In fact there's not really enough light to read by during the daytime either. It is a large garden full of nooks and crannies, with chairs and tables in them, but wherever you sit the foliage is so thick around you and over your head that the light scarcely gets through – and though you're sitting in shade it doesn't feel like shade, in the sense of being protected from the sun, because the atmosphere is heavy and fetid and gives you a headache which is intensified by the strain on your eyes as you struggle to make out the print. I like Mahfouz's trilogy too much to attempt it in these conditions, so there it is, the third volume, marked at page 6, probably to be so marked until we're on the plane home.

This horrible house is entirely my own fault. Last year we had a house high up on the hillside, overlooking the sea. It was a lovely thing at night to sit at the long table on the terrace and gaze down at the bright specks of sea-taxis zipping across the darkness, seemingly so haphazard in movement, but full of purpose – I remember sitting at that table in a white plastic chair, looking out and writing the scene down – but the steps up to the house from the side of the beach were so steep and rough-hewn that it was a real labour to make it to the top, my heart would be pounding, my face covered in sweat, my breathing short and raspy, I had to take short breaks with a cigarette to recover myself, then onwards, upwards, almost collapsing when I got to the door. That was the part I most remembered when we thought about where to stay when we decided to come back for a fortnight this year. I remembered the steps and the exhaustion, not the terrace and looking down at the cool blue sea in daytime, the speeding, winking boats at night, which is why I am crouched in the fetid and oppressive darkness of the courtyard outside our bedroom, scribbling this down with my right hand while with my left, which should be holding a cigarette, I scratch at my ankles, bitten every few seconds by midges, mosquitoes, etc., interrupting myself only to stare at the wild cats that peer back at me through the foliage or leap down from the roof or the wall and arch their backs and spit hissingly at me. Of course the other house had cats too. A mother, two adolescent sons, and three kittens, they were dark ginger and white, with small, alert, intelligent heads on long necks, with long, thin bodies and long, prancing legs. They were exceptionally agile, high jumpers, sometimes leaping through the kitchen window, and sometimes through the living-room window, and one of them or even some of them came in one day and crapped all over the sofa, but there was no doubting their pedigree. They were royalty. While these cats, these cats are like rats, at least I respond to them as if they were rats, and believe I would actually kick at one if it came near me, which would be most unfair as their behaviour is scarcely their fault. The people of Spetses have a history of dealing badly with cats, and one year wiped them all out by poisoning, clubbing, drowning them, then were astonished to find the island overrun by rats. They had to bring cats back. But I suppose the distinction between cat and rat is now a fine one in Spetses. The inhabitants would treat the cats like rats if there were no rats, and perhaps many of the cats behave accordingly.

A lost bag gets more and more lost as one tells off the contents – Victoria's Filofax, my sponge bag containing the only nail clippers, all my summer shirts, my iPod – my seven pairs of espadrilles, why did I pack them all, I thought, even as I put them in, you can't possibly need seven pairs of espadrilles, and then I thought, but they're new, you haven't tried them on, perhaps only two or three pairs will fit, besides it's not BA's business how many pairs of espadrilles you take, your taking a surplus doesn't entitle them to confiscate them, and on top of it all, all my medication, again why did you have to bring six weeks' supply when you're only planning to be away for two weeks, again I cannot answer the question except to say that it's easier to pour the whole lot into a carrier bag and stuff it in your suitcase than to count the requisite number of pills, furthermore I must have thought it's better to be safe than sorry – hah! – but you're travelling BA should have been my next thought, BA may or may not make you safe, they'll almost certainly make you sorry – now there'll be days or anyway hours of endless phone calls, visits to Spetses chemists, how long can I survive on one pair of trousers, two shirts, one pair of espadrilles –

I have just finished the third volume of the Cairo trilogy under the glare of a lamp I've rigged up in an overhanging bush. A light wind has shaken petals off the bush. I've no idea what the flower is. I'll ask Victoria in the morning. They're very big petals and they're scampering about like mice under the table I'm writing on – I keep catching them out of the corner of my eye, the petals and their shadow, and though I know them for what they are, and therefore know that they're not mice, my feet twitch nervously every time a petal brushes against them, but even if my feet think the petals are mice, what are they afraid of? Mice don't bite, do they? No, but they scamper up your trouser leg if frightened, will you be able to assure your trouser leg that it's a petal and not a mouse, which anyway wouldn't bite you? But if the petal got to your crotch, would it find teeth and sink them into you? There's no doubt that I'm quite spooked out here at 4 a.m., now a few minutes past 4 a.m., out here in this dank, unwholesome night air, compressed almost into the bush from the branches of which sharp-toothed petals are tumbling, tumbling –

It's time I went to bed, but I'm afraid that the damp has got into the wiring of my lamp, and that when I switch it off I'll electrocute myself. On the other hand if I don't switch it off, what then? But I can't bear to think of it glaring on into the dawn, though in this garden it would be a dark dawn – I really hate it here, on the other hand, again on the other hand, I'm glad I've read Mahfouz – almost all the first volume, and sections of the two other volumes, have the transparency of a great novel, you seem to go straight into the characters without being conscious of the words that take you there – and this in translation, as with Tolstoy – and you feel the alien world of Cairo during the First World War becoming utterly familiar to you, habits and customs that would be disgusting when reported to you out of the context he creates come to seem quite natural, so that one accepts, for instance, the prosperous merchant's attitude towards his wife and daughters even when shocked by it. He's a wonderfully sympathetic creature, this merchant, majestic, epicene, wise, intolerant, devout, unfaithful. When he behaves badly, which he does quite often, we find ourselves wishing quite simply that he wouldn't, as we do with our friends, the close ones that we can't allow other people to judge, and when we judge them ourselves it's with the proviso that the judgement should carry no penalties. Very few novelists can do this, it seems to me, make us make close friends with characters we wouldn't hope, or even want, to understand if we came across them outside the novel. Mahfouz brings comfort – for which my gratitude and blessings here in this uncomfortable garden, with dawn possibly approaching above the incarcerating foliage, how would I know? – bed, bed, bed, bed, bed with you.

LOST IN TRAFFIC

It's five in the afternoon. See that half-naked elderly man sitting in the outside bar of the Klimis hotel. He's half naked because he has taken off his sopping shirt and hung it over the top of his basket, which contains a wet towel, wet swimming trunks, two packets of purple Silk Cut, a mobile phone, some money in a strange woollen wallet (local produce) that he purchased this morning, and also in this wallet are his false teeth. The swimming trunks he is wearing are cold and damp, as is his stomach, which hangs down over the top of his trunks. His sodden espadrilles are on the floor beside his feet. He is smoking, sipping coffee, spooning down lumps of chocolate cake – altogether a poignant and grotesque spectacle to both tourists and people indigenous to the island, they avert their eyes from him as they pass by, as did the slovenly young waiter who served him. He is in this condition because he has just returned in a small sea-taxi from Zogheria, his favourite beach in the whole world – about halfway back the seas became tumultuous, pitching the little taxi up and down, sheets of spray slapping over the body, face and hair of the elderly man who likes to sit outside the cabin, on a bench beside the one-eyed helmsman, Michaelis, rather than inside the cabin with Victoria, his silly little goose of a wife, who prefers to be warm, safe and dry – he was smoking, of course, as the first large wave rose up against him, pasting his cigarette across his lips and almost washing it down his throat before he managed to gag it back into the water – when they were about five minutes from port a voice blared urgently out at Michaelis from his radio, and he swung the boat around in an arc, heading back to Zogheria, or so the elderly man thought, but then Michaelis bounced over some particularly high waves to a cement promontory on which a cluster of people were failing to get into a sea-taxi, which was listing sideways and clearly had something wrong with it – Michaelis swerved towards them, lined his boat up, helped aboard a group of four, led by a fat and furry young man in bathing trunks and sandals, with inward-slanting teeth and enormous glasses – the elderly man rose with his customary courtesy from his bench to let the group pass easily into the cabin, whereupon the furry young man sat down in the elderly man's place, leaving the elderly man the bench on the windward side it might be called nautically, anyway the side facing the open sea, which lashed furiously at him, sending its spray into his face and over his shirt as the boat rocked unsteadily off towards the harbour –

So now, safe on land, he sits, dilapidated, looking washed up and out, gobbling down the cake for the sugar to restore his strength, gulping down black coffee and cigarette smoke to restore his nerves, waiting for his wife Victoria to return from the shops with fresh fruit, yogurt and honey for tomorrow's breakfast. The waiter is pulling down sheets of plastic to protect the café from the waves that are beginning to come up over the seawall and are rushing across the pavement. The wind is strong, it's quite cold now, but the sun is shining, here comes his wife Victoria, holding three heavy plastic shopping bags, and really it was a marvellous afternoon in Zogheria, the water calm there, glowing in the sun, the taverna and the family just as when last seen – so the old guy, cold and wet, victim of a callous man in furry skin with inward-sloping teeth, can still consider himself among the blessed.

Sitting in the *amaxi*, the horse cantering along, the carriage rocking and swinging, my arm around Victoria, I had the feeling I've had so often in Spetses, of regality and freedom, jaunty, debonair, my straw hat in my hand, when suddenly, and quite unaccountably, the memory of the dead from all the summers here – Piers. Alan. Roger. Peter Payne. Roxannie. Joanna.

I've become frightened of almost everything on this small island where I am used to being at my ease. At night enormous motorbikes roar up and down the narrow alleys, driven by extra-large young men with boisterous thighs – they seem Brobdingnagian, and I, shredded by nervousness, a Gulliver, no, a Lilliputian – when I hear a motorbike's noise from afar, or from a distant alley, I jump and clutch at Victoria's arm, but if it actually appears in the alley we're walking down, coming at us from behind or its headlights like golden fists as it bears down at us, it being a combination of the large man on the large machine, with a bundle behind him that usually turns out to be a girl, her slim legs raised, with her knees clamped against his hips, her arms wrapped around the monster's usually enormous stomach. Likely as not he's bald-headed, he wears a black string vest and trunks but never a crash helmet. I assume there is no law forcing him to, so I ask myself – so careless of his own life, how can he be careful of ours?

This morning along the front rode a paterfamilias on a motor-bike at a terrific speed, on his handlebars a child, on his lap another child, on his pillion a woman with a child in her lap –

ILLUMINATIONS

Just back from dinner at the house of a friend of Alex, on a large terrace overlooking the sea. We had a magnificent view of the annual pageant, in which is re-enacted the destruction of a Turkish warship by a host of locals in their fishing boats. The Turkish boat is dragged into the middle of the harbour and the small boats encircle it, setting light to it. As it bursts into flames fireworks go off in the harbour, magnificent explosions of colour that hang in the air then fade down, then more magnificent explosions, plumes, haloes, stars, dragons of lights. As we were watching this, at about midnight, awe-struck and exclaiming, Victoria's mobile rang. Andie from BA to say that our bags had been found and would be in Spetses at midday tomorrow – so, with all that splendour in the sky, we felt a rush of gratitude, love in fact, for good old BA, dear old BA, who had got our bags back from themselves and were returning them to us. I'd be getting my toenail clippers back, the only clippers I've ever had that worked on my fingernails. Something exotic in purple, orange and green flowered above us, and down in the harbour everybody suddenly burst out singing, and we were filled with such delight –

In previous Spetses summers, when the water was warmer or the body-heat younger, we would swim for hours off Zogheria – well, two, sometimes three hours, out across the small bay to the line of rocks that runs beneath the pine wood, then swim around the point into the large bay where lay the water-boat, a long, broken-backed half-sunk vessel, painted grey-green, like a battleship – we would swim past it, it wasn't really swimming it was a kind of strolling on our sides or on our backs through water that was so soft and velvety and warm. We would swim to the end of the bay, roll around, and swim back, sometimes stopping at a small cove with a church above it, climb up to the church and walk back through the pines to the taverna, or we would swim back to our beach. There seemed no difference in temperature when in the water and when out of it, almost no change in our sense of the elements. But now – now the water isn't cold precisely, but it has a cold edge to it.

This evening, after it had stopped raining, we went down to the harbour and took an *amaxi* to Nata's for dinner. I used to love riding in an *amaxi* – the wonderful strength and agility of the horses pulling us along, the clip-clop of their hooves, the regal swing of the carriage – in early years in Spetses, when I had a very bad back and walked with a stick, I took them extravagantly – I would doff my straw hat to familiar and even unfamiliar faces in way of celebration as I bounced and swayed, clip-clop, clop clop clop, on the road that runs along the sea's edge, the roguish majesty of it. But this evening when we set out and surged through the streets all I could think about was the motorbikes, the Vespas, the motorized tricycles accelerating around us to pass us or coming straight at us with a last-second swerve. How could the horse, a lovely white creature with a high head and a swinging mane, but all flesh and blood, sinews, nerves, muscles, sensitivity – how could it bear the noise, the brightness, the constant relentless assault, the threat. There was a moment when a furious and enormous motorbike came straight at us, then bullied past us on one side, while a Vespa with two middle-aged men overtook us on the other side. Our driver paid no attention, sitting slouched with his whip resting above his horse, which trotted steadily on, clip-clop, clop clop, head held high, mane swinging, but I became frightened – pathetic, I thought – but when the horse slipped and buckled at the knees and the carriage dipped, I gripped Victoria's knee and shrank in terror, and I didn't think my reaction was at all pathetic, it seemed to be the most natural reaction in the world – the three humans thrown on to the cobbles, the horse rearing and shying, the wheels running over us as the hooves came down on our heads, faces, our lives ended in the cold damp of this September evening in Spetses –

It was warm in Nata's dining room and I felt ill. I went out on to the terrace, sat with my feet against the low wall and listened to their voices, Victoria's mingling in the laughter, and I worried about my future, would my currently shaky limbs be strong enough to carry me into it, would I be continent when I got there – home? home? where is home? and went quite blank, as if the metaphorical and rhetorical question had become a particular one, and I didn't know where my home was for that night, where I was to lay my head. Victoria came out and smiled down at me, so there I could see quite clearly where I would be laying my head that night, and for all the nights of my life to come, I hoped. She led me home, a slow journey through the dark, as we went down passages too narrow for motorbikes.

I PRACTISE MY PROFESSION

I keep failing to mention the bulletins I receive by email every night from New York, sent after the rehearsals of *Butley*, and signed by one Michael McGoff, the stage manager. We receive them on a kind of combined computer-mobile phone sort of device, called a BlackBerry, that somehow collects all the emails sent to both Victoria and myself in London, and to which, on this same BlackBerry, we reply – at least Victoria does, as I can't really manage the keyboard, it is too cramped and fiddly for my fingers, which are not contorted by arthritis, as they might well be at my age, but are so plump – overweight, really – from under-use and from lack of exercise that when I try to pick out the letters I invariably hit two or three of them at the same time. So now every night before Victoria goes to bed, we have a little session – it's become a ritual, really – in the garden or in the bedroom, depending on the weather. I light a cigarette and sit comfortably, a glass of Diet Coke in my hand, while she summons up the day's emails and reads out those addressed to me, and some of those addressed to her.

Sometimes I have to reply, and I admit I rather enjoy the lordliness of it, dictating a few sentences as if she were my secretary – it makes me feel as if I'm on a yacht, for some reason – I suppose from scenes in films, a fat elderly man, generally a mobster, reclines on the deck of a yacht anchored off Cuba. He has a cigar in his mouth, there are two or three of his lieutenants, minor hoods who are usually wearing suits – he of course is wearing swimming trunks and a cap and between his legs there is a fishing rod, its line going over the stern, so he has half an eye out for the swirl of a fin, a big fish, a tuna, and half an eye on the girl in a bikini, who has a notepad on her knee – I'm not sure I've ever seen a film with that exact scene in it, and now, when I try to visualize it, the man I see is familiar, not a mobster, and not at all like myself – he is burly with a lot of thick grey hair on his chest, he has the cigar but it's clamped between his jaws, which are stretched in a grin, he has a grey beard, a square, bullish face, something stupid about it, and aggressive, and his posture is also aggressive, he is standing with his legs apart and the hint of sucked-in bloat about the stomach, and the fishing rod held out as if it were a weapon – the memory of this image, which I know I have seen in newspapers or books, is somehow distressing. I think it's because I think it's phoney in some way. Who is it, who is it? Someone famous. A film star, probably. Clark Gable? Who ever talks about Clark Gable these days?

Well, back to the BlackBerry, and opening and answering emails from Michael McGoff, the stage manager of *Butley*. Usually I enjoy his emails, they invariably contain titbits of interesting information – for example, a week or so ago we learnt that one of the actors wanted to wear the shoes that he or she – I'm not specifying the sex of the actor, as I want to conceal his or her identity – on the other hand I don't want to write he or she, his or hers every time I mention him or her by pronoun, so from now on I shall write she and her on the strict understanding that I might really mean he and his – anyway she wanted to wear in rehearsal the shoes that she'd be wearing in performance, to give her feet a chance to get used to them – she has awkward feet, apparently, and wanted to be sure that she would be able to move easily about the stage when it mattered i.e. in front of a paying audience – so for the following couple of nights Michael McGoff would include in his bulletins a sub-bulletin on how the actor was getting on with his shoes, which had been specially, and at great expense, made for him. It was quickly apparent that these specially made and expensive shoes were causing her a lot of pain, and having a crippling effect on her acting, would have to be dumped, and a new pair cobbled – and then came the news that she was going back to her own, old shoes, the shoes that he'd been wearing in the first days of rehearsal, he would continue wearing them through rehearsals, and then wear them in performance. Then the day before yesterday came a brief sentence to the effect that the management had negotiated a weekly rate for the rental of her shoes in performance – so the management will be paying him for wearing her own shoes, which would certainly turn out to be far more expensive than buying him custom-made shoes – which, of course, the management has already done, and discarded. Now what, I wonder, has happened to those shoes? On whose feet will they end up? Would they fit me if they are a man's, or Victoria, if they are a wife's?

Hemingway! The man with the beard, the cigar, the stupid grin and the belly, fishing on a boat off Cuba for tuna is Ernest Hemingway! And that's who I reminded myself of when I was dictating to Victoria on her BlackBerry. Odd, because I don't think I have anything at all in common with him, not even the belly – his thrusts, mine droops.

Well, as I've said, when the emails are a stage manager's reports about an actor making money out of the use of her own shoes, that sort of thing, they're amusing, and also make me feel that I'm a part of what's going on over there, in New York, that I'm valued, in other words, and important, but don't actually have to do anything – what could be nicer for a man on holiday? But the last few nights the emails have become slightly ominous, furthermore they're not general rehearsal reports, they're addressed specifically to me. One of the actors, the young actor playing the part of Gardner, who has a single scene at the very end of the play, which makes it an important scene, is having trouble mastering an English accent, is there any chance, the slightest chance, that I can figure out a way to help him? In the latest email Michael McGoff says that Nicholas Martin, the director, will be phoning me to discuss this problem further.

I TELL MY WIFE TO RUN ALONG

The director, Nicholas Martin, phoned this afternoon our time, early morning his time, to discuss the problem and to propose a solution, which he said was simplicity itself. That we, or rather I, should rewrite the scene, turning Gardner from an English undergraduate into an

American exchange student. In fact, we could make Gardner come from anywhere in the States that suited us, we could give him any accent we liked, including the accent that he actually has – Midwestern, I think Nicholas Martin said – if we made him an exchange student. The actor playing Gardner – let me call him Eric – Eric is a really gifted and charming young actor, Nicholas Martin said, who has a touch of 'something special' about him, he was sure I would see the point of casting him when I met him and saw him in action, it was just that when I heard him I would also see the point of the phone call, the English dialect coach had worked really hard with him, in every rehearsal he'd shown a marked improvement, but not marked enough to make him convincing and – and – and well, he, Nicholas Martin, and our leading actor, Nathan Lane, and all the rest of the company along with the producers, and no doubt the stage management and the man on the street, were deeply fond of this delightful and – and – to cut it short, nobody could bear the thought of having to let him go, he was sure I would understand.

I did understand, I said, I really did, but I also really didn't think rewriting the scene, which had been written almost forty years ago and not been tampered with since, would come easily to me. I wasn't the same chap that had written the play. Nowadays I saw myself more as the chap who collected and spent the royalties on behalf of that other, almost forty years ago chap who'd written the play. I did actually say all this, in an even more roundabout way, because I was wondering if I had it in me to say what I suspected I really needed to say, which was: 'No, no, on no account will I tamper with this venerable old scene! Fire the delightful young actor from the Midwest now! Recast the part and have done with it – the longer you leave it etc. etc. – and above all, please, please have it done with before I come over there, so I won't have to have anything to do with it!' That's really what I needed to say, complete with exclamation marks!! What I said instead was, yes, I said, yes of course I'll have a go at rewriting, couldn't bear to think of the alternative, of course I couldn't, why the very idea of replacing this fine young man who was so very, very talented, Good God, of course we mustn't etc. – He thanked me profusely on behalf of everybody, including the stage management, man on the street etc. – and we hung up in a salvo of loving farewells, speak soons etc. – The thing is I like Nicholas Martin very much, and think he did a very good job on *Butley* in Boston three years ago, and have every confidence in him, his judgement on such matters, but –

I gave Victoria the gist of the conversation, rather grimly, I expect, said the least I could do was to have a crack at it, and then realized I didn't have a copy of the play with me, and couldn't possibly remember the scene apart from the central fact of it, which is that Butley, who is a self-destructive lecturer in English Literature, hands Gardner T. S. Eliot's *Four Quartets*, and asks him to read out loud a passage from the second quartet, *East Coker*, the passage that begins – 'In that open field/ If you do not come too close, if you do not come too close,/ On a summer midnight, you can hear the music/ Of the weak pipe and the little drum' – one of my favourite passages in the whole of English poetry. I hope, I said to Victoria, that I wasn't expected to translate this passage into an American accent, and I suddenly became very indignant and quite noisy at having agreed to tamper with the scene, a scene that had always worked very well, it was a shocking suggestion, unprofessional, why had I let him talk me into it? Why had I given in and agreed? – on I went, and on a bit, with shameful phrases like 'bloody Americans' thrown in – though of course, now I come to think of it, Eliot was an American until he got himself naturalized – and though I can't remember whether he was legally American or legally English when he wrote *Four Quartets*, I don't believe it matters whether it's read in an English or an American accent as long as it's read with understanding and feeling, and as they insist that Eric is a fine young actor I'm sure he'll find the understanding and feeling for the poetry if he's allowed to do it American – so all I have to do is to get them to send over the dialogue, the very little dialogue before and after the passage from *East Coker*, change a few words in his lines so that they sound American – so what was I making all the fuss about? Why all those dark feelings and indignation about the venerable old scene, I won't be compromising the venerable old scene here, certainly not sufficiently to justify all the fuss and nonsense – is it a symptom of the ageing process, or have I always made this sort of fuss and nonsense over this sort of thing?

I got Victoria to BlackBerry the stage manager, Michael McGoff, requesting that he email the scene over, not omitting the passage from *East Coker*, as I haven't brought *Four Quartets* with me, in fact the only poetry I've brought to Spetses is some Wyatt and some Coleridge, how stupid not to bring a decent anthology. As soon as the scene arrives I'll get to work, if altering a few words can be called work.

Victoria is out in the town, doing some essential shopping – fruit, cold ham, bread and most importantly, bars of chocolate to help me through my addiction, spasms that start at two in the morning, that I defy until about 2.30, and then defeat by cramming bar after bar in my mouth until about 2.45, when I sit slumped, satiated, bloated, here, where I'm sitting now, except it will be in the moonlight, what there is of it when filtered through the heavy foliage, as opposed to the feeble twilight, what there is of it now, as filtered through the heavy foliage dripping with dew. But by then, by cramps-in-the-stomach chocolate time, I hope I will have completed my task of Americanizing the young English character Gardner for the sake of the young American actor whose name I keep forgetting, oh yes, I decided to call him Eric, after little by little – it has turned out to be a more complicated business than I imagined, not simply a matter of Americanizing a few words and phrases. I did that in five minutes flat, in fact before Victoria went out to shop, in fact she was heading towards the gate with her basket on her arm, wearing her straw hat aslant over one eye and her gypsy smile, as if eager for an expedition into the heart of Spetses town at its most bustly period, and I was just about to say, 'Hey wait a minute! Why don't you BlackBerry this off to New York before you go?' In fact I got the first bit out, 'Hey, wait a minute' – so that she turned, her hand on the gate latch, and she smiled and waited, reminding me of Eliot's 'La Figlia che Piange' – 'so I would have had her turn and smile', no, that's not the line, I always mess the line up when I try to remember it, anyway I was looking at her standing at the gate, and misremembering the line from 'La Figlia che Piange' when the thought struck me, sometimes thoughts do actually seem to strike one like a fist, thwack! In the middle of the brain's solar plexus. 'No, no,' I said. 'It's all right,' I said. 'You run along!'

'Run along?' she said.

So we had a brief conversation about what I meant by telling her to 'run along', and off she went, with the high, prancing gait of a fiery steed just untethered – actually she just walked with her usual grace around the gate, her hat atilt, and out of sight – leaving me to deal with the thought that struck me right in the middle of the brain's solar plexus – that Gardner is talked about by other characters regularly throughout the play, and now that I'd Americanized him he'd have to be talked about quite differently – not as a bolshie, troublemaking English undergraduate, but as a bolshie, troublemaking American exchange student, which, at London University in 1970, when American exchange students were famously humble and shy (i.e. educationally retarded) was almost a contradiction in terms, and would certainly require from the playwright a modicum of explanation. In other words I couldn't just have him come on at the end and be American, I had to have him American before he comes on, when first referred to, and have his American-ness alive whenever he is discussed, which will involve backtracking through the whole play.

The whole bloody play was there this morning when Victoria checked, it was actually there, in the BlackBerry, not just the scene I asked for, but the whole bloody play, in microscopic print. For some reason – oh yes, the computer was down in the rehearsal room, the stage manager, McGoff, had had to phone the producer's office and have them do the scan and email and all that stuff, and it had been impossible – here's where we get to the 'for some reason' – a technological reason, I assume, but it might have been a human one, laziness, inattention or malice perhaps, it had been impossible to scan and email just the relevant passage, they'd had to send the whole bloody play, and in almost invisible writing – Victoria set to work reading the instructions for the BlackBerry and fiddling with the keyboard and finally succeeded – she has some of the magical powers I associate with the older woman, though in reality, in years as well as in other ways that really count, she's much younger than me – she succeeded so brilliantly that she initially over-magnified, instead of having several microscopic unreadable pages, we had half a word – three or four gigantic letters filling the screen – so more fiddling, peering, fiddling, until finally the whole play became readable, but only at four or so lines on the screen at a time, she couldn't get it any smaller without reducing it back to microscopic.

It was an interminable business, scrolling backwards and forwards three or four lines at a time to find the places where Gardner was referred to, but not as interminable as trying to think of new lines for the other characters, because of course – something else I hadn't anticipated but should have – new lines demanded different responses, and so whole patches of dialogue, even though quite short, had to be changed, and this in its turn had a knock-on, and sometimes knock-backward, effect – a changed small patch of dialogue in a scene in the middle of the play involved looking again at, and slightly changing, a small patch at the beginning of the play, and that, when slightly changed, made me look again at the small patch in the middle and change it slightly, and then to a small patch towards the end of the play, just before Gardner enters, and a slight change there. So back and forth, forth and back I went, until I began to fear that at any moment I would start in on other, unrelated scenes, and in no time I'd be performing major and almost certainly life-threatening surgery on this venerable old play that had been resting neglected in attics and basements for nigh on forty years, and resting quietly in my writer's soul for nigh on forty-two years. I've done such stupid things before, rewritten old plays until they become not-quite new ones, sort of Frankenstein mutants really, that are unproduceable in themselves because they're reminiscent of the play that they're derived from, and also prevent the revival of the play they're derived from because producers read one and then the other and think about them in relation to each other until they're not sure which characters belong in which play and so move on to a play with no siblings or half-siblings and not written by me – I believe that Michelangelo had the same problem, or was it Leonardo? Whichever it was, it is generally now considered to be the consequence of his botched sexuality, or his anal retentiveness, anyway something like that, which prevented him from letting go, never considering a piece finished and done with and so forth – I also share the problem with many lesser figures, I suspect axe murderers might suffer from a version of it, the swing of the axe being the desperate, but deeply satisfying last step in letting go, or making let go. Simon Gray, Axe Murderer, has a convincing ring to it, as a potential headline, though probably of a small item on an inner page. I've often, when trapped in the mire of writing a play, with drafts on drafts half done or phonily completed and totally hopeless therefore, longed to murder myself, and violently, but I don't see how one could do it with an axe, how get the leverage and balance required to swing the heavy blade in on oneself – except for the crotch, that would be the only easy target area – no, I've just tried it, stood with my legs apart and head down like a golfer, then swung a phantom axe upwards, and it turns out that the easiest slice would be right between the buttocks, and how would one guarantee that it would be fatal, and how attempt to explain it if one survived it? One would end up not in a headline but in one of those can-you-believe-it columns that report real-life misadventures, like the cross-dressing burglar who couldn't shed the high-heeled boots while fleeing from the police, he was also impeded by the tight skirt and constricting undergarments, or the flasher who stepped out of a dark doorway and found himself pointing his penis at his female boss – he subsequently claimed that he was tendering his resignation by cocking a snoot, or perhaps snooting his cock at her – you can follow him into the future with your imagination, the sex offenders' register, unemployment, alcoholism, homelessness, or of course rehab on television, acclaim and a fortune to waste –

You can never tell whether these stories are true, or whether someone like me is making them up, as a way of avoiding the issue, which for me, this evening, in an insalubrious garden in Spetses, is the suspicion that I have probably messed up my play by Americanizing one of the characters in it, and all to save the job of Eric, which isn't even the real name of a young actor I've never met, and am already hoping I shall never have to meet, or if I do meet him, it will be as a perfectly acceptable English undergraduate, circa 1970 – him, I mean, not me – how treacherous grammar is, if you don't keep an eye on it. But where is Victoria, is the question? Where is my wife, is the big question? She's been gone for hours, it seems to me – where is she?

She is lying on the bed, reading. I went in on the off chance, and there she was, looking surprised to see me looking surprised, she came back some time ago, didn't I remember, we'd had a brief conversation about where we'd go for dinner, surely I remembered? I said I did, now that she'd reminded me, but the truth is I didn't remember, I have no idea where we're going for dinner, but when we come back I shall have her BlackBerry the new lines to New York, about twenty of them there must be, and only a few of them spoken by Eric (Gardner), the rest spoken by the other characters about him.

A RASPBERRY ON A BLACKBERRY

We had dinner in the old port. The restaurant is set on a concrete and narrow promontory that stretches out to sea – we had a table at the end, there was a high wind and – actually I don't really want to go into it much, the food and the service, because it's owned by a good friend, he's been kind to us over the years, taking me up to and from his restaurant on the back of his motorbike when I had a bad back and could scarcely walk ten yards without having to sit – this was about fifteen years ago, when he had a different restaurant, up in the hills. He's much younger than me, shares a birthday with Victoria in fact, and looks like Yves Montand, some years like a rather fleshy Yves Montand, other years like a rather lean Yves Montand. He has a very troubled relationship with women, especially Scandinavians, who find him immensely attractive – they're always very attractive themselves, and intelligent, and well educated, and sophisticated – they are all these things to a slightly higher degree – honesty compels me to say it – than he is, but they are also doting and motherly and want to look after him and settle down with him, yes, willing to give up good jobs as teachers or solicitors back in Copenhagen or Oslo, and settle down with him in Spetses, help him run his restaurant and no doubt bear his children, and then they're gone, and when we ask him, let's call him Luka – he speaks very good English, by the way, as do his girlfriends, they speak to him in English – hey, Luka, we say, where is Ingrid? although by now we know the answer – and he smiles sheepishly but radiantly, it's actually a rather boastful smile, and he spreads his hands and says that it's very sad, she wanted more than he could give, he is very sorry, he misses her – but now there is another girl, she comes from Norway, he met her while holidaying in Rome at Christmas, she's arriving next week, he's looking forward to showing her to us, she's very, very nice – but really his tone is much the same when a new girlfriend is about to arrive as when an old one has just left, already rueful and regretful, with a sparkle in the eye that could be a kind of contempt, when you review his history – Odd how I don't mind writing all this down about Luka, but wouldn't dream of writing down what I think about the food and the service in his restaurant, because I would feel disloyal, although I suppose I've just done that, too, at least by inference.

As soon as we were back from dinner we set about BlackBerrying, but there was simply too much, far too much, for Victoria to tap out, especially as there were little bits of stage direction that had also occurred to me when rewriting and adding the dialogue, so finally I waited until 3 a.m. our time, and did it the old-fashioned way, by telephone. Thank God I had the sense, for once, to get Nicholas Martin to phone me straight back, so that the producers will have to pay for the call – the Spetses–New York rates are very high, our friends here tell us. It took me an hour or so to dictate the twenty or so new lines that I had made up in the complicated process of Americanizing Gardner as played by Eric. Nicholas Martin was excited, above all relieved. He said he was convinced that it would work out very well. I said I was worried that the other actors might not like having their lines changed, and he agreed that there might be a little trouble there, but on the whole everybody was so keen not to damage this young man at so early a stage in his career, they were determined that he should keep the part – and that spoke eloquently for the company spirit, did it not? I said yes, I supposed it did. We ended in a burst of anecdotes, gossip and laughter, and finally on the goodbyes appropriate to each other's different time zones, I wishing him a good morning's work, he wishing me a good night's sleep. But I'm too restless to go to bed tonight, the conversation with Nicholas Martin, hearing his voice, has made the whole prospect of going to New York likely and I wish it weren't. I wish we were going from Spetses to our cottage in Suffolk for our usual few weeks instead of just a few days. A few days in Suffolk, a few days in London, then to New York for five weeks. Five weeks in New York. Christ!

*

This is the next morning, and on the BlackBerry there is a message from Michael McGoff, on behalf of all the actors as well as from the stage management and the man in the street, thanking me for my prompt and helpful response to a young colleague in distress. However, the new lines I'd provided for the Americanizing of Gardner had seemed to threaten and confuse Eric, furthermore the new lines for the other actors really rather – I forget what word he used for what the new lines did to them, but it was something like 'irritate' – anyway a word with that sort of feel to it – and they didn't think they should spend rehearsal time on unlearning lines that had seemed to work perfectly well, in order to learn lines that came strangely off the tongue and didn't seem to make much sense – those weren't his precise words, but that was his gist. Well, yes, I said to Victoria, hadn't I said! Hadn't I guessed! Hadn't I known! Yes, she said, you had, and you had, and you had – but here is the odd thing, I felt mortified, yes, really a touch mortified that the lines I'd worked on so hard, and for so many characters, along with my new thinking about stage directions, had been turned down by the actors, rather as if I'd been submitting a new play, and there flashed into my mind the actors' comments as they tried my new lines out – hey, this doesn't work, why does he make me say this, this is crap, crap! and so forth – he, she, all of them, aye, joining in to denounce me for expecting them to work on this crap – no doubt even Eric, who in the manner of actors everywhere, especially insecure ones, would speak from a profound understanding, gained through the strange new mystical attachment he's developed to his character – yes, his would be the loudest, the most dismissive voice – I managed to muffle the throb of shame that went through me, that always accompanies this sort of rebuff, and managed to dictate a reply in which I said I was glad and most relieved to get their message, no good could come of changing lines at this stage of rehearsal, no good could come of firing an actor at this stage of rehearsal either, it would upset the whole company, but now that the whole company – he, she, all of them aye! – knew to what lengths the director and playwright were prepared to go to prevent the dismissal – so please give Gardner, a.k.a. Eric, my best wishes and the best of luck – as Victoria sent this message off, she noticed that she'd earlier failed to notice a PS to the stage manager's last message – that they were happy to let us know that Eric has suddenly taken a massive leap forward in his Englishness, thanks to some further intensive sessions with the dialect coach, he is now quite on top of the poetry – the crisis is over, they looked forward to seeing us in New York. So I can console myself with the thought that if my freshly minted American lines appalled him so much that with the help of his dialect coach he's made a gigantic leap into true Englishness, then what does it matter that I've been wounded in my writer's vanity, all that matters is that rehearsals were back on track, a delightful youth's career has been saved – so we went down to the town beach light of heart, though I scowling slightly.

Home tomorrow and I'm coming to the end of this pad. I won't start a new one, I'll just sit here and smoke. To think that last year I came to Spetses intending to give up smoking, and here I am, in Spetses almost exactly a year later, still smoking. Well, perhaps next year in Spetses. Or next week in New York. Yes, in New York, where they've banned smoking in bars, restaurants, offices, and no doubt rehearsal rooms, it should be easier, more natural –

BUTLEY – ITS PLACE IN MY FUTURE, ITS PLACE IN MY PAST

In a few hours' time we set off for New York for the first previews, that's its place in my future, my immediate future. Its place in my long-term future, if I have one, will depend on whether it's a success or a failure – the truth is that it's possibly my last chance to make enough money to see me through until – see you through until what? Why, see you through until either you need more money again, or will never again need more money, indeed any money at all. As for the past, the man who once wrote *Butley*, where is he now? Well, he's here, writing this, that's where he is, but if I look back –

Sometimes I see him as if he were framed, like a figure in a composition, a man in his very early thirties, with a round Welsh sort of face, a prominent nose that his mother was always certain he would one day 'grow into', small hazel eyes that look smaller than they actually are because of his over-bushy eyebrows, and a chin that usually had a few small red holes in it, razors then being not what they are now, you had to throw away the blades after at the most five shaves, and some seemed to go blunt as you were shaving with them for the first time. I have no idea what sort of character his face expressed or suggested then, as I have no idea what sort of character my face expresses or suggests now. All I know about my face now is that it's a successful liar because it doesn't announce in any aspect, or when all those aspects are viewed together as one countenance, all the sins of commission and of omission, all the forgetfulnesses, unkindnesses, small acts of deliberate let alone accidental cruelty along with the larger acts of cowardice and evasion that it would have to express or suggest if you could see the soul's history in the face – but it's also an honest face now and therefore most likely was so then, to this limited extent at least, that it's quite obviously not the face of a gentleman in whom you would put an absolute trust – there is a furtiveness to the small hazel eyes, it seems to me, whenever I meet them – or try to meet them in the mirror – yes, that's my point, my eyes can't meet my eyes in the mirror unless I will myself to stare unblinkingly at myself, and even so, however hard I stare, the eyes in the mirror are always edging away from the eyes I'm looking at them with – and there's something not quite *comme il faut* about my hair, it looked unnaturally black and glossy back then, when he shampooed it every other day, and is still as black and as glossy now, when I don't shampoo it at all, and only wash it, or rather let it wash itself, when I swim in the sea – it has been unnaturally natural-looking all my adult life – there's a gesture that I make regularly as I sit here, trundling my pen over the page, that he used to make just as regularly when he worked on his Olympia portable typewriter, clackety-clackety, clackety-clackety, sweeping back with the right hand a lock of hair that flops over the left eye – I imagine him doing it then as I do it now – both of us simultaneously, I trundling, he clacketing – clackety-clackety –

But the important thing for me now, at seventy, peering back to that man in his early thirties, is that the man in his early thirties is pounding, stabbing and beating out on his Olympia portable typewriter the play that is going to take me to New York in a few hours' time. All those hours in that little room – such physical hours, drinking, smoking, pushing the hair back, clackity-clackity, and the then wife – who is now seventy years old – asleep, and the son who was then not yet two years old and is now thirty-nine, thirty-nine years old and – and –

Well. Our beginnings never know our ends, as Butley says once or twice in the play, quoting T. S. Eliot – and it seems to me that it's probably also true that our ends never know our beginnings – well, how can we? As we can never know when our beginnings began. I don't mean just the seminal fuck, which is often the end of something else, a vile row or a stretch of leisurely wooing, or something that neither party remembers happening because it happened when they were both virtually asleep and one rolled into the other for comfort during a bad dream, I mean the years before that, when one thing led to another and conclusions were somehow reached before choices were made, when you became a man in an altered condition as a result of a slip of the tongue, or a moment of inattention. They felt more like lapses than choices – one lapsed into the future as possibly one lapses into infidelity, or into bankruptcy, or into death –

PART SIX

AND THERE WAS TINY TIM AT THE ALCOTT

Today, our first full day in New York, we went for a walk. Our intention was to make it a short one, to get our bearings while buying a couple of cellphones, as they're called over here, because our mobiles, as we call them over there, don't work too well. No, that's not right, they do work perfectly well, but they're enormously expensive because every time I want to phone Victoria, say, when I'm, say, on 45th Street, where the Booth Theatre is, and she's on, say, 63rd Street, where our hotel is, the signal goes all the way from 45th Street to England, bounces itself off some mast or other there back to 63rd Street, in other words crosses the Atlantic twice in order to reach its destination a few blocks away – I'm writing all this down in order to persuade myself that it's true – I know it's true, several people have explained it to me, but I still don't quite believe it. But then I don't believe that mobile phones, cellphones, whichever you choose to call them, actually work. It defies reason and common sense, though obviously not science, just as it defies reason and common sense that if you use a mobile phone rather than a cellphone in New York, it will cost you fifty dollars rather than ten cents to phone somebody almost within shouting distance.

We got our cellphones from a shop where a very understanding and pretty Hispanic girl fixed them so that they would work immediately.

We noticed how Sunday morningish New York seemed, it brought back memories of long-ago Sunday mornings in New York, with the sun shining and everything moving at an idle, easy pace. We were suddenly pleased to be where we were, and felt mildly adventurous. Where we were, by the way, when we were outside the shop, was on 65th and Broadway. 'I know,' I said. 'I know what we'll do, let's go up to the Promenade, and see what's on there.' The Promenade is the theatre that had housed my greatest success in New York, *The Common Pursuit*, which I had directed myself, and then a few years later had housed my biggest flop in New York, *The Holy Terror*, which I'd also directed myself. I suppose I ought to have mixed feeling about it, therefore, but I don't, I've always loved the memory of the Promenade, such a neat, unassuming little off-Broadway theatre – off-Broadway signifying its status, not its location, because actually it's on Broadway, but with 499 seats – one more seat would have made it on Broadway, and everything, including the tickets, would have cost much more.

So we strolled up Broadway to 74th Street, or 75th, anyway which-ever street the Promenade is on the corner of, except it isn't any more, it's gone – not yet physically gone but in the process of being transformed, so a notice on the wall told us, into dance studios. What was strange was that though the façade and the architecture haven't yet been destroyed, or even seriously disturbed, the spirit of the building was quite different, it used to have a timid lustre about it, a withdrawn grandeur, it knew its place along the avenue, it was the Promenade, both off Broadway and on it, a theatre the playwright and the actors were proud to be in, the audiences too – but the lobby had no atmosphere, no ghosts, you couldn't imagine the theatre audiences that had once buzzed, buzzed, buzzed about in it, it was seedy and desolate, with small, handwritten notices tacked up on the walls – the sort of place that people went into to get out of the rain for a few minutes, or to do quick deals with packages – Well, no doubt in due course it will be remodelled and reshaped, just right for dancers who lead cheerless and ascetic lives and prefer stark workplaces until the music begins – and one day years from now an elderly couple who used to dance in the studios will stand where Victoria and I stood, and look around in dismay, saying the sort of things that we said – 'How could they have let it—!' and 'But what can have happened—!' It won't occur to them that it had a history before theirs, just as it didn't occur to us that before we knew it the Promenade might have been – what? What could it have been, but the theatre that put on notable triumphs, like *The Common Pursuit*, and notable flops, like *The Holy Terror*.

It was quite a blow, really, quite a blow. You expect things to change all the time, you think you're used to it, you approach every remembered and once-loved building with an almost deliberately cultivated dread, in anticipation that it will have been knocked down or made into something else, but you're never sufficiently prepared, besides it's always the ones that you've taken for granted, that it doesn't even occur to you to fear for, that are gone.

Well, look, I said to Victoria, while we're in the neighbourhood, why don't we check out the Alcott, I didn't say 'the dear old Alcott' though that was my tone. The Alcott was the hotel in which we'd lived for about two months when I was directing *The Holy Terror*. It was the strangest hotel either of us had ever been in – its foyer was grand, magnificent, and dilapidated, like the abandoned set of a film made in the 1950s, a Busby Berkeley musical, possibly, although it had too an atmosphere of violence, not small personal violence, muggings etc., but lavish, old-fashioned violence, as if men on horseback might canter into it, swords or pistols in their hand, or from the film of *War and Peace*, King Vidor directing, was that his real name, King Vidor? A Czech, I suppose – there must have been a reception desk, but I don't remember it, or any of the management, come to that, but I remember our suite – five rooms, plus two bathrooms, plus a large kitchen, and cheaper than any single room I'd stayed in previously in New York. From the room I made into my study there was a view of rooftops, charmingly domestic, tubs of flowers and garden furniture – more Paris than New York. Most of the time the Alcott seemed to be uninhabited, apart from ourselves and Tiny Tim, a once upon a time pop star, who introduced himself to us in the elevator, which was big enough for cattle – Tiny Tim, and an actor, a very fine actor whose name I forget but he was the private detective in *Psycho*, the one who is tiptoeing confidently up the stairs when the little old lady who is Anthony Perkins pretending to be his own mother comes screeching at him from nowhere and stabs him to death. He was also in *Twelve Angry Men*, playing the slow, serious one with a frown. Any film he was in was a classy film, he made it so, and the thing about him, the thing we were told about him, was that he had come to the Alcott from an apartment just around the corner where he'd lived happily with his wife but – but he was an alcoholic and he was drinking himself to death, and he'd decided that there was nothing he could do to stop himself, it was out of his hands, but he didn't want his wife to endure the witnessing of it. So he set up in the

Alcott and proceeded to do what he couldn't help doing, or so he believed. Does this count as suicide? Not really very different from my brother Piers's story, in its bare bones. He too set up around the corner from his loved ones, and calmly drank himself into his early grave. I've often thought of it as a kind of suicide. Although I don't think that death was consciously part of his plan, I do think he was consciously relinquishing his grip on life, on every aspect of his life but his drinking life. Does that count as suicide? Does it matter what word we give to it? If you don't believe in an afterlife then all judgements stay in the here and now, in which case how we behave, whether well or ill, doesn't matter very much – except, of course, in the here and now. But what judgement can I possibly make on Piers, whom I loved? If I hadn't loved him I might have judged him with confident indifference. He drank his life away, silly bugger! Or – converting it to a general principle – people haven't the right to drink their lives away. Why not? I can't think why not, other than that they wound the people they leave behind, who also suffer because they miss them. So it always comes back to the same thing – if no God and no afterlife, no afterlife and no God, then no judgement. Judging is simply another form of grieving, and all you really mean is: he shouldn't have done it because it's not fair on me. Izaak Walton described Donne, after the death of his wife, as being like the pelican in the wilderness – pelicans being thought to tear at and rend themselves from grief – and yet Donne was a man of God who triumphed in the thought of his own death because 'Then Thou hast done!' – 'hast Donne' – how is it then that he couldn't triumph in the thought of his wife's death? Surely he should have exclaimed triumphantly, 'Then Thou hast Mary!' Mary? Why do I think her name was Mary? It was Anne, surely? Anne Donne? He wrote it on the kitchen door, on the day of his marriage. 'John Donne, Anne Donne, Undonne.'

All this stuff about death, Piers, judgement and grieving – yet all I meant to say was that when we got to the Alcott, it too, like the Promenade, had gone – or rather it too, like the Promenade, was in the process of becoming something else – in its case, one of the workmen told us, an apartment block – which would be an excellent commercial move, I should imagine, certainly make more sense than a hotel vacant except for an alcoholic actor and Tiny Tim, the decaying pop star. Oh and – I suddenly remember – a bridge club. No, two bridge clubs. Another eccentricity of the Alcott, that its top floor was reserved for two bridge clubs. The members didn't live in the Alcott, they just played bridge there once or twice a week. Like the Promenade, its lobby was so far undisturbed, though scattered about its floor were sinister humps of tarpaulin, under which presumably the drills, mechanical hammers, small bundles of explosives, whatever, needed for destruction – well, partial demolition.

MY LIVES ON BROADWAY

There we were then, on a Sunday morning in New York, in the bright New York sunshine, wondering if we dare risk a visit to any other building that still survived intact in our memories.

We ambled down Broadway, ambled and ambled, without much sense of purpose, past our hotel on 63rd, and then we were into the 50s, I ambling less and less fluently as my feet began to ache and my legs to weary. In fact I had my arm hooked around Victoria's and was leaning on her slightly, and moaning not entirely under my breath. Around 50th Street, as we stood waiting at the traffic lights, she wondered whether I was sure I wanted to go on, and I nearly said no, I didn't want to go on, I wanted to go back to the hotel and lie down, but instead I said yes, yes, I did want to go on, there was something I wanted to look at, and wanted her to look at, although it had only really occurred to me as I spoke – I was suddenly full of purpose, because I did, in fact, know where we were going, though I still needed her arm to get us there.

Broadway from 48th Street on was Broadway almost as I remembered it, from my first visit nearly forty years ago, the same garish and seedy façades, seemingly the very same bars and doughnut and hamburger joints, the same sort of people standing around in clusters shouting to each other in Italian, Spanish and unidentifiable tongues, and the same sense of milling – people milling about, almost aimlessly, it seemed – but really it wasn't the same at all. In the old days, the days of my youngish manhood, the millers-about always seemed to have an end in view, and were threatening – you walked carefully, in case you jostled a man with a temper or a cause or a head full of drugs and bad dreams, it was a dangerous place, and if you hung around there at night, in Times Square at one or two in the morning, dipping into a bar or a sleazy movie house or a pornographic bookshop on the lookout for Miss Goodbar or whatever might come your way, you knew that something very bad was also likely to come your way, a terminal mugging, for instance – Of course I was usually drunk, no, I should say that I was always drunk late at night in New York, in those days, drunk and full of contradictory desires and an underlying restlessness that was like desperation – what was it I wanted? I couldn't have put a name to it, it had no exact form, possibly what I wanted was what I had, fear, excitement, anticipation – also the sense of being quite alone, without attachments or responsibilities, available. That was how I spent many nights in New York, from my late twenties to my late forties, every time I came back I brought with me more attachments and responsibilities, but I shed them as easily as ever, after a certain hour, when I'd had enough to drink, in Times Square.

Times Square this afternoon, when I ambled into it, limping and supported by my wife, was only dangerous in that it was crowded. It was like Leicester Square, perhaps, in the mass of bodies moving along the pavements and across the streets, but not at all like in that nobody was drunk, nobody shouted, if you bumped into somebody, which you did constantly, because they were rather clumsy and not very aware, they apologized immediately, with anxious, eager smiles, and they all seemed to be Americans or tourists, but they mostly seemed to be American tourists, out-of-towners with children, babies in prams, elderly relatives attached to zimmer frames, or like me to their spouses' arms. So many of them in the sunshine, so good-humoured and slow of movement and almost passive as they trudged around and around, as if being there were the sole point of being there, a bit like the closing scene of *The Invasion of the Body Snatchers*, or was it *The Night of the Living Dead*? – no, that's not right, they seemed to be alive within, if sweetly and passively, so more like cattle, perhaps, with Times Square their pen, and the police placed at various strategic points, visible and watching, to protect and control them, their shepherds and herdsmen.

I couldn't remember seeing police in Times Square before except once, on one of my first visits, two of them handcuffing a middle-aged black man in a red dress and a silver wig, while a third rummaged through his handbag. I remember being struck by the casual, almost lackadaisical manner of it, as if it was something all of them did on a regular basis, also I remember the wig fell off, and one of the policemen picked it up and patted it back on the black man's head, but inaccurately, so that it slipped over one eye –

It took an age to jostle around the square to Shubert Alley. I wasn't sure of my bearings, and we kept finding ourselves back on the corner of 45th Street, waiting for the lights to change, and then it came to me that we had to go towards Eighth Avenue, along 45th Street between Times Square and Eighth Avenue lay our destination – some several thousands appeared to have the same destination in mind, though doubtless without the same reason, in fact among all those thousands and thousands of zombies, mutants, cattle-people, decent American souls I was the only one – I hoped – who could reasonably expect to see his name on placards and hoardings, on the walls of a theatre and even – if my agent had done a proper job – above the theatre. In lights! In lights! On Broadway! My name!

We stood in Shubert Alley, where a strange cold wind appeared to have arisen. It was still a sunny day, quite warm in all the other parts of New York we'd visited, including the small stretch on 45th, between Eighth and Times Square, but in the little arc of an alley between 45th and 44th there was a wind. I suppose the alley itself must have formed a wind tunnel, but if there wasn't wind anywhere else where did it come from to be tunnelled by Shubert Alley?

Nevertheless I stood and pointed, Napoleonically.

'There!' I said.

'What?' She was half turned against the wind and had trouble hearing me.

'There! There!' I heaved her around to face the façade of the Booth Theatre, the bit of it that's in Shubert Alley.

'There!' I said. 'Look!' I pointed at the row of posters on the wall. They were for quite a few shows, *Chicago, A Chorus Line, Spamalot* – actually I'm not sure there was one for *Chicago*, it just popped into my head as a likely candidate, but I am sure about *A Chorus Line* and *Spamalot*, and there were other posters, presumably for the plays in all the other theatres owned by the Shuberts outside their personal alley, in other spots on Broadway – but two of the posters were for *Butley*, my name distinctly where it ought to be, under the title of the play, and almost a half, well almost a quarter the size of Nathan's. A bit less than a quarter, possibly –

'Yes!' she said. 'Wow!'

I pointed above the theatre, where there was a gigantic sort of frame, in which light bulbs could be screwed, is how I imagined that the electrical side of it was done. 'And in a few days, up there. In lights.'

'Wow!' she said again. 'Your name in lights! Wow!'

We looked up at it for a short while, hunched there in the wind, our heads at an unnatural angle, trying to imagine it, my name in lights, winking, glittering, sparkling, towering over Broadway, possibly visible from the extreme edges of the city, or across the water in New Jersey – all the way to New Hampshire, Connecticut, New Orleans, Los Angeles – from London, with one of those new AstroAge telescopes it could almost certainly be picked out – really the wind should have dropped, the orchestra struck up, and she and I, and I and she, we and me, and she and he, have hoofed our way down Shubert Alley, along 45th into Times Square – to what tune though? What tune?

We took a cab back to our hotel, and I went straight to bed. It was nearly five in the afternoon, well past my usual daytime bedtime.

When I woke up we went for a meal at a large Chinese restaurant we'd taken note of on our walk. We'd both eaten there, separately and together, in our previous lives in New York, and from the look of it and the feel of it I'd say that nothing much had changed – not that either of us remembered it very well, it was just that it felt and looked as if nothing much had changed in it for many decades – that the same waiters, at the same ages then as they were now had served us – or for the stretch of about an hour, failed to serve us. This is a characteristic of Chinese restaurants, I think, that they give the impression of being rooted and permanent until one day you go along as usual and it's simply not there, even if it was there last week, and you were, or thought you were, a familiar, indeed favoured customer who would be kept informed of any changes in its circumstances. Of course, as has been well known in the West for centuries, the Chinese are an enigmatic people, who talk in riddles and pass messages about in cookies, but they're also capable of searing and salutary frankness, as was experienced by friends of ours, a family of four, two distinguished adults and two comparatively placid sons under ten, who went regularly to a restaurant some distance from their home because they enjoyed both the delicious food and the speed of service. They were nonetheless slightly puzzled by the gravity of the management's and waiters' demeanours – though they were never rude, they never smiled, or even greeted them as if they'd ever seen them before. Finally, after several years of this, the man, a distinguished lawyer then, and now a judge, let's call him Cravenwood, decided to unravel what had come to seem to the whole family a bit of a mystery. On their way out on what would prove to be their last visit, Cravenwood stopped at the door where the head waiter was loitering, and put it to him: 'Look', he said, 'look, we really, really like your restaurant, the food is excellent, and the service so efficient, and yet you, none of you, give us as much as a smile or a hello, not once in all these years, not even to the boys,' gesturing to them, 'so we can't help wondering, is there any particular reason?' The manager thought for a moment, then said, 'We don't like you.' There's not much you can say to that, really, all you can do is wish you hadn't asked – and not go back, of course. But now I've put it down and given it a little thought, it occurs to me that I wasn't that keen on the Cravenwoods myself, although not being inscrutable, it would never occur to me to tell them so. Besides, it may be illegal these days not to like people, or to say to their faces that you don't like them.

The waiters at the Chinese restaurant we went to tonight would never say they didn't like you, not to your face, they were exceptionally merry, patting me on the back soothingly when I asked if there was any chance of getting soon the dish we'd ordered well over half an hour before – which when it finally arrived wasn't up to much. So perhaps that's the way it works, you can either have good food and speedy service without smiles and hellos, or poor food and virtually no service, but lots of hellos and smiles.

*

Victoria's gone to bed. She'll be fast asleep. If I listened hard I'd hear low voices, or low music, or possibly low gunfire coming from the television set that's suspended above the foot of our bed. Perhaps they'll mingle into her dreams, become comforting, to make up for the absence of George and Toto on either side of her. In a moment I shall go in and turn the television off, kiss her on the brow, then take a sleeping pill, maybe two, as it's our first night in New York, and tomorrow I have to go to the Booth to watch the dress rehearsal.

On the other hand I might come back in here and write for a while, to keep my mind off various problems, the most pressing of which is what to do about this hotel we're in. If it is a hotel.

GUNFIGHT AT BARNES AND NOBLE

The dress rehearsal was only mildly depressing. I went down to it in a cab with the director, Nicholas Martin. He is a small man, a very short man, a year or so younger than myself, probably. He has spectacles, and a lot of grey hair that is swept back but often gives the impression of standing straight up, partly because he has an air of constant surprise – something to do with his eyebrows, which are naturally on the lift. He is a non-smoking teetotaller, which I assume indicates a rich and varied, possibly even tumultuous past, and we get on very well – at least I get on very well with him, it's almost impossible not to, as not only is he intelligent and funny, he is also very sociable – so sociable, in fact, that you can't always keep a hold on him, one moment you're engaged in close conversation and there is a sudden blur, you blink and look around, and there he is, you spot him over there, engaged in close conversation with someone else, and when you next look he's with someone else, and then somebody else, and suddenly he's back with you, picking up where he left off – whenever I have anything urgent to discuss I make a point of resting a hand on his shoulder or elbow, as a way of restraining him, but he's so quick and agile that you could only be sure of keeping him if you could clamp him – When I discussed this aspect of his behaviour with him, he explained that it was a skill, political really, that he'd developed during his time as artistic director of the Huntington Theatre in Boston, one of the most comfortable and beautiful theatres I've ever been in, designed by the man who designed the London Haymarket but requiring for its survival the support of the good and the great of Boston, who in their turn require a great deal of attention, especially at functions like first nights, where so many of them turn up and stand about in singles, pairs and small clusters, waiting to be noticed – if not noticed offence might be taken, financial contributions cancelled, obstacles raised at board meetings, etc. I expect that this explanation is true, but I also suspect that there is a something in his nature, a kind of from-flower-to-flower bumblebee something that takes over whenever he finds himself in company – it's in its way very engaging, and can also be quite infuriating, especially on those occasions when, like the bumblebee on a particularly balmy day, one flower leads to another flower, and one garden to another, and he doesn't come back to pick up where you left off, and you have to phone him on your mobile – actually, this can be quite fun, you watch him as you punch in his number, he is smiling into someone's face, his arm around their shoulder, then he stiffens, his hand shoots to his pocket because it can't help itself, he clasps the mobile to his ear, so that you can see his expression as you whisper, 'As we were saying about the Edna scene—' and he throws back his head and laughs, and keeps the conversation going on the mobile as he bustles over to you.

I learnt all this when Nicholas directed *Butley* at the Huntington three years ago. Nathan was quite extraordinary and I thought the play was almost perfectly cast, no, perfectly cast, even the actor who had trouble remembering the lines, and would fall into fleeting vacancies, was otherwise quite perfect – in other words I loved the production, as did much of Boston – and it played there for a limited run of six weeks, and was packed every night, with standing at the back etc. – and was reviewed so favourably, as was the play itself, as above all was Nathan – the *New York Times* said it was a perfect meeting of actor and part, that Nathan was the rightful successor to Alan Bates – and *Variety* said much the same – that a Broadway production became inevitable. It might have been best if it had moved straight away, just as it was, but Nathan had previous commitments – the film of *The Producers* immediately, and then when that got under way something else popped up – as I remember he stepped into a play written by a friend when an actor dropped out unexpectedly, and then was seduced into doing a revival of *The Odd Couple*, with Matthew Broderick his other half – and so three years passed, and here we are, about to open on Broadway, with only Nathan and Pamela Gray (no relation) in the part of Anne, his wife, from the original Boston cast.

Nicholas is staying at the same hotel, in rooms identical to ours on the floor below. He likes his rooms, which he says suit him perfectly – as why shouldn't they, as he is a small man and on his own, while I am quite a large man with a normal-sized wife, which is why our rooms don't suit me. Furthermore – no, the hotel can wait, this is about the dress rehearsal, which was, as I said, only mildly depressing – I've never been to a dress rehearsal that wasn't depressing, the only question being to what degree depressing – mildly is somewhere near the top, absolute top is 'encouraging' followed by 'OK', for the bottom you find yourself rummaging through your vocabulary for words like 'grisly' or 'ghastly' or 'catastrophic' – I was going to describe the dress rehearsal, that's what I sat down to do, in fact, but you know I can't be bothered – tomorrow there's a dress rehearsal in front of an invited audience, and then we're into previews, and I simply haven't got it in me to chart the course of the previews night after night right up to the first night, it's as if – this is quite an odd thought, and would be worrying if I were worried by it – as if I didn't care very much. There. It's out. I want the play to be a success because I want the money, nay, need the money and I love Nathan and don't want him to fail, but beyond that it doesn't matter very much, I really don't care –

I wrote that before we went out to dinner, over which I talked relentlessly to Victoria about the dress rehearsal, then back we came, I still talking about the dress rehearsal, then as we entered this room I was still talking about the dress rehearsal, talking about it when my eye caught this pad on the table and talking about it as I picked the pad up and talking about it as my eye took in the last sentence 'I really don't care –', to which my behaviour all evening has given the lie. So given that I do care, here is the gist of what I said to Victoria, more than several many times – from the dress rehearsal I could see that there was nothing much wrong with the production that a few sackings wouldn't put right. No, only joking etc., not a few sackings, just one – it's Eric, of course. Eric, the fine young actor who plays Gardner and whose career I thought I'd saved by sending in from Spetses new lines of American dialogue so ghastly that he'd virtually transformed himself – with the help of a dialect coach – into an Englishman born and bred, to avoid saying them. If only he didn't come on in the last scene of the play – in fact if he came on anywhere else you wouldn't think there was much wrong with him, rather you wouldn't notice that there was anything wrong with him, you would just assume that the drop in dramatic temperature – assuming it was reasonably high – was because you, you being a normal member of the audience, had lost interest, as you often tend to do during the course of a play, or that the play had become less interesting – as all plays tend to do here and there over a two-hour or so stretch. The truth is that audiences don't really know miscasting when they see it, why should they, as they have no idea how the part should be cast, not knowing the play, so if this actor, the one I've got so used to thinking of as Eric – in fact the name slipped out when I was having a very pleasant chat with him at the interval, outside the stage door, where we'd both gone for a smoke – he corrected me the first time with a gently wrinkled brow and a puzzled smile, the second time with a rather worried laugh – 'Yes, I'm sorry, I don't know why I keep calling you Eric,' I said. 'I don't know any Erics' – I almost said 'any other Erics' – if Eric had turned up anywhere else in the play, he would have slipped past you, to be forgotten until he turned up at the curtain to take his bow, and even then you might not have placed him clearly, because his would have been a brief and early bow, and almost at once the more prominent actors would have been flowing in from either wing to bow and curtsy big-time – and he wouldn't, in short, have had to be sacked. But as I say, and kept saying to Victoria in Spetses, he comes on in the last scene, which automatically makes him important, and furthermore we've heard a great deal about him at regular intervals during the play, how he behaves, even what sort of clothes he wears and we know that Butley is, or says he is, intensely interested in him, so we want to know what effect he has on Butley – we sense that the direction of the rest of Butley's life, the life he's going to lead after the curtain comes down, so to speak, is going to depend on what transpires between the two of them – particularly when he reads out the lines from *Four Quartets* – 'In that open field/ If you do not come too close' – but I went into all this in Spetses, before I'd met him – now that I have I can confirm as accurate everything that Nicholas said in that long conversation on the telephone about his talent and his charm, but the point about Eric is not that he isn't a good actor, nor that he isn't charming – he has an exceptionally sweet and easy manner, a sympathetic face – but he is wrong for the part. His sweetness, easiness and charm, indeed his talent, are all rendered irrelevant by the simple fact of his not being able to be, in speech or gesture, a student at an English university in 1970. Every other actor in the play can assume the necessary Englishness, and assume it naturally – anyway, so that it seems natural – but Eric is modern, American, anomalous – and made more anomalous with every line of verse he reads out – he can't make sense of it, not only because his accent is ineradicable – apparently it's still being much worked on by the English dialect coach – but because his sensibility is almost visibly at odds with it – the words are coming out of the wrong sort of mouth, and it's unfair, unfair to Eliot, because his great lines sound feeble and enwizened, unfair to the play, because it comes to a halt just as it should be reaching its climax, unfair to Nathan, who doesn't know how to play the scene with an actor who isn't there as the character, and unfair to Eric, who shouldn't have been there as Gardner, should never have been offered the part.

The windows of our hotel suite's tiny sitting room and tiny bedroom are enormous, and through them, directly across the street, I can see into the vast windows of a vast Barnes and Noble, I can see the customers going up and down the escalators, walking between the shelves, if you have excellent eyesight you could probably make out the titles on the covers of the larger books, well, the titles on the posters anyway, and there's a cafeteria, I can see people at tables, making gestures – I like this aspect of our suite, to be a spectator of so much lively movement, the colours of the clothes, people's heads vanishing and reappearing, it's almost as if one were seeing into a city, or a human hive. But there lurks the thought that if we can see into the human hive, we can be seen into from the human hive –

Of course Barnes and Noble is brightly lit, its contents highly visible, and I am sitting in a corner of our sitting room in darkness, for modesty's sake, as I am wearing only my vest and underpants, so I hope that if any part of me can be seen from Barnes and Noble it is only the tip of my cigarette. I shall sit like this writing rancorous thoughts and glancing through the windows, until midnight, when the shop closes. After that there will be only a few people moving about, cleaning and clearing up . . .

I am now looking at a completely empty shop, the lights have been lowered but not turned off, and it seems to ride there, on the other side of the street, like a great ship, abandoned and ghostly – and here are two figures come into view, walking towards each other from opposite ends, many racks of books between them, I wonder if they can see each other, from here it looks as if they must, but there's something about the way they move and keep turning their heads, as if they have no sense of another presence, or perhaps they're so used to each other – yes, that's probably it, they're wearing blue uniforms and one has a cap on, so they're security guards – do they have guns in holsters, I must look the next time we're in the shop. If they came across each other unexpectedly, would they go for their guns and shoot, die in a hail of bullets, there among the books?

I looked in on Victoria, who's tucked up in bed watching television on a plasma screen – it gives a wonderfully clear picture, she said, but the commercials interrupt every few minutes, and it's difficult therefore to grasp a narrative that's really just made up of bits – we wondered if this means that Americans have had to develop formidable powers of concentration in order to keep all the bits in mind and connect and then reconnect them, or is it that their powers of concentration have rotted away, so they no longer care whether they have a consecutive narrative – we talked crap like that for a short while, while we put off discussing what was really on our minds: can we spend five weeks – now four and half – in these tiny quarters, or should we find somewhere else? We agreed that either tomorrow I'd phone the producers and make a fuss, or I wouldn't.

We've moved into a hotel further downtown. When we arrived the lobby was full of people sitting on their luggage, there were a lot of children, some of them crying, others running around in that meaningless way common to children – they looked as if they were waiting to be evacuated but I suppose they were either departing guests waiting for their transport, or arriving guests waiting for their rooms –

Our rooms were ready. We're on the 110th floor, and thus have some fine views towards the river from one set of windows, towards downtown from the other set. There is a very large sitting room with a television, a decent-sized bedroom with a television, a kitchen and eating area, and two bathrooms, and though it's somewhat tacky in its furnishing and underlit and neither television works properly and the armchairs and sofa are uncomfortable, it's fine, fine, and not to be written about because today –

A LUCKY MAN

Tom Stoppard is in New York, for rehearsals of his play *Rock 'n' Roll*. No, for his trilogy *The Coast of Utopia* – *Rock 'n' Roll* is coming over later. He phoned this morning to say he had some important news, he'd found a restaurant which I mustn't name for legal reasons where you can smoke – not in the main part of the restaurant, but in a small room off, where – if they think you're OK – they'll bring out ashtrays and give you the nod. I told him about the various places I'd found, not much use to him as they're all in this area where he's very unlikely to have business, and anyway they're all legal because they're outside – so his discovery of what is in fact a smoke-easy is an altogether different kettle of fish, as Harold might have put it in the days when he a) smoked and b) came to New York – we agreed to meet up at the restaurant this evening, after *Butley* comes down – It'll be nice to see him – it's always nice to see him, but it'll be particularly nice to see him in a restaurant with a small room in which we can smoke.

*

The restaurant is stylish and comfortable, with two kinds of waiters, one lot young and pretty and eager to please, the other old and creaky but not unwilling to serve, and the food was very good, or so Victoria says, I have no judgement on food, thinking if I can chew it and it slips down my throat it will do – altogether we liked it very much, although it's irritatingly close to our previous hotel, about a three-minute walk, in fact, so we kept saying 'If we'd known'. The only problem was the little room Tom Stoppard had spoken of, or rather its absence, and also the absence of Tom Stoppard, so that it struck us that perhaps we'd come to the wrong address, and were in this charming restaurant entirely by accident. I got up and went to the lavatory by a very circuitous route, allowing myself to misunderstand the directions offered by several waiters, but couldn't see in any corner that I visited a little room, or even a door, except the door to the lavatory, and surely he can't have meant 'little room' as a euphemism for lavatory, that he'd found a restaurant where we could have a smoke in the lavatory – I visited the lavatory, which was certainly very little, especially by New York standards, with two urinals, one cubicle, and no visible ashtray, I couldn't imagine the two of us standing there like a couple of ancient schoolboys – I went back and was reporting to Victoria when my mobile went off, I had one of those awful lurches in the stomach, my first thought that it was tragic news from London, my second that it was bad news from the Booth Theatre, my third that it was Tom Stoppard because there was his name on the little screen of my mobile – 'I was just wondering how long you're going to be,' he said, 'because I don't think I'm going to hang about much longer' – I asked him where he was. 'Well, waiting in the restaurant,' he said, which he then named, and was the restaurant that we were in. 'I'm in the little room,' although he wasn't, he was now coming through the restaurant with his slightly floppy walk, putting his mobile into his pocket, smiling rather mysteriously, as if he'd performed a sort of vanishing act in reverse – but in fact it was all quite simple, the little room he'd come from wasn't in the actual restaurant, it was in the lobby, quite easy to find if you knew where to find it, he said, but he realized now that he should have explained. As we hadn't finished our meal he stayed at the table and we talked about his rehearsals, my previews. I find his calm in these situations almost preternatural, as if, a benevolent man himself, he has become used to benevolent outcomes in his journey through life. I remember asking him, a few months ago in London, whether he thought he was a lucky man. He thought quite hard about the question, considered it properly, in fact, and decided that yes, he thought he was – not had been, but was – let me put that in clarifying tenses, direct speech therefore – 'Tom, do you think you're a lucky man?' Pause for consideration. 'Yes, I think I am.' Not 'I have been', is my point, but 'I am', which some-how includes the future tense – 'I am in a continuous state or condition of being lucky' – this seems to me, from the superstitious point of view, a very sensible answer – if he feels that he is lucky but denies it, as most lucky people probably would, the Fates might take offence and decide that a reversal or two might be good for his soul, while a frank declaration of his debt – yes, I am successful, lovable, rich, talented, and lucky therefore – would endear him to them even more, and they would feel inclined to reward him with a further clutch of honours, although it's hard to think what honours are left for them to give him – he has a knighthood and an OM and doubtless countless honorary degrees – well then, reward him with a further clutch of rave reviews, and a map showing the location of every smoke-easy in New York, and one for London next year, when the ban comes into effect – it is actually one of Tom's achievements that one envies him nothing, except possibly his looks, his talents, his money and his luck. To be so enviable without being envied is pretty enviable, when you think about it.

On the way out Tom showed us the little room, tucked discreetly, as he'd said, into the opposite side of the lobby. He opened the door with a sweeping gesture, as if upon a personal treasure trove, and there indeed, to feast our eyes on, were two large men sitting at a small table smoking cigars, and three women at another small table smoking cigarettes – it looked and smelt extremely unwholesome, one's eyes watered and stung, one scarcely dared breathe, and one certainly couldn't help wondering whether this sort of thing shouldn't be banned. We walked Tom halfway back to his apartment, which, as he described it, was an apartment suitable to a man of his luck and talents, then got a cab back to where we are now, I at the table writing this, Victoria in bed, asleep.

*

Oh. One thing suddenly comes back from the dinner with Tom the other night, he asked me how I was getting on with my producer, by which he meant the single, active, on-the-job producer, as opposed to the many merely money-contributing producers, and I said, 'Oh you know what it's like with American producers,' and he said yes, he did know, which one was it? And I couldn't remember – not only the name, but the face, anything, really, except the gender – but it did come to me after a moment or two of foolish gestures and mumbles – 'McCann,' I was able to declare triumphantly, 'Liz McCann.' I think the reason I forgot her was that, as yet, I hadn't put down anything about her, and still haven't, and so –

A BARING OF BREASTS

I first met her in about 1976, when she produced *Otherwise Engaged* on Broadway, with her then partner, Nell Nugent. Liz was plump and curly blonde, Nell curly dark and plump, they were in their early forties I suppose, a bit older than me and a bit younger than Harold (who was directing), and seemed, or anyway were thought of as, inseparable, being known about town as 'the girls'. They were also known for their roguish charm by some, and as a pretty tough couple of cookies by others, though there's no reason I can think of for their not being both – there was an incident that I always remember when I think about them in those days that was a fair example of their modus operandi – there is a scene in *Otherwise Engaged* in which an ambitious and intellectual young woman has a drink thrown over her by her lover, who then departs, leaving her alone on stage with the character played in London by Alan Bates and here in New York by Tom Courtenay – she peels off her soaking blouse and for the rest of the scene, for about twenty minutes in fact, she struts and stalks about the stage bare-breasted, speaking with an unattractive cogency of her literary ambitions and her sex life. It was her casual matter-of-factness that shocked and amused audiences back in 1975 (oddly enough, audiences seemed more shocked, and laughed less freely, in fact slightly furtively, in a recent revival at the Criterion Theatre in London a couple of years ago). Now we – that is the playwright and the director, both men of fierce good taste and astringent judgement –

were determined that the scene shouldn't become a sort of vulgar treat in what was intended to be a rather classy comedy of manners, and had insisted in London, and now insisted again in New York, that it mustn't be used for publicity purposes, and never, under any circumstances, photographed. 'Absolutely not!' Harold said to the girls, when they raised the possibility, 'Absolutely on no account!' in a tone that they might have felt was almost insultingly emphatic, 'Under no circumstances!' and he made it clear that he didn't intend to discuss it further, and they made it clear that he didn't need to – 'We won't say another word about it,' they said, or words to that effect – and they didn't, until they had to explain why half a dozen or so photographers were found loitering behind pillars and crouching behind seats at the dress rehearsal, just before the topless scene – it was one of the most exhilarating passages of my life, when Harold and I seized and smashed their cameras, ran the rascals out of the theatre by the seats of their trousers and the napes of their necks – two girl photographers we treated more circumspectly, the hand for their neck's napes went around their titty-pops – whoppers, whoops, whoa there, here I am, an old man in a dry month etc. – the fact is that I don't remember what happened after we found the photographers – I know that they didn't get their pictures, I suppose somebody – presumably the stage manager – got them to leave, and we then got on with the dress rehearsal. I do remember a meeting with the girls that evening, though it might only have been one of them, ice and contempt from Harold, but not that much grovelling from the girl or girls, indeed there was a touch of contempt in their own manner, not for themselves, but for the over-fastidious director and his sidekick playwright – although actually I suspect from what I know of him the sidekick playwright wouldn't have minded his play being publicized by photographs of a bare-breasted girl smoking a cigarette –

Strange to think that when I began writing the scene I had no idea that Davina was going to take her blouse off, nor that when she did she'd have nothing underneath it but her breasts. It just popped into my head after I had Jeff throw his drink over her, and I think I had Jeff throw his drink because I couldn't think of anything for him to say in response to a withering paragraph from her – so one thing led to another, within a matter of seconds I went from a fully clothed to a half-clothed Davina on the page, and a few months later there was a half-naked Davina on the stage – I met a middle-aged man not long ago who told me that he was taken to *Otherwise Engaged* by his mother when he was thirteen, and that the Davina scene had given him twenty of the most difficult minutes of his life, he had never been quite so conscious of his mother, at the interval he didn't know where to look and hoped his mother didn't either, it remained one of his life's most vivid memories – to think that I did that to a thirteen-year-old, just by rattling off a few sentences on my typewriter. That was over three decades ago, when boys were boys, and went to theatres with their mummies. Nowadays – nowadays – but what do I know about nowadays?

PICK-UP IN THE BAR OF THE MERIDIEN HOTEL

I don't think I saw Liz McCann again after *Otherwise Engaged* until a few months ago, when I met her in the bar of the Meridien Hotel, Piccadilly, to discuss the forthcoming production of *Butley* – really it wasn't so much a discussion as a reintroduction – 'Here I am again, Liz, after all these years!' and 'Here I am again, Simon!' I don't know what she expected to see, but probably not me – I mean, people don't change in our memories, we can't add on the changes that life has wrought on them during all the years we haven't seen them, and even if we could it wouldn't be any good, they'd be the wrong changes – we'd look for wrinkles and the skin would be shinier, we'd expect eyes dulled by fatigue and defeat (a dire marriage, troublesome children) and find instead (an unexpected widowing, delightful grandchildren) a sparkle in the eye, a strut in the step; and there are dewlaps, and there are wattles, which I never bargain for – well, who sees in one's thirty-year-old friend intimations of the pouches to come – we seem to take our imagining of ageing from literature or films – whitened hair, wrinkles around the eyes, a stoop or even a shuffle, linear and almost childish ageing, while, well to take the obvious case, the case from which I started, in the bar of the Meridien, in Piccadilly, where I anticipated, vaguely anticipated, a woman who had only aged by being slightly worn down from staying roughly the same for over thirty

THE COMPLETE SMOKING DIARIES

years, plump and blondely curly, with a frisky manner and bright blue eyes, one half of 'the girls' –

The Meridien bar off Piccadilly is rather like the New York bars I remember from my early visits, very comfortably furnished but dimly lit, so if you come down to it from a bright outside, you find it difficult to see anyone distinctly, at least at first, but my eyes went straight to the nearest unaccompanied elderly female. 'Hello, Liz,' I said to the rather slovenly and mountainous heap that was stretched out in an armchair that looked too small for her, in fact it looked as if she'd clipped it on to the underneath part of herself, a prosthetic addition to her buttocks, to save her the trouble of finding a seat when she wanted one. Her short legs stuck out in front of her, her heels resting on a leather stool. So it was to this rather formless and shapeless being that I said, 'Hello, Liz.'

'Hello?' she said in that American way, 'hello?' like a question. I sat down beside her, thinking that I always thought of her, though perhaps incorrectly, perhaps it was Nell I thought of, as a bit of a dresser – feminine, floral dresses kind of thing – and here she was, in a shirt and trousers that produced an odd and contradictory effect, they seemed loose and baggy and far too big for her, and yet she also seemed to be spilling out of them, folds of flesh visible at the waist and around the armpits, and elsewhere one suspected, if one cared to look. 'Nice to see you – it's been a long time,' I said. 'Well,' she said, 'I don't know about that.' 'More than thirty years,' I said, trying to examine her face for a something that would make her familiar to me, but really in that light her face was almost without features, just a white blob with a white blob of a nose and dents for eyes and mouth, and I couldn't say anything about her hair except that she might have had some on her head, some of which might have been hanging down the sides of her cheeks, though that might have been a scarf. 'Yes, more than thirty years,' I repeated, smiling and nodding at her and trying to be a little romantic by resting my hand lightly on what I hoped was her knee – well, what harm in a little show of caring, of *tendresse*, this was my producer, after all –

It turned out that this wasn't my producer after all, my producer was sitting deeper into the bar's shadows with my agent, Judy Daish, who has sharp eyes and hailed me before I got any further in my seduction of this somewhat bloated and elderly American lady, to whom, of course, I apologized. 'So sorry,' I said, 'I thought you were the lady over there, sitting with – the other lady over there, so sorry.' 'No, that's OK,' she said, 'I was getting quite interested. Gonna ask ya if ya wanted my room number.' And she gave me a charmingly husky cough of a laugh – a fifty-a-day laugh, I'd say, and quite a lot of gin to go with them.

Now the irritating thing is that this encounter with the elderly American lady who wasn't Liz McCann has become my memory of meeting Liz McCann, she usurped the experience so completely that the trifling business of going over to join Judy Daish and the genuine Liz McCann is blocked by it, as is the ensuing conversation apart from a little patch in which she said how much she was looking forward to producing *Butley* on Broadway and then said something else that suggested that she hadn't yet read the play, which pleased me. I have an innate faith in producers who don't read my plays, it means that they're putting their faith in something that's probably more reliable – in this case in the star, Nathan Lane, which makes complete sense – but that's really all I remember of the meeting, I suppose she turned out to be so completely appropriate to the Liz of my memory or my curiosity about her was completely used up by the lady who wasn't her – Supposing Judy hadn't called out, would she really have given me her room number? Well, I suppose I could have passed it on to someone in need.

What about Liz McCann now, here, in New York, the currently active producer of my play, what do you make of her? Not much, not much to make. I see that she's been active, in that everything that should have happened has happened, Nathan Lane's in lights, his face and his name dominate the ads, the previews have been running smoothly enough, though there's trouble from the next-door theatre, which spills its audience into Shubert Alley before our show has ended, and they shout and even sing and sometimes swear and reel about, of course the swearers and reelers-about may be revellers from the nearby bars, but if they're not, if they're actually coming out of the theatre shouting and swearing and reeling about, then that must be quite a show they have next door to *Butley*, I must make a note of what it is, it might be worth a visit – I have an idea it's *A Chorus Line*, does that seem likely? Anyway, the point is that Liz is responsible for preventing these people, whoever they are, from disturbing our previews, and I have no doubt that she will find some way of doing it, by re-routing them, or bringing in the police, or perhaps coming to speak to them herself, with the full force of her personality – no, no, she can't do that, unless she's brought along in her wheelchair, oh yes, that's what I've forgotten to mention, Liz McCann has been physically absent as a producer because she damaged her leg just as *Butley* was going into rehearsals – apparently she was somewhere in the Caribbean, resting up, preparing herself mentally and emotionally for the stress of a Broadway production, when there was an incident of some sort, I don't think I've been told the details, just in general terms that she slipped and overturned herself, but the good news is that she is making a rapid recovery, and should shortly be visiting the theatre in person, rather than through her representatives, who are, I have to say, about as prepossessing as – no, I don't have to say, so I won't.

CRUEL AND USUAL BEHAVIOUR ON BROADWAY

Let me go through today as quickly as possible, because it's been quite unpleasant, and will in a sense still be going on while I'm writing it down, until I've written it down, when I suppose I can count it as over at last. The nub of it is that the young actor I think of as Eric has been sacked at last – or rather, it has at last been decided that he is to be sacked, although he himself won't learn of it until we've found a replacement – the plan, as far as I can make it out, is to search out potential Gardners, arrange for their auditions, choose one, rehearse him a few times, and while this is being done continue with the already posthumous Gardner, paying him compliments when he comes off stage, issuing him with notes before he goes on stage, as if he were an abiding member of the company – if the new one isn't ready by next Tuesday, the current one, his head still stuffed with reassurances, as he's constantly in need of them, and asking for them – 'How did I do tonight? Is my reading the poem better? Am I doing that bit where I sit down right? And when I stand up again? – Oh, really? Oh, thanks, I was a bit worried about that – Gee, great, thanks, well, see you tomorrow' – is the type of exchange that follows his every appearance – will be sacked on Thursday, I think it's agreed, Thursday or Friday, one of those, immediately after the performance, so when he approaches the stage manager or Nathan or whoever relevant is to hand – 'Hey, how did I do? What about the poem?' – Nicky will manifest himself between them, so to speak, lay a compassionate hand on his shoulder and say something like, 'I think you did really great tonight, under the circumstances, the circumstances being that you're completely wrong for the part, sorry, my mistake in casting you, you're a fine young actor, one of the finest, as you know I know, because we've worked together before, that's why I cast you, and will cast you again some time in a part that we both hope you'll turn out to be right for, but as for your immediate future, you won't be going on tomorrow, could you clear your dressing room tonight, our love goes with you, your agent has been notified.' And if his replacement is still not ready, then the understudy will go on until he is. Anyway, we'll have a new Gardner quite a few performances before opening night if the plan goes according to plan, as I'm sure it will, as it's been used so often, in so many Broadway productions, and it's always worked. It always works.

At least as far as the shows are concerned. One has no idea how it works for the dismissed actor, who has to explain to all the people he's told – parents and brothers and sisters and friends – 'Yeah, that's right. Broadway. I'm gonna be on Broadway – Booth Theatre – with Nathan Lane! We open Oct 25th. Yeah, Oct 25th! How about that! All right!' – that in fact, come Oct 25th, he himself won't after all – won't after all – all the phone calls he'll have to make, or won't be able to face making, all the familiar bars he'll have to go into, the eager faces, the smiling enquiries – will it be a consolation to know that he's one in an endless line, to the crack o' doom and back again, the ghosts of sacked actors, living and dead –

It came about like this, the decision to sack Eric. They were rehearsing his scene, the last – as I keep noting – scene in the play. So there was

Eric, as Gardner, on the stage, Nathan as Butley up there on the stage with him, and there, in about the fourth row of the stalls, were the director, Nicholas Martin, his assistant, Michael – a tall, easygoing young fellow who stays close to Nicholas Martin, writing his muttered observations and asides down in a notepad – he reads them back to him at the end of the day's work – almost as useful as a memory, when you think about it, and far less effort than working with your own pad and pen, furthermore a vital means of blocking people from talking to you, when the playwright wants to have a word with you, for instance, all you have to do when he approaches is swing your head towards your assistant, who begins to write, and the playwright, ever deferential, returns to his place at the back of the stalls – but let this pass, let this pass, on with the sacking of Eric – So Nicholas Martin in the fourth row – beside him, his body arched with super-attentiveness towards him, pad and pen at the ready, was his assistant, Michael, and all kinds of supernumeraries, God knows who they were, really, assistant thises and thats to the stage manager, the lighting designer, the costume designer, who knows who, a large pack of them, and then yet other figures scattered out in the darkness of the stalls, probably some of them producers – there are about twenty producers, as far as I can make out, twenty producers scattered into the darkness! – and me, standing at the very back, with my elbows on the balustrade, my hands wrapped over my ears, as a way of supporting my head, which felt both very heavy and completely empty, and also as a way of making it difficult, and if possible impossible, to hear Eric's reading from *East Coker* – 'In that open field/ If you do not come too close, if you do not come too close' – and though it was difficult it wasn't impossible, not nearly impossible enough, in fact, as is often the way, the more I squeezed my hands against my ears, the more sensitive to the spoken word they seemed to become.

They got to the end of the scene and they went back and started it again, which I'd hoped they weren't going to do, but I took it as a portent – they were going to go on doing the scene again and again until I paid it proper attention – I don't think this was a conscious plan, I don't think Nicholas Martin put it to himself that he'd go on and on doing the scene until finally someone, the playwright, for instance, was forced to look at it properly, and then, having looked at it properly, was in duty bound to object. I expect he hoped that if he went on doing it again and again it would somehow right itself, although it can be taken as a rule on the stage, as in life, that the more often you do something wrong the more difficult it becomes to accept that you're doing something wrong, even if you go on sensing that it's somehow not quite right. Well, what struck me on seeing it this second time around was that there were two scenes going on, in two different areas of the stage – centre stage, by the desk, was Eric, frail, feeble and charming, doing the scene as he always did it, out towards Nicholas Martin, and Nicholas Martin's assistant, and all the supernumerary assistants and producers scattered through the stalls, and there in a space on the stage only a few feet away from Eric was Nathan, who'd turned his back physically as well as metaphorically on Gardner and was addressing the lines he should have been giving to him to an empty bit of the stage, thus giving the impression that he was either talking to himself or to a ghost – this was not without a certain emotional effect, quite a powerful one, if surreal, particularly when he declaimed the Beatrix Potter nursery rhyme:

> 'Ninny Nanny Netticoat,
> In a white petticoat,
> With a red nose, –
> The longer he stands
> The shorter he grows.'

Thus he describes Gardner to Gardner, not just as a candle, but a candle of clownish aspect, dwindling before his very eyes, it's quite a violent insult, really, and of course, must be spoken straight at Gardner, not with his back to him, or it won't seem like an insult, it will seem like a nursery rhyme, summoned with no clear intention, out of affectation or whimsy –

So it is again, only in reverse, when Eric/Gardner reads from *East Coker*, so thinly and ineptly, with so little sense of what it's about, that we assume that Butley cuts him off because of the offence to T. S. Eliot, and not – as is intended to be the case – because he can't bear the weight of feeling in the lines. In the final moments of the scene, when Butley dismisses Gardner in language that is uncompromisingly brutal, Nathan had found a way of doing it, gulpingly and sorrowfully, and without meeting Eric's eye, so that we know that in his heart he isn't really telling Gardner just to fuck off, he's really calling out to Joey, his ex-protégé, who during the course of the play has been defecting as his flat-mate, his office-mate, his play-mate – to come back, come back! is Nathan's inaudible but visible cry to the absent Joey, as he stands with his back to a therefore dramatically absent Gardner –

I can see now, and could even see at the time, that this was a difficult situation for both Eric and Nathan to be in, but it also seemed to me then, and still does now, a pretty disgusting situation for the playwright to be in, confronted with either having to watch Nathan playing the scene against its grain, and so having the curtain fall on Butley as a self-pitying wreck, or coercing Nathan into playing the scene as if with the grain but without its spirit, and so having the curtain fall on Butley as a self-pitying bully. Both curtains false, and equally unattractive.

I'm only going on about this because I can't face putting down what happened this afternoon after the scene had been rehearsed several times, to no evident purpose. Finally there came a hiatus, with everyone frozen – no, that puts it too dramatically – they weren't frozen but they went quiet and still, as if fallen into a stupor. I seized the moment, I'd felt it welling up inside me, and now I seized it, or it seized me, and there I was, tramping down the aisle towards the stage, coughing and making the little retching noises that I tend to make in times of crisis, which are audible only to myself – when I had got to the aisle at the end of which Nicholas and his assistant were sitting, their heads together but not quite touching, as if each were waiting for the other to propose something helpful – marriage, or a mug of hemlock – I bent down and whispered – 'The thing is,' I said, 'the thing is, can we go somewhere quiet and talk?'

'Sure,' said Nicholas, 'sure. But what do you want to say?'

'I don't want to say it here,' I whispered.

Nathan pattered lightly down the steps from the stage, and joined us. Nicholas moved along a couple of seats, his assistant moved along a couple of seats, I sat down in one of the vacated seats, Nathan sat down next to me. The four of us were in a line, going from left at the end of the aisle – leading man, playwright, director, assistant to the director. There was a bustling and hustling sound from behind, as all the other assistants, and the numerous producers, moved forward to sit directly around and behind us. Eric/Gardner stood alone on the stage, facing us, smiling wistfully – he made me think suddenly of a stricken colt, though I've never seen a stricken colt, probably he wouldn't look at all like Eric/Gardner, he'd have four legs, for one thing, though Eric/Gardner probably wished he had another two just at the moment, to help him stay upright while being the observed of all observers.

'Simon wants to say something,' Nicholas said to Nathan, leaning across me.

'Yes, but not here!' I whispered.

'What?' said Nathan. 'What does he want to say?' Then turning to me, 'What do you want to say?'

'Well, not here.'

Eventually it was agreed that I didn't want to say what I had to say there, in front of the actor that I was going to propose that we sacked, with the rest of the company plus producers and assistants and surplus assistants sitting around and behind us, and we went somewhere else –

First, to the back of the stalls, and then to a bar across the road from Shubert Alley. What I said was pretty well what I've written above, although leaving out the bit about sacking Eric.

'Well, what do you think we should do?' Nicholas asked.

I put in the bit about sacking Eric.

They both knew, of course, that it was going to come to this, and said so. They'd just been waiting, really, for someone to come along and say it out loud. How lucky, we all agreed, that I'd come along and said it out loud.

I wish I'd said it out loud down the telephone in Spetses, instead of wasting hours working up some bogus Americanized dialogue and emailing it across on that bloody thing, what was it, the blueberry thing – but then I couldn't say it out loud until I'd seen the performance, could I? And how would I have seemed – the elderly and malevolent English playwright sunning himself on a Greek isle while blueberrying requests for the dismissal of some desperate, hard-working and lovable young American actor I hadn't even seen? On the other hand the desperate, hard-working and lovable young actor would have been gone by the time I arrived, he would have been gone and long forgotten, nobody would have blamed me for something they wouldn't have remembered – There is a moral in all this, quite an obvious one, that may serve me well when I get into my eighties, and a similar situation arises – but then a similar situation never arises, there's always an element in it that makes all the difference and – in other words you can learn nothing from experience, at least in my experience.

TOM AND JERRY – BUT WHICH IS WHICH?

Although this hotel is geographically closer to the Booth Theatre than our last hotel was, it takes longer to get there, because the traffic is worse – from the other hotel the cab could go straight downtown, it took on average ten minutes, from this hotel the cab has first to go across town, and then downtown, and it takes, it can take – well, last night, for instance, when I wanted to get to the theatre a little earlier than usual for a meeting with Nicholas Martin, it took me forty minutes to get within a ten-minute walk of the Booth – it would be a one-minute walk if it weren't for the people, most of whom look like immigrants and tourists from the land of the Fattipuffs, there are thousands and thousands of them, they're slow and fat and wheezy, they waddle along right in front of you and right beside you, waddle waddle waddle, hemming you in on all sides, and then it strikes you – at least it does if you're me – that you're just like them, you too are overweight, you're slow and you wheeze, and if you didn't have a limp you too would waddle – but I do have a limp, my legs have become very odd these last few days, almost as if they were disjointed, my left one more than my right one, so I sort of list – yes, there I was yesterday evening, dragging myself down Broadway, listing to the left, reminding myself of a character in a gangster film I once saw, waddle-limping to his death by gunfire. Unlike me, he wore a trilby.

When I got to Shubert Alley there was an enormous queue at the box office, always a gratifying sight for a playwright, and restorative, at least for a moment or two – I sidled further down the alley, to my favourite spot opposite the stage door, with my back to the wall, and a hamburgery sort of place on one side, and a small store that seems to specialize in bottled water on the other. This is where I stand, smoking, before the curtain goes up, and then in the interval – and then sometimes for a few minutes after the curtain's come down. I feel anonymous there, and almost invisible except to those who know me, who also know where to look for me – the director, for instance, comes over to join me as soon as he's seen me arrive. The flaw in this scheme is that those who don't know me feel free to speak freely if they happen to veer out a little as they leave the theatre – a few nights ago, at the third or fourth preview, a middle-aged woman came out of the theatre backwards, and kept coming backwards in my direction until she swung, still going backwards, away from me, down Shubert Alley. A little mob of other women with an elderly man mixed in was following as she instructed them, in a fierce, honking voice, what they were to feel about my play. 'You can't care about those people, you can't care a single heartbeat about people like that! Horrible, disgusting people!' She was still walking backwards as she spoke, backwards down Shubert Alley, and they were still walking forwards, towards her, people coming in the opposite direction had to step out of their way. 'Didn't you just hate the lot of them!' she honked, as she pedalled backwards, and voices called out from her followers, her pursuers, 'Hated them, just hated them!' – I kept my eye on the elderly man, but he didn't speak, just made vaguely belligerent gestures with his arm – There was something faintly sinister about it, probably because it looked simultaneously spontaneous and organized, like the very first stage of a political demo, I suppose, or of a lynch mob – but I expect they were one of those preview theatre study groups – and there was another night – but that was my fault for not getting out of the theatre quickly enough, a small man of about fifty, I should think, in a grey sweater with a long scarf and a blue cap which I thought had the word Crap on it, just above the peak, but it can't have been Crap, perhaps it was Gap, I have a blue cap at home that has Gap on it, so let's assume I misread it, to make it conform to what he was saying, or rather chanting, 'Bor-ing, bor-ing, bor-ing' was what he was chanting, low and to himself. That was the worst part of it, that not only did he not intend the playwright to hear, he didn't intend anyone to hear, he was obviously and simply overwhelmed by the need to express himself, it was his true and heartfelt judgement on the evening therefore – and there was something about him, the schoolboy aspect of his behaviour, that was undoubtedly sympathetic, and I thought that if we'd met at a party, for instance, I'd probably have liked him.

I should put in here that I've heard some very nice things, too, but compliments never seem to stick in quite the same way, they become generalized in the memory, as pleasant experiences tend to do, while unpleasant experiences never seem to slip their particularity – so of the woman who actually spotted me, recognizing me from the programme and came up to me and said, 'Mr Gray, I just wanted to tell you that *Butley*'s one of my favourite plays of all time,' I remember nothing more than that she was a woman, and was quite big, and might have been my sort of age, perhaps a decade or two younger.

But to get back to last night, and my firstly admiring the long queue at the box office, and secondly going to my special spot between the hamburger type of place and the water-selling store, and lurking there with a cigarette, anonymously and invisibly. Well, it soon became apparent that tonight not only was I anonymous and invisible to strangers, but also to people who knew me quite well – Nicholas Martin, the director, among them. He was standing by the stage door, sort of sideways on to me, talking to his tall young assistant. I saw his alert and agreeable eye take me in from around his tall young assistant's elbow, then he reached up and put his hands on his tall young assistant's shoulders and swivelled him around, blocking my view of him – and probably more to the point, blocking his view of me. I took a few steps sideways, until I had him in my sights again, and again his hands went up to his tall young assistant's shoulders, and he readjusted their positions. I told myself that this couldn't be what it seemed to be, waited a few minutes, took out my mobile and phoned him. I heard the phone ring, and ring some more, then it stopped. 'This is Nicholas Martin, why don't you leave me a message?' his voice said, with a hopeful, upward inflection on 'message'. I left him a message bidding him good evening and informing him that I was a few yards away, and at his service with my thoughts about that scene that we'd arranged to meet and discuss. I was watching the assistant's back, waiting to see if Nicholas Martin would emerge from behind it. Nothing happened for a moment and then the assistant walked quickly towards the stage door and went inside, and there was absolutely nobody where Nicholas Martin ought, by all known rules of nature etc., to have been. I wondered for a moment whether he'd somehow attached himself to the front of his assistant's body, and thus been smuggled by him through the stage door, it was just possible, he was short enough, the assistant's spine long enough – but then I saw him much further along the alley, up at the box-office end, wedged in between a young couple that he turned into a kind of human tunnel that he scaled, like an old-fashioned chimney-sweep, so that he could hug them simultaneously around the neck, then he shinned down and was into the box office where I knew there was a door to take him backstage. I thought of going through the stage door in the alley, trapping him in the corridor as he came down the stairs, but he might whip past me, or turn around and run back up the stairs, what would it look like if the large – elderly, but large – playwright were seen chasing the younger – small but younger – director around the insides of the theatre, and what would I say to him? 'Nicky, Nicky, why are you running away from me?' in that tone Marlon Brando adopts in the back of the car with Rod Steiger in *On the Waterfront*, when Rod Steiger – who is his brother – pulls a gun on him. It's a lovely and sorrowful moment, but I didn't think it would work with Nicholas Martin unless he pulled a gun on me, and if he did, I'm not sure I would get the tone right, I'd turn and run, and we'd be off again in reverse, cinematically more Tom and Jerry or the Marx Brothers than Brando and Steiger –

MR POOLE REVISITING

So I went in and stood in my usual spot at the back of the stalls, and when all the audience was in and the curtain was going up, Nicholas Martin slipped in and stood some way down from me, by the door, through which he shot just under an hour later as the curtain came down. I went out and hung around in my usual spot, smoking, at the interval, not really expecting him, and feeling distinctly unwanted and unpopular – people who have been saluting me, well, they don't actually salute, but they wave with kindliness and respect, come in and out of the stage door quite clearly refraining from looking to where they know I'm to be seen at the interval, it was as if I were someone both shameful and shaming. Now what distinction am I making here? What is the difference between being shameful and being shaming? I must have assumed a difference or I wouldn't have said I was both. The suffix -ful and the suffix -ing, think of other uses. Well, hateful and hating – if someone is hateful it's because they fill other people with hate, whereas hating, it's difficult to think of an ordinary use, except by Apu in *The Simpsons*, who might well say, 'We are hating all the noise Mr Simpson is making', otherwise it turns up mainly as a gerund, isn't that what it's called, when a verb is made into a noun? 'He couldn't abide all the hating that went on between Apu and Simpson etc.', though Apu isn't much of a hater – none of this is helping me to distinguish between being 'shameful' and being 'shaming' but there was a time when I understood, or understood for a brief moment – when Mr Poole, at Portsmouth Grammar School – I was about nine years old, in the infirmary with flu. I had to pee, and the nearest lavatory was corridors on corridors away, it seemed endless, the wavering totter down these cold corridors in my pyjamas, my bladder bursting and thinking that I was going to fall over any second because my legs were wobbly and I was shivering. But I made it, and oh the relief, the joy of it, in spite of the cold and also feeling so hot. When I finished and opened the door there was Mr Poole standing there, tall and bald-headed and looking down at me through his glasses with his usual irritation. He stepped aside to let me pass, then went into the lavatory, and back I went, along the corridors on corridors to the infirmary, and climbed into bed. There were three or four other boys in the infirmary, so it must have been one of the flu epidemics – how appalling, though, that there wasn't a lavatory in the room, or just off it – but there must have been an OK matron, because I don't remember her, just as I don't remember who the other boys were, or whether they were younger or older, in fact, all I remember is being back in bed, so glad to be back in bed with an empty bladder, and shivering, and then there was Mr Poole there standing over me, looking down at me with considered and thoughtful anger – he spoke at me from the foot of the bed in a voice that, though it was conversational, he intended to carry to the other beds, and no doubt to matron. He said it had been disgusting to follow after me in the lavatory, there was wet on the floor and on the seat – I still remember now that I couldn't remember then having peed on the floor and on the seat, but I expect I did, he wouldn't have been making it up, after all, Mr Poole never made things up, and his disgust was 'real' and 'felt', to use a Leavisite vocabulary, 'felt' and 'real', and it was in this context that I first came across the use of 'both shameful and shaming', he said that it was both shameful and shaming that a boy in the boarding house of Portsmouth Grammar School should have so little consideration for others, should be so lazy and disgusting in his personal habits, should be so this and that, that and this, shameful, shaming, should be ashamed, disgusting, it seemed to have no end, his peroration – well, that's anger for you, it quickly becomes addictive, one angry sentence leads into another and then into paragraphs, it becomes exhilarating, and difficult to bring to a conclusion. It's very possible, though, that Mr Poole only spoke for a very brief time, but at the time – and in memory – it was interminable, lying there at attention under the covers, head straight on the pillow, staring obediently at Mr Poole's implacably disgusted and contemptuous face. When he'd done I burrowed under the bedclothes and hoped I'd never have to meet the gaze of any of the other boys in the san, or of the matron. But I have an idea now that nobody said anything about it – and it was a tough enough school, where you were likely to be held to loud and sneering account, with descriptive nicknames and so forth, if you were at the centre of an incident considered unsavoury.

Well, I'm not saying that I felt last night as I felt sixty-odd years ago when I hid under the bedclothes, in fact the fact is that though I can identify such feelings, mortification, embarrassment etc., they're not really feelings in the old sense of the word, in the days when I had feelings I could feel, they're more like reminiscences of feelings, they're so faint and thinned out, and I cared far more about having my cigarette than I did about my shame.

ALL'S WELL THAT ENDS

I went back in for the second act and in he slipped as the curtain went up, and out he slipped an hour later as it was coming down. I stayed for the applause because there was so much of it, some of it even being for the play, and for Nathan there were bravos. Bravo, bravo, bravo! they cried, yippee, yippee! as if he were taking his bows on a horse in a rodeo. Then I went backstage and spent half an hour with Nathan in his dressing room. He was hot and shiny from his shower, and looked terribly young, like a boy almost, his eyes very bright, but his eyebrows were lifted and his voice growly and drawly, which meant that he was worried, and wanted notes – I've never known him not worried after a performance, not wanting notes. I thought of asking him about Nicholas Martin, was there something he knew which would explain his reluctance to have contact with me, but thought I'd better not, thought I'd better not worry him with it. So I came back here and worried Victoria with it, over a supper we had sent up from room service – a perfectly edible supper, brought up by very pleasant whatdoyoucallems, not bellhops, waiters I suppose, one of each sex, male for the main course, female for the pudding, or can you still say waitress, in which case a young South American waiter and a young black New York waitress, both very charming and wearing easy smiles – a pleasant meal with the New York night glittering below us, and I fretting and fretting on about Nicholas Martin, why was he avoiding me or was it my usual paranoia? Victoria thought it might be both – that he was probably avoiding me, and that I was paranoid about it, which seemed to me reasonable, and still does. But still – Victoria's gone to bed, and I'm sitting in a corner of the couch, with a portable music player playing Mozart piano sonatas and writing this on a pad on my lap, and as it's all about Nicholas Martin avoiding me, I must be still worrying about it. Well, actually, I wasn't worrying about it while I was writing it down. Now that seems to me important, that writing down my worry was a completely unworrying experience, and not because it was therapy, that sort of crap, but because it was fun. Yes, I had fun writing down all my worry. I wonder how far one could take that. If one were due to be hanged in the morning could one conceivably find any fun in the writing about it – Chidiock Tichborne was very young when he wrote the poem on the eve of his execution, which was not just a hanging affair but a drawing and a quartering affair too – it's no good pretending his poem is fun to read, it isn't, it's a desolate lament, very much on one note – 'And now I live, and now my life is done' is pretty well the whole content, the burden of his song – there are nine cigarette ends in the ashtray, all since Victoria went to bed –

Spent a harmonious if sometimes excitable afternoon here, in the apartment, going through the play scene by scene with Nicholas Martin. By excitable I mean that we both enjoyed it, and laughed a great deal. He has a hooting and highly contagious laugh, he's also very observant, and remembers and is good at describing gestures and expressions. Although I love things that make me laugh, I rather wish I didn't actually have to laugh, the physical part of it has become quite difficult, no doubt because of my smoking – the noise I make is a wheeze, that I try to keep shallow – the moment it goes deep into my lungs I begin to cough, the cough goes on and on, then I become dizzy, light-headed and I think I'm going to faint. Anyone who wanted to murder me would simply have to say three funny things in a row, so that I couldn't get my breath back long enough. Or perhaps I'd go into a coma, and stay in it for years, somehow that would be more ignominious than actually dying of laughter, and far worse for Victoria, who would find herself having to explain to people how it had come about that I was lying there alive but to all intents and purposes quite dead – 'It happened because he laughed too much at something that Nicholas Martin said' – and supposing they found the nerve to ask what Nicholas Martin had said, and supposing she'd actually been there and had heard the jokes and witticisms and seen me laugh, then collapse laughing, then lapse into unconsciousness, making dreadful little gasping-wheezing-laughing noises, and then supposing that she told them what he'd said – what would they do? They could scarcely rock with robust, healthy-lunged laughter, it would be unseemly, surely, but they couldn't not laugh, it would make my coma even more pathetic if it had been caused by my laughing at something that other people didn't find at all funny. I imagine they'd have to laugh politely while nodding sombrely, quite a difficult trick to pull off. Probably Victoria would suggest, without actually lying, that I'd become comatose from an excess of thought for others, or from worrying about the state of the world.

Anyway it's good to be back on terms with Nicholas Martin – at least not to feel that he'd scale any nearby person just to avoid talking to me. I accompanied him down in the elevator and saw him into a cab. Just as I was closing the door on him he said something very quickly to the effect that he was sorry he'd been 'mad' at me, and then the cab sped off. I went to the smoking alley beside the hotel, and sat at the table I always sit at, opposite the side door into the hotel, with a Diet Coke, wondering whether I would ask him this evening why he'd been 'mad' at me, or would it be better to leave it? It was very pleasant sitting in the alley, it was mild with a light breeze, and people were coming up and down, they were all colours, shapes, sizes, such a variety that would once have struck me as typical of New York and one of the things about it that I most loved, but now of course it's also typical of London, it was just as if I were sitting at my usual table on Holland Park Avenue. I felt the same sort of mood, that suspended mood when you know there's much to worry about but you can't quite remember what it is – not exactly serenity, more a gentle vacancy of spirit.

UP IN LIGHTS AND FURTHERMORE

We went downtown together, Victoria and I, though we were going to different theatres – I to the Booth to see *Butley* for the sixth or seventh preview, she to a neighbouring theatre, just around the corner from the Booth, to see the new production of *A Chorus Line*. We got off at the corner of Eighth and 45th, and stood there, quite still, holding each other by the hand as we stared up at the frame that towered from the roof of the Booth that was infinitely more imposing even than the last time we'd gazed at it and had tried to imagine how it would look when lit up, my name in lights – because now at last it was actually lit up, and there, glittering and sparkling, were the words NATHAN LANE, and underneath that the word IN, and underneath that the word

BUTLEY. 'So,' I said calmly, trying not to squeeze my wife's hand more savagely than was absolutely necessary, 'so. There you have it. My name not up in lights, after all.' 'Still, the play's in lights,' she pointed out. 'Although,' she added, 'they could scarcely just put Nathan Lane. They'd have to put that he's in something.' I admit that I was childishly disappointed. I really had longed to see my name in lights. But why 'childishly' come to think about it? It seems to me a perfectly proper and adult disappointment. In fact, I can't imagine children wanting to see their names in lights, well, not normal children, anyway, by which I mean of course children of my generation. Children of today, who are brought up almost from birth to crave celebrity, and are mostly abnormal by the standards of my day, would no doubt love to see their names in lights, although whether they would be able to recognize their names without having them read out is another matter. Anyway, I've decided not to be ashamed of wanting to see my name in lights, although I must try to get over being ashamed of not seeing it in lights. It seems to me, however I look at it, that I must have failed somewhere along the line, that I'm caught in a kind of vicious circle – my name doesn't go up in lights because, quite frankly, I'm not famous enough, and therefore not worthy of the bulbs, electricity, space, etc. But the reason I'm not famous enough is because my name never goes into lights. I'm convinced that if people got used to seeing my name in lights they would begin to recognize it in other spheres of life. In fact, their eyes would light up from the memory of a lit-up name when I was being introduced to them, and we would be spared, on both sides, the kind of ghastly conversation that proceeds from my having to identify myself as a playwright – 'Might I have seen anything you've written?' someone will ask, which forces me to offer a list of plays – and with each title they dip their heads in embarrassment at not recognizing it, or occasionally exclaim – 'Oh yes, I think I saw that one, it had Peter O'Toole in it, didn't it?' and no, I say, no, no, it didn't have Peter O'Toole in it – and if I name the actor who was in it, they might say, 'Oh, how odd that I missed it – I generally make a point of seeing anything with him in it, one of my favourite actors!' and with luck we can move on to remembering all the plays the famous actor has been in.

*

Victoria went off to see *A Chorus Line*, I stood between the hamburgers and the bottled water and talked to Nicholas Martin – really going over the conversation of the afternoon, reminding ourselves of the moments we wanted to pay particular attention to. We stood companionably near each other during the first act, which went well – or well enough, given that three mobile phones went off in the stalls that I could hear. It's a pretty good rule of thumb or whatever that twice as many mobile phones go off than I hear, as there are parts of the stalls, in the front to the far left and right, which are inaudible to those of us standing in the back. If I wrote about my feelings about every mobile phone I heard during a performance – how dark, bloody, murderous my thoughts – the most appalling thing about the people responsible is that they're not even embarrassed – one man, fleshily into his fifties with a thick mop of yellowish hair and a lissom young man beside him who might have been his nephew, in as much as he bore a resemblance – Fleshily's mobile went off just as the Edna scene was getting under way, it made a piercing chirruping noise, like a mad bird – he extracted it in leisurely fashion from his inner breast pocket, and handed it, without glancing at it, to Lissom, who looked at the screen, fiddled coolly, then muttered something to Fleshily as he handed it back to him. But apart from that – this was the thing – they seemed quite involved in what was going on on the stage, laughing and looking towards each other in appreciation. In other words I wouldn't have minded a whole theatre full of Fleshilies and Lissoms, minus their mobiles – cellphones, they're called here, don't forget. Or just cells. I sometimes wonder whether members of the audience cell each other during the performance to discuss the jokes, or the meaning of a line, or perhaps to remind each other of where they're going to have dinner.

In the interval we went to a nearby bar whose name I can never remember as it's too complicated, both a Christian name and a surname, and both of them quite ordinary. I can't say I like it much as it's generally crowded, every table full and everybody at every table shouting and laughing at the tops of their voices, with people also standing between the tables, also shouting and laughing at the tops of their voices – or it's completely empty apart from, say, a couple of tables, and another couple sitting at the bar, and a surplus of waiters, all talking in low voices, so that you feel that you have to talk in a low voice too, otherwise you will be overheard by showbiz journalists, who like, or so it's rumoured, to sit on the fringes of the rooms, in the shadows, hoping to pick up bits and pieces of conversations that they can publish to embarrassing effect – but in fact this evening it was, for once, just right – just enough people to ensure that you could speak at a normal level. I think we both felt very comfortable as we sat over our Diet Cokes and traded cellphone experiences, then discussed a few patches of Act One that needed attention, then aspects of Nathan's performance and then rose to go back to the theatre and then sat down again instead. We'd both, I think, had enough of previews for a while – or at least for this evening – or at least for the very next bit of it, because we agreed we'd go back sort of halfway through the second act, avoid the tension of waiting with the audience for the curtain to go up while overhearing things we didn't want to hear – It seemed like a good opportunity, if there's ever really a good opportunity for such matters – and so I said, 'You said this afternoon, when you were getting into the cab, that you were sorry you'd been mad at me yesterday.' 'Well, yes, I am,' he said. 'I am sorry.' 'Yes, well, that's good. I'm glad. But what were you mad at?' 'Oh,' he said. 'Oh. Well, yesterday I had to tell Eric he was fired. And it was pretty terrible. His parents and his friends were all coming to the first night. You know – none of them's even been to a Broadway show before, and so – he cried, and said, "What am I going to tell my mum?"' I thought about this. 'But do you think he shouldn't have been fired?' 'Oh, he had to be fired. No question of it. And I should have done it before you came. And then I kind of hoped he'd be all right. I kept telling myself he was getting better, and believing it, until you spoke up. And I knew it was true. Everybody knew it, really.' 'Well,' I said, 'if I'd been here from the beginning of rehearsals and got to know him I probably wouldn't have spoken up.' I really don't know if this is true or not. Certainly it had helped that I'd only had one conversation with Eric, although that had been one conversation too many, as I'd found him touching and likeable. As I suppose one would find any young man who was in a sense already posthumous. Like Chidiock Tichborne, really, when you think about it. Anyway, Chidiock Tichborne was long dead, Eric had left the building, Nicholas Martin had had a rotten day which he'd been unable not to share with me – and so the conversation moved on, to other things, and eventually he went back to the Booth, and a few minutes later I followed, smoking a cigarette along the way, and got in and sidled to a spot along the back, and watched the new Gardner come on stage, where he looked eerily like the old Gardner, the way he stood, his expressions, the same blond hair, and almost the same voice – the difference was he was in every respect stronger, more present – even his blond hair was blonder, more assertive, and Nathan was seeing him and playing to him, and therefore I felt much better about the end of the play. He got a good hand, the new Gardner, and even one or two low-key bravos and the yip in yippee! But that might have been family, of course, or a partner. Fleshily and Lissom gave him a good clap – no, unfortunately put – applauded him vigorously, as they did all the actors, then went wild when Nathan took his curtain – not bravos or yippees, but both of them clapping their hands above their heads and thrusting out their chests, and I don't think they were family, Fleshily and Lissom, wrong physical types, but there was no doubt they'd enjoyed their evening. I found myself looking on them with doting eyes as I slipped out behind them. They had a limousine waiting on the kerb on 45th, with a man in a peaked cap holding the door open for them. As they clambered in Lissom put the cell to his ear, then passed it to Fleshily as the car slid into the traffic.

SKIDDING ON VOMIT

Most of the recent nights I've come back to the hotel, and sat with a pad in front of me, thinking about how to describe the day, or whether I want to. I put down a few words, then stop, look out of the window, down at the little dots of the car lights going up and down the street – our street – and the sight stirs a memory that doesn't stay, as if it's nudging me to a memory beyond it, and so I flounder, look down at the traffic, then put on the Mozart and wait for Victoria if she's out, or for Stephen Hollis, an old friend who put on several of my plays when he was artistic director at the Palace Theatre, Watford, in the 1970s, then directed three, I think it was, in London, and three or four in New York, where he now lives, still directing and teaching drama at a university in a town nearby. Stephen sometimes joins us for dinner, sometimes afterwards, at the large, outside café on the corner of 50th Street which takes its style from Parisian pavement cafés. You can get wine, beers, Cognacs, *pâtisseries* and coffees, then sit over them for as long as you want. In the section we go to, which is the one in which you are almost sure to find a table straight away, you are allowed to smoke. There are always clean ashtrays on the tables, and the people who come to use them are mostly regulars, who don't bother to hang about until the *maître d'* comes to escort them, they stroll straight on through, their cigars and cigarettes unlit but ready between their lips. They never come in smoking, they relish sitting down first, then lighting up with a degree of ceremony, but there are a few who have become so furtive and cowed that they don't really believe, in spite of the evidence provided by a dozen or so tables of smokers, that it's allowed. They stand at the entrance apprehensively, waiting for the *maître d'*, who after midnight tends to be a robotic but quite pretty Russian girl, and they ask her, 'Hey, is it all right to smoke?' and she smiles in a friendly, slightly unseeing fashion, and says, 'Yes, yes, you can smoke, yes, it's OK, yes', and leads them to a table, and when she's sat them down she moves the ashtray a few inches, then turns it around a few times, not complete revolutions but partial revolutions almost as if it were a combination lock and the top of the table the door of a safe. It sometimes makes me think of chastity belts, though I doubt if chastity belts have combination locks, they'd have neat little padlocks, I'd guess, made of gold with pearls inlaid – well, the female ones, I can't imagine the male ones – anyway, she creates the sense, with these needy and ill-at-ease smokers, that whatever had to be opened has been opened, they may now smoke, but they check several times before taking out their cigarettes and lighters. Perhaps they'd relax and light up with more of a flourish if they weren't conscious of being closely watched by an ill-kempt, elderly man, I suspect that I'm a clumsy and ostentatious observer, I know that I stare directly at people. When Victoria catches me at it she says that it's more like a glare than a stare, an accusing glare that must be alarming to those it's fixed on – the fact that I'm smoking clearly doesn't reassure them, perhaps they see me as an *agent provocateur*, I don't know what they see me as, probably just an ill-natured old man, a sort of Evelyn Waugh but with small, malevolent eyes instead of protuberant, indignant ones.

I wrote too soon about Liz McCann being on the way to recovery. I suppose it was having written about her that made me think of her when I went to the matinée – I was hanging about in my usual spot, smoking, when a young lady from the McCann office came over with an envelope containing my tickets – I always have trouble finding something to say to her, she's small and pleasantly brisk in her manner, but she always, on giving me the envelope with the tickets in, stands rooted, as if waiting for me to say something to follow the thank you that I've just said. We sometimes stand there for up to a minute, she staring up at me, I bending over her. Then she says, 'Well, I'd better get back,' and goes through the stage door or towards the lobby. This afternoon, though, I said thank you, and then I said, 'Oh, and how's Liz getting on?' and she said, 'Oh, didn't you know, she's broken her leg.' 'Yes,' I said, 'but it's getting better, isn't it?' 'No,' she said, 'she's had another accident,' and she told me that a few evenings ago, at her home, Liz had skidded on some cat vomit and taken a tumble down the stairs. I think she said down the stairs, or have I just added that because that's how I imagined it – Liz McCann heaving herself along on her crutches, coming to the top of the stairs, putting her foot down on an unnoticed puddle of mess, then whoops! and crash. But it may have happened quite differently, of course. I don't think the ticket lady told me how it happened. I could scarcely pursue the matter once I'd got the essential fact of her skidding on cat vomit.

Apart from that, I enjoyed the play very much.

THREE SCORE AND TEN

It's nearly four in the afternoon and I'm sitting at a low table in our hotel suite, Suite 1410, writing this down into a pad on my lap while a youngish man, short and dark, with a ragged goatee and holes in his socks and a broad Boston accent, is taking photographs of me – posed photographs – he keeps putting me into completely phoney and unnatural positions, and when I break free to do something that is actually natural, e.g. lighting a cigarette, he stabs a word out – a word like 'Freeze!' or 'Hold!' – while I'm in the middle of the action – he's a very courteous, slightly anxious-mannered man of Greek origin, and you wouldn't think he had such sharp peremptoriness in him, but he has managed to keep me frozen in positions that become phoney immediately I've taken them up, and he keeps me in them until every part of me begins to ache, and reminding me of the various punishments to which I was subjected by my powdered and pouchy-eyed prep-school teacher Mr Burn, who most particularly liked to keep me in positions that were no doubt eloquent for him. He would walk, slightly crouched, around and around me, watching me, much like this photographer, but of course my reactions now are totally different – instead of shy and furtive and tortured pleasure, a kind of self-mangling self-love, I feel a terrible weariness, the ache is the ache of age protesting, aged muscles, creaking limbs, stiffening back – the difference between being eleven and knowingly desired and seventy and being photographed – vanity the only connecting element –

Actually I wasn't actually quite seventy when I wrote the above, but I am now, and have been since midnight four hours ago. We celebrated my becoming it at a restaurant called La Miseria, something like that anyway, on 48th Street, between Broadway and Eighth. It was recommended by Nathan, who'd had one of his forties birthdays there a few years back, and it seemed OK when we explored it. The staff, or cast really, were entirely Italian – I mean, not simply every one of them, but every bit of every one of them, no one spoke English fluently, some of them seemed not to speak it at all, and the portly, no, roly-poly laughing Italian who was in charge of parties spoke lots of half phrases and clichés that he managed to make adequate to his needs and ours – so his reply to our anxious enquiries as to whether there was really enough room in the back half of the restaurant which was where he proposed we should hold our party was 'OK. Sure. Yeah. Be all right on the night, trust yes?' and there was so much merriness in him, he shook and rolled about with it, that we took him at his word, the one that mattered, and we did indeed trust – well, Victoria did indeed, I only did in patches – 'I'm sure it'll be all right, as he says, just don't see how we're going to fit nearly fifty people in that small space', to which, from Victoria, 'He's very experienced, and he wants to do it, and he won't want to let Nathan down.' 'People who let people down don't usually want to' was my usual answer to this – in fact I can't think of anyone out of all the many I personally have let down that I actually wanted to, or set out to, let down. So this *maître d'* etc. certainly seemed determined to let us down on the night of the party. Victoria and Stephen Hollis and I arrived at just after 10 p.m. Most of our guests were at the theatre, either watching *Butley* or acting in it, and as the curtain comes down at 10.15 and it's a five-minute walk from the theatre they could be expected from around 10.30 on. So what did we see in the back part of the restaurant, the set-apart-for-the-party part, at 10.15 but two long tables at which were sitting, at each table, about a dozen diners. Italians. Of the sort that roll spaghetti around their forks while raising glasses and shouting loving messages across the room, some of them sounded like loving birthday messages – yes, two long tables of birthday revellers in the space reserved for my forty or so birthday guests.

My brother Nigel and his wife, Barbara, had flown in from Toronto, and had come along early, with Stephen, to help seat the guests and settle my nerves. So there were five of us waiting to receive forty-eight – I''ve just checked with Victoria – it was forty-eight guests. Well, minus the five of us, come to think of it. So forty-three guests in a room currently occupied by about twenty noisy Italian diners, celebrating, from the sound of them, a birthday per head.

I went out on the pavement and smoked, not being allowed, of course, to do it anywhere else, even on my birthday. *Signor il padrone* came out on the pavement and smoked with me, not anxiously, as I did, but patiently and benevolently, a man who enjoyed his cigarette wherever he might be, and in whatever company – in this case a suppuratingly angry man of exactly seventy years of age – now here is an odd thing about age, this proprietor, let me call him Giuseppe, no, that's too long, can't be bothered to write that out each time, what about Gino? Yes, Gino, Gino was about, I should say, fifty years old, no more, perhaps a month or so less, yet I had the distinct sense that he was older than me by more than a few months, by about thirty years, in fact – I don't mean that I felt him to be a hundred, but that I felt that he was my senior, in responsibility, in authority, in the kind of maturity that counts, in life as opposed to years, as it were, and therefore, though I was livid with him –

No, let me go back to that thought, about my being in physical terms about twenty years older, but feeling in real terms, in life terms, that I was thirty years his junior – I realize, now I've put it down, that this has become quite a common experience with me, and it's not a recent one, to do with my being seventy. I've had it most of my adult life, as if at a certain stage I just stopped adding years to my sense of my self, and have gone on seeing people, people I don't know, from a constantly juvenile perspective. But what do they see? What did Gius – no, Gino see, but a seventy-year-old – he knew my age to the day, as he was organizing the party that celebrated it – a seventy-year-old Englishman being petulant and ill-tempered on the pavement. Or did he see a noble wreck of an English gentleman, irritated and impatient but only in a manner that became his years? 'Eet weel be OK. They are frands,' he kept saying to me. 'They weel be gone in tree four meenits.' The most infuriating thing about him was his smiling certainty, which turned out to be completely justified – I went for a very short walk, about three, four minutes, and when I got back Gino was holding open his restaurant door and ushering his frands on to the street, and beyond him, in the back part of the restaurant, his waiters were converting the two long tables into four smaller tables, moving all the other small tables out of the wings and into place, putting down the tablecloths, the knives and forks etc., and at the upstairs table, in the alcove, I could see Victoria laughing and relaxed with Nigel, Barbara, Stephen –

So it should have been all right. How now to explain that it wasn't – not in my soul it wasn't. It wasn't really the problem with Gino or the unwanted diners, it wasn't simply that I didn't want to be seventy – it was as if I wasn't there, or as if I was at an oblique angle to what was going on, an oblique angle to my birthday, to the event itself and the people who'd come, a number of them from far away. The food was very good, everybody said, and there was certainly enough to drink, perhaps more than enough if the strange suggestions and propositions put to me by an actress I was once very close to were anything to go by. And it passed, it all passed, this too has passed –

Perhaps the problem for parties with me is mundane – that I no longer drink, I'm not allowed to smoke, therefore etc. But what is unarguably true about this particular party is that now that it's over and retrospective I find that not only can I enjoy it at last, but that I'm moved by the memory of it, and grateful that people came, that friends came, and that I have a wife like Victoria to organize it. What do I mean, a wife like Victoria? She is not like Victoria she is Victoria. Is my wife.

ALAN, NATHAN AND ALAN

Something else from the party that has stuck like a burr in my mind, and that I wish I could dislodge – several people who had seen Alan's Butley on stage in London or New York or who have seen the film, and who have now seen Nathan's Butley, came up to me and asked, in rather too low and intimate a manner, as if they were prying into family matters, which Butley I preferred, Nathan's or Alan's. And in fact I felt that they were prying into family matters – being asked to choose between two blood relatives or – or – absurd, of course, because it's a reasonable question to ask, even though it's one I can't answer reasonably, at least not in terms of preferences, although I could, perhaps, in terms of comparisons, elementary comparisons, starting with Nathan. His performance is extraordinary, not because it's immensely funny and full of bravura comic moments with impeccable timing – the things that one would expect from Nathan, the great comedian – but because there's a darkness and a loneliness to it as of a man living out the last hours of his life. One feels that for this Butley the loss of Joey is a death of the spirit, from which there can be no resurrection. For Alan, not only an attractive man but a beautiful one, in whose eyes the light never quite went out, one felt that tomorrow – no, not tomorrow, he'd be too hung-over, and the next day too and perhaps the day after that – but anyway before the week was out he'd be on the rampage once more, back at his desk despoiling students' essays, at his office door blocking their entrance, on the telephone buggering up the college's administration, above all in and out of Joey's new office – back in his life, turning it into a chaos. Alan's Butley was an exhilarating experience, really, his triumphant curtain calls an extension of his last moments on the stage – on Broadway women came armed with flowers, which they flung at him as he bowed and beamed, and whatever you thought the character would be doing the next evening, you knew the actor would be back for his flowers. It seemed to me a miracle that Nathan was back for the next performance, I would have looked for him where I would have looked for his Butley, exhausted and drained, adrift in the night. Well, these are extravagant and generalized statements, I know, and subject to mundane qualifications – some nights, when the mischief is on him, Nathan is more Alan, just as some nights Alan prefigured Nathan in his final moments of desolation, clutching at the curtain-call bouquets as if he'd been thrown lifesavers, wrapping his arms around them, and hugging them to his stomach. It would be meaningless to say which of the performances was better. If one had been able to see them on alternate nights over a couple of weeks one couldn't have kept a scorecard, they were different experiences that emanated from different cores, and when they were bad, they were bad as I would expect them to be bad, with Nathan demanding more pity from the audience than the audience had at its disposal, Alan coasting along with too many flourishes and sometimes the hint of a smirk –

Well, of course I didn't go into any of this at the party, muttering vaguely to the effect that really the only performance I could see at the moment was Nathan's, it blocked out all other performances, even Alan's, especially while we were in preview, and indicated that perhaps there were other topics of conversation, indeed other plays. And it was a bit odd, really, to have people asking whether I preferred Alan's or Nathan's Butley with Nathan sitting only just out of earshot and highly visible, having just a short while ago given his performance. There was an elderly actor with a withering tendency when discussing other actors, and who has become slightly deaf, and you would think from his behaviour slightly blind too, as he seemed to be looking straight towards Nathan when he said – 'But Alan's performance is on film. I've got the DVD. I'll send it over to your hotel, if you want.' I said, rather tersely, that I couldn't imagine why I would want it. 'So you can compare the two performances. You can come back from Nathan's in the theatre and put on Alan's on film, see them consecutively.' I said yes, and there was probably some way I could get the film up on my mobile, so I could actually watch Alan's film performance and Nathan's stage performance simultaneously. I think he thought this a pretty stupid idea.

Alan though –

Of course I have the DVD at home, somewhere in the basement, along with a lot of other memorabilia. The film was meant to be – in accordance with the avowed intention of Ely Landau, the somewhat messianic producer – a filmed record of the stage performance, but given cinematic authenticity by being filmed in a studio, where the camera could travel to all the secret nooks and crannies of the specially built office, as well as the nooks and crannies of the actors' faces. It wasn't, in other words, a mere static filming of one of Alan's theatre performances, but a scrupulous rendering of the performance in cinematic terms. I saw it on its first public showing and remember having only one clear critical thought – that the playwright should have turned himself into a screenwriter at least to the extent of cutting twenty minutes or so out of the script, but I don't believe I knew then, and certainly don't know now, which twenty minutes. I've never been tempted down to the basement to forage around for the DVD because the thought of having it in my hand, putting it in the DVD player, then sitting calmly watching Alan alive, breathing, laughing, subsiding exhausted, remembering the days I sat in the studio observing the various takes, then sat with him during the interminable settings-up between scenes – it was odd enough at the time, just to be in what was an exact reconstruction of my daily office, but when I sat beside Alan he would be wearing a version of the suit I wore to my office, and when he entered my office he was wearing a copy of my mackintosh and carrying in his hand my actual briefcase, as he'd done every night on stage at the Criterion Theatre, it had become for him a sort of talisman, my briefcase. He'd also borrowed my walk, some of my gestures and my manner of talking, so I was told – who knows how they appear to walk, what habitual gestures they make, how their voice sounds when they speak, but I had an odd sensation about which I can't be precise – I didn't feel I was being stolen from or imitated or in some sense doubled, nor that there was some conspiracy between the actor and the director which involved me from which I was also excluded – actually what I felt was an extremely heightened sense of the shame that I always feel when a piece of my writing is being acted out, the only approximate image for which is a variation on the familiar nightmare of discovering oneself naked in a public place, the variation being the element of deliberate intent – that one of me has positively and arrogantly strutted naked on to a public stage, while another of me is an aghast spectator, unable to speak out confessionally and penitentially. The result is a jumbled self, yes, that's me, look at him, isn't he something! Please, please forgive me, I know not what he does – that sort of jumble of self, of selves really – well now, that's a heightened version of the heightened version of shame that I experienced when I watched Alan giving his version of me in the filming of *Butley*. It wasn't happening in a dream or a nightmare, it was happening in a recognizable world of everyday consciousness, and when someone, usually Harold, asked me what thoughts I had about what I was seeing, I answered in a composed enough fashion, and probably tried to demonstrate my eye for detail – 'Just wondering whether those essays look right on Butley's desk, a bit too neatly piled, mmm?' and Harold would run an alert eye over the essays, shuffle them about a little. Sometimes Alan and I would go to the canteen, where he would have me buy for him three or four large chocolate biscuits rather gaudily packaged in the shape of wagon-wheels that he was too embarrassed to buy for himself. So we both had our embarrassments, but Alan being Alan passed them on in uncomplicated fashion.

In some obvious respects I could never be confused with Alan, especially by myself. He was the most beautiful and attractive man, of course, but there was also the sexual mystery of him. Such a solid, purposeful-seeming, peasant-like body, so male, but the suggestion of something soft and feminine in his smile, the subtle and pleasing physical expression of the cruder psychological truth, that Alan was all over the place emotionally. He had long, painful affairs with men and longer, more painful affairs with women, and sometimes with both simultaneously. It was as if he never knew, from one minute to the next, what his sexual direction was, or as if the sexual nature of his next, intended partner was incidental to a greater need, the precise nature of which left him baffled but not particularly tormented. The painfulness of his affairs with both men and women came from trying, almost immediately after starting them, to find a way of ending them. He would emerge from the protracted and ghastly struggle of separating himself from her or him with exhausted triumph, like a football player whose team has just won the cup, while the other party – well, it would depend on which sex they were. As a matter of fact I can't really speak of the men, I only met them long after the tumultuous part of the relationship was over, sometimes years and years after, when they would pop up again in Alan's life and be introduced with impersonal warmth, as if they were distant cousins rather than the ex-lovers that he'd imitated, analysed and caricatured with comic and bitter brio that would give way to irritable confusion – 'What did they want? Why did they start it?' From time to time he would attribute base motives – they were after material goods (a car, perhaps?) or a connection with his glamorous reputation. These dark speculations would usually conclude in a comic gesture of resignation, and the admission of a suspicion that perhaps he himself wasn't really very interested in sex, except as the giving and receiving of short bursts of affection and pleasure. I think that was the truth of it, that he liked men's and women's bodies mostly for the comfort they could give him, physical intimacy bringing a more intense form of the companionship he loved – and of course for some years after his wife Victoria's death his only companions at night were his two spaniels, who slept on his bed I think, and to whom he was devoted. One, a marvellously fluid runner, perished under the wheels of a car when chasing a cat across the road. The other survived to a considerable age, becoming incontinent and senile. He would say when he went home at night to first the pair of them, and then to just the one of them, something along the lines of – well, what more did a man want after all, but creatures who were unchanging in their needs and affections. The thought of his preference for dogs over lovers made him laugh sardonically but cheerfully – and always there was his work on stage and screen, where he was such a complicated and romantic presence –

But really, what do I know? The above is merely gossip, or more accurately merely a report of Alan's gossip about himself, and it leaves out entirely the main story of his life, the death of his wife Victoria, his devotion to his twin sons, Tristan and Benedick, the death of Tristan – there was an afternoon one Easter in Lyme Regis. My first wife, Beryl, and I in my father's house in the town, Alan and Victoria in small hotel just up from the Cobb. It was a gorgeously soft and warm afternoon, Beryl and I were walking on the beach when they suddenly appeared, running hand in hand down the slope towards us, they had come looking for us, had something to tell us. 'We're very happy,' Victoria said. 'Aren't we, Alan?' Alan said that they were, and his beam confirmed it. 'You see,' Victoria said, 'we've just made love.' They spoke of it as of a rare and mysterious event. And in truth it was, as it had scarcely ever happened before – they'd been married about a year – and was, according to Alan, never to happen again – and it was right that their manner should have been both ecstatic and ceremonial, because what they were announcing turned out to be not only an almost unique act of love but a conception. They were for those few hours on the beach unambiguously happy and proud, they looked almost as if they belonged to each other.

THE PRODUCER CALLS

I had a brief encounter with Liz McCann this afternoon, at the matinée. She was in a wheelchair, in Shubert Alley, outside the box office. There were several people clustered about her, among them Nicholas Martin, whose head when standing was on a level with Liz's when sitting, which at least made conversation between them physically easy. Nicholas Martin was talking a lot and laughing a lot, he has a way of throwing his head back when he laughs, have I described this before? His spectacle lenses seem to glitter with mirth and his teeth, which he bares, sparkle with it – he is, when he laughs, a completely laughing creature. I couldn't tell whether Liz McCann was laughing with him, as she had her back to me, and I couldn't tell who was pushing her wheelchair when the little party moved towards the theatre lobby, it was almost as if she were being propelled collectively, by a small mob. I finished my cigarette and went in. She had been rolled to the head of an aisle at the back of the stalls. Her partner, a stout and very pleasant English woman of about Liz's age, I should imagine, who coincidentally walks with a stick, was standing beside the wheelchair. She called me over and bent to Liz McCann's ear, to tell her that here I was, standing behind her – given her position it was difficult to get into her line of vision, she had to twist her head at an awkward angle to see me. I asked her how she was, and she said, 'Coming along, coming along,' slightly irritably, clearly tired of the question. I said I hoped she would enjoy the show, she said she hoped she would too. It was a bit strained, this exchange, I had the feeling that she was angry about something – well, who could blame her, to skid on cat vomit and break your leg just as you were recovering from a broken leg – anyway, I didn't try to stretch the conversation, and moved away in search of Nicholas Martin. I spotted him an instant before the lights went down. He was sitting at the end of an aisle, whispering anxiously to his tall young assistant, who was taking notes – but about what? The show hadn't begun – perhaps on the conversation he'd had with Liz McCann?

It was the usual full house, with people standing beside me at the back. I thought the show was distinctly sluggish in places – some pauses that had been cut reintroduced themselves, in the way that pauses do, they're often as hard to exterminate as a virus, if you get them out of one scene, they turn up in another, where they've never been before, which sometimes makes one feel that they actually breed. Nevertheless it was OK really, it seemed to me, and is certainly much better, much more fully expressed than it was, say, four nights ago – previews don't get better from performance to performance, in my experience, but in fits and starts, with occasional little steps backwards before forwards again. The audience was fine at the curtain, with yips, bravos etc. for Nathan, but as for Liz McCann and her reaction –

I kept half an eye on the back of her head during both acts, but it didn't tell me much – it didn't seem to bob about when the audience laughed, though, and once or twice I saw it shake, slowly and possibly negatively, but body language is difficult to read when you don't have the front of the body to work with – Liz McCann might have been smiling and even chortling all through the show until we got to Nathan alone and forlorn, when she might have wept a little – still, it seemed to me wise to keep out of sight at the interval and speed off at the end – Nicholas Martin can deal with Liz McCann, it's his job, after all –

Hah! I've just put down the phone on Liz McCann. I don't mean I hung up on her, it's my policy never to hang up on people, however offensive you think they're trying to be, because it's almost a physical act, like a blow. I don't believe she hung up on me, either, it's just that her goodbye and the clicking-off noise were almost simultaneous – well, the 'good' and the click off were simultaneous, I'm taking the 'bye' as understood – she's probably in a considerable amount of pain from her leg, and also there'll be the painkillers – so hurting and a bit muzzy would explain why she was so curt, she couldn't cope with a long conversation – what there was of it went like this: 'Simon, it's Liz McCann.' 'Hello, Liz, how –' 'Simon, I think you better get out your scissors and make some judicious cuts.' 'Oh, really? Well, where exactly should I –' 'Don't know. Just make some judicious cuts. Better do it straight away, Simon. Good –' click. 'Bye' understood. Although perhaps it was boy, as in 'good boy' as in 'There's a good boy!' In a moment I'll phone Nicholas Martin, and tell him what she said, although I expect he knows already, they probably discussed it after the show yesterday. I'll also tell him that I've no intention of making any cuts, as far as I'm concerned any cuts would be completely injudicious. Now. Do it now.

Done it. He agrees with me. We discussed the need to close down further on pauses and to speed up various passages and speeches, in other words to go on as we're going on – and to hell with Liz McCann really, when it comes down to it, though we didn't actually say that out loud, at least not to each other.

QUESTIONS. PERTINENT AND IMPERTINENT, FROM MY WIFE

The other night, after she'd come to a preview, Victoria said that she thought *Butley* was probably the most misogynist play that she'd ever seen. Also she thought it was strongly homosexual in its feelings and sensibility. I asked her if she thought it had therefore been written by a misogynistic homosexual, and would that therefore strike her as an accurate description of her husband. I didn't say this in a particularly abusive or threatening manner or in a misogynistic or homosexual manner, at least I don't think I did, because I was quite anxious to pursue the subject a little, having – I admit it – been coming to something like the same thoughts myself. I can't say that in myself I detect any impulses that I could categorize as homosexual or misogynistic – on the other hand, by his fruits shall ye know him, and there is my fruit, early fruit, in the form of a play that has as its central story the desperate attempt of a male university lecturer to maintain emotional possession of a younger and homosexual male colleague, furthermore the play teems with – that can't be the right phrase, 'teems with', 'is rife with' doesn't seem appropriate either, but get to what it teems with, or is rife with, and let's face it, if it's not misogyny it's the next best thing – So let's leave it at that, after all the early fruit is not the only fruit, there are lots of later fruits, mature, which are full of love for women, compassion for them too, and as for the works of my dotage, the fruit that follows the mature fruit – yes, better leave it at that.

A LETTER TO NATHAN

It's all over, really, this New York experience, apart from the reviews, which are already out, but which we haven't yet read. Victoria's in bed, asleep, I've turned off my mobile and told the hotel operator not to put any calls through, as I don't want news of the reviews until tomorrow, I want first of all to write a letter to Nathan, and then, when I've done that, to get on with this – an account of the first night. But I may skip that, write the letter to Nathan, and go to bed. Or sit smoking, and listening to Mozart.

I've written the letter to Nathan. I've smoked three cigarettes. I've listened to half a CD of Mozart. I've also taken a sleeping pill and two co-proxamol. I feel tired and am a little dizzy, but here I am, nevertheless, with my pen in my hand, and a befuddled sense of a duty yet to be completed. Begin at the end is perhaps the best route, going backwards from here, rather than forwards from there, partly because I can't really work out which is the appropriate there to start from, every backwards point from which I might go forwards immediately suggests another backwards point, so that ultimately I'd start from my birth, or go backwards from there to my parents' birth, it would therefore take me more than a few lifetimes to get forward to the moment when I sat down to write to Nathan at the round table in the kitchen area of this preposterous apartment with its views over New York, which is obscurely magnificent at four in the morning, a triangle of deep caverns at the bottom of which specks of light move up and down, and across – oh Nathan, Nathan!

It was actually a bit like that – oh Nathan, Nathan! – the impulse to write to him – it was something to do with the way he looked at the party, not at all like an accomplished and experienced performer of some fifty years – his suit looked so smart, and his face so clean and his hair so shiny – really he looked like a spruced-up, anxious child at an adult's very important birthday party – and actually it was difficult to say who was giving the party – there seemed to be a lot of elegant young women and men who greeted us once we'd got into a dining room the size of a banqueting hall – they greeted me as if they knew me, though I'm sure I've never seen any of them before, and ushered us to one of the large round tables which had my name on it, then pointed to long tables to the side where there was food and drink in abundance, and so perfectly arranged that though a lot of people were busying themselves with plates and glasses, there wasn't the hint of a queue – I have simply no idea how many guests' tables there were, sixty, seventy, a hundred? – the eye couldn't take it all in, the sweep and glitter of it, table after table with winking cutlery and sparkling glasses and there was enough space between the tables so that people could move easily about, dropping in on friends here and there – it was, the whole thing, I was going to say magnificent, and it was, and it was also grotesque, and it kept reminding me of a scene that I knew well but couldn't quite place, from a book, I think, and not a film, not simply because of the opulence on display, and the opulence of the people, most of them sumptuously dressed in dinner jackets and gowns and so forth – I mean one's seen scenes like that in lots of films, and generally something momentous happens to disturb the vibrant, worldly and organized glamour – a gun is fired, a man collapses with a red spot on his otherwise spotless shirt front, women scream, men yell and dash about, some of them with guns they've had concealed in holsters under their armpits, and then a little gang of men run with their arms around a shrouded bundle who is in fact the president of the United States being hurried away from an attempted assassination – of course *In the Line of Fire*, Clint Eastwood as the president's bodyguard and John Malkovich the leisurely psychopath with a grudge against the government and a self-damaging fondness for the Clint Eastwood character – and of course *Towering Inferno*, when another, equally magnificent banquet with famous character actors scattered around the tables, thrillingly unready for the fire that the audiences know will presently sweep on to the screen and burn everything up, including a large handful of the famous character actors – much of the fun of the film comes from 'a spot the survivor game' – which of these famous actors will go first, which will be there, drenched and sooty, at the end – really one wishes they'd made many versions of the film, each one with a different schedule, and possibly a very limited edition, a collector's item, in which Steve McQueen and William Holden are crisped in the fire's first moments, and that actor with the atrocious wig is left standing on the pavement, surveying the hosed-down rubble of what was once – well, two hours ago – the proudest and tallest building in San Francisco. I'm not saying that at the *Butley* first-night party one found oneself yearning for a blazing gun, or a purging blaze, but there was something one yearned for, something there was that wasn't there – I think this is why it reminded me more of a book than a film – I mean although I've only managed to remember *In the Line of Fire* and *Towering Inferno*, I could think without stirring my brain of at least five more films with imperilled banquets – Buñel's *Exterminating Angel*, any film made about the Battle of Waterloo or Napoleon's invasion of Moscow, *Giant* (the peril there being James Dean's performance) – but none of these quite caught the atmosphere of uncompleted luxury, of almost irrelevant opulence and display, the sense that the real story hadn't arrived, or perhaps that the real purpose hadn't arrived and never would, whatever narrative there was, was the narrative of separate tables – all the producers' tables, one imagines ten or so, the lighting designer's table, the set designer's table, the various actors' tables – all kinds of things could be happening at those tables, marriages breaking up, new adulteries developing, children planning their parents' anniversary parties or deaths, so forth and so forth, they might have been terrifically interesting stories in all sorts of ways, far beyond the reach of my imagination, but they weren't subplots to a strong, coherent narrative because, as I've already said, there wasn't one – it's almost as if there would have been no clear answer to the question, 'Why are we here?' although the ostensible answer would, of course, have been, 'To celebrate the first night of *Butley*.' So perhaps what was predominantly missing that one yearned for was the spirit of celebration – there was a lot of noise, people shouted and clapped their hands at each other and embraced and laughed but these didn't seem like celebratory acts, more like tribal routines. We'd come into this remarkable restaurant, if it was a restaurant, by way of an enormous lobby, walking down a passage formed by two ropes, on either side of which were showbiz journalists and photographers, most of them quaint and middle-aged, with academic stoops or hunched-up shoulders – not at all like the occasions I've seen on television, which were all hustling intimacy and a 'Hey, Si, whaddya think of Nay-tan?' sort of approach, instead these journalists had a formal, rather stilted way of addressing you: 'Please, Mr Gray, could I just have a word?' – and I would be escorted over the rope, a matter of raising first one foot and then the other higher than comes naturally to me, and then standing still and smiling with a few cameras aimed at my face while replying to a number of carefully thought-out but dowdy questions. In fact, I had the feeling that I was attending a rather austere postgraduate ceremony rather than a high-octane first-night fanfare – I had to do about six of these almost identical interviews, the middle-aged, bespectacled man being replaced by a middle-aged bespectacled woman, and then a drooping sort of woman followed by a drooping sort of man. I found it quite easy to relax into the role of playwright emeritus, and wouldn't have minded a gown and a mortarboard, a scroll in my hand – it did cross my mind that this might be an elaborate trap to catch another preening, clapped-out, opportunistic Brit but it clearly wasn't, because for two of the interviews Nathan was brought to my side – he'd done a dozen or so on his own before we arrived, and there was no change of tone when we were interviewed jointly, Mr Gray and Mr Lane was how it went, with discreet enquiries into our relationship, when and where had it started? How it had come to this blossoming? – so a quick trudge back to New Haven where we'd first met, on to Los Angeles, where we'd suffered together at the Matrix Theatre, ninety-nine seats and nobody gets paid, on to our triumph in New York, at the Promenade Theatre, 499 seats and a steady income for months and months – we'd both told the tale in separate interviews before the opening, and now we were telling it together before going off to our separate tables – he to sit with his two brothers and various friends, I to sit with my brother Nigel, his wife Barbara, my nephew Chris, my wife Victoria, and one of her nieces, Alice – I was very dull company, I expect, I wasn't at all hungry and all that glamorous-looking food made me feel queasy, and as I couldn't smoke, I had only my Diet Coke to occupy my hands, which were twitching, as if they wanted to do violence to somebody, perhaps just to myself – occasionally I looked over to Nathan's table, I could see his face, red, shiny, laughing too much – once I got up and went over, we met in a no man's land between tables occupied by elderly people, producers from the look of them – have I noted down how many producers there are on *Butley*, I mean I can't actually note down how many, I mean it rhetorically, how many producers! On the trip from the lobby to our table I was accosted by half a dozen who rose from their tables to thank me and congratulate me on their being where they were, at the first-night party of *Butley* – and then you think of all the tables you didn't pass at many of which producers almost certainly sat and you can say with confidence that there were probably two herds of them –

What Nathan and I talked about in this interlude was the reviewers – it wasn't really a conversation, but a series of interrogatives – 'Have you heard anything?' from him, 'No, have you?' from me, and then from him, 'Who do we know who might have heard?' and from me, 'Well, there's that friend of yours who does publicity – do you think she's heard?' and from him, 'Who, Jackie, no, I just asked her, and she hasn't heard a thing, isn't there somebody –?' and so it went, repetitiously, until Jackie happened up to us, smiling underneath her controlled and dead-pan eyes, giving Nathan the opportunity, which he took, to ask her if she knew anything. 'No,' she said, 'no more than I knew five minutes ago.' A flash of doubt befuddled Nathan's innocently enquiring expression. 'Surely somebody must know something, for God's sake!' Jackie took off her glasses, so to speak, though I don't think she wears glasses. 'I would never,' she said intensely, 'ever hold back on anything with you, Nathan, for the sake of our friendship.' Probably not precisely those words, but absolutely that meaning. Off she went, leaving us to hang around for a few minutes longer, to eye the great scene, all those guests sitting at all those tables eating all that food and drinking all that drink and wearing all that money, all because of us – yes, it is the case that if Nathan hadn't been born some fifty years ago and become a Broadway star who wanted to do *Butley*, and if I hadn't been born seventy years ago and written *Butley* before I'd lived for half of them, then neither he nor I nor the hundreds upon dozens of producers would have been wherever it was we were this evening (must find out its name and address) waiting, some of us, for news of the *New York Times* review. Neither of us expressed this thought, nor indeed any particular thought, as we stood together for a bit longer, then we smacked each other on the shoulder and laughed both at and with each other, as if diverted by our feebleness and fear, and went back to our tables – producers rising to both of us as we passed – now here's the thing I'm getting to –

I knew for a fact that the main review, the *New York Times* review, was out, in the sense that its content was known to quite a few people in the room, doubtless to at least a few of the producers and I was going to write 'almost certainly' as 'almost certainly' is a kind of writing tic of mine that I am aware of and can't control – well, that's the nature of a tic, after all – but in this case 'almost certainly' won't do, the words you have to write down are 'most certainly' as in – Jackie, the publicity girl, 'most certainly' knew the content of the *New York Times* review, and furthermore knew that it was bad, when she stood among the tables and told Nathan that she knew nothing, and would never jeopardize their friendship by withholding information from him.

Now how is it I knew what seemingly other people, far more experienced in the ways of Broadway and New York reviews, didn't know – or at least didn't know that they knew? I think Nathan knew.

He'd been on stage in New York very regularly over the last decade, had been through the whole business again and again, and would surely have understood, at a higher level of certainty than mere guesswork, that information about the review would have been in circulation before he arrived at the first-night party, but probably he persuaded himself that there would be an unusual explanation for the unusual delay – for instance that the review was so intensely favourable that it had to be vetted by specialist policemen for signs of a conspiracy – bribery, corruption etc., or that the reviewer had delayed publication because he wanted to insert some extra compliments that had occurred to him just as the paper was going to press, or that the reviewer had shot the editor or the editor the reviewer in a crime of passion and revenge – anyway he persuaded himself, against all previous experience, to hope for the best, or at least postpone facing up to the worst until it was plonked directly in front of him and there was no escaping it. That's the thing about a certain sort of hope, it's merely despair delayed by an act of will. But as I say, I think he knew all right, he just hadn't got around to acknowledging it yet.

My own case is slightly different. I am always eager to acknowledge the worst, and well in advance of the evidence. My temperament is to assume it, in fact, which is not to say that I welcome it, although there's possibly a bit of that perversity in it – I blame the usual suspect, my mother's womb, which is where I first learnt of disappointment – though whether in the being in it or in the getting out of it I can't really say, probably a case of out of the frying pan –

So we begin with my predisposition to suppose that there was a bad review in the *New York Times*. We add to that my sense of the improbability of the contents of this review not being known by someone or other by 10 p.m. on the night before its publication. We heap on top of that my conviction that a publicity person who begins a sentence with 'I'd never ever' is already more than halfway through the beginning of a lie. Underneath all that was my feeling that there was something awry – 'awf' or 'orf', as some of my older and classier English friends would put it – in the festive atmosphere, something uneasy circulating around the hall, possibly in the form of a muttered piece of gossip or even hard news. Then perch on the very top of that this fact:

That at the interval I'd sloped away from the theatre to the small bar where they allow you to smoke in the passageway leading to the front door, where they have four tables and two stand-up ashtrays. I sat at one of these tables with a Diet Coke and gaped vaguely towards the pavement, thinking of nothing in particular but admiring Nathan's performance in a grateful and hazy sort of way, when a young lady came around the corner from the pavement and into the passageway. She had her cellphone to her ear and a stricken look on her face, as if hearing something she didn't want to hear, and when she saw me at the table she looked aghast, as if seeing something she didn't want to see. She did a little skid and spin and went back around the corner – just that glimpse I had, that glimpse of Jackie the publicity lady on her cellphone, looking first stricken and then aghast – there was a pause and then she reappeared, the cellphone no longer visible. 'Hi, Simon,' she said, as she squeezed past me, 'having a Diet Coke?' I said I was, yes. Had she been in for the first act? 'No,' she said, she'd had some business to see to. Was she going in for the second act? No, not until the last moments, for the curtain call, she had to see some people – she gestured towards the door to the bar, and let the gesture carry her towards it, and then through it, a bit like a ballet dancer leaving the stage, really, except not on her toes, and not particularly gracefully, so not like a ballet dancer at all, although that was the image that came to mind, it must have been the gesture with the arm and the way her body followed on –

I sat for a few minutes, trying to imagine how Victoria would have dealt with my suspicions: 'Oh, really! She could have been talking to anyone, her mother, her boyfriend, her girlfriend, her dogsitter – some domestic worry.' Yes, I would have said, but then why was she so upset to see me? 'Actually,' she might have replied, 'people are often upset to see you, especially when they're not expecting to. And she was probably embarrassed at missing the performance, the first night –' No, I would have said, it was the review. The *New York Times* review. 'Oh, really!' and on like that, for a bit, but her protests would have got feebler because she would have known I was right. I usually am, on such matters. I got up to go back to the theatre, then thought I'd better have a pee, and went into the bar. It was quite empty except for a table by the lavatory. There were half a dozen people, men and women, I didn't really take them in because I was firstly conscious that there was one of those silences that happen when people suddenly stop talking because somebody who is connected to what they're talking about has suddenly appeared, and secondly that Jackie the publicity lady was sitting at the head of the table, rather formally, as if she were chairing an urgent meeting. I raised my hand in salute as I went into the lavatory, she raised hers, smiling radiantly, and she was still smiling radiantly, the table still in complete silence, when I came out. Of course it's possible that this group of people were always silent, they may simply have liked sitting with each other, not saying anything because wise to the many disasters, violent death etc., that are among the consequences of speech. On the other hand they could have been people who had clustered together to discuss the *New York Times* review and its implications, and naturally fell silent when one of the subjects of the review passed and repassed their table, on the way to and from a pee.

I hung about outside the Booth for about twenty minutes, smoking in the wind – it was really very windy, and I spent most of the time hunched, to protect the cigarette. Then I went in, with my head down so that I wouldn't see anyone coming out, and they wouldn't see me – there was a bit of activity around the door to the auditorium as I approached it, it opened and closed several times, quite violently, as if a rather feeble person were trying to leave, and a stronger person preventing him or her – perhaps a child and a parent? But would any sensible parent bring a child to the first night of *Butley*, and then forcibly stop him or her from leaving? When I opened the door myself, to sidle in, there were no signs of disruption, and no discernible explanation for the door's behaviour. In fact, there was an attentive row of people standing at the back of the stalls, and an attentively packed house, no one had failed to come back from the interval, not even Victoria, who was settled comfortably in her aisle seat, brave and concentrating, in fact as far as I could see, there were no empty seats, unless some of the audience were doing what we call in the trade 'double-shuffling' – i.e. and e.g. a chap uses his ticket for the first act, hands it to his wife at the interval who uses it for the second act – a variation on what we call 'single-shuffling' – i.e. and e.g. when a chap uses the same ticket for both acts, which happens more often than you would think, and is profitable to the management, although not as profitable as the 'single shuffle twice over' – i.e. and e.g. a husband and a wife with a ticket each sitting through both acts, which is nothing like as profitable as the 'double booking times X', X being the number of tickets the management can sell twice – apart from the possible financial gain, the confusion and rows that break out in the auditorium can lead to excellent publicity, with i.e. and e.g. 'They're fighting for seats at the Booth Theatre, where Simon Gray's *Butley*, starring etc. etc. –'

Well, the fact is that the play was mightily well received, with bravos and yippees and assorted screeches, screams and howlings at the curtain – I tried to join in but my husky rattlings went unheard except by the plump young man next to me, who turned away with what might have been revulsion. Nevertheless he yipped and clapped his way to the exit – he might have been one of the producers, of course, eager to get on to the party.

We went in a small van hired by the management – Victoria and I and Michael Musso, a small, pleasant man who is the chief administrator of the Huntington Theatre in Boston, where the production had originated three years before. He considered the evening to be a total triumph, and smiled and chatted calmly and confidently of what it would mean for the Huntington, which had a share in the royalties, and for his close colleague Nicholas Martin. Then we arrived at the place I've described above, I still can't remember its name or its precise location but it seemed to be right downtown, around 20th Street, anyway in an area I'd never visited before, at least to my knowledge – but in New York who knows where I've been at other times in my life? Then we did all the stuff in the lobby, then we sat at the table and then I got up and had that conversation with Nathan and Jackie the publicity lady and then we left and came back here – oh, one thing I've forgotten to put down, that shortly after the conversation with Nathan I went out to the pavement with Victoria's niece, Alice, for a cigarette. Alice is tall and blonde and very pretty, has just finished at Oxford and gets into the English papers now and then because she has an active social life in London of a sort that is incomprehensible to me, because in my day, etc. and so forth, modern youth so forth and etc. Anyway, though, she is vastly more sophisticated at twenty than I am at seventy. But perhaps not when I was forty. I have a sense that I've become less sophisticated in the last ten years or so, less at ease in company, I find conversation more difficult and am sometimes awed and even frightened by the prospect of meeting people I don't know – but then it's ten years since I stopped drinking, so perhaps that explains it. Anyway it would have been pleasant on the pavement, smoking and chatting with Alice, and looking for resemblances to her father, a very intelligent and charming man who died young and unfulfilled in life – pleasant to note his expressions in hers, his gestures in hers, if I hadn't been conscious of people exiting from the party. They walked quickly, in couples and threes, their heads together, their voices low, like conspirators – not quite like the exits from my first Broadway first-night party, which had taken place on the top floor of Sardis, the famous – more famous then than now – show-business restaurant, in 1969 – the room had been crowded and abuzz when I slipped out for a pee and virtually empty when I returned a few moments later, guests scampering past me in the hallway and down the stairs. 'Why, what's happened, what's going on?' I asked the producer, who sat slumped at the head of the table. 'The *New York Times*,' his wife said in a dead voice, as she left the room. Well, as I say, it wasn't quite like that tonight, people weren't leaving in an unseemly rush, it was more like a dignified and measured withdrawal from a slightly unseemly event, but still there was something in their manner that reminded me of my first night thirty-nine years ago.

We stayed on at the table, I longing to go because I felt tired and couldn't eat, Victoria keeping an alert eye on me as she continued in a lively and unworried vein. Nathan came over and we had the same conversation again, almost word for word – 'Have you heard?' 'No. Have you heard?' and then I said I was thinking of leaving, what did Nathan think? Yes, he said, he'd give it a few more minutes and then he'd leave. We agreed not to wait for each other, as we were going in opposite directions.

So we went back to our respective tables and stayed a few more minutes, and then a few more, and a few more after that, and then Victoria and I left, after a quick embrace with Nathan. We'll talk in the morning, we said.

*

Victoria and I had some coffee sent up, lolled about going over the evening. I kept my suspicions to myself for once, although I suspected she suspected them. She went to bed, and I turned off my mobile, phoned down to the operator, had a 'do not disturb' on our lines, and then wrote my letter to Nathan. I started from the premise, which I didn't state, that the *New York Times* review was going to be, at the least, a disappointment. I could have gone on to say how much I admired his performance, but I'd already said it, in Boston and in New York, and in the end he knew what his performance was, and nothing that the *New York Times* printed would alter that – at least I hoped it wouldn't. What I really wanted to write to him about was something quite different, and for me, as I've been feeling these last few days, far more important than the first night, or the immediate future of the revival of an old play. I hope I've written all that I wanted to write, but the thing is – the thing is – I can't at this moment remember a single sentence. It's as if I'd written in a trance, not easily and flowingly, but very meticulously – knowing how difficult my handwriting is to read, I'd made each letter as distinct as I could – that's actually my memory of the letter, finished only an hour or so ago, the careful grip on my pen as I laboured for legibility. But what exactly did I say? Now I have the letter in front of me, in an envelope, sealed and with Nathan's name on it. It would be perfectly easy to open the envelope, read the letter – but I don't think I have another envelope, I'd have to go down to the lobby and ask at the front desk – down 110 floors, at what is it? 4.13 in the morning – go to the front desk and ask for an envelope. Or I could try and reseal this one – but it wouldn't look right, it would look slightly grubby around the flap, as if I'd opened it and resealed it. Besides it would be wrong to change anything, whatever I wrote was full of feeling and intention, the fact that I no longer remember what it was apart from its being an expression of friendship, and of gratitude to the play for bringing me three close, true and good friends, the other two being Alan, of course, and Harold – without *Butley* I'd never have met them, and my life would have been completely different, in almost every respect.

Oh yes, well that's what it was, that's all it was, a simple and natural thing, no wonder I've had trouble remembering it.

NO MORE HEYDAYS

It's the end of the next day, not quite one in the morning, which actually, I suppose, makes it the beginning of the day after, in other words tomorrow. But can you ever be in tomorrow? Can you ever be out of today? But then what the hell is one in the morning, neither today nor tomorrow in any way that makes sense. I'm back from dinner with Nathan, Victoria is still not back from dinner with friends in Brooklyn, so it's just me, here in Suite 1410, determined to write about a day I'm unwilling to think about. Do it quickly. See if you can get it done before Victoria gets back.

When we got up at about eleven, we ordered breakfast and the *New York Times* – we've made it a rule over the last few years never to read reviews of my plays, but this morning had to be an exception, the concern being Nathan and his feelings rather than me and mine. We noticed that the messages light was winking on the telephone, but we decided not to listen to them until we'd found out what they'd be saying.

We ate breakfast with the *New York Times* lying unopened on the table between us, then I lit a cigarette, Victoria poured us each a cup of coffee, we went into the loungey half of the room, I sat in a corner of the sofa, she sat in an armchair beside me, I opened the arts section, and there was the review, a lot of it in the sense that there were quite a few paragraphs and a photograph of Nathan, but somehow laid out so as not to be eye-catching, in fact sort of squeezed in and lumpish-looking, and finishing over the page where you can't find it without searching. It's mostly bad for Nathan, and while it's good for the play it mainly mentions it parenthetically, or compliments it as a way of insulting Nathan – Nathan not being up to the part of Butley being the main theme, with side dashes at the other actors for not being up to their parts either, and for working so hard at their English accents that they're all accent and no character – this is odd, really odd, as Julian Ovenden, who plays Joey and virtually shares the stage with Nathan for most of the evening, is English born and bred, is in fact an Old Etonian, and all the other actors were assumed by all our English friends who saw the play on my birthday to have been imported from

England specially, so natural and easy and unlearnt did their English accents sound – but the *New York Times* chap clearly has an ear of his own, and knows his English accents as other men know their French wines –

Well, what's to be said? what's to be said? I said to Victoria, who said, that what was to be said, all that could be said, really, was that this chap Ben Brantley wasn't really reviewing Nathan at the Booth Theatre, really he was reviewing the review of his colleague Bruce Webber, who'd been sent by the *New York Times* to review *Butley* at the Huntington Theatre in Boston three years earlier, arguing with him and contradicting him, sometimes almost by the sentence – Webber, for example, had said that Nathan and Butley were a perfect match, that Nathan was, in a sense, Alan's heir apparent, it was worth the thirty-five-year wait – while for Brantley, but I've already written down what Brantley said about Nathan, wrong for the part, not up to Alan etc. – Webber admired Nicholas Martin's production, Brantley therefore despised it.

I picked up the messages from the telephone. They were from Nathan and Nicholas Martin and were grave in tone and disappointed, though both, being the men they were, also laughed quite a lot. I phoned them both up and we talked at length and purposelessly, so much the usual conversation when there's a bad review – happily Brantley has an unhappy prose style, aiming to be simultaneously colloquial and elegant it comes out in a bit of a muddle, here snobbish and there vulgar, and sometimes both in the same sentence, so again we laughed quite a lot – but really it was a bit like finding comedy in the deformities of a man who has harmed you, a bit schoolboyish, really, but I suppose the point is that though Brantley can't help the way he writes, any more than he could help it if he speaks with a lisp or a slur, for instance, he's still responsible for the opinions he expresses, and there's no getting away from it, Brantley's opinions are the official opinions of the *New York Times*, and might do us harm at the box office.

According to my American agent, Charles Kopelman, who has just phoned, the Brantley review won't do us much harm, if any. The box office is ticking away, the advance is huge. He also said that there were lots of very good reviews for Nathan, including one from Clive Barnes, in the *Post*, who had reviewed Alan in both the original London production and the subsequent Broadway production for the *New York Times* – there was also going to be a rave in the forthcoming *Newsweek*. The producers were already preparing a monster ad, full of marvellous quotes, to appear in the *New York Times* on Saturday, I think he said.

I phoned Nathan again to report my conversation with Kopelman, but I don't think it cheered him up particularly, he knows the box office is OK, what is depressing him is the thought that the *New York Times* review will be most audiences' only preparation for the show, they will bring the memory of it in with them, and they will actually look for him to disappoint them, because Brantley has promised them he will.

We arranged to have dinner after the show, which means I shall have to see it, half of it at least, actually I think I might enjoy it – of course I shall have the advantage of not expecting to be disappointed. I must remember to take the letter – it hasn't moved from the table where I left it last night, but already has a slightly shop-soiled look, as if somebody has opened it and resealed it. I've just examined the back of the envelope – it has a smudge at the apex of the flap, as of a thumb pressing into a spot of moisture, now dry – a teardrop, perhaps, but if so, whose?

I thought Nathan was terrific. The first few moments, appearing as a silhouette at the door and then coming on in the dark, the intricate stage business with the lights, were pretty awful, he said afterwards, when I went up to his dressing room, he felt that the audience for the first time in his experience of the play was tentative and ill at ease, probably cursing themselves for having bought tickets before the *New York Times* review came out, now having to sit through the evening out of respect for the money they'd paid and a grudging politeness to the star – that's how it felt to him, anyway, with the review stinking away in his consciousness, but gradually, by concentrating on the performance moment by moment, keeping his eyes and ears fixed on the other actors, he forgot the audience and the review and began to enjoy himself – and as so often happens the enjoyment became contagious, the audience relaxed, Nathan became free, the evening took off – perhaps not into full flight, as in the best of the previews, but sufficiently for Nathan to feel that the worst was over, that it hadn't been too bad, nothing like as bad as he'd expected, in fact it had been OK, tomorrow he'd be OK too, and one evening soon he'd be better than OK.

Just before we left his dressing room to set out for dinner I handed him my letter. He took it from me with an odd, set smile, as if he knew what it contained, and then ripped it across, rolled it between his hands until it fitted into his fist, and then threw it across the room, into the wastepaper basket behind the sofa, a perfect shot. 'Olé,' he said, 'and to hell with your crappy letter.' Well, no he didn't. He took the letter, with a serious little smile, put it in his pocket and said he'd read it when he got home. But one has these fantasies of rejection, one should express them sometimes, as a way of knowing oneself better.

We had dinner in the restaurant in which we'd had my birthday party. The waiters were subdued and the portly owner, with whom I'd smoked cigarettes on the pavement while he assured me that all would be well, came over bowing gravely and shook us by the hand – he was in undertaker mode, quite unsuited to his personality, but perhaps he'd read something in Nathan's expression, or something in this morning's *New York Times*, anyway the service was compassionately attentive and the food was good. Nathan's account of the evening came out in spontaneous fits and starts, interspersed with digressions of an inevitably vituperative nature on the subject of Brantley, and the old absurdity of it – that really Brantley was merely Brantley, no doubt the sort of chap whose opinions you'd greet with a concealed scowl if he tried to press them on you over a dinner table, especially if he speaks as he writes, but by virtue of his job he ceases to be the socially unwelcome B. Brantley and becomes the fearsome Ben Brantley of the *New York Times*, or consider it another way around, if Bruce Webber, who'd reviewed us in Boston, and writes readable and literate as well as glowing prose, had instead reviewed us in New York, Nathan would now be the toast of Broadway, instead of merely the apple of the playwright's eye –

Here's the sound of the door opening, Victoria back – and has now gone to bed. She says she had a good time over there in Brooklyn, it's really lovely, gardens, trees, flowers, you must try and see it, you'd love it – yes, I said, I must, it sounded really lovely, I'd heard that trees grew there, in Brooklyn, but flowers too, eh? This was formulaic, we both knew that there was as little chance of my getting to Brooklyn as the sisters had in getting to Moscow. I told her about Nathan's performance, the dinner etc., and then she went to bed, and here I am again, thinking that what I'd really like is to go into the bedroom, wake her up, and say, 'Hey, why don't we go home? Go home immediately? Go home tomorrow?'

We're all packed, the limo to take us to the airport is due in half an hour, Victoria is having a shower, and I'm sitting at the table in the kitchen writing this. In front of me is the *New York Times*, open at the page in which there is the promised advertisement for *Butley*, and I have to say that it's mightily impressive – the compliments for Nathan snake on and on, down the length of the page, a full page in the *New York Times* concluding with the name of the play in bold black type – BUTLEY – there it is! what playwright could wish for more, apart perhaps for a quote for himself, or if not that, for the play, and if not that, then at least to have the play ascribed to him. In justice it has to be added that, as in the lights above the theatre, it hasn't been ascribed to anyone else instead, it has no authorship whatsoever, as if self-generated. Of course there's a theory in modern literary criticism that the author is merely the accidental point at which historical trends and influences meet, and that he should therefore be treated as if he were anonymous. It's entirely possible that the producer of *Butley* subscribes to this theory, and is putting it into practice both on Broadway in lights and in the *New York Times*, though like the authors of the theory she herself likes to be named. There it is, her name, for all the world to see. And there is the bellhop to take down our bags. And there is my wife, wearing a towel and a top hat, ready for flight, and here are the last words I shall write in New York. It was a vile month. There. I've got it down. It was a completely vile month. I don't think there was a day in it that I enjoyed. The New York of my splendid heyday, of my thirties, forties and early fifties, has vanished, no doubt about that.

No, no, let's face it, the truth is more likely that the I of my splendid heyday has vanished – the bellhop has gone with the bags, and my wife, fully dressed, is standing by my chair, waiting to assist me to my feet, and the returning home has begun.

We're home. Got in this morning, very early. It would have been earlier, if the specially cheap airline – let's call it Soar – the producers had put us in hadn't lost one of our bags, the one with my nail clippers in it. A woman who started off by being very calm – 'Don't worry, we'll have it in a minute or two, it's somewhere about' – ended with panic in her eyes – 'It's never happened before, we've never lost a bag before.' I said it might be the computer, Soar had installed a new one at Kennedy airport, which is why we'd had such trouble boarding – She said she hadn't heard about the computers, that had never happened before either – Hints of accusation emerging in her tone, as if she were putting two and two together and coming up with us – the couple that caused things to happen to Soar, the specially cheap airline, that had never happened before. We left Stansted without the bag, which somehow we know we'll never get back, but we're home now, George and Toto, Errol and Tom all well, so who cares about the bag with my nail clippers in it?

PART SEVEN

ANCESTORS

We've been back a week now, I've spent most of it in bed with a version of flu, I suppose it's flu, my head aches and my nose is running and my eyes are red and smarting – these might not be the symptoms of physical flu, but of moral flu, anyway of a contagion picked up in the course of the month in New York, I cut an altogether disgusting figure to myself and to others – although very few others, as I've scarcely been out, except once or twice, up to the Renaissance for coffee, sitting outside at one of the tables because they've banned smoking inside – so in a sense I'm repeating an aspect of my life in New York, sitting outside in the cold in order to enjoy a cigarette – it must be merely a coincidence that I could smoke inside the Renaissance until I went away to New York, that I've spent a month dreaming of being back in my favourite and personal coffee shop in Holland Park Avenue, that I've actually trudged with weary, flu-drained limbs through the cold, up Holland Park Avenue, to my personal and favourite coffee shop, to find that I'm returned so to speak to New York, where I used to sit at a table on a cold pavement dreaming of being back in the Renaissance, while now I sit at a cold table on the pavement outside the Renaissance dreaming of being back inside it – but the old Renaissance is a month ago, never to return. Actually this is flu-generated self-pity, I never sat inside the Renaissance if I could help it, even on the coldest days I chose the outside, just as I did at the New York café, which I believe was called Café Maison. I suspect it was at the Café Maison that I picked up the cold in my chest that turned to flu when I got home.

I'm sitting in front of a new computer, these are my first words on it, and I worry that they may be my last – it really is so neat and compact, compact – yes, that's the word – no, the word the man who sold it to us used was 'sexy' and indeed it's a ladylike thing that reminds me of face powder in small containers, silk stockings, a pistol half the size of the slim and dainty hand that holds it, a knife in an especially fitted thigh-clasp, a poisonous lipstick, and a two-way mirror, not to mention a two-way bra and a pussy-whip – perhaps that's what he meant when he called it sexy, a sexy little computer, the sexiest on the market, because all these images from the flowering of my adolescence swarm into my consciousness – but then they swarm out once the lid is lifted and I see a keyboard and a screen and a pad and I wonder again at my folly – for years I've had a perfectly good system of working, I type out my first drafts on my typewriter if they're plays, and scribble them down on yellow pads if they're random musings that come to me where no technological help is available i.e. when I'm an unadorned writer in need only of the simplest of implements, I like to believe I could make out with a sliver of flint and the bare wall of a cave, as my ancestors did, although I'm not sure if at that stage of my evolution I would have had a vocabulary, I might have had to make do with pictures, which would be difficult, as I have no gift for drawing, no sense of perspective – but then nor did they, from examples I've seen of their work, which has mainly been in newspapers or in cartoons in the *New Yorker* – odd thought, that, that the cartoons on a cave wall from many, many thousands of years ago become the subject of cartoons in a shiny metropolitan magazine of today – what was he doing? What did he think he was doing as he scratched the outline of three bison, for instance, on his wall, was he keeping accounts, but if so, of what? Three live bison herded, three dead ones stored, three eaten, three dreamt of, hoped for, regretted – the fact is that we don't have a clue what he was doing in his cave, if it was a he – but why not she, alone with the babies, anxious, bored, scratching a dream on the wall of the cave, figuratively a stomach's dream, but perhaps not figuratively, the bison embodiments of an impulse, a prayer, a message to the *New Yorker* –

I would have needed sounds, however brutish and short, to record the narrative of my life, and more complicated sounds than grunts, groans and yodellings – what was the first word spoken, what can it have sounded like? There must have been a first word, chronologically, a sound uttered for the very first time that wasn't simply an angry or satisfied or terrified expulsion of air, a sound that had a content and was directed towards a fellow creature, perhaps it was a sound that meant 'help!' and that could be understood to mean 'help!' – When did we first laugh, what made us first laugh? In films and novels and so forth people are constantly laughing in happiness, but I have never heard or seen anyone laugh in happiness, though in joy – physical joy, yes, when the body is suddenly liberated from itself, in sex, say, or tobogganing downhill in a Montreal park when I was six or seven, or in the water, the first time in a warm sea after months of overcoated land-life, I have sometimes let out a yelp of joy, but not a laugh, really –

And when he heard himself laughing for the first time, what did he make of it, this ancestor of mine, of yours, of everybody's, who has given rise to so much laughter in the pages of the *New Yorker*, when presented as a cartoon? And why do I resent the *New Yorker* for it, it's not reasonable, really –

Nathan phoned to say that business is very good and that the houses are full, if sometimes of eccentric composition – at one of the matinées, halfway through the first act, a gang of middle-aged women, evidently from out of town, began to dispute among themselves in the stalls, at the tops of their voices, the ushers had to come in and calm them down. Apparently they kept away from each other during the interval, coming back in separate little groups, but ten minutes or so into the second act they started again, standing up and bawling at each other, even aiming slaps and punches until the ushers descended once more – Nathan couldn't give a completely clear account as each time he'd gone on playing the play, not daring to look out front – the good news though was that their rage was with each other, and not with the actors or the playwright – or so the ushers told the stage management. Or so the stage management told the actors.

He said he'd had one extraordinary performance, when the role had taken him over so completely that he seemed not to be acting but just happening – he'd never experienced anything like it, nor expected to again.

HITS AND MISSES

I was sitting where I am now, doing the sort of thing I'm doing now, when I heard Victoria scream – well, it wasn't exactly a scream, rather a shocked calling out of something I couldn't hear properly, but my name came into it somewhere, I could hear it distinctly, but I went on doing what I am now doing, on the rather lunatic, I now see, assumption that if she could call out my name, in however much alarm, it couldn't be for too serious a reason, it would only be serious if she couldn't call out my name, besides I had a sentence to finish – when I finished it I noticed that she was still calling my name, so I went to see what it was she wanted –

She was standing at the top of the stairs, outside the bedroom, with the almost serene look people sometimes assume when they have a calamity to announce. 'The ceiling's just fallen in,' she said, in a tone that made it clear that she wasn't speaking metaphorically. Rose, our elegant young cleaning lady, was standing just behind her, also looking calm, but with a graze on one of her arms, which she was dabbing at with a handkerchief. Apparently she'd been putting a garment into the chest of drawers, and from some instinct, had done a little skip-skip sideways just as the ceiling dropped, yes, it just dropped, dropped from whatever ceilings are attached to, in a cascade of heavy plaster, a small lump of which had caught, only very lightly, her arm – She was lucky, she said, with one of her brilliant smiles, she wears quite a lot of lipstick and has fine white teeth so her smiles are often radiant – She said it had happened to her in a café she'd worked in, a few years ago, when for the same 'some reason' as in our bedroom she'd found herself taking a little skip into the only spot in the café the ceiling didn't fall on, it had fallen all around her but on that occasion she hadn't even been grazed – I thought this was interesting, was there any possibility that we were getting it the wrong way around, that the skipping had caused the ceiling to fall by first arousing it with what it might have interpreted as an invitation, or a challenge, or an act of hubris? – was it something peculiar to Rose, that she possessed unknowingly, a kinetic power that contained within it another power that guaranteed her safety? – after all twice, twice in a few years, while surely for most people who live in an earthquake-free area once in a lifetime would still be well above the average – but there's nothing about Rose that suggests that she has an intense inward relationship with inanimate matter – inanimate matter? Is that a tautology, or can matter be animate? – Well, poets, novelists, playwrights, musicians, mystics, all those types, talk of the spirit of place, so why not be particular and talk of the spirit of a place's ceiling, and if of its spirit, then why not of its will? And then of a will that exhausts itself and collapses from the sheer strain of *being*, to put it in existential terms, and especially from the sheer strain of being a ceiling, and a bedroom one, at that? – But what am I doing? Why am I writing about matter and spirit and ceilings collapsing from boredom etc.? I'm completely missing the thing I should surely be thinking about – that the ceiling could have collapsed during the night while Victoria and I were underneath it, in bed – if you take eight hours as the average time in bed – actually it doesn't work like that in our case, as our sleeping overlaps, Victoria is generally in bed from 1 a.m. to 9 a.m., I am generally in bed from 5 a.m. to 1 p.m., so there are four hours in which we could have been buried in rubble together, and eight hours in which one of us could have been buried in rubble, so that makes a total of twelve hours in which one or both of us could have been buried in rubble, therefore there was a 50 per cent chance – Christ, 50 per cent! One in two! Doesn't bear thinking about, which was probably why I wasn't thinking about it – but now that I am thinking about it, I notice that I wrote that to have a ceiling fall on you once in your lifetime would be well above the average, but I've just remembered that when I was a child of about six in Montreal, residing at 4047 Vendome Avenue, I was sitting on the lavatory one day when the ceiling did in fact fall down, filling the little room with lumps of plaster and a cloud of dust, but leaving me unscathed, like a little prince enthroned on a battlefield is how I like to think I looked –

I wonder how many other near misses I've had, not just from ceilings but from all conceivable sources, that I can't remember, or possibly never knew about, or was too drunk to notice – the ones I can recall are probably routine, appropriate anyway to an Englishman who has lived most of his three score years and ten in peacetime, but an eighteen-year-old Englishman born in 1897 and dispatched to Mons, Marne, Ypres might have been able to list five times as many near misses by the end of a morning and not lived through the afternoon – although many of even the youngest soldiers apparently believed there was no such thing as a near miss, every bullet reached its correct destination, and it was either you or it wasn't.

*

I could say that I'm lucky to have been born in 1936, and not forty-five years earlier, in good time for World War One, or not fifteen years earlier, in good time for World War Two – I hit what might turn out to be a parenthesis, because I also sense that I'm lucky not to have been born fifteen or forty-five years later either – I have a sense, from what I've glimpsed of it, that the future's not going to be my kind of period, well, it will be a different century and a different country after all, they'll do things differently there –

DO I BELONG ON THE SEX OFFENDERS' REGISTER? AND OTHER WORRIES

And they're already doing them differently here, so perhaps the present's no longer my kind of period either – why today, this very day, in fact here, underneath my desk where I've thrown it, there's a copy of today's *Evening Standard* with a headline and a front-page story about a new law that is being proposed to the effect that women who give consent to sex when they're drunk can withdraw the consent after the event, when they've sobered up, and have the man involved – assuming it's a man they consented to have sex with – charged with rape. There's no mention of what happens if it's with a woman – presumably, if both women are drunk, then they could both withdraw their consent, and charge each other with rape. The story is followed up by an editorial of almost stupefying stupidity celebrating the probability of vastly increasing the number of successful prosecutions for rape – or that form of rape which could I suppose best be described as non-consensual consensual sex – actually I see it as yet another major step in the infantilizing of women, one of the bizarre consequences of the woman's liberation movement – but in the name of equality, which I've ever championed, I'd like to enter a plea for a quid pro quo infantilizing of men – let me reach into my own rubbish bin of experience and draw out a memory of something appropriate – well, there are several along these lines: when I was a research student at Cambridge I went one evening to a reception for a professor newly appointed from a provincial university, where I met a young woman, a Cambridge graduate and an assistant lecturer in the professor's old department, who was known to be his mistress – he was married, with a child or two. She was lively and attractive, with an easy laugh and a soft, shapely manner, about twenty years younger than the professor, and about eight older than me. There was something about me that appealed to her, mostly I think that I listened to her with close attention and apparent sympathy when she spoke of how Cambridge's gain was her loss, she there in the provinces, he here – and here he certainly was, in the centre of the room, his large, shaggy head inclined towards attentive young faces, his cheeks popping to the commands of his celebrated pipe, which he had once, in the middle of a seminar, crammed still alight into his jacket pocket along with his half-open box of Swan Vestas – the ensuing explosion, his attempts to scuffle off his smouldering jacket while still pursuing his thoughts on *Antony and Cleopatra* were the stuff of his legend – endearingly and comically absent-minded, yes, but with all-obliterating powers of concentration – a short, stooping man with visible dandruff and bad teeth, yes, but he held full lecture halls entranced, students mesmerized, he had genius and animal magnetism – this was the nature of her conversation, though I have to admit that the dandruff and bad teeth are my contributions, inserted here, out of spite. She was slightly drunk when we began our conversation and three times drunker by the time she suggested we take our leave and have coffee somewhere, what about my flat? It wasn't altogether my flat, I said, I shared it with two other chaps, and didn't mention that they were both away. She said that was all right, she'd like to meet them, let's go, why not, or did I have an objection to introducing her – ? She wasn't exactly aggressive and I wasn't exactly sober, but though I was no longer completely new to sex – see various *histoires* above – I was completely new to the prospect of having sex with someone I didn't know. So we set off through the soft Cambridge night – something of a phenomenon in nature, most nights in Cambridge were hard, very hard, even in warm weather – she clinging to my arm and talking now of her departing professor, now of other men in her life, perhaps to reassure me that I was not to take this, whatever it was going to be, too seriously, I was to see myself as a trifle, a toy in the blood etc. – My tactic was to lead her around and about, this way and that, until she was worn out and wanted to get back to where she was staying the night, but I'd only managed a few diversions when she did that thing that drunks sometimes astonish us by doing, she achieved a complete concentration on what she wanted – 'I thought you said you lived in Green Street,' she said, pulling me by my arm in a circle, 'We're going the wrong way.' 'It's a nicer way,' I said, 'we're going around by the Backs, for a peek at the river.' 'No,' she said, 'we're going to Green Street, to see your friends.' We got to Green Street in no time, it seemed to me, and then we were up the stairs and into the flat, which consisted of a small sitting room, three bedrooms, a kitchen and no bathroom, not even a lavatory, which was off the stairs on the way up to the flat, and contained as a washing facility only a small sink – we took our baths, when we had them, in our respective colleges. At this moment I can remember the disposition of the flat very well, because she led me from room to room, on a tour of inspection, rather as if she sensed there'd be nobody there but us. 'Back any moment,' I said, 'they're always around when you least want them.' Or never around when you most want them, would have been at that moment a more accurate way of putting it. She lay on the sofa, which was a squat ragamuffin of a thing, and spilled voluptuously over it. I went to make some coffee, and when I brought it back she had adopted a new position, in the centre of the room, and her clothes were everywhere but on her. I handed her a mug, and sat down. I'd ruined the previous occasion when a woman had undressed on my behalf by explaining that I was a virginal sort of man – i.e. inexperienced and probably inept, but very, very willing – I believe I've gone into the incident somewhere else, but the point is that here, with this girl, let me call her Mo, for Maureen, say, also out of spite, I was not a virginal sort of man, I was a quarter drunk, was a little more than half willing, out of primeval excitement, but then again almost half not, because she really was a little too excitable, a little too determined, a little too drunk and there was the professor and all the other chaps she'd told me about somehow somewhere in the room, and I wasn't sure she wasn't mistaking me for one of those – well, not the pipe-puffing, dandruff-headed genius of a professor, of course, but one of the subsidiaries, many of them known to me as serious men who read literature with moral intent, but now also known to me as men who'd been laid by Mo – as I might soon become known to them. Would being laid by Mo elevate me into a morally serious reader? was not a thought that was occupying me when Mo launched herself at me in a flurry of fists and kisses – I won't claim that I was passive, or that I remained fully dressed for long, but I still retained the top part of my clothing when we hit the floor. There was a slip-shod chaos between our legs, terrible farmyard sounds (poultry section) as we rolled on top of each other, and then away from each other. She came unsteadily over to me on her hands and knees, her face hovered over me, cheeks white and eyes staring as if she had an urgent message most of which she then delivered over my exposed chest, and the rest of it over my genitals, which were already in a fairly depressed state. Ever the gentleman, I went to the sink in the lavatory off the stairs, while she made do with the sink in the kitchen. I can't remember much in the way of conversation as we got dressed. I like to think I walked her to wherever her bed for the night might have been, but I have a strong suspicion, based on what I have come to learn of my character, that I probably merely offered to – in mitigation I should say that the streets of Cambridge weren't particularly dangerous in those days, except for men like me when women like Mo were about in them.

A few days later a letter arrived, in which she apologized in a deft and witty manner for the 'rather shameful incident the other evening', she'd had 'rather more than far too much to drink', for one thing she'd been 'grieving', for her the reception had been a little like a funeral as it marked the loss of her professor from her daily life. She went on to make a few penetrating remarks about the state of English studies in the provinces, with particular reference to her own province, and hoped we'd meet again some day. There was an indecipherable squiggle at the end, to serve as 'sincerely', 'ever', 'best wishes', whatever I chose to make of it, followed by her first name – Mo, if we're still sticking to Mo, and then, oddly, her surname in brackets.

We never met again, although I heard of her now and then, her steady rise up through English departments in this university and that, until she became in due course a professor herself, in the States, somewhere in the Midwest, I believe, and then I have the impression that a few years ago I heard that she was dead, but I'm not altogether sure about that. One's always thinking one's heard that someone's dead, and then they turn out to be alive, and vice versa, of course.

But to return to the reason I found myself recalling my night with Mo: the headline in the *Standard*, announcing that a parliamentary committee had proposed new legislation to the effect that a woman who has sex with a man when she's drunk can change her mind when she's sobered up, call the police, and have him charged with rape – this followed up in an imbecilically pious editorial insisting that such legislation was necessary to increase the number of rape convictions, and so reverse the current tendency of juries to hold women responsible for their own actions when drunk. Under this new law, should it come to pass, Mo could have pressed charges, I might have found myself in court, then quite plausibly convicted of rape, and the Crown Prosecution Service – Service! Can that be right? Crown Prosecution Service, the accused now seen as a customer, as passengers on the railway services are now seen as customers? Will convicts become customers of the prison services? Well, whether as customer or convict the Crown Prosecution Service would have added me as one more statistic in their successful drive to increase the number of convicted rapists in the nation, and one more name on the sex offenders' list to congratulate themselves on. Thus would a life have been destroyed – well, no, you can't say that, not for sure, my life as a convicted rapist and listed sex offender would certainly have been different from my life as, say, an unconvicted rapist and unlisted sex offender, which is what I am, really, when you think about it, thanks to the historical accident of having come to my sexual prime decades before the proposed new law was even a malevolent glint in the eye of the future – and anyway who can argue with authority that my life would have been destroyed by being convicted and listed? My writing, if I'd chosen to continue as a writer, might have been richer for its being darker, profounder for its being more pessimistic, and more commercial, far more commercial for its being brewed out of suffering and injustice. At least I could put my middle-class public school and university education behind me. I would have had a best-seller story to tell. Or perhaps I wouldn't – if the parliamentary committee has its way there would be too many like me with pretty well the same story to tell.

But what about Mo's life? Let us fast-forward Mo into a quite other creature, a young woman of today as hoped for by the Crown Prosecution Service – a young woman who is a fearless drinker and an equally fearless fucker, for what has she to fear on either count? On either count, drinking and fucking, the only consequence will be the pain, or will it be the pleasure?, of ruining the life of her drinking and fucking partner. They did the same thing, but she's a woman, so it doesn't count for her, it's not her fault, she's a woman. They did the same thing but he's a man, it does count for him, it's his fault, he's a man. In fact the woman doesn't really exist, at least in name – she's a nameless, anonymous victim and remains so until the end of her life. The man is named the moment he's charged, and remains so until the end of his life, whether convicted or acquitted. He can be listed, named, shamed, acquitted, with possibly many months in jail after he's listed, named, shamed, and before he's acquitted.

Come back to my own case. I would submit that if there was a victim it was myself. I tried, within the gentlemanly and therefore limited means at my disposal, to prevent Mo from coming back to my flat. I was reluctant to have sex until it became positively discourteous to refuse, by which time my penis, head-strong in the way that penises tend to be (in this respect they resemble C. S. Lewis's dog, who never obeyed him, but sometimes agreed with him. If only men could train their penises as they frequently manage to train dogs – Down boy! Stand! Sit! Beg! Down, I said!). Anyway, my view would be that I could certainly claim, in an imaginary world where men were as equal before the law as women, that Mo pretty well raped me. An adequate lawyer could make the case, furthermore, that her vomiting over my chest and genitals was a serious abuse of my human rights, and what's more, what's more you are seventy, and you sound it, so stop it, stop it! The fact is that you don't drink any more so you won't even get yourself to the first stage, the Mo stage, therefore you're most unlikely to appear in court or on the sex offenders' list – besides there are far more serious and complex issues around, which might touch on you personally and affect the course of your life in your remaining years, why don't you worry about them – ?

Because I don't think you can be a selective worrier, or – in another of those phrases I hate so much – 'cherry-pick' your worries, this business of non-consensual consensual sex has grown and grown in wherever it is in my consciousness that is the seat of worry – seat of worry? Well, what is worry, anyway? – I mean, what is its relation to memory and imagination, is it a separate faculty, how do we come by it? What would we be like if we didn't worry? It seems to me that my stream of consciousness is really a stream of worry, from the moment I awake, when I contemplate getting out of bed – is somebody other than Victoria in the house? Can I potter down to my lavatory naked, which is what I really want to do – no, perhaps slip downstairs to the kitchen, pick up a newspaper, slip back up – slip? Slip? Hah! Plod, plod down naked, plod back up the stairs, potbelly swinging – they will say, how his arms and legs are grown thin – no, they won't, if the girl who walks the dogs is in the hall and looks up the stairs and sees you coming down, she won't think how his legs are growing thin, she'll think, how disgusting ees thees man – she's Spanish, South American, anyway she speaks English with a Spanishy accent – thees man, with his beeg belly swinning thees wye and thees wye – but no, she won't think in English with a Spanish accent, she'll think in Spanish with a Spanish accent, or will she? Do we actually think in words, come to think of it, well, however she thinks she'll probably be thinking of not walking our dogs again, or if she's an advanced and practised child of our time she'll think of calling the police – sexual harassment, *si, si* – or a lawyer, she'll sue me, *si, si, si por favor* – very shameful, embarrassing for Victoria – back on the sex offenders' list – what do you mean back, you haven't been on it yet, this continual, in fact almost continuous fretting about being on the sex offenders' list is perverse, to say the least, you haven't done anything for years and years that would qualify you – and do you think of committing a sex crime as a qualification for a distinction? like getting an honour, Simon Gray, *quondam* playwright, was honoured in the New Year sex offenders' list, his autograph and photograph are available from a police station near you – or is it the sad dry form that an old man's sexual fantasy now takes, is this what I've come to? fretting or dreaming about getting on the sex offenders' list while still in bed at – oh Christ, it's half past one, Victoria's out, where's she out, the dogs are out, you're alone, I'm alone, he's alone – we're all alone – and I have to write, I'm a writer, writers write – but what about? – get up, get up, need a pee – incontinence, yes, when does that begin? Or will death snatch me first? I really and truly don't want to be incontinent, Alzheimer's, incontinence, look at him shuffling naked down the stairs for his first pee of the day – but it's amazing that you can get through six, seven, sometimes even eight hours of sleep without needing a pee, especially when you consider all that Diet Coke you drink, all those cigarettes you smoke, and yet here you are at seventy, continent – but for how long?

That's pretty well how it goes, something like that, in that vein anyway, when I have nothing specific to worry about.

PART EIGHT

SOME BEWILDERMENTS

We've got through Christmas without anything bad happening. We had the usual Boxing Day dinner with Harold and Antonia. Harold looked wonderfully well above the table, but he said that beneath it his legs were creaky and painful. He said it cheerfully, though, and got angry once or twice.

Here comes the New Year. 2007. What an unlikely number. The question, though, is whether you're going to make yet another promise to yourself to give up smoking. Let's start by putting down yet again all the reasons for giving up. No, let's not. Let's sit by the window, light a cigarette, and see if we can see the fox in the garden. It's a bright night, the sort of night that foxes like. The one I'm looking for sometimes strolls along the back wall, laughing. At least it sounds like laughter. It may be a mating cry, or desperation.

Last night was the last night of *Butley*. Nathan phoned to say it had gone very well, the company relaxed and at its best, the house packed, terrific reception. Afterwards there had been a party to celebrate the success of the run – we'd actually made a profit, very rare for a straight play on Broadway these days – it had been a pleasant and slightly melancholy party, only slightly marred by the late arrival of the producer, Liz McCann, who'd spent the evening at *A Chorus Line* rather than at *Butley*, which she hadn't looked in on since its opening night. I asked whether by any chance she was still in her wheelchair. He said he hadn't noticed, he thought not. We agreed that whether she was or not she might be again very soon, unless she'd got rid of the cat, of course.

We hung about on the line for a while, mixing inconclusive sentences with laughter, then finally said goodbye, we'd keep in touch, and of course we will – we might even celebrate another birthday together, one that falls somewhere between Nathan's sixtieth and my ninetieth, why not?

When Nigel first saw me he was sixteen months old, and I was three days old. According to our mother he looked at me for a while, then slapped her face. Nevertheless, he was as kind an older brother as a man could have. He died last night in Oakville, Ontario, of heart failure, and I am suddenly all at sea, a brotherless man – there are many of us, of course, but I have never been one before.

I have a tumour in my lung, discovered by accident during the annual scan of my aneurysm, which itself has apparently grown or swollen apace and will have to be dealt with in due course – if there is a due course, which will depend, I suppose, on the tumour and whether it's confined to the lung or has come from somewhere else. If from somewhere else, would it explain why a lymph gland on my neck is swollen and has to be investigated? Or has that come from the lung? So. So ahead of me – biopsies, scans, tests, consultations, more scans, an operation if I'm strong enough and lucky, otherwise radiotherapy or chemotherapy, or both, so forth and so forth, but absolutely certainly, one way or another, I'm coming up to the last cigarette.

Well –

I went there this afternoon. Piers's little section was *en fête*, quite extraordinary, not simply the abundance of flowers on every grave, including Piers's, but flags, bunting, balloons, dolls, as if transformed into the setting for a party, a victory party, where was the music, one wondered, and where the voices? – because it was as quiet as it usually is, with just the sound of a car or a mower in the distance, and it was as sunny as it usually is – there's always bright sunshine when I visit Piers, not at all a coincidence or a mystical harmony between me and the weather, it's simply that I never go there unless the sun is out, partly to make sure that I associate his grave with cheerfulness and brightness, though not entirely with warmth, as my favourite time is on a cold, bright winter midday, and partly because I never want to go unless the sun is out, in fact the impulse only comes with the sun, and

I can see myself now, as I write this – yes, there I am, an elderly man, sitting on the bench in the sunshine. I am smoking a cigarette, coughing slightly and perhaps, if you catch me at the right moment, slightly squinting so that I have the verses on the next-door tombstone in the corners of my eyes. I have half a newspaper on my lap. The other half – the business, travel and property sections – is under my buttocks, to cushion them against the wood of the bench. I imagine that the few people who pass by, usually in clusters of three or so, would take me for what I am, a brother visiting a younger brother, rather than a husband grieving for a wife, or a father for a lost child. I don't know what precisely would make this evident, it wouldn't really be anything in the detail, more a general effect, but one can always distinguish the brothers from the husbands and the fathers, at least I can, I think, and I therefore assume others can as well, but we might all of us be wrong, I might be identified, for instance, as one of those creatures who likes to visit graveyards, I was going to say 'strange creatures', but when I think about it I see nothing strange in it, there are few more interesting places in London than Kensal Green Cemetery, and few more enchanted and eloquent spots than Rowan Gardens, or more vivacious, at least on an afternoon when the bunting and the flags are out, and balloons floating, and there is the sense of victory in the air, not grim and forceful victory, as in 'Death, be not proud –', but a jolly victory, a celebration as of a – what? I can't think what sort of event would be collectively celebrated in Rowan Gardens Cemetery in a manner that made it look like a village fair from a different age – how come the balloons and flags? and who put the flowers on Piers's grave? there were two bunches, a bunch of fresh daffodils and a bunch, a clutch, really, of artificial poppies, they must have been laid by different hands – now, as I sit here writing this, I realize that none of it makes sense – if it was in memory of a momentous event, a great battle won or a country liberated, they would leave a sign, surely – it begins now to feel like a hallucination, the question being whether I had the hallucination when I visited Piers this afternoon or am having it now, in memory, in memory decorating with flags, bunting and balloons that sedate and pleasant place I know so well.

THE
SMOKING
DIARIES

Volume 4

Coda

Victoria – without whom, nothing

LONDON

GRINNER WITH A KNIFE

It's coming up to 4 a.m. on a Friday morning, and I've just promised myself, a self loaded with and lightened by a couple of sleeping pills, that I will go on with this tomorrow – just get a first sentence, I told myself, and when you are ready tomorrow look at it, and then continue into another sentence, and if you can another one, and if you're lucky you'll catch up with yourself in what you understand, at 4 a.m. on this Friday morning, will be an account of what you've been told, on good medical authority, is the beginning of your dying.

A demain, therefore.

Demain has arrived, and I'm going on with this, the beginning of my dying – now, is that merely a perverse way of writing the end of my living – the ending of my life? I don't think so – the perverse part of my situation is that, apart from the fact – not yet completely authenticated – that I'm dying, I feel really quite well, physically better than I've felt in a long time, for the last year almost, so really it's not that I'm dying, rather that I'm being killed off by a tumour that so far hasn't announced itself by an overt presence on its host – my body, more specifically my lung – but has been discovered –

It's like this, at least in my imagination – you come back home one evening, the house is dark, as you expect it to be, you switch on a light, an extra light, one you didn't know you had, and unexpectedly your eye goes to a corner of the room that you've never seen illuminated before, and in it is crouching a grinning man holding a knife – and then the light goes off, normal lighting is resumed, there is no one in the corner as far as you can see, but you know that if the light came on again you would see him again, see him in more detail, the teeth, one particular and prominent tooth, the completely confident intent in the eyes, the compactness, wholeness, distinctive of his intent to murder you – and you can't get out of your house, which was once your protection and the most comforting place in the world – it is now your prison, inhabited by you and the creature in the corner, who might also be slipping into other rooms, to catch you there, or there, or there – in his own good time. You are his good time, in waiting. So I am living in a state of terror and cowardice – I am waiting to be murdered in my house by the grinning murderer with the knife – that is sort of how I feel about the tumour in my lung. Almost I want to give myself over to him – there, there you are, do it, do it now – but mostly I want to run and run, as if running will carry me away from him, and not carry him along inside me, there for the ride, enjoying it.

A RUN IN THE CHURCHYARD

And indeed an hour or so ago I went to the churchyard at the end of our street, unlocked the gate, and walked around and around for an hour without stopping, a very rapid plod, head lowered so I don't have to meet the look of anyone else strolling along the paths, keeping my eyes off any dogs with affectionate, trouser-pawing tendencies – I felt my body surging along, even if rightly I've called it a plod, I felt a looseness in my legs, an easy swing in my arms, and at one point, having made sure that there was no witness but a bunched-up woman with two corgi-type dogs who was as determined to avoid me as I was to avoid her, I went to the top of the path and set out on a jog. It was as if I'd never run before in my life.

I feel a need to interpolate here a brief history of my athletic career, which entails, I think, a brief history of my mother's career – she was a fine athlete, outstanding in the broad jump, a competition long ago eliminated as an international event – you stood still on a board embedded in the ground, swung your arms, heaved yourself through the air into a pit of sand – a stationary version of the long jump, which involves a very fast sprint to a board embedded in the ground, from which you take off into a pit of sand – Mummy also did that, the long jump, as well as the high jump, and won some medals at international level – there was a photograph in an album of her receiving a medal from the King of Sweden, not long before the last war, although I can't remember for which event, or whether it was gold, silver or bronze – but anyway there she was in the photograph, a medal-winner and acknowledged as such by Swedish royalty – I have an idea that it was King Gustav, but have no idea whether Sweden ever had a king called Gustav, it's just that the name Gustav has attached itself to the memory of a small man with a beard holding something out to Mummy, who is stooped in a sort of bow – but what was she wearing? I have a memory of her position but not of her clothes – I wonder what happened to the photograph, and how old I was when I saw it – I do remember clearly that it embarrassed us, Nigel, my older brother, and me – we didn't like looking at it, or hearing about her athletic achievements, they seemed inappropriate for a mother, even a long-legged mother who swam and played tennis, and would race after us to deliver a kick or a blow, up and down the stairs or across the garden – I've described elsewhere her combative nature, her readiness to meet perceived impertinence or foolishness with a cuff or a kick, and how, after five years of separation – we were evacuated to Canada during the war when I was three, Nigel four – we relished the excitement and drama she brought into our lives, as well as the reassuring intimacy of casual and only accidentally painful violence – when our reflexes failed, for instance, and we stumbled into rather than away from the swiping hand.

But the idea of her running about and jumping in public was strange and distasteful, her winning medals somehow made it worse, it seemed much more respectable and normal that she'd been a gym teacher and coached lacrosse and hockey at a girls' school until she met and married my father, a Canadian doctor, a locum at her father's practice – actually he was engaged to her sister until Mummy returned from her school in Shropshire and took him for herself – but why am I going back into all this history? I've already written about it elsewhere – I think to establish that being good at running and jumping, football and cricket was in my genes, and that the memory of being good seemed to be lingering in my body like a taunt, as if my legs themselves had a memory of a time when they could lift and stretch, and I could fly along the top of the ground with no need of muscles or bones or lungs, all those parts of me that have become more and more noticeable as they've served me less and less well, like bad waiters – a ridiculous analogy, it would make my body into a restaurant, but it gets me back to the sentence that I interrupted about being in the churchyard just a few hours ago feeling that I could walk, was in fact walking, with power and authority, so how could I be terminally ill? and deciding to test myself further with a little run – and I tried, and – I wrote – 'It was as if I'd never run before' and really the sentence should have gone on 'which is probably why I couldn't do it', because the fact is that I couldn't, not even for three steps, for all my legs' memory of once having sped and flown etc., they'd forgotten – I've forgotten – how to run.

I tried to work it out, the mechanics of it, and after a bit of lifting my legs and pumping my arms while stationary, I tottered forward and managed a jerky little passage of about fifteen steps of something that was more complicated and more urgent than a walk, but also made me feel ill with exhaustion and shame, as if I'd been struggling uphill with a great weight, which was I suppose the weight of my self, accumulated over seven decades – I thought I must get home and lie down, and headed towards the gate, which the two-corgis woman seemed to be holding open for me but wasn't, she was holding it open for her dogs, just as I got to it she let it swing closed behind her, and hurried off with her head down, the dogs scampering playfully around her, and I had to fumble for my key, locate the lock, heave it open – and here I am, having rested on the bed for a while, writing it all down and thinking as I do so that this is not the way a man should confront the fact that he's dying, how can writing of his failure to run about in the local churchyard possibly help him, and what if I'd succeeded? What if I'd sped and flown up and down the paths as once I could have done, once, once upon a time I could have done?

A SHORT HISTORY OF FAILURE

I keep sitting down to go on with this, again and again and again, night after night after night, but it's no good. I suppose that I'm the writing equivalent of dumb-struck.

It's been weeks now – a month even, the whole of July, and I still can't do it.

*

That's August gone, the summer almost over. I haven't the will is the truth of the matter. Perhaps it's been zapped by the radiotherapy. Every time I pick up my pen I write into my yellow pad either a squiggle or that I can't write, and put the pen down again.

We've planned to go to Crete. In fact we should have been there on Friday, and then again yesterday, but I wasn't well enough – washed out and frail, the effect of the radiotherapy. We're now booked on a flight tomorrow afternoon. If we get there perhaps I'll be able to put something down.

OK, here we are, and I'll try. The thing is, it's all so haphazard in memory that I can't do it chronologically, or in any sort of order, probably, I'll just have to let it happen as it happens. If it happens.

Well now.
    Take it easy.
    Go from where you're sitting, why not?
    Yes, but not today.
    Tomorrow. I'll start tomorrow.

As it happens, then.

It's tomorrow again.

So tomorrow I'll start. Tomorrow I'll let it happen as it happens.

CRETE

AS IT HAPPENS AT LAST

As it happens, I am sitting at a long blue table with my back cushioned against the wall of a small white chapel. I think this table is actually a part of a restaurant and not the chapel, because just beyond it are small, square tables with canvas chairs, some of them under a makeshift roof, and then there is a kitchen and a section enclosed to make a dining room, and an outside grill and bar arrangement – so really, while all the currently highly sensitive and emotional part of me clings to the notion that I've attached myself physically to a chapel, the truth is likely to be that I'm sitting in an empty restaurant. I've been pretending I don't know it's a restaurant, that really it's a complicated extension of the chapel, serving a religious function for the feasts of the saints' name days, for example, and that all the people of the neighbourhood attend it and then eat appropriate dishes, or eat appropriate dishes before attending it, served by assigned parishioners or members of a holy order, but it's no good, the fact is that I ate here myself, last night, with Victoria of course. The food was delicious, at least Victoria says it was, and actually I did manage to eat a little of it – eating is a bit tricky at the moment as a) I'm a bit short of an appetite since the radiotherapy and b) I seem to have lost my sense of taste since the radiotherapy and c) I have trouble fitting my dentures into my mouth since the radiotherapy – it's as if my lower and upper jaw have been realigned by the rays to give me a differently shaped mouth from the one my dentist worked from. On the other hand I could see that the food was at least popular, because everybody at the surrounding tables ate it with real enthusiasm, and made appreciative if charmless noises – grunting and going 'mmmm'. There was a French couple at the table next to ours, neat and low-voiced, young middle-aged and gravely happy – he looked a bit smooth and film-starry until he suddenly addressed the waiter on the subject of the pieces of cheese fried in batter they'd just consumed – his clear, tight little film-starry face became vulpine, you could see all his teeth – such was his grinning enthusiasm for the pieces of fried cheese in batter, a Crete speciality, apparently, and offered as a pudding because the batter is soaked in honey. His wife or mistress was a charming though not very pretty mess of a woman, farouche might be the word, short black hair tangled, and the sleeves of her wind-breaker down over her wrists. She was, like him, a hearty and appreciative eater. They were both heavy smokers. It was what I noticed first about them. During the course of the meal she had five, he had four, cigarettes, but the odd thing was that they shared the pack – no, she was the keeper of the pack, kept it just above her plate, and he would reach over, take the pack, shake out a cigarette, light it with the lighter she kept on top of the pack, then put both back in front of her. In my experience, heavy smokers like to have their own pack and lighter, so there was probably something symbolic in their arrangement. He liked the sense of her being in charge, she liked the sense of being his handmaiden. I don't think it was simply that he'd forgotten his cigarettes and lighter, it looked habitual, a relaxed and intimate ritual that might one day, when recollected by one or other of them, be charged with pathos, even grief.

It was very pleasant and peaceful sitting under the Cretan night sky, the sound of the waves lapping at the beach below, the murmur of voices and quiet laughter, well, that is until a trio of elderly northerners, Yorkshire from their accents, suddenly appeared and sat down at a table near us – two women and a man with a finely structured, noble face, with crinkly eyes and a furrowed brow who looked unnervingly like Sean Connery – the impersonation helped by the grey spade beard, heavy eyebrows and balding head, but in his speech, in the level of his conversation – it's not simply that he was boastful and loud but he appeared to be retarded in some way. I don't believe he was drunk, but he shouted and bellowed out laughter as if he were in a crowded pub. At one point he told a joke that involved imitating a hen, so he 'did' the hen with flappings of his arms and squawks and bouncings up and down in his chair – the two women, one of whom could be mistaken for an academic – cropped grey hair, serious spectacles, a blinking, murmuring manner, short and squat of figure, but with a piercing laugh that, once started, went on and on – the other was fat, slovenly, coarse-haired, hoarse-voiced – the three of them, especially when they were simultaneously in full flow, the two women screaming out their laughter, he raising his voice to be heard above it, seemed to have come from a mid-twentieth century that only existed in the cinema and in novels – *Saturday Night and Sunday Morning, Room at the Top* and so forth, and yet here they were last night at a table a few yards away from the little chapel, against the wall of which I'm resting my back as I write this –

My tendency is to go on writing this, and this sort of stuff – about the hotel, its restaurants, the sea, Crete, to which we've come in late September – as a way of avoiding what is most on my mind to write about, which is that I have a year to live. No, three months ago I was told that I had a year to live, so now I have nine months to live. Well, medical predictions, even when delivered with an off-hand matter-of-factness, can't surely be precise even to the month. Everybody knows some-body who knows somebody who was given six months to live, and here they are, only just dead, eight years later. Or, in exceptional cases, here they still are, eating oysters and boring the shit out of people. Eight years, I've noticed, tends to be the outer limit of an incorrect prognosis. There was that remarkable woman who died a few weeks or so ago, she rode bicycles around the world, took part in marathons, walked across continents, all while undergoing chemotherapy etc. and had only just completed some astonishing run or walk or cycle three days before she died, which was eight years later than had been authorised for her. One wonders how the doctor who made the prognosis felt about her continued, and very public – often saluted in headlines – survival. Did he feel a bit of a charlie, and harbour dark thoughts, especially at the beginning of her so-to-speak post-mortem career, find himself wishing, and then willing, her out of the newspapers and off the television screens into the spot he'd assigned to her? I don't think the prognosticating doctor's name was ever mentioned – a pity, really, it would have been amusing to read that 'Julia Hobday, who seven years ago was told by Dr Angus McDuff of the Middlebury Cancer Hospital that she would be dead in six months, came fourth in yesterday's Chelsea–St Ives Marathon. Dr McDuff, when asked for his comment, said that –'

*

Well, what would he say? 'I'm only human' is the currently favoured excuse for failure. Footballers offer it after losing football matches, politicians after costing lives, journalists after ruining reputations, policemen after mowing you down in their pandas, and I suppose that's pretty well what I would say if asked why I should think I could smoke sixty cigarettes a day for fifty odd years without getting lung cancer – well, I'm only human, which would be, of course, not my excuse for the smoking, but for not expecting, or willingly accepting, the consequences. 'I'm only human,' I say to myself, and to prove to myself that I am add, 'It's not fair!'

Actually, it would be only human for the many doctors I've seen over the last six weeks to say, 'You've smoked sixty cigarettes a day for the last fifty years, and written boastfully about it! What did you expect! Everybody told you, warned you, indeed threatened you with exactly what's happening to you! Talk about serves you right! Talk about own fault! And now you come to us and you ask us to make you well again! How can we make a man well from over fifty years of sixty a day! I should hope we can't! Yes, I'm glad we can't, it would make nonsense of cause and effect, crime and punishment, if ever a man deserved to die from lung cancer, that man is standing before us now, cap in hand! Hah!' Actually, it would be fag in hand, if only I had the nerve. I've never needed cigarettes more than when getting the news that I'm dying from them.

In fact, they register my answer to the question 'Are you a smoker?' – always put in neutral – with an equally neutral smile. Not one of them has suggested, in tone or gesture, a hint of reproach. They've all been – what? The trouble is that there have been so many of them that they've concentrated themselves into a single figure, young-to-middle-aged male, spruce, in a neat suit, greeting me with gloomy courtesy, and at some point in the conversation making brief but significant physical contact – a squeeze on the shoulder, a touch on my wrist. The gloomy courtesy and the shoulder or wrist squeeze or touch I came to recognise. I think I recognised it the first time it happened, actually, as a kind of mimed proclamation of my death sentence.

A GLIMPSE OF MY UNDERTAKER

Sentence, yes, as I was writing the last sentence, lo! three of these doctors suddenly came into focus. One of them, the first, was Indian or Pakistani by complexion, and had a Persian-sounding name, but in every other respect he was English – his accent was what used to be called Essex, the sort of accent deployed to conceal an expensive education, which his casually sophisticated syntax and vocabulary exposed. And he knew how to pause. At one point in our third – and so far last – conversation, when all the medical evidence was in, and it was finally established that the tumour on my neck was a secondary from the tumour in my lung, he engineered one of these pauses – difficult to know how he did it, created a space in the conversation that was an actively solemn invitation to ask a question, and not simply a question, but *the* question, the only possible question – which Victoria and I resolutely refused to ask. We had agreed – no, we hadn't had to agree, it was understood between us – that the answer to this question that we weren't going to ask contained information that we didn't want to possess. So on and on and on went the pause, and then he frowned – he had a fine but undistinguished, or do I mean indistinctive, face, with an innately melancholy tinge to its dusky hue – what do I mean? How can a face have an 'innately melancholy tinge', especially when its hue is dusky? All I mean is that he somehow exuded melancholy without visibly, in the play of his features etc., expressing it. It might have been a professional acquisition, a product of his medical training, this ability to create a melancholy atmosphere simply by sitting still and smiling pleasantly, he might be equally adept at summoning up a carefree, indeed merry atmosphere without apparent effort when a different patient, with a longer future, entered his office – anyway, back to the silence, which Victoria and I were determined not to fill until he broke it himself by interpreting it for us – 'Ahem,' he said, and that's not a device on my part, he said it in two syllables – 'Ah' and then 'hem', as if 'hem' were a noun, but an abstract one. So – 'Ah-hem' (pause) 'Is there anything you perhaps want to ask me?' (little pause) 'At this time.' We didn't speak, we made negative sounds and gestures, little shakes of the head, so forth. 'Well then,' he said, getting up from behind his desk, standing there until we got up, then crossed the room and laid a hand quietly on my shoulder before moving on to open the door. As we left the room I had the feeling that we had just conferred with my undertaker.

AND ON TO A PARTY

I remember that we went home befuddled, not quite able to speak to each other yet, perhaps not wanting to speak about the pause and its implications, and then realised, almost before our front door closed behind us, that we had to go straight out again, to a drinks party for Ian Jack, my editor at Granta, who was retiring from the publishing side of his life. We'd become close since he'd asked me to contribute something to the magazine, and then encouraged me to make a book out of it, and really, it seemed to me that we had to go to the party. After all, I might be dying but I wasn't actually ill, at least I didn't feel it. So we went to a mansion in Holland Park set in magnificent grounds, with a grand and fine lawn at the back where the party was mainly taking place. It was a quite gorgeous evening, and of course there were a lot of people that we knew, and of course I was asked, in an entirely social way, how I was, and I replied either in an entirely social way, 'Very well, thanks, how are you?' or 'Actually, I've just been told that I've got lung cancer, a possible secondary here,' touching the lump on my neck. I don't know why I did this, or what my selection principle was, if there was one. I think it must have been that to people I knew very well, friends, I gave the second answer, and to people I only meet on this kind of occasion, I gave the sociable answer, but it might easily have been the other way around, I was in such a muddle of thoughts and feelings at the time, and it's still all a bit of a muddle now. I have an idea, though, I'd half decided that it was better to come out with the news and get it over with, also that if I told a few people I wouldn't have to go on telling people, word would get around, it always does – though there's the chance, I suppose, that at a party where there was champagne and fine wine and publishing and literary gossip in the air, as well as possibly other stuff, like romance, sex, jealousy, envy – who knows what goes on at literary parties? So who knows whether my news was taken in, or held on to long enough to get passed on? Perhaps it would be dimly remembered by some the next day, but would they get the right illness? Yes, yes, they would, the word cancer always sticks, but then would they get the right victim, would they remember the cancer but fish for a name to go with it? Well, the problem didn't occur to me then, and now it seems less a problem than a comic possibility – people in the pink of health being greeted with compassionate smiles and averted eyes, or even avoided altogether – there are people who tend to avoid the ill, not out of hardness of heart or fear of contamination, but out of embarrassment – not knowing what to say, what attitude to take.

Well, as I say, I have no idea who I told, and what confusions I may have caused, I have so little clear memory of particular moments, though there were a few people who came up to me, knowing me to be a smoker, and asked for a cigarette, although I wasn't smoking myself, for once I didn't want a cigarette – I refrained from saying as I held out the packet and then lit their cigarette, 'Oh, by the way, that reminds me, I've got lung cancer.'

Looking back on the party now, I see it as if it were a painting, all those people on the great lawn in the dying light of a soft summer evening, it's a lovely picture, although, unlike the Doge of Venice, I can't see myself in it.

A PATRIARCH CALLS

It's one thing to go about at a party, telling people in a slapdash sort of way that you've got lung cancer, quite another to tell the people who have a right to know, and to do so with due care and attention. 'I must tell my children,' I said to Victoria. Normally I would have named them, as in, 'I must tell Ben and Lucy that my email is down/that we're going away for a week,' whatever. They're both parents themselves after all, and have provided me with four magnificent grandchildren – from Ben two boys, Josh and Louis, both into their teens, in fact Josh almost out of them; and from Lucy two girls, Madeleine into her teens, Georgina on the fringe. Nevertheless, 'my children' seemed the appropriate phrase for the circumstances. It embraced them all, children and grandchildren, with the suggestion of generations to come. It was patriarchal. Biblical. I remember reminding myself before I phoned, Ben first and Lucy immediately after – I think, in accordance with seniority – that I must be honest without being worrying. They have worries enough of their own – who doesn't?

Lucy has a warm, chuckly voice, a delight to listen to, even when she's vexed, which isn't often, while Ben has many voices, which he uses for many effects, some of them comic, even when he's vexed, which is quite often. My dead brother Piers, Ben's uncle, was also a gifted mimic. I hear his voice in Ben's when he's imitating a policeman, for instance, but never when he's just being himself.

Talking to the children on the phone, especially consecutively, often provides almost opposite experiences, Lucy a calm one, Ben a tumultuous one, but on this occasion they were remarkably similar. I tried to keep my own voice at the casual murmur they know so well, but I could hear that it was hoarse, and possibly too low. They had to keep saying, 'What? What did you say, Dad?' and asking me to speak up. I got through all the medical stuff fluently enough – tumour here, tumour there, both small, etc. – mentioned radiotherapy and chemotherapy as likely treatments, and was able to say, when asked stumblingly what was the prognosis, that there hadn't been one, absolutely not, and didn't add, 'And there won't be, not if I can help it.'

As I muttered gutturally on they relaxed into a sort of parental sympathy, offering advice about diet and exercise, and when I said, 'And you know, when you get to my sort of age, these things happen,' neither of them said, 'Especially if you smoke, Dad.' And both said, 'But you're not old Dad, not really!', which was soothing, with a bit of a twinge in it, because I now suspect that 'old' isn't just how far you are from the beginning, but how close you are to the end.

At the earliest possible point I switched the subject – always a good tactic if you do it abruptly enough – and eventually the conversations became almost routine, the one with Ben ending in jokes and laughter, the one with Lucy in her having to hang up, it was time to collect the girls from school.

So. So I had told my children, and was quite light-headed with relief.

I remember wondering though about Maddie and Gee-Gee, who were coming to lunch on a Sunday soon. Would they be told in their turn – yea, unto the next generation? – and if so what would they feel about having a cancerous Granddaddy? Would I see it in their eyes, their expressions, the way they talked to me?

DOCTOR NUMBER TWO: MUMMY'S DELIGHT

The second doctor, who came after the Persian-named doctor, had a Welsh name but was a magnificentlooking specimen of Anglo-Saxon manhood, though not of his own generation. He might have been an admired young friend of my parents, say ten years younger than they were when they were in their middle years. Mummy would have adored him, he was so shy and yet so easy in his manner, and his eyes had the right amount of exhaustion in them, as if he'd just come off duty – an arduous round in the hospital ward after a long morning at the operating table, nevertheless, nevertheless here he was, at our service, full of mumblingly decent apologies for having kept us waiting, half guessing that we'd noticed the way his eyes had avoided ours as he'd crossed the otherwise empty waiting room, his face lowered urgently into his mobile on his way to his office. So we waited there for half an hour before he sent for us. You could tell that he had colleagues to consult, patients to respond to, almost certainly a young wife and two or three small ones, and who knows what other obligations clamouring for his attention. He was slightly sloppy in that old-fashioned public school sort of way, his youthfully grey hair flopped down over his eye and his tie flopped out of his jacket and yet so much of him so slightly awry and askew somehow contributed to the effect of great competence – an amateur in private life, needing to be mothered and pampered and teased by his girlfriends, but a professional in his profession, magisterial with a scalpel and forceps, effortlessly masterful with the nurses.

This is all guesswork and possibly nonsense. I've no idea what he's really like, I know nothing about him except that I didn't like him, and that's probably relevant information about me and not about him, my reaction to his causing me physical distress and what came after it.

He made me sit on a stool in the corner of his office and tilt my head back and then he threaded through one of my nostrils a stiff wire with a camera at the end, and then wiggled and jiggled it down my throat. As he did this he explained that he was looking for signs of cancer in my tonsils and such places. Well, of course I hated him while he was doing it, it was worse than painful, one's nostrils and throat belong so completely to oneself – and he'd given no warning – just asked me to sit on the stool, tilt my head back and then performed the other-end-of-the-body version of a colonoscopy, and it was almost, though of course not quite – nothing could be – as foul an invasion of one's most tender and childish self – but I didn't go on hating him after he'd done it, or even disliking him. Why I disliked him then, and still do now, was that as he put the instrument away, he said, 'Well, there's nothing bad, nothing cancerous going on down there, which is reassuring.' A lie, you see. Not, I mean, that there was 'nothing bad, nothing cancerous going on down there' – doubtless true, apart from the rawness and bruising occasioned by himself – the lie was in his pretending that this was 'reassuring'. I wanted, indeed desperately hoped, that something bad was indeed going on down there. It would have meant that I had an independent cancer that would explain the tumour in my neck. With cancer two is better than one, two tumours from two separate cancers can be operated on separately, and separately eliminated. However, if the two tumours are from one cancer, they can't be operated on at all. If the tumour in the neck is from the tumour in the lung, the cancer cells are in the blood therefore, and nothing can be done. I knew all this because the first doctor, with the Persian-sounding name – let me call him Omar from now on – had not only explained it to me but in fact sent me to the present doctor precisely in the hope that he would find something cancerous going on.

But this Welsh-named doctor, let's call him Morgan Morgan and be done with it, thought – well, what did he think? Oh, I suppose only that he could delude us into thinking that bad news was good news – after all, it sounded like good news – no sign of cancer down there, rejoice! whoopee! – then he could avoid the sort of conversation that would follow giving the bad news as bad news – 'I'm very sorry, no sign of a cancer there, you're a dead man' – that sort of conversation. We didn't quite have that sort of conversation, though in fact I let him know that I understood the real significance of what he'd said. 'But we wanted to find cancer there, didn't we, surely?' I asked, not tremblingly, quite calmly. For a moment he faltered, skidded so to speak into his mumbling shyness, punctuated by apologetic laughs and abstracted hand gestures, then got himself into the clear by refusing to find his own findings conclusive – 'You never know what's there until you've had a proper look. The best thing is for me to operate. Then we'll know for sure' – and then on to suggesting dates and so forth. 'The sooner we know for sure, the quicker we can get on with it.' Getting on with it being – what exactly is the 'it' we'd be getting on with? 'Ah. That will depend on what we find.' The pause that followed wasn't engineered by him Omar-style. He wanted it as little as we did, and when he ended it with, 'Now, if there's anything you'd like to ask me?' he wasn't inviting a question, he was finishing the meeting, he was rising from his desk, he was opening the door, and the brush of his hand on my shoulder, while not exactly a push, made me feel that I was being gently encouraged out of his sphere of attention. To Victoria he gave his hand, tentatively, with a mumbling of soft farewells, and the sweetest of smiles. Yes, Mummy would have adored him. Morgan Morgan knows his onions when it comes to women, 'a bit of a lady's man, my dear, such a charming manner!'

And such a charming glimpse I suddenly had of his ruin, headlines in the *Daily Mail*, with a photo of Mr Floppy Morgan Morgan on his way to court, and inset, photos of the women he'd betrayed, some of them while under anaesthetic – all of them now emotionally dead, or dying, or at the very least in tatters as a consequence of his favourite lie – 'Oh no, don't you worry, child, nothing bad going on down there – that's the reassuring thing about me, you know, the good news about me, look you, that nothing bad ever goes on down there – married? children? who told you that? It's a bloody untruth, you know, look you!'

AN IDEAL PASSENGER

We've already settled in to being here. This morning Victoria hired a car and we went for a short spin – first along the coast road and then into town, Agios Nikolaus, which looked extremely lively, not only a tourist town but a town in its own right, part of it built around a harbour, and another part built around a lake, but we couldn't investigate it properly because we couldn't find anywhere to park, the one-way system is immensely confusing, so that we kept turning down streets that we then had to back out of, we really had to do some very skilful manoeuvring, and put up with impatient honking and unnecessarily aggressive gestures. Under the circumstances, in the bedlam of a busy Greek town, we remained remarkably calm, imperturbable. I say 'we' in this grand way because, though I don't actually drive, I take on my share of the responsibility. I sit in the passenger seat, staring out of the window and exclaiming on matters of interest – 'Hey, look at that couple over there! They must be Brits! Scots I'll bet. Only the Scots could wear shorts like that, with legs like that, both of them, and their tattoos, what's his say, on his arm?' And, 'Hey, there's a shop that sells English newspapers, and I can see the *Herald Tribune*, I wonder if they get the *Spectator*, why don't you pull over?' In other words I do my best to keep her entertained, and never let her glimpse my impatience and frustration at her inability to follow my impulses and commands.

After we'd found ourselves going down the same street for the third time, we decided to go back to the hotel and swim. We've already had a lot of swims – we start off by going down to the beach before breakfast. Victoria used never to do this, and I suspect that she's only doing it now because she's not sure how my strength will hold, and wants to keep an eye on me, if she can't see me she'll worry about me – a version of what I feel in London, when it's time to walk the dogs at night and I hate the thought of going out, but hate the thought of her going out on her own even more, knowing that every minute she's gone I'll worry that some London foulness, a twelve-year-old with a knife or a rampaging police car, will befall her. Of course, once we're out on the pavement I'm pleased I've come, although I can't say I love doing it as much as Victoria now loves our early-morning swims. We're usually the only people on the beach, and always the only people in the water, which is actually warmer at that hour than later in the day. Or is that an illusion, to do with body heat and so forth? This morning it was so still and warm and clear that after we'd got out and dried ourselves we found ourselves going back in again, without really intending to. I wish there were a way of just dissolving in the sea, without having to go through the business of drowning first.

UNCLEAN! UNCLEAN!

We spent the three weeks before the operation in Suffolk, during the only part of the summer that was like summer. It was beautiful, fresh and green and yet warm, and the light soft, like a dream, really, a dream of England that only the previous months of bad weather could have given us. We walked every evening for an hour or so, swam in the mornings and sometimes the afternoons in a friend's swimming pool, and at night – at night –

At night I tried to write but couldn't, because, well, what was the point? And I tried to stop smoking, but again, well, what was the point? Nevertheless, I cut down to about fifteen a day, and felt proud of myself.

I read familiar things that comforted me, mainly Wordsworth, Edward Thomas, Hardy, and Larkin's essays, and sometimes I sat in the garden in the moonlight, or as the dawn came up. There is no silence like a Suffolk night, in my experience, until the birds come, to shred your nerves. One night I sat for a long time at my desk in my study without doing anything at all until I suddenly began to beat myself about the head, I think in an attempt to make myself cry. I know I quite often wanted to cry, as if crying would bring release, but release from what? There was nothing to be released from. I wasn't in any pain. In fact I hadn't felt so well, physically, for a long time, not for a couple of years. Knowledge, perhaps. Yes, it must have been knowledge that I wanted to be released from.

About a week before the operation, we were still in Suffolk, my mobile rang, and a pleasant voice, female, middle-aged, practical, asked me if I was Mr Simon Gray. I said I was. 'Oh, good,' she said, and asked me if I knew that I'd got – I couldn't make out at first what it was that she wanted to know if I knew I'd got, it didn't actually seem to be a word, or a group of words – actually it turned out to be a group of letters, which she translated for me as methicillin-resistant *Staphylococcus aureus* bacteria, otherwise known as the infamous MRSA. 'What do you mean?' I said. 'I've got MRSA! How can I have got MRSA? You get it from hospitals, don't you? And the only hospital I've been to is yours.' She explained that I hadn't got it in the hospital, I'd brought it in with me, they'd found it when they'd taken a swab from one of my nostrils. I suddenly recalled having a nostril swabbed, done so swiftly and matter-of-factly that I'd scarcely registered it. 'How disgusting!' I said. 'I'm sorry, I had no idea, no idea –' 'Oh, it's quite all right, Mr Gray,' she said very pleasantly. 'About 50 per cent of the people in this country have MRSA. It doesn't do them or anyone else any harm, except when they come into a hospital. But it never comes into our hospital. We make sure of that. That's why we swab you. But you'll have to get rid of it before your operation.' Then she told me to surrender myself, so to speak, to a local doctor, she would email to him or her the necessary information, and then I was to follow the following instructions: I was to shampoo my body, with particular attention to my armpits, my chest, and between my legs three times a day; gargle three times a day; take antibiotics three times a day; if I performed these things for five consecutive days, the MRSA would be gone by the date of my operation. The gargle, the shampoo and the antibiotics would be prescribed by the doctor, and would be available from any chemist. If by any chance I forgot the instructions, the doctor and the chemist would be able to remind me of them. Was that all right, Mr Gray? I said it was. 'Then we'll see you for your operation as scheduled.' She added, 'And don't worry. It's all quite usual, Mr Gray.' When I thought about the conversation afterwards I felt there was something slightly odd about it, not simply the subject, but her manner, her tone, what was it? And eventually I realised it was the way she'd addressed me, not only formally, as Mr Gray, but regularly, slipping it into almost every sentence. I remembered that on my first visit to the hospital I'd been asked whether I wanted to be called by my first name or as Mr, and I'd said 'Mr'. Her using it so often in such a brief conversation on such a subject could have seemed satirical, but in fact it had been calming, positively soothing. I'd really felt almost dignified when confirming that I understood what I must do to render my body hygienic, and to prevent it from being a source of possibly fatal sickness to others. I wondered if she'd been trained in tact, or came by it naturally. Either way, I was grateful, and reminded myself of it as I applied the obnoxiously powerful shampoo to my pubic hair and gargled with the vile pinkish mouthwash, and so kept at bay certain scenes from films, I think American prison films of the 1940s, when the convicts are forced to de-louse themselves, whether they have lice or not, as part of a humiliation ritual –

The operation was scheduled –

but I mustn't forget the local doctor, who gave me the prescriptions for the shampoo, mouthwash and antibiotics. He has his practice, with which Victoria had had dealings since she had first come to Suffolk, in an old and elegant house in the nearby market town. His office looks out on the main square, it's a large and civilised room, and the swish modern computer on the handsome and antiquey desk is at odds with it, but his hands played skilfully over its keyboard as he brought up the details sent from the London hospital. He was a slight man, very young by my standards, somewhere in his late forties, I'd guess, and mildly elegant, in a countrified sort of way, with a shy manner of speaking, and a trace of a Suffolk accent. He looked at the screen for a while, then turned and let his gaze settle between Victoria and myself, sitting in nice chairs, facing him. 'You have cancer?' 'Yes,' I said. 'In the lung?' 'Yes,' I said, and added, 'And possibly the neck. Though it might be a secondary.' 'Yes,' he said. 'You see, I had to ask, before I could write the prescription.' There was a little pause, and his eyes came towards me, shyly. 'I'm sorry,' he said. 'I'm very sorry.' I couldn't really think of anything to say. I was touched, of course, because it was so feelingly said, but also shocked, because it was so feelingly said. I'd got into the habit, during our time in the country, of thinking of my illness as a secret. Well, not exactly a secret but as belonging to another aspect of my life, not shared with anyone but Victoria and the people in the hospital in London. In the last few days I'd even found, not a serenity exactly, certainly not at night, alone in my garden study, but during the day, during our walks and after them – they were such perfectly beautiful days, long and tender and bright days – and now in the doctor's office a decent and kindly young man had, without intending to, unravelled me, and there was the disbelief, the inner gaping at the impossible, as of hearing the news for the first time. 'Is there anything else I can do?' he asked, as he handed me the prescription. 'Are you all right for – well, sleeping, anxiety, depression – that sort of thing, what are you taking for them?' I couldn't remember, but Victoria could. 'Well, that sounds all right. If you run out of anything just give me a ring.'

We walked across the square to the chemist, where we got the shampoo, mouthwash and antibiotics. The town looked old in the evening, old and well used, and the hotel where Dickens and Mr Pickwick had stayed – sometimes you look at familiar places as if you've never seen them before, or will never see them again – perhaps it's the same sort of look.

INCRIMINATING EVIDENCE

The day before the operation I had to go in and be tested, to make sure that the shampoo, the mouthwash and the antibiotics had cleaned the MRSA out of me. We were very nearly late, as the traffic was appalling, and then the road beside the hospital, where we park, was blocked off for cars for the usual London reasons, so I got out and hurried down it, having arranged to meet Victoria at the pub where we always went after one of my appointments – in fact I passed the pub on my way down the street, and had a momentary jolt when I saw a man sitting at one of the tables on the pavement – he looked very like one of the doctors that I had routine dealings with until the cancer made him irrelevant – a short, very handsome Yorkshireman, with a lopsided smile, bright blue eyes and a wry, charming manner – let me call him Dr Mumby – Victoria thought Dr Mumby very attractive and I liked him too – when he was warning me about my smoking, he would do it in a murmuring, shoulder-shrugging sort of way, sympathetic – his father was a chain-smoker, he said, so he knew how difficult it was to give up, and to get people to give up, this with a smile to Victoria and a nod at me – well, the man sitting outside the pub, talking intensely to a middle-aged woman in a white coat, looked, as I've said, very like this doctor, so like in fact that I couldn't understand how I knew it wasn't until I realised that he was smoking, indeed he was talking around his cigarette in a very practised manner, almost like a gangster in an old movie, so I didn't shout a greeting as I went past, and when I looked back just before I went in, I could see clearly that it wasn't Dr Mumby, it wasn't just the cigarette that looked gangsterish, but the whole of him, his posture, his clothes, the cut of his jib.

All the test amounted to was a swab-taking, and there was something else, I think, I can't remember, but I didn't have to wait, it was done, the swab and whatever else they did to me, within minutes of my arrival, and then I had to wait a while, sitting on a hard chair in the corridor, for the result. I don't think that took long, but I felt very tense, as if waiting to hear whether I was rid of a sexually transmitted disease. A nurse came and told me that I was OK – I don't remember what she looked like because I avoided looking at her, I didn't want her to see the relief on my face. I went out, and there was Victoria, I could see her sitting at the table next to the one at which the pseudo-Mumby had sat. 'It's fine,' I said as I approached her. 'No more MRSA,' or words to that effect. 'Good,' she said. 'Guess who was here a moment ago, he's just left.' 'No,' I said. 'It wasn't Dr Mumby. He was smoking.' 'Yes, it was Dr Mumby,' she said. 'He recognised me. And he wasn't smoking. At least –' she got up and together we looked under his table. There was a cigarette end, half smouldering. 'Well well,' we said. 'Well well well.' Victoria looked quite pleased, probably because the thought of him furtively dropping the cigarette under the table on spotting the wife of a chain-smoking patient made him seem engagingly naughty and boyish, and I felt pleased too, though I don't quite know why.

I SENSE AN OPPORTUNITY FOR
SELF-IMPROVEMENT

The operation was scheduled for 1.30 p.m., no food or water for eight hours before. I had a little room at the end of a ward, a sombre little room, no doubt clean in fact but grubby in atmosphere, with a history of death, or so I felt as I stood by the bed holding my overnight bag, which contained pyjamas, toothbrush, books, writing pad and pens. 'Yes, it has a history of death,' I said to Victoria, nodding to the walls as if I could see on them the outlines of dreadful stains, and nodding to the bed and the ghostly line of corpses that lay on it, and then nodding around the room as a whole, at the memory of all the grieving relatives – or no grieving relatives, just the necessary functionaries cleaning and folding up the bodies of men and women of my sort of age who'd arrived clutching their overnight bags –

It was a miserable business, lying on the high, narrow bed waiting for an operation that was postponed, and again postponed, and then again postponed, becoming light-headed from hunger and dehydration. By the time I got to the knife I'd been without food and water for thirteen hours, no time at all, I realise, for the many heroes and victims that pass through all kinds of epic ordeals in war zones, no time at all for the many elderly NHS patients abandoned on trolleys in hospital corridors, forgotten, unnoticed, unfed, unwatered, unchanged, lying in their own excrement and urine, some for days on end, 'here – here and in England' – but for me, pampered as I've always been by circumstances and by the love, care and attention of others, this short period of deprivation, during which I could at least keep myself clean, was – well, it was a miserable business – made worse by my absolute conviction that Morgan Morgan had seen as much as he needed to see when he pushed his camera down my throat by way of the wire he threaded through my nostril – further gouging about with scalpels and such would tell him only what he already knew, and that I knew he knew – for him the consolation for the waste of effort would be a fee, for me that I'd been taught a lesson, a lesson in patience, humility, fortitude, all departments of the moral life in which I'm weak – if I hope to get up to the required standard in the time left to me, I shall have to do some cramming, so start by being grateful to Dr Morgan Morgan for bringing you to that forlorn little room, and letting you linger there, in hunger and thirst –

HIS SPURS AND TROUSERS, MY SHOES – A DIGRESSION

Like any good and happily married man, I share my sufferings, as much as I can, with my wife. There's not much Victoria can do about the sheer blank terror and disbelief – the self alone with the self – so she does all the things I can't, for lack of will and morale, do myself – fixing and remembering all the appointments, packing up the overnight bag, organising the taxi, getting me to the right hospital entrance, to the right admissions desk, to the right ward. I sometimes wonder if she had all these skills before I entered her life, or has she had to acquire them as we went along? She does it all with such consideration, tact, kindness and grace – such charm and softness and delicacy – all these on my account, for me. And in return she has a bewildered, angry, blustering, ungrateful – yes, frequently ungrateful – shameful to write it down, how ungrateful I've been, am being, for all that she gives me that helps me get through all the things I have to get through in order to get to the end, the only end of all this.

And when I get there, have got there, am gone, what will it be like for her? Going into my study, for instance. Well, I should think it'll be quite – quite – I can't imagine it. I suppose I mean that I don't want to imagine it –

Well then, what about others, people who know me but have never seen my study? What will they make of it? Can I imagine that? Well, I have experience to draw on. For instance, when I visited Ian's flat after his death, because I was told that he wanted me to have something, a book or a print – in fact, I took his straw hat, which he'd worn to cover his balding and blotched head during chemo – I was moved by the atmosphere of dedication as well as of loneliness. He'd moved into it as a halfway house between his marriage with Ahdaf and their two sons, and his intended marriage to Patchy, by whom he had two young children, a daughter and a son. It didn't look like the flat of a man who'd ever lived with anyone else, it was neat and organised in a bachelor's way. Most striking were the number of television sets, all with fairly up-to-date systems, and recording devices – one in every room, and in one room two sets – can that be right? – so that he would never miss a football match, whichever room he was in. He watched virtually every match shown on television, he told me, which even five years ago was an enormous number, but then football was his passion. Well, Tottenham Hotspur, Spurs, was his passion and football in general the context in which his passion flourished and smouldered. I remember once he wanted to change the evening for a dinner because Spurs were playing Newcastle in a cup tie but for reasons I can't remember I was determined to keep him to the arrangement. I told him I would record the match, then after dinner – we always met at Chez Moi, a little restaurant almost opposite our house – we'd watch it in my study. He felt anxious about this, was sure something would go wrong, but I said I'd recorded hundreds of matches, it wouldn't go wrong, why should it? So he agreed, slightly mutteringly, that that's what we'd do. I set the video timer just before crossing the road to Chez Moi, then, to make sure all was well, I recorded something, I don't remember what, and played it back. The screen filled with white dots on a blank background. I tried to phone Ian to tell him not to come, to stay at home and watch the match. I was too late. He'd already left and I got the answering machine. I almost panicked, then had a moment of inspiration – I phoned Philip, who has a car hire firm and has taken us, Victoria and me, to airports and first nights and special occasions for many years now and has become a friend who furthermore often records things for us when we're away. He promised to tape the match and as soon as it was finished to bring it to the restaurant. I crossed the road to Chez Moi and found Ian already ensconced. He listened with suspicion as I explained what had happened, and what I'd arranged to rectify it, and when I'd finished he looked uneasy and impatient. 'It'll be all right,' I said. 'Philip never lets me down, he'll be here with the tape as promised, we'll see every moment of the match.' He shook his head and muttered that the evening was beginning to have a smell of calamity. He was probably on the verge of taxiing back to his flat and watching what was left – he'd get most of the second half – but he didn't. He got through the meal restlessly, constantly checking his watch and then, pretty well the minute he judged the match to be over, eyeing the door and saying things like, 'Where is this Philip of yours?' – and I kept saying things like, 'Give him a chance, he lives twenty minutes away.' In fact, he turned up with the tape before we'd finished our coffee, and said that he'd tested it to make sure it had come through clearly, and then wound it back to the beginning, it was set, ready to be played. Ian and I went back to my study, I put a drink and an ashtray beside him, turned on the television, put in the tape, sat down, got up again as Ian groaned aloud, the groan of a man who'd known all along that there was no hope. The screen was black, with white dots. Instead of cursing Philip, in whom I had complete faith, I sauntered in a confident manner to the video, checked that the tape was in properly, checked that the set was on the right channel, pressed a few buttons at random and suddenly there it was on the screen, a perfect picture, the sound also perfect. Ian lit a cigarette and settled tensely in his chair. I sat watching from my desk, also smoking and at first offering observations and bits of analysis until I realised from his answering grunts and silences that they weren't wanted, indeed that he found them irritating because they interfered with his concentration. So it was in full, uninterrupted concentration that he watched Newcastle score one, then two, then three, then four, then five goals. Spurs scored none. When the match was over, frowning commentators discussed whether Spurs had finally reached rock bottom. Before they'd finished Ian got up. I walked him to Holland Park Avenue, where he hailed a taxi. 'Thanks,' he said, in a dead tone as he got in. 'Thanks a lot.' I'd always thought of myself as a man who loved football and watched it avidly, but I supported the team that played the sort of football that I most enjoyed watching, and it tended to change from season to season, sometimes within the season. That evening with Ian made it clear that there was a world of difference between a man who followed the game and a man who followed a club. In Ian's eyes, I realised, I was little more than a dilettante, while he was a man who had given his heart and his loyalty to Spurs, who had just been beaten 5–0, and had hit rock bottom.

It wasn't a surprise, then, to find so many television sets in his flat, but it was poignant to see them there, so tactically arranged. It gave one a glimpse into his habits, with the piercing thought that he'd never turn them on again, just as he'd never sit at his desk again. There were papers spread on it, a couple of open books. And then there was his bedroom, with a single bed, neatly made, the whole room, the whole flat was neat, have I already said that? neat and orderly, so unlike his emotional and financial life. Over the chair in his bedroom was draped a pair of trousers, looking as if they were waiting for him to get into them.

But to get back to my own case, my study after my death, what would people see? Well, there are the books chaotically everywhere, the desk with my typewriter on it and some papers, the other desk with my computer and probably some yellow pads full of illegible writing, the portraits on the wall, Schubert and Dickens, a couple of cricketers by Spy, a lovely watercolour of a frog, done by the father of a good friend. All in all, pretty well what you'd expect of a man who does the sort of things I did, but oh yes, except for the shoes, of course, all my shoes lined up against the wall of my study – I've just counted them in my head, got up to twelve pairs, most of them worn only once or twice as they'd changed size the moment after I'd bought them, others that I've used for over twenty years, and somehow look as if my feet are still in them even when they're empty, and there are the espadrilles with holes in the toes and flattened-down heels, and there's a round box with more shoes in them, sneakers and trainers and sandals, and up in the bedroom closet a couple of pairs of shiny black shoes, for smart occasions, they pinch and squeeze my feet and I only put them on if I know I'll be able to sit down for most of the evening, or best of all kick them off under the dinner table –

What will it be like for her, all those shoes to deal with, with all of them, even the unworn ones, having a sort of history to them? I wonder if I shouldn't start getting rid of them when we get back, a pair or so at a time, so that Victoria won't notice. But where would I take them? Oxfam? Put them in carrier bags and taxi them up to Oxfam, say two bags a week. But supposing she went into Oxfam, as she does sometimes, and saw all the shoes lined up against the wall there – what would she think? what would it mean, that I'd been secretly disposing of my shoes? But why secretly? Surely I could say, 'Darling, don't you think it's time –' No. Stop there. You couldn't say that. So let's move on from shoes to ties, because a) I've only got three or four of them and b) I never wear them anyway.

A VISIT FROM MUMMY'S DELIGHT

I woke from the operation some time after midnight with a bursting bladder. It took me several minutes to get out of bed and into the bathroom, where I discovered that my bladder wouldn't empty, and nor would my bowels. Both were becoming painful. I passed this information on to a nurse, who passed it on to a mortifyingly pretty doctor (female), who came in with a gadget that I recognised from some ten years ago, after an operation on my stomach had left me with the problems that I now had again. She was deft, as well as pretty, the doctor. She had curly black hair, an olive complexion, alert brown eyes and a mouth that would have looked even more delightful if she'd allowed it to smile. It took her about three minutes to insert my penis into the catheter, or is it technically the other way round, and I only screamed once, though at length. She went out and returned immediately with a nurse, who hitched me up to a drip. So there I was for the night – the tube of a catheter in my penis, my right hand attached to a drip, my throat – my throat was in waiting, underneath the painkillers. The next morning, shortly after Victoria arrived with newspapers, an oddly shifty little nurse, I took her to be, poked her head around the door and said something so incomprehensible that I knew it must be English. I looked to Victoria to translate and, when she couldn't, asked the nurse if she'd mind – I hadn't quite understood. This time she spoke slowly and clearly, if rather nervously.

'Dr Morgan Morgan is doing his rounds and would like to visit you if you have no objections.'

I said of course I had no objections, was indeed anxious to have a few words with Dr Morgan Morgan.

'That's very kind of you,' she said, and withdrew.

'How strange,' we thought, that the doctor who'd operated on me should seek permission to speak to me. Or perhaps he'd been informed of my catheter-bruised penis, my drip-tube imprisoned arm, my swollen bowels, and felt responsible for them, as indeed he was, although only accidentally, at least I assumed accidentally.

Morgan Morgan came in a few minutes after the shifty little nurse-figure had withdrawn, and he came in accompanied by the shifty little nurse-figure, who I now realised was actually a shifty little doctor-figure, a junior doctor or trainee doctor, as were the eight or nine young men and women who stood there with her, all of them looking shifty – at least in relation to me, none of them able to meet my eye. Of course, what the shifty little doctor-figure had really been asking was whether Morgan Morgan could bring in his students and display me to them, for educational purposes. I didn't feel humiliated so much as humbled – brought low – an object of study and later of discussion. Morgan Morgan stood in the middle of his semicircle and wondered how I was. I said I was fine, really, under the circumstances, apart from a sore throat and – I gestured with my unattached hand towards my attached one, but decided not to mention the catheter. 'Well,' he said, seemingly at a loss, 'that's good. And – well – we didn't find anything bad in your throat, except a slightly septic tonsil, which I took out. But that was all. Nothing wrong down there, no cancer is the good news.' Yes, there he was, doing it again – delivering unbearably bad news as if it were good news – I almost expected him, wanted him even, to say, 'Look you,' as in my caricaturing impersonations of him. Of course I hadn't been foolish enough to harbour a hope, though hope, as we all know at bitter times in our lives, is an eager ally of foolishness, and the truth is that I had now and again, before the operation and in the uncomfortable hours since, found myself daring to harbour – such an odd phrase, to harbour a hope, as if hope drifts about in search of a haven, a resting place –

There were all those students' eyes that couldn't look at me.

'I thought,' I said, 'that the good news would be if you found cancer.'

He gave me a confused smile, as if I were being too clever for him.

'Your not finding cancer in my throat means that the cancer on my neck is a secondary from the cancer in my lung.'

'Well, yes,' he agreed, 'there is that.' He tried to think of something else to say. 'Thank you,' he said, 'for letting us come in to see you.' He went out, his students trailing after him, one or two of them achieving nice, apologetic smiles – apologies on behalf of youth and health to age and illness.

Victoria and I sat for a while. We didn't have much to say to each other. I thought it was odd, though, that Morgan Morgan hadn't examined me or questioned me, apart from asking me how I felt. What exactly had he been showing his junior doctors or trainees or what-ever they were? What was there to see except a seventy-year-old man in a bed on a drip? They couldn't see the catheter, and wouldn't have needed to anyway, as they surely knew what a catheter was and did.

From where they stood they couldn't have seen the tumour on my neck, so what was it he was showing them? Why did he want them to look at me? Unless, of course, I was his straight man in a little demonstration, or skit even, on how to dress dreadful news up as its opposite. On the other hand, perhaps there was a complicated lecture, part of which he gave before they came in, the other part after they'd gone out – 'I want you particularly to note the distinctive shape of the nose, characteristic of the heavy smoker destined for lung cancer' and then 'Which one of you would care to make an observation about the relationship between the smallness of his eyes, the lowness of his brow, and the probable sites of his third, fourth, fifth and sixth tumours?'

LITERARY WHEELING AND DEALING – NO WONDER THERE'S A SMELL!

The next morning a nurse called Anita told me I could go home. She was a rather stern-looking woman of about forty-five, and was from Barbados. She had tended to me – emptied my urine out of the flask, adjusted the position of the drip needle in the back of my hand, taken my temperature and blood pressure etc. – in a solemn and unforgiving manner. I felt uneasy every time she came into the room, she confirmed my sense that I was there in foul circumstances – catheter, drip, tumours – because I deserved to be. When she told me that she was now going to take out the drip and the catheter tube, she made me feel that these unsavoury duties were forced upon her as the consequence of my unsavoury behaviour – and of course she was right, if you trace the thought far enough back. If I hadn't smoked I wouldn't have cancer, wouldn't have had a throat operation, wouldn't have required a drip and a catheter, neither of us would be where we now were, me in a hospital bed, she at the foot of it, staring at me. 'Are you still writing?' she asked. For a moment I wondered whether one of us had made a mistake, that either she'd said or I'd heard 'writing' instead of 'smoking', but then I noticed that her expression, though as serious as usual, was also interested, possibly even self-interested. So I said yes, I still wrote, though not much at the moment.

'I write,' she said. 'I am a writer too.'

I was very pleased to hear this. I wanted the person who was going to take the catheter tube out of my penis to want something from me, and I could sense that Anita wanted something. I couldn't wait to promise it to her, whatever it was.

'What have you written?' I asked eagerly.

It was a novel about herself and her adventures. She'd had an adventurous life, she said, strange things had happened to her since her escape from Barbados.

'You escaped from Barbados?'

'I thought I would call it *Dangerous Escape*, or *My Dangerous Escape*.'

'"My" is better,' I said. 'It makes it more personal.'

'*My Dangerous Escape*.' She seemed to like the sound of it. She said it several times more, lengthening it slightly: '*My Dan – ge – rous Es – cape*.'

'What were you escaping from?' I asked. For me Barbados was one of the places I escaped to, and never wanted to leave.

'From Barbados,' she said.

Well, I suppose if you were born there, with the prospect of spending the rest of your life there, you might come to feel that you were on too little land in far too much water – and then there would be the family – parents, brothers and sisters, cousins, aunts, uncles – and the church – there are lots of churches of so many denominations that it would be hard not to belong to one of them, yes, a God-fearing people, a neighbour-fearing people, too, probably – so a perfect place for clapped-outs like me, who yearned for the England of the 1950s, but for Anita when she'd been young it might have seemed like a prison.

'Well, I suppose it's all in the book,' I said. 'Why you wanted to escape.'

She said it was. Along with all the things that had happened to her since. She'd had a difficult and exciting life, the escape from Barbados to Canada, and then from Canada to London. She had a son growing up and had a husband somewhere. She also had a good friend, a clever woman younger than herself who had advised her to write the book, and had helped her in the revising of it. Her friend thought that there was still a little work to be done on it, and then it would be ready for publication. What did I think?

I said it sounded very promising.

Yes, she said. It was. Very promising.

Her tone through all this was slightly friendlier than before, but still forbidding. I kept thinking of her fingers working the tube out of my penis, and longed to speak words that would make them gentle, coaxing, caring, loving, above all painless.

How, she asked, could she get *My Escape from Barbados* published?

I told her that it was very difficult these days to get books published, at least in my understanding of the situation. I didn't say that if she were twenty years or so younger and possibly a mite prettier – though she'd really be quite pretty, Anita, if only she'd stop frowning – actually, it was almost a scowl – so if she'd stop almost scowling – and there was a moment when she laughed, all white teeth and sparkling eyes, and her face came alive and was better than pretty – in other words I didn't tell her that her chances of getting *My Escape from Bermuda* published were minuscule unless her story included rape, alcoholism, drug addiction, racial abuse, sexual servitude.

'Best thing to do is to get an agent,' I said.

'An agent?'

'An agent will know all the publishers. She'll know which one to send your book to.'

'You have an agent?'

I said I had.

She didn't say anything, just stood there, keeping her level, authoritarian gaze fixed on me.

'Hey,' I said eventually, 'I've got an idea. Why don't I –?' and gave her my agent Judy Daish's address and several of her phone numbers, reminding myself that Judy was always superb in a crisis, and that the removal of a catheter was a crisis. Anita took a pad out of her pocket, and a pen, wrote down the address and the phone numbers, read them out to me twice, put the pen and the pad away. She didn't thank me, or smile acknowledgement, she accepted it as her due, something that I in some way owed her. I wonder, though, how she knew I was a writer.

She took the tube out in a simple, straightforward manner, very practised, but not particularly sensitively – I mean, she didn't seem either touched or irritated by my scream of pain. After this one conversation she didn't refer to *My Escape from Barbados* again, though she was in and out of my room quite often, for pulse and temperature etc., and the next day, when she came in to tell me that I could go home, and I wished her luck with the book, she said, 'Thank you,' in an indifferent and blank sort of way, closing off the subject.

While we were hanging about in the corridor, waiting for a doctor to come and sign the document that made it OK for me to leave, an exceptionally pretty Indian nurse came up to us. With a dazzling smile to Victoria, she turned to me and said in an intimate and caring voice, 'I hope you won't mind my mentioning it, but you smell of urine.' I suppose that once or twice, when I was a child, an adult had said something like that to me, and perhaps as a child I was mortified, but now, as an elderly adult in dire straits, I felt nothing except a dull curiosity. 'Are you sure?' I said. 'I can't smell anything,' and asked Victoria whether she could smell urine on me. 'I don't mean to offend you,' the nurse said. 'I was worried that if you go home by bus or on the tube people will say something, and you will be embarrassed. Please don't mind my mentioning it,' and she went off gracefully, on long and shapely legs, her charming head held high. 'Do I smell of urine?' I asked Victoria again. She sniffed around me, and said that I didn't, but that she'd been aware of a strong uriney smell coming from the room opposite. Its door was open and two old men lay on beds, propped up on pillows, facing each other, asleep. They were both sallow, gaunt and bald, so similar to each other that they looked related, twins almost, though I don't expect they were.

All the stuff in the hospital – the operation, Morgan Morgan, Anita, the catheter, smelling or not smelling of urine – it's all quite trivial, really, in the grand scheme of things – even in the very small grand scheme of things which is me and the rest of my life. Why, then, do I not only remember it but insist on writing it down?

WELL, WHAT SHOULD I BE WRITING?

Wisdom? But I have none. Consolation? But I am inconsolable. I have no faith that is – in one of the current phrases I hate so much – 'fit for purpose'. No faith that isn't 'fit for purpose' either. But do I have any sort of faith, even a small, uneasy one, not perhaps 'fit for purpose' but a helpful guide through the moment-by-moment moments that I have left to live through? Of course not. I have only the self that I've been stuck with all my life. Odd that I should think that I am an I that has a self, as if I and my self weren't identical. I certainly behave as if I were in some way double, if not actually plural, especially in the last few years when I talk to myself almost continuously when on my own, and sometimes when I'm not, and also have the sense that I'm in the audience, a commentator or a judge of a debate when the dialogue becomes quarrelsome, which it frequently does. Recently, since the news, we've spoken lamentations to ourself, 'Oh, poor Simon,' we say, or 'Poor old Si,' quite affectionately, as to a dog. Or 'You stupid bugger, stupid, stupid bugger!' Or struck myself savagely in the face, as I did that night in the garden in Suffolk, swearing at myself, 'Fuck, shit, arsehole! What a stupid, fucking arsehole!' – and though I suppose I mean, specifically, for having smoked myself to death, I also mean more generally, for being a creature that dies – thinking that the relationship between me and my mortal self was a sort of arranged marriage, the fundamental terms of which I never agreed to. Could I believe that that deceived and coerced 'I' is in fact my soul, my soul 'fastened to a dying animal/It knows not what it is' – from Yeats, surely, but I can't remember which poem, and of course he believed in the soul almost as a physical being – 'unless/Soul clap its hands and sing, and louder sing/For every tatter in its mortal dress'. But no, my self isn't my soul, there's too many of it, and it's grubby and it can't sing, it's probably what I have instead of a soul, and it's not soulful, it's helpless and angry –

Does this mean, then, that I never expected to die?

Actually, I think I'll try to come back to this question later. For now let me just say that actually it's a heavenly day –

PLEASANTRIES AND OTHER PLEASURES

Yes, a most heavenly day. Warm, with the mildest of breezes, the sea calm and the surrounding mountains visible, with the distinct hint, like large thoughts not yet thought, of mountains beyond them, and beyond. I'm sitting at the table, as has become my habit, with my back resting against the chapel wall. In front of me are the tables and chairs of the restaurant, and then the esplanade and the steps down to the beach. It's the sort of day that helps people to be friends, almost everyone who passes by me nods or smiles, some say a few words, the routine words – 'Isn't it lovely here!' and 'What a beautiful day,' or more personally, 'You look comfortable there in the shade.' An elderly Scotsman with a verra thick accent has just loitered to discuss the charms of the hotel, it's his first time in Greece, usually he goes to Portugal 'and such', he tries to learn the language of the country he holidays in, but he's finding Greek 'verra, verra difficult' – he's been here a week, going back on Tuesday, so he doubts that he'll master it on this visit, at least – Well, it was a nice conversation, cheerful and easy. Then he was down to the beach and a few minutes later up again with a stately, heavy-treading silver-haired wife, who continued on her way while he paused to tell me to send him a cheque, a blank cheque, any sort of cheque would do as long as it was blank. I laughed and nodded, but couldn't think what to say because I didn't understand the joke, if it was a joke. Yes, it was a joke, his countenance and the tone of his voice announced it as such, but what was its point? I'm going to go for a swim, why not?

Victoria was on the beach, lolling on a sunbed, reading. I sidled up to her, reached for her hand to lead her into the sea, but coughed before I could surprise her. That's the thing about this cough. It's not the free and easy, loose and phlegmy, and on the whole controllable cough of health. It's a tight little cough, a bit of a rasper, that comes when it chooses. It's a cancer cough, as the swelling on my neck is a cancer swelling, one the audible, the other the visible sign of my condition.

Victoria has become used to the cough. As soon as she heard it she looked up, then held out her hand – and so, though I didn't succeed in surprising her, I did nevertheless lead her into the sea, which was clear and still, with only one other couple swimming, but lots of small black fish scampering near the surface. We sported about in the shallows, as I haven't yet the courage to go out of my depth. I'm not sure of my strength, whether it won't suddenly give out, as it's started to do now and then on land, when I have to pause, stoop to recover my breath, my legs heavy and weak, my shoulders sagging. If that happens in the water I can probably roll on to my back and float. On the other hand, well, there are worse deaths, some of them in bed.

Eventually Victoria went off for a proper swim and I stayed near the shore, the water just up to my neck. If I bent my knees I had the feeling of being suspended. It was really very pleasant, hanging about in the water, watching her steady breaststroke taking her away from me until the fuzz of her hair was too far out for my liking. The familiar anxiety clutched at my heart, and, as if responding to it, she turned and headed back. We got out – a nice, easy beach to get out on to, thank God – and went to the shower, an unusual shower in that it delivers the water with such force that it hits the skin like needles, and the top of one's head is sore for a few moments afterwards. Then she returned to the sunbed and her book, and I walked to the steps, intending to come back here to the chapel. But I didn't come back here, I turned around, and without actually concealing myself from Victoria slipped back into the water without her seeing me. I think I wanted to test myself out. I did all the things I've been doing since I was five or six, underwater somersaults, spiral dives, corkscrews. I went through my repertoire grimly, as if I were auditioning, then more and more freely until suddenly, without at first being conscious of it, I was enjoying myself – splashing and sporting, diving and twirling, holding my breath underwater for quite long stretches. Then I did the more taxing stuff, the two backstrokes, the sidestroke and the crawl. The backstrokes were fine, the sidestroke OK, but the crawl wasn't right. Something was out of alignment, in the small of my back or at the base of my spine. And the fact is that although I could do all the other strokes properly, I couldn't do any of them for very long, almost as if, when it came to purposeful swimming, my body had a weak will or a short attention span – it's not that I slowed down or wore myself out, I just stopped – perhaps it was to catch my breath, perhaps my lungs had abruptly emptied. But that's all right, really, perfectly all right, because I had so much pleasure from the breath that kept me afloat – yes, think of it that way, a new way, for you, of thinking about things.

As I was writing the above a young Frenchman with a perpetual half-smile and a perpetual stubble – it's been the same length for three days now, how does he do it? – stopped by to confide that he was leaving this afternoon, he was very sad, going back home to Tours, did I know Tours? I said I did, which was a lie, and a foolish one – my plan was to stop him telling me about Tours, its history, its architecture, its restaurants, after all there would be no need for him to tell me if he thought that I already knew – but he was so astonished that I knew Tours that he wanted to know when I'd been, why, and what did I think of it? So I said, 'Oh,' I said, 'it was a long time ago, and it might have been Lourdes, come to think of it, yes, Lourdes, not Tours.' He did a polite little French gape, eyebrows up, mouth pursed, at the thought that anyone, even an Englishman, could confuse going to Lourdes with going to Tours, but then pressed on to what he really wanted to talk about, which was his new car. He was picking it up in Paris on his way to Tours, it was an English car, a beautiful car, it was a Jaguar!

'Wow!' I said.

We beamed proudly at each other, he because of his new car, I because I come from the country that made it. Then he passed on, up the path to the hotel and – I think I can say with confidence, though of course you never know – out of my life for ever. He's not somebody I would mind meeting again, he was so friendly and pleased with everything.

DOCTOR NUMBER THREE: CHIPMUNK OF DOOM

I was just about to settle back against the wall of the chapel, stop writing for a while and smoke what would be only my third cigarette of the day. Only! Only your third! Yes well but – three months ago it would have been my twenty-third, thirtieth even – no, it wouldn't, it's not midday yet, three months ago you wouldn't even have been up, so you wouldn't have smoked any cigarettes, none – I've actually managed to put the cigarette back in the pack, but in order to keep it there I've got to go on writing, and I don't really want to, as I'll almost certainly find myself writing about the third doctor, the one that came after Omar and Morgan Morgan, the one I keep putting off writing about –

He wore the same sort of clothes as Omar and Morgan Morgan, dark suit, shirt, tie, but in their cases the clothes seemed both to confer authority and to imply deference. I think I described Omar as looking like an undertaker, and though Morgan Morgan gave the impression of being dishevelled the dishevelment was in his personality, he was still in absolutely the right clothes, the clothes were right for the man and the clothes were right for the job, ergo the man was right for the job, was how it worked in the cases of both Omar and Morgan Morgan. The third doctor looked wrong in all three respects, though my first impression, physical and before thought, was that he was a chipmunk, a massive chipmunk, and then the second one, when he'd formed into a man, that he was in the wrong clothes, that they were too grown-up for him. In fact, he looked like an exuberant prep-school boy, circa the period I went to prep school. His eyes popped boisterously behind the lenses of large spectacles, his straw-coloured hair stood straight up from his head as if in jubilation, and his round, pink face wore a worried, an actively worried, expression, as if knowing that it wasn't the expression required, which should have been responsible, grave, kindly, an expression along those lines. All through the conversation he gave the impression of being simultaneously surprised and at a loss, as if he'd been caught out doing something not exactly against the rules, but against some code he wasn't yet quite grown-up enough to understand. So when he said, once he'd got behind his desk, that he was very sorry, it really did sound as if he was apologising for some misdemeanour of his own, which prevented it from being the chillingly serious opening that he'd probably intended it to be. He probably wanted to start from an absolutely clear understanding of my situation – that it demanded and deserved profound commiserations, and we would proceed from there.

In fact, we didn't seem to be proceeding towards much of consequence. He pretty well repeated what Omar and Morgan Morgan had said – i.e. there were two possibilities: 1) that the tumour on my neck was an independent tumour, the two tumours could be treated separately, in both cases either by surgery or by chemotherapy; 2) that the tumour on the neck was a secondary of the tumour in my lung, which would mean that the cancer cells were in my bloodstream, and the treatment, by radiotherapy, would be palliative, a matter of keeping the cancer in check, but not curing it. The question as to whether we were confronted by 1) or 2) would be answered by the operation to be performed by Dr Morgan Morgan – 'Now, is there anything you want to ask me?' It came out very abruptly, not at all the hesitant invitation of Omar and Morgan Morgan. It was almost a challenge. There was a brief pause, during which he – let me give him a name – Len Rootle let me call him, Dr Rootle – So –

'Now, is there anything you want to ask me?' asked Dr Rootle.

Then came the brief pause. During it he sat behind his desk ogling us. We indicated that there was nothing we wanted to ask him.

'Well,' he said, 'would you like a prognosis? I mean, if the operation to be performed by Dr Morgan Morgan doesn't reveal a cancer in the throat, would you like a prognosis?' It was most peculiar, most peculiar, the way he got this out, awkward, impetuous and alarmed, with a throb of excitement in it.

'No,' Victoria said firmly. No, for her part, she certainly, most certainly didn't want to hear a prognosis.

Dr Rootle nodded inattentively, his ogle was fixed on me.

The word 'prognosis' made me dizzy. Especially as we hadn't yet had a definitive diagnosis, which couldn't be made until after Dr Morgan Morgan's operation, surely – how long would it take them after Dr Morgan Morgan's operation to reach a definitive diagnosis? I wondered.

'How long –' I began, and stopped, thinking that I didn't really want to prolong the conversation, really it was time to go home. Dr Rootle decided that 'How long?' was the whole of my question, which was in response to his own question, so, yes please, he took me to mean, give me your prognosis, how long do I have before I die? 'About a year.' The words came out of the side of his mouth, low but clear.

I believe I said, 'Christ!' I looked at Victoria, who shrank, looked small and white.

I wanted to say, 'But I didn't ask that question, so kindly withdraw your answer.' I also wanted to swear at him, 'You stupid fucking awful fucking moron' sort of stuff, and for a moment or two, as I stared at his face, now for the first time befittingly calm and solemn, with a certain satisfaction in it – 'Mission accomplished! Difficult deed done, and out of the side of my mouth too!' – I wanted to kill him. I wanted to kill him and say just as I pulled the trigger, thrust the dagger, whatever, 'That's a year longer than you have, matey.' The thing I think I understood immediately, before I'd even thought about it, was that a doctor who tells you that you have a year to live has taken the year away from you – from the moment the sentence was delivered – the sentence that delivered the sentence – the knowledge would never be cleared from my consciousness, the last thought at night, the first in the morning, for the rest of my life –

I really don't remember much about how it went after that.

MY STRUGGLE TO ESCAPE – PART ONE

It is one o'clock in the morning, I am sitting at a table on the patio that separates our room from our small private swimming pool, and I am becoming maddened by the walls that hem me in. At the end of the pool there is a row of jagged rocks, cemented together with a gap in the middle to give a view of the sea, which is pitch black. In the morning it's the most marvellous blue, the sea stretches out, you can see boats in the distance, and there is a sense of space, ease, freedom and I leap into the pool, naked, and swim about – this morning, for instance, we went to the beach and swam in the sea, it was almost transparent, it was lovely, then walked back along the garden paths to our room, to find breakfast on the table I am now writing at. I took off my trunks and into the pool I went. It's a saltwater pool, quite cold, cold and cramped, and I don't quite know why I do it, especially after a proper swim in the sea, but it's now become a ritual – sea swim, pool swim, shower, breakfast, and over breakfast the view of the sparkling blue, and the yachts and their sails –

But at night I feel trapped by the walls, the blackness of the sea, so impenetrably black, no lights of passing ships, nothing to distinguish it from the black sky, and my lungs feel as if they are contracting, I begin to cough and wheeze, and panic sets in – panic is setting in now, as I write – I find myself hating the hotel that I like so much in the daytime, and particularly hating the manager –

The wall to the right is so high that it is impossible to see over it. The wall to the left is lower, and if I stand up I can see into the neighbouring pool and the patio and even into a bit of the room next door, and beyond, over their low wall, I can see all the way to the beach, and the little chapel where I sit writing in the daytime, and then the hill above the hotel, with the lights of the cars moving along the roads – the sea is bright, little boats bobbing up and down, and the waves rippling – it is a charming and a painful sight – painful because now I passionately covet the room next to ours that commands this view from its patio, and this morning we were offered it by the manager, and I turned it down. Why did I? Why did he let me? Why didn't he insist on my taking it? What a fool I am! Fool! Sitting here at the table, in my pitch-black cell, my cancer cell – this is hysteria.

That was hysteria.

I calmed down by going to the wall I could see over, the left wall, and breathing in the view, the beach, the little white chapel where I sit, the hills and the lights moving up and down and across. Then I came back here, to the table, and smoked a cigarette.

Now I'm going to write it down in a sensible fashion.

The reason I didn't accept the next-door room that I now covet only just this side of lunacy is because the manager wouldn't let us have a rather splendid bungalow on the other side of the hotel, with accommodation for six people, with the swimming pool set on a large lawn, and most importantly, from the patio where I would sit at night, there was an expansive view of the sea. It's been unoccupied for several days, according to the young Italian couple in the small suite next to it, and will probably remain unoccupied until the end of the season, and is very expensive, expensive even for four, therefore preposterously expensive for two. I asked the manager if he would give us a discount – no, let's get this absolutely right, for some reason I was worried that he would be upset – his feelings would be hurt – if we

wanted to change rooms without explanation, he would think we
didn't like our room, which, he'd confided to me, was the best room
in the hotel, the one that he, personally, liked the most – he's a rather
freaky looking guy, about fifty I suppose, short, with a rosy
complexion and glistening black eyes and black plastered-back hair
and a high-pitched voice – a lot of Cretans, we've noticed, have high-
pitched voices and are quite short – he wears trousers that look as if
they're made of tweed, hitched high up on his body, to almost his
armpits, and has a rapid, disjointed walk. When we arrived at the
hotel last Sunday, at around midnight, it was pouring with rain. A
savage wind lashed at us as we got out of the taxi. He came dashing
out of the rather grand entrance into the rain and wind to welcome
us with an umbrella and to escort us down to an empty restaurant,
where a meal had been arranged. The hotel has four restaurants that
all close before 11 p.m., which is depressing and completely un-Greek,
in our experience, but still, it was thoughtful of him to have a meal
ready and waiting, though actually it was spooky, the two of us sitting
there in an otherwise totally empty restaurant, the wind howling, the
rain beating at the large glass doors.

A very nice man in a suit, plump and avuncular, though about
twenty years younger than me, a maître d' figure, I suppose, brought
us an assortment of dishes I couldn't eat, so Victoria had to be politely
hungry for two. 'Oh, my fran, no food, why no food?' the maître d'
kept saying, gazing miserably down at my untouched plate and
caressing my shoulder until I was desperate to get away from him, his
wounded eyes and the threat of further dishes – perhaps he'd cooked
them himself – and said how tired we were, sleepy, and backed it up
with imitations of myself sleeping, snoring noises and so forth, but still
he insisted on bringing us some terrible Greek puddings. It was a great
relief when the manager reappeared, and we could leave the table with
fulsome thank yous to the maître d' and scurry after the manager
through the rain to our room. It was then that he told me of his love
for it, that it was his favourite room etc. and it was just after he'd gone,
while Victoria was unpacking, that I took in these oppressive walls. 'We
can't stay here,' I said, although it was obvious that we'd have to, at least
for the night –

which I got through by taking two sleeping pills, and two co-proxamol, and half a dozen cigarettes. I sat outside on the patio, not completely protected from the rain by a sliver of roofing, and not at all from the wind, which came whistling and howling through or over the walls in a way that seemed quite personal, as if it were seeking me out, in fact. 'Hey! Go get the cancer guy smoking his cigarettes. He's in a daze or a doze from his sleepers. See if you can shake him up a bit. Make him scream out or cry like when we did the old guy back on the heath. See if he's got any "Blow, winds, and crack your cheeks" sort of stuff in him. Cancer, cigarettes, chemicals. Talk about a deserving case!'

At some point before dawn I climbed into bed and clung to my wife.

MY STRUGGLE TO ESCAPE – PART TWO

It wasn't raining when we woke up, but the wind was still at it, and the skies were grey. In the evening the sun came out, and we had a swim from the little beach. It was surprisingly pleasant in the water, but chilly getting out of it, the wind had dropped a little, but seemed to have become colder, and the few other people on the beach were huddled on sunbeds, under layers of towels. Now and then we discussed the question of changing rooms, then moved on to the question of changing islands, from Crete back to England. If the weather was going to remain like this, what was the point? – confined to a single room, with a cold swimming pool at the end of it? It was a day of depression, really, and of yearning for a few years ago, when I had health, or a few months ago, when I had ignorance.

Then the next day and we were here, saw in its proper weather what a beautiful place it is, so perfectly spread out, with charming walks and so much sea to look at, gentle and kindly, and the surrounding mountains – it was then that I spotted the bungalow, walked up to it, checked it out, and spoke to the Italian couple in the suite next to it – so we went up to the hotel and asked to speak to the manager, hitherto unnamed in these pages, though I remember he'd named himself when he'd first greeted us, in the rain. 'I am Nikos,' he'd said, as he ushered us under his umbrella. 'Is that Mr Nikos?' 'No, no, not Mister, only Nikos,

Nikos, so that I can be close to you.' Now he came bustling out of his office in a flurry, clapping his hands and asking how we were, were we happy, could he help? all this in his high, piping voice, his black, marblish eyes slightly at odds with his words – well, as I've said, we couldn't bring ourselves to tell this small man with the pulled-up trousers, plastered-back hair and reedy voice that we didn't like the room he'd put us in, the room he loved most, his favourite in the hotel – instead we went into a fiction we'd concocted that we had friends coming to join us, would need a larger place, really we needed to move to it straight away as these friends never made fixed plans, they turned up when they turned up and we had to be available with accommodation at the ready, what did he have, perhaps one of the rooms on the other side of the hotel, that bungalow perhaps? He said the room next to ours would be free by the end of the day, we would be very near to each other – no, no, we said, we really all had to be in the same quarters, it was our tradition, no, the bungalow would be better, there were certain things we did together at night – actually I was thinking of how when we'd holidayed with James and Dena Hammerstein many years ago, every night we'd played a card game, Hearts, which is a sort of bridge for the retarded, but the way I put it – 'certain things we did together at night' – suggested even less wholesome pursuits, wife-swapping or gay-husbanding and such. He gave me a quick marbly look, perhaps checking on my age, or for evidence of corruption in my face, and said the bungalow would be available in a day or so, and named the preposterous figure. I did something I've never managed to do before. Usually, when told that something I want costs more than I can afford, I smile proudly and take it, a way of affirming my status, I suppose, my financial manhood. But with Nikos I bargained. I said that for much of the time there might only be two of us, indeed our friends were such harum-scarum folk that they were quite likely to arrive after we'd left, so it would be better to proceed on the understanding that there would be just the two. He made a swift calculation.

We could have it with 10 per cent off, the 10 per cent to go straight back on if our friends arrived. He then deducted the 10 per cent out loud, in English, in an impressive display of racing mental arithmetic.

When he announced the sum that was left it actually sounded larger than the sum originally proposed – I suppose because the original sum was a round sum, and the amended sum was an awkward sum, which took longer to say. I wondered what his response would have been if I'd said, 'Look, Nikos, according to Dr Rootle I've only eight, nine months at most, to live, couldn't you let me spend two weeks of them in the bungalow at, say, half price?' Instead Victoria and I looked at each other briefly, then said we'd take it, which didn't seem particularly to please him, in fact, he looked slightly fed up, and asked us to phone him with our decision later in the day, and we didn't insist that we'd already made it.

We went down to the beach, had a swim and then considered the matter calmly. Victoria's position was that under the circumstances I was entitled to whatever I wanted, even if we couldn't afford it. As this has been my position for most of my life, it was hard for me to understand why I should resist it now – it may be some sad and childish notion that the more I make myself go without, the more extra time I'll be awarded.

So we rejected the room, and came clean about our reasons for wanting to change. We didn't actually admit that we'd lied about our vagabond friends turning up on the doorstep, but slipped in a query about the availability of a room with a more open view. Victoria spoke movingly about my claustrophobia and my night-time working habits. Visibly controlling his impatience, he led us down all the familiar paths until I felt sure he was going to show us our own room, but he swerved at the last minute and trotted down the steps that led to the next-door room, the one that had the view I had to crane over the wall to enjoy, that got the sun all afternoon – ours went dark well before evening – and had a pool that you could walk around – apart from a brief, narrow strip of paving on the right, ours was hemmed in by the walls – and it was being offered at the same price, he would need to know our decision in half an hour, he had someone waiting for either this room or our room, depending on which one we chose, and with a hitch of his trousers and a cold-eyed smile and a piping farewell he left us to it. Victoria turned the decision over to me, and I – with the proud common sense that has marked such moments in my life –

rejected the offer, on the grounds that it was almost certainly the room that would most suit me –

Hence my breakdown, my railings against fate and my intense loathing of the young man – a German, I think, who has moved into it – indeed never moves out of it, his DO NOT DISTURB sign is on permanent display – and he can be glimpsed, through chinks in the wall, lounging naked on the sunbed by the pool – I don't want him to catch me eyeing him through these chinks, reporting me to the management – I'd have to explain to Nikos that it's not lust but homicidal envy that keeps drawing me back to the chinks. On the other hand the way that he lies, so abandoned, with his knees spread apart, suggests that he's an immodest young fellow, or even that he's offering himself to his neighbours, the male or the female, or possibly both. I would say that his face has a depraved and carnal look, but I haven't seen his face yet, am familiar with only the lower part of his body, his private parts, as they used to be called, which he doesn't keep at all private, at least from me, when I happen to glance through the chink.

He's here for the rest of our stay, according to reception, when I phoned to enquire when his room would become available – I've thought of squirting noxious liquids at him through the chink, or perhaps honey, to attract wasps, but I suppose it would be traced to me pretty quickly, and I'd find myself spending my last months in a Cretan prison – or I could try and do it with a kiss, one of the methods prescribed by Oscar Wilde, or like the Chinese woman I read about in the *Herald Tribune* this morning – she murdered her lover by slipping a pellet of rat poison into his mouth while kissing him – it slipped down his throat and into his stomach without his noticing, and he died a few hours later. The woman said at her trial that she and her lover had a pact that if either was unfaithful, the other had the right to kill him or her, and she had noticed him talking in a suspicious manner to a young woman of the village. Apparently murder by rat poison is quite common in China. I suppose it was the decisiveness of her action that impressed and appalled me. I'd bet that the pact was her idea, which he understood to be merely a metaphor for their love, while secretly the thought of it gave him an erotic charge he probably boasted about to his friends – 'She said she'll kill me if I as much as talk to another woman, and I can do the same to her! Hey! What about that!' – but really, from the moment he agreed to the pact his fate was sealed, not only was he bound – honour-bound, in a way – to talk to another woman, she was bound to catch him at it – such a pledge has meaning only if it's fulfilled – and what a kiss it must have been, for him not to notice the pellet in his mouth and then sliding down his throat! – unless of course she'd made a habit of passing something from her mouth to his, to add texture and mystery to a kiss, sometimes a little peppermint or an aphrodisiac, so that he was actually anticipating, his tongue probing eagerly for the expected surprise – but rat poison? I've always imagined death by rat poison to be very painful. Would she have told him, as he writhed in his death throes that she'd merely kept her side of their bargain, so it was his own fault, but oh how she loved him, his present and final agony was a testimony to her love for him. Anyway, she's going to be executed as the Chinese justice system has no place for *crime passionnel*, if that is what it was.

OPPORTUNITY KNOCKS

This morning after breakfast I was sitting by the pool, thinking about nothing in particular as far as I knew, but Victoria must have seen something in my face because she asked me whether I was all right. I came back from wherever I'd been speaking a jumble of words that made no sense to either of us, and stopped, feeling as bewildered as she looked. These little fits – stupors followed by fluent incoherence – have occurred several times since we've been here, and I don't know whether they're the result of the cancer, the radiotherapy, or simply ageing – a form of Alzheimer's, possibly, though I don't think it's Alzheimer's, or any of its variations. Victoria says that it's probably shock – that I'm still in the process of taking it in. She may be right, but it seems to me odd that I haven't grasped at every level of my being – except in my immortal soul, which will remain delusional until the last possible moment, that's its job after all – that I'm dying. I'm at an age I would have settled for when I was twenty, fifty, even sixty, even sixty-five come to that – and I should have died from alcohol at the end of my drinking life – one more glass would probably have done it. And then there's the smoking. So why should I be surprised, let alone shocked? Yet I think Victoria's right. I was completely unprepared for the news, and still am. Perhaps I am always unprepared, at least when it comes to my health – well yes, consider this, that though you'd been feeling really ill for about a year, you hadn't expected to be told that you were actually ill. Certain events happen annually – Christmas, birthdays, wedding anniversaries – that you have to observe, and in early July, for the last ten years, there have been your medical tests. Yes, it's true that I'd come to treat them as irritating interruptions, and certainly as a formality that had nothing to do with how I actually felt – and why not? as every year the results were pretty much the same, with the sorts of problems that had to do with age – there was cancer of the prostate, but so far it was still in the prostate, and there was an aneurysm that had to be measured and would have to be operated on, but not yet – neither prostate nor aneurysm was treated by the doctors as alarming, and neither was thought about much by me. The tests were a once-a-year humdrummery, and still seemed so this year, although the blood test showed cancerous activity – my GP and my urologist both assumed that it was the prostate cancer stirring at last, but I wasn't to worry, they were prepared, they knew what had to be done and sent me for a scan that would show what the prostate was up to, and also a scan to show how the aneurysm was doing, and also for a scan to make sure that there was no cancer in my bones, and I was having the bone scan, an exceedingly boring business – one has to lie on one's side on a narrow bed while a machine inches over one's body at what seems like ten minutes per inch – I was very tired on the afternoon of the scan, for some reason, but pleased to be so because I fell into a light doze, and stayed there until a disembodied voice roused me with the news that I was done. I got off the bed, put on my clothes, and stumbled out, still a bit sleepy, leaden-limbed and ill at ease. I spotted Victoria standing by a door at the top of the stairs, listening on her mobile. She saw me just as the conversation was evidently finishing. I lumbered towards her, lighting a cigarette as we went out into the alley behind the clinic. 'Who was that?' I said, without much curiosity. She took my hand. I can't remember who it was, or rather which one it was – urologist, GP, aneurysm man, stomach and liver man, all of whom, it turned out, were in possession of the information that one of them had just passed on to Victoria and she was now passing on to me in a voice that was, like her face, calm on the outside. 'They've found something in your lung. On the aneurysm scan.' So not in the prostate, where they were looking for the cause of the cancer activity in the blood tests, but in the lung. It was what they call an 'opportunistic' finding.

So.

So I received the news with mumbled swear words, the words that I was to use quite regularly over the coming weeks and which I've already quoted several times, and are interesting to me, and probably not at all to anyone else, as indications of a poverty of vocabulary in times of crisis, or maybe it's a poverty of actual responses – one simply, no, I simply didn't know what to say when confronted with facts for which I had no reference point – no preparation in myself whatsoever. Even now I wonder if there are moral standards I am failing to meet, and if there are, where am I to find out about them? I can't imagine what I should have said to the first piece of bad news, and the words that spring to mind now are the words that sprang to mind then – but then perhaps such words, along with stupors and bursts of nonsensical eloquence, are the symptoms of shock, and from then on there's been no time, no time –

A BURST OF ADULT BEHAVIOUR – BUT WHY?

I still can't sort out the following weeks, they were a muddle of scans, consultations, biopsies, further scans, more consultations, until the discovery of a swelling on my neck and the confirmation that it was cancerous – it was odd this, in that it hadn't been there, at least I hadn't noticed it, until the scan detected it, whereupon, as if given permission, it became tangible and visible, a shiny little lump the size of a walnut. Then came the meetings with the three doctors, Omar, Morgan Morgan and Rootle, followed by the hiatus in Suffolk, the long walks in the evening sunshine, the horses in fields that were so green and fresh in an autumn that was like spring, and then the phone call announcing that I had MRSA, then to London for the ghastly operation that established what everybody already knew, that the walnut on the neck was a secondary.

And now here we are in Crete, another hiatus before the next phase begins. When we get back I have to go for a scan to see what effect the radiotherapy has had on the two tumours. All I can say at the moment is that I felt much better before the radiotherapy. In Suffolk I could walk two miles without feeling particularly tired, I could swim eighty-five lengths underwater, I could hurdle fences, I could scuttle up trees and down dales, I could write sonnets in Greek and Latin and translate them into Turkish – I could – but what does it matter what I could do before the radiotherapy? It seems, now, like a dreamtime, as does all my life before Dr Rootle said out of the side of his mouth, 'About a year.'

What occupies me now, as I sit once again with my back against the chapel wall – there is a strong wind, I have to hold the page of my pad down with my left hand as I write, a strong wind and a strong sun, whitecaps racing across the dark blue sea – it's beautiful, really, though the wind is making me shiver a little –

Yes, what occupies me now, as I sit here writing this, is what am I to do with the 'about a year' that is shrinking day by day and now stands at about nine months. What to do with the nine months? In the adult world, represented by novels, films, plays and so forth, people in my position set about 'putting their affairs in order', but I did that very thing, Victoria and I did it, in the months before I learned I was ill. We did it, having postponed it so long – 'We really must,' we kept saying, 'we must really –' until one day, with a sudden sense of urgency, almost somewhat frantically, as if there were a deadline, we began to do it. Neither of us could understand why the urgency, why we chivvied a rather slow, overcareful – so she seemed to us – solicitor with emails and phone calls and faxes, bustled to offices in taxis. When it was complete, as far as we could see, we collapsed with a sort of bewilderment – what, then, was that all about? we asked each other, why all the panic? But still, we said to each other, 'I'm glad we've got it done, aren't you? Now we need never think about it again, now we can relax –'

So now my affairs are in order, there's nothing for me to do unless I change everything on a whim, disorder them in order to reorder them, like one of those spiteful old people in novels, Miss Havisham for instance – no, I don't think Miss Havisham changed her will, come to think of it, she just implied that it actually contained what Pip's imagination supplied it with. On the other hand, I have so little to leave – the contents of my two studies, one in London and one in Suffolk, and that's about it, apart from my copyrights, not all of which I own, and which are of uncertain value –

DIALOGUE BETWEEN A THICKO AND A SICKO

How do you value them, as a matter of interest, your copyrights?

Who?

You.

Aka me?

Yes. Aka you. You personally. You, Simon Gray. The author of your plays. What value do you put on them?

Financial, do you mean?

Whatever. Emotional, ethical, sentimental, financial –?

How can I put a value on my own work? It's for others to do – for others to buy or not buy an option, to stage them or not stage them, and if staged, for other others to say whether they were worth the price of a ticket. The world can tell you the value of my plays by the way it treats them.

You're lying. You have a very clear idea of whether your plays are any good or not.

That's not the same thing as how I value them.

Yes, it is. You're coming to your end, there are going to be obituaries, assessments of your life and work, work and life, by people whose judgements you'd think about if they were being made about somebody else. Now is the chance to put your case.

My CASE!

Yup. Go on. Your case. Defend your career as a writer.

I can't because that's exactly the point I missed, really – that writing is a career. You don't just write and that's the end of it, you have to look after your writing, promote it, cherish it in the world. You have an obligation to get it the help it needs. As people do in all professions – as they do for their children. I was, as far as my work is concerned, a neglectful parent. Furthermore –

Furthermore?

Furthermore I suspect that this failure comes from a more profound weakness than mere neglectfulness. Neglectfulness could be, often is, a matter of laziness, or careless impetuosity – 'There, that's finished with, on to the next, and then the next, what's done is done, let it look after itself' sort of attitude – but my neglectfulness was more active than that, it was almost a disowning, and was – is – perhaps still is – the consequence of shame, from which I can never cleanse myself.

Cleanse yourself?

Well, you know what I mean.

No, I don't. Give me some instances.

Instances! I'm thinking theologically, I can't remember any instances.

Try, for God's sake!

Well, let's say my reactions when I happen to overhear wounding remarks about my work.

You mean you think you are intended to overhear them? An act of divine will or something, to make you ashamed?

No, of course not. What I'm talking about is my reaction, not the circumstances. It's merely bad luck or bad judgement that I place myself next to people who then say unpleasant things. I'm not meant to overhear them, after all. I'm sure they'd be horrified if they knew I had. They're as much victims of my bad luck or judgement as I am.

Are you sure?

Yes. Of course. You don't think they come looking for me, plant themselves beside me, say these things deliberately for me to hear, do you?

It's possible.

It's ridiculous. Give me an instance.

I thought you didn't want instances.

Thank you. I knew you couldn't.

Well, only that taxi driver.

What taxi driver?

The one who came to pick you up when you were a lecturer at Queen Mary College, in the East End, to take you home to Highgate.

Lots of taxi drivers came to pick me up at Queen Mary and take me home to Highgate.

You saw this one talking to the porter when you went to find him at reception. Surely you remember.

I left both Queen Mary and Highgate twenty years ago, how could I possibly remember!

They both looked at you as you were coming towards the desk. The taxi driver said something and the porter laughed.

He had a wart on the back of his neck, did he?

Which one?

The driver, of course.

So you do remember?

I am now in the process of remembering it. The moment you mentioned the wart, you set my memory off. Memory is a creative faculty. I am a creative writer. It only takes one small thing, one detail. Your wart was my madeleine, so to speak.

It's not my wart, it's yours. I didn't remember it, I didn't mention it. You did.

Oh. Well – well – it's not surprising, is it, as it's all I had of him in the back of his cab, the wart on his neck, and his voice.

Saying –

What?

What was he saying?

Oh, only that – that he'd been to see my play –

He and his wife. Don't leave out his wife. So – he and his wife – they'd been to see your play Otherwise Engaged the night before and – and –

He was rather abusive.

But what exactly, mmm?

Oh, just the usual sort of thing. That he hadn't cared for it. So forth.

Really? They hadn't cared for it? Those were his words?

That was his meaning.

He gave you an honest opinion. He spoke his mind. Is that what you mean by abusive?

I didn't ask him to give his opinion. Or to speak his mind.

Still, it's pretty mild, 'didn't care for it'. Now if he'd said something like, 'It was terrible, terrible, terrible, my missus said we should ask for our money back, what a waste of money, she said, what a waste of an evening, the only evening we've had out for months, a disgrace, how does a thing like that get on the stage, and at those prices!' – if he'd said something like that – did he?

Possibly along those lines.

And how did you silence him?

I didn't dignify him with a response. I was almost certainly trying to concentrate on an upcoming lecture – probably on Wordsworth, I lectured on Wordsworth most terms, I could do a whole hour on the 'Lucy' poems, half an hour alone on 'A slumber did my spirit seal;/I had no human fears:/She seem'd a thing that could not feel/The touch of earthly years./No motion has she now, no force;/She neither hears nor sees;/Roll'd round in earth's diurnal course' –

'As for the bastard who wrote that shit! What wouldn't I give to get my hands on him!' – Sorry, didn't mean to interrupt, probably a rotten imitation, eh? I don't think I caught the note of delirious venom, astonished joy – that he actually had the bastard who wrote the shit in the back of his cab – the sheer luck of it!

And what about the sheer luck of it for me? I phone for a taxi and of all the drivers available in London I get the only one, surely the only one, who'd gone to my play the night before – he has a chance conversation with the porter – says to the porter, for want of anything else to say, that he'd had a – a – rather disappointing night at the theatre – and the porter says –

'Here comes the man you're looking for, the very man that wrote the shit!' You think that sort of coincidence is luck, do you, simple bad luck? It's not just a case of standing next to somebody in a pub, or hearing somebody as they're leaving the theatre. As you've said yourself, so many different elements came together.

What do you think it is?

You tell me. You're the theologian. The shame-seeker. The man who needs a good cleansing. Perhaps it was you who sought him out, not the other way around.

How could I? How could I possibly? The odds were hundreds of thousands to one – possibly millions – unless you think I phoned for a taxi and said, by the way, I want a driver who took his wife to Otherwise Engaged last night and hated it.

Not heavy odds against the last bit. Perhaps he was the answer to your prayers, as you were to his. He wanted the bastard who wrote the shit in the back of his cab, you wanted the humiliation, the shame – God works in mysterious ways to get these match-ups. You've fallen strangely silent, as Mummy used to say to Daddy when she'd embarrassed him. Well, it's only me, not even Mummy. You can't be embarrassed by only me.

I'm not embarrassed. I'm trying to work it out. The truth is that I didn't feel abused, I felt unmasked. Yes, that's the truth.

That he was right? Your play was shit? You deserved, as well as needed, to hear it? Eh?

Yes, but – whether Otherwise Engaged was shit or not is irrelevant. In my soul –

Your soul?

Soul, yes – don't worry about the word, it's theological jargon, as is the rest of what I'm about to say. In my soul I believe I am one of the fallen, and that my natural and proper condition in the world is that of a man who needs –

Cleansing?

Yes.

Well, go on, on into shame, humiliation, the rest of it. Your voice is developing that throb. It's your confessional voice. You've got a palpable design on my emotions, haven't you, you little devil you!

I hate anyone – anyone! – who has a palpable design on the emotions, you know I do.

Even a child?

Children don't.

Really? Too innocent?

Yes – well, let's say too ignorant.

I know a child. Let me tell you about him. The sort of thing he used to do. An instance, *if you like, of the sort of thing he used to do.*

It's a beautiful day. I'd really rather –

It'll only take a minute. Have a cigarette. Go on. You need and deserve one, just the one. One can't hurt you. Here. Let me light it for us.

A CHILD WITH A PALPABLE DESIGN

It is 1942. He is standing on a street corner in downtown Montreal, outside a post office. He has a letter in his hand, to send to his parents back there in England, and he is upset because he can't find the money his Auntie Gert had given him for the stamp. He begins to cry. A grown-up stops to ask the little chap what the matter is, and he explains, holding up the envelope. The grown-up smiles at how small mishaps seem great tragedies for children, rumples the little chap's hair, gives him money for the stamp, and a little bit over, from the pleasure of giving. After the little chap had posted the letter he went home, thought awhile then, without consulting his older brother Nigel, wrote another envelope, returned to the corner and burst into tears. Men and women stopped regularly to ask him what the matter was. He showed them the envelope, told them he'd lost the money for the stamp for the letter for his mummy and daddy in England. It was amazing what delicate chords he touched in passers-by. In time he grew bold and impatient. Instead of standing passively shedding tears and waiting to be consoled and rewarded, he began to accost people, holding out the envelope, sobbing and asking if they could help him, his letter to his mummy and his daddy, in England – well, a weeping child, his parents in the war-torn and valiant mother country, he stoppeth one in nine, or eight, even, and even a very large, ill-tempered-looking man striding along, who nevertheless paused to enquire tenderly, 'What's the matter, son?' and the little chap trembled and whimpered out his answer, whereupon the large man, looking no longer ill-tempered, lowered himself to the little chap's height and cupped his vast hands around the little chap's cheeks, smiled into the little chap's eyes and informed the little chap that he was a policeman, and if it wasn't that he was off duty and going home, he'd take the little chap down to the station and have him put in jail for swindling, fraud, etc. He stood up and addressed the passers-by, 'Don't give money to this kid, he's a liar! A liar and a cheat! I'd arrest him if I had the time!' and went on his way back to his family, a Samaritan of some sort, and the little chap ran home, doubtless thinking that, well, all good things come to an end, his pockets were full of money for cigarettes, candy, comics – so how's that for a child with a palpable design? And not only on the emotions but on the emotions for the money? Pretty well what he did when he grew up and

*became a playwright, eh? Same sort of trick, when you think about it –
and same sort of comeuppance, except it comes from critics, and not from
a policeman.*

You've missed out the real end of the story. I ran home in a shock of
shame. A shock. Of shame.

Because you were caught.

Of course. But also for what I'd done. The two things were mixed into
each other. I knew that I deserved –

*And needed – don't forget needed – you deserved and needed to be caught,
right? Just as you deserved and needed to get bad reviews, right? And
deserved and needed to be abused by the cab driver, right? And so deserved
and needed to get cancer is the next thought, eh? Right?*

THE NEXT THOUGHT

Well, actually, it's not quite as if cancer were an off-duty policeman
and I a swindling child, but not altogether not that – there is certainly
a sense of shame that makes me feel that I'm at a moral disadvantage
when discussing my condition – I have been caught out, they (the doctors)
have caught me out – but in what? Well, of course in my smoking, but
really, when it comes to it, I don't believe my cancer is the result of
smoking, or rather the much more important question is what my
smoking is the result of. What in my nature made me a smoker? What
in my nature allows me – sometimes it feels more like insistence – to
go on smoking? The thought of dying terrifies me, the thought of
dying of cancer particularly terrifies me, and yet – and yet – destiny
is too grand a word, what I want is a word that has the meaning of a
meeting up between the something in me that needs to smoke, call
it a genetic disorder or call it original sin, and the something in me
that needs the consequence, call it an effect, as in the law of cause
and effect, or a punishment. When it comes to thoughts of this sort,
this contradictory sort, I remember that not only am I a great-great-
grandchild of the Enlightenment, which was itself the father of chaos,

but also that I'm descended on my father's side from a long line of Scots Presbyterians, on my mother's from a long line of Welsh Anglicans, i.e. Anglicans who, because of their Welshness, believed in sin, original sin and sin ever since. In other words, what a mess.

One of my fears in life has always been that other people are as bad as I am. Then what hope for the world? I think. What's more –

Hey – no more 'what's more's' and 'furthermore's', all this stuff about guilt, shame, sin, in fact all the stuff since I asked you your opinion of your contemporaries, it's all evasion.

Actually, you asked me for my opinion of myself. And I gave it.

No, you didn't. You went into an account of how you'd mishandled your career. You claimed it was from a holy innocence, an innate and genuine belief in the need to behave with integrity –

No, I didn't. I said it was from stupidity, a failure to understand what the world is, how it works. There are two entirely unrelated activities. One is writing, the other is getting on in the world. There is nothing shameful in knowing how to get on in the world and there is something shameful in my not knowing – it's wilful. And vain in the sense of conceited ignorance, the assumption that my modesty will come to be associated with my work, almost a subtle manifestation of its virtues.

But if you're going to be dead soon, then the sooner you stop suppurating about the injustices and dishonesties of the world – of which you claim you're a victim – the more time you'll have to suppurate about the things that matter. Like the triumphs of your contemporaries.

I'm not suppurating about anything. That's what I'm trying to tell you. If you listen to me properly you'll hear the voice of a man who is learning to accept his death with composure and even serenity.

Then why does it squeak?

It's a physical thing, in my lungs. Not a psychological thing. I want to talk about Chekhov.

Chekhov?

Yes, Chekhov.

Would you like to run with that?

Well, his plays are about – oh, you know – love and the failure of love, friendship and the failure of friendship, about brotherhood and parenthood, about the work people do, how they see themselves, their fear of how others see them, their fear of loss, illness and death. That sort of play.

And politics?

Politics?

Chekhov had an interest –

Some of his characters did. They had visions of the future, yearnings for the past. But there was censorship, of course, that defined the limits of discussion. But no one, I hope, comes out of a Chekhov play talking first of all about the light it sheds on Russia at the turn of the century, although you might get around to that in due course – see it in relation to the Revolution etc., but in the end it's the feeling that every conversation in the plays is somehow sub specie aeternitatis that makes them now funny and now sad, often both at once.

So you think of yourself as Chekhovian?

Not in the usual meaning of the word, which is to do with atmosphere, the mixture of the touching, the comic and the melancholy, fin de siècle, I suppose one could call it, that meaning of Chekhovian – but I aspired to write plays, dreamed of writing plays that leave audiences with the experience of having looked in on other lives, other conditions, and have them see much that's the same as and much that's different from their own lives. All I'm really saying is that sort of theatre seems to me true theatre, in that sense Chekhovian, the kind of plays that I tried to write, and wish I'd written.

Well now, perhaps you'll come out with it.

With what?

How you value yourself.

I think I'm better than my reputation. Possibly I'm the best playwright in English of the second half of the last century, well, at writing the sorts of plays I wanted to write, but then I suspect that nobody else wanted to write those sorts of plays, so being the best at it –

What about some titles?

Quartermaine's Terms, Close of Play, The Common Pursuit, The Rear Column, The Late Middle Classes, Japes and so forth.

And so forth? What about the two early plays, the ones that made you briefly rich, and more briefly famous? Butley *and* Otherwise Engaged.

Yes, well I'm not denying them. They were revived recently, *Otherwise Engaged* in the West End and *Butley* on Broadway. Both were well received and played to good houses and it was quite pleasant to be in the audience, but I didn't really feel they had much to do with me, I've lost contact with the man who wrote them, I've no idea, really, what they came out of, they seem to be about waste, self-waste and partly self-disgust. But I may be quite wrong, they may be about something else entirely. All I really remember is being astonished by their success at the time. And also by the anger they aroused. One theatre critic, I think of the Oxford newspaper – both plays had their premieres in Oxford – wrote that he hoped to meet up with me so that he could punch me in the stomach. And I got some letters from women along the same lines, though knees into balls was more how they looked forward to greeting me. It must have been the climate of the times, there was nothing of that sort of response in the recent revivals, or if there was, it wasn't passed on to me.

But the later plays – Quartermaine's Terms, Close of Play, The Common Pursuit, The Rear Column, The Late Middle Classes, Japes *and so forth – you're still in touch with the man who wrote those?*

Yes. But less so and less so. I'm losing touch with – Excuse me.

Where are you going?

For a swim.

But we haven't finished.

I have. It's a lovely afternoon, and I can't afford to spend it on a grubbing journey through my work, defending and puffing it, what will survive will survive and so forth, and whether it does or doesn't I shall never know and there's the sea, all a-sparkle, and there'll be Victoria down there on her sunbed, half waiting for me, and I may not have many more afternoons like this, not many more swims with my wife, *carpe diem, carpe diem*!

BACK TROUBLE

It's been three days since I've written, three days of sunshine and cool, calm evenings. I've become languorous and physically at ease, I have no sense that there is anything wrong with my body at all, apart from my slight hack of a cough, which is infrequent and socially much less noticeable than the coarse and liquid brute that used to revolt those around me. I've been swimming about six times a day, and furthermore I haven't smoked until the evening, when I smoke ten, well, say a dozen to be on the safe side, as opposed to the old sixty or more a day, could this be one of the reasons I've been feeling better? so much better that I don't want to ruin it by writing about the second meeting with Dr Rootle, without which this record of my recent medical history is incomplete. Every time I've thought of beginning, pulling my yellow pad towards me and picking up my pen, I settle back for a moment against the chapel wall, and drift, drift along, leaving Dr Rootle and his importunate knees – he sat so close to me while he talked that our knees almost touched – well, as I put that down I feel myself inclined to sit back again, put down the pen, push the pad away and drift, drift, and think anyway that it's nearly lunchtime, time for another swim, we like to have three before lunch, but as yet haven't been in since our pre-breakfast dip, hours ago, hours and hours ago it now seems, though in fact it's only – what? two and a half hours. Perhaps in a minute I shall write about Dr Rootle.

*

We had dinner again at the restaurant by the chapel. Only three of the other tables were taken, and the people at them were as low-voiced as we were. It was a lovely still evening, a perfect temperature for eating out, the moon bright and the sea shimmering. We talked of this and that, comfortably but not altogether aimlessly. Underlying all our conversations is the thought of the future, but on the whole we try to stay away from it, so I don't really know why I suddenly began to talk about the way I wanted certain things disposed of, those copyrights I still own and one or two items, not valuable but with a meaning for me, and I hope for the people I want them to go to – then my back began to hurt, as it has done occasionally since the radiotherapy. I got up, walked about, then went to the railing and looked out over the sea, listening to the waves – it was the most soft and gorgeous evening, I forgot what I'd been saying, and turned to go back to the table, to say to Victoria come, come and have a look at this! when I saw that her head was bent and she had a hand to her face – I suppose it was the matter-of-factness of my manner, the assumption, and the assumption that she shared it, that my death is fairly soon and inevitable – but the truth is that I don't really know even quite elementary things about myself, my wants and needs, until I've either written them down or spoken them – still, it was very thoughtless of me, stupid, stupid – I couldn't get through this, if that's what I'm doing, without her, I couldn't have done anything over the last twenty years without her, I've for so long taken what sureness and confidence I have from her undemonstrative strength that I don't ever think what a strain it must be for her, and now more than ever – I must be more careful, must be more careful – but she wouldn't want me to be careful, would she? so I must also be careful not to seem careful.

REFLECTIONS OF A SMOKING ANTI-SMOKER

I suppose I should remind myself that I smoked one or two cigarettes at the restaurant last night, something I swore to myself I wouldn't do while we're in Crete, and that I will no longer be able to do in restaurants in England – well, not strictly accurate, it'll be permitted at tables outside – here you can smoke inside too – I can see from here that in the restaurant, in the enclosed bit, there are ashtrays on the tables, two on each table.

It's astonishing how quickly strange new social customs are developing in London because of the ban – for instance, at Kensington Place the table we always sit at is next to the window and beside the revolving door, so I have a comfortable view of diners who now go out to smoke on the pavement – some of them go to the bus stop a few yards down the road, because it has a bench to sit on and a bit of roof to protect them when it's raining – others go round the other side to an alley, and are usually out of sight – but quite a few can't be bothered to go anywhere, they stay right by the restaurant window in clusters, sometimes so close to our table that only the pane of glass separates us. I'd never realised before how unattractive groups of people are who are only there for the smoke. I suppose it's because they're not doing something else while smoking, or smoking without noticing, as they used to, they're there for one purpose only, to smoke, and it makes smoking a bit disgusting – after all, it's an activity that should be subsidiary to other activities, and to do it for its own sake makes it seem like an affliction or a degrading personal habit. Like nose-picking for instance, it should be done in the utmost privacy, and though it's possible that all kinds of exciting things – engagements, adulteries, divorces and even murder – might follow on from accidental relationships formed on the pavement, it most often looks a dismal and solitary affair, people who don't know each other standing apart, heads bent over their cigarettes with a shifty or an agitated air, as if they were outside a courtroom, awaiting the verdict and sentencing. Mainly that's the social effect one notices of the smoking ban, the outside-on-the-pavement effect, but the other day, at a fairly large dinner party – about twenty people or so, also at Kensington Place – I noticed for the first time the inside-the-restaurant effect – it was really a very pleasant evening, everything seeming to be going well and comfortably, the people knew each other, the food was good, the wine was flowing, the chattering and laughter festively loud, when suddenly one of the men stood up, looked around the table in a knowing manner, and raised two fingers to his mouth in a smoking gesture, whereupon about eight people – five or six men and a couple of women – got up and trampled out in a little pack or herd, pack is probably the right word, inasmuch as a self-appointed leader had given the signal. Several people were left stranded at the table with empty chairs on either side of them, one woman had no one on either side of her and no one opposite her either, it was as if she were being ostracised, or in quarantine – she sat there smiling in a falsely dignified sort of way, what else could she do? After about ten minutes the pack, no, herd seems the right word here, because in they trampled like cattle, though they didn't look sheepish, which would have been appropriate, but as if they thought they were charmingly naughty, which also made them seem rather pleased with themselves. Eventually the table picked up, everything flowed along until there he was on his feet again and with his fingers to his lips. It happened twice more during the evening, and I felt – I have to admit it – that their behaviour was – well, loutish. And selfish, actually. Of course it's easy for me, in that my lung cancer makes me positively relieved to be in places where I'm not allowed to smoke, but I hope, I really do hope, that even if I were healthy and back on sixty a day I would have remained seated until the end, looking forward to smoking when I got home – but alas, alas, alas and further alas, I have a ghastly feeling that not only would I have gone out to the pavement, but I would have competed for leadership of the pack – or herd, whichever – and no doubt thought myself naughty and charming, while in fact being selfish and loutish.*

Oddly, or perhaps not oddly, come to think of it, the smoking ban came into effect about three days after I discovered I'd got cancer. Yes, now I do come to think of it, it seems more than odd, it seems eerily consequential, suggesting among other possibilities that I am so innately, organically obedient that my whole physical system submitted to the law in spite of my habits and inclination, and that my inner opposition to it was immediately met by the most appropriate and natural punishment.

On the night before you could no longer smoke inside a restaurant we had a long-prearranged dinner with Ronald and Natasha Harwood,

---

* A short while after writing this I joined the smokers on the pavement. However, I have not yet thought myself naughty and charming.

smokers of a quantity and intensity to equal my own, at a restaurant in Piccadilly, one of the very few restaurants that still allowed smoking right up to the last day – a lot of restaurants had introduced their own ban months before – so it was on that night a particularly popular spot, they'd put three or four ashtrays on each table, and the clientele all had their cigarettes and lighters on display in a here-we-stand spirit, perhaps there was even a flavour of Dunkirk about it, heroic and defiant defeat. Now, the thing was that at that time I really couldn't bear to smoke, each inhalation made me dizzy and nauseated, but the desire – the need – to smoke was as strong as ever, and the knowledge that I had lung cancer made me – what was it? Defiant? No, no. I think anxious to show that nothing of major importance had changed in my life, so not defiant, stupid. Stupid to sit there with lung cancer smoking cigarettes I didn't want and that made me feel sick for a cause I no longer believed in – the cause being the right of smokers to fill a restaurant with smoke and a smell that many people can't abide, and makes some of them feel actually ill.

So it was altogether a weird evening at the place in Piccadilly, it was the Wolseley I now remember, of course it was the Wolseley, spent with very good friends whose company I always enjoy – a weird and also horrible evening, the evening before the first day of the smoking ban, the last evening when it was still legal to smoke inside restaurants and people hadn't yet developed the habit of standing on the pavement and irritating diners by the windows as they do at Kensington Place.

Actually, there are very few restaurants that have windows as large as Kensington Place, where all the diners, not only the ones sitting next to the window, can see out on to Kensington Church Street, and everyone in Kensington Church Street – pedestrians, as well as people in cars, buses and taxis – can see into the restaurant, can actually see quite distinctly the faces of the diners with our snouts in our troughs and the waiters scurrying about, obedient to our appetites. It's a sight that could start a revolution. Who, if poor, hungry, unemployed, wouldn't feel like heaving a brick through the window? lots of bricks through the window? the thought of all that glass shattering, splinters flying into our bowls of soup, our venison, our puddings, our faces – and then the mob unleashed, hurdling through the holes with more bricks for close-up and personal. In fact, the more I think about it the more I wonder whether it's safe and sensible to sit at our particular table. It's quite difficult not to catch the eye of pedestrians, and indeed sometimes a pair or a trio of yobs pause, rap their fists on the windows and dance jigs and pantomime obscenities. We try to smile aloofly back at them, as if we were at a distance and invulnerable – I think we ought to find out whether the glass is shatterproof, whether bricks would bounce off it or smash through it. If the latter what should we do? Take our custom to a restaurant with smaller windows? Or, less radically, move to one of the tables on the other side, against the wall, which no brick, however powerfully thrown, could reach? And yet – and yet the charm of our table is its location, we're slightly cut off from the other tables and have the best acoustics, we enjoy watching the parade through the vast windows in spite of being threatened and jeered at by intoxicated louts and – and you must stop this, what have smokers outside Kensington Place and imaginary yobs throwing bricks through the window got to do with what's happening to you and where you are? Why not think about our being here, the simple pleasure of our being here in Crete?

Right. Tomorrow back in Crete.

No, tomorrow back to Dr Rootle. Your last meeting.

Then you can have Crete.

DR ROOTLE'S KNEES

His secretary summoned us to a meeting at the hospital, to a different waiting room, very large, with several coffee machines and a counter where you could buy sandwiches and chocolate bars. It had several doors, from which elegant, usually Asian nurses would appear, call out a name, and somebody would rise eagerly and hurry forward. It wouldn't have seemed at all like a hospital waiting room if there weren't so many people, of all ages, with sticks and crutches, bandages on their wrists and ankles, the most striking being those who had bandages around their necks with a circular hole in front, and a bit of tube that obviously went into the throat. There was a bulky and frankly rather brutish-faced man and, like a biker in a film, he had cropped hair, tattoos on his arms, a black leather waistcoat and black leather trousers. Although he was very big, massive biceps and a bull neck, he was quite unmenacing. I don't think it was just the circumstances that made him unmenacing. He had a soft, slightly abstracted smile and a vague, unseeing but rather tender way of looking around at the rest of us as he waited on his partner, a raddled-looking woman in a shapeless yellow dress, with stringy black hair and a peaky face, and most noticeably a throat bandage with a plug in it – he kept bringing her various items from the counter, a mug of coffee and then a sandwich, which she put in her pocket, and then a chocolate bar, and then another chocolate bar, one of which she put in her pocket, the other she shared with him. They also each had a packet of cigarettes, Marlboro, and a lighter each, which they kept on the arms of their chairs, very visibly, but seemingly quite unconscious of the – what? inappropriateness, I suppose is the right word – in the waiting room of a famous cancer hospital, with those signs all around showing struck-off cigarettes, and strategically placed racks with pamphlets announcing the relationship between smoking and cancer – and yet there they were, sitting beside their cigarettes. At one point he said something to her and they both opened their packets and began to count the contents with their fingers, he plucked two of his out and gave them to her, she squeezed one of them into her packet, which seemed already pretty full from where I sat, and kept the other one between her fingers – there was an exciting little passage when he picked up the lighter as if to light her cigarette, but he just bounced it up and down on his palm, whispering endearments to her, and she nodded and nodded, it was hard to keep one's eyes off the cigarette between her fingers, the black tube in her throat – I wondered if she could speak, and also wondered whether she actually smoked, and if she did, did she plug the cigarette into the plug in her throat? It didn't bear thinking about, really. And nor did the fact that I had a packet of Silk Cut and a lighter in my own pocket, and as soon as we were out of the hospital I would light up – would I, if I ever had to have a plug in my throat, would I even then? When I was called at last, by an exceptionally neat and pretty Chinese nurse, the man smiled in his pleasant, slightly absent way, and put his hand on the woman's, as if to say, 'Your turn soon,' and she –

No, time for a swim.

*

It's past midnight, and I'm on the patio, one hand clamped on my pad to keep the pages down in the strong wind, which I'm determined to ignore because I want to pick up where I left off, before our swim. Actually, it wasn't much of a swim, this wind had already –

No. To the meeting.

The nurse led us down a corridor and showed us into a small room, in which there were three chairs – no, two chairs, one with a stool in front of it. The nurse said, 'Dr Rootle will be with you shortly,' and went, leaving the door into the corridor open. There was another door, which wasn't quite closed, into another room, from which came men's voices, loud, jolly, slightly argumentative. Their voices also came at us along the corridor, so that they were twice as loud as they would have been with only one of the doors open, but they somehow overlapped and drowned themselves out. It was almost as if they were in the room with us, shouting out incomprehensible sentences, it was impossible to make out any word clearly except one, which seemed to detach itself and ring out separately. My name. Every few seconds, in the excited, humorous babble, a cocktail party sort of babble, my name, followed once or twice by a little silence, and then a murmur, a little laugh. This went on for about ten minutes, it was quite hellish, until at last Victoria cried out, 'We can hear you!' in fact cried it out several times, but there wasn't a flutter of silence or uncertainty from the next room, the shouting, the laughter, the good-humoured quarrelling continued at full throttle, even when she went out into the corridor and called out from there. We'd pretty well decided that we'd show ourselves at one of the doors – simultaneously, one at each door, might have been a better idea – when the voices stopped and almost immediately Dr Rootle strode exuberantly into the room by the connecting door, followed seconds later by Dr Morgan Morgan from the corridor door – virtually doing to us what I've just imagined doing to them. There was some fervent hand-shaking in a muddled sort of way – it really was a small room, too small for four people to do the social things without jostling each other – and then Dr Morgan Morgan said he was just looking in for a moment to say hello, then he'd leave us, leave us – he gestured to Dr Rootle – but first if he could just glance – just a quick glance – into my throat, to make sure that the operation – I sat there with my wife to one side of me, Dr Rootle to the other, while Dr Morgan Morgan went down my throat for a quick glance, and then came up again, and said, he really did say, I had some difficulty believing it, and still do, he said, 'The good news is that it's all clear down there, not a sign of anything wrong, and there was no cancer in the tonsil I took out, it was just slightly infected.' And I said again, I really did say, though I had no difficulty believing it, 'But that's not exactly good news, is it? It would have been better if it had been cancerous, the tonsil, wouldn't it?' 'Ah,' he said, 'well, there is that.' He offered me his hand, and I shook it. He offered it to Victoria, who shook it. 'Now,' he said, smiling shyly at Dr Rootle, 'over to you, um,' and off he went, out into the corridor and then on to the canteen or to a ward or to a woman or to his wife, closing the door behind him. Dr Rootle closed the door into the other room, then sat down on the stool in front of me. As I've mentioned elsewhere, I think, our knees almost touched. Also he leaned forward, so that his face was close to mine. I could feel his breath on my face, wholesome and clean – I was anxious about my own, that it wasn't full of nicotine and other impurities. As he was on the stool, he was lower than me, but I had the impression that he was towering above me. I felt myself hunching, like a schoolboy having an unhappy session with his hyperactive housemaster – I've discovered that being told you're dying sometimes distorts your view of people, you sometimes feel very small, which makes them seem very large. I was completely hypnotised and cowed by Dr Rootle's physical proximity, he was all teeth and spectacles, large, gleaming teeth and flashing spectacles, and there were his knees, I had to force myself not to look down at them as he spoke in a warm, clear and urgent fashion – all I really took in was that he'd arranged for me to start a course of radiotherapy quite soon. He explained what its purpose was, what effect it would have, and other stuff which I hoped Victoria was assimilating. The one thing I managed to grasp was that he didn't once mention his previous prognosis, that he was confining himself to my immediate future, and that he managed to make it sound pretty lively, and when Victoria asked him whether it would be all right to go away on a holiday, he said enthusiastically that yes, why not if I felt well enough, just go on doing all the things

I usually do, why not? – that came right at the end, before he got up and left the room.

'Is it over?' I asked Victoria, who smiled comfortingly as if she'd understood everything, which she evidently had, because she said, 'No, no, he's just gone to sort out the dates for the radiotherapy.'

'Did he ask us if we wanted to ask him anything?'

'No.'

When he came back he had a paper in his hand, with the dates, days, hours and venue on it, and handed it to Victoria – clearly he'd understood the difference between the person he was obliged to talk to and the one who understood what he was saying. When they'd finished there was one of those short, uncertain pauses that precede goodbyes between people who don't know each other, then he said to Victoria, 'If there's anything you think I can help you with, don't hesitate to get in touch,' and gave her his email address. They shook hands. He turned to me, held out his hand, and as I took it, in all its capability and power, the hand of a grown man, a true adult, he rested his other hand on my shoulder and said, gently, almost sotto voce, 'Don't worry. We'll take care of you.'

Afterwards, sitting at a lopsided table on the awkward chairs outside the pub, Victoria took me through my appointments, which were to begin the following Tuesday, when I would have my chest and neck marked with little tattoos, to show where the rays had to be aimed, then Wednesday, Thursday and Friday and the following Monday and Tuesday for the actual radiotherapy. I remember we felt relaxed, almost jolly. Victoria's eyes were bright and so was her voice, possibly my own were too – and this wasn't simply because I hadn't taken in most of what he'd said, because Victoria had explained it to me on the way out of the hospital, it was all quite simple and unthreatening, the treatment might hurt slightly, causing a burning sensation at the spots where the rays penetrated, but then again it might not. I would be likely to feel tired for a week or two after the treatment, but would then begin to feel better, much, much better.

'But better than what? I haven't been feeling ill.'

'Even so, you could probably feel better.'

This was undeniably true. One could always feel better, and there was a strong possibility that I'd got so used to feeling ill that I no longer noticed it.

We stayed at the pub for quite a while, free of tension, in fact quite uplifted – a tribute on Victoria's part to Dr Rootle's energy and confidence, and on mine to his physical and moral dominance. I felt such relief at having escaped from it, yes, exactly like a schoolboy who'd learned that there was to be no punishment after the interview, that the interview itself was the punishment – if indeed it was a punishment, it might even have been intended as a benefit. We went on to discuss our holiday. We'd have almost four clear weeks before we had to be back, there was a christening that we absolutely had to go to, Toby and Annie-Lou Stephens's newborn son, Eli. We'd been asked to be his godparents, were honoured to be asked. After that there would be the scan that would show what effect the radiotherapy had had.

I smoked a cigarette or possibly even two during this, as we decided that we'd go to Greece, but where in Greece? Perhaps to our usual island, Spetses – but Spetses wasn't reliable in its weather in early October, it could be beautiful, warm but fresh, the sea at its most perfect for swimming – I wasn't sure I was up to Spetses emotionally, if it turned out to be as lovely as we hoped, with the soft light fading in the evening, and all the familiar people in the familiar bars and cafés, it might feel like a leave-taking, harrowing – so what about Crete? – yes, Crete, we'd look into Crete, we'd been there once in early summer and liked it, and it was known to be at its best late in autumn and we had no ties to it, we could just enjoy it for what it was. I had a severe thought, and presented it to Victoria. 'Look,' I said, 'do you think it's quite right for me to be Eli's godfather, given my situation? Shouldn't he have somebody who's likely to be around for him? I mean, that's the point of a godfather.' She was unusually sharp with me, saying that Toby and Annie-Lou had been aware of my 'situation' when they asked me, they wanted me to be a godfather, that's all there was to it. She didn't say, 'Subject closed,' but it was. Anyway, I remembered that Toby and Annie-Lou were Catholics, there were probably all kinds of contingency plans in their church, an edict or a bull could sort the matter out, when the time came.

Just before we left, or it might have been when we were on our way to the car, I said, 'What did he mean, they'll take care of me? "Don't worry, we'll take care of you," he said. And he put his hand on my shoulder. What did he mean by it?' Victoria said she hadn't heard him say it. 'He said it in a low voice. When he put his hand on my shoulder.' She said that he certainly didn't mean anything sinister by it, he certainly only meant that he'd make sure I got the right treatment. Still, the phrase and the gesture troubled me, as they do now that I think about them, sitting here, on the patio, at two in the morning. The wind's dropped, it's quite still, and through the break in the wall I can see a small boat in the moonlight, just the one, rocking gently, and a dark figure bunched at the end, by the bow, fishing I suppose – I can't see clearly what he's doing, he may be asleep, or just sitting, possibly watching me. I must be very visible, because I got the management to clamp a couple of extra lamps to the roof, angled to shine down on the patch where this table is – yes, he can certainly see me if he's looking in this direction, see what I look like and what I'm doing. I think I'll stop writing now, have a cigarette and just sit, watching the boat, and hope that he stands up and moves about, that he waves to me. I'd like that.

THE BUNDLES ON THE BEACH

The beach looked completely deserted at 9 a.m. this morning when we had our swim, except for two bundles of clothing on adjacent sunbeds that had been left behind from the evening before, or had been put down as markers, to reserve the places until the day got warmer. There was an autumnal nip in the air, which is perhaps why there was no one else on the beach, or it might be that a lot of guests left yesterday evening and will be replaced by a new lot tonight, when the planes come in from London, Manchester, Paris, Milan –

We had our swim, quite a brief one, and headed for the shower, passing on our way the two beds with the bundles of clothing on them, which turned out to be two elderly women – quite a bit older than me, into their eighties, I should think – in their overcoats, collars up to their chins, scarves wrapped around their necks and more scarves over their feet. They both wore glasses and were both smoking.

One of them was curled on her side, and nestled against her stomach was a dachshund. 'Good morning!' we said to them, wet, cold, but unfailingly polite, as many English feel obliged to be, when abroad, to show that we don't intend to punch and kick people just because they're old and on a beach, for instance. I added a loving chuckle for the dog. The two ladies looked at us not exactly with malevolence, but with hostility and a soupçon of contempt, then spoke to each other in hoarse voices in what sounded suspiciously like German but wasn't German. Then they laughed, drew on their cigarettes and puffed smoke affectionately towards each other's faces. We wondered whether they were related – they were alike in appearance, attitude and voice, but they might have been partners, is the correct word I think, who through many years of cohabitation have come to resemble each other – perhaps met as girls at school, begun what in those days had to be a covert but was nevertheless a passionate romance, then as laws changed and the world relaxed sexually into its unhappy-go-unlucky muddle of righteousness and libertinism, came together for life as it were, finally sealing their relationship in a registry office or even a church, depending, of course, on the mores of whatever country they come from. Their unattractively united front in sneering dismissal of a gentle and courteous English couple might be a defensive habit acquired during their early years, years of wounding humiliation – on the other hand, they might merely be nasty pieces of work, lacking in manners and ordinary human decency, and now I write about them I realise that they reminded me most of all of Marge Simpson's twin sisters but without the sisters' wayward charm and sense of fun – they weren't as pretty as Marge's sisters, either, and the inert dachshund looked bogus and unpleasant, perhaps it was stuffed, or drugged, perhaps it wasn't theirs, they'd stolen it –

READING MATTERS

I'm rather puzzled by the books we've brought with us. For the first time ever we had our luggage sent ahead because I can't stand for long, my legs tend to buckle and my breathing becomes laboured. Victoria would have had a bad time keeping an eye on me as we waited for our bags to come through, and then getting them and us to the taxi and so forth. Realising that we wouldn't have to deal with our bags made us carefree in filling them, especially with books – too many of them, in fact, because I can't find any principle in my own selection, apart from the poetry, two editions of *The Oxford Book of English Verse* (Gardner and Ricks), two of *The Oxford Book of Modern Verse* (Yeats and Larkin), an edition of Hardy, selections of Wordsworth, Yeats and T. S. Eliot, all the basic stuff I yearn to have to hand on holiday, plus an edition of William Barnes, but the rest of it, the prose, seems completely arbitrary – there are even a couple of thrillers, but it's been a long time since I've been able to read a thriller, and now, now, when I feel I've got to make every book count, I can't bear the thought of reading a book that won't be helpful or appropriate. But in what way could a book be helpful or appropriate? I see that I've stuck in *The Death of Ivan Ilyich* – well, I can see how that's appropriate, but can't see how it could be helpful – in fact, its appropriateness, the story of a mediocre man coming to terms with his death, makes it far too appropriate and therefore positively unhelpful. And then there are a lot of biographies of people in whom, suddenly, I'm no longer interested – Samuel Butler, Clough, Disraeli – I think they're there because I had a plan to write a play about Florence Nightingale and simply forgot that I'd abandoned it. There are some novels by people I've heard of but never got around to reading, Musil's *The Man without Qualities*, which I've promised myself, or is it threatened myself with, since people first mentioned him at Cambridge fifty years ago. He's in three paperback volumes, is over a thousand pages altogether, and I've read about a hundred of them twice, the first time when I was in my fifties, the second time recently, in fact it was the book I was reading when I got the cancer news – I found I couldn't go on with it, I doubt if I could have gone on with any book, really, but I suspect I'd have dumped *The Man without Qualities* if I'd been in good health, it's so dazzlingly intelligent, so felinely observant, so casually erudite, and so completely static that it made me dizzy with admiration and boredom, a hundred pages and no discernible story, no glimmering of a plot, not even the feeblest narrative thrust – it's a book for patient and philosophical minds, I think, and not therefore for me – so why did I bring them, all three volumes? Oh, because I had room for them, of course. And room for *Middlemarch*. I thought it might bring comfort, as I know it so well, and there is George Eliot's voice, guiding you through her story and possibly guiding you through this time in your life when you feel such a need for wisdom and comfort. I started it last night, and didn't get far and didn't want to go further, I remembered it too well, and was afraid I wouldn't care enough, even about Lydgate, and his 'fatal spot of commonness'. So what does that leave? All these books, and not one of them, not a single one of them, attracts. Didn't I put in a novel by Stefan Zweig, with a title that reminded me of a Jacobean play, *Women Beware Women*? – 'Beware' comes into it –

Yes, I've got it. *Beware of Pity*, by Stefan Zweig. Why this? Now let's think – yes, I picked it up at Daunt's partly because the cover caught my eye – I'm looking at it now – it's the Klimt of Schubert at the piano, Schubert clothed in black with an abundance of black hair and a long, thick black sideboard, but his face in profile is pink and pudgy. Beside him a woman is singing, she is young and pretty, with a halo of pink and brown air that looks like – it may even be – a hat, and beside her another young woman listens intently, with her head bowed towards perhaps a candle, perhaps a slender vase of flowers – all my perhapses and qualifications are because, though it's a charming and suggestive picture, it's slightly muzzy, and one can't tell whether that's true of the original or has been exaggerated in reproduction. Either way it's eye-catching. In fact I might well have bought the book simply for its cover, but I also wanted to find out about Stefan Zweig. His is one of those names that's always been on the periphery – I mean for me – an early twentieth-century Viennese intellectual would have been my guess, from dimly recalled and un-assorted titbits, and I see from the first sentence of the tiny biography that indeed he was, born in 1881, of a wealthy Austrian-Jewish family, but it doesn't say what else he wrote, how irritating, how very irritating. When did he die? Good God, he died in 1942, 'he and his wife were found dead in bed in an apparent double suicide'. What does that mean, apparent? What would the alternatives be? An accident? A murder and a suicide, either way around? Did he or they leave a note? Here's a photograph of him on the back of the bio page, taken in his late forties, his expression is pleased and eager. Long fine nose with a serious moustache under it, alert eyes, thinning hair and a high forehead. He looks very like Adolphe Menjou, who was Irish-American, I think, and Anton Walbrook, who was Viennese, I think. I really wish we had a computer with us, so that I could google Stefan Zweig. And Adolphe Menjou and Anton Walbrook, come to that. Anyway, Zweig's face on the photograph doesn't strike one as being the face of a suicide, in that it's not only 'pleased and eager', as I observed above, but it's also positively complacent, in a sympathetic way, a modest man who knows that he's famous and important. Why, then, would he commit suicide, that is if it was a real as opposed to an 'apparent' suicide? Did he have a terminal illness? Cancer? But then he wouldn't take his wife with him, just for the sake of her company, I hope. Let's look at the bio again – oh, in Brazil, he died in Brazil – well, of course in 1942 he would have been in exile, Austria in the clutches of another Austrian. As a Jew Zweig's books would have been banned, probably burnt, his whole world in flames and about to become rubble, enough reason at sixty-two to kill himself, and his wife might have felt the same. Or, assuming that she was also Austrian, she didn't want to be a homeless widow. As soon as I get home I'll find out all about him – in the meantime I might as well read *Beware of Pity*. Try it, at least.

No, I don't think so. I think I'd really rather read poetry tonight. One of the Oxford books, the Helen Gardner for once, I've thumbed through the Ricks so often that I always seem to dip into the same pages, read the same poems again and again, all the Donne, all the Herbert, then skip to Pope's 'Letter to Arbuthnot' and the Fourth Book of *The Dunciad*, then Wordsworth's 'Immortality Ode', his poem in memory of James Hogg, some Coleridge – always 'Frost at Midnight' and 'Dejection', then occasionally something exotic and opium-driven, 'Kubla Khan' or 'The Ancient Mariner' – they're never really right for my mood, but once started they're hard to stop, on to Keats, 'Autumn', 'Nightingale' and 'Urn', ending with the fragment from 'The Fall of Hyperion – A Dream', and then nothing much until Hardy, Edward Thomas, Yeats, Eliot, really my own personal anthology, and never breaking new ground, although it's rich enough, especially when in the state I'm in now, when I don't really want to break new ground, but to be comforted by the poems that have always brought me comfort – still, I'll have a quick go at the Gardner, open it anywhere and see what happens – actually I find I've picked up the Yeats *Modern Verse*, ages since I've looked into that.

And it'll be ages until I look into it again, which means I'll never look into it again, what a disgrace of a selection, what a shabby, mean-spirited, pompous – how could a great poet have done such a thing? And the Introduction! I'd forgotten how vague, self-important and prejudiced – his dismissal of the war poets, not a poem by Owen, not a single poem, but pages of Edith Sitwell and Lascelles Abercrombie and Laurence Binyon, and Edwin John Ellis and lots of other poets with three names, William Henry Davies, Thomas Sturge Moore, George William Russell, and some of them OK, W. H. Davies for a minute or two, but none of them should be in an Oxford anthology, oh, here's one with four names, you'd expect to come across them on a tombstone – Leonard Alfred George Strong – here's this from him:

> I sweep the street and lift me hat
> As persons come and persons go,
> Me lady and me gentleman:
> I lift me hat – but you don't know!
> I've money by against I'm dead:
> A hearse and mourners there will be!
> And every sort of walking man
> Will stop to lift his hat to me!

Yes, that and no Owen, Rosenberg, Sassoon – and one poem by Edward Thomas, one poem! and not really a very good one, I suppose Yeats decided that Thomas was just and merely a war poet – but enough of this, your time has become precious, don't forget, and you're wasting it on bile, just remind yourself of what Yeats himself wrote, and how much of him you love to read, toss his anthology aside, and plunge into the Gardner –

I trawled along very enjoyably, profitably, I think – I opened on Marvell, which was a stroke of luck, because there they were, the ones I would have wanted, which are probably in the Ricks but I've never looked, and of course I should have – 'To His Coy Mistress', 'The Garden', 'The Definition of Love' and best of all, because I haven't read it for years and years, 'The Picture of Little T.C. in a Prospect of Flowers' – and then straight into Henry Vaughan, 'The Retreat' and 'Peace' and 'The World' with that opening –

> I saw Eternity the other night,
> Like a great ring of pure and endless light,
> All calm, as it was bright

but I didn't hang about in that neighbourhood, or nip back to Donne and Herbert, I did a big jump with my eyes closed, taking an oath that I would read all the poems by whichever poet I arrived at, and almost reneged when I landed in the middle of Sir Walter Scott – the thing is that I've never been able to read his novels – I bought a whole set when I was at Cambridge, over fifty years ago, for about a pound, and they're still in my study, a whole shelf of small red books with small print and pages that cling to your fingers when you try to turn them over – I've come across articles by Alan Massie and A. N. Wilson that persuade me that Scott is a great writer, but it's no good, as soon as I pick up a volume with one hand, the other hand snatches it away and puts it back on the shelf – as for his poems, well, I always think I know them because I learned one or two at school, prep school I think, for patriotic reasons –

> Breathes there the man with a soul so dead,
> Who never to himself hath said,
> 'This is my own, my native land!'

my ten-year-old chest swelled when I recited it – my chest hasn't swelled often since, except when I take Casodex for my prostate, and then it's a different swelling of my chest, into bosoms really –

*

and of course there was

> O, young Lochinvar is come out of the west,
>> Through all the wide Border his steed
>>> was the best.

and so forth, and so forth, that and a few others were Scott's poetry for me, but I stuck to my pledge and read through them and was pleased to do so, finding them rather thrilling, in fact, and then just towards the end, the last poem but one and immediately after 'The Rover's Farewell' there was this, which made my hair shift on my scalp –

> *Madge Wildfire's Song*
> Proud Maisie is in the wood,
>> Walking so early;
> Sweet Robin sits on the bush,
>> Singing so rarely.
> 'Tell me, thou bonny bird,
>> When shall I marry me?'
> 'When six braw gentlemen
>> Kirkward shall carry ye.'
> 'Who makes the bridal bed,
>> Birdie, say truly?'
> 'The grey-headed sexton
>> That delves the grave duly.
> 'The glow-worm o'er grave and stone
>> Shall light thee steady;
> The owl from the steeple sing,
>> Welcome, proud lady!'

'NO!' TO A BARE BODKIN, BUT –

– at some point, at any point, come to think of it, I can pull out – refuse radiotherapy, refuse chemotherapy, refuse to see Drs Omar, Morgan Morgan and Rootle, accept that I have a terminal illness and let it all happen as it happens. Or I can drop out when the pain becomes too much to bear – I have a low threshold when it comes to pain – 'drop out', a euphemism for kill myself, why not put it un-euphemistically – I can always kill myself as soon as I find that living is an agony, but how? is the question I've put to myself quite often over the last months, how exactly does one kill oneself in a fashion that causes the least distress to those one loves – and the least inconvenience to many people that one doesn't love, but has no right to inconvenience? I've often been infuriated by having a journey interrupted by 'a body on the line', thinking how selfish and thoughtless, and then making myself remember Anna Karenina, and the agony of despair, akin to madness, that drove her to throw herself in front of the train – also it may not be a planned act, it might be a coincidence of despair striking at a railway station, the realisation that one step, one small step – it comes hurtling along so invitingly, you'll be caught up in all that rush and noise and you'll be gone, you'll be gone, you'll be gone – I used to have the impulse at Highgate Tube Station, and had to press myself against the wall of the tunnel between the two platforms, the southbound and the northbound, although it was always the southbound train I was inclined towards, the trains that went to Camden Town, Tottenham Court Road, Waterloo, Morden – I remember that, too, whenever I'm exasperated by a body on the line – or is it 'person' they say, 'person on the line'. Or possibly 'customer' these days – 'a customer on the line'.

The fact is that I don't want to die violently, even by self-inflicted violence, it would seem more like an act of murder, and though I have serious misgivings about my character and much of my behaviour over the last seventy years, I don't hate myself enough to want to punish myself with death. I'm merely thinking of how I can escape months of pain, at the same time releasing Victoria from the burden of having to deal with it. I've seen three people die of cancer – my mother, and two of my closest friends. My mother, a tall, athletic woman with a fiery nature and a strut to her walk, even at the age of fifty-nine, became in three months so shrunken and gaunt that I couldn't bear to look at her. The doctor took pity on her and on her husband and their three sons by administering a final dose of morphine, so that she died virtually mid-hallucination –

The first friend to die of cancer was Ian Hamilton, fine poet and critic, at the age of sixty-four. He became aware that something was wrong with him on the opening night of my play *Japes*. He told me the following day that at the interval he'd gone for a piss, and out had shot a jet of blood with bits of matter mixed in it – he'd no idea it was coming, he'd felt well – in fact, never better, he'd said, and his trip to the lavatory hadn't been particularly urgent, he'd just felt that he'd better go, because it was the interval. I asked him what he thought caused it, this fount of blood instead of urine, he said he had no idea. He seemed both amused and shocked by it. He was seeing a doctor very soon, at the hospital I now go to, as a matter of fact, a woman who was presumably in the same unit or team as my lot and therefore probably quite young. She opened the interview by handing him his scan. He could make nothing of it, though he studied it carefully – he didn't really know what he should be looking at, or for, and said that it reminded him of his breakfast. She took the scan from him and said, 'You'll probably be dead in three months. Now do you think it's funny?' He escaped as soon as he could, went down to the car park and smoked a cigarette, knowing only one thing with any certainty, that he could never, under any circumstances, see that brute of a doctor again. He went to a different hospital, where the doctor, a woman, kindly and sympathetic, who wasn't offended by his attempts to find courage in jokes, took him on. It turned out that he had a tumour near his bladder, hence the jet of blood instead of urine, and he had tumours in his lungs and his liver. I don't know whether he thought smoking was a primary cause, actually I don't think he much cared, for him his cancer was a fucking nuisance, and therefore an enemy, a personal enemy – but then Ian was by nature combative, a bit of a warrior, and in his early years positively enjoyed making enemies – in his last months he was unrecognisable, only recently a sturdy and handsome man, he had been made bloated and bald by chemotherapy, in his last days he could scarcely walk or talk, though he found immense energy at the very end, his partner Patchy told me, angry and defiant and tormented, trying to heave himself up and grapple with death as if in a bar-room brawl with it.

The second friend to die of cancer was Alan Bates, fine actor and famously beautiful man. He remained beautiful to the last, and seemed not to mind the dying, he felt he'd had a successful life, and a good one – but then Alan was never ashamed of his cancer, he thought of it as possibly just a mistake on, presumably, nature's part, and he accepted it with tolerance, almost as if it weren't a personal matter. I suppose if I could die like him, serenely and for the most part painlessly – but I doubt if I would, as these things are also a matter of temperament, I suspect, and Alan was by nature amiable and conciliatory, in many of his relationships a touch passive – completely unlike Ian –

Well, what are you? Yes, what are you, what sort of death would you make, do you think? How can I answer that? I don't know, but you should try to think, shouldn't you, because surely the kind of death you imagine is in store for you will help you decide whether you kill yourself or let nature and medicine have their way. So?

SICKO AND THICKO DISCUSS THE ORIGINS OF THE MORAL SENSE

So?

Well, are you by nature conciliatory or are you combative?

Both. Generally alternately. Combative until I meet resistance, and then I become conciliatory.

A bully and a coward, then?

Well – yes.

Come on, come on, admit it, admit it, you're a bully and a coward, and a coward and a bully, admit it!

Yes yes, a coward and a bully, a bully and a coward, so please leave me alone now, please.

I'm just getting started.

I'm not going on with this unless you stop shouting.

OK.

Oh, thank you, thank you.

Not at all, not at all. A pleasure. Now explain to me, if you would, how being a bully and a coward works in practice, in your daily life.

Well, let me think. Yes. I'm often caught between a desire to please people and a desire to tell them the truth, so end up by doing neither.

You equate being a bully with telling the truth and desiring to please people with cowardice?

Presumably these basic characteristics, drives, whatever they are, manifest themselves in complicated ways in my social behaviour. Bullying and cowardice are somewhere near the murky bottom of my self.

Somewhere near? And at the very bottom?

Greed and fear, I assume. That's the Hobbesian view, and I've always thought it to be the right one.

On what evidence?

From what I feel going on in myself, and what I understand from what I observe in other people.

So really you're saying you're only human.

On the other hand, what a piece of work is man. I believe that, too. Greed and fear are refined by consciousness, and further refined, until the initial impulses are disguised, and even nearly lost. So we have table manners, Mozart, Chekhov –

And Shakespeare and so forth and so forth, eh?

Actually, the thing about Shakespeare – the thing about him –

Is what? What is the thing about Shakespeare?

That he never loses touch with the initial impulses – for instance, when Hamlet forces himself to believe that he can kill, and then kills the wrong man, and then decides the wrong man will do for starters, when Macbeth finds out what it means to kill a king, and then kills him anyway, or when Lear discovers where his life is when he discovers Cordelia dead – they're almost like physical throbs, these moments of understanding. Shakespeare's above all the great poet of the particular, so in fact his greatest poetry isn't his, it belongs to Hamlet, Coriolanus, Macbeth, Lear – to this particular man at this particular moment in these particular and devastating circumstances – there are no great truths in Shakespeare that aren't wrung from the immediate, which is why you can also find their perfectly truthful opposites somewhere in his work – people are always quoting the saying – all art aspires to the condition of music – but really I think that all art aspires to the condition of literature –

Which doesn't have a universal language. Which music has.

Yes, that's why it's an aspiration. Literature is rooted in the particularity of language. No other art has that particularity. On the other hand, all other arts can be universal, in the way that literature can't be. But an Englishman who can't read Russian or French can still have a strong sense of what Raskolnikov and Pierre, or Emma Bovary and Julian Sorel go through, while music can't give us a Raskolnikov or a Pierre or a Madame Bovary or a Julian Sorel. So even in translation there's a certain universality about literature. Some literature. Not poetry. For instance, nobody who reads Baudelaire in translation would think for a moment that he's reading great poetry.

So really, apart from Shakespeare, you're talking about novels?

Yes, well they touch our sympathy, the best of them, even in translation.

Sympathy? That's an odd word, coming from a man who believes that Hobbes is right, that at our murky bottom we're composed of greed and fear.

But I also believe that Hume is right, that we have sympathy – a faculty of sympathy.

So what it comes down to is that your personal philosophy is an amateurish synthesis of Hobbes and Hume?

I haven't got a personal philosophy. I'm merely using Hobbes and

Hume as a way of describing my understanding of myself – of the way I've felt, of the way I've behaved –

And this faculty of sympathy that you read about in Hume?

It's the recognition of other people's feelings through the awareness of those feelings, or the possibility of them, in myself.

You sympathise with other people's fear and greed because you're frightened and greedy yourself?

That puts it very crudely.

Yes, but then it's pretty crude.

Sympathy, the faculty of sympathy, or the power of sympathy, seems to me a wondrous thing. It's the dove in us, according to Hume, as opposed to the serpent. Also, it's essential both for self-preservation and for the preservation of society. Every good act comes from it, as do the feelings that cause us so much distress and so – sometimes – manage to stop us from doing bad things to people, or from doing them again – sometimes.

What feelings are those?

Guilt, shame, remorse – you know perfectly well.

And those come from which? Greed or fear? Or both?

Well, fear, historically speaking. We form society because it's safer, societies depend on laws and customs for their survival, and laws and customs depend for their survival on rewards and punishments – gradually this primitive system becomes internal and increasingly complicated, our rewards come in states of consciousness, peace of mind – for instance, the satisfaction of helping others – while the punishments –

Guilt, shame, remorse, etc.?

Exactly. Look, I really haven't got a head for this sort of thinking. That's why I've stuck to writing plays.

OK. Then let's get back to your own particularity, shall we? Your claim that you're a bully and a coward. Or is that just a boast?

I wish it were, but right from childhood – well, when I went to school in Montreal at the age of six I was bullied because I was different. For one thing I still had an English accent. I was beaten up by the school gang on a daily basis. There is a gap in my memory, I don't know how I got to the next stage, but the next stage was being taken into the gang that beat me up, and being allowed to join in the beating up of other boys who were different, mainly Jews and Catholics. Eventually I became one of the beaters-up in chief. There's a very good account of the process in Sartre's *Childhood of a Leader*, about the birth of an anti-Semite.

But you grew out of it?

I hope so. But you never know. Things stir sometimes. And like many of my generation I've never been put to the test. I thank God that I wasn't a German in 1930, for example. Or a Russian at that period. Or a dependant of a slave-trader. I'm always amazed at the ease with which people now assume – as a matter of course – that they would have rebelled against the moral norm of other times, other countries. How long did it take the abolitionists to win over the House of Commons? Years and years and then more years. I think most MPs now are as morally supine and as greedy as the MPs then, and if you could perform some magical time switch, so that they kept their current personalities but were otherwise adjusted historically, they would have mostly voted against abolition. And if you stuck them in Hitler's Germany or Stalin's Russia you'd find them in equivalent positions to the ones they occupy here and now – promulgating race laws, scrambling for a position in the politburo. I'd like to stop this. I really don't want to spend the time I have left on anything but the life I have left.

OK. Where were you?

Considering whether I ought to be planning suicide.

WILL SOMEBODY PLEASE TELL ME WHICH
AND HOW MANY?

The temptation will be to keep postponing it until it's too late. But choosing the right time will also depend on the how. If I rule out violence, jumping from the Clifton Suspension Bridge, throwing myself under a train, cutting my throat, thrusting a knife into my heart, and try to sort out a tranquil and painless method, I imagine I'd have to come in the end to pills. Well, I've more than thought about pills – I've been storing them ever since I got the news. Zimovane (my sleeping pills) and co-proxamol, which is an analgesic that doesn't affect the liver or the stomach. Now when Dr David Kelly, the UN inspector of weapons of mass destruction who reported on Iraq, was found sitting dead under a tree in a field, he was at first declared to have committed suicide by taking an overdose of co-proxamol and then slitting his wrists, and I remember even then, long before the discovery of my cancer, that this was useful information to have about co-proxamol, should the need ever arise etc., but later it came out that he'd vomited up most of the co-proxamol undigested and that a number of experts, medical experts I assume, claimed that there wasn't enough left in his system to have killed him, nor had he lost enough blood to cause his death, and recently there have been rumours that he was murdered. This is depressing for many reasons, among them my own personal reason – as I've said, I've no intention of cutting my wrists, the thought of it makes them tingle with dread – but I had hoped that co-proxamol was a sure thing. Now I have to accept the possibility that I'd just vomit the pills up. Also I have no idea how many you'd have to keep down to do the job. I suppose if I washed down say fifteen with a bottle of Scotch, the Scotch might help to absorb them into my system. On the other hand, I'm not sure I could drink a bottle of Scotch, or even a glass of it, or even a teaspoonful – I've come to loathe the smell of alcohol. There's an irony to be foraged out of this, I think, that I gave up alcohol because it was killing me, and now that I want to kill myself I can't take it up again. Well, what about the sleepers, zimovane? I've been taking them for years and they seem jolly effective – one generally puts me out, and on occasional bad nights two will do the trick. Of course they're much helped in their work by Victoria, who always puts her arms around me shortly after I come to bed, the combination is so soothing, so lulling. But I can't ask Victoria to put her arms around me when I've taken an overdose, she might find herself charged with a criminal offence, assisting with a suicide possibly, so I'll have to rely on the zimovane alone. But how many? And actually, are they the right sort of sleeping pills? You hear and read stories of people who've gobbled down bottles of sedatives but instead of dying they turn into vegetables – whenever I hear or read that phrase, 'he turned into a vegetable', I always think of a marrow or a cucumber. Well, it would be awful if I turned into a cucumber or a marrow, and Victoria had to tend me – watering me, cleaning me, and settling me down – although in reality I would just be an inert lump, with tubes sticking out of me, my chest rising and falling with mechanical regularity. She couldn't grieve over me because there I would be, technically alive, a drain on her emotions and eventually her health.

So really, yes, it's a bit of a problem. It's one thing to see coolly the need to kill myself at some point in my dying, quite another thing to work out how to do it. The obvious person to provide information would be a doctor, but there's doubtless some code of professional ethics that would prevent him from spilling the beans. I could try to pretend that I'm writing a thriller, 'There's a chap I want to knock off at the end, it's got to look like a suicide, what would be the best sleeping pill, would zimovane do it, and how many precisely?' but would he believe me? If I found the right doctor he could pretend to believe me. Well, for the moment all I can do is make sure that I always have a lot of co-proxamol and zimovane to hand, and hope that someone will turn up who'll give me the right information. And when I've got that sorted out, I'll have to work out where, and at what time of the day or night, so that nobody is inconvenienced or embarrassed, and so that it is in some way supportable for Victoria. I'll want her by me, and she's said she wants to be by me, right up to the end, but I can only let her in so far as it's legally possible.

A NIGHT ON THE TOWN AND AFTERWARDS

We took a taxi into Agios Nikolaus for dinner this evening. We stopped at a Vodafone place to see if we could get the BlackBerry to work, but a rather indolent and ill-tempered girl said they could do nothing with it, the signals had been set wrong for Greece, which didn't make sense as we'd used it in Spetses last year. The owner of the shop, or perhaps he was the manager, came out from the back, and took a politer and more concerned view. He opened the BlackBerry up, made a phone call which lasted a long time and caused him to smile and laugh often – the taxi ticking away through all this – then hung up, closed the BlackBerry and handed it back, saying there was nothing they could do, the signals were set wrong for Greece. We returned to the taxi and asked to be taken to the nearest supermarket, as I needed to stock up on white chocolate, to which I'm addicted – in fact, I can't get to sleep unless I've gulped down at least half a bar of a large Green & Black's. It was a strangely tortuous and complicated journey, from the Vodafone place in the centre of town to the outskirts. The supermarket was as ghastly as our local Tesco's in London, but less busy, not at all busy. Actually, we were virtually the only customers, so it had a mortuary feel to it – and at least our local Tesco's sold Green & Black's white chocolate. This supermarket didn't sell any white chocolate at all. I had to make do with milk chocolate, which usually makes me feel sick and gives me a headache. I bought ten bars of it – enough to last me, I hope – then back to the taxi. We asked to be taken to the lake, where the young man at reception had told us there were many restaurants, and indeed there were many, many restaurants. We walked along, peering into them, not seeing much difference between them in the seating arrangements, and not much difference in the menus, large versions of which were posted outside, with photographs of the dishes on offer. The lurid colours of heaps of bright red spaghetti and scarlet crabs and violent green salads and corpse-white squares of feta cheese made the food look disgusting, and when we turned away from it we invariably found ourselves facing the – I don't know what he was – maître d' doesn't sound right, but he was more than just a waiter – he was a sort of pimp, actually, he was pimping his restaurant, 'Allo, yas, good ivnin, lovely and licious plates ere, you like, you come in, yas, come in,' and when we smiled apologetically and moved off, he would shout after us, 'Tankyewverraverramush, sir, madame, tankyewverraverramush,' not sarcastically but mechanically, and the thing was these pimps all looked the same, short and burly, unshaven, in baggy grey trousers and messy white shirts, though one or two had stained white and blue aprons, but they all had the same blank eyes, never looking at you even when they described in an intimate voice the specialities of the house.

In the end we sat down at a table that was more on the pavement than in the restaurant, not that we chose it but the pimp was broader and fatter than his rivals, and instead of following us with invitations in a fairly loud voice and then dropping away to track another client, he stepped in front of us and spoke in a low, insinuating murmur, which made him sound more salacious than the others, indeed slightly perverted, as if he were at the gastro-paedophile end of the market, and he also extended his arm. It could have been a conversational gesture, but it prevented us from walking deafly ahead. Trudging politely around him, we also crossed the line, so to speak, into his establish-ment, which began at the edge of the pavement. He pulled a chair out for Victoria, who hesitated, we shrugged at each other and sat down. There was no doubt that it was a lively position – all nationalities, English, Welsh and Scottish, passed by in what frequently looked like the costumes of their countries, the Scotidge were dumpy men in tartan shorts and shirts, the dumpy men in nursery jumpsuits I took to be the Welsh. The English wore a combination of the infantile and the threatening – cut-off trousers with chains looping out of the pockets and shirts that had no sleeves but were tattered at the shoulder, as if they'd been ripped in a drunken rage, although were no doubt sold that way, and were probably expensive – these were the young men, and mainly the young women, but the middle-aged and elderly were merely inelegant and dowdy, the women in unbecoming tracksuits and shapeless dresses or – if they were fat – shorts and T-shirts with slogans on them. In all of them, whatever their age and costume, was an innate courtesy that made it impossible for them to get past the pimps without apologising, explaining that they'd eaten already or were going to meet friends or – in one case, a North Country couple in their sixties – that they were still recovering from a bit of stomach trouble they'd picked up the other night, but tomorrow they hoped to be over it and they would certainly like to try this restaurant, as it wasn't the restaurant that had caused the trouble, it was one a little further down – the pimp patted them both on the arm without looking at them, 'Tankyewverramush,' he said, 'tankyewverraverramush,' and as the couple went off they gave each other a grin, so they'd obviously delivered a prepared alibi – there were other nationalities, of course, French, Dutch, German, and the pimps were presumably saying in their language the sort of thing they said in ours. There were also groups and couples of Chinese and Japanese – I think this is the first time I've ever seen Chinese and Japanese in Greece – the Japanese stood politely listening to the pimps, and asked questions in English, while the Chinese, I suppose more used to the huckstering and pimp approach, went past with fixed smiles, or took photographs, which our particular pimp actually posed for, beside his menu, then watched them turn into the next restaurant and sit down – watched, I might say, without rancour.

The lake is small – more like an enormous puddle – but it has a few ducks on it, and a few rowing boats also, and then there are the lights reflected in the water, and the sounds drifting across from the other side, all the bustle and animation. It was fun sitting there, and remained fun even when the food arrived. But then you don't come to Greece for the food, just as you don't come to England for the people –

A toothsome, high-breasted but slightly grubby waitress cleared the overflowing plates away and we paid the bill – preposterously cheap when you consider how much had been put in front of us, preposterously expensive when you consider how little we'd been able to eat – and strolled off, the pimp's farewell 'Tankyewverramush' soiling our ears. We went around the lake and up one of the very busy streets, looking into the shop windows. They were full of luxury goods, fashionable underwear, expensive watches. One had shelves on shelves of cigarettes, it was called Tobacco Warehouse. It was like any street now, I suppose, in any European tourist town. We couldn't see shops selling specifically Greek things, but what are specifically Greek things, things you'd want to buy because they were made in Greece, by Greeks? I can't think of a single thing that you look forward to buying in Greece, except cheap cigarettes.

As we strolled along I began to feel that oddness, when all energy goes out of me, just like that, my legs begin to buckle. I had to catch Victoria's arm and cling to her to stay upright. The taxi driver who'd brought us in had dropped us close to a rank, so we knew where to go. It wasn't far, no more than fifty yards or so, but I couldn't make it, and sank on to a café chair on the pavement, feeling on the edge of consciousness, my legs watery, my breathing short and abrupt. The lump on my neck was throbbing. I kept plucking at it, and then stroking it, to soothe it. Victoria ordered a couple of espressos, and we sat with her hand on mine. When the coffee came I had trouble lifting the cup to my lips, but managed a sip, and it was delicious – the most delicious taste since we came to Greece. I began to feel better, whether it was the wonderful espresso or the resting, I don't know, but some energy and strength came back. I tried to explain what had happened and how it felt – the question really being, was it the work of the cancer or of the radiotherapy, the illness or the treatment? If the latter, then perhaps these collapses are actually good signs –

Back at the hotel, we looked in at the bar for another coffee. It was full of English and Scottish, noisy and mostly drunk, not nasty drunk but jolly and singsongy and laughter-at-the-top-of-the-voice drunk. There was a man playing something that looked like a piano but was actually one of those music machines that produce all kinds of instrumental effects, organ, violin, flute, trumpet – when we went in he was producing a combination of them, and singing loudly enough to be heard over the din. The room stank of cigarette smoke and I realised that I'd come to loathe all cigarette smoke except my own – but then one doesn't smell one's own cigarette smoke, or not in the way that one smells other people's.

We went out on to the terrace, where there was only one other couple, young, English and elegant, she blonde and pretty, in a shimmering silver skirt, and he dark and handsome in a pouty and illtempered sort of way. He was talking into his mobile, breaking off to snarl something to the woman, who would avert her head contemptuously. They were in the middle of a row, obviously, that had nothing to do with the conversation on the mobile. Their voices were too low for me to hear, though I tried, but I imagined, of course – the two of them coming to the rancorous end of an affair, perhaps one of them married but they both looked too – what? – childish? unused? to have a husband or wife somewhere – so an office romance, I guessed, a couple of moneymaking high-flyers, hedge-funders and such. If so, it would be ugly when they got back, lawsuits and harassment charges etc. Suddenly he raised his voice and said, 'So now you go to bed, darling, and here's Mummy to say goodnight,' and passed her the mobile, and she said, one could tell from her expression though not actually hear, all kinds of sweet and loving things. When she'd finished, she handed him the mobile, he tucked it into his shirt pocket and sat with his hands behind his head, sealed off, oblivious, and she sat in that way that women do, hunched and her arms crossed, hands tucked into the armpits, as if it were cold, which of course it wasn't. Then he said something, she said something, he looked at her, she laughed, he laughed and put his hand on her knee, and lit a cigarette, which they shared. So that was all right then. When we got up to leave, after a feeble, virtually caffeine-free coffee, they suddenly noticed us, she smiled prettily but he scowled, which made him look prepubescent, and as if he thought we were interlopers or eavesdroppers, for God's sake!

Now I'm sitting on the patio beside our swimming pool, there's no moon, and it's dark beyond the pool. I can't see the sea between the rocks, in fact I can't distinguish the rocks from the darkness, and I'm getting jittery, the walls-closing-in experience, not as bad as previously, but it's unsettling, and makes me think about my collapse this evening, which hasn't become a memory so much as an apprehension – It's – what is it? Nearly 3 a.m., I think I've got to get away from here, I'm too awake to go to bed, I'll go for a walk, slip out without telling Victoria, she'd worry – the key, make sure you've got your key.

I'm back. I walked along the dimly lit paths to the chapel where I sit in the daytime, and sat there, with my back against the wall, listening to the sea, its steady lapping. There were no other sounds at all, no lights in the rooms or buildings. The hotel was like a dormant town, and I would say peaceful, but I wasn't at peace, I was trying too hard, I expect, telling myself that here, in this still Cretan night, I could think awhile, accept my condition as the common condition of all living things, but my eyes were darting about, locating the bushes that I knew were there, and my ears were straining, and suddenly there came from the beach a man's laugh, clear and cruel, and a yelp, a boy's or a woman's, then another yelp and the sound of scampering and a man's voice again, this time low, urgent and angry. I got up and walked back along the paths, not running exactly, because I'm not capable of it, but at speed, swaying a bit and stumbling. I had a difficult time with the door, which jammed, as it often does, and I had pretty well to kick it down to get in. I made a dreadful din, and expected to find Victoria sitting up in shock, clutching a sheet to her breasts, as on the cover of those books I used to love, but she was deeply asleep on her side, her glasses on the tip of her nose, her book in her hand. I slipped her glasses off, which involved tilting her head a bit, took the book from her hand, put it on the table beside her bed. She mumbled something, burrowed under the sheet, and I'm here, on the patio, with a sleeping pill and two co-proxamol inside me and *The Oxford Book of English Verse* – Christopher Ricks edition – I feel OK about the walls now, which is the main thing, at least tonight.

A DISGUSTING NEW HABIT

The newspapers come at around midday. *The Times*, the *Telegraph* and the *Guardian*, but we don't look at them until we have lunch in a café above the beach. It has a marvellous setting, the sea directly below and the mountains unfolding in the distance. Every lunchtime, though, it's a slightly different view, sometimes range after range of mountains, as far as the eye can see, sometimes just the nearest range and then clouds beyond, through which a tip rises. It would be a perfect place for lunch, with that view and comfortable chairs and efficient service, but it's ruined by the dreadful music, which is played full blast, and by the foulness of the food – enormous hamburgers with meat the texture of chewing gum, and club sandwiches you can hardly lift, let alone fit into your mouth, and when you manage a bite it takes a very long time, especially if you have teeth like mine, to convert it into swallowable pulp, which is of course quite tasteless except for a slight flavour of dust. Victoria says the salads are OK but I can't eat lettuce or greens or any of that stuff – it's not quite an allergy I have, but it's a strong aversion – but the point about the lunch is not the food, it's the newspapers, and more precisely, for me it's the obituaries.

It began in London, this new habit of turning to the obituaries first and then reading them all the way through, whether I knew the deceased or know of them or know nothing about them, going through them very quickly first of all to find out how they died, with an eye open for cancer and most particularly lung cancer – just occasionally you're not told, apart from 'died at home after a short/long illness', which always gives the impression that whether it was long or short it was the kind of illness the nearest and dearest don't want people to know he or she died of – but what I'm most interested in is how long? how long did they live, these painters, politicians, actors, sailors, soldiers, civil servants, headmasters, criminals, television presenters? how many years did they manage? If they died at seventy or under I feel a little surge of uplift, joy really, as if I'd beaten them in some tournament. But if they got beyond seventy-one I feel an envy and bitterness at the unfairness of it, and we're always told – or so it seems to me – that those who persisted to a great age did so with grace and style and full of energy, still climbing mountains at eighty-three, conducting symphonies at ninety-one, full of mirth at 106 – I think, what right did they have? who decides these things? the injustice of it! and go back to look at the piece on someone who went in his fifties, feeling not only triumph on my own account, but sympathy and indignation on his or her account. Actually I mind much less about women living longer, feeling that they have a natural and moral claim on extra years. I'm glad to note that I am distressed when I read of anyone cut down unduly young, I manage not to compare their term with mine, and feel that I have a kinship with them, especially if they knew that they were dying, and I feel sad and angry for their families. Quite a pleasant feeling, in a way, that's the awful thing.

I've tried to stop doing this, tried going first to the sports pages, as I always used to do, then to the editorials and letters, but it's no good, I can't stop, I can only delay, and so when I finally get to the obituaries my reactions have been sharpened by self-restraint and impatience, and I find myself almost gloating at the account of well, for instance, in today's – a distinguished City accountant and a gardening expert, one who made it to sixty-eight and the other who got to seventy – Christ, look at my vocabulary, 'made it to' and 'got to', yes, exactly as if they were competing, as if we're all competing, and not in terms of contribution, not how did he spend his years? what did he give to the world? how good a man was he? but for how long, for how many years?

And actually it's worse than this, my new habit or addiction. I find myself doing it almost automatically when I come across any mention of a life in the newspapers or a book blurb. I count the years between the date of birth and the date of death, usually getting very muddled, as I'm poor at mental arithmetic, but I keep at it, checking and checking again until I've established whether I'll outlive them or not. Whether I'll outlive the dead, in fact, would be the grotesque but accurate way of putting it – as I did with Stefan Zweig the other night, when studying that tiny bio. Born in 1881, died in 1942. So he would have been twenty-nine in 1900, add forty-two to twenty-nine comes to – comes to seventy-one, well, that's all right, look again, no, no, sixty-one, killed himself when he was sixty-one, that's more than all right! On the other hand, does the fact that he killed himself alter the statistics, he exercised a choice after all – but you're thinking of exercising a choice – yes, but it's a choice that's been forced on me, I'll only be lopping off a few months, Zweig might have pulled off another fifteen or twenty-nine – 'pulled off' – Christ!

I wonder if he left a letter, that's one of the first things I'm going to do when I get home, google him and find out all that I can, because now I'm into *Beware of Pity*, I want to know everything there is to know about its author. It's a quite astonishing novel, unique, I think, in what it undertakes, which is pretty well declared in the title – well, I'm only halfway through, but how grateful I am for the impulse in Daunt's that made me pick it up, it's already crammed a lot of life into a few hours of reading – so here's to you, Stefan Zweig, long life to you!

*

I was just thinking – apropos my current obsession with obituaries and the length of people's lives – that I don't feel pleased that people close to me died before me and had shorter lives – Alan at sixty-nine, Ian Hamilton and Ian MacKillop and Roger Gard in their early to mid-sixties, Clive Goodwin before he was fifty, my younger brother Piers at forty-nine, James Hammerstein at sixty-seven, my mother at fifty-nine – and nor do I feel bitter and envious that others who are older than me will probably outlive me, but that's because I miss the first lot so much, and need the second lot so much, a matter of selfishness, then, triumphing over competitiveness. Or possibly the idea that you leave some part of you behind with the survivors and so have a – what? a form of afterlife in this world that is not actually you, and can't be appreciated by you, but is an idea of you that will last as long as they last.

And with luck somebody now and then might put on one of my plays or pick up one of my books, and will hear my voice, which is a consoling thought as I write it down. But will it be a consolation after I'm dead? is the real question, and the answer is obvious, so it stops being a consolation now. But at least I'll be in a true democracy for the first time in my life, where no one is more equal than anyone else – though you never know.

Actually I do feel bitter and envious that my father will have lived longer – he died at seventy-six – perhaps because I feel he had a paternal duty to make sure that I had more than he had, or perhaps because ours was an uneasy relationship, I think neither of us knew what he wanted or hoped for from the other, he depending on his wife and I on my mother to point the way – 'Your father loves you, he may be quiet and shy about it, but never forget that!' she would say to me, and sometimes, possibly, she said much the same to him – 'Simon loves you, you know, James, he may be sneering and conceited when he's with you, but in his heart he adores and admires you, James, I hope you know that!'

And there is this: that my older brother, sixteen months older brother, Nigel, died at seventy-two, just before I was told about my cancer, which left me almost no time to grieve for him before I began to grieve for myself, it seemed to be intertwined grieving, but then I've always felt that, in spite of our differences in temperament, our fates were in large matters also intertwined. He died a week before his birthday, in June. Would it be optimistic to suppose that I might be allowed until around my next birthday, thus keeping to the sixteen months of separation? It's asking for a few months more than Dr Rootle predicted, but he may not be infallible, at least to the month.

A GREAT ADVENTURE

It was very windy today, so after lunch we decided to drive towards the town, as I thought I'd glimpsed a beach or two along the way, and about halfway between the hotel and Agios Nikolaus there was indeed a beach, the public beach, so we drove into the parking area, which was both neatly organised and commodious – what does that mean, commodious? Well, I think I merely mean that though there were a lot of cars we found a space to park in quite easily. There was none of the usual rubbish you see lying about in a parking area in England. Furthermore the beach was clean, even though it was crowded – people on sunbeds, sprawled on towels, horsing about with balls and Frisbees, the atmosphere jolly and pleasant. The sand was soft, the kind you can shake off once your feet are dry, and the sea was clean, shallow enough for children to play in quite a long way out, and then deep enough to have a proper swim. There was an elegant little café on stilts, where Victoria sat and read while I went off for a stroll along the promenade.

I went quite a long way, past cafés and restaurants, noting that the sea got deeper and deeper. There were cement squares from which you could dive straight in and a ladder to climb down. I was thinking how delightful it all was when I suddenly began to feel hot, too hot, and a bit dizzy and realised that I ought to get back to Victoria in the café and the shade but couldn't face the walk. I wondered whether I had the nerve to swim. I thought I probably hadn't the energy and strength, and therefore hadn't the nerve, and then I thought, well, what the hell, what the hell, went to some nearby steps, and climbed down into the sea, which was cool and refreshing.

I took it very slowly, very gently, on my side, leisurely strokes on my side, thinking that I could always turn back to the ladder, until suddenly it was too late, I was as far from the ladder as from the beach. There was nothing for it but to toil on, to assume a calm and easy air, turning my arm over languidly, as if really I were idling along on my side, but my stroke was getting feebler and my legs kept dropping under me, to the vertical – getting them up again was becoming a conscious and laborious act, but still I was all right, making sure that my breathing was steady and regular, strolling, strolling along in the water, not panicking. A middle-aged couple walking arm in arm along the path stopped, and looked down at me. What did they see? A brave and classy swimmer making his smooth if leisurely way towards a possibly glamorous destination, or an elderly fool of a man labouring out of his depth, with a certain look in his eyes that could be identified as fear, or even as a plea. The man said something to the woman and they hurried on – and who could blame them? if they'd asked me whether I was all right I might have said, 'No, no, please help me, I can't go on much longer,' and then what could they have done? I suspect that if the positions had been reversed I'd have done what they did.

And of course if the positions had been literally reversed there'd have been two of them in the water and only one of me on land, so I would most certainly have hurried off, unseeing and deaf, leaving them to their own devices and fates. I imagined them clinging to each other and either bawling for help or wrestling each other to their deaths, possibly both, first bawling and then drowning, they'd looked attached to each other, husband and wife walking arm in arm, perhaps they'd be happy to drown arm in arm, or even better in a close embrace – a good way to go, though probably several decades earlier than they'd wish. I rolled on my back and looked up at the sky, letting my body drift, drift, and sort of knew that I was drifting, drifting away from shore, out to sea, there was a slight tightening in one of my calves, from cramp, and so the first stirrings of real panic. I let myself hang loosely so that I was atilt, my head above water, my body trailing out under it but comfortable, floating, drifting, the pain eased in my calf, and I had that feeling I have sometimes in the sea of wanting to go on drifting and on, until I drift far away, finally drifting underwater without noticing a change, simply a slipping out of two elements into one, seeping into

806 THE COMPLETE SMOKING DIARIES

the sea, scarcely a death, really, and so much better, so much better than rotting in bed like Freud, for instance – at the end his mouth stank so much of cancer that his dog wouldn't go near him – so much better than that sort of death, but I couldn't, not now, leaving Victoria reading in the café, alone in Crete, having to arrange to take my body back if it washed ashore, or waiting weeks for me to turn up, wrapped in seaweed, what was left of me, after the fish had had their fill – and so forth the thoughts rolled, as I lay tilted upwards in the water, with the sun beating down on my head, and without planning it I began to haul myself back towards shore, and then towards the beach, arm over, arm over, arm over, la la la, la la – I had a bit of difficulty with the cement jetty that stuck out at the end of the promenade, and had to swim out again to get around it, and then I was among people, first of all the grown-ups in singles or in pairs, then mothers and fathers playing with their children and teaching them to swim or dunking the babies, and then I was on the beach – almost the most difficult part, getting to my feet and wading to the shore. I plodded across the hot sand, around recumbent young couples who were holding hands with their faces turned towards each other, went into one of the dressing rooms, sat on the bench in a collapse, went really into a sort of coma for a while. At last it occurred to me that I'd been gone quite a long time, Victoria might have begun to worry. As I picked my way across the sand, I was actually rather proud of myself. I climbed the steps to the café and saw Victoria standing up at the table, the book in her hand, staring anxiously along the promenade. I wanted to boast – 'I've walked and then I swam for, oh, miles and miles –' though I hadn't, more like half a mile each way, well, perhaps half a mile altogether. Anyway, I didn't say anything other than 'I'm back.' 'Where have you been?' 'Oh, walked along the path a bit, went in for a dip –' I picked up a towel and went off to shower and change, and then we had lunch there, Victoria a health-giving salad and I multiple layers of bread with nothing identifiable between them, but it was pleasant, shady and peaceful, lots to look at on the beach, and no music – no music, so who cared what was in the sandwich?

On our way back we stopped out of curiosity at a hotel that we suspected might be rather grand behind its dowdy front, and indeed it was grand, the lobby spacious and cool, with a long reception counter, comfortable-looking armchairs and sofas, a bar off, and in front open glass doors through which we sauntered with the casual aplomb of paid-up guests into an enormous and jungly garden which had little white cottages scattered about in it. We went down one of the paths that led to a large lawn and the sea, and a tree-shaded walk with ladders into the water, and at intervals small beaches. We settled on one of the beaches and went for a swim. Really, it was more like a paddle than a swim, and it would have been perfect if I hadn't made a hash of trying to change discreetly, caught my foot in my trunks as I was stepping out of them and toppled over. Victoria had to hold a towel up while I got into my trousers, protecting the people on the beach from a sight of my naked front, but exposing to the people on the lawn a distasteful view of my buttocks. Actually, I haven't seen my buttocks for ages, they might be rounded and muscular, for all I know, the buttocks of a bullfighter, for instance – well, an ex-bullfighter.

In fact, nobody paid us the slightest attention, there appeared to be no security whatsoever, there'd been no cameras in the lobby and there were none peeking out of the foliage or sticking out of the sea, and nobody walked about in police-type clothing. We realised the same was true of our own hotel – it seems to me wonderfully relaxed and typically Greek, until somebody gets mugged or murdered, of course, when it will seem to me shockingly negligent and typically Greek.

By the time we got back it was early evening, the sun was still strong and the wind had dropped. We went to our room by way of the beach, and on impulse, without really discussing it, went in for a swim, a sedate and careful swim in my case, no further out than my chest.

It's now getting on for 2 a.m., I've been writing away ever since we got back from dinner. I'm tired but it's a tiredness that is actually a pleasure, unlike the tiredness that attacks me without warning during the day, when I feel as if the blood is draining out of my soul. Here, now, as I write this, it seems impossible that I'm dying, at least until I feel the lump on my neck, which I am now doing. They said in the radiotherapy place that it would shrink after treatment, but to my fingers it's still the same size, the size of a walnut. Perhaps it's softening a bit, perhaps just a bit, but I'm not sure. I wish, I do wish, that I could stop myself fingering it. The problem is that I'm acutely conscious of it, even when it's not throbbing or tingling, and I'm sensitive to its visibility, especially on the beach, where I've noticed a couple of other people with very similar lumps on their necks – a lean hawk-like German of about my age, and a fraught English woman who is an exploited grandmother, I think – she screams anxiously to her two grandchildren, a boy and a girl of twelve, thirteen, that sort of age, warning them not to swim out so far, to come in where she can see them – then she sits smoking with a book on her lap, but her eyes are drawn to the children, and she's back on her feet, then forcing herself to sit down – well, my point is that I don't notice anyone else noticing her lump, which is closer to the ear than mine is, and I think a bit larger, or the lean hawk-like German's, which is exactly where mine is, and looks roughly the same sort of size, so I tell myself that therefore nobody notices mine, or wouldn't do if I could stop touching it. Which I will now do, and smoke a cigarette instead. The real point, the important point, is that it's been a lovely day, an adventurous one, and we've been happy, the two of us. How good that we came to Crete.

GHOSTS AND EXILES

We went for a spin this afternoon, late afternoon, motored along the coast road with no particular destination in mind, although we thought we might get as far as Elounda, and have a drink there, but were through it and past it before we noticed it, and went through a couple of smaller towns until we got to Plaka, which is where the road ended. Plaka, and after Plaka nowhere, as far as we could make out. So we stopped there, just on the edge of the town, in an empty car park on the edge of the sea. It was getting on for six o'clock, the light beginning to thin, the air to cool, and before we'd got to the centre a brisk wind had sprung out of nowhere, as if it had been waiting for us to turn up. We passed a little group of three, three women who looked English and as if they taught courses in discrimination awareness and gender disability, that sort of thing. They were all three of them short and slightly bulky, with hair – grey, grey, brown – cut short and they had worried, kindly expressions. As we went by they nodded and smiled and so did we. I thought I recognised one of them, and also thought I saw a glimmer of recognition in her eyes, and when I looked back she was looking back – 'Do you think we might have come across them before, one of them anyway, the one at the end?' Victoria said yes, not just the one at the end, but all three of them. We puzzled at it for a while, offering each other different contexts, mainly from our teaching days at Queen Mary College, and then agreed that they were probably a genre, so to speak, we'd met dozens like them in all sorts of contexts – in fact walking down Holland Park Avenue to two of the most serious shops in London, Daunt's bookshop and its neighbour Lidgate the butcher – you could easily imagine them coming out of Lidgate with their organic sausages and wheeling straight into Daunt's for the latest pamphlet on Jane Austen and the abolition of the slave trade.

The reason we talked about them so much, also speculating on where they were staying in Plaka, was because they'd turned off a path that seemed to lead towards a field, then rough countryside and eventually the mountains, and they hadn't been dressed for adventure, nor were they built for it, nor did they seem inclined to it, so where were they going? The other reason we talked about them was because they were the only people we saw in Plaka until we reached the centre of town, where there appeared to be no tourists or visitors but ourselves, and the few natives that were visible were silent. They were hanging out washing or sweeping the fronts of their houses and cafés, mainly they were middle-aged women, within easy speaking distance of each other, some of them, but not speaking, as if they were so used to each other they were no longer aware that they were there.

We went along the main street, which consisted of the usual Greek seaside shops, selling the usual seaside things, there was a small supermarket and several electrical shops and so forth. Outside most of these shops the owner or manager was standing smoking, or sitting in a chair smoking or reading a paper or with his hands on his knees. They were all men, of different ages, and apart from them the street was empty – again, not a single tourist, not a single customer on the street, only the two of us walking along it and making a point of not glancing into the windows and arousing expectations – but none of them looked as if they believed or hoped we might go in and make a purchase, they looked as if, to all intents and purposes, their shops were closed and they were only sitting or standing in front of them because they had nothing else to do, nowhere else to go.

There was only one other proper street in Plaka, it met the main street at a crossroads, and then did a little loop and ran along the side of the beach. It stretched for about a hundred yards and on both sides there were restaurants, and only restaurants, right next to each other and sometimes seeming to overlap into each other, so you couldn't tell where one ended and the other began. They had outside them large menus with photographs, as in the restaurants beside the lake in Agios Nikolaus, and also, as by the lake in Agios Nikolaus, a man outside, pimping. But there was none of the ebullience, the hectoring and imploring, of Agios Nikolaus – hardly surprising, I suppose, as again we were the only other people on the street. It was grim and slightly unnerving walking down it, right in the middle of the street, and only just hearing from our left and our right low murmurs in English offering us lamb, chicken, pasta, salads, fresh fish. There was no belief in their voices, no enthusiasm, actually no real interest, and there were no customers inside, not one table in all these restaurants was occupied, and there seemed to be no staff either. We scarcely dared raise our eyes, from embarrassment or even a kind of shame, we seemed to be intruding on a display of failure and defeat. It was a relief to get to the end and walk along the promenade. The sea was grey and miserable, the wind was now quite cutting, altogether it was such an unexpected and eerie experience – well, spooky, actually, and depressing – the grey hostile sea and the sense that we'd just walked through a ghost town, even the shop-owners and the restaurateurs were like ghosts, as if they weren't real even to themselves. We were getting cold, but just as we were about to turn back we came to a quay and a sign in English giving the times of the ferry to Spinalonga, the small island which had been used for a leper colony in the first half of the twentieth century. I knew a little about it from a marvellous book on leprosy by my old and dear friend Tony Gould, and Victoria had a fresher knowledge, having read not only Tony's book, but a recent and successful novel called *The Island* set in Plaka and Spinalonga. We stared across at the island, which was huddled in dreariness just a short boat ride away, and said well, we must come back on a warmer day and look at the little town where the lepers had lived out their lives, see their homes, their shops and their restaurants and imagine what it was like to have been carried across this short stretch of sea to your final home, everyone in your life now a leper like yourself. From its shore you'd be able to see the healthy mainland, people moving about their business and their pleasure. Yes, we must certainly come back and make the trip, we said, as we hurried to the car and drove away, we really must, perhaps in a couple of days, put aside a whole afternoon before we go home, make a proper outing of it – but I think we both knew we wouldn't, we'd seen something of Plaka when nobody else was looking and that was quite enough.

On the way back we stopped at Elounda, a charming little town, lively and colourful and full of luxury-goods shops, among them a shop that sells Canadian fur coats at low prices – there was one in the window, at what seemed a very high price to me, but how odd to think of someone buying a fur coat in a tourist town in Crete. Do they wear it through customs and immigration, to avoid paying duty, or do Greeks buy them, does it get that cold in Athens in winter that you'd wear a Canadian fur coat?

We didn't stay long in Elounda as I had one of those near-fainting episodes, just managed to get back to the car. As soon as we were in our room I went to bed, and slept. I'm all right again now, in a moment I'll dip into Larkin's Oxford anthology and smoke one, perhaps two, I hope not three cigarettes.

IF YOU CAN'T SEE HER LEGS, DON'T ASK HER FOR A DANCE

I haven't so much as looked at this pad recently, not at night, when I've been on the patio, nor during the day, when I've been at my usual place – at the table with my back against the chapel wall. They've been beautiful days, and I would like to have written that down about each of them. We've been going to the hotel down the road, with the lawns and the marvellous water you can ladder down into or walk gently into from one of their beaches – very good lunches in a delightful restaurant that overlooks the bay, hot and cold buffets or a mixture of both with not much Greek stuff in it apart from stuffed peppers and such. We have a swim before lunch, and a swim after lunch – they have showers and changing rooms, everything you need – and then back to the hotel in the late afternoon for another swim. Sometimes we go back to the other hotel for dinner. And sometimes we eat here, at the restaurant by the chapel or the swanky restaurant with tables around the swimming pool where there's a small band and a middle-aged male singer – he has an OK voice with sad eyes and a smarmy delivery. There is also a young female singer – she has a lousy voice that sets your teeth on edge. She likes to sway and screech on the edge of the pool, and so interferes with your meal as you keep watching her in the hope that she'll fall in. A few of the guests dance, mostly the elderly ones, and they're really rather good, with complicated steps and twirls, the ladies in long dresses, high heels, necklaces, earrings, the men in short-sleeved shirts and loose trousers. The other night there was a man in canvas shorts and a see-through shirt. He was small and burly, with no hair on his chest, like me, and with a chubby, rather sweet face – what you could see of it behind his large sunglasses, the ones that look like wings – and he was wearing shiny black shoes, his dancing pumps, I suppose. His wife was taller by some inches, handsome with a mass of grey hair piled up, a pearl choker and a long, trailing dark red gown, the whole effect of her fine and Edwardian. They made an eccentric-looking couple, though they danced well, he particularly, he was properly dominating, swinging her about and making her crouch to run under his arm and then he twirled her. I'd like to have seen them do something racy and dangerous, one of those homicidal Spanish or South American numbers.

So that's all we've been doing in the last few days. For many hours together I've almost forgotten about the cancer and the prognosis. It's there only as a faint stain on my consciousness except at night, when it becomes more than that, but there seems no point in writing that down. The great thing is that if I turn to Stefan Zweig's *Beware of Pity*

I can escape for as long as I'm reading it, which is why I've been going so slowly. Also it's too good to read except with the closest attention, and so painful that I have to put it down constantly.

The story is really very simple. Anton Hofmiller, an Austrian cavalry officer stationed in a remote garrison town in the months before the First World War, goes one evening to a party given by the richest landowner in the area, a widower. He has a splendid time showing off and being enjoyed by his host and fellow guests, and when the meal is followed by dancing he disports himself with gusto, and is about to depart euphoric and triumphant when he suddenly realises that he's been a bit amiss in not asking his host's daughter to dance with him. In fact, he hasn't exchanged a word with her as they were sitting at opposite ends of the table during dinner. He finds her in a small room, seated at a table and attended by her companion and other ladies, and with great charm presents himself and asks her to dance with him. Her response is a hysterical fit – mad laughter, wails, screams etc. – and she has to be taken away – half dragged and half carried out – and he sees that she is paralysed from the waist down.

Appalled by his monstrous gaffe, Anton spends hours in an agony of shame and self-recrimination. The following day he sends her flowers and she invites him back to the house. He and the girl – though she's emotionally somewhat turbulent, she has intelligence and charm – develop a rapport. The father, a Jew who was once a moneylender and financial opportunist, has been devastated by first the untimely death of his wife and then the illness of his daughter. He welcomes Anton into the household and encourages him to become a regular visitor, looking on hopefully as his daughter falls in love. And so it unfolds from there, the story of a young man betrayed by his own unwanted impulses, his own timid decency. Zweig tells it with extraordinary concentration, he follows every bounce-bounce of feeling, from Anton's increasingly desperate attempts at disentanglement back to guilt-ridden and resentful submission. It's entirely Anton's story. We only know the girl from his point of view, though there are two other characters with whom he has dealings, the father, whose determination to fulfil his daughter's emotional needs is both moving and repellent, and a doctor who is half secular saint, half gluttonous parasite. They're both sympathetically done, but with an odd, sometimes comic, sometimes sinister edge. But really it's the way that the novel single-mindedly, almost obsessively, illustrates and analyses the destructive power of a single emotion that makes it unique, at least in my experience. I've only the last twenty or so pages to go, catastrophe looms for Anton, the girl and her father – I long for it not to, just as I long for the novel not to end, but then all things, good and bad etc. and so forth –

So there is this at least about going home, I'll find out more about Stefan Zweig, and read other things by him – we go – when? Oh, Christ, the day after tomorrow – but no need to think about that until the day after tomorrow. Well, until tomorrow anyway – anyway not tonight, when it's clear and still, and in the moonlight through the gap between the rocks I can see two little motorboats, one of them possibly the boat I saw the other night. It's the same size and shape, and there's the same large lump in the bow. The other boat is slightly larger, more obviously a fishing boat with a small hutch, a cabin, I suppose, in the middle. I can't see anyone. Can there be a bed in the cabin? There they are, rocking and swaying gently in the water. I like them there, they look attached to each other, like brother and sister – oh, something's just splashed near the side of the smaller boat, a fishing net going in, a fish jumping –

SO HOW MUCH SHOULD WE TIP OUR DOCTORS?

We've just come back from our last swim of the holiday, of the year. Who knows when we'll have another? It wasn't a great swim, the wind is quite biting, the skies grey, rather like our first day here, so perhaps there's rain in the offing, and the sea is beginning to turn cold. Still, there were quite a lot of people on the beach, and quite a few in the sea, there must have been a batch of arrivals last night – it's the cheap end of the season, with special deals and so forth. There were young couples, some of them honeymooners, and young parents with babies, but no children over about five, no schoolchildren. There was also a fresh batch of older people, most of whom had the air of regulars, a 'yes, here we are again, good to be back' air. The only people we've seen before were the Marge Simpson twins, huddled under coats and towels, lying in the same postures as on the morning we first saw them, on their sides, smoking into each other's faces, with the dachsund settled into the curve of the stomach of one of them. Our bags are packed and have gone off. In two hours or so a taxi will come and take us to Heraklion and the airport. Victoria is in our room, packing the on-flight bags, and I'm sitting with my back against the chapel wall for the last time, writing this. I'm dreading going home but more immediately I'm dreading leaving here. For one thing there's the tipping. I've put wodges of euros in one of my trouser pockets for the restaurant people, and another wodge for the café people, and more in my top shirt pocket – I'm not at this moment wearing the trousers and shirt, they're hanging in the wardrobe in our rooms – in the shirt pocket are euros for the taxi and, oh yes, in the back pocket of my trousers I've put surplus euros in case we bump into someone that we've forgotten about. The chambermaids and the waiter who brings us our breakfast we've already tipped. We gave them theirs in envelopes, which they didn't open in front of us, so we don't know whether they're pleased or indignant – we generally overtip, knowing that if you ever get it right – give in Italy what the Italians give, in Greece what the Greeks give and so on – you're probably undertipping, as the standards for foreigners are higher, unless you're German, according to a recent article on the subject in one of the papers, when they're lower, or non-existent. Now I can tell myself that I've really got it sorted out – how could I not have, with so many contingency pockets full of euros? There's nothing else really to worry about. We've ordered the taxi for far earlier than necessary, so if it threatens to be late we'll be able to order another one and still be in good time. The airport business is always a dread – although in fact when we arrived here we got through customs and immigration in no time, the airport was completely empty except for the passengers from our plane and it gave the impression of being underused, a lonely place. The flight itself, of course, is not in our hands, so there's no point in planning for it – a drunken pilot, a defective engine, a suicide bomber, a flick of Zeus's finger – all those are the responsibility of Miracle Airlines, who have a policy of losing your bags, I hope in a kind of pact with Zeus and the rest not to lose your life –

My real dread isn't going home but being home. There will be all the compensations, the dogs George and Toto, the cats Errol and Tom, my study where I can play music again – ten days is a long time without decent music – and seeing friends, above all. I hope I won't be so embarrassed now that I've had time to get used to having cancer and they've had time to get used to my having it. My embarrassment is really a probably unjustified anticipation of their embarrassment, and this anticipation comes from shame. I know I've gone into this before, probably lots of times, but it perplexes me, this shame. I don't really believe that because I'm a smoker the cancer is self-induced. I have more than a hunch that I'd feel shame if the cancer were of the pancreas, like Alan's – there are surely no vices that result in cancer of the pancreas – although some arsehole of a government doctor will doubtless claim there is, that pancreatic cancer is caused by being famous, or not being famous when you want to be, or by being famous when you don't want to be. Or from drinking too much tea with lemon in it, or from bacon, of course – over the years many illnesses have been brought back to bacon. There's something about bacon that offends the medical profession at government level, but you have to remember that any doctor who is any good as a doctor wouldn't be working for the government, he would be doing something useful. Doctors with no sense of vocation and possessed of political skills are very dangerous, I think – look at their opposition to Chadwick and his belief in drains, sewers and hygiene in the middle of the nineteenth century, their opposition to the use of anaesthetic for operations at the start of the Crimean War, their refusal to admit that cholera was carried by contaminated water, and so forth, so forth. Oh oh! Here comes the hotel manager! He's coming down from the hotel –

WHITHER ERNESTO?

– he's walking along the path towards me with his trousers hitched up to his chest and his odd, disjointed but speedy gait, he's carrying a briefcase – he's seen me, for a second he slowed down, then quickened his step, does he think he can go so fast that he can get past me in a kind of blur?

No, he stopped, came to a full stop right in front of me, the briefcase swinging. He gave me his fullest smile. 'Now you go today, yes?'

'It is sad for us. For me.'

'Thank you. For us, too. Have you had a nice holiday?'

'Very nice, thank you.'

'Good. I am very happy.'

He moved off, duty done and courtesies observed, and I was about to return to my pad and report the conversation and describe again the unlikely rosiness of his complexion and the shininess of his black hair pasted flat on his scalp, when he stopped, came back and asked me whether I had arranged our taxi for the airport.

I said that I had, or rather that reception had.

'If I think of anything I can do to you, I phone you in your room, of course,' he said.

I didn't quite laugh at the thought of the various things he might think he could do to me. 'That's very kind of you, really very kind, Ernesto.'

He stopped smiling, as if there was something in my expression he didn't like, his black eyeballs had a glint in them, and he walked off abruptly, down the steps to the beach. I went to the rail to watch him. He looked anomalous, hurrying along the beach in his heavy trousers and shiny shoes and shiny hair with his shiny briefcase, passing guests in trunks and bikinis coming wet from the sea or towelling themselves. I wondered who he was going to see, why he needed his briefcase. One of the Simpson twins spotted him, sat up and called him over. The other twin sat up. From where I stood they both seemed to be talking to him at the same time, gesturing ill-temperedly with their cigarettes, evidently making a complaint. When they'd finished he spoke briefly, then made a loving reach for the dachsund, which the twin pulled away and hugged protectively to her chest. He made a little bow, then he was on his way, right to the steps at the other side. He climbed them rapidly, was gone from my sight briefly, then emerged on the path to the hotel and headed back up to it. In other words he'd made a brisk, businesslike circuit for no apparent reason. It was mysterious, what was he up to? I wondered, what was in his briefcase? but then there was something about Ernesto that never made sense, his motives were always obscure, his behaviour –

Ernesto – oh, Christ! Did I call him that? Yes, here it is, I've actually written it down. It can't be his name, Ernesto's an Italian name, surely – I'll look back and see if –

Nikos. His name is Nikos. What on earth made me call him Ernesto? It must be his personality, his hair and briefcase, his trousers – *The Importance of Being Ernesto*. Better not think of the things he'd like to do to me. Better instead to sit back in this sheltered spot and wait for Victoria to come down, I always love seeing her come along the path, her hat aslant, her straight, graceful walk, and she has a couple of very fetching wrap-arounds to cover her swimsuit – oh, but she'll be in her London clothes, and she'll tell me that it's time for me to change into mine. Socks and shoes instead of espadrilles, underpants and trousers instead of swimming trunks, a long-sleeved shirt – if only we could spend another week or two, or some months, or years, or for ever, being here, being as we've been over the last ten days – but the hotel closes at the end of the month, all the hotels in this part of Crete close, and we have a christening and a scan to go home to, a sort of life to get on with.

PRIVILEGED TREATMENT

Yes, yes, well we're back. We got home before midnight, and spent yesterday recovering from the flight, though actually the flight itself wasn't too bad. Cramped, of course, business class and cramped, but you expect that from MA, that sort of almost criminal – no, completely criminal, in my view – swindling, but it was in fact such a relief to be on the plane, and in the air, because the airport, Crete airport at Heraklion, which had seemed so desolately empty when we arrived that I felt quite sorry for it and the people who worked in it, was chaos. There was a queue that came out on to the street and along the pavement and out of sight. It wasn't a thin and orderly queue, people standing in a single or double line, it was a swollen and turbulent queue, people jostling each other, shouting, in a panic. We wondered what flight this was, or rather the nationality of the airline as there were far too many people for it to be for just one flight. Inside the noise was extraordinary – all those people trying to go through passport control and customs, for which there was only one gate. We looked up at the flight board to see if our flight was on time and where it went from, and saw that there were seven flights leaving in the next half an hour. So the queue was seven flights' worth, with just one gate to let them through. We checked in fairly quickly. A briskly efficient girl told us that we should now go through passport control, although we had an hour and a quarter to wait – Victoria pointed this out to the girl, who said, 'Yes, yes, but it's better to go through now, it will get worse perhaps.' It was obviously hopeless. The queue was not only enormous, it seemed never to move. That was the worst thing, one didn't seem to see people actually getting through, they were wedged against the barrier, shouting, waving their tickets, children were crying, and behind them thousands more – as I've said, right through the airport and out on to the street – it was like an evacuation, with the enemy at the gates and the last planes about to take off. We sat down on a bench for a while, to rest from the shock, really, it was so unexpected, one really had hoped that this sort of thing was confined to Heathrow.

I spotted a man with a label on his shirt lapel and a walkie-talkie, into which he was talking without much urgency, quite serenely, in fact, as if he were making a call to his wife about domestic matters – but he'd do that on a mobile, surely, I thought, not on a walkie-talkie so he must be an airport official. I went over to him and waited, trying not to look too importunate. I also tried to read the writing on his label, but it was in Greek. He made a soothing gesture, to let me know that he knew I was there, went on with his conversation for a minute, then put his walkie-talkie into his belt, and gave me a charming and attentive smile. He was very good-looking in a relaxed, casual and good-humoured sort of way, a bit like Al Pacino but a foot or two taller, normal-sized in other words. 'How can I help, sir?' His English was good. I wondered why he used it before I spoke, do I look English? English-speaking? Or is the assumption that all foreigners speak English these days, and whatever I was, I couldn't be mistaken for a Cretan – too dishevelled, for one thing. And my hair. 'Well,' I said, 'I was wondering what the matter is. The queue – all the people.' I gestured towards them. 'They are going through passport control.' 'Yes, but why is it like this? Is it always like this?' 'It is often like this,' he said.

'For one reason or another. This evening, it is because there is only one police officer looking at the passports.' 'Won't a lot of them miss their planes?' He thought about it. 'Sometimes it happens. Sometimes yes.' I tried to find a tactful way of asking what his official position was – he was so friendly and easy – 'What do you do,' I asked, cleverly I thought, 'if people get left behind?' 'What do I do?' he said with a shrug of his shoulders and his friendly smile. 'I do nothing. What can I do? This is Greece.' He took his walkie-talkie out of his pocket and listened, then said something in a Scandinavian language, fluently and slightly flirtatiously – but then he was obviously by nature flirtatious.

I went back to Victoria and said that all I'd gathered was that this shambles was quite usual, that sometimes people missed their planes, but I couldn't vouch for the source of this information, as I had no idea who he was or what he did, or even his nationality. 'Are you all right?' she said. 'Yes,' I said, but I wasn't, my legs were dissolving under me, and I felt as if I was going to fall down. 'Here,' she said, 'sit down.' She gave me her seat, as someone had taken mine, a pleasantly impassive Oriental girl. I slumped there, looking at the queue that hadn't changed, the same people still seemed to be at the front of it, still holding up their tickets and clamouring, and once again it had got fatter, now almost double the size it had been when we arrived – Well, there was one thing I knew for certain, I couldn't join it, I suspected I couldn't stand by myself for long, I could hardly keep my head up.

Victoria brought me a chocolate bar. I tore its wrapping off and guzzled it down with uninhibited greed, behaving as I behave every night when alone, a disgusting spectacle. I didn't look up to see whether I was being observed and when I finished I demanded another one. 'Sorry, darling, need another one,' is what I think I said. She'd bought three, and I ate them all, the third one rather more decorously, and though I felt sick when I'd finished, and had a headache, I felt stronger. I could stand up and walk a few paces, not exactly steadily, but in a steady direction at least. I sat down again and Victoria went off to get some water. She also suggested she get me a wheelchair – there was a time, before my hip replacement, when I'd had to go through airports in a wheelchair, and I'd hated it, believing it was more honourable to totter along with a stick and the support of my wife – it was one of the

CODA 821

many pleasures of being able to walk properly again that I could deal with airports like a normal passenger – so I said no, I can manage, I'll be all right – though really I knew this was nonsense – but I also thought that, well, we could always spend the night in Heraklion, leave tomorrow.

Victoria brought the water. She also brought a pretty young woman, blonde, in an MA uniform, with a harsh, bossy voice, who told me to wait where I was, went off for a few minutes and returned leading a wheelchair procession – young people with casts on their legs and necks, an obese man in his fifties with curly grey hair who was wearing red swimming trunks and a soiled white T-shirt with an image of a bare-breasted girl riding a motorbike stamped on it, and several elderly and frail-looking men and women, clasping sticks. Behind each wheelchair was a pusher, presumably a partner, though some looked ill-assorted – in the case of one of the frail old men there was a seemingly much frailer old woman pushing him, and the obese man with the T-shirt was being pushed by a campy young fellow in purple trousers and a yellow shirt who kept fluting, 'Hold on there, Rodge, we'll be on in a jiff!' while Rodge chortled and mumbled to himself, possibly he was drunk or brain-damaged. Well, this lot was my cortège, so to speak. I walked at the head of it, Victoria at one side and at the other, just in front of me, the blonde MA girl, who shouted instructions in her hoarse, abrasive voice, in both English and Greek, in English 'Out of the way please, out of the way,' and in Greek presumably much the same. The people at the head of the queue surged towards us mutinously and then fell away when they saw what we were, it was a sort of miracle, really, as if I were leading a group of ill and maimed to Lourdes, so much respect, amounting to reverence, did this hitherto desperate and panic-stricken mob give us, watching us with sorrowful eyes as we passed through them. I don't know what they made of me, looking tanned and healthy, even if I was drooping a little. Perhaps they assumed I was there in a medical capacity.

We went straight through passport control, where two officers, not just one, were studying every passport with academic thoroughness as we approached, but hardly glanced at ours, then security and customs – and we were on the other side, where we could settle down and wait calmly for our call. It came punctually. We left on time. I fell asleep at once, before we were in the air – the first time in my life I've slept through an entire flight – and was scarcely awake during the drive from Gatwick.

When we got home I said hello to all the animals, and went to bed, where I stayed for much of yesterday. Now I'm up and about. Tomorrow is Saturday, the christening. I would think that Crete was a dream, if I didn't remember the time at the airport so vividly. And then there's the tan, visible on my arms below my rolled-up shirt sleeves and on the backs of my hands, as I sit writing this –

LONDON

ELI TAKES CENTRE STAGE

The christening was at Farm Street Church, a famous and fashionable Catholic church in Mayfair, which I hadn't been to before. It looked very swanky at three o'clock this afternoon, bathed in sunlight with little groups of well-dressed people, many of the ladies in hats and one or two of the gents in morning suits – relaxed and elegant, there was a touch of Ascot about it, not that I've been to Ascot. At the bottom of the street, waiting in the wings, so to speak, were Toby, his wife, Annie-Lou, and in Annie-Lou's arms their baby son, Eli. Annie-Lou looked sensational in a sensationally short skirt and a very elegant top which I didn't really notice as I couldn't take my eyes off her legs, they were so long and shapely. Toby was wearing a natty suit and a waistcoat, I think – perhaps it was a morning suit. We stood outside the church on the pavement watching them come towards us. I honestly don't think I've seen such a beautiful couple, a beautiful trio, really, because Eli, as yet only a scrap at five months, has a beautifully shaped head off which the sun seemed to strike so that it glittered. We did some kissing and so forth and then went inside. Dame Maggie Smith, the fortunate grandmother to Eli, emerged from behind a pillar to say hello, and then we – Victoria and I – were led to our pew, the godparents' pew, right at the front on the left facing the altar, on the other side of the aisle from the parents and Eli. There was another godparent, a smiling young woman, a cousin – well, I think cousin – of Annie-Lou already ensconced. She seemed pleased to see us, and we were certainly pleased to see her. None of us had acted as Catholic godparents before,* none of us being Catholic, but at least we could give each other moral support – in fact I always look to Victoria in this sort of situation, believing that she has an innate understanding of the ceremonies of life,

* Victoria has many other godchildren and I have one, Simon Hammerstein, of many years' standing.

even though, like me, it's a long time since she's been in a church – we used to go every Christmas to our local, at the top of our street, but gave up when one year at the end of the service the vicar asked us to handshake and cuddle fellow members of the congregation, most of whom I didn't like the look of, and one of whom, a distraught, middle-aged woman, threw herself into people's arms, tears of love and joy running down her cheeks – 'Bless you, bless you,' she cried, as she bounced from bosom to bosom – so we felt slightly ill at ease being back in a church again, even one where you could expect calm and dignified behaviour. In fact the atmosphere, though calm and dignified, was also cheerful and relaxed, with people meeting up and chatting in the aisle, and children skirmishing at the front and sides, and popping out from behind the pews. Under the circumstances it was quite difficult, even for inexperienced and unrehearsed godparents, to feel nervous and in fact all that really worried me was that I might have to hold Eli, and have a sudden weak spell and drop him on the stone floor, head first – It would be difficult to live that down, a godfather who killed his godchild at the christening. I decided, if by any chance Eli was passed to me, I'd pass him straight on to Victoria, whatever the convention. The vicar came in, no, presumably not the vicar, the priest, whatever – and moved about, shaking hands and being sociable, then went to the front and, in an easy, conversational manner, began the service – service, I suppose that's the right word for it. The priest – let's call him that – the priest was astonishingly like the English film actor of many years ago, Wilfrid Hyde-White, noted for his hooded eyes and his sleazy charm. But the priest's eyes were only slightly hooded and his charm wasn't in the slightest sleazy, the resemblance was more in the appearance, same height, same hair, same sort of age that Wilfrid Hyde-White always appeared to be – about sixty, even when young – and same timbre of voice. He was beguiling, especially in his concentration on five-month-old Eli. He addressed everything important directly to him and not to the congregation, and Eli, now in his beautiful mother's arm, returned the compliment by fixing his baby gaze on him with rapt and devoted concentration – it was both funny and moving, the loveliest sight I've ever seen in a church, the elderly man and the wide-eyed baby in earnest consultation, the elderly man speaking a language that the rest of us recognised and understood, and yet seemed to contain within it another and private language recognised and understood by the baby –

The godparents' turn came about halfway through. We had first of all to give a number of solemn undertakings. I can't say I felt easy about any of them, even the basic ones of resisting the temptations of the devil, and making false promises. I suspect that there are one or two temptations I would be quite pleased to have the devil offer me at the moment, and I really don't see how you can manage a career as a playwright without making a false promise now and then, after all so many are made to you – by actors, directors, producers, who insist that one day, absolutely certainly one day, they'll do this or that play of yours – equally, one day, I say, I'll write a play you'll want to do, I know I will. So really I felt a bit odd about not making false promises, suspecting that I'd actually made one in undertaking not to. But the most difficult bit was when we, the two godmothers and the one godfather, were asked whether we were prepared to make sure that Eli was brought up in the Catholic faith. There wasn't a distinct sound from any of us, just an ambiguous mumble, and then the priest, probably knowing the situation, passed fluently on. Eli loved the actual baptism, which was – cunningly – with warm water. He gurgled with pleasure and it was a joy when it was my turn to dab his forehead and have him gurgle at me. And that was it, really, my godfatherly duty had been to speak lies before God and then to stand at the font and lie again in dumbshow by assisting in a religious ceremony that had, for me, no spiritual significance. And yet very little in these last few years has given me so much pleasure and made me so proud, and Victoria, I know, feels the same, and though we can't do anything for the Catholic side of Eli's life, we've made a start on the many other sides by presenting him with specially bound copies of the whole of Shakespeare, with his initials on the spine.

Afterwards we went to Annie-Lou's parents' place for drinks and such. I began to feel tired, had an attack of weakness and had to sit down. Annie-Lou introduced Victoria to a friend of her parents, a very lively and intelligent woman who knew a great deal about the treatment of cancer in America, and particularly of a man in California, a specialist in a new form of chemotherapy. Someone else had told us about this man and had spoken as highly of him as did this woman, whose husband had been treated by him. Victoria told me afterwards, because I wasn't able to concentrate properly, that she said that he was remarkable. Unlike so many doctors he had a wide range of interests, including an interest in his patients, what they did, what they thought about, what they read, their favourite music, that sort of interest. Furthermore he was a genius and a miracle worker. Her husband, who'd gone to California to be treated by him, had gone to him far too late and refused a final course of chemo because he needed to get home to England to die, but right to the end had shared his wife's enthusiasm for the man in California.

SERVITUDE

We left and came home and I went to bed, but couldn't sleep. I got up and here I am, the established godfather of Eli, writing this – and now there is something making a disturbance at my door, it's a soft noise, difficult to describe, but it's as if someone were beating a small cushion against it, causing it to tremble slightly. I know perfectly well who it is. It's Errol, our big black bushy cat who came out of nowhere one day, intruded himself through the dog flap and set up as a lodger. He made an immediate and close friendship with our half-westie bitch, George, but was hostile to Tom, our elderly black and white female cat, treating her as if she were an undesirable squatter and sitting bulkily in front of the dog flap whenever she went out to stop her coming in again.

On the other hand, when we introduced a second dog, a terrier called Toto, into the household Errol welcomed her and made a fuss of her, eating as affectionately from her bowl as from George's, sleeping sometimes between her paws, at other times between George's, a dog's cat, you might say, although he's good with humans too. Now, some six years later, he and Tom get on reasonably well. He's prepared to defer, I think, to Tom's great age – she's twenty-one. They touch noses when they meet in the hall, and lie side by side on the warm spot on the floor outside the kitchen and when in a minute or two I go to the door which Errol is butting with his head, I will find Tom sitting beside him, waiting. When I open the door Tom will screech at me ill-temperedly, then turn and follow Errol downstairs to the kitchen, occasionally looking over her shoulder to make sure I'm following, and, if I'm slow or too far behind, give another screech. I will go to the larder and take out a packet of jellied meat for Errol, and hoist up a large sack of nodules for Tom and put it on the table. Tom's and Errol's bowls are on the counter of the dresser. I will fill Errol's bowl with the jellied meat and then – in spite of the fact that he can climb to the counter by way of a chair placed there for that very purpose, and in spite of the fact that he can scale and leap like a mountain goat when food is his quest – I will have to bend down and pick him up and place him in front of his bowl. Then I will have to pick up Tom, who is also perfectly capable of reaching the counter on her own, and put her in front of her bowl, which she refuses to touch, even if it's half full or completely full of nodules, until I have put, or pretended to put, more nodules in it. Then I can leave them to themselves and go back to my study. I have no idea why they both insist on being picked up. I suspect it's something to do with dominance, their need to keep me in my place as both provider and servant. Sometimes I don't mind, in fact the ritual is reassuring, but these days I find Errol a real weight, bending down and lifting him has made me feel faint once or twice, and I resent it. Tom is an easy lift, her body is light with age and she lies almost weightless in my hand, but – well, I've caught myself looking at her when she creaks as if broken-backed up the stairs, or wakes from one of her long sleeps and stumbles about before finding her balance – 'Yes, but for all that –' and I've said it aloud to her, quite bitterly, 'for all that, you'll be here, creaking about, when I'm gone.'*

A LIVING BOWER? OH, FOR GOD'S SAKE!

I had the scan this afternoon. Really it was simple and efficient, only a five-minute wait and then I was under the machine, a voice calling out from a protected booth when to breathe and when to hold my breath, and I was finished and joining Victoria at a table outside the pub. The bad part of it is that Dr Rootle is away – it's half-term, apparently, so he might be on a holiday with the wife and kids, or he might be at a conference in Beijing, for example – all I know is that it's a week and

---

* She won't. She died shortly after I wrote that passage.

a day until we see him, and find out the results of the scan – whether I am to have more radiotherapy, or am promoted to chemotherapy, or go on as I'm going on at the moment.

Before we left the pub we discussed whether to give me a birthday party. We'd given them now and then over the years, and usually I'd enjoyed them enormously when they were over, thinking that they would be markers in my memory – not so much little tombstones on the way to the final, big tombstone, but milestones on a winding, complex journey of ever-extending length, or living bowers of remembrance or some such – and in fact when I do look back on them I have a general sense of muzzy, unfocused pleasure for most of them, with sharp, painful details sticking out from some of them – there was one in my fifties, for instance, when a young fan of a guest, more stalker than fan, happened to be in the club where the party was being given, and invaded it for a while. He was drunk and full of pot, the personification of malice, envy and worship all mixed up – the worship unsatisfied as the guest who was the object of it, a famous actor, sent him on his way with gentle authority. He responded with mutinous obedience in that he took his humble leave of the famous actor but then went lurching from table to table delivering his opinion of all the people in the room he recognised, and also of those he didn't recognise but whose appearance stimulated his venom. I knew him quite well, and finally got him outside on the pavement. I smoked cigarettes while he smoked joints, and we made vile, conspiratorial conversation until I lured him into a taxi and sent him into the night. He only took up half an hour of a party that began at nine and ended in the early hours of the morning. I doubt if anyone else would remember him, or took much notice of him at the time – a stoned and hostile young man who intruded briefly at your table was not a significant event unless you were the host – but, as I've said, he's all I remember with any distinctness, and as for the rest of the evening, all I can say is that I believe it went well enough but I can't be sure.

The fact is that a party given on my behalf makes me nervous, and then as the date grows closer I actively dread it – more even than I dread a first night – but then a first night is a shared responsibility, you, the director, the actors and the producers are all in it together, at least until the reviews come out to separate you – frequently and specifically me, the playwright, with such sentences as, 'Not even Oliver Gilboy playing three parts can save a play that should be booed, hooted and raspberried off the stage.' But from then on you can conceal yourself, stay indoors for a year or two or go to restaurants where people won't have read the reviews because they never read the reviews of anything and may not be able to read anyway, as opposed to your usual restaurants, where there will be people who will have read the reviews several times but who will pretend not to have, and will call out, 'Simon, how did it go, what were the reviews like? Madge was telling me about the ones in the *Guardian* and *The Times* and the *Telegraph*, but I can't remember what she said they said –' and if you claim – as has been true in recent years – that you don't read them, they will reply, 'Good for you, because I gather from what Madge said that they weren't worth reading.' But my point is that even the anticipation of a first night and the next day's reviews is better than the anticipation of a party, a birthday party above all, and what – according to Dr Rootle – would be a birthday party on my last birthday. I feared I might find myself looking around at all the familiar, beloved (well, many of them) faces, thinking sombre thoughts and possibly bursting into tears when my health was proposed – that sort of thing. This would make it memorable, though not to me, of course, as I wouldn't, again given Dr Rootle's estimate, be around long enough to make it a memory. But perhaps it's a pleasing thought that my guests would remember it, making the doleful but moving connection – 'Just fancy, his last birthday was his last ever and he knew, of course! How very, very, very moving!' – we went over the pros and cons for a while, and before we left I think we settled it that we'd either have a party or we wouldn't, we'd talk about it again later, or perhaps we wouldn't –

A DISASTER REMEMBERED

Harold came out of hospital a couple of days ago but is still, Antonia said, very weak, couldn't go out, but would welcome a visit, she thought. I phoned him and though he sounded thin and far away, he said he'd like it if I looked in. He was in his usual armchair, with a fire blazing in the grate, its flames orange and blue. I gave him a book I'd brought for him, then sat in the armchair opposite, on the other side of the fire. He looked into the book, Keith Miller's autobiography, written over fifty years ago, which I bought second-hand over forty years ago and is long out of print. I thought Harold would like and be touched by the photographs, the sort you don't see any more, grey and white and one-dimensional, the men with Brylcreemed hair and smiling, shiny faces, and the clothes, of course – the cricketers either in long-sleeved white shirts and creased white flannels belted tightly at the waist, or in drab grey suits with fedoras and trilbies. The prose is cheerful and kindly, lots of anecdotes but no gossip, nothing revealed but the spirit of the age and the modest decency of the writer, who was, in fact, also a gambler and a womaniser, one of Princess Margaret's lovers and a bit of a home-wrecker and so forth, as well as a war hero – an incomparable man, really.

Harold dipped into a few places, smiled and grunted, put the book down and we looked at each other. So here we were, two elderly and ailing men who'd known each other for half our lifetimes. We talked bitterly about the things that were most on our minds – sickness, hospitals, colonoscopies, catheters, the sheer helplessness and humiliation of it all. His voice got stronger the longer we talked, and we both got more cheerful, the absurdity of it, that such things could be happening to us, who in so many important respects hadn't yet reached our maturity, we still had miles to go before we slept, miles to go.

After we'd been at it for about an hour or so I thought he must be getting tired. I was feeling a little tired myself and was on the point of getting up when he reached for the book. 'Thanks for this,' he said, opened it, looked closely at one of the photographs, and remarked that there was going to be the annual meeting of his cricket club, the Gaieties, in a few days' time, he wouldn't be able to go himself, he said, wouldn't be up to it, but they'd asked him if he'd do a little speech on video, and he'd decided that this was what he was going to tell them –

That in one of his first matches as captain the opposing side's best batsman was in, and going ominously well until he skied a catch, very high, with Harold directly under it. He mimed himself gazing anxiously upwards, then jerking from side to side to get into the right position, then cupping his hands, then watching the ball as it fell through his hands and dropped at his feet. The next ball the batsman repeated the shot, the ball went up, came down through Harold's hands to land once again at his feet. The batsman went on to make a hundred. It came to the Gaieties' turn to bat. Their best batsman was going promisingly well, with a big score and possibly victory in sight, when a wicket fell and Harold came out to join him. In no time Harold had run him out. A few balls later Harold was bowled neck and crop. The Gaieties lost by an enormous margin, entirely because of Harold's versatile performance.

It was as if we were suddenly many years ago, back having a boozy lunch in our favourite restaurant, L'Epicure, Romilly Street, a week before rehearsals. He finished with a broken cry of despair, as if he could still see the ball at his feet, hear the stumps rattle behind him, and we both laughed and laughed until we both coughed and coughed, laughed and coughed –

WHY I BOUGHT SO MUCH CHEESE

Walking home from Harold's down Holland Park Avenue, I felt quite sprightly, yes, really quite sprightly. I saw Annabelle outside Tesco's, tootling her recorder, her dog at her feet. Annabelle is a local beggar, no, one of the two local beggars. They're partners, I think, although in what sense of the word isn't really clear. I know she has grand-children but not whether he's the grandfather. They seem to have a fairly intense and complicated relationship, working within fifty or so yards of each other, he sitting on the pavement, with competent if insipid watercolours of beaches and harbours, meadows and woodlands, she with her recorder and dog. They're often in earnest, whispering confabulation together, and just as often having hateful exchanges, standing not facing each other but sideways on, speaking out of the sides of their mouths, and then one or the other flounces off. Though to me they're Annabelle and Hyacinth, I have no idea what their real names are – I forget why I called her Annabelle, just from a desire to name her, I suppose. I called him Hyacinth after the Henry James character Hyacinth Robinson in *The Princess Casamassima* for reasons now obscure to me as I no longer remember the novel. I could see that she'd seen me. Her eyes were now fixed on me. She was expecting me to come to her with a handful of cigarettes or some money.

For once I wasn't in the mood for Annabelle. She can have a lowering effect on my spirits, particularly in the soft evening sunshine, and though she never asks for anything, she is somehow importunate, she aims her recorder at you, and her eyes search out yours. Hyacinth is easier, as he's down on the pavement, below one's eye level, and one can pretend he's not there. If he croaks out a greeting one can lift one's hand in vague but benevolent salute as one scoots past. In fact, I didn't spot him in the vicinity this evening. There was just Annabelle, expectant. So I thought, oh well, give her something and get it over with, and then realised that as I no longer carry cigarettes in my pocket, and as I had no money apart from a twenty-pound note, I had nothing to give her, so without consciously planning to I swung into Tesco's. There was nothing I wanted in Tesco's, there is never anything I want in Tesco's. If occasionally they introduce a line that actually appeals to me they withdraw it the moment they know I've begun buying it. So I didn't go right into the shop, I stood to the side of the door, out of her sight, and waited for her to trap someone else and then I'd slip out, was my vague plan.

Actually she's quite a popular figure, Annabelle. People know her and stop to exchange a few words, give her a coin, pass on, but this evening, perhaps because it was so lovely, people felt as I did and gave her a miss. One couple even crossed the road to avoid her, because I saw them cross back again at the next traffic lights. The security chap by the door began giving me quick, appraising glances. Of course these days, an elderly man hanging about on his own in a busy shop must be up to no good, almost certainly about to practise some senile form of sexual deviance. I had the feeling that he was going to come over and question me at any moment, so I decided to get on with it, take my chances with Annabelle. I'd make a brisk enquiry after her health and be on my way as she was answering me. I went out, she moved a step or so towards me, lowering the recorder and with one hand extended – she's quite pretty, Annabelle, have I said that? young-looking for a grandmother, at least her face is. She keeps it blank when just standing waiting and when receiving money even from people she knows well, just saying in a lifeless mutter, 'Thank you very much, I reelly appreciate it,' but if she's engaged in a proper conversation her face becomes animated, her previously dull, almost lifeless eyes glint with humour, sometimes sly and malicious humour, and she becomes, well, not exactly attractive but –

Well, actually it's impossible to talk about her body as she's made it bulky and shapeless by the dark bits and pieces in which she clothes herself, they don't look like garments, but like large pieces of cloth ripped from larger pieces of cloth. She wears them in layers, wrapped around the top part of herself and hanging from her waist, and one or sometimes two wrapped around her head and tied under her chin.

Anyway, there she was, coming towards me, with her hand extended, not in an actual begging position. I've never heard either Annabelle or Hyacinth ask for anything except the time – a tactic for stopping people, luring them into conversation, a situation from which donations may flow – but even so there was the sense of an appeal in the way she was holding out her hand, an emotional appeal, for help and comfort in distress, perhaps, though the truth is I couldn't bear to look at it properly, her hands are the worst thing about her, visibly, anyway – they're filthy, as are the fingernails, broken and jagged and dark yellow from nicotine, the nicotine stain seems to go right into the palm of the hand, a hand you hope you will never, ever, have to touch, and the sight of which made it easier for me to hustle around her with, 'Evening, how are you? OK are you, eh?' and then I was away, smoothly enough.

I sensed rather than heard her pattering up behind me, and then she was muttering in my ear – 'He's dead. He's dead, you see, Simon.' Well, of course, I had to stop, turn around and face her. 'He's dead,' she said again, with exactly the blank expression and in exactly the toneless voice that she uses when she says, 'Thank you very much, I reelly appreciate it.' Her hand was still held out, and it struck me that she was asking me to take it, clasp it. 'Who's dead?' 'My friend,' she said. 'What, Hyacinth!' I exclaimed. 'Good God!' Her blank expression went blanker, from bewilderment. 'Who?' 'Oh, I mean your friend – um?' 'Yes,' she said. She named him. I can't remember what name, I was confused with embarrassment, really, at having forgotten that I'd never told Hyacinth and Annabelle what their names were. 'I'm dreadfully sorry,' I said. 'So very sorry, how exactly did he –?' She said his liver had given out, he'd collapsed, been rushed to St Mary's, Paddington, and died there three days ago. 'We been friends thirteen years,' she added, or was it seventeen, anyway it was an odd number, not a rounded one, and she made it sound very specific, as if it were important. Thirteen as opposed to fourteen or twelve, or seventeen as opposed to sixteen or eighteen. So for thirteen or possibly seventeen years they'd been friends. Her cupped hand, which had the appeal of a soiled lavatory bowl, was still cupped and wagging itself at me. 'Well, I'm so sorry,' I said again, thinking, Oh, Christ, I'll have to do something! 'Look,' I said, 'look, I'll see you, eh?' and stepped away from her, and walked down Holland Park Avenue wondering whether I should give her the twenty, and then thinking that no, I shouldn't, because a) it might seem that I was trying to pay her off for her grief and b) I didn't want to, it was too much.

I went into Jeroboams and looked at the cheeses, my intention being, not to buy her cheese for consolation but to buy myself a cheese and give her a few quid from the change – it's a long time since I've bought cheese, and I've never known much about them, so I selected rather randomly, pointing to a French goat's cheese because it looked like one I used to eat in Clermont-Ferrand, where I taught English to trainee chefs and waiters in 1956, and then a Cheddar, then a blue and white one, then a round Dutch one. I got into the swing of it, overcoming my usual indecisiveness by pointing at any cheese that caught my eye. The problem was that I had no idea, when it came to cutting them into portions, how much I wanted, as the question was put to me in terms of weight. I finished up with an enormous carrier bag of cheeses plus some luxury chocolate bars and a bag of ginger snaps, I hope they are, and as it came to just over twenty quid I had to pay with my credit card and so still had nothing for Annabelle.

She was back standing outside Tesco's, talking to an old-fashioned middle-aged man in a suit. He was fumbling in his pocket, and she was looking impassively past him, straight at me. I went a few yards down, into the newsagent, and bought a packet of cigarettes, Silk Cut, and got back a ten-pound note and under five pounds in change. I walked towards Annabelle, who pretended not to see me. She put the recorder to her lips and tootled at it unmusically. I couldn't help suspecting she was being satirical. When I got to her she put the recorder down, and I put into her hand the change, which she put into a bag at her waist, 'Thank you very much, I reelly appreciate it,' she said in her receiver's voice. I handed her the packet of cigarettes and, though she didn't change her tone or vocabulary, she added my name. 'Thank you very much, Simon. I reelly appreciate it, Simon,' and then, 'He was my friend for seventeen years, Simon' – though, as I've said, it might have been thirteen years, thus directly and uncomplicatedly connecting my gifts to Hyacinth's death. Well, I'd rather give her cigarettes and money than write her a letter of condolence about Hyacinth's passing, I thought, as I went on down the avenue, swinging the heavy bag of assorted cheeses. Thank God Victoria loves cheese, though I have an idea she's trying to stop eating it as she suspects it's bad for her, has, in fact, stopped buying it –

The thing about Hyacinth is that the last time I saw him, about four days ago, he was in a floral shirt and jeans, his hair tied back in a pigtail, he was foraging in a litter bin and looked appalling, scrawny and gaunt, his eyes so sunk that his face seemed to be all jaw and brow and his body was trembling and I thought the sort of thought I've been having about Tom, our ancient cat – yes, well, you've been there before, Hyacinth, at the grave's edge, but you'll be back on the pavement with your feeble watercolours eventually, and you'll outlive me, won't you? and the thought made me angry, not with him, but with who knows what, whatever is responsible for these things.

WHAT IF, ONE DAY, HE'S NOT THERE?

There's a small bearded man in a peaked cap with a bent-forward walk, as if he's battling strong winds, who passes by Kensington Place at roughly the same time every evening – well, every evening we've been there, and as we sometimes go to Kensington Place two or three times a week and have been going there for the last ten years, it's not logically correct but perfectly reasonable to assume that he goes past our table every evening, whether we're sitting at it or not. Very often, but not always, we also see him coming back about half an hour later, walking with the same bent-forward walk, which is how I know that he's not battling the wind, unless the wind changes to the opposite direction for the specific purpose of blowing against him. He has a very peaceful if determined face, rather philosophical, and it's possible that like Immanuel Kant he takes a constitutional at the same time and follows the same route every day, although one night –

We pointed him out to friends who frequently eat with us at Kensington Place. One night the four of us went to another restaurant in the same neighbourhood, but at a considerable distance from it. When we came out and were standing on the pavement kissing goodnight and so forth, he suddenly appeared at the top of the street, bending forward as usual, and walked past us. We froze, the four of us, in astonishment, believing for the moment that his usual route must actually be any route that took him past us, wherever we happened to be. Then we wondered if he weren't a hallucination that had belonged first to Victoria and me, and now to anyone who joined us for a meal in Notting Hill, and then of course it occurred to us that it was a simple coincidence, that his was a long looping constitutional that took him past Kensington Place, then on past this restaurant and then round and back past Kensington Place –

So everything we need to understand about this man is now understood. There is no mystery or need for a supernatural explanation. He is simply a man of mechanically regular habits. I long to know what work he does, whether he's married and has children. He seems a solitary, a lifelong solitary, not a widower. I have begun to worry about him. Now when we go to Kensington Place I keep an eye out, and I get increasingly anxious until he appears. He hasn't failed me yet, but I wonder what I'll feel if one night he doesn't come. I suspect that I've attached my fate to his continuing to trudge, bent forward and resolute, along the pavement past our table –

He came tonight, thank God, his scarf flowing behind him – I don't think I've mentioned his scarf, it's grey and very long, and sometimes almost horizontal, as if to emphasise the strength of the wind he is battling against. The reason I was so relieved to see him is that tomorrow we go to Dr Rootle for the results of the scan, but not until late in the afternoon. How will I get through the hours leading up to it?

Dr Johnson said that knowing you're going to be hanged in the morning concentrates the mind wonderfully. Supposing you won't know until the morning whether you're going to be hanged in the morning? What does that do to the mind?

A DISTRACTION FROM DISTRACTION: TONIGHT

Well, right now I'll keep myself distracted by writing about – by writing about – oh yes, Stefan Zweig, why not? I've spent the last week or so reading as much of him as I could get my hands on and I've looked him up on Google, where I discovered that he was an immensely popular and successful author in the 1920s and early 1930s, a worldwide bestseller, particularly loved and admired in France, in Germany and in his native Austria – and he still is in France, where you can buy translations of his short stories and novellas at railway stations and airports. He also did well in the United States, but was never quite taken up by the English – I don't know why and my source in Google offers no explanation. Now I'm English, can I offer an explanation? Well for one thing he likes to write about women, he has a feeling for their feelings – *Twenty-four Hours in the Life of a Woman*, for instance, is about a composed and attractive widow who spots a young man gambling in a casino at a fashionable resort, is struck by the intensity of his play, catches the despair in his eyes and on impulse follows him when he runs out, to find him sitting on a bench contemplating suicide. She determines to save him, spends the night with him in a turmoil of sex and sacrifice, and then gets together some money and gives it to him, after making him promise that he'll give up gambling, return to his family and pay off his debts. And then – and then – well, the end is predictable almost from the first moment that she sees him, and in spite of the urgency of the writing – even in translation Zweig is a fluently urgent and impassioned writer – one doesn't care much. The fact is that gamblers, like all addicts, are pretty boring in that their lives tend to follow one of two narratives, they either struggle heroically to give up and succeed, or they struggle less heroically and fail, there is very little room for variety in either tale, and the thing about Zweig's storytelling is that he is so earnestly insistent, sometimes almost pleading with us to feel as the woman feels, care as she cares – and of course the more he insists and pleads the more we resist – and yet there's such decency and kindness in his writing, his tone of voice I mean, that one feels a touch mean-spirited – and one resents that too, a bit – one really wishes one didn't find him somewhat phoney and melodramatic – Christ, it's past dawn, there's sunlight and the birds, the bloody birds – bed, bed, must go to bed, two co-proxamol and a sleeper, no, two sleepers – no, try and make do with one.

THE SAME DISTRACTION FROM THE SAME DISTRACTION

I've been up for an hour, two hours to go before we leave the house, if I could trust myself I wouldn't go, I'd say I feel OK, not exactly well but not really ill, let sleeping tumours lie etc., but of course I've got to find out for sure – he's bound to give me bad news, probably reduce my life expectancy, which according to his previous prediction is now down to eight months – I should think I've used up two or three of those in destructive emotions but now, this morning, I feel, apart from the fear, abnormally calm, accepting that whatever the news there is nothing I can do to change it – I can neither make it worse by smoking a couple of panicky cigarettes nor make it better by not smoking them, so now the second one is smouldering in my ashtray, I lift it to my lips sometimes as I write this, but don't draw the smoke deep in my lungs, I let it swirl in my throat and linger there before blowing it out – now where did I stop? On what? Oh yes, Zweig, my last sentence was about, oh yes, *Twenty-four Hours in the Life of a Woman* – that I didn't really believe any of it – now what other stories have I read? There's – oh yes, *Amok*, well, I didn't believe that, either, I remember that much, but what was it about? Think now. Concentrate.

Ah yes. The narrator is travelling on a steamer from Calcutta to Europe, he comes across a fellow passenger skulking about the deck at night, drinking and distraught and desperate to tell his story, which our narrator passes on to us exactly as it was told to him, in fact in direct speech, I think, only inserting himself to set the scenes of their various meetings and to describe the man's tone of voice, his glittering eye, his frantic manner – the story the man tells is this: that, yes, that eight years ago he'd been a successful young doctor with a good post in a big hospital in Leipzig, had met a beautiful woman with an imperial manner and an icy heart, for whom he had stolen money from the hospital funds. The scandal was hushed up by an uncle who found him a job in a wretched and swampy outpost of the colonies – Dutch East Indies, I think – where he festers away from drink, loneliness and boredom, nothing but animals and natives for company until one day an English woman of evident class and breeding and with a somewhat haughty manner turns up, having come all the many miles from the colonial capital. She has somehow heard of his skills and hints that she's after an abortion.

The doctor, out of a confusion of unruly feelings along with a perfectly understandable desire for revenge on coldly beautiful women, says he will help her only if she a) asks him outright for what she wants from him, i.e. an abortion, and b) gives him what she knows he wants from her, i.e. her body. She refuses and sweeps indignantly off.

He sets out to find her and when he does so (at a society ball in the colonial capital) mumbles out abject apologies for the foulness of his behaviour and begs her to let him perform the operation before it becomes dangerous, it's already nearly too late – she rejects his offer and evades his overtures until it's actually too late, then sends her Chinese servant, who has, if I remember correctly, a 'moist, dog-like but determined gaze', to bring him to a squalid backstreet hideaway, where she is lying blood-soaked and in agony from a botched abortion. He and the Chinese dog-like boy clean her up – no, no, I can't go on with this.

The truth is that even as I write the plot down every sentence strikes me as so preposterous that I can't believe that I'm remembering it accurately – but then I found it pretty preposterous when I was reading it, it's chock-a-block with the sort of coincidences that only happen in life, should never happen in fiction – what's the time?

THIS AFTERNOON: THANK YOU, STEFAN ZWEIG, THANK YOU

So. So. Yes, there's something I said above, to the effect that often with Zweig I don't trust the narrator – it's a peculiar thing about quite a few of the stories I've read, they're not told directly by Zweig, they're told to him by someone he meets, and then passed on to us in a first-person narrative that is therefore in inverted commas – this is true of Amok and also of *Beware of Pity*. It's as if Zweig needed to shift the responsibility for his imagination on to someone else – and this odd sort of evasiveness is there in his autobiography, what's it called, terrible title, hopelessly unmemorable, anyway he presents himself so completely as a representative figure of his age, born and nurtured in the golden and dying days of the Austro-Hungarian Empire, with no sense at all that his Jewishness separated him from the world of Viennese culture – then came the First World War and its havoc, followed by a decade of peace that for him was a decade of growing success and international fame, and then suddenly, inexplicably, there was Hitler, and Zweig's highly acclaimed and immensely popular books made part of the bonfire, and then there were the concentration camps, which plucked from their homes his colleagues and friends and were reaching out for him too, for after all he was known to be a Jew, even if he hadn't really known it himself until then – not even his collaboration with Strauss, Hitler's favourite living composer, could save him, and anyway, when it came to it, he didn't want to be saved, not in that sense – so what was left but flight and exile?

He went to London, then to Bath, then to America, and from there to Brazil – why Brazil, when he had so many friends in New York? The edition I have ends with his suicide letter, written in Petropolis in 1942, in which he thanks the people of Brazil for welcoming him into their midst, states that he's leaving the world while still in full possession of his health and faculties because all he sees for the future of Europe, his spiritual home, is nightmare – death the only refuge. In fact he sees himself as a forerunner, others will surely follow, he will await them, although he doesn't say exactly where – although perhaps I've misremembered that bit. Anyway, it's a stately and gracious letter, more like a letter of resignation than a suicide letter, with only glancing reference to his much younger wife, and after all he took her with him – or she elected to go with him, let's rather say. They were found dead in their bed from an overdose of barbiturates, their hands clasped – is that right, about their hands, or have I added it in? Victoria's just rung from her study to say that we have to leave in half an hour, am I ready? I said yes, yes I am –

Now where – yes, well, so what's disconcerting about the book – it's called *Tomorrow's World* – no, no, it can't be, fat-head, *Yesterday's World* is what it's called, of course, *Yesterday's World* – what's disconcerting about *Yesterday's World* is its reticence. He divorced his first wife, who evidently adored him, to marry his secretary, who also evidently adored him, but you have no sense of a marrying and divorcing man in the autobiography, I don't mean in the citing of personal facts, I mean in the communication of a living and contradictory self – he speaks for civilisation, it's almost saintly, his voice, in its modest and humane authority – he knew every famous writer, musician, artist, and he describes them all with meticulous kindness and sensitivity, with what one could call, I suppose, a writer's eye, and yet they seem to fade from view even as you're reading – you don't think for a minute that he's lying, exactly, just that he's too well trained in himself to tell – or perhaps see, or sniff – the coarser grain, the tackier substance of the inner life of others, so it's really the authorised autobiography, and you have to feel your way behind its impeccable surface to realise what a sad and wounded and lost creature he must have been when he wrote it – and then you realise that the surface is itself the achievement, without it he couldn't have written at all about his times, the early ones and their charms, and then the later ones and their horrors, which for him could have no end, his world was over – and don't forget – don't forget what? Have I time to remember? Remember what?

Oh yes, yes, and there's his biography of Balzac, he thought of it as his life's great work although it was still unfinished at his death – but even unfinished and in translation it's a quite wonderful book, free and easy in its manner – the extravagant French genius who died of coffee, overwork and above all crazy impulses, falling hopelessly in love with women who wrote him fan letters, stalking them with sexual yearning and urgency until he was humiliated by them or tired of them, often first one and then the other – all his sexual and emotional luck came when he was a very young man, with good and experienced older women who made love to him and mothered him – yes, Zweig tells it all with charm and zest and something more – a joy in celebrating a man who was, I would think, temperamentally his opposite – so – so there's his biography of Balzac and of course his novel *Beware of Pity*, two books for a writer to be proud of – he was a good and honourable man, I think, in ways which we no longer know much about, but finally no man can speak for the turmoil of his time unless he speaks from the turmoil of himself –

Victoria again. Time to go. Right. I must have a pee first. When I come back I'll write about Zweig's account of Balzac's marriage to the ghastly Madame Hanska and of his grotesque death, Zweig tells it superbly, the pathetic and the farcical in perfect balance – no, no I won't, I'll simply write down what Dr Rootle says, and whatever it is, that had better be the end of this, this whatever it is, they will be my last words, my last written words on the subject of myself – off you go – I've only smoked three cigarettes today, will that be taken into account? Off, off you go, off we go.

I FALL IN LOVE

I haven't been here doing this for four days, since the morning of the day that we went to see Dr Rootle, to get the result of the scan, and to find out what my immediate future would be. I don't know why I've postponed writing about it, it almost feels like a moral lapse, a kind of laziness. I've pulled the pad towards me, picked up my pen, I see I actually wrote a few words, in such a scrawl that I'm still not sure I can read them correctly, but I think they are: 'He came into the waiting room and went to the receptionist's desk directly behind us.'

I can't remember much before that, all the business of getting to the hospital, finding the right area – oh, I do remember it wasn't the usual hospital, it was somewhere even nearer to us, it took almost no time to get there, and then we – what? Yes, we walked about outside for a few minutes, then went into the lobby, which was like a combination of a Hilton Hotel and an airport departure lounge, people sitting on sofas and on chairs in postures of attention, hands on their knees and leaning forward, or whispering to their partners, as if waiting for their flight to be called – there were lots of Arabs, I remember, outnumbering the other patients – we went to one of the reception desks and were told that Dr Rootle's office was downstairs in the basement. As we were early we hung about where we were. I had several pees in a clean and comfortable lavatory, nervous pees or rather pees from nervousness, and I thought, as I always do in tense situations, first nights and such, that I must be careful not to dribble down my trousers or over my shoes – I would have been wearing espadrilles, as I've worn them all week, dark blue espadrilles, I doubt if they'd have shown any stains but of course one can't be too careful, one wants to be at one's most self-possessed when receiving life/death-type news.

When we had five minutes to go we went down in the lift to the basement and – and it was a small waiting room, there were only three or four people sitting about, I don't remember anything about them or much else until – try and pick up from the one sentence I wrote down – 'He came into the waiting room and went to the receptionist's desk directly behind us.' Yes, that's right. He came out of a door that opened on to the waiting room, so there he was, suddenly, abruptly really, one second walking towards us, and seemingly smiling a welcome so that I stood up, and then he was past us, at the counter and talking to the receptionist in a low voice, so I sat down again, and then he was around in front of us, and I was on my feet again and he was shaking Victoria's hand, then mine, and he led us into his office, where we sat on two hard-backed chairs facing his desk, and he stood behind it, looking down at a folder, my folder I assumed, took out what looked like an X-ray, my scan I assumed, then sat down. He put the scan back into the folder and smiled, a huge smile as he has huge teeth, huge and white, that could make you feel like Little Red Riding Hood.

What followed was very confusing, and I can't recall, though I've tried, the exact words. In fact I have an idea that I didn't understand them, nor did Victoria, and we looked at one another for help. Part of the problem was Dr Rootle's manner, it seemed playful, almost teasing, his eyes sparkled and bulged behind his spectacles, and his teeth continued to flash – he looked more than ever like a large schoolboy – and then we realised, almost simultaneously, that he thought we knew the results of the scan – we said no, no, that's why we were here, to be told the results. He looked surprised, slightly disbelieving, but then our own surprise must have persuaded him that we weren't teasing him back. He didn't stop smiling as he explained that the scan showed that the radiotherapy had shrunk both tumours, furthermore there were no signs that the cancer had spread – although there was no question but that the cancer was still there, in the blood, and would eventually return. There were two ways of dealing with someone in my situation, the American way, which was to press on immediately with aggressive treatment, probably an intensive course of chemotherapy, which might prolong my life but perhaps by no more than a month or so, and would be very uncomfortable, if not downright miserable. The second way was the way that they favoured in this hospital, the English way, so to speak, which was to encourage the patient to lead as full a life as possible for as long as possible, and not to resort to intensive chemo-therapy until it was absolutely necessary – towards the end, in other words, which in my case might be as far away as eighteen months or even two years. What did I think? I thought that I was in love with Dr Rootle, he was the most delightful man I'd ever met, I adored him, but I didn't say so. I said instead that it was better news than I'd dared hope. And then thought, let's get out of here now, immediately, no need to prolong the conversation into qualifications and so forth. I stood up and held out my hand. He shook it, then shook Victoria's hand, and came around the desk to open the door for us. I noticed that he didn't put his hand on my shoulder or clasp and squeeze my elbow, which I took to be a confirmation that I was out of the compassion zone for eighteen months or even two years – two whole – Victoria drove us home. I've no idea what we said. We were both in a kind of stupor – I mean, two years, two whole – well, eighteen months then, yes, let's keep it at eighteen months, in order to avoid disappointment.

ACKNOWLEDGEMENTS

My thanks to

Ian Jack, for the time and care he has given to my memoirs, and for the great pleasure of his company

Dinah Wood, the editor of my plays, unfailing in her support and encouragement

Hugh Whitemore, always one of the first and most valuable readers of my writings

three true friends.